1-2-3® for Business
2nd Edition

Douglas Ford Cobb
Leith Anderson

Revised for Release 2.01
by David Maguiness

Que™ Corporation
Carmel, Indiana

1-2-3 for Business, 2nd Edition.
Copyright © 1987 by Que™ Corporation.

Library of Congress Catalog No.: LC 86-063834

ISBN 0-88022-283-2

91 90 89 88 87   8 7 6 5 4 3

Interpretation of the printing code: the rightmost double-digit number is the year of the book's printing; the rightmost single-digit number, the number of the book's printing. For example, a printing code of 87-4 shows that the fourth printing of the book occurred in 1987.

Screen reproductions were produced with *Inset*, a graphics-and-text-integrator program from American Programmers Guild, Ltd.

About the Authors

Douglas Ford Cobb

Douglas Ford Cobb received his B.A. degree, magna cum laude, from Williams College and his M.S. in Accounting from New York University's Graduate School of Business Administration. He coauthored *Spreadsheet Software: From VisiCalc to 1-2-3; Using 1-2-3;* and *1-2-3 Tips, Tricks, and Traps;* all published by Que Corporation. He is president of The Cobb Group, Inc., a microcomputer information firm in Louisville, Kentucky.

Leith Anderson

Leith Anderson is a business consultant doing strategic planning for small businesses. He holds a B.A. degree in American history from Stanford University and a J.D. from Indiana University Law School. He is president of Ryan-Hunter, Ltd., and editor of *Leather Goods*, a publication he originated.

Acknowledgments

The authors wish to thank these people for invaluable assistance in completing the first edition of this book:

Gena B. Cobb

Rex Hancock, ComputerLand of Indianapolis

Additional thanks to Terrie Solomon and Timothy S. Stanley for assistance in completing the second edition of this book.

Editors

Betty White
Gail S. Burlakoff

Technical Editors

Wally Bryant
Cheryl Watson
Linda Flanders
Terry Thompson

Production

Dan Armstrong
Kelly Currie
Jennifer Matthews
Joe Ramon
Lynne Tone

1-2-3 for Business, 2nd Edition,
is based on Lotus 1-2-3 Release 2.01
and can be used with 1-2-3 Release 2.

Table of Contents

Introduction

Part I An Overview

---

1 **An Overview of *1-2-3 for Business*, 2nd Edition**

Part II Managing Cash

2 Managing the Checkbook

3 Projecting Cash Flow

4 Managing Cash Flow

5 Managing Accounts Receivable

Part III Using Financial Statements

6 General Ledger Accounting

7 Interactive Financial Statements

8 Performing Ratio Analysis

9 Calculating Growth Capacity

Part IV Managing Debt

10 Tracking a Line of Credit

Part V General Management Applications

14 Managing Time

15 Project Management

Trademark Acknowledgments

Introduction

1-2-3® for Business, 2nd Edition, presents 14 spreadsheet applications that you can apply to common business tasks, using the best-selling software program, Lotus® 1-2-3. Each application, or model, can be tailored to your business situation to improve your firm's efficiency and productivity.

The book is intended for the intermediate or experienced 1-2-3 user who needs help in developing a specific business spreadsheet application. Even though *1-2-3 for Business*, 2nd Edition, should not be considered a reference book, most readers will benefit from the 1-2-3 techniques and methods presented.

Those of you who have been using the first edition of *1-2-3 for Business* will note substantial differences in this second edition.

Improved Models

The models are basically unchanged from the first edition of the book. But wherever possible, 1-2-3's Release 2 features have been included to make the models more efficient. The Release 2 features are designated by an R2 symbol in the margin of the page. In addition, the second edition features a greater number of optional macros you can use to reduce time spent on routine tasks and accelerate the spreadsheet construction process.

The applications also have been revised to reflect the changes in tax regulations, as encompassed in the Tax Reform Act of 1986. Most notably affected are Chapters 12, "Lease versus Debt," and 13, "Fixed Asset Management," because the investment tax credit has been eliminated and depreciation schedules have been lengthened.

(Note: Although we have made every effort to accurately reflect the new tax laws, Que Corporation cannot be held responsible for any omission, error, or misrepresentation contained in this book. Because tax regulations continue to be subject to official interpretation, we strongly suggest that you consult your accountant, attorney, or the Internal Revenue Service if you have questions or concerns.)

Conventions Used in This Edition

Several conventions are employed in *1-2-3 for Business*, 2nd Edition, to help you use the applications effectively. Some of the more important conventions are discussed briefly here.

Each chapter contains a 1-2-3 spreadsheet model that details each section, or module, of the application. At the top of the spreadsheet, a three-row area displays the name of the application and the Que Corporation copyright notice. You can use the two blank rows in this section for entering notes, instructions, or other information about the application.

If you use 1-2-3's **/W**orksheet **/W**indow **H**orizontal command to lock the screen at the bottom of the header (usually around row 5 or 6), this section of the application will always be visible on the screen.

Those of you who are familiar with the first edition of *1-2-3 for Business* will note a change in the presentation of section titles, such as "Criterion Range" or "Analysis." To make the text more readable, only the first letter of each word in the section titles has been capitalized in the second edition.

Text to be typed is shown in *italics*, but commands are presented with initial capital letters in boldface:

   /Data **Q**uery **I**nput

Although you type only **/DQI**, the commands are presented as whole words for clarity.

All function keys are printed in capital letters and enclosed in parentheses: F9 (CALC). Special-purpose keys are enclosed in braces: {EDIT}. The Enter key is shown with an initial capital "E" or with the tilde (~).

Text Arrangement

The second edition is organized by specific business activity into four parts: Managing Cash, Using Financial Statements, Managing Debt, and General Management applications.

Each chapter contains a completely revised explanation of the model and, for clearer understanding, the text is divided into three major categories:

   • Creating the Model, which tells you precisely how to set up the model. Included in this discussion are columns requiring width adjustment, cell formula locations, cell formatting, and range naming. New tables have been incorporated into the text to help you with these procedures.

- Understanding the Model, which discusses the operation of each spreadsheet module, or section, and how the modules interact with one another. New figures show you what your screen should look like after you have created each section. This background information, which is essential to realizing the application's full potential, will help you to modify the model.

- Using the Model, which shows you how to use the model in your business. Included is an explanation and/or table where your data should be entered, the correct sequence of keystrokes to use to run your model, and suggestions of ways to modify the application.

New with this edition are figures showing each section of the spreadsheet. You can use these figures as a reference when building your own model. To further assist you in creating the application for your business, separate tables of range names, formulas, column-widths, and formats have been added to the text.

A summary of the *1-2-3 for Business,* 2nd Edition, models follows.

Managing Cash

Chapter 1, an overview, describes how to use this second edition of *1-2-3 for Business.* The chapter describes the computer equipment and knowledge you need to create and use the models. A summary of the major 1-2-3 commands is provided. Also included is a description of a 1-2-3 macro utility library file that you can create to help you develop your spreadsheets. (This file is included on the *1-2-3 for Business* disk.)

Chapter 2, "Managing the Checkbook," discusses two applications. The Checkbook Manager can balance and reconcile your checking account. The optional Accounting Summary uses 1-2-3's **D**ata **T**able commands, and provides you with an accounting system for use at home or for a small business.

Chapter 3, "Projecting Cash Flow," is a comprehensive model designed to project your company's cash flow. The model incorporates the relationships between sales and inventory, accounts receivable, accounts payable, and cash to provide you with a twelve-month cash flow forecast.

Chapter 4, "Managing Cash Flow," is a cash flow planning and management tool. You use your actual cash receipts and disbursements to determine your business's monthly cash requirements and thus gain control over this important asset.

Chapter 5, "Managing Accounts Receivable," records your sales invoices and collections and generates an Aging and Sales Summary Report from this data. This application also uses 1-2-3's **D**ata **T**able commands.

Using Financial Statements

Chapter 6, "General Ledger Accounting," is a new application for this edition. The model provides a full accounting system and generates financial statements for a small or medium-sized business. This application relies on Release 2 features, the @DSUM function, and range names. The General Ledger model, which was developed by Que Corporation's Accounting Manager, Wally Bryant, CPA, is the book's most practical application.

Chapter 7, "Interactive Financial Statements," is another planning tool you can use to forecast your company's future. Because the balance sheet and income statement are interdependent, your forecast will reflect the relationships between the two. This application demonstrates 1-2-3's iterative recalculation capability and lends itself well to "what-if" analysis.

Chapter 8, "Ratio Analysis," can calculate key ratios from your financial statements and provide you with useful information about your company. The model includes two simple but useful macros, a database, and graphing capability.

Chapter 9, "Calculating Growth Capacity," contains an application that can determine how quickly your firm can grow without additional external financing. This is another useful "what-if" tool.

Managing Debt

Chapter 10, "Tracking a Line of Credit," describes a simple but useful model that provides you with daily information about your line of credit. Using 1-2-3 @functions, the application also calculates important statistics about your short-term financing.

Chapter 11, "Amortizing a Loan," contains a sophisticated loan amortization calculator that can amortize both fixed- and variable-rate loans. The application also has an optional database capability so that you can review your payment history for a specific time period. This is one of the book's most useful models.

Chapter 12, "Lease versus Debt," determines whether purchasing or leasing will provide your lowest-cost financing alternative for capital assets between loan and lease options. The model and 1-2-3 can do this important task quickly and easily.

Chapter 13, "Fixed Asset Management," presents a small-business fixed-asset management system. However, large companies can use the principles of this model to create a similar system. This model is structured for assets acquired after December 31, 1986. The application contains two optional macros to speed entry of acquisitions and disposals to and from the model's summary area.

General Management

Chapter 14, "Managing Time," provides a system to help you control that most elusive of resources, your company's time. Because of the Tax Reform Act of 1986, this application will have special appeal to accountants and attorneys. Even if you do not need a time management system, understanding the operation of this model will give you valuable insight into 1-2-3's **D**ata **T**able functions.

Chapter 15, "Project Management," is another new application. The Project Manager supplies you with information about the costs and duration of your company's projects. The model displays this information dramatically with 1-2-3's graphics.

In short, this practical text shows you how to save time and money with carefully designed models that will work for you and your business.

To develop or refresh your understanding of 1-2-3, turn to Chapter 1 of *1-2-3 for Business*, 2nd Edition.

An Overview

1

An Overview of *1-2-3 for Business*, 2nd Edition

Introduction

This chapter is designed to help you create and use the updated and revised models in this book. Although this discussion is not a substitute for the Lotus documentation or *Using 1-2-3*, you should find it a valuable reinforcement of 1-2-3 principles and spreadsheet methods.

What You Need To Use This Book

Experience with 1-2-3 is a prerequisite for using this book. You should have basic knowledge of the 1-2-3 commands, formulas, formatting, and so on before you attempt to create these models. And, of course, you will need appropriate hardware and software.

If you have limited or no experience with 1-2-3, practice using the program with the reference manual provided by Lotus. Que's best-selling books, *Using 1-2-3* and *1-2-3: Tips, Tricks, and Traps*, are valuable resources that can help you fully understand and use this powerful business tool.

To use Chapter 6, "General Ledger Accounting," correctly, you need at least an introductory level knowledge of accounting. If you haven't had accounting experience, or if you feel uneasy around debits and credits, you may want to turn this application over to your accountant.

Finally, this chapter discusses some of the frequently used 1-2-3 commands in the applications, and a macro utility library file that you can use in developing your spreadsheet and other models.

The Hardware

The models presented in this book were revised using a COMPAQ 286® computer with 640K of random access memory (RAM) and a 20-megabyte hard disk. You will need a personal computer that can run Lotus 1-2-3 and that has two disk drives, or one floppy and one hard disk drive. Those of you who use dual-floppy drive systems will use the A-drive for the Lotus System disk and the B-drive to create, save, and retrieve your spreadsheets. To benefit fully from the models, we recommend at least 320K of RAM, or as much as you can afford.

To print a report, you will need a dot-matrix printer that is supported by 1-2-3. A 132-column, or wide-carriage, printer is preferable, because some of the models are quite large.

To print the graphs displayed in this book, you'll need a dot-matrix printer or plotter supported by 1-2-3. Contact your computer sales representative if you have a question or concern about your system configuration.

The Software

Needless to say, you will need Lotus 1-2-3, Release 2 or 2.01, to use these applications. If you want to use Release 1A, you'll have to modify the models—especially the macros. For example, 1A users should replace **/R**ange **V**alue with {EDIT}{CALC}.

Planning

In general, the models in this book are examples of concepts. Unless a model precisely fits your company's needs, you need not always enter the model directly from the book. In the sample model in Chapter 6, "General Ledger Accounting," for instance, space considerations caused us to omit many of the accounts commonly found in most businesses (such accounts as Salaries Payable, Taxes, and so on). The principle of the application is what's important.

However, some models, such as Chapter 11's Loan Amortization Calculator, can be taken directly from the book (or disk) and used by your company with little or no modification. In summary, some preplanning will help you to develop a model that's suited to your particular business situation. If you plan, you can avoid frustration later on and take advantage of the program's considerable flexibility.

With all of these elements in place, you should have few problems developing and using your models.

The following sections present an overview of some of the 1-2-3 commands and functions that are used frequently in this book. In a sense, you might consider the next section as "1-2-3 for Business: Tips, Tricks, and Traps."

Worksheet Commands

The number of /Worksheet commands is large and beyond the scope of this chapter. The commands used most commonly in this book are /Worksheet Insert Row and /Worksheet Column Set-Width. These commands can be included in your model as macros.

All of the models (except the Line-of-Credit Tracker in Chapter 10) have been set on manual calculation with the /Worksheet Format Recalculation Manual sequence of commands. The small but useful model in Chapter 10 should be left at the default setting of Automatic Recalculation.

Finally, using the /Worksheet Titles command options will give you a helpful reference while you create your model, especially if you are far from your column headings and row titles.

The Range Commands

The Range commands cover many options. If you study the command chart carefully, you will notice that the bulk of these commands are Format and Name options. We have used these two commands often, including the two new /Range features: /Range Value and /Range Transpose.

When formatting cells, this book attempts to reflect basic accounting convention. Therefore, only the first and last cells in a column have been formatted with a dollar sign, using /Range Format Currency 2 commands. All other values usually have been formatted with /Range Format Comma 2. We believe that too many dollar signs clutter the worksheet and make the report difficult to read. Feel free, however, to format your model to your liking or according to your company's policy.

R2

Most of the dates in the models appear as **D**ate **1**. In Chapter 14, the
Time Manager has been formatted with the **/R**ange **F**ormat **D**ate **3**
command, however, to show you the month and year. Note also that
1-2-3 will do the formatting for you. Thus, we recommend that before
you enter the model's formulas you format your worksheet. Enter a
formula, format, then copy it.

This book also takes advantage of three new Release 2 features, using
/Range **F**ormat **H**idden to format many of the @DSUM functions in
models with data-table modules. The models in Chapter 2, "Managing
the Checkbook," and Chapter 14, "Time Management," are examples.
We find this approach more visually appealing than displaying a section
of the @DSUM function in a cell. Be careful if you decide to follow this
approach. The only way to determine whether a formula is in a Hidden
cell is to place the cursor at that cell location, or to issue the
/Worksheet **S**tatus command while you are at that cell location.

Chapter 13, "Fixed Asset Management," draws on Release 2's **/R**ange
Value and **/R**ange **T**ranspose commands. When you use the **/R**ange
Value command, be sure to specify a separate *TO:* range from the
FROM: range, as we did in Chapter 13. Otherwise, you will lose the
formulas you had before you started the operation.

Using range names is a handy way to move around your worksheet. To
move the cursor in this manner, all you need to do is press F5, the
(GOTO) key, input the range name, and press Enter. The cursor will be
whisked instantly to that cell location.

Using range names also simplifies your formulas and macros by
referencing a name rather than a lengthy range location. Be sure to
save a step when you name your macros: use the **/R**ange **N**ame **L**abel
Right command. Range names, a frequently overlooked feature of
1-2-3, can enhance and simplify your spreadsheets.

Copy and Move

Whenever possible, use the **/C**opy command to enter formulas and
separator lines. Doing so will greatly reduce the time required to re-
create the models. Although this book does not use the **/M**ove
command frequently, be careful if you use either **/C**opy or **/M**ove
commands with cells that contain formulas—the commands may
produce unwanted results. In Chapter 15, for example, the Project
Manager model contains formulas that require absolute cell references
to result in a correct **/C**opy operation.

File Operations

It is important to remember that you should **/F**ile **S**ave your model before ending a 1-2-3 session, retrieving another file, or attempting a risky or experimental operation. This point cannot be stressed too strongly. Use a file name that is different from the template. For example, save your April, 1987, accounting data under the name "APR87" rather than under the model's name "GL". In this way, your blank model will always be ready to use when the next reporting period rolls around.

You will need one other command in this category—the **/F**ile **C**ombine **C**opy **N**ame/Specified **R**ange command sequence mentioned in Chapter 6, "General Ledger Accounting." Be sure to use a range name that has meaning for you; this will help you copy the correct range and file.

Printing

To create a report, you must at least designate a range to be printed. If you want to print the entire worksheet and if your print range begins at cell A1, press the . (period), End, and Home keys. In this manner, you can easily have 1-2-3 print your entire worksheet file. Also, consider naming the area of the worksheet that you want to print. Then, when 1-2-3 asks you for the range to be printed, all you need to do is enter the name of the range and press Enter.

After you have done this, all you need to do is issue the **/P**rint **P**rinter **A**lign **G**o command. The combination of keystrokes and 1-2-3 default printer settings will provide you with a basic report.

However, for a presentation-quality report, select **O**ptions from the Print menu. You can add **H**eaders and **F**ooters with these options, and specify the size of print by using the **S**etup command. If you use the **M**argins command, you can choose where your report is to be printed. This is useful if you want your report printed on a specific area of the paper or if your paper is a different size from that in the default margin settings.

Establishing a report format and the corresponding printer settings can take many sequences of 1-2-3 print commands. Instead of doing this each time you want to print a report, enter your print commands once and then **/F**ile **S**ave your model. Then you need only type **/P**rint **P**rinter **A**lign **G**o to print your document. The commands can be incorporated into the following print macro that is used throughout the book:

```
\p   /ppagq~~
```

Finally, as an aid to debugging your model, you can print a cell listing similar to the one found at the end of each chapter. To do this, issue the **/P**rint **O**ptions **O**ther **C**ell-Formulas command. Each cell that contains an entry will be printed, one line at a time.

Graphing

The Graph option is another set of commands too numerous to discuss thoroughly. You should experiment with different Graph Types, Titles, Legends, and so on, because some graph formats are more suitable than others. For example, displaying a "percent of total"-type report lends itself well to the pie graph.

When working with 1-2-3 graphics, however, don't forget to:

- **/G**raph **N**ame **C**reate
- **/G**raph **S**ave
- **/F**ile **S**ave

Many users who forget to do this experience unnecessary frustration.

Data Commands

1-2-3's Data Management capability is probably the program's most overlooked feature. Some users feel intimidated by the database component; others feel that, because it is not a dedicated data-management program, it is not powerful enough. This is unfortunate because 1-2-3's database functions can create an extremely powerful spreadsheet application.

For example, the **/D**ata **F**ill command is a handy data-management feature. You can use this command to quickly and easily enter a series of numbers, such as the months of the year. Consider using **/D**ata **F**ill the next time you create a model with consecutive numbers.

The **/D**ata **Q**uery command is another data-management tool used frequently in this book. **/D**ata **Q**uery, a data search, is made up of the **F**ind, **E**xtract, **U**nique, and **D**elete subcommands. To perform any of these, 1-2-3 requires an Input Range, a Criterion Range, and (for **E**xtract and **U**nique operations) an Output Range.

In most cases, the Input Range will be the area that contains all your records, or data, and your field names, or headings. The Criterion Range forms the criteria, or rules, that 1-2-3 will follow when it looks for a match between your database records and your criteria. Because your Criterion Range generally will be a duplicate of your Input Range headings, you can /Copy these field names to create a Criterion Range. Remember that the maximum width for a Criterion Range is 32 columns and at least two rows, with the first row containing the field names of your search criteria.

Sometimes the criteria are complicated and may include a formula rather than a blank cell location. For example, by calculating an equation, 1-2-3 will substitute the first Input record into an equation located in the Criterion Range to determine whether the record meets the criteria, continuing this process until each record in your database has been used. The application in Chapter 14, "Time Management," relies heavily on this process.

The Output Range functions as a destination point at which 1-2-3 can place extracted database records. To perform an Extract or Unique operation, you must have an Output Range, with headers that exactly match your Input Range headers. To reduce the possibility of omission or error, use the /Copy command to create your Output Range headings.

Be sure to select an unused portion of your spreadsheet for your Output Range, because the extracted data will be written over any data present in the planned Output Range location.

After you have designated your Input, Criterion, and Output ranges, you will be ready to do any of the Query operations. Because these parameters have been set, any subsequent operation can be repeated with the F7 (QUERY) key.

The /Data Table command is another powerful 1-2-3 feature that is used frequently in the book, particularly in the Time Manager. Like a /Data Query operation, table building requires input values, a criteria range, and a table (or output) range.

Table building, which is used frequently for "what-if" analysis, can automate a multiple analysis. Thus, we have combined 1-2-3's table-building capability with an @DSUM function in the table range to generate reports. To grasp the capability of this feature, refer to Chapter 14, "Managing Time," which explains one- and two-variable data tables. And be sure to use the /Data Table Reset command upon completion of each data-table process.

Finally, if you frequently rely on /Data Table functions, you may want to add an 8087 or 80287 math coprocessor to your computer. Data-table calculations can take time, depending on the size of your model, and this microchip will greatly reduce your calculation time.

Function Keys

The special function keys are another 1-2-3 feature that you will find useful for creating and using the models. Located on your keyboard's left side, these keys can be used for some of the more burdensome tasks and repetitious keystrokes.

The F2 (EDIT) key, for example, is extremely useful for correcting lengthy formulas. You can use this function key to correct an equation rather than reenter it.

If you choose to use the F2 key while you are in edit mode, pressing the Home key will move the cursor quickly to the beginning of the formula. Pressing the End key while you edit will take the cursor to the end of the formula.

Consider also using the /Copy command to copy formulas, such as those with relative references. You can then use the F2 key to edit and correct these formulas rather than entering them individually, thus saving time. Use this technique if you plan to use the model from Chapter 15, "Project Management," in your business.

The F4 (ABS) key will reduce the number of keystrokes needed to enter or edit a formula with absolute or mixed addresses. If, with the cursor on the cell address, you press the F4 key while you're doing one of these operations, the result will be

First time	$A$1
Second time	A$1
Third time	$A1
Fourth time	A1

Don't overlook the F4 key as you construct equations and formulas with mixed or absolute cell addresses.

Other function keys that we used frequently while working with the applications were F5 (GOTO), F7 (QUERY), F10 (GRAPH), and (because all of the models except the Line of Credit Tracker are in manual calculation mode) F9 (CALC).

The F5 key is convenient for moving rapidly around the spreadsheet. You just press F5, type the cell address or range name, and press Enter. Your cursor will be moved instantly to the desired spreadsheet location.

F7 and F10 are repeat-type keys. After you have set the parameters for a /Data Query and /Graph operation, respectively, you can repeat the previous operation by pressing the appropriate key instead of reentering the entire sequence of keystrokes.

These are only a few of the ways you can put the 1-2-3 special function keys to work for you. Keep these keys in mind whenever you use 1-2-3.

Macros

Because of the way the applications in this book were developed, use of the macros is not mandatory. They have been included only for your convenience.

The macros are fairly simple (the best kind, in our opinion). However, they are a definite spreadsheet aid that will make your 1-2-3 session more enjoyable and take advantage of all Release 2 features.

When you develop or re-create the macros, don't forget to use the tilde (~) after each line that requires one, so that your macro will execute properly. Conversely, remember that you'll need to use an apostrophe (') at the beginning of each line of your macro. Finally, don't forget to Name your macro using the /Range Name Labels Right command.

For an in-depth discussion of macros, refer to Que's *1-2-3 Macro Library* and *1-2-3 Command Language* .

The Macro Library Utility File

The macro utility file in table 1.1 was developed as another spreadsheet tool to help you create your models.

Study these macros carefully. They are listed in an order that you might use to create your models. Although these macros are optional, using some or all of them will make your 1-2-3 sessions more enjoyable and less tedious. Remember to use the macro utility file whenever you develop an application. Then /File Save your model under a different file name.

The \e macro deserves special attention. If you place the cursor two lines below the first dashed line in a range, and then type Alt-E, 1-2-3

Table 1.1
1-2-3 for Business Macro Library Utility File

Name	Macro	
\a	'/wcs{?}~~	
\b	'/wir~~	
\c	'/cAF5~.{?}~	-----
\d	'/cAF7~.{?}~	=====
\e	'/cAF7~.{UP 2}{END}{RIGHT}{DOWN 2}~~	
\f	'/rfd~~	
\g	'/rfc0~.{?}~	
\h	'/rfc2~.{?}~	
\i	'/rf,0~.{?}~	
\j	'/rf,2~.{?}~	
\k	'/rfp0~.{?}~	
\l	'/rfp2~.{?}~	
\m	'/ppagq~~	

will draw a double-underline beginning at your cursor's current cell location and ending with the column at the end of your dashed line. Accountants and financial analysts will find this macro especially useful for creating multiperiod actual and budget reports.

Conclusion

This chapter has taken a look at some of the ways to easily create and use the 1-2-3 for Business models, as well as ways to develop good spreadsheet habits. The chapter has presented a worksheet file that you can use whenever you create a 1-2-3 application, thereby reducing preparation time and lessening some of your more burdensome tasks. You should now be ready to incorporate these models into your business.

II

Managing Cash

2

Managing the Checkbook

Introduction

All businesses have one task in common: balancing and reconciling checking accounts. This repetitive task is an important one because cash must be managed and controlled accurately. The 1-2-3 Checkbook Manager can help you simplify and automate the checkbook-balancing process.

The 1-2-3 Checkbook Manager performs all the traditional checkbook-balancing activities that you're probably doing with paper and pencil—adding, subtracting, balancing, and so on.

But the Checkbook Manager, like many models in this book, is an *integrated* application. The information in your check register is used to summarize by account (in another section of the worksheet) your company's income and expense transactions. In addition, the Checkbook Manager separates tax-deductible and nondeductible expenses.

To manage your checkbook, the model uses six sections: the Check Register, Accounting Codes, the Accounting Summary, Outstanding Items, Reconciliation, and Macros \d and \i. An overall display of the model is shown in figure 2.1.

```
     A      B        C          D        E       F        G        H       I         J        K      L      M         N            O       P         Q
 1 =========================================================================================================================================================
 2
 3 CHECKBOOK MANAGER          Copyright (C) Que Corporation 1987
 4
 5 =========================================================================================================================================================
 6 CHECK REGISTER                                            ACCOUNTING CODES                              ACCOUNTING SUMMARY
 7 =========================================================================================================================================================
 8 Beginning Balance:       $3,479.13
 9                                                                                                                                Jan-87     Feb-87
10 Check or                                                                                               Payments      1      $1,884.00   $942.00
11 Deposit  Date                    Running                                                               Interest      2         0.00      17.00
12 Number  Written      Payee      Amount   Balance  Cleared  Account1  Amount1  Account2  Amount2                      0         0.00       0.00
13   101  01-Jan-87 Telephone     (79.90)  3,399.23    1       101     (79.90)             0.00                         0         0.00       0.00
14   102  02-Jan-87 Electric      (35.67)  3,363.56    1       101     (35.67)             0.00                         0         0.00       0.00
15   103  02-Jan-87 Gas           (12.65)  3,350.91    1       101     (12.65)             0.00                         0         0.00       0.00
16   104            Void                    3,350.91    1                0.00               0.00                         0         0.00       0.00
17     1  02-Jan-87 Deposit       942.00   4,292.91    1         1      942.00             0.00       Total Income             1,884.00     959.00
18   105  04-Jan-87 Office Leasing Inc. (855.00) 3,437.91  1    401    (855.00)            0.00
19   106  04-Jan-87 K&D Enterprises (344.00) 3,093.91  1       601    (344.00)            0.00                                   Jan-87     Feb-87
20   107  05-Jan-87 Acme Tool & Die (267.11) 2,826.80  1       601    (267.11)            0.00       Utilities     101       (128.22)      0.00
21   108  09-Jan-87 USA Computer   (75.68)  2,751.12    1       201     (75.68)            0.00       Comp Hdwe     201        (84.22)      0.00
22   109  12-Jan-87 Amalgamated Widget (27.00) 2,724.12 1      601     (27.00)            0.00       Comp Sftwe    301       (319.95)      0.00
23   110  14-Jan-87 Software Corp  (300.00) 2,424.12    0       301    (300.00)            0.00       Office Rent   401       (855.00)      0.00
24   112  15-Jan-87 Que Corp       (19.95)  2,404.17    1       301     (19.95)            0.00       Office Supp   501       (100.00)    (46.12)
25     2  16-Jan-87 Deposit        942.00   3,346.17    1         1     942.00             0.00       Inventory     601       (661.11)      0.00
26   113  19-Jan-87 Triangle Machine (23.00) 3,323.17  1       601     (23.00)            0.00                        0          0.00       0.00
27   114  25-Jan-87 Quill & Pen Inc. (100.00) 3,223.17 1       501    (100.00)            0.00                        0          0.00       0.00
28   115  27-Jan-87 General Micro   (8.54)  3,214.63    0       201      (8.54)            0.00                        0          0.00       0.00
29   116  01-Feb-87 Nat'l Off Supply (46.12) 3,168.51  1       501     (46.12)            0.00                        0          0.00       0.00
30     3  01-Feb-87 Deposit        942.00   4,110.51    0         1     942.00             0.00                        0          0.00       0.00
31     4  03-Feb-87 Account Interest 17.00  4,127.51    1         2      17.00             0.00                        0          0.00       0.00
32                                           4,127.51                                     0.00                        0          0.00       0.00
33                                           4,127.51                                     0.00                        0          0.00       0.00
34                                           4,127.51                                     0.00                        0          0.00       0.00
35                                           4,127.51                                     0.00       Total Expenses           (2,148.50)   (46.12)
36                                           4,127.51                                     0.00
37                                           4,127.51                                     0.00
38                                           4,127.51                                     0.00                                   Jan-87     Feb-87
39                                           4,127.51                                     0.00                        0          0.00       0.00
40                                           4,127.51                                     0.00                        0          0.00       0.00
41                                           4,127.51                                     0.00                        0          0.00       0.00
42                                           4,127.51                                     0.00                        0          0.00       0.00
43                                           4,127.51                                     0.00                        0          0.00       0.00
44                                           4,127.51                                     0.00                        0          0.00       0.00
45                                           4,127.51                                     0.00                        0          0.00       0.00
46                                           4,127.51                                     0.00                        0          0.00       0.00
47                                           4,127.51                                     0.00
48                                           4,127.51                                     0.00       Tax-Deductible Expenses     0.00       0.00
49                                           4,127.51                                     0.00
50                                           4,127.51                                     0.00       Net Income/(Loss)        ($264.50)   $912.88
51                                           4,127.51                                     0.00                             ========   ========
52                                           4,127.51                                     0.00
53                                           4,127.51                                     0.00
54                                           4,127.51                                     0.00
55 OUTSTANDING ITEMS                                    RECONCILIATION
56 =======================================================================================================================  Written   Account1  Account2
57 Cleared        Total Outstanding:   $633.46
58    0
59                                          Ending Checkbook Balance:        $4,127.51
60 Check or                                 Less: Checks and Deposits Outstanding  633.46
61 Deposit   Date                                                                --------
62 Number  Written      Payee      Amount   Adjusted Checkbook Balance       3,494.05
63   110  14-Jan-87 Software Corp  (300.00) Less: Adjustments to Bank Balance     0.00
64   115  27-Jan-87 General Micro    (8.54)                                   --------
65     3  01-Feb-87 Deposit        942.00   Bank Balance                    $3,494.05
66                                                                           ========
```

Fig. 2.1. The Checkbook Manager.

	R	S	T	U	V	W	X	Y	Z	AA	AB
	Mar-87	Apr-87	May-87	Jun-87	Jul-87	Aug-87	Sep-87	Oct-87	Nov-87	Dec-87	Total
	$0.00	$0.00	$0.00	$0.00	$0.00	$0.00	$0.00	$0.00	$0.00	$0.00	$2,826.00
	0.00	0.00	0.00	0.00	0.00	0.00	0.00	0.00	0.00	0.00	17.00
	0.00	0.00	0.00	0.00	0.00	0.00	0.00	0.00	0.00	0.00	0.00
	0.00	0.00	0.00	0.00	0.00	0.00	0.00	0.00	0.00	0.00	0.00
	0.00	0.00	0.00	0.00	0.00	0.00	0.00	0.00	0.00	0.00	0.00
	0.00	0.00	0.00	0.00	0.00	0.00	0.00	0.00	0.00	0.00	0.00
	0.00	0.00	0.00	0.00	0.00	0.00	0.00	0.00	0.00	0.00	2,843.00
	Mar-87	Apr-87	May-87	Jun-87	Jul-87	Aug-87	Sep-87	Oct-87	Nov-87	Dec-87	Total
	0.00	0.00	0.00	0.00	0.00	0.00	0.00	0.00	0.00	0.00	(128.22)
	0.00	0.00	0.00	0.00	0.00	0.00	0.00	0.00	0.00	0.00	(84.22)
	0.00	0.00	0.00	0.00	0.00	0.00	0.00	0.00	0.00	0.00	(319.95)
	0.00	0.00	0.00	0.00	0.00	0.00	0.00	0.00	0.00	0.00	(855.00)
	0.00	0.00	0.00	0.00	0.00	0.00	0.00	0.00	0.00	0.00	(146.12)
	0.00	0.00	0.00	0.00	0.00	0.00	0.00	0.00	0.00	0.00	(661.11)
	0.00	0.00	0.00	0.00	0.00	0.00	0.00	0.00	0.00	0.00	0.00
	0.00	0.00	0.00	0.00	0.00	0.00	0.00	0.00	0.00	0.00	0.00
	0.00	0.00	0.00	0.00	0.00	0.00	0.00	0.00	0.00	0.00	0.00
	0.00	0.00	0.00	0.00	0.00	0.00	0.00	0.00	0.00	0.00	0.00
	0.00	0.00	0.00	0.00	0.00	0.00	0.00	0.00	0.00	0.00	0.00
	0.00	0.00	0.00	0.00	0.00	0.00	0.00	0.00	0.00	0.00	0.00
	0.00	0.00	0.00	0.00	0.00	0.00	0.00	0.00	0.00	0.00	(2,194.62)
	Mar-87	Apr-87	May-87	Jun-87	Jul-87	Aug-87	Sep-87	Oct-87	Nov-87	Dec-87	Total
	0.00	0.00	0.00	0.00	0.00	0.00	0.00	0.00	0.00	0.00	0.00
	0.00	0.00	0.00	0.00	0.00	0.00	0.00	0.00	0.00	0.00	0.00
	0.00	0.00	0.00	0.00	0.00	0.00	0.00	0.00	0.00	0.00	0.00
	0.00	0.00	0.00	0.00	0.00	0.00	0.00	0.00	0.00	0.00	0.00
	0.00	0.00	0.00	0.00	0.00	0.00	0.00	0.00	0.00	0.00	0.00
	0.00	0.00	0.00	0.00	0.00	0.00	0.00	0.00	0.00	0.00	0.00
	0.00	0.00	0.00	0.00	0.00	0.00	0.00	0.00	0.00	0.00	0.00
	0.00	0.00	0.00	0.00	0.00	0.00	0.00	0.00	0.00	0.00	0.00
	$0.00	$0.00	$0.00	$0.00	$0.00	$0.00	$0.00	$0.00	$0.00	$0.00	$648.38

	AE/AF	AH/AI/AJ
\I	{PANELOFF}{WINDOWSOFF}~	Control Panel & Windows Off
	{GOTO}BOTTOM~	Go to cell named Bottom
	/rndBOTTOM~	Delete range name Bottom
	{DOWN}~	Move cursor down one cell
	/wir~~	Insert row
	/c{ESC}{UP}~~	Copy column E formula
	/rncBOTTOM~	Name cell Bottom
	{PANELON}{WINDOWSON}~	Control Panel & Windows On
\D	{GOTO}INCOME_TABLE~	Go to the first table
	{CALC}{INDICATE WAIT}	Calculate/Mode = WAIT
	{PANELOFF}{WINDOWSOFF}	Control Panel & Windows Off
	/dtr/dt2	Data table Reset/Start Table calc
	INCOME_TABLE~	Assign Table Range
	IN1_1~IN_2~	Assign Input Cells
	/dtr/dt2	Data table Reset/Start Table calc
	EXPENSE_TABLE~	Assign Table Range
	IN1_1~IN_2~	Assign Input Cells
	/dtr/dt2	Data table Reset/Start Table calc
	TAXDDUCT_TABLE~	Assign Table Range
	IN1_2~IN_2~	Assign Input Cells
	{INDICATE}	Reset Mode Indicator
	{PANELON}{WINDOWSON}	Control Panel & Windows On

Creating the Model

Before you start to build the model, consider the number of monthly transactions and accounts your business has. The example shown in figure 2.1 has seven income, fourteen expense, and eight tax-deductible expense accounts. Your firm may have more accounts than the model, or you may want to practice using more accounts. Adapt the model to meet your needs.

You can use your company's account codes or create your own chart of accounts for the Accounting Summary. If your accountant or another financial professional is doing this task, you may not need the Accounting Summary. You can use the Checkbook Manager as a stand-alone model. Whatever your situation, by planning before you begin the session you'll increase the model's benefit and eliminate the need for later modifications.

Now you are ready to begin creating the Checkbook Manager model.

Setting Column Widths

Begin with a blank 1-2-3 worksheet. Change the column widths to match these specifications:

Column	Width
A	8
B	10
C	20
D, E, F, G, H, I, J	11
K	5
L, M	11
N	12
O through AG	11
AH	16

Entering the Model

Next, enter column headings, row titles, and other labels. You can use table 2.1 as a guide for entering labels and borders. To speed up entry of the separator lines, use the \= and \- trick.

Table 2.1
Row Titles and Column Headings

Enter into cell:	Original label:	Copy to:
	Model Headings	
A1:	\=	B1..AB1 A5..AB5, A7..AB7, A56..M56
A3:	'CHECKBOOK MANAGER	
	Check Register	
A6:	'CHECK REGISTER	
A8:	'Beginning Balance:	
A10:	^Check or	A60
A11:	^Deposit	A61
A12:	'Number	A62
B11:	' Date	B61
B12:	' Written	B62
C12:	^Payee	C62
D12:	' Amount	D62
E11:	'Running	
E12:	'Balance	
	Accounting Codes	
F12:	'Cleared	
G12:	^Account1	
G6:	'ACCOUNTING CODES	
H12:	^Amount1	
I12:	^Account2	
J12:	^Amount2	
	Outstanding Items	
A55:	'OUTSTANDING ITEMS	
A57:	'Cleared	
C57:	'Total Outstanding:	

Enter into cell:	Original label:	Copy to:

Reconciliation

G55:	'RECONCILIATION	
G59:	'Ending Checkbook Balance:	
G60:	'Less: Checks and Deposits Outstanding	
L61:	' --------	L64, P17..AB17, P35..AB35,P47..AB47, P49..AB49
G62:	'Adjusted Checkbook Balance	
G63:	'Less: Adjustments to Bank Balance	
G65:	'Bank Balance	
L66:	' ========	P51..AB51

Accounting Summary

N6:	'ACCOUNTING SUMMARY	
N18:	'Total Income	
N36:	'Total Expenses	
N48:	'Tax-Deductible Expenses	
N50:	'Net Income/(Loss)	
AB9:	' Total	AB20, AB38

Macros

AD1:	'\l
AE1:	'{PANELOFF}{WINDOWSOFF}~
AH1:	'Control Panel & Windows Off
AE2:	'{GOTO}BOTTOM~
AH2:	'Go to cell named Bottom
AE3:	'/rndBOTTOM~
AH3:	'Delete range name Bottom
AE4:	'{DOWN}~
AH4:	'Move cursor down one cell
AE5:	'/wir~~
AH5:	'Insert row
AE6:	'/c{ESC}{UP}~~
AH6:	'Copy column E formula
AE7:	'/rncBOTTOM~
AH7:	'Name cell Bottom

Enter into cell:	Original label:	Copy to:
AE8:	'{PANELON}{WINDOWSON}~	
AH8:	'Control Panel & Windows On	
AD10:	'\D	
AE10:	'{GOTO}INCOME_TABLE~	
AH10:	'Go to the first table	
AE11:	'{CALC}{INDICATE WAIT}	
AH11:	'Calculate/Mode = WAIT	
AE12:	'{PANELOFF}{WINDOWSOFF}	
AH12:	'Control Panel & Windows Off	
AE13:	'/dtr/dt2	
AH13:	'Data table Reset/Start Table calc	
AE14:	'INCOME_TABLE~	
AH14:	'Assign Table Range	
AE15:	'IN1_1~IN_2~	
AH15:	'Assign Input Cells	
AE16:	'/dtr/dt2	
AH16:	'Data table Reset/Start Table calc	
AE17:	'EXPENSE_TABLE~	
AH17:	'Assign Table Range	
AE18:	'IN1_1~IN_2~	
AH18:	'Assign Input Cells	
AE19:	'/dtr/dt2	
AH19:	'Data table Reset/Start Table calc	
AE20:	'TAXDDUCT_TABLE~	
AH20:	'Assign Table Range	
AE21:	'IN1_2~IN_2~	
AH21:	'Assign Input Cells	
AE22:	'{INDICATE}	
AH22:	'Reset Mode Indicator	
AE23:	'{PANELON}{WINDOWSON}	
AH23:	'Control Panel & Windows On	

Specifying Cell Formats

Format the rows, columns, and individual cells according to table 2.2, but remember that these are only guidelines. You'll want to tailor the model to your specific needs. For example, you may prefer to format the @DSUM functions with the Text or other format rather than with Hidden format.

Table 2.2
Cell Formats

Check Register

Format	Cell or Range
/rfc2	C8
/rfd1	Column B
/rf,2	Column D
/rf,2	Column E

Outstanding Items

/rfc2	D57

Reconciliation

/rfc2	L59
/rf,2	L60
/rf,2	L62
/rf,2	L63
/rfc2	L65

Accounting Codes

/rf,2	Column H
/rf,2	Column J

Accounting Summary

/rfh	O9
/rfd3	P9..AA9
/rfc2	P10..AB10
/rf,2	P11..AB16
/rf,2	P18..AB18
/rfh	O20
/rfd3	P20..AA20
/rf,2	P21..AB34
/rf,2	P36..AB36
/rfh	O38
/rfd3	P38..AA38
/rf,2	P39..AB46
/rf,2	P48..AB48
/rfc2	P50..AB50
/rfh	N57

Naming Ranges

Range names are an integral part of the model because several formulas, which you will include in the model later, rely on them. Remember that a macro name is really nothing more than a range name, and that macros and range names are created in the same way. Macros, however, have one different naming convention: their names are limited to two characters, and the first character must be a backslash (\). From the list in table 2.3, enter the range names (with the macro names included) for this model.

Table 2.3
Range Names

Name	Cell or Range
BOTTOM	E54
EXPENSE_TABLE	O20..AA34
IN1_1	O57
IN1_2	P57
IN_2	N58
INCOME_TABLE	O9..AA16
REGISTER	A12..J55
TAXDDUCT_TABLE	O38..AA46
\D	AE10
\I	AE1

Entering Formulas

Now that you've entered the cell widths, column headings, row titles, cell formats, and range names, the next step is to enter the model's formulas. Table 2.4 lists all the formulas used in the Checkbook Manager model. If you have included extra unassigned accounts, be sure to enter a zero in column O so that the @DSUM equation will calculate properly.

Compared to other models in this book, the Checkbook Manager uses relatively few equations. But be sure to use the /Copy command for column E (the Running Balance column) in the Check Register, and for rows 18, 36, 48, and 50 of the Accounting Summary.

Table 2.4
Formulas and Functions

Enter into cell:	Original formula:	Copy to:
	Check Register	
E13:	+$C$8+D13	
E14:	+D14+E13	E15..E54
	Accounting Codes	
H13:	+D13-J13	H14..H54
	Outstanding Items	
A58:	+F13=0	
D57:	@DSUM(A12..F55,3,A57..A58)	
	Reconciliation	
L59:	+BOTTOM	
L60:	+$D$57	
L62:	+L59-L60	L65
	Accounting Summary	
N57:	@MONTH(B13)=@MONTH($IN_2)	
O9:	@DSUM($REGISTER,7,N56..O57)	
P9:	@DATE(87,1,1)	P20, P38
Q9:	+P9+31	R9..AA9, Q20..AA20, Q38..AA38
P18:	@SUM(P10..P17)	Q18..AB18
AB10:	@SUM(P10..AA10)	AB11..AB16, AB21..AB34, AB39..AB46
O20:	@DSUM($REGISTER,7,N56..O57)	
P36:	@SUM(P21..P34)	Q36..AB36
O38:	@DSUM($REGISTER,9,N56..P57)	
P48:	@SUM(P39..P46)	Q48..AB48
P50:	+P18+P36+P48	Q50..AB50

Now that you have created the model, you are ready to examine the operations of the Checkbook Manager.

Understanding the Model

In this section, you examine the model to understand each of the modules and how they interact with one another. Again, the modules are the Check Register, Accounting Codes, the Accounting Summary, Outstanding Items, Reconciliation, and Macros \i and \d.

The Check Register

The first Checkbook Manager module, the Check Register, is located at cells A5 through F54. Figure 2.2 shows a section of this module.

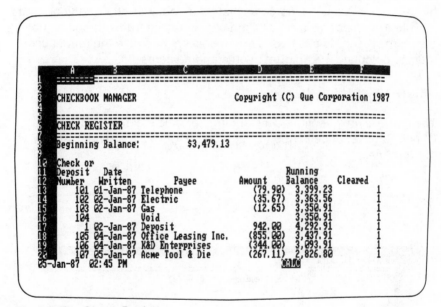

Fig. 2.2. The Check Register.

The Check Register's first five columns are similar to the register in your checkbook. Column A is used to record your check number; column B, the date your check was written. Make a mental note now that you MUST use the 1-2-3 @DATE function

   @DATE(YY,MM,DD)

when entering the date. For example, you would enter April 1, 1987, as @DATE(87,4,1). Column C shows you who your check was written to, column D shows the amount of the check, and column E provides your current checking account balance. To compute the current balance, the model uses the following formula in cell E13:

E13: +$C$8+D13

This formula is the sum of your first transaction and your beginning checkbook balance. The next equation, in cell E14, is

E14: +D14+E13

This formula adds the transaction in cell D14 to the current balance in cell E13 to arrive at a new total. This logic is repeated down column E.

Column F is used to indicate whether a transaction has been processed by your bank. A one (1) indicates that your check or other debit or credit has cleared the bank; a zero (0) indicates that the transaction has not been processed. These codes are necessary because the model uses them to calculate the amount of outstanding items.

Outstanding Items

The model's next section, Outstanding Items, is located below the Check Register at cells A55 through D62. Figure 2.3 provides a view of this module.

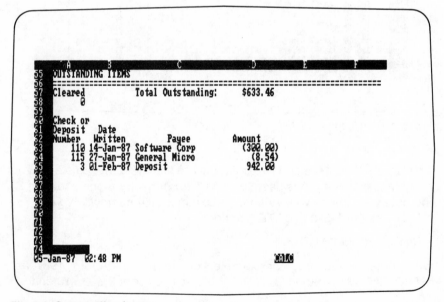

Fig. 2.3. Outstanding Items.

Outstanding Items identifies and summarizes the outstanding checks, deposits, and other transactions in transit that cause your checkbook and bank statement to disagree. To perform these tasks, Outstanding Items uses several of 1-2-3's Database functions.

For example, cells A57 and A58 form a criterion range, in which the formula in A58 is

   A58: +F13=0

With this formula and the /Data Query command (discussed later in this section), 1-2-3 will be able to retrieve every transaction that has not cleared the bank. These transactions, which are indicated by a zero (0) in column F, will be totaled in cell D57 with the formula

   D57: @DSUM(A12..F55,3,A57..A58)

In this formula, the range A12 through F55 is the database to be scanned by 1-2-3, column D is the offset column, and A57 and A58 are the search criteria.

You can obtain a list of outstanding items by issuing a 1-2-3 /Data Query command. The list of transactions will begin in cell A63. (This operation is discussed in the "Using the Model" section of this chapter.) After listing any outstanding items, the model will reconcile your checkbook and bank statement.

As stated, the /Data Query command will Extract any outstanding checks to an "output" range, where you can verify them. In fact, after the appropriate ranges are set up, outstanding checks can be Extracted by pressing F7 (Query).

Initially, however, the ranges must be set up correctly. To do so, follow these steps:

1. Press /Data Query Input.

2. Type A12..F55 and then press Enter.

3. Press Criterion.

4. Type A57..A58 and then press Enter.

5. Press Output.

6. Type A62..D62 and then press Enter.

7. Press Extract Quit.

At any time, you can extract all outstanding checks by pressing F7 (Query).

Reconciliation

The model's Reconciliation section begins at cell G55 and continues to cell L66 (see fig. 2.4).

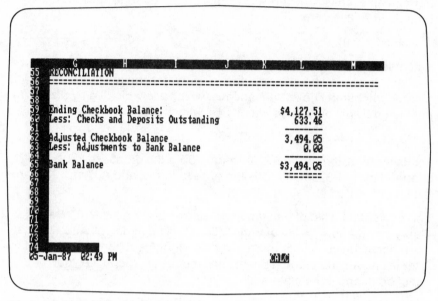

Fig. 2.4. Reconciliation.

Reconciliation, like your bank statement's reconciling worksheet, includes outstanding checks, deposits-in-transit, and adjustments to your bank balance. The ending checkbook balance in cell L59 references your running balance:

L59: +E54

Similarly, the checks and deposits outstanding in cell L60 reference the previous module's outstanding item balance:

L60: +$D$57

Your adjusted checkbook balance will be the difference between these two amounts. The formula in cell L62, therefore, is

L62: +L59-L60

Cell 63 has been included to accommodate bank errors. The bank balance in cell L65 is the difference between your adjusted checkbook balance and any bank errors:

L65: +L62-L63

In summary, 1-2-3 and the Checkbook Manager have done all your routine checking-account tasks quickly and easily.

Accounting Codes

The first section of the income and expense summary, Accounting Codes, begins at cell G5 and continues, in this example, to J31 (see figs. 2.1 and 2.5). In this section, you code your checking account transactions so that income and expenses (tax deductible and nondeductible) can be summarized by account for your review and analysis in the Accounting Summary.

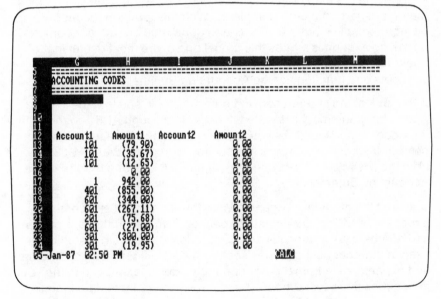

Fig. 2.5. Accounting Codes.

Consider cell H13 (refer to fig. 2.1). This cell's value is entered automatically by the formula

H13: +D13-J13

The formula ensures that unless you intervene, the full amount of the check in cell D13 will be copied to cell H13. This formula structure is similar for all cells in column H of this module.

However, you may have checks which require that part of the amount be coded to deductible and part to nondeductible expense. The tax-deductible portion of the payment is entered in cell J20; the nondeductible portion will be calculated by the formula in cell H20

H20: +D20-J20

D20 is the total payment, J20 is the tax-deductible amount, and H20 is the nondeductible portion. In this manner, your payment amounts are coded properly for use by the Accounting Summary.

Accounting Summary

Up to this point, the Checkbook Manager is similar to other electronic spreadsheet checkbook models. However, the ability to account for your business's expenditures on a monthly basis sets the Checkbook Manager apart from other templates. With this function the model is a bit more complex, but the information generated about your company's operating expenses makes this model one of the most useful in the book. The following discussion should help you understand the concepts and functions of the Accounting Summary.

If you look at the spreadsheet in figure 2.1, you'll see that the Accounting Summary is located at cells N1 through AB51, to the right of the Accounting Codes. As you can see, the module is larger than your computer screen. To access this section, you press the {TAB} key twice from the {HOME} cell location (A1). Figure 2.6 shows a portion of the Accounting Summary.

Note that the module is organized into three categories: Income, Expenses, and Tax-Deductible Expenses. The account descriptions and numbers (in columns N and O, respectively) should match those used in the Accounting Codes section. 1-2-3 will retrieve your income and expense data from the Accounting Codes section, and using your transaction account numbers, build three two-variable data tables, which comprise the Accounting Summary. The account numbers in column O are the *first* of these variables. The *second* variable will be based on the dates in rows 9, 20, and 38, starting in column P. The formula which utilizes the two variables is located at cells O9, O20, and O38.

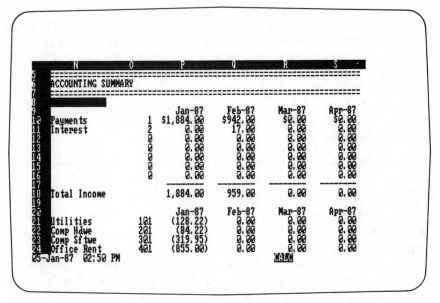

Fig. 2.6. The Accounting Summary.

The formula in cell O9:

   O9: @DSUM($REGISTER,7,N56..O57)

for example, computes monthly totals for your income accounts. The formula instructs 1-2-3 to scan your Check Register ($REGISTER, located in cells A12..J55), and selects those items in column H that meet the criterion in cells N56 through O57. Note that Release 2's Hidden format has been used in 09, 020, and 038 because the formula doesn't need to be shown.

Cell N57 of the criterion range contains the formula

   N57: @MONTH(B13)=@MONTH($IN_2)

This formula will select from the database only those items for which the month portion of the date in column B is equal to the month portion of the date in cell N58, which has the range name of IN_2.

Cell O56 and range name IN1_1 (cell O57) form the other part of the criterion range. The model selects only those records whose entries in column G match cell O56 and range IN1_1.

You'll notice that in the example in figure 2.1, ranges IN1_1 and IN_2 are blank. These ranges will be used as the input cells for the **/D**ata **T**able **2** command. When you invoke the **/D**ata **T**able command, each account number in column O will be placed into range IN1_1 and each date into range IN_2. In this manner, 1-2-3 will select from the designated criteria only those Check Register transactions that are income items for the month in which they occurred. To have 1-2-3 post your transactions, all you have to do is set the appropriate **/D**ata **T**able ranges and use the **/D**ata **T**able **2** command.

For example, if you were to enter all the data ranges from figure 2.1 and activate the data table, the first amount in the Account1 column is substituted into range IN1_1, and the date function @DATE(87,1,1) is substituted into range IN_2.

The combination of account number and date will cause the criterion range to select two records for processing: Deposits 1 and 2, both coded to Account1 and both entered during January. The total of these two deposits ($1,884.00) is entered in cell P10. The table will continue to process until all combinations of account numbers and dates are considered by the model. At the end of the process, the @DSUM function in cell O9 will recalculate.

NOTE: In this **/D**ata **T**able **2** process, the column of variables (in this case, the Account numbers) is denoted as variables for input cell 1. The variables in column B (Dates, in this case) are denoted as variables for input cell 2.

Your annual account totals are calculated by the formula in AB10:

   AB10: @SUM(P10..AA10)

In a similar fashion, monthly income totals are computed by the formula:

   P18: @SUM(P10..P17)

Although this particular formula computes the totals for January, formulas for other months contain the same logic.

The second and third data tables (Expenses and Tax-Deductible Expenses, respectively) use similar table-building functions. The only difference is the @DSUM equation used in the Tax-Deductible table. This formula is

   O38: @DSUM($REGISTER,9,N56..P57)

The range REGISTER is the same as in the earlier example, but the offset column is now column J, the amount of your tax-deductible expense. Furthermore, because you want 1-2-3 to select your tax-deductible accounts, Account2, N56..P57, is included in the criterion range.

Your business's monthly income or loss is determined by subtracting the two expense totals from your total income for the month. For January, this formula is

    P50: +P18+P36+P48

in which P18 represents your total income, P36 your total expenses, and P48 your total tax-deductible expenses.

The \d Macro

The \d macro is located at cells AD10 through AJ23, although the actual macro starts at cell AE10. Figure 2.7 shows the \d macro.

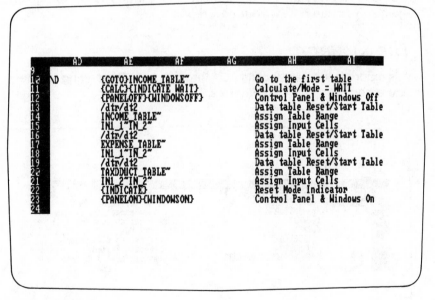

Fig. 2.7. \d Macro.

The \d macro reduces the tedium of building the Accounting Summary's data tables. Calculating the three Accounting Summary data tables ordinarily takes several keystrokes and a great deal of time, depending, of course, on the number of transactions in your Check Register. If you wish to calculate all three data tables, simply invoke the macro by pressing Alt-D. Then you can sit back and relax. The macro will make all the proper assignments for you.

The \d macro uses range names. For instance, the entire Check Register (cells A7 through J55) has the name REGISTER. Each table has a name (INCOME_TABLE, EXPENSE_TABLE, and TAXDDUCT_TABLE) as do the Input Cells (IN1_1, IN1_2, IN_2).

When you invoke the macro, the cell pointer moves to the first table. Then the mode indicator is changed from READY to WAIT, because the macro will turn off the control panel and windows in the next step. 1-2-3 will now assign table ranges and input cells, and calculate each data table in sequential order.

After the macro has calculated all three tables, the mode indicator returns to READY, and the control panel and windows are turned on again so you can review your new report.

The \i Macro

This macro is located at cells AD1 through AJ8. The coding for the macro begins in cell AE1. Figure 2.8 shows macro \i.

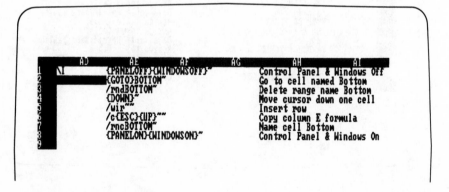

Fig. 2.8. \i Macro.

Although using the \i macro is optional, think of the macro as your insurance policy against inserting a row in the wrong place. The first time you use \i, the macro inserts a row below row 54. The location at which the row is inserted is important, because inserting rows above row 54 will damage the model.

To use \i, simultaneously press Alt-I. The macro first turns off the control panel and windows. Next, the cursor moves to the range name BOTTOM. (If this is the first time you've used the macro, BOTTOM will be located at cell D54.) The macro deletes the range BOTTOM, moves the cursor down one cell, inserts a new row at this location, and copies the column D formula from the cell immediately above the inserted row. The new cell location is renamed BOTTOM, in case you need the macro again. The macro then reactivates the control panel and windows.

The \i macro can save time and minimize frustration if you need to add rows later.

Using the Model

If you understand the way in which the Checkbook Manager operates, you should have no trouble using the model. To use the Checkbook Manager, you need your most recent bank statement, cancelled checks, and checkbook.

If you are using the model for the first time, enter your reconciled checkbook balance in cell C8. Then enter your bank deposit and other checking account information in the Check Register. If your payment has a tax-deductible portion, enter your check data in columns A through D, and in column J. (See table 2.5 for a summary of the data the model requires.)

You may want to consider making the Checkbook Manager part of your bill-paying process by entering your payment data as you write your checks.

You'll need your bank statement at this point. Enter any bank service charges or interest earned into the model. Be sure to code your transactions by placing in column F a 1 (one) for transactions that have cleared the bank or a 0 (zero) for those that have not. After you have coded your checks, press F7 (QUERY) and then F9 (CALC). Your running balance, outstanding items, and reconciliation will be computed for you.

Table 2.5
Data Entry

Description	Location
Check Register	
Beginning Balance	C8
Check Number or	Column A
Deposit Number	
Date Written	Column B
Payee	Column C
Amount	Column D
Cleared	Column E
Reconciliation	
Adjustments to Bank Balance	L63
Accounting Codes	
Account1	Column G
Account2	Column I
Amount2	Column J

If you notice a difference between the amount of the bank balance in the model and that in your bank statement, make sure that you have properly entered all transactions affecting the account. If you are confident that you have entered all the information, make an appointment to see your friendly banker and dazzle him or her with a printout of your 1-2-3 Checkbook Manager.

If you have decided to use the Accounting Summary, you already have supplied the model with the data it requires to generate this report. Using the Accounting Summary is a five-step process that relies on 1-2-3's **/D**ata **T**able **2** command.

The first step is to press F9 (CALC) to ensure that all the formulas needed for the data tables contain correct values. Imagine what the results would be if you were to begin computing with invalid values.

To compute your income for the month, select **/D**ata **T**able **2**. The table range in the example (refer to fig. 2.1) will be O9..AA16, or its range name, INCOME_TABLE. Input 1 will be cell O57 and Input 2 will be cell N58. After you input this data, the data table will be built. Then the

@DSUM function will calculate your account totals automatically. During this process, you may want to get a cup of coffee or return a telephone call. 1-2-3 needs a few minutes to perform this routine.

To construct the expense table, you issue the **/D**ata **T**able **R**eset command, followed by the **/D**ata **T**able **2** command. This time, the table range will be O20..AA34 or EXPENSE_TABLE, the expense accounting range. Input 1 will be cell O57, Input 2 will be N58.

For your tax-deductible expenses, invoke the **/D**ata **T**able **R**eset command and then **/D**ata **T**able **2**. As you probably have guessed, the Table range will be O38..AA47 or TAXDEDUCT_TABLE. Input 1 will be cell P57, and Input 2 will be cell N58. These Data Table commands will retrieve, add, and correctly enter all your income and expense transactions in the month in which they occurred.

The final step is to press F9 (CALC) to calculate your monthly income and expense totals. Now you should have a complete summary of all your financial transactions for the month.

Remember that you can use the \d macro instead of going through this five-step process.

Modifying the Model

Modifying the model is not difficult if you have planned your Checkbook Manager in advance. If you need more space in the Check Register, use the \i macro or the **/W**orksheet **I**nsert **R**ow command and then adjust the @DSUM equations accordingly. Consider also using **/W**orksheet **T**itles **H**orizontal at row 12. You'll be able to use the column headings as a reference when you enter your checking account transactions throughout the year.

You may want to include your account codes and descriptions in an area of your worksheet—below or to the right of the Accounting Summary, for example. Then, if you forget an account number, you will have a list to refer to. One cell of this range can be named CHART, for example, so that you can move quickly to this area by using F5 (GOTO). Be sure to experiment with the application to tailor the model to your business's particular needs.

Conclusion

The Checkbook Manager is an application of 1-2-3 that you can apply immediately to a common (and necessary) financial task—that of balancing and reconciling your company's checking account. Used with the Accounting Summary, this model provides you with a small but useful and inexpensive accounting system. Implementing the Checkbook Manager in your reporting cycle will help you to gain insight into the income and expenses of your firm.

A1: [W8] \=
B1: [W10] \=
C1: [W20] \=
D1: [W11] \=
E1: [W11] \=
F1: [W11] \=
G1: [W11] \=
H1: [W11] \=
I1: [W11] \=
J1: [W11] \=
K1: [W5] \=
L1: [W11] \=
M1: [W11] \=
N1: [W12] \=
O1: [W11] \=
P1: [W11] \=
Q1: [W11] \=
R1: [W11] \=
S1: [W11] \=
T1: [W11] \=
U1: [W11] \=
V1: [W11] \=
W1: [W11] \=
X1: [W11] \=
Y1: [W11] \=
Z1: [W11] \=
AA1: [W11] \=
AB1: [W11] \=
AD1: [W11] '\I
AE1: [W11] '{PANELOFF}{WINDOWSOFF}~
AH1: [W16] 'Control Panel & Windows Off
AE2: [W11] '{GOTO}BOTTOM~
AH2: [W16] 'Go to cell named Bottom
A3: [W8] 'CHECKBOOK MANAGER
D3: [W11] 'Copyright (C) Que Corporation 1987
AE3: [W11] '/rndBOTTOM~
AH3: [W16] 'Delete range name Bottom
AE4: [W11] '{DOWN}~
AH4: [W16] 'Move cursor down one cell
A5: [W8] \=
B5: [W10] \=
C5: [W20] \=
D5: [W11] \=
E5: [W11] \=
F5: [W11] \=
G5: [W11] \=
H5: [W11] \=
I5: [W11] \=
J5: [W11] \=
K5: [W5] \=
L5: [W11] \=
M5: [W11] \=
N5: [W12] \=

O5: [W11] \=
P5: [W11] \=
Q5: [W11] \=
R5: [W11] \=
S5: [W11] \=
T5: [W11] \=
U5: [W11] \=
V5: [W11] \=
W5: [W11] \=
X5: [W11] \=
Y5: [W11] \=
Z5: [W11] \=
AA5: [W11] \=
AB5: [W11] \=
AE5: [W11] '/wir~~
AH5: [W16] 'Insert row
A6: [W8] 'CHECK REGISTER
G6: [W11] 'ACCOUNTING CODES
N6: [W12] 'ACCOUNTING SUMMARY
AE6: [W11] '/c{ESC}{UP}~~
AH6: [W16] 'Copy column E formula
A7: [W8] \=
B7: [W10] \=
C7: [W20] \=
D7: [W11] \=
E7: [W11] \=
F7: [W11] \=
G7: [W11] \=
H7: [W11] \=
I7: [W11] \=
J7: [W11] \=
K7: [W5] \=
L7: [W11] \=
M7: [W11] \=
N7: [W12] \=
O7: [W11] \=
P7: [W11] \=
Q7: [W11] \=
R7: [W11] \=
S7: [W11] \=
T7: [W11] \=
U7: [W11] \=
V7: [W11] \=
W7: [W11] \=
X7: [W11] \=
Y7: [W11] \=
Z7: [W11] \=
AA7: [W11] \=
AB7: [W11] \=
AE7: [W11] '/rncBOTTOM~
AH7: [W16] 'Name cell Bottom
A8: [W8] 'Beginning Balance:
C8: (C2) [W20] 3479.13

AE8: [W11] '{PANELON}{WINDOWSON}~
AH8: [W16] 'Control Panel & Windows On
O9: (H) [W11] @DSUM($REGISTER,7,N56..O57)
P9: (D3) [W11] @DATE(87,1,1)
Q9: (D3) [W11] +P9+31
R9: (D3) [W11] +Q9+31
S9: (D3) [W11] +R9+31
T9: (D3) [W11] +S9+31
U9: (D3) [W11] +T9+31
V9: (D3) [W11] +U9+31
W9: (D3) [W11] +V9+31
X9: (D3) [W11] +W9+31
Y9: (D3) [W11] +X9+31
Z9: (D3) [W11] +Y9+31
AA9: (D3) [W11] +Z9+31
AB9: [W11] ' Total
A10: [W8] ^Check or
N10: [W12] 'Payments
O10: [W11] 1
P10: (C2) [W11] 1884
Q10: (C2) [W11] 942
R10: (C2) [W11] 0
S10: (C2) [W11] 0
T10: (C2) [W11] 0
U10: (C2) [W11] 0
V10: (C2) [W11] 0
W10: (C2) [W11] 0
X10: (C2) [W11] 0
Y10: (C2) [W11] 0
Z10: (C2) [W11] 0
AA10: (C2) [W11] 0
AB10: (C2) [W11] @SUM(P10..AA10)
AD10: [W11] '\D
AE10: [W11] '{GOTO}INCOME_TABLE~
AH10: [W16] 'Go to the first table
A11: [W8] ^Deposit
B11: [W10] ' Date
E11: [W11] 'Running
N11: [W12] 'Interest
O11: [W11] 2
P11: (,2) [W11] 0
Q11: (,2) [W11] 17
R11: (,2) [W11] 0
S11: (,2) [W11] 0
T11: (,2) [W11] 0
U11: (,2) [W11] 0
V11: (,2) [W11] 0
W11: (,2) [W11] 0
X11: (,2) [W11] 0
Y11: (,2) [W11] 0
Z11: (,2) [W11] 0
AA11: (,2) [W11] 0
AB11: (,2) [W11] @SUM(P11..AA11)

AE11: [W11] '{CALC}{INDICATE WAIT}
AH11: [W16] 'Calculate/Mode = WAIT
A12: [W8] 'Number
B12: [W10] ' Written
C12: [W20] ^Payee
D12: [W11] ' Amount
E12: [W11] 'Balance
F12: [W11] 'Cleared
G12: [W11] ^Account1
H12: [W11] ^Amount1
I12: [W11] ^Account2
J12: [W11] ^Amount2
O12: [W11] 0
P12: (,2) [W11] 0
Q12: (,2) [W11] 0
R12: (,2) [W11] 0
S12: (,2) [W11] 0
T12: (,2) [W11] 0
U12: (,2) [W11] 0
V12: (,2) [W11] 0
W12: (,2) [W11] 0
X12: (,2) [W11] 0
Y12: (,2) [W11] 0
Z12: (,2) [W11] 0
AA12: (,2) [W11] 0
AB12: (,2) [W11] @SUM(P12..AA12)
AE12: [W11] '{PANELOFF}{WINDOWSOFF}
AH12: [W16] 'Control Panel & Windows Off
A13: [W8] 101
B13: (D1) [W10] @DATE(87,1,1)
C13: [W20] 'Telephone
D13: (,2) [W11] −79.9
E13: (,2) [W11] +$C$8+D13
F13: [W11] 1
G13: [W11] 101
H13: (,2) [W11] +D13−J13
J13: (,2) [W11] 0
O13: [W11] 0
P13: (,2) [W11] 0
Q13: (,2) [W11] 0
R13: (,2) [W11] 0
S13: (,2) [W11] 0
T13: (,2) [W11] 0
U13: (,2) [W11] 0
V13: (,2) [W11] 0
W13: (,2) [W11] 0
X13: (,2) [W11] 0
Y13: (,2) [W11] 0
Z13: (,2) [W11] 0
AA13: (,2) [W11] 0
AB13: (,2) [W11] @SUM(P13..AA13)
AE13: [W11] '/dtr/dt2
AH13: [W16] 'Data table Reset/Start Table calc

A14: [W8] 102
B14: (D1) [W10] @DATE(87,1,2)
C14: [W20] 'Electric
D14: (,2) [W11] -35.67
E14: (,2) [W11] +D14+E13
F14: [W11] 1
G14: [W11] 101
H14: (,2) [W11] +D14-J14
J14: (,2) [W11] 0
O14: [W11] 0
P14: (,2) [W11] 0
Q14: (,2) [W11] 0
R14: (,2) [W11] 0
S14: (,2) [W11] 0
T14: (,2) [W11] 0
U14: (,2) [W11] 0
V14: (,2) [W11] 0
W14: (,2) [W11] 0
X14: (,2) [W11] 0
Y14: (,2) [W11] 0
Z14: (,2) [W11] 0
AA14: (,2) [W11] 0
AB14: (,2) [W11] @SUM(P14..AA14)
AE14: [W11] 'INCOME_TABLE~
AH14: [W16] 'Assign Table Range
A15: [W8] 103
B15: (D1) [W10] @DATE(87,1,2)
C15: [W20] 'Gas
D15: (,2) [W11] -12.65
E15: (,2) [W11] +D15+E14
F15: [W11] 1
G15: [W11] 101
H15: (,2) [W11] +D15-J15
J15: (,2) [W11] 0
O15: [W11] 0
P15: (,2) [W11] 0
Q15: (,2) [W11] 0
R15: (,2) [W11] 0
S15: (,2) [W11] 0
T15: (,2) [W11] 0
U15: (,2) [W11] 0
V15: (,2) [W11] 0
W15: (,2) [W11] 0
X15: (,2) [W11] 0
Y15: (,2) [W11] 0
Z15: (,2) [W11] 0
AA15: (,2) [W11] 0
AB15: (,2) [W11] @SUM(P15..AA15)
AE15: [W11] 'IN1_1~IN_2~
AH15: [W16] 'Assign Input Cells
A16: [W8] 104
C16: [W20] 'Void
E16: (,2) [W11] +D16+E15

F16: [W11] 1
H16: (,2) [W11] +D16-J16
J16: (,2) [W11] 0
O16: [W11] 0
P16: (,2) [W11] 0
Q16: (,2) [W11] 0
R16: (,2) [W11] 0
S16: (,2) [W11] 0
T16: (,2) [W11] 0
U16: (,2) [W11] 0
V16: (,2) [W11] 0
W16: (,2) [W11] 0
X16: (,2) [W11] 0
Y16: (,2) [W11] 0
Z16: (,2) [W11] 0
AA16: (,2) [W11] 0
AB16: (,2) [W11] @SUM(P16..AA16)
AE16: [W11] '/dtr/dt2
AH16: [W16] 'Data table Reset/Start Table calc
A17: [W8] 1
B17: (D1) [W10] @DATE(87,1,2)
C17: [W20] 'Deposit
D17: (,2) [W11] 942
E17: (,2) [W11] +D17+E16
F17: [W11] 1
G17: [W11] 1
H17: (,2) [W11] +D17-J17
J17: (,2) [W11] 0
P17: (C2) [W11] ' --------
Q17: (C2) [W11] ' --------
R17: (C2) [W11] ' --------
S17: (C2) [W11] ' --------
T17: (C2) [W11] ' --------
U17: (C2) [W11] ' --------
V17: (C2) [W11] ' --------
W17: (C2) [W11] ' --------
X17: (C2) [W11] ' --------
Y17: (C2) [W11] ' --------
Z17: (C2) [W11] ' --------
AA17: (C2) [W11] ' --------
AB17: (C2) [W11] ' --------
AE17: [W11] 'EXPENSE_TABLE~
AH17: [W16] 'Assign Table Range
A18: [W8] 105
B18: (D1) [W10] @DATE(87,1,4)
C18: [W20] 'Office Leasing Inc.
D18: (,2) [W11] -855
E18: (,2) [W11] +D18+E17
F18: [W11] 1
G18: [W11] 401
H18: (,2) [W11] +D18-J18
J18: (,2) [W11] 0
N18: [W12] 'Total Income

P18: (,2) [W11] @SUM(P10..P17)
Q18: (,2) [W11] @SUM(Q10..Q17)
R18: (,2) [W11] @SUM(R10..R17)
S18: (,2) [W11] @SUM(S10..S17)
T18: (,2) [W11] @SUM(T10..T17)
U18: (,2) [W11] @SUM(U10..U17)
V18: (,2) [W11] @SUM(V10..V17)
W18: (,2) [W11] @SUM(W10..W17)
X18: (,2) [W11] @SUM(X10..X17)
Y18: (,2) [W11] @SUM(Y10..Y17)
Z18: (,2) [W11] @SUM(Z10..Z17)
AA18: (,2) [W11] @SUM(AA10..AA17)
AB18: (,2) [W11] @SUM(AB10..AB17)
AE18: [W11] 'IN1_1~IN_2~
AH18: [W16] 'Assign Input Cells
A19: [W8] 106
B19: (D1) [W10] @DATE(87,1,4)
C19: [W20] 'K&D Enterprises
D19: (,2) [W11] -344
E19: (,2) [W11] +D19+E18
F19: [W11] 1
G19: [W11] 601
H19: (,2) [W11] +D19-J19
J19: (,2) [W11] 0
AE19: [W11] '/dtr/dt2
AH19: [W16] 'Data table Reset/Start Table calc
A20: [W8] 107
B20: (D1) [W10] @DATE(87,1,5)
C20: [W20] 'Acme Tool & Die
D20: (,2) [W11] -267.11
E20: (,2) [W11] +D20+E19
F20: [W11] 1
G20: [W11] 601
H20: (,2) [W11] +D20-J20
J20: (,2) [W11] 0
O20: (H) [W11] @DSUM($REGISTER,7,N56..O57)
P20: (D3) [W11] @DATE(87,1,1)
Q20: (D3) [W11] +P20+31
R20: (D3) [W11] +Q20+31
S20: (D3) [W11] +R20+31
T20: (D3) [W11] +S20+31
U20: (D3) [W11] +T20+31
V20: (D3) [W11] +U20+31
W20: (D3) [W11] +V20+31
X20: (D3) [W11] +W20+31
Y20: (D3) [W11] +X20+31
Z20: (D3) [W11] +Y20+31
AA20: (D3) [W11] +Z20+31
AB20: [W11] ' Total
AE20: [W11] 'TAXDDUCT_TABLE~
AH20: [W16] 'Assign Table Range
A21: [W8] 108
B21: (D1) [W10] @DATE(87,1,9)

C21: [W20] 'USA Computer
D21: (,2) [W11] -75.68
E21: (,2) [W11] +D21+E20
F21: [W11] 1
G21: [W11] 201
H21: (,2) [W11] +D21-J21
J21: (,2) [W11] 0
N21: [W12] 'Utilities
O21: [W11] 101
P21: (,2) [W11] -128.22
Q21: (,2) [W11] 0
R21: (,2) [W11] 0
S21: (,2) [W11] 0
T21: (,2) [W11] 0
U21: (,2) [W11] 0
V21: (,2) [W11] 0
W21: (,2) [W11] 0
X21: (,2) [W11] 0
Y21: (,2) [W11] 0
Z21: (,2) [W11] 0
AA21: (,2) [W11] 0
AB21: (,2) [W11] @SUM(P21..AA21)
AE21: [W11] 'IN1_2~IN_2~
AH21: [W16] 'Assign Input Cells
A22: [W8] 109
B22: (D1) [W10] @DATE(87,1,12)
C22: [W20] 'Amalgamated Widget
D22: (,2) [W11] -27
E22: (,2) [W11] +D22+E21
F22: [W11] 1
G22: [W11] 601
H22: (,2) [W11] +D22-J22
J22: (,2) [W11] 0
N22: [W12] 'Comp Hdwe
O22: [W11] 201
P22: (,2) [W11] -84.22
Q22: (,2) [W11] 0
R22: (,2) [W11] 0
S22: (,2) [W11] 0
T22: (,2) [W11] 0
U22: (,2) [W11] 0
V22: (,2) [W11] 0
W22: (,2) [W11] 0
X22: (,2) [W11] 0
Y22: (,2) [W11] 0
Z22: (,2) [W11] 0
AA22: (,2) [W11] 0
AB22: (,2) [W11] @SUM(P22..AA22)
AE22: [W11] '{INDICATE}
AH22: [W16] 'Reset Mode Indicator
A23: [W8] 110
B23: (D1) [W10] @DATE(87,1,14)
C23: [W20] 'Software Corp

D23: (,2) [W11] -300
E23: (,2) [W11] +D23+E22
F23: [W11] 0
G23: [W11] 301
H23: (,2) [W11] +D23-J23
J23: (,2) [W11] 0
N23: [W12] 'Comp Sftwe
O23: [W11] 301
P23: (,2) [W11] -319.95
Q23: (,2) [W11] 0
R23: (,2) [W11] 0
S23: (,2) [W11] 0
T23: (,2) [W11] 0
U23: (,2) [W11] 0
V23: (,2) [W11] 0
W23: (,2) [W11] 0
X23: (,2) [W11] 0
Y23: (,2) [W11] 0
Z23: (,2) [W11] 0
AA23: (,2) [W11] 0
AB23: (,2) [W11] @SUM(P23..AA23)
AE23: [W11] '{PANELON}{WINDOWSON}
AH23: [W16] 'Control Panel & Windows On
A24: [W8] 112
B24: (D1) [W10] @DATE(87,1,15)
C24: [W20] 'Que Corp
D24: (,2) [W11] -19.95
E24: (,2) [W11] +D24+E23
F24: [W11] 1
G24: [W11] 301
H24: (,2) [W11] +D24-J24
J24: (,2) [W11] 0
N24: [W12] 'Office Rent
O24: [W11] 401
P24: (,2) [W11] -855
Q24: (,2) [W11] 0
R24: (,2) [W11] 0
S24: (,2) [W11] 0
T24: (,2) [W11] 0
U24: (,2) [W11] 0
V24: (,2) [W11] 0
W24: (,2) [W11] 0
X24: (,2) [W11] 0
Y24: (,2) [W11] 0
Z24: (,2) [W11] 0
AA24: (,2) [W11] 0
AB24: (,2) [W11] @SUM(P24..AA24)
A25: [W8] 2
B25: (D1) [W10] @DATE(87,1,16)
C25: [W20] 'Deposit
D25: (,2) [W11] 942
E25: (,2) [W11] +D25+E24
F25: [W11] 1

G25: [W11] 1
H25: (,2) [W11] +D25-J25
J25: (,2) [W11] 0
N25: [W12] 'Office Supp
O25: [W11] 501
P25: (,2) [W11] -100
Q25: (,2) [W11] -46.12
R25: (,2) [W11] 0
S25: (,2) [W11] 0
T25: (,2) [W11] 0
U25: (,2) [W11] 0
V25: (,2) [W11] 0
W25: (,2) [W11] 0
X25: (,2) [W11] 0
Y25: (,2) [W11] 0
Z25: (,2) [W11] 0
AA25: (,2) [W11] 0
AB25: (,2) [W11] @SUM(P25..AA25)
A26: [W8] 113
B26: (D1) [W10] @DATE(87,1,19)
C26: [W20] 'Triangle Machine
D26: (,2) [W11] -23
E26: (,2) [W11] +D26+E25
F26: [W11] 1
G26: [W11] 601
H26: (,2) [W11] +D26-J26
J26: (,2) [W11] 0
N26: [W12] 'Inventory
O26: [W11] 601
P26: (,2) [W11] -661.11
Q26: (,2) [W11] 0
R26: (,2) [W11] 0
S26: (,2) [W11] 0
T26: (,2) [W11] 0
U26: (,2) [W11] 0
V26: (,2) [W11] 0
W26: (,2) [W11] 0
X26: (,2) [W11] 0
Y26: (,2) [W11] 0
Z26: (,2) [W11] 0
AA26: (,2) [W11] 0
AB26: (,2) [W11] @SUM(P26..AA26)
A27: [W8] 114
B27: (D1) [W10] @DATE(87,1,25)
C27: [W20] 'Quill & Pen Inc.
D27: (,2) [W11] -100
E27: (,2) [W11] +D27+E26
F27: [W11] 1
G27: [W11] 501
H27: (,2) [W11] +D27-J27
J27: (,2) [W11] 0
O27: [W11] 0
P27: (,2) [W11] 0

Q27: (,2) [W11] 0
R27: (,2) [W11] 0
S27: (,2) [W11] 0
T27: (,2) [W11] 0
U27: (,2) [W11] 0
V27: (,2) [W11] 0
W27: (,2) [W11] 0
X27: (,2) [W11] 0
Y27: (,2) [W11] 0
Z27: (,2) [W11] 0
AA27: (,2) [W11] 0
AB27: (,2) [W11] @SUM(P27..AA27)
A28: [W8] 115
B28: (D1) [W10] @DATE(87,1,27)
C28: [W20] 'General Micro
D28: (,2) [W11] −8.54
E28: (,2) [W11] +D28+E27
F28: [W11] 0
G28: [W11] 201
H28: (,2) [W11] +D28−J28
J28: (,2) [W11] 0
O28: [W11] 0
P28: (,2) [W11] 0
Q28: (,2) [W11] 0
R28: (,2) [W11] 0
S28: (,2) [W11] 0
T28: (,2) [W11] 0
U28: (,2) [W11] 0
V28: (,2) [W11] 0
W28: (,2) [W11] 0
X28: (,2) [W11] 0
Y28: (,2) [W11] 0
Z28: (,2) [W11] 0
AA28: (,2) [W11] 0
AB28: (,2) [W11] @SUM(P28..AA28)
A29: [W8] 116
B29: (D1) [W10] @DATE(87,2,1)
C29: [W20] 'Natl Off Supply
D29: (,2) [W11] −46.12
E29: (,2) [W11] +D29+E28
F29: [W11] 1
G29: [W11] 501
H29: (,2) [W11] +D29−J29
J29: (,2) [W11] 0
O29: [W11] 0
P29: (,2) [W11] 0
Q29: (,2) [W11] 0
R29: (,2) [W11] 0
S29: (,2) [W11] 0
T29: (,2) [W11] 0
U29: (,2) [W11] 0
V29: (,2) [W11] 0
W29: (,2) [W11] 0

X29: (,2) [W11] 0
Y29: (,2) [W11] 0
Z29: (,2) [W11] 0
AA29: (,2) [W11] 0
AB29: (,2) [W11] @SUM(P29..AA29)
A30: [W8] 3
B30: (D1) [W10] @DATE(87,2,1)
C30: [W20] 'Deposit
D30: (,2) [W11] 942
E30: (,2) [W11] +D30+E29
F30: [W11] 0
G30: [W11] 1
H30: (,2) [W11] +D30−J30
J30: (,2) [W11] 0
O30: [W11] 0
P30: (,2) [W11] 0
Q30: (,2) [W11] 0
R30: (,2) [W11] 0
S30: (,2) [W11] 0
T30: (,2) [W11] 0
U30: (,2) [W11] 0
V30: (,2) [W11] 0
W30: (,2) [W11] 0
X30: (,2) [W11] 0
Y30: (,2) [W11] 0
Z30: (,2) [W11] 0
AA30: (,2) [W11] 0
AB30: (,2) [W11] @SUM(P30..AA30)
A31: [W8] 4
B31: (D1) [W10] @DATE(87,2,3)
C31: [W20] 'Account Interest
D31: (,2) [W11] 17
E31: (,2) [W11] +D31+E30
F31: [W11] 1
G31: [W11] 2
H31: (,2) [W11] +D31−J31
J31: (,2) [W11] 0
O31: [W11] 0
P31: (,2) [W11] 0
Q31: (,2) [W11] 0
R31: (,2) [W11] 0
S31: (,2) [W11] 0
T31: (,2) [W11] 0
U31: (,2) [W11] 0
V31: (,2) [W11] 0
W31: (,2) [W11] 0
X31: (,2) [W11] 0
Y31: (,2) [W11] 0
Z31: (,2) [W11] 0
AA31: (,2) [W11] 0
AB31: (,2) [W11] @SUM(P31..AA31)
E32: (,2) [W11] +D32+E31
J32: (,2) [W11] 0

O32: [W11] 0
P32: (,2) [W11] 0
Q32: (,2) [W11] 0
R32: (,2) [W11] 0
S32: (,2) [W11] 0
T32: (,2) [W11] 0
U32: (,2) [W11] 0
V32: (,2) [W11] 0
W32: (,2) [W11] 0
X32: (,2) [W11] 0
Y32: (,2) [W11] 0
Z32: (,2) [W11] 0
AA32: (,2) [W11] 0
AB32: (,2) [W11] @SUM(P32..AA32)
E33: (,2) [W11] +D33+E32
J33: (,2) [W11] 0
O33: [W11] 0
P33: (,2) [W11] 0
Q33: (,2) [W11] 0
R33: (,2) [W11] 0
S33: (,2) [W11] 0
T33: (,2) [W11] 0
U33: (,2) [W11] 0
V33: (,2) [W11] 0
W33: (,2) [W11] 0
X33: (,2) [W11] 0
Y33: (,2) [W11] 0
Z33: (,2) [W11] 0
AA33: (,2) [W11] 0
AB33: (,2) [W11] @SUM(P33..AA33)
E34: (,2) [W11] +D34+E33
J34: (,2) [W11] 0
O34: [W11] 0
P34: (,2) [W11] 0
Q34: (,2) [W11] 0
R34: (,2) [W11] 0
S34: (,2) [W11] 0
T34: (,2) [W11] 0
U34: (,2) [W11] 0
V34: (,2) [W11] 0
W34: (,2) [W11] 0
X34: (,2) [W11] 0
Y34: (,2) [W11] 0
Z34: (,2) [W11] 0
AA34: (,2) [W11] 0
AB34: (,2) [W11] @SUM(P34..AA34)
E35: (,2) [W11] +D35+E34
J35: (,2) [W11] 0
P35: (C2) [W11] ' --------
Q35: (C2) [W11] ' --------
R35: (C2) [W11] ' --------
S35: (C2) [W11] ' --------
T35: (C2) [W11] ' --------

U35: (C2) [W11] ' --------
V35: (C2) [W11] ' --------
W35: (C2) [W11] ' --------
X35: (C2) [W11] ' --------
Y35: (C2) [W11] ' --------
Z35: (C2) [W11] ' --------
AA35: (C2) [W11] ' --------
AB35: (C2) [W11] ' --------
E36: (,2) [W11] +D36+E35
J36: (,2) [W11] 0
N36: [W12] 'Total Expenses
P36: (,2) [W11] @SUM(P21..P35)
Q36: (,2) [W11] @SUM(Q21..Q35)
R36: (,2) [W11] @SUM(R21..R35)
S36: (,2) [W11] @SUM(S21..S35)
T36: (,2) [W11] @SUM(T21..T35)
U36: (,2) [W11] @SUM(U21..U35)
V36: (,2) [W11] @SUM(V21..V35)
W36: (,2) [W11] @SUM(W21..W35)
X36: (,2) [W11] @SUM(X21..X35)
Y36: (,2) [W11] @SUM(Y21..Y35)
Z36: (,2) [W11] @SUM(Z21..Z35)
AA36: (,2) [W11] @SUM(AA21..AA35)
AB36: (,2) [W11] @SUM(AB21..AB35)
E37: (,2) [W11] +D37+E36
J37: (,2) [W11] 0
E38: (,2) [W11] +D38+E37
J38: (,2) [W11] 0
O38: (H) [W11] @DSUM($REGISTER,9,N56..P57)
P38: (D3) [W11] @DATE(87,1,1)
Q38: (D3) [W11] +P38+31
R38: (D3) [W11] +Q38+31
S38: (D3) [W11] +R38+31
T38: (D3) [W11] +S38+31
U38: (D3) [W11] +T38+31
V38: (D3) [W11] +U38+31
W38: (D3) [W11] +V38+31
X38: (D3) [W11] +W38+31
Y38: (D3) [W11] +X38+31
Z38: (D3) [W11] +Y38+31
AA38: (D3) [W11] +Z38+31
AB38: [W11] ' Total
E39: (,2) [W11] +D39+E38
J39: (,2) [W11] 0
O39: [W11] 0
P39: (,2) [W11] 0
Q39: (,2) [W11] 0
R39: (,2) [W11] 0
S39: (,2) [W11] 0
T39: (,2) [W11] 0
U39: (,2) [W11] 0
V39: (,2) [W11] 0
W39: (,2) [W11] 0

X39: (,2) [W11] 0
Y39: (,2) [W11] 0
Z39: (,2) [W11] 0
AA39: (,2) [W11] 0
AB39: (,2) [W11] @SUM(P39..AA39)
E40: (,2) [W11] +D40+E39
J40: (,2) [W11] 0
O40: [W11] 0
P40: (,2) [W11] 0
Q40: (,2) [W11] 0
R40: (,2) [W11] 0
S40: (,2) [W11] 0
T40: (,2) [W11] 0
U40: (,2) [W11] 0
V40: (,2) [W11] 0
W40: (,2) [W11] 0
X40: (,2) [W11] 0
Y40: (,2) [W11] 0
Z40: (,2) [W11] 0
AA40: (,2) [W11] 0
AB40: (,2) [W11] @SUM(P40..AA40)
E41: (,2) [W11] +D41+E40
J41: (,2) [W11] 0
O41: [W11] 0

P41: (,2) [W11] 0
Q41: (,2) [W11] 0
R41: (,2) [W11] 0
S41: (,2) [W11] 0
T41: (,2) [W11] 0
U41: (,2) [W11] 0
V41: (,2) [W11] 0
W41: (,2) [W11] 0
X41: (,2) [W11] 0
Y41: (,2) [W11] 0
Z41: (,2) [W11] 0
AA41: (,2) [W11] 0
AB41: (,2) [W11] @SUM(P41..AA41)
E42: (,2) [W11] +D42+E41
J42: (,2) [W11] 0
O42: [W11] 0
P42: (,2) [W11] 0
Q42: (,2) [W11] 0
R42: (,2) [W11] 0
S42: (,2) [W11] 0
T42: (,2) [W11] 0
U42: (,2) [W11] 0
V42: (,2) [W11] 0
W42: (,2) [W11] 0
X42: (,2) [W11] 0
Y42: (,2) [W11] 0
Z42: (,2) [W11] 0
AA42: (,2) [W11] 0
AB42: (,2) [W11] @SUM(P42..AA42)

E43: (,2) [W11] +D43+E42
J43: (,2) [W11] 0
O43: [W11] 0
P43: (,2) [W11] 0
Q43: (,2) [W11] 0
R43: (,2) [W11] 0
S43: (,2) [W11] 0
T43: (,2) [W11] 0
U43: (,2) [W11] 0
V43: (,2) [W11] 0
W43: (,2) [W11] 0
X43: (,2) [W11] 0
Y43: (,2) [W11] 0
Z43: (,2) [W11] 0
AA43: (,2) [W11] 0
AB43: (,2) [W11] @SUM(P43..AA43)
E44: (,2) [W11] +D44+E43
J44: (,2) [W11] 0
O44: [W11] 0
P44: (,2) [W11] 0
Q44: (,2) [W11] 0
R44: (,2) [W11] 0
S44: (,2) [W11] 0
T44: (,2) [W11] 0
U44: (,2) [W11] 0
V44: (,2) [W11] 0
W44: (,2) [W11] 0
X44: (,2) [W11] 0
Y44: (,2) [W11] 0
Z44: (,2) [W11] 0
AA44: (,2) [W11] 0
AB44: (,2) [W11] @SUM(P44..AA44)
E45: (,2) [W11] +D45+E44
J45: (,2) [W11] 0
O45: [W11] 0
P45: (,2) [W11] 0
Q45: (,2) [W11] 0
R45: (,2) [W11] 0
S45: (,2) [W11] 0
T45: (,2) [W11] 0
U45: (,2) [W11] 0
V45: (,2) [W11] 0
W45: (,2) [W11] 0
X45: (,2) [W11] 0
Y45: (,2) [W11] 0
Z45: (,2) [W11] 0
AA45: (,2) [W11] 0
AB45: (,2) [W11] @SUM(P45..AA45)
E46: (,2) [W11] +D46+E45
J46: (,2) [W11] 0
O46: [W11] 0
P46: (,2) [W11] 0
Q46: (,2) [W11] 0

R46: (,2) [W11] 0
S46: (,2) [W11] 0
T46: (,2) [W11] 0
U46: (,2) [W11] 0
V46: (,2) [W11] 0
W46: (,2) [W11] 0
X46: (,2) [W11] 0
Y46: (,2) [W11] 0
Z46: (,2) [W11] 0
AA46: (,2) [W11] 0
AB46: (,2) [W11] @SUM(P46..AA46)
E47: (,2) [W11] +D47+E46
J47: (,2) [W11] 0
P47: [W11] ' --------
Q47: [W11] ' --------
R47: [W11] ' --------
S47: [W11] ' --------
T47: [W11] ' --------
U47: [W11] ' --------
V47: [W11] ' --------
W47: [W11] ' --------
X47: [W11] ' --------
Y47: [W11] ' --------
Z47: [W11] ' --------
AA47: [W11] ' --------
AB47: [W11] ' --------
E48: (,2) [W11] +D48+E47
J48: (,2) [W11] 0
N48: [W12] 'Tax–Deductible Expenses
P48: (,2) [W11] @SUM(P39..P47)
Q48: (,2) [W11] @SUM(Q39..Q47)
R48: (,2) [W11] @SUM(R39..R47)
S48: (,2) [W11] @SUM(S39..S47)
T48: (,2) [W11] @SUM(T39..T47)
U48: (,2) [W11] @SUM(U39..U47)
V48: (,2) [W11] @SUM(V39..V47)
W48: (,2) [W11] @SUM(W39..W47)
X48: (,2) [W11] @SUM(X39..X47)
Y48: (,2) [W11] @SUM(Y39..Y47)
Z48: (,2) [W11] @SUM(Z39..Z47)
AA48: (,2) [W11] @SUM(AA39..AA47)
AB48: (,2) [W11] @SUM(AB47..AB39)
E49: (,2) [W11] +D49+E48
J49: (,2) [W11] 0
P49: [W11] ' --------
Q49: [W11] ' --------
R49: [W11] ' --------
S49: [W11] ' --------
T49: [W11] ' --------
U49: [W11] ' --------
V49: [W11] ' --------
W49: [W11] ' --------
X49: [W11] ' --------

Y49: [W11] ' --------
Z49: [W11] ' --------
AA49: [W11] ' --------
AB49: [W11] ' --------
E50: (,2) [W11] +D50+E49
J50: (,2) [W11] 0
N50: [W12] 'Net Income/(Loss)
P50: (C2) [W11] +P18+P36+P48
Q50: (C2) [W11] +Q18+Q36+Q48
R50: (C2) [W11] +R18+R36+R48
S50: (C2) [W11] +S18+S36+S48
T50: (C2) [W11] +T18+T36+T48
U50: (C2) [W11] +U18+U36+U48
V50: (C2) [W11] +V18+V36+V48
W50: (C2) [W11] +W18+W36+W48
X50: (C2) [W11] +X18+X36+X48
Y50: (C2) [W11] +Y18+Y36+Y48
Z50: (C2) [W11] +Z18+Z36+Z48
AA50: (C2) [W11] +AA18+AA36+AA48
AB50: (C2) [W11] +AB18+AB36+AB48
E51: (,2) [W11] +D51+E50
J51: (,2) [W11] 0
P51: [W11] ' ========
Q51: [W11] ' ========
R51: [W11] ' ========
S51: [W11] ' ========
T51: [W11] ' ========
U51: [W11] ' ========
V51: [W11] ' ========
W51: [W11] ' ========
X51: [W11] ' ========
Y51: [W11] ' ========
Z51: [W11] ' ========
AA51: [W11] ' ========
AB51: [W11] ' ========
E52: (,2) [W11] +D52+E51
J52: (,2) [W11] 0
E53: (,2) [W11] +D53+E52
J53: (,2) [W11] 0
E54: (,2) [W11] +D54+E53
J54: (,2) [W11] 0
A55: [W8] 'OUTSTANDING ITEMS
G55: [W11] 'RECONCILIATION
A56: [W8] \=
B56: [W10] \=
C56: [W20] \=
D56: [W11] \=
E56: [W11] \=
F56: [W11] \=
G56: [W11] \=
H56: [W11] \=
I56: [W11] \=
J56: [W11] \=

K56: [W5] \=
L56: [W11] \=
M56: [W11] \=
N56: [W12] ' Written
O56: [W11] ^Account1
P56: [W11] ^Account2
A57: [W8] 'Cleared
C57: [W20] 'Total Outstanding:
D57: (C2) [W11] @DSUM(A12..F55,3,A57..A58)
N57: (H) [W12] @MONTH(B13)=@MONTH($IN_2)
A58: [W8] +F13=0
G59: [W11] 'Ending Checkbook Balance:
L59: (C2) [W11] +BOTTOM
A60: [W8] ^Check or
G60: [W11] 'Less: Checks and Deposits Outstanding
L60: (,2) [W11] +$D$57
A61: [W8] ^Deposit
B61: [W10] ' Date
L61: (C2) [W11] ' --------
A62: [W8] 'Number
B62: [W10] ' Written
C62: [W20] ^Payee
D62: [W11] ' Amount
G62: [W11] 'Adjusted Checkbook Balance
L62: (,2) [W11] +L59-L60
A63: [W8] 110
B63: (D1) [W10] 31791
C63: [W20] 'Software Corp
D63: (,2) [W11] -300
G63: [W11] 'Less: Adjustments to Bank Balance
L63: (,2) [W11] 0
A64: [W8] 115
B64: (D1) [W10] 31804
C64: [W20] 'General Micro
D64: (,2) [W11] -8.54
L64: (C2) [W11] ' --------
A65: [W8] 3
B65: (D1) [W10] 31809
C65: [W20] 'Deposit
D65: (,2) [W11] 942
G65: [W11] 'Bank Balance
L65: (C2) [W11] +L62-L63
L66: [W11] ' ========

3

Projecting Cash Flow

Introduction

Your company's cash flow is as important as its profitability, especially if your firm is just starting out, growing rapidly, or dependent on seasonal sales.

You need to know when to expect payment from a sale and when to increase inventories. You need to know the impact on your cash flow of future financial obligations, such as line-of-credit payments. And the Tax Reform Act of 1986, which eliminates many deductions and credits for business, further emphasizes the importance of cash.

The 1-2-3 Cash Flow Projector will help you to determine whether your company will need outside financing. You can use the model to project future cash flows AND to predict sales, collections, and disbursements.

Designed to project cash flows for a business with five profit centers, the model can be modified to meet the needs of your business. The Cash Flow Projector creates a twelve-month cash flow projection based on your assumptions about and experience with sales, accounts receivable, inventory, expense disbursements, and loan repayments.

This chapter explains how you can put 1-2-3 to work for you. After looking at the Cash Flow Projector's modules and functions, the chapter explains how to create the model, and then discusses understanding, using, and modifying the model.

Don't let the size of the Cash Flow Projector model (which may seem overwhelming at first) intimidate you. You can greatly reduce the time spent creating the model, for example, if you use the **/C**opy command to create most formulas.

CASH FLOW PROJECTOR

Copyright (C) 1987 Que Corporation

BALANCES IN WORKING CAPITAL ACCOUNTS

	Dec	Jan	Feb	Mar	Apr	May	Jun	Jul	Aug	Sep	Oct	Nov	Dec
Assets													
Cash	$17,355	$31,643	$34,333	$36,657	$35,614	$29,146	$20,000	$20,000	$20,000	$76,623	$186,131	$337,995	$582,796
Accounts Receivable	493,151	510,780	533,597	551,287	577,314	614,997	641,802	750,544	819,271	989,501	1,097,616	1,170,646	1,218,036
Inventory	163,833	169,209	176,671	189,246	206,788	228,828	269,990	296,527	324,230	345,629	352,687	358,926	358,926
Liabilities													
Accounts Payable	125,000	130,754	139,851	150,186	163,731	180,350	203,669	225,085	243,320	258,740	267,621	272,747	275,041
Line of Credit	0	0	0	0	0	0	1,834	8,327	2,035	0	0	0	0
Net Working Capital	$549,339	$580,878	$604,750	$627,003	$655,984	$692,620	$726,289	$833,659	$978,146	$1,153,013	$1,368,812	$1,594,820	$1,884,718

SALES

	Oct	Nov	Dec	Jan	Feb	Mar	Apr	May	Jun	Jul	Aug	Sep	Oct	Nov	Dec	Total
Profit Center 1	$27,832	$23,864	$26,125	$31,336	$37,954	$43,879	$51,471	$56,953	$53,145	$54,140	$53,614	$52,015	$48,902	$44,091	$42,536	$570,036
Profit Center 2	13,489	21,444	20,140	22,572	24,888	25,167	32,588	40,140	37,970	34,587	33,463	28,939	24,153	27,060	26,701	358,228
Profit Center 3	126,811	124,382	123,618	131,685	129,044	131,723	139,221	141,879	147,108	147,032	153,440	149,990	145,198	150,510	150,510	1,716,633
Profit Center 4	94,285	92,447	89,010	95,473	98,008	96,986	95,318	103,538	108,146	108,642	106,065	110,401	112,018	111,956	107,522	1,254,073
Profit Center 5										115,000	115,000	225,000	300,000	325,000	350,000	1,490,000
Total Sales	$262,417	$262,137	$258,893	$281,066	$289,894	$297,755	$318,598	$342,510	$349,064	$459,477	$515,174	$569,795	$635,063	$653,305	$671,269	$5,388,970

Percent of Collections: Cash 10% / 30 Days 20% / 60 Days 50% / 90 Days 20%

Cash Collections	Jan	Feb	Mar	Apr	May	Jun	Jul	Aug	Sep	Oct	Nov	Dec	Total
	$263,437	$267,077	$280,066	$292,571	$304,827	$322,258	$330,735	$386,447	$459,566	$526,948	$580,275	$629,878	$4,664,085

PURCHASES

Cost of Goods Sold

	%	Oct	Nov	Dec	Jan	Feb	Mar	Apr	May	Jun	Jul	Aug	Sep	Oct	Nov	Dec	Total
Profit Center 1	33%	$9,185	$7,875	$8,621	$10,341	$12,525	$14,480	$16,985	$18,794	$17,538	$17,866	$17,693	$17,165	$16,138	$14,550	$14,037	$188,112
Profit Center 2	29%	$3,912	$6,219	$5,841	$6,546	$7,218	$7,298	$9,451	$11,641	$11,011	$10,030	$9,704	$8,392	$7,004	$7,847	$7,743	$103,886
Profit Center 3	50%	$63,406	$62,191	$61,809	$65,843	$64,522	$65,862	$69,611	$70,940	$74,902	$73,554	$73,516	$76,720	$74,995	$72,559	$75,255	$858,317
Profit Center 4	67%	$63,171	$61,939	$59,637	$63,967	$65,665	$64,981	$63,863	$69,370	$72,458	$72,790	$71,064	$73,969	$75,052	$75,011	$72,040	$840,229
Profit Center 5	30%										$34,500	$52,500	$67,500	$90,000	$97,500	$105,000	$447,000
Total Cost of Goods Sold		$139,673	$138,224	$135,908	$146,696	$149,930	$152,621	$159,910	$170,745	$175,908	$208,741	$224,476	$243,746	$263,189	$267,507	$274,075	$2,437,543

Inventory Purchasing Schedule:
- 0 Days in Advance 5%
- 30 Days in Advance 50%
- 60 Days in Advance 30%
- 90 Days in Advance 15%

Inventory Purchases	Oct	Nov	Dec	Jan	Feb	Mar	Apr	May	Jun	Jul	Aug	Sep	Oct	Nov	Dec	Total
	$138,873	$141,363	$148,015	$152,072	$157,391	$165,196	$177,452	$192,785	$217,071	$235,277	$252,180	$285,145	$270,247	$273,747	$274,075	$2,632,637

Payment Schedule: Cash 30% / 30 Days 40% / 60 Days 30%

Payment for Purchases	Jan	Feb	Mar	Apr	May	Jun	Jul	Aug	Sep	Oct	Nov	Dec	Total
	$142,612	$147,237	$152,451	$158,137	$166,531	$178,375	$195,471	$215,247	$234,886	$250,999	$262,786	$269,766	$272,795	$2,504,680

OPERATING EXPENSES

#	Item		Oct	Nov	Dec	Jan	Feb	Mar	Apr	May	Jun	Jul	Aug	Sep	Oct	Nov	Dec	Total
77	Profit Center 1		$20,458	$20,760	$20,963	$21,529	$22,329	$22,802	$23,108	$24,099	$24,422	$24,431	$25,060	$25,646	$26,515	$26,639	$26,881	$293,461
78	Profit Center 2		14,377	15,002	15,587	15,946	16,790	17,355	17,739	18,195	18,610	19,412	19,546	20,348	20,860	21,729	21,785	228,315
79	Profit Center 3		25,921	26,393	27,339	27,554	28,286	28,464	29,275	29,292	29,578	30,246	30,358	31,041	31,680	32,048	32,525	360,347
80	Profit Center 4		13,922	14,885	15,801	16,130	16,800	17,651	18,039	18,789	19,704	20,400	20,939	21,589	21,833	22,024	22,154	236,052
81	Profit Center 5						10,000	14,000	18,000	20,000	22,000	22,470	22,837	22,995	23,364	24,023	24,806	224,495
83	Corporate Overhead		14,944	15,262	15,801	16,332	16,474	16,933	17,616	18,575	18,640	19,278	19,544	20,225	21,142	21,565	22,378	228,702
85	Total Expenses		$89,622	$92,302	$95,491	$97,491	$110,679	$117,205	$123,777	$128,950	$132,954	$136,237	$138,284	$141,844	$145,394	$148,028	$150,529	$1,571,372
87	Payment — Cash		70%	70%	70%	70%	70%	70%	70%	70%	70%	70%	70%	70%	70%	70%	70%	
88	Schedule — 30 Days		20%	20%	20%	20%	20%	20%	20%	20%	20%	20%	20%	20%	20%	20%	20%	
89	60 Days		10%	10%	10%	10%	10%	10%	10%	10%	10%	10%	10%	10%	10%	10%	10%	
91	Total Payment for Expenses				$94,266	$96,572	$106,523	$113,928	$121,153	$126,741	$131,236	$134,852	$137,342	$140,571	$143,973	$146,883	$149,515	$1,549,288

CASH FLOW SUMMARY

#	Item	Dec	Jan	Feb	Mar	Apr	May	Jun	Jul	Aug	Sep	Oct	Nov	Dec	Total
97	Collection of Receivables		$263,437	$267,077	$280,066	$292,571	$304,827	$322,258	$350,735	$386,447	$459,566	$526,948	$580,275	$629,878	$4,664,085
98	Other Cash Receipts		0	0	0	0	0	0	0	0	0	0	0	50,000	50,000
100	Cash Disbursements														
101	Payment for Purchases on Credit		147,237	152,451	158,137	166,531	178,375	195,471	215,247	234,886	250,999	262,786	269,766	272,795	2,504,680
102	Operating Expenses		96,572	106,523	113,928	121,153	126,741	131,236	134,852	137,342	140,571	143,973	146,883	149,515	1,549,288
103	Long-Term Debt Service		0	0	0	0	0	0	0	0	0	0	0	0	0
104	Interest Payment on Line of Credit		0	0	0	0	0	0	20	94	23	0	0	0	137
105	Interest Rate	13.50%	13.50%	13.50%	13.50%	13.50%	13.50%	13.50%	13.50%	13.50%	13.50%	13.50%	13.50%	13.50%	
106	Payment		0	0	0	0	0	0	0	0	0	0	0	0	
107	Income Tax Payments		5,340	5,413	5,677	5,930	6,179	6,532	7,109	7,833	9,315	10,681	11,762	12,767	94,538
108	Other		0	0	0	0	0	0	0	0	0	0	0	0	0
110	Total Cash Disbursements		249,149	264,387	277,742	293,614	311,295	333,238	357,228	380,154	400,908	417,440	428,411	435,077	4,148,643
112	Net Cash Generated This Period		14,288	2,690	2,324	(1,043)	(6,468)	(10,980)	(6,493)	6,293	58,658	109,508	151,864	244,801	565,441

ANALYSIS OF CASH REQUIREMENTS

#	Item	Dec	Jan	Feb	Mar	Apr	May	Jun	Jul	Aug	Sep	Oct	Nov	Dec
118	Beginning Cash Balance		$17,355	$31,643	$34,333	$36,657	$35,614	$29,146	$20,000	$20,000	$20,000	$76,623	$186,131	$337,995
119	Net Cash Generated This Period		14,288	2,690	2,324	(1,043)	(6,468)	(10,980)	(6,493)	6,293	58,658	109,508	151,864	244,801
121	Cash Balance before Borrowings		31,643	34,333	36,657	35,614	29,146	18,166	13,507	26,293	78,658	186,131	337,995	582,796
122	Minimum Acceptable Cash Balance		20,000	20,000	20,000	20,000	20,000	20,000	20,000	20,000	20,000	20,000	20,000	20,000
124	Amount above/(below) Minimum Acceptable Balance		11,643	14,333	16,657	15,614	9,146	(1,834)	(6,493)	6,293	58,658	166,131	317,995	562,796
126	Current Short-Term Borrowings		0	0	0	0	0	1,834	6,493	(6,293)	(2,035)	0	0	0
127	Total Short-Term Borrowings		0	0	0	0	0	1,834	8,327	2,035	0	0	0	0
129	Ending Cash Balance		$31,643	$34,333	$36,657	$35,614	$29,146	$20,000	$20,000	$20,000	$76,623	$186,131	$337,995	$582,796

Fig. 3.1. The Cash Flow Projector.

An Overview of the Model

This useful model is so comprehensive that you may want to think of the application as six separate modules: Working Capital Accounts, Sales, Purchases, Operating Expenses, Cash Flow Summary, and Analysis of Cash Requirements. Figure 3.1 shows the Cash Flow Projector.

If you're familiar with these main modules, you'll better understand the steps needed to create the model. Each module introduced here is discussed more fully in the "Understanding the Model" section of this chapter. As you read the following brief descriptions, refer to figure 3.1 to get a feel for the structure of the application.

The Working Capital Accounts module, located in cells A5 through S20, contains the combined current assets and liabilities from a typical firm's balance sheet. (For a more detailed discussion of balance sheet basics, see Chapter 7, "Interactive Financial Statements.")

The Sales module, cells A21 through T41 (directly below the Working Capital Accounts module), contains the sales data used to project how much cash your business will receive each month.

The Purchases module, cells A42 through W73, lists your costs of goods sold. These figures are used to project monthly inventory purchases and payments.

The Operating Expenses module in cells A74 through T93 summarizes product or service overhead expenses.

The Cash Flow Summary module, located in cells A94 through T114 (directly below the Operating Expenses module), summarizes all monthly cash transactions.

The Analysis of Cash Requirements module begins at cell A115 and continues through cell S130. This module analyzes your company's cash flow to determine the amount of cash that is needed on a monthly basis.

The six modules work together to help you project monthly cash flow requirements. Now that you've been introduced to the model's main components, you can begin to create the worksheet.

Creating the Model

The model is designed to project cash flows for a business with five profit centers, and as a first step you should create all five for your model also. After you have accurately created this application, you'll be able to customize it for your own business.

Setting Column Widths

To create the model, begin with a blank 1-2-3 spreadsheet. You'll leave columns A through D set at the default width of nine, and you'll set all other column widths at eleven. To make this task easier, set the global column width to 11 by typing **/W**orksheet **G**lobal **C**olumn-Width **11** and then pressing Enter. Next, to set columns A through D, type **/W**orksheet **C**olumn **S**et-Width **9**.

A list of the column widths follows:

Column	Width
A	W9
B	W9
C	W9
D	W9
E through W	W11

Specifying Cell Formats

Using table 3.1, specify the cell formats for the model. You can use formats other than those listed, where appropriate.

Entering the Model

Enter the row titles, column headings, and labels according to figure 3.1 and table 3.2. Be sure to use the \= trick and the **/C**opy command for the separator lines.

Table 3.1
Cell Formats

Balances in Working Capital Accounts

/rfc0	G9..S9
/rf,0	G10..S15
/rfc0	G17..S17

Sales

/rfc0	E24..T24
/rf,0	E25..T28
/rfc0	E30..T30
/rfp0	E33..S36
/rfc0	H38..T38

Purchases

/rfp0	E46..S46
/rfc0	E47..T47
/rfp0	E48..S48
/rfc0	E49..T49
/rfp0	E50..S50
/rfc0	E51..T51
/rfp0	E52..S52
/rfc0	E53..T53
/rfp0	E54..S54
/rfc0	E55..T55
/rfc0	E57..W57
/rfp0	E60..W63
/rfc0	E65..T65
/rfp0	E67..S69
/rfc0	G71..T71

Operating Expenses

/rfc0	E77..T77
/rf,0	E78..T83
/rfc0	E85..T85
/rfp0	E87..S89
/rfc0	G91..T91

Cash Flow Summary

/rfc0	G97..T97
/rf,0	G98..T103
/rfp0	G105..S105
/rf,0	H106..T108
/rf,0	H110..T110
/rfc0	H112..T112

Analysis of Cash Requirements

/rfc0	H118..S118
/rf,0	H119..S126
/rf,0	G127..S127
/rfc0	H129..S129

Table 3.2
Row Titles and Column Headings

Enter into cell:	Original label:	Copy to:

Opening Headings

A1:	\=	B1..W1, A5..W5, A7..F7
		A21..T21, A23..D23,
		A42..T42, A44..D44,
		A74..T74, A76..D76,
		A94..T94, A96..F96,
		A115..T115, A117..F117

A3:	'CASH FLOW PROJECTION	

Balances in Working Capital Accounts

A6:	'BALANCES IN WORKING CAPITAL ACCOUNTS	
G6:	^Dec	
H6:	^Jan	
I6:	^Feb	
J6:	^Mar	
K6:	^Apr	
L6:	^May	
M6:	^Jun	
N6:	^Jul	
O6:	^Aug	
P6:	^Sep	
Q6:	^Oct	
R6:	^Nov	
S6:	^Dec	
G7:	' =========	H7..S7, G18..S18,
		E23..T23, E31..T31,
		H39..T39, D44..T44,
		E58..T58, G72..T72,
		E76..T76, G92..T92,
		H96..T96, H113..T113,
		G117..S117, H130..S130

A8:	'Assets	
A9:	' Cash	
A10:	' Accounts Receivable	
A11:	' Inventory	
A13:	'Liabilities	

Enter into cell:	Original label:	Copy to:
A14:	' Accounts Payable	
A15:	' Line of Credit	
G16:	' --------	H16..S16, E29..T29, H37..T37, E56..T56, G70..T70, E84..T84, G90..T90, H109..T109, H111..T111, H120..S120, H123..S123, H128..S128
A17:	'Net Working Capital	

Sales

A22:	'SALES	
T22:	'Total	
A24:	'Profit Center 1	
A25:	'Profit Center 2	
A26:	'Profit Center 3	
A27:	'Profit Center 4	
A28:	'Profit Center 5	
A30:	'Total Sales	
C33:	'Cash	
A34:	'Percent of	
C34:	'30 Days	
A35:	'Collections	
C35:	'60 Days	
C36:	'90 Days	
A38:	'Cash Collections	

Cell	Copy From	Copy To
E22:	Q6..S6	E22
H22:	G6..S6	G22

Purchases

A43:	'PURCHASES
A45:	'Cost of Goods Sold
A46:	' Profit Center 1
A48:	' Profit Center 2
A50:	' Profit Center 3
A52:	' Profit Center 4
A54:	' Profit Center 5
A57:	'Total Cost of Goods Sold

Enter into cell:	Original label:	Copy to:
A60:	'Inventory	
C60:	' 0 Days in Advance	
A61:	'Purchasing	
C61:	'30 Days in Advance	
A62:	'Schedule	
C62:	'60 Days in Advance	
C63:	'90 Days in Advance	
A65:	'Inventory Purchases	
A67:	'Payment	
C67:	'Cash	
A68:	'Schedule	
C68:	'30 Days	
C69:	'60 Days	
A71:	'Payment for Purchases	

Cell	Copy From	Copy To
E43:	E22..T22	E43

Operating Expenses

A75:	'OPERATING EXPENSES	
T75:	^Total	
A77:	'Profit Center 1	
A78:	'Profit Center 2	
A79:	'Profit Center 3	
A80:	'Profit Center 4	
A81:	'Profit Center 5	
A83:	'Corporate Overhead	
A85:	'Total Expenses	
A87:	'Payment	
C87:	'Cash	
A88:	'Schedule	
C88:	'30 Days	
C89:	'60 Days	
A91:	'Total Payment for Expenses	

Cell	Copy From	Copy To
E75:	E22..T22	E75

Enter
into
cell: Original label: Copy to:

Cash Flow Summary

A95:   'CASH FLOW SUMMARY
A97:   'Collection of Receivables
A98:   'Other Cash Receipts
A100:   'Cash Disbursements
A101:   ' Payment for Purchases on Credit
A102:   ' Operating Expenses
A103:   ' Long-Term Debt Service
A104:   ' Interest Payment on Line of Credit
A105:   '   Interest Rate
A106:   '   Payment
A107:   ' Income Tax Payments
A108:   ' Other
A110:   'Total Cash Disbursements
A112:   'Net Cash Generated This Period

Cell   *Copy From*   *Copy To*
H95   H75..T75   H95

Analysis of Cash Requirements Headings

A116:   'ANALYSIS OF CASH REQUIREMENTS
A118:   'Beginning Cash Balance
A119:   'Net Cash Generated This Period
A121:   'Cash Balance before Borrowings
A122:   'Minimum Acceptable Cash Balance
A124:   'Amount above/(below) Minimum
         Acceptable Balance
A126:   'Current Short-Term Borrowings
A127:   'Total Short-Term Borrowings
A129:   'Ending Cash Balance

Cell   *Copy From*   *Copy To*
G116   G75..T75   G116

Next, study the formulas and functions in table 3.3. Then, to create the model, enter the information as it is listed.

Note the number of times the **/C**opy command can be used to enter the formulas—most can be entered once and then replicated across the model. When you have a feel for the model's structure, enter the equations into the application.

Table 3.3
Formulas and Functions

Enter into cell:	Original formula:	Copy to:
	Balances in Working Capital Accounts	
H9:	+H129	
H10:	+G10+H30-H38	
H11:	+G11+H65-H57	
H14:	+G14+H65-H71+H85-H91	I14..S14
H15:	+H127	I15..S15
G17:	+G9+G10+G11-G14-G15	H17..S17
	Sales	
T24:	@SUM(H24..S24)	T25..T28
E30:	@SUM(E24..E29)	F30..T30
F33:	+E33	F33..S33
E36:	1-@SUM(E33..E35)	F36..S36
H38:	+E30*E36+F30*F35+G30	I38..T38
	*G34+H30*H33	
	Purchases	
F46:	+E46	G46..S46
		F48..S48
		F50..S50
		F52..S52
		F54..S54
		F60..S62
		U60..W62
		F67..S68
E47:	+E46*E24	F47..S47
		E49..S49
		E51..S51

Enter into cell:	Original formula:	Copy to:
E47:	+E46*E24	E53..S53
		E55..S55
T47:	@SUM(H47..S47)	T49, T51, T53, T55
E57:	+E47+E49+E51+E53+E55	F57..T57
U57:	+S57	V57..W57
E63:	1-@SUM(E60..E62)	F63..S63
		U63..W63
		E69..S69
E65:	+E60*E57+F61*F57+G62 *G57+H63*H57	F65..S65
T65:	@SUM(H65..S65)	T71
G71:	+E69*E65+F68*F65+G67*G65	H71..S71

Operating Expenses Formulas

T77:	@SUM(H77..S77)	T78..T81, T83, T85, T91
E85:	@SUM(E77..E84)	F85..S85
F87:	+E87	F87..S88
E89:	1-@SUM(E87..E88)	F89..S89
G91	+E89*E85+F88*F85+G87*G85	H91..S91

Cash Flow Summary

H97:	+H38	I38..S38
H101:	+H71	I101..S101
H102:	+H91	I102..S102
T97:	@SUM(H97..S97)	T98, T101..T103, T107, T108, T110, T112
H105:	+G105	I105..S105
H106:	+G105/12*G127	I106..S106
H110:	@SUM(H101..H104)+ @SUM(H106..H109)	I110..S110
H112:	+H97+H98-H110	I112..S112

Enter
into
cell: Original formula: Copy to:

Analysis of Cash Requirements

Cell	Original formula	Copy to
H118:	+G9	I118..S118
H119:	+H112	I119..S119
H121:	+H118+H119	I121..S121
I122	+H122	J122..S122
H124:	+H121-H122	I124..S124
H126:	@IF(H124<0,@ABS(H124), @IF(G127>0,@IF(G127>H124, -H124,-G127),0))	I126..S126
G127:	+G15	H127..S127
H129:	+H121+H126	I129..S129

As you can see, the Cash Flow Projector is a complex model. Be sure that you understand the model thoroughly before you attempt to use the application.

Understanding the Model

Because the model begins with Working Capital Accounts, the discussion of the model also will begin with this module.

Working Capital Accounts

As mentioned earlier, working capital is your current assets and liabilities from your balance sheet. (See Chapter 7, "Interactive Financial Statements," for a discussion of the balance sheet.) Figure 3.2 shows the Working Capital Accounts module.

Working Capital Accounts is one of the model's financial reporting sections. Your firm's sales, purchases, inventory, expense activity, and decisions concerning these accounts affect these balances. Therefore, most of this module depends on formulas found in other areas of the model.

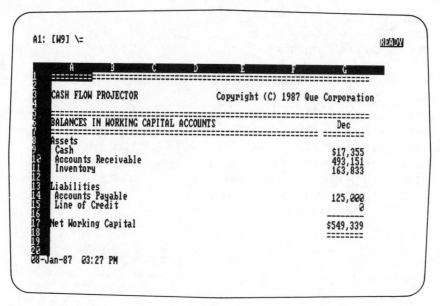

```
A1: [W9] \=                                                        READY

        A       B        C        D        E        F        G
1  ==================================================================
2
3  CASH FLOW PROJECTOR              Copyright (C) 1987 Que Corporation
4
5  ------------------------------------------------------------------
6  BALANCES IN WORKING CAPITAL ACCOUNTS                          Dec
7  ------------------------------------------------------  =========
8  Assets
9   Cash                                                      $17,355
10  Accounts Receivable                                       493,151
11  Inventory                                                 163,833
12
13 Liabilities
14  Accounts Payable                                          125,000
15  Line of Credit                                                  0
16                                                          ---------
17 Net Working Capital                                      $549,339
18                                                          =========
19
20
08-Jan-87  03:27 PM
```

Fig. 3.2. Working Capital Accounts module.

For example, the first working capital account, Cash, is derived from the Analysis of Cash Requirements module's Ending Cash Balance for the months January through December. For January, the formula is

> H9: +H129

The second account, Accounts Receivable, is defined as the prior period's receivables balance plus sales less cash collections. In the model for January, this formula would be

> H10: +G10+H30-H38

G10 is the receivables balance for December, H30 is total sales, and H38 is the total amount of cash collections, both for the month of January.

The third current asset account, Inventory, uses similar logic to calculate this account balance. Inventory is defined as the prior month's inventory balance plus total inventory purchases less cost of goods sold. For January, this is computed by the formula in H11

> H11: +G11+H65-H57

In this formula, G11 is the company's inventory balance from December. H65 is total inventory purchases, and H57 is total cost of goods sold, again, both for January.

Accounts Payable builds on the relationship by adding the previous month's accounts payable to total inventory purchases and then subtracting the current month's payments for purchases.

However, because the model accommodates inventory purchases and overhead expenditures, you need to include your total operating expenses and any payments for these expenses for the current period. For example, the January accounts payable balance in cell H14 is calculated by the following formula:

H14: +G14+H65-H71+H85-H91

The Line of Credit account references row 127 for its balance. For January, the equation to compute your outstanding line of credit is

H15: +H127

In summary, working capital accounts depend on your sales, purchase, inventory, and operating expense accounts. The following sections discuss these independent variables in greater detail.

Sales

The Sales module contains the sales data you need to project monthly cash collections. You'll note that the sample module shown in figure 3.3 includes monthly sales data for five profit centers. In this book, a profit center is defined as a product, store location, division of a company, and so on. When you customize the model for your business, you may need to increase or decrease the number of rows. 1-2-3's @SUM function is used to compute Total Sales.

Collection of payment data comprise the next section of the Sales module. The model gives you the opportunity to build a customized collections pattern based on your business's collection experience.

In the example, 10 percent of sales are for cash, 20 percent are collectible in 30 days, 50 percent are collectible in 60 days, and the remaining 20 percent are collectible in 90 days. The 90-day percentage is a calculated value; the formula for January is

H36: 1-@SUM(H33..H35)

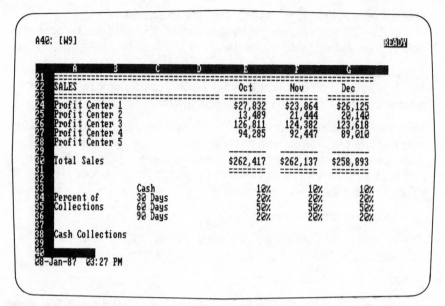

Fig. 3.3. Sales module.

This equation, also used in the Purchases and Operating Expenses modules, subtracts the cash, 30-, and 60-day percentages from one (100 percent) to arrive at the 90-day collection percentage.

Row 38 calculates monthly cash receipts based on your earlier sales data input and the percentage of collections on those sales. The amount that will be collected in any month is the sum of the current month's cash sales plus collections on the previous month's credit sales. Collection of your receivables is calculated by multiplying the sales for each previous month by the appropriate collection percentage. For example, the cash collection for January is

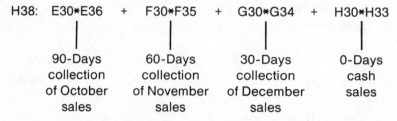

To project cash collections for the month of January, this equation draws on the sales data for October, November, and December, and on the collection percentages for those months.

The Sales module displays the cash inflows to your firm. The next two
modules, Purchases and Operating Expenses, capture your cash
outflows.

Purchases

The Purchases module comprises the cost-of-goods-sold data used to
project monthly purchases and payments for inventory. A section of this
worksheet is shown in figure 3.4.

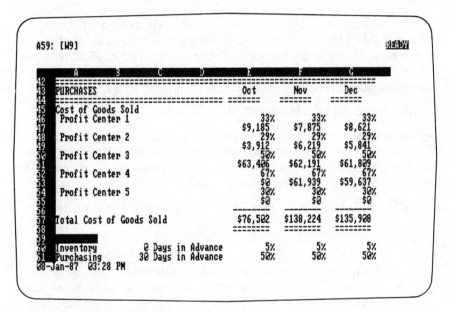

Fig. 3.4. Purchases module.

The historical cost of goods sold for each of the five profit centers is
represented as a percent of sales. Beneath each percentage is the
dollar amount of the cost of goods sold. For Profit Center 1, the amount
for January is calculated by the formula

H47: +H46*H24

This equation multiplies the sales amount by its cost of goods sold
percentage to arrive at a dollar amount for January. The total cost of
goods sold is computed by adding all of these values from every profit

center. For example, January's total is calculated by the following formula:

H57: +H47+H49+H51+H53+H55

The length of the formula depends on the number of profit centers at your business.

The next section of the Purchases module addresses the firm's inventory purchasing pattern. As you know, raw materials must be purchased before the finished goods are produced and the sale realized.

The model accommodates the time lag between inventory purchases and final sale. You can enter the percentages of purchases that will be made zero, 30, 60, and 90 days in advance of your sales. Furthermore, the 90-day value is calculated for you. For example, the 90-day percentage for January (in cell H63), is computed by the formula

H63: 1-@SUM(H60..H62)

which is similar to the formula in January's Percentage of Cash Collections. From these percentages and the monthly cost-of-goods values, the model projects your inventory purchasing requirements. For example, the cost of inventory for January is

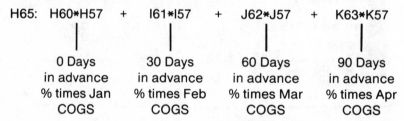

This formula (1) multiplies the 0-day percentage by January's cost of goods sold, (2) adds the product of the 30-day percentage and the February cost of goods sold, (3) adds the product of the 60-day percentage and the March cost of goods sold, and (4) adds the product of the 90-day percentage and the cost-of-goods value for April.

Note the similarity between this formula and the formula in cell H38. One is the inverse of the other, collections being a cash inflow and inventory purchases a cash outflow.

Based on your firm's payment policy (as percent), the module's Payment for Purchases worksheet area estimates the payments for inventory purchases. In the sample module, 30 percent of all purchases are paid for with cash, 40 percent by 30-day credit, and 30 percent by 60-day credit.

This section and the inventory section are similar in structure and contain the same arithmetic logic. For example, the 60-day percentage for January is calculated for you with the equation

H69: 1-@SUM(H67..H68)

You can see that this formula is similar to the one used to compute the 90-day percent of inventory purchases and of the Sales module's cash collections.

Payment for Purchases projects your cash outflow for inventory purchases. January's Payment for Purchases is calculated by the now familiar equation:

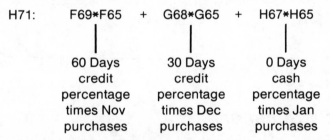

H71:   F69*F65   +   G68*G65   +   H67*H65

| | |
60 Days   30 Days   0 Days
credit   credit   cash
percentage   percentage   percentage
times Nov   times Dec   times Jan
purchases   purchases   purchases

This formula multiplies the 60-day percentage by November's purchases, adds the product of the 30-day percentage and December's purchases, and then adds the product of the cash payment percentage for January's purchases.

Operating Expenses

The Operating Expenses module summarizes your expenses for your product or service and for your overhead. Figure 3.5 shows the structure of the operating expense categories.

In this module, which is similar to the Sales module, monthly Operating and Overhead Expenses for each profit center are entered manually. The @SUM function is used in row 85 to total these expenses.

The Payment Schedule and Total Payment for Expenses portion of the module duplicates exactly the functions and equations found in the Purchases module. (For an explanation of how these values are calculated, refer to the Purchases module section in this chapter.)

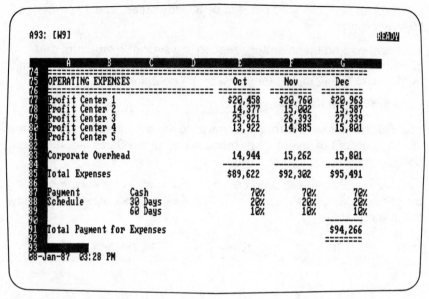

Fig. 3.5. Operating Expenses module.

Cash Flow Summary

The Cash Flow Summary module is shown in figure 3.6.

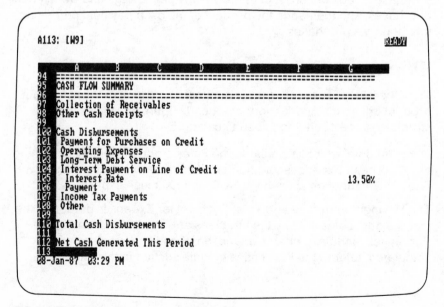

Fig. 3.6. Cash Flow Summary module.

As its name suggests, the Cash Flow Summary module is a report that recaps all of your monthly cash transactions. The Summary first lists all cash inflows, then lists and totals all cash outflows, and then subtracts cash disbursements from cash receipts.

The first cash inflow is the Collection of Receivables in row 97, which is linked to the Sales module's Cash Collections in row 38. For January, the formula for the Collection of Receivables account is

H97: +H38

In row 98, Other Cash Receipts, you can enter additional cash received during the month.

The first cash disbursement, or outflow, is payment for inventory purchases. For January, this is defined as

H101: +H71

Cell H71 is the payment for inventory in the Purchases module. Similarly, Operating Expenses is linked to the total payment in the Operating Expenses module. For example, the equation for January will be

H102: +H91

The example assumes no long-term indebtedness. However, your firm may have a monthly or other periodical long-term debt payment. In that case, the amount should be entered in the appropriate cell in row 103.

The interest rate on your line of credit appears in row 105. This value is used by row 106 to compute the monthly payment, if any, on your line of credit. For January, the formula is

H106: +G105/12*G127

The payment amount is calculated by first dividing your interest rate by 12 to arrive at a monthly value and then multiplying the result by the previous month's line of credit balance, found in row 127.

The previous month's balance is used to avoid a circular reference in the model. If you prefer to use the current month's line of credit balance, substitute H127 for G127.

Your quarterly federal income tax payments are entered into row 107, and the model gives you the opportunity to enter additional cash disbursements in row 108.

Two @SUM functions are used to compute Total Cash Disbursements. January's total, for example, is derived from the equation

H110: @SUM(H101..H104)+@SUM(H106..H109)

This formula adds all of the cash disbursements (except the line of credit interest rate, in cell H105) in column H of the Cash Flow Summary.

Finally, row 112 computes your net cash generated in each period by subtracting disbursements from receipts. A positive value indicates that cash was generated for that month. A negative balance indicates the amount of cash reserves that were depleted from your firm. Net cash generated for January is calculated by the formula

H112: +H97+H98-H110

After summarizing your company's cash activity, the model analyzes your cash requirements.

Analysis of Cash Requirements

The sixth and final section of the model, the Analysis of Cash Requirements module, is shown in figure 3.7.

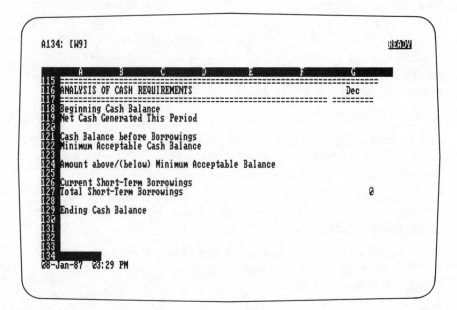

Fig. 3.7. Analysis of Cash Requirements module.

The purpose of this module is to analyze your company's cash flow on a monthly basis and to determine the amount of cash, if any, that is required to meet your firm's financial obligations.

Similar to the Cash Flow Summary, the Analysis of Cash Requirements section depends on data from other areas in the model to perform its calculations. For example, row 118 is January's Beginning Cash Balance, which is linked to the Working Capital Accounts worksheet:

H118: +G9

The next line, Net Cash Generated this Period, is the same as the balance from the Cash Flow Summary. Thus, row 119 for January is defined as

H119: +H112

The Cash Balance before Borrowings, then, is the sum of these two line items. Your January total is calculated by the equation

H121: +H118+H119

For Minimum Acceptable Cash Requirements, the model needs your input of the minimum amount of cash you must have available on a monthly basis. You need only to enter this value in cell H122 and it will be copied across for you, or you can enter an amount for any month you want.

In the next row, the Amount Above or Below your Minimum Acceptable Cash Balance is calculated. This amount is simply the minimum cash balance you will accept, subtracted from your cash balance before borrowings. For January, this total is computed by the formula

H124: +H121-H122

Row 126, Current Short-Term Borrowings, contains the model's most challenging equation. The equation determines the amount your firm will need to borrow on a short-term basis. With some study, you should have no difficulty understanding its concept. For example, your borrowing needs for January are calculated by the following equation:

H126: @IF(H124<0,@ABS(H124),@IF(G127>0,@IF(G127>H124, -H124,-G127),0))

This formula translates: If the minimum acceptable balance for January (H124) is less than zero, borrow this amount. If not, are your December (G127) borrowings greater than zero? If not, you don't need to borrow money, and zero is returned in cell H126.

If so, are your December borrowings greater than the amount above January's minimum acceptable cash balance? If so, the amount above January's minimum acceptable cash balance will be repaid (H124). If not, your entire short-term loan will be repaid (G127). Figure 3.8 represents this process.

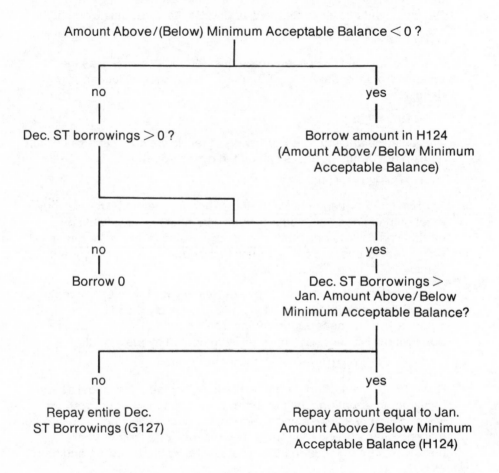

Fig. 3.8. Analysis of December borrowings.

Next, your Total Short-Term Borrowings is computed. This is the sum of your previous line-of-credit balance, if any, and the current month's borrowings. For example, January's total is calculated by the formula in H127:

H127: +G127+H126

Your Ending Cash Balance equals the Cash Balance before Borrowings, plus Total Short-Term Borrowings. To compute this total, your company's January Ending Cash Balance uses the following equation:

H129: +H121+H126

You are now ready to put the Cash Flow Projector to work for your firm.

Using the Model

Because of its complexity, this model requires a significant amount of your business data. Information concerning sales, purchases, and interest rates should be entered in the appropriate section. If the model is to operate properly, you need data similar to our example as it appears in figure 3.1. Enter the data outlined in table 3.4. You may also want to refer to the complete cell listing at the end of this chapter.

Table 3.4
Data Entry

Description	*Location*
Working Capital Accounts	
Cash	G9
Accounts Receivable	G10
Inventory	G11
Accounts Payable	G14
Line of Credit	G15
Sales	
Profit Centers 1-5	E24 through S28
Cash Sales	E33
30 Days	E34
60 Days	E35

Description	*Location*

Purchases

Cost of Goods Sold

Profit Center 1	E46
Profit Center 2	E48
Profit Center 3	E50
Profit Center 4	E52
Profit Center 5	E54

Inventory Purchasing Schedule

Cash	E60
30 Days in Advance	E61
60 Days in Advance	E62

Payment Schedule

Cash	E67
30 Days	E68

Operating Expenses

Profit Center 1	E77 through S77
Profit Center 2	E78 through S78
Profit Center 3	E79 through S79
Profit Center 4	E80 through S80
Profit Center 5	E81 through S81
Corporate Overhead	E83 through S83

Payment Schedule

Cash	E87
30 Days	E88

Cash Flow Summary

Other Cash Receipts	H98..S98
Long-Term Debt Service	H103..S103
Int Pymt on Line of Credit	H105
Income Tax Payments	H107..S107
Other	H108..S108

Analysis of Cash Requirements

Minimum Acceptable Cash Balance	H122

Depending on the number of profit centers in your company, however, your model may require more or less data.

You can accelerate your data entry by borrowing a concept from Chapter 7, "Interactive Financial Statements." If your firm is fortunate enough to have sales growth of one percent per month, for example, 1-2-3 can calculate these monthly amounts for you. Use Column D to indicate the growth rate percentages in the Sales section. (The column heading should be changed accordingly.) Enter the following formula into cell F24:

F24: (1+$D24)∗E24

This formula will multiply the October sales amount by the growth rate indicated in cell D24 to arrive at the November sales value, as shown in figure 3.3. If you /Copy this equation to all subsequent months and then press F9 (CALC), monthly sales for the entire year will be calculated for you. You also can use this technique for the Purchases and Operating Expenses modules.

After the data has been entered, simply press F9 (CALC), and review the results.

Modifying the Model

You can perform "what-if" analysis on your business's cash flow by changing sales values, interest rates, and so on.

Use the /Worksheet Insert Row command to add rows, and add more detailed information about your profit centers. For more detailed reporting and analysis, you may want to use a separate Cash Flow Projector for each of your company's products or profit centers. Then use 1-2-3's /File Combine Add command to consolidate your individual cash projections into a summary statement.

Conclusion

Although the 1-2-3 Cash Flow Projector is complex, it is one of the most useful business management applications. The model will provide you with important financial information about your company to help you make better, and better informed, decisions. Include the Cash Flow Projector as part of your management information system.

A1: [W9] \=
B1: [W9] \=
C1: [W9] \=
D1: [W9] \=
E1: [W11] \=
F1: [W11] \=
G1: [W11] \=
H1: [W11] \=
I1: [W11] \=
J1: [W11] \=
K1: [W11] \=
L1: [W11] \=
M1: [W11] \=
N1: [W11] \=
O1: [W11] \=
P1: [W11] \=
Q1: [W11] \=
R1: [W11] \=
S1: [W11] \=
T1: [W11] \=
U1: [W11] \=
V1: [W11] \=
W1: [W11] \=
A3: [W9] 'CASH FLOW PROJECTOR
E3: [W11] 'Copyright (C) 1987 Que Corporation
A5: [W9] \=
B5: [W9] \=
C5: [W9] \=
D5: [W9] \=
E5: [W11] \=
F5: [W11] \=
G5: [W11] \=
H5: [W11] \=
I5: [W11] \=
J5: [W11] \=
K5: [W11] \=
L5: [W11] \=
M5: [W11] \=
N5: [W11] \=
O5: [W11] \=
P5: [W11] \=
Q5: [W11] \=
R5: [W11] \=
S5: [W11] \=
T5: [W11] \=
U5: [W11] \=
V5: [W11] \=
W5: [W11] \=
A6: [W9] 'BALANCES IN WORKING CAPITAL ACCOUNTS
G6: [W11] ^Dec
H6: [W11] ^Jan
I6: [W11] ^Feb
J6: [W11] ^Mar
K6: [W11] ^Apr

L6: [W11] ^May
M6: [W11] ^Jun
N6: [W11] ^Jul
O6: [W11] ^Aug
P6: [W11] ^Sep
Q6: [W11] ^Oct
R6: [W11] ^Nov
S6: [W11] ^Dec
A7: [W9] \=
B7: [W9] \=
C7: [W9] \=
D7: [W9] \=
E7: [W11] \=
F7: [W11] \=
G7: [W11] ' =========
H7: [W11] ' =========
I7: [W11] ' =========
J7: [W11] ' =========
K7: [W11] ' =========
L7: [W11] ' =========
M7: [W11] ' =========
N7: [W11] ' =========
O7: [W11] ' =========
P7: [W11] ' =========
Q7: [W11] ' =========
R7: [W11] ' =========
S7: [W11] ' =========
A8: [W9] 'Assets
A9: [W9] ' Cash
G9: (C0) [W11] 17355
H9: (C0) [W11] +H129
I9: (C0) [W11] +I129
J9: (C0) [W11] +J129
K9: (C0) [W11] +K129
L9: (C0) [W11] +L129
M9: (C0) [W11] +M129
N9: (C0) [W11] +N129
O9: (C0) [W11] +O129
P9: (C0) [W11] +P129
Q9: (C0) [W11] +Q129
R9: (C0) [W11] +R129
S9: (C0) [W11] +S129
A10: [W9] ' Accounts Receivable
G10: (,0) [W11] 493151
H10: (,0) [W11] +G10+H30-H38
I10: (,0) [W11] +H10+I30-I38
J10: (,0) [W11] +I10+J30-J38
K10: (,0) [W11] +J10+K30-K38
L10: (,0) [W11] +K10+L30-L38
M10: (,0) [W11] +L10+M30-M38
N10: (,0) [W11] +M10+N30-N38
O10: (,0) [W11] +N10+O30-O38
P10: (,0) [W11] +O10+P30-P38
Q10: (,0) [W11] +P10+Q30-Q38

R10: (,0) [W11] +Q10+R30-R38
S10: (,0) [W11] +R10+S30-S38
A11: [W9] ' Inventory
G11: (,0) [W11] 163833
H11: (,0) [W11] +G11+H65-H57
I11: (,0) [W11] +H11+I65-I57
J11: (,0) [W11] +I11+J65-J57
K11: (,0) [W11] +J11+K65-K57
L11: (,0) [W11] +K11+L65-L57
M11: (,0) [W11] +L11+M65-M57
N11: (,0) [W11] +M11+N65-N57
O11: (,0) [W11] +N11+O65-O57
P11: (,0) [W11] +O11+P65-P57
Q11: (,0) [W11] +P11+Q65-Q57
R11: (,0) [W11] +Q11+R65-R57
S11: (,0) [W11] +R11+S65-S57
A13: [W9] 'Liabilities

A14: [W9] ' Accounts Payable
G14: (,0) [W11] 125000
H14: (,0) [W11] +G14+H65-H71+H85-H91
I14: (,0) [W11] +H14+I65-I71+I85-I91
J14: (,0) [W11] +I14+J65-J71+J85-J91
K14: (,0) [W11] +J14+K65-K71+K85-K91
L14: (,0) [W11] +K14+L65-L71+L85-L91
M14: (,0) [W11] +L14+M65-M71+M85-M91
N14: (,0) [W11] +M14+N65-N71+N85-N91
O14: (,0) [W11] +N14+O65-O71+O85-O91
P14: (,0) [W11] +O14+P65-P71+P85-P91
Q14: (,0) [W11] +P14+Q65-Q71+Q85-Q91
R14: (,0) [W11] +Q14+R65-R71+R85-R91
S14: (,0) [W11] +R14+S65-S71+S85-S91
A15: [W9] ' Line of Credit
G15: (,0) [W11] 0
H15: (,0) [W11] +H127
I15: (,0) [W11] +I127
J15: (,0) [W11] +J127
K15: (,0) [W11] +K127
L15: (,0) [W11] +L127
M15: (,0) [W11] +M127
N15: (,0) [W11] +N127
O15: (,0) [W11] +O127
P15: (,0) [W11] +P127
Q15: (,0) [W11] +Q127
R15: (,0) [W11] +R127
S15: (,0) [W11] +S127
G16: [W11] ' --------
H16: [W11] ' --------
I16: [W11] ' --------
J16: [W11] ' --------
K16: [W11] ' --------
L16: [W11] ' --------
M16: [W11] ' --------
N16: [W11] ' --------

O16: [W11] ' --------
P16: [W11] ' --------
Q16: [W11] ' --------
R16: [W11] ' --------
S16: [W11] ' --------
A17: [W9] 'Net Working Capital
G17: (C0) [W11] +G9+G10+G11-G14-G15
H17: (C0) [W11] +H9+H10+H11-H14-H15
I17: (C0) [W11] +I9+I10+I11-I14-I15
J17: (C0) [W11] +J9+J10+J11-J14-J15
K17: (C0) [W11] +K9+K10+K11-K14-K15
L17: (C0) [W11] +L9+L10+L11-L14-L15
M17: (C0) [W11] +M9+M10+M11-M14-M15
N17: (C0) [W11] +N9+N10+N11-N14-N15
O17: (C0) [W11] +O9+O10+O11-O14-O15
P17: (C0) [W11] +P9+P10+P11-P14-P15
Q17: (C0) [W11] +Q9+Q10+Q11-Q14-Q15
R17: (C0) [W11] +R9+R10+R11-R14-R15
S17: (C0) [W11] +S9+S10+S11-S14-S15
G18: [W11] ' ========
H18: [W11] ' ========
I18: [W11] ' ========
J18: [W11] ' ========
K18: [W11] ' ========
L18: [W11] ' ========
M18: [W11] ' ========
N18: [W11] ' ========
O18: [W11] ' ========
P18: [W11] ' ========
Q18: [W11] ' ========
R18: [W11] ' ========
S18: [W11] ' ========
A21: [W9] \=
B21: [W9] \=
C21: [W9] \=
D21: [W9] \=
E21: [W11] \=
F21: [W11] \=
G21: [W11] \=
H21: [W11] \=
I21: [W11] \=
J21: [W11] \=
K21: [W11] \=
L21: [W11] \=
M21: [W11] \=
N21: [W11] \=
O21: [W11] \=
P21: [W11] \=
Q21: [W11] \=
R21: [W11] \=
S21: [W11] \=
T21: [W11] \=
A22: [W9] 'SALES

E22: [W11] ^Oct
F22: [W11] ^Nov
G22: [W11] ^Dec
H22: [W11] ^Jan
I22: [W11] ^Feb
J22: [W11] ^Mar
K22: [W11] ^Apr
L22: [W11] ^May
M22: [W11] ^Jun
N22: [W11] ^Jul
O22: [W11] ^Aug
P22: [W11] ^Sep
Q22: [W11] ^Oct
R22: [W11] ^Nov
S22: [W11] ^Dec
T22: [W11] ^Total
A23: [W9] \=
B23: [W9] \=
C23: [W9] \=
D23: [W9] \=
E23: [W11] ' =========
F23: [W11] ' =========
G23: [W11] ' =========
H23: [W11] ' =========
I23: [W11] ' =========
J23: [W11] ' =========
K23: [W11] ' =========
L23: [W11] ' =========
M23: [W11] ' =========
N23: [W11] ' =========
O23: [W11] ' =========
P23: [W11] ' =========
Q23: [W11] ' =========
R23: [W11] ' =========
S23: [W11] ' =========
T23: [W11] ' =========
A24: [W9] 'Profit Center 1
E24: (C0) [W11] 27832
F24: (C0) [W11] 23864
G24: (C0) [W11] 26125
H24: (C0) [W11] 31336
I24: (C0) [W11] 37954
J24: (C0) [W11] 43879
K24: (C0) [W11] 51471
L24: (C0) [W11] 56953
M24: (C0) [W11] 53145
N24: (C0) [W11] 54140
O24: (C0) [W11] 53614
P24: (C0) [W11] 52015
Q24: (C0) [W11] 48902
R24: (C0) [W11] 44091
S24: (C0) [W11] 42536
T24: (C0) [W11] @SUM(H24..S24)

A25: [W9] 'Profit Center 2
E25: (,0) [W11] 13489
F25: (,0) [W11] 21444
G25: (,0) [W11] 20140
H25: (,0) [W11] 22572
I25: (,0) [W11] 24888
J25: (,0) [W11] 25167
K25: (,0) [W11] 32588
L25: (,0) [W11] 40140
M25: (,0) [W11] 37970
N25: (,0) [W11] 34587
O25: (,0) [W11] 33463
P25: (,0) [W11] 28939
Q25: (,0) [W11] 24153
R25: (,0) [W11] 27060
S25: (,0) [W11] 26701
T25: (,0) [W11] @SUM(H25..S25)
A26: [W9] 'Profit Center 3
E26: (,0) [W11] 126811
F26: (,0) [W11] 124382
G26: (,0) [W11] 123618
H26: (,0) [W11] 131685
I26: (,0) [W11] 129044
J26: (,0) [W11] 131723
K26: (,0) [W11] 139221
L26: (,0) [W11] 141879
M26: (,0) [W11] 149803
N26: (,0) [W11] 147108
O26: (,0) [W11] 147032
P26: (,0) [W11] 153440
Q26: (,0) [W11] 149990
R26: (,0) [W11] 145198
S26: (,0) [W11] 150510
T26: (,0) [W11] @SUM(H26..S26)
A27: [W9] 'Profit Center 4
E27: (,0) [W11] 94285
F27: (,0) [W11] 92447
G27: (,0) [W11] 89010
H27: (,0) [W11] 95473
I27: (,0) [W11] 98008
J27: (,0) [W11] 96986
K27: (,0) [W11] 95318
L27: (,0) [W11] 103538
M27: (,0) [W11] 108146
N27: (,0) [W11] 108642
O27: (,0) [W11] 106065
P27: (,0) [W11] 110401
Q27: (,0) [W11] 112018
R27: (,0) [W11] 111956
S27: (,0) [W11] 107522
T27: (,0) [W11] @SUM(H27..S27)
A28: [W9] 'Profit Center 5
N28: (,0) [W11] 115000

```
O28: (,0) [W11] 175000              S31: [W11] ' ========
P28: (,0) [W11] 225000              T31: [W11] ' ========
Q28: (,0) [W11] 300000              C33: [W9] 'Cash
R28: (,0) [W11] 325000              E33: (P0) [W11] 0.1
S28: (,0) [W11] 350000              F33: (P0) [W11] +E33
T28: (,0) [W11] @SUM(H28..S28)      G33: (P0) [W11] +F33
E29: [W11] ' --------              H33: (P0) [W11] +G33
F29: [W11] ' --------              I33: (P0) [W11] +H33
G29: [W11] ' --------              J33: (P0) [W11] +I33
H29: [W11] ' --------              K33: (P0) [W11] +J33
I29: [W11] ' --------              L33: (P0) [W11] +K33
J29: [W11] ' --------              M33: (P0) [W11] +L33
K29: [W11] ' --------              N33: (P0) [W11] +M33
L29: [W11] ' --------              O33: (P0) [W11] +N33
M29: [W11] ' --------              P33: (P0) [W11] +O33
N29: [W11] ' --------              Q33: (P0) [W11] +P33
O29: [W11] ' --------              R33: (P0) [W11] +Q33
P29: [W11] ' --------              S33: (P0) [W11] +R33
Q29: [W11] ' --------              A34: [W9] 'Percent of
R29: [W11] ' --------              C34: [W9] '30 Days
S29: [W11] ' --------              E34: (P0) [W11] 0.2
T29: [W11] ' --------              F34: (P0) [W11] +E34
A30: [W9] 'Total Sales             G34: (P0) [W11] +F34
E30: (C0) [W11] @SUM(E24..E29)      H34: (P0) [W11] +G34
F30: (C0) [W11] @SUM(F24..F29)      I34: (P0) [W11] +H34
G30: (C0) [W11] @SUM(G24..G29)      J34: (P0) [W11] +I34
H30: (C0) [W11] @SUM(H24..H29)      K34: (P0) [W11] +J34
I30: (C0) [W11] @SUM(I24..I29)      L34: (P0) [W11] +K34
J30: (C0) [W11] @SUM(J24..J29)      M34: (P0) [W11] +L34
K30: (C0) [W11] @SUM(K24..K29)      N34: (P0) [W11] +M34
L30: (C0) [W11] @SUM(L24..L29)      O34: (P0) [W11] +N34
M30: (C0) [W11] @SUM(M24..M29)      P34: (P0) [W11] +O34
N30: (C0) [W11] @SUM(N24..N29)      Q34: (P0) [W11] +P34
O30: (C0) [W11] @SUM(O24..O29)      R34: (P0) [W11] +Q34
P30: (C0) [W11] @SUM(P24..P29)      S34: (P0) [W11] +R34
Q30: (C0) [W11] @SUM(Q24..Q29)      A35: [W9] 'Collections
R30: (C0) [W11] @SUM(R24..R29)      C35: [W9] '60 Days
S30: (C0) [W11] @SUM(S24..S29)      E35: (P0) [W11] 0.5
T30: (C0) [W11] @SUM(T24..T29)      F35: (P0) [W11] +E35
E31: [W11] ' ========'             G35: (P0) [W11] +F35
F31: [W11] ' ========              H35: (P0) [W11] +G35
G31: [W11] ' ========              I35: (P0) [W11] +H35
H31: [W11] ' ========              J35: (P0) [W11] +I35
I31: [W11] ' ========              K35: (P0) [W11] +J35
J31: [W11] ' ========              L35: (P0) [W11] +K35
K31: [W11] ' ========              M35: (P0) [W11] +L35
L31: [W11] ' ========              N35: (P0) [W11] +M35
M31: [W11] ' ========              O35: (P0) [W11] +N35
N31: [W11] ' ========              P35: (P0) [W11] +O35
O31: [W11] ' ========              Q35: (P0) [W11] +P35
P31: [W11] ' ========              R35: (P0) [W11] +Q35
Q31: [W11] ' ========              S35: (P0) [W11] +R35
R31: [W11] ' ========              A36: [W9] '
```

```
C36: [W9] '90 Days                              Q39: [W11] '  ========
E36: (P0) [W11] 1-@SUM(E33..E35)                R39: [W11] '  ========
F36: (P0) [W11] 1-@SUM(F33..F35)                S39: [W11] '  ========
G36: (P0) [W11] 1-@SUM(G33..G35)                T39: [W11] '  ========
H36: (P0) [W11] 1-@SUM(H33..H35)                A42: [W9] \=
I36: (P0) [W11] 1-@SUM(I33..I35)                B42: [W9] \=
J36: (P0) [W11] 1-@SUM(J33..J35)                C42: [W9] \=
K36: (P0) [W11] 1-@SUM(K33..K35)                D42: [W9] \=
L36: (P0) [W11] 1-@SUM(L33..L35)                E42: [W11] \=
M36: (P0) [W11] 1-@SUM(M33..M35)                F42: [W11] \=
N36: (P0) [W11] 1-@SUM(N33..N35)                G42: [W11] \=
O36: (P0) [W11] 1-@SUM(O33..O35)                H42: [W11] \=
P36: (P0) [W11] 1-@SUM(P33..P35)                I42: [W11] \=
Q36: (P0) [W11] 1-@SUM(Q33..Q35)                J42: [W11] \=
R36: (P0) [W11] 1-@SUM(R33..R35)                K42: [W11] \=
S36: (P0) [W11] 1-@SUM(S33..S35)                L42: [W11] \=
H37: [W11] '  --------                          M42: [W11] \=
I37: [W11] '  --------                          N42: [W11] \=
J37: [W11] '  --------                          O42: [W11] \=
K37: [W11] '  --------                          P42: [W11] \=
L37: [W11] '  --------                          Q42: [W11] \=
M37: [W11] '  --------                          R42: [W11] \=
N37: [W11] '  --------                          S42: [W11] \=
O37: [W11] '  --------                          T42: [W11] \=
P37: [W11] '  --------                          U42: [W11] \=
Q37: [W11] '  --------                          V42: [W11] \=
R37: [W11] '  --------                          W42: [W11] \=
S37: [W11] '  --------                          A43: [W9] 'PURCHASES
T37: [W11] '  --------                          E43: [W11] ^Oct
A38: [W9] 'Cash Collections                     F43: [W11] ^Nov
H38: (C0) [W11] +E30*E36+F30*F35+G30*G34+H30*H33  G43: [W11] ^Dec
I38: (C0) [W11] +F30*F36+G30*G35+H30*H34+I30*I33  H43: [W11] ^Jan
J38: (C0) [W11] +G30*G36+H30*H35+I30*I34+J30*J33  I43: [W11] ^Feb
K38: (C0) [W11] +H30*H36+I30*I35+J30*J34+K30*K33  J43: [W11] ^Mar
L38: (C0) [W11] +I30*I36+J30*J35+K30*K34+L30*L33  K43: [W11] ^Apr
M38: (C0) [W11] +J30*J36+K30*K35+L30*L34+M30*M33  L43: [W11] ^May
N38: (C0) [W11] +K30*K36+L30*L35+M30*M34+N30*N33  M43: [W11] ^Jun
O38: (C0) [W11] +L30*L36+M30*M35+N30*N34+O30*O33  N43: [W11] ^Jul
P38: (C0) [W11] +M30*M36+N30*N35+O30*O34+P30*P33  O43: [W11] ^Aug
Q38: (C0) [W11] +N30*N36+O30*O35+P30*P34+Q30*Q33  P43: [W11] ^Sep
R38: (C0) [W11] +O30*O36+P30*P35+Q30*Q34+R30*R33  Q43: [W11] ^Oct
S38: (C0) [W11] +P30*P36+Q30*Q35+R30*R34+S30*S33  R43: [W11] ^Nov
T38: (C0) [W11] @SUM(H38..S38)                  S43: [W11] ^Dec
H39: [W11] '  ========                          T43: [W11] ^Total
I39: [W11] '  ========                          A44: [W9] \=
J39: [W11] '  ========                          B44: [W9] \=
K39: [W11] '  ========                          C44: [W9] \=
L39: [W11] '  ========                          D44: [W9] \=
M39: [W11] '  ========                          E44: [W11] '  =======
N39: [W11] '  ========                          F44: [W11] '  =======
O39: [W11] '  ========                          G44: [W11] '  =======
P39: [W11] '  ========                          H44: [W11] '  =======
```

I44: [W11] ' =======
J44: [W11] ' =======
K44: [W11] ' =======
L44: [W11] ' =======
M44: [W11] ' =======
N44: [W11] ' =======
O44: [W11] ' =======
P44: [W11] ' =======
Q44: [W11] ' =======
R44: [W11] ' =======
S44: [W11] ' =======
T44: [W11] ' =======
A45: [W9] 'Cost of Goods Sold
A46: [W9] ' Profit Center 1
E46: (P0) [W11] 0.33
F46: (P0) [W11] +E46
G46: (P0) [W11] +F46
H46: (P0) [W11] +G46
I46: (P0) [W11] +H46
J46: (P0) [W11] +I46
K46: (P0) [W11] +J46
L46: (P0) [W11] +K46
M46: (P0) [W11] +L46
N46: (P0) [W11] +M46
O46: (P0) [W11] +N46
P46: (P0) [W11] +O46
Q46: (P0) [W11] +P46
R46: (P0) [W11] +Q46
S46: (P0) [W11] +R46
E47: (C0) [W11] +E46*E24
F47: (C0) [W11] +F46*F24
G47: (C0) [W11] +G46*G24
H47: (C0) [W11] +H46*H24
I47: (C0) [W11] +I46*I24
J47: (C0) [W11] +J46*J24
K47: (C0) [W11] +K46*K24
L47: (C0) [W11] +L46*L24
M47: (C0) [W11] +M46*M24
N47: (C0) [W11] +N46*N24
O47: (C0) [W11] +O46*O24
P47: (C0) [W11] +P46*P24
Q47: (C0) [W11] +Q46*Q24
R47: (C0) [W11] +R46*R24
S47: (C0) [W11] +S46*S24
T47: (C0) [W11] @SUM(H47..S47)
A48: [W9] ' Profit Center 2
E48: (P0) [W11] 0.29
F48: (P0) [W11] +E48
G48: (P0) [W11] +F48
H48: (P0) [W11] +G48
I48: (P0) [W11] +H48
J48: (P0) [W11] +I48
K48: (P0) [W11] +J48

L48: (P0) [W11] +K48
M48: (P0) [W11] +L48
N48: (P0) [W11] +M48
O48: (P0) [W11] +N48
P48: (P0) [W11] +O48
Q48: (P0) [W11] +P48
R48: (P0) [W11] +Q48
S48: (P0) [W11] +R48
E49: (C0) [W11] +E48*E25
F49: (C0) [W11] +F48*F25
G49: (C0) [W11] +G48*G25
H49: (C0) [W11] +H48*H25
I49: (C0) [W11] +I48*I25
J49: (C0) [W11] +J48*J25
K49: (C0) [W11] +K48*K25
L49: (C0) [W11] +L48*L25
M49: (C0) [W11] +M48*M25
N49: (C0) [W11] +N48*N25
O49: (C0) [W11] +O48*O25
P49: (C0) [W11] +P48*P25
Q49: (C0) [W11] +Q48*Q25
R49: (C0) [W11] +R48*R25
S49: (C0) [W11] +S48*S25
T49: (C0) [W11] @SUM(H49..S49)
A50: [W9] ' Profit Center 3
E50: (P0) [W11] 0.5
F50: (P0) [W11] +E50
G50: (P0) [W11] +F50
H50: (P0) [W11] +G50
I50: (P0) [W11] +H50
J50: (P0) [W11] +I50
K50: (P0) [W11] +J50
L50: (P0) [W11] +K50
M50: (P0) [W11] +L50
N50: (P0) [W11] +M50
O50: (P0) [W11] +N50
P50: (P0) [W11] +O50
Q50: (P0) [W11] +P50
R50: (P0) [W11] +Q50
S50: (P0) [W11] +R50
E51: (C0) [W11] +E50*E26
F51: (C0) [W11] +F50*F26
G51: (C0) [W11] +G50*G26
H51: (C0) [W11] +H50*H26
I51: (C0) [W11] +I50*I26
J51: (C0) [W11] +J50*J26
K51: (C0) [W11] +K50*K26
L51: (C0) [W11] +L50*L26
M51: (C0) [W11] +M50*M26
N51: (C0) [W11] +N50*N26
O51: (C0) [W11] +O50*O26
P51: (C0) [W11] +P50*P26
Q51: (C0) [W11] +Q50*Q26

```
R51: (C0) [W11] +R50*R26
S51: (C0) [W11] +S50*S26
T51: (C0) [W11] @SUM(H51..S51)
A52: [W9] ' Profit Center 4
E52: (P0) [W11] 0.67
F52: (P0) [W11] +E52
G52: (P0) [W11] +F52
H52: (P0) [W11] +G52
I52: (P0) [W11] +H52
J52: (P0) [W11] +I52
K52: (P0) [W11] +J52
L52: (P0) [W11] +K52
M52: (P0) [W11] +L52
N52: (P0) [W11] +M52
O52: (P0) [W11] +N52
P52: (P0) [W11] +O52
Q52: (P0) [W11] +P52
R52: (P0) [W11] +Q52
S52: (P0) [W11] +R52
E53: (C0) [W11] +E52*E27
F53: (C0) [W11] +F52*F27
G53: (C0) [W11] +G52*G27
H53: (C0) [W11] +H52*H27
I53: (C0) [W11] +I52*I27
J53: (C0) [W11] +J52*J27
K53: (C0) [W11] +K52*K27
L53: (C0) [W11] +L52*L27
M53: (C0) [W11] +M52*M27
N53: (C0) [W11] +N52*N27
O53: (C0) [W11] +O52*O27
P53: (C0) [W11] +P52*P27
Q53: (C0) [W11] +Q52*Q27
R53: (C0) [W11] +R52*R27
S53: (C0) [W11] +S52*S27
T53: (C0) [W11] @SUM(H53..S53)
A54: [W9] ' Profit Center 5
E54: (P0) [W11] 0.3
F54: (P0) [W11] +E54
G54: (P0) [W11] +F54
H54: (P0) [W11] +G54
I54: (P0) [W11] +H54
J54: (P0) [W11] +I54
K54: (P0) [W11] +J54
L54: (P0) [W11] +K54
M54: (P0) [W11] +L54
N54: (P0) [W11] +M54
O54: (P0) [W11] +N54
P54: (P0) [W11] +O54
Q54: (P0) [W11] +P54
R54: (P0) [W11] +Q54
S54: (P0) [W11] +R54
E55: (C0) [W11] +E54*E28
F55: (C0) [W11] +F54*F28

G55: (C0) [W11] +G54*G28
H55: (C0) [W11] +H54*H28
I55: (C0) [W11] +I54*I28
J55: (C0) [W11] +J54*J28
K55: (C0) [W11] +K54*K28
L55: (C0) [W11] +L54*L28
M55: (C0) [W11] +M54*M28
N55: (C0) [W11] +N54*N28
O55: (C0) [W11] +O54*O28
P55: (C0) [W11] +P54*P28
Q55: (C0) [W11] +Q54*Q28
R55: (C0) [W11] +R54*R28
S55: (C0) [W11] +S54*S28
T55: (C0) [W11] @SUM(H55..S55)
E56: [W11] ' --------
F56: [W11] ' --------
G56: [W11] ' --------
H56: [W11] ' --------
I56: [W11] ' --------
J56: [W11] ' --------
K56: [W11] ' --------
L56: [W11] ' --------
M56: [W11] ' --------
N56: [W11] ' --------
O56: [W11] ' --------
P56: [W11] ' --------
Q56: [W11] ' --------
R56: [W11] ' --------
S56: [W11] ' --------
T56: [W11] ' --------
A57: [W9] 'Total Cost of Goods Sold
E57: (C0) [W11] +E47+E49+E51+E53+E55
F57: (C0) [W11] +F47+F49+F51+F53+F55
G57: (C0) [W11] +G47+G49+G51+G53+G55
H57: (C0) [W11] +H47+H49+H51+H53+H55
I57: (C0) [W11] +I47+I49+I51+I53+I55
J57: (C0) [W11] +J47+J49+J51+J53+J55
K57: (C0) [W11] +K47+K49+K51+K53+K55
L57: (C0) [W11] +L47+L49+L51+L53+L55
M57: (C0) [W11] +M47+M49+M51+M53+M55
N57: (C0) [W11] +N47+N49+N51+N53+N55
O57: (C0) [W11] +O47+O49+O51+O53+O55
P57: (C0) [W11] +P47+P49+P51+P53+P55
Q57: (C0) [W11] +Q47+Q49+Q51+Q53+Q55
R57: (C0) [W11] +R47+R49+R51+R53+R55
S57: (C0) [W11] +S47+S49+S51+S53+S55
T57: (C0) [W11] +T47+T49+T51+T53+T55
U57: (C0) [W11] +S57
V57: (C0) [W11] +U57
W57: (C0) [W11] +V57
E58: [W11] ' ========
F58: [W11] ' ========
G58: [W11] ' ========
```

```
H58: [W11] ' ========        A62: [W9] 'Schedule
I58: [W11] ' ========        C62: [W9] '60 Days in Advance
J58: [W11] ' ========        E62: (P0) [W11] 0.3
K58: [W11] ' ========        F62: (P0) [W11] +E62
L58: [W11] ' ========        G62: (P0) [W11] +F62
M58: [W11] ' ========        H62: (P0) [W11] +G62
N58: [W11] ' ========        I62: (P0) [W11] +H62
O58: [W11] ' ========        J62: (P0) [W11] +I62
P58: [W11] ' ========        K62: (P0) [W11] +J62
Q58: [W11] ' ========        L62: (P0) [W11] +K62
R58: [W11] ' ========        M62: (P0) [W11] +L62
S58: [W11] ' ========        N62: (P0) [W11] +M62
T58: [W11] ' ========        O62: (P0) [W11] +N62
A60: [W9] 'Inventory         P62: (P0) [W11] +O62
C60: [W9] ' 0 Days in Advance Q62: (P0) [W11] +P62
E60: (P0) [W11] 0.05         R62: (P0) [W11] +Q62
F60: (P0) [W11] +E60         S62: (P0) [W11] +R62
G60: (P0) [W11] +F60         U62: (P0) [W11] +S62
H60: (P0) [W11] +G60         V62: (P0) [W11] +U62
I60: (P0) [W11] +H60         W62: (P0) [W11] +V62
J60: (P0) [W11] +I60         C63: [W9] '90 Days in Advance
K60: (P0) [W11] +J60         E63: (P0) [W11] 1-@SUM(E60..E62)
L60: (P0) [W11] +K60         F63: (P0) [W11] 1-@SUM(F60..F62)
M60: (P0) [W11] +L60         G63: (P0) [W11] 1-@SUM(G60..G62)
N60: (P0) [W11] +M60         H63: (P0) [W11] 1-@SUM(H60..H62)
O60: (P0) [W11] +N60         I63: (P0) [W11] 1-@SUM(I60..I62)
P60: (P0) [W11] +O60         J63: (P0) [W11] 1-@SUM(J60..J62)
Q60: (P0) [W11] +P60         K63: (P0) [W11] 1-@SUM(K60..K62)
R60: (P0) [W11] +Q60         L63: (P0) [W11] 1-@SUM(L60..L62)
S60: (P0) [W11] +R60         M63: (P0) [W11] 1-@SUM(M60..M62)
U60: (P0) [W11] +S60         N63: (P0) [W11] 1-@SUM(N60..N62)
V60: (P0) [W11] +U60         O63: (P0) [W11] 1-@SUM(O60..O62)
W60: (P0) [W11] +V60         P63: (P0) [W11] 1-@SUM(P60..P62)
A61: [W9] 'Purchasing        Q63: (P0) [W11] 1-@SUM(Q60..Q62)
C61: [W9] '30 Days in Advance R63: (P0) [W11] 1-@SUM(R60..R62)
E61: (P0) [W11] 0.5          S63: (P0) [W11] 1-@SUM(S60..S62)
F61: (P0) [W11] +E61         U63: (P0) [W11] +S63
G61: (P0) [W11] +F61         V63: (P0) [W11] +U63
H61: (P0) [W11] +G61         W63: (P0) [W11] +V63
I61: (P0) [W11] +H61         A65: [W9] 'Inventory Purchases
J61: (P0) [W11] +I61         E65: (C0) [W11] +E60*E57+F61*F57+G62*G57+H63*H57
K61: (P0) [W11] +J61         F65: (C0) [W11] +F60*F57+G61*G57+H62*H57+I63*I57
L61: (P0) [W11] +K61         G65: (C0) [W11] +G60*G57+H61*H57+I62*I57+J63*J57
M61: (P0) [W11] +L61         H65: (C0) [W11] +H60*H57+I61*I57+J62*J57+K63*K57
N61: (P0) [W11] +M61         I65: (C0) [W11] +I60*I57+J61*J57+K62*K57+L63*L57
O61: (P0) [W11] +N61         J65: (C0) [W11] +J60*J57+K61*K57+L62*L57+M63*M57
P61: (P0) [W11] +O61         K65: (C0) [W11] +K60*K57+L61*L57+M62*M57+N63*N57
Q61: (P0) [W11] +P61         L65: (C0) [W11] +L60*L57+M61*M57+N62*N57+O63*O57
R61: (P0) [W11] +Q61         M65: (C0) [W11] +M60*M57+N61*N57+O62*O57+P63*P57
S61: (P0) [W11] +R61         N65: (C0) [W11] +N60*N57+O61*O57+P62*P57+Q63*Q57
U61: (P0) [W11] +S61         O65: (C0) [W11] +O60*O57+P61*P57+Q62*Q57+R63*R57
V61: (P0) [W11] +U61         P65: (C0) [W11] +P60*P57+Q61*Q57+R62*R57+S63*S57
W61: (P0) [W11] +V61         Q65: (C0) [W11] +Q60*Q57+R61*R57+S62*S57+U63*U57
```

R65: (C0) [W11] +R60*R57+S61*S57+U62*U57+V63*V57
S65: (C0) [W11] +S60*S57+U61*U57+V62*V57+W63*W57
T65: (C0) [W11] @SUM(H65..S65)
A67: [W9] 'Payment
C67: [W9] 'Cash
E67: (P0) [W11] 0.3
F67: (P0) [W11] +E67
G67: (P0) [W11] +F67
H67: (P0) [W11] +G67
I67: (P0) [W11] +H67
J67: (P0) [W11] +I67
K67: (P0) [W11] +J67
L67: (P0) [W11] +K67
M67: (P0) [W11] +L67
N67: (P0) [W11] +M67
O67: (P0) [W11] +N67
P67: (P0) [W11] +O67
Q67: (P0) [W11] +P67
R67: (P0) [W11] +Q67
S67: (P0) [W11] +R67
A68: [W9] 'Schedule
C68: [W9] '30 Days
E68: (P0) [W11] 0.4
F68: (P0) [W11] +E68
G68: (P0) [W11] +F68
H68: (P0) [W11] +G68
I68: (P0) [W11] +H68
J68: (P0) [W11] +I68
K68: (P0) [W11] +J68
L68: (P0) [W11] +K68
M68: (P0) [W11] +L68
N68: (P0) [W11] +M68
O68: (P0) [W11] +N68
P68: (P0) [W11] +O68
Q68: (P0) [W11] +P68
R68: (P0) [W11] +Q68
S68: (P0) [W11] +R68
C69: [W9] '60 Days
E69: (P0) [W11] 1-@SUM(E67..E68)
F69: (P0) [W11] 1-@SUM(F67..F68)
G69: (P0) [W11] 1-@SUM(G67..G68)
H69: (P0) [W11] 1-@SUM(H67..H68)
I69: (P0) [W11] 1-@SUM(I67..I68)
J69: (P0) [W11] 1-@SUM(J67..J68)
K69: (P0) [W11] 1-@SUM(K67..K68)
L69: (P0) [W11] 1-@SUM(L67..L68)
M69: (P0) [W11] 1-@SUM(M67..M68)
N69: (P0) [W11] 1-@SUM(N67..N68)
O69: (P0) [W11] 1-@SUM(O67..O68)
P69: (P0) [W11] 1-@SUM(P67..P68)
Q69: (P0) [W11] 1-@SUM(Q67..Q68)
R69: (P0) [W11] 1-@SUM(R67..R68)
S69: (P0) [W11] 1-@SUM(S67..S68)

G70: [W11] ' --------
H70: [W11] ' --------
I70: [W11] ' --------
J70: [W11] ' --------
K70: [W11] ' --------
L70: [W11] ' --------
M70: [W11] ' --------
N70: [W11] ' --------
O70: [W11] ' --------
P70: [W11] ' --------
Q70: [W11] ' --------
R70: [W11] ' --------
S70: [W11] ' --------
T70: [W11] ' --------
A71: [W9] 'Payment for Purchases
G71: (C0) [W11] +E69*E65+F68*F65+G67*G65
H71: (C0) [W11] +F69*F65+G68*G65+H67*H65
I71: (C0) [W11] +G69*G65+H68*H65+I67*I65
J71: (C0) [W11] +H69*H65+I68*I65+J67*J65
K71: (C0) [W11] +I69*I65+J68*J65+K67*K65
L71: (C0) [W11] +J69*J65+K68*K65+L67*L65
M71: (C0) [W11] +K69*K65+L68*L65+M67*M65
N71: (C0) [W11] +L69*L65+M68*M65+N67*N65
O71: (C0) [W11] +M69*M65+N68*N65+O67*O65
P71: (C0) [W11] +N69*N65+O68*O65+P67*P65
Q71: (C0) [W11] +O69*O65+P68*P65+Q67*Q65
R71: (C0) [W11] +P69*P65+Q68*Q65+R67*R65
S71: (C0) [W11] +Q69*Q65+R68*R65+S67*S65
T71: (C0) [W11] @SUM(H71..S71)
G72: [W11] ' ========
H72: [W11] ' ========
I72: [W11] ' ========
J72: [W11] ' ========
K72: [W11] ' ========
L72: [W11] ' ========
M72: [W11] ' ========
N72: [W11] ' ========
O72: [W11] ' ========
P72: [W11] ' ========
Q72: [W11] ' ========
R72: [W11] ' ========
S72: [W11] ' ========
T72: [W11] ' ========
A74: [W9] \=
B74: [W9] \=
C74: [W9] \=
D74: [W9] \=
E74: [W11] \=
F74: [W11] \=
G74: [W11] \=
H74: [W11] \=
I74: [W11] \=
J74: [W11] \=

K74: [W11] \=
L74: [W11] \=
M74: [W11] \=
N74: [W11] \=
O74: [W11] \=
P74: [W11] \=
Q74: [W11] \=
R74: [W11] \=
S74: [W11] \=
T74: [W11] \=
A75: [W9] 'OPERATING EXPENSES
E75: [W11] ^Oct
F75: [W11] ^Nov
G75: [W11] ^Dec
H75: [W11] ^Jan
I75: [W11] ^Feb
J75: [W11] ^Mar
K75: [W11] ^Apr
L75: [W11] ^May
M75: [W11] ^Jun
N75: [W11] ^Jul
O75: [W11] ^Aug
P75: [W11] ^Sep
Q75: [W11] ^Oct
R75: [W11] ^Nov
S75: [W11] ^Dec
T75: [W11] ^Total
A76: [W9] \=
B76: [W9] \=
C76: [W9] \=
D76: [W9] \=
E76: [W11] ' =========
F76: [W11] ' =========
G76: [W11] ' =========
H76: [W11] ' =========
I76: [W11] ' =========
J76: [W11] ' =========
K76: [W11] ' =========
L76: [W11] ' =========
M76: [W11] ' =========
N76: [W11] ' =========
O76: [W11] ' =========
P76: [W11] ' =========
Q76: [W11] ' =========
R76: [W11] ' =========
S76: [W11] ' =========
T76: [W11] ' =========
A77: [W9] 'Profit Center 1
E77: (C0) [W11] 20458
F77: (C0) [W11] 20760
G77: (C0) [W11] 20963
H77: (C0) [W11] 21529
I77: (C0) [W11] 22329
J77: (C0) [W11] 22802
K77: (C0) [W11] 23108
L77: (C0) [W11] 24099
M77: (C0) [W11] 24422
N77: (C0) [W11] 24431
O77: (C0) [W11] 25060
P77: (C0) [W11] 25646
Q77: (C0) [W11] 26515
R77: (C0) [W11] 26639
S77: (C0) [W11] 26881
T77: (C0) [W11] @SUM(H77..S77)
A78: [W9] 'Profit Center 2
E78: (,0) [W11] 14377
F78: (,0) [W11] 15002
G78: (,0) [W11] 15587
H78: (,0) [W11] 15946
I78: (,0) [W11] 16790
J78: (,0) [W11] 17355
K78: (,0) [W11] 17739
L78: (,0) [W11] 18195
M78: (,0) [W11] 18610
N78: (,0) [W11] 19412
O78: (,0) [W11] 19546
P78: (,0) [W11] 20348
Q78: (,0) [W11] 20860
R78: (,0) [W11] 21729
S78: (,0) [W11] 21785
T78: (,0) [W11] @SUM(H78..S78)
A79: [W9] 'Profit Center 3
E79: (,0) [W11] 25921
F79: (,0) [W11] 26393
G79: (,0) [W11] 27339
H79: (,0) [W11] 27554
I79: (,0) [W11] 28286
J79: (,0) [W11] 28464
K79: (,0) [W11] 29275
L79: (,0) [W11] 29292
M79: (,0) [W11] 29578
N79: (,0) [W11] 30246
O79: (,0) [W11] 30358
P79: (,0) [W11] 31041
Q79: (,0) [W11] 31680
R79: (,0) [W11] 32048
S79: (,0) [W11] 32525
T79: (,0) [W11] @SUM(H79..S79)
A80: [W9] 'Profit Center 4
E80: (,0) [W11] 13922
F80: (,0) [W11] 14885
G80: (,0) [W11] 15801
H80: (,0) [W11] 16130
I80: (,0) [W11] 16800
J80: (,0) [W11] 17651
K80: (,0) [W11] 18039

```
L80: (,0) [W11] 18789
M80: (,0) [W11] 19704
N80: (,0) [W11] 20400
O80: (,0) [W11] 20939
P80: (,0) [W11] 21589
Q80: (,0) [W11] 21833
R80: (,0) [W11] 22024
S80: (,0) [W11] 22154
T80: (,0) [W11] @SUM(H80..S80)
A81: [W9] 'Profit Center 5
I81: (,0) [W11] 10000
J81: (,0) [W11] 14000
K81: (,0) [W11] 18000
L81: (,0) [W11] 20000
M81: (,0) [W11] 22000
N81: (,0) [W11] 22470
O81: (,0) [W11] 22837
P81: (,0) [W11] 22995
Q81: (,0) [W11] 23364
R81: (,0) [W11] 24023
S81: (,0) [W11] 24806
T81: (,0) [W11] @SUM(H81..S81)
A83: [W9] 'Corporate Overhead
E83: (,0) [W11] 14944
F83: (,0) [W11] 15262
G83: (,0) [W11] 15801
H83: (,0) [W11] 16332
I83: (,0) [W11] 16474
J83: (,0) [W11] 16933
K83: (,0) [W11] 17616
L83: (,0) [W11] 18575
M83: (,0) [W11] 18640
N83: (,0) [W11] 19278
O83: (,0) [W11] 19544
P83: (,0) [W11] 20225
Q83: (,0) [W11] 21142
R83: (,0) [W11] 21565
S83: (,0) [W11] 22378
T83: (,0) [W11] @SUM(H83..S83)
E84: [W11] ' --------
F84: [W11] ' --------
G84: [W11] ' --------
H84: [W11] ' --------
I84: [W11] ' --------
J84: [W11] ' --------
K84: [W11] ' --------
L84: [W11] ' --------
M84: [W11] ' --------
N84: [W11] ' --------
O84: [W11] ' --------
P84: [W11] ' --------
Q84: [W11] ' --------
R84: [W11] ' --------
S84: [W11] ' --------
T84: [W11] ' --------
A85: [W9] 'Total Expenses
E85: (C0) [W11] @SUM(E77..E84)
F85: (C0) [W11] @SUM(F77..F84)
G85: (C0) [W11] @SUM(G77..G84)
H85: (C0) [W11] @SUM(H77..H84)
I85: (C0) [W11] @SUM(I77..I84)
J85: (C0) [W11] @SUM(J77..J84)
K85: (C0) [W11] @SUM(K77..K84)
L85: (C0) [W11] @SUM(L77..L84)
M85: (C0) [W11] @SUM(M77..M84)
N85: (C0) [W11] @SUM(N77..N84)
O85: (C0) [W11] @SUM(O77..O84)
P85: (C0) [W11] @SUM(P77..P84)
Q85: (C0) [W11] @SUM(Q77..Q84)
R85: (C0) [W11] @SUM(R77..R84)
S85: (C0) [W11] @SUM(S77..S84)
T85: (C0) [W11] @SUM(T77..T84)
A87: [W9] 'Payment
C87: [W9] 'Cash
E87: (P0) [W11] 0.7
F87: (P0) [W11] +E87
G87: (P0) [W11] +F87
H87: (P0) [W11] +G87
I87: (P0) [W11] +H87
J87: (P0) [W11] +I87
K87: (P0) [W11] +J87
L87: (P0) [W11] +K87
M87: (P0) [W11] +L87
N87: (P0) [W11] +M87
O87: (P0) [W11] +N87
P87: (P0) [W11] +O87
Q87: (P0) [W11] +P87
R87: (P0) [W11] +Q87
S87: (P0) [W11] +R87
A88: [W9] 'Schedule
C88: [W9] '30 Days
E88: (P0) [W11] 0.2
F88: (P0) [W11] +E88
G88: (P0) [W11] +F88
H88: (P0) [W11] +G88
I88: (P0) [W11] +H88
J88: (P0) [W11] +I88
K88: (P0) [W11] +J88
L88: (P0) [W11] +K88
M88: (P0) [W11] +L88
N88: (P0) [W11] +M88
O88: (P0) [W11] +N88
P88: (P0) [W11] +O88
Q88: (P0) [W11] +P88
R88: (P0) [W11] +Q88
S88: (P0) [W11] +R88
```

C89: [W9] '60 Days
E89: (P0) [W11] 1-@SUM(E87..E88)
F89: (P0) [W11] 1-@SUM(F87..F88)
G89: (P0) [W11] 1-@SUM(G87..G88)
H89: (P0) [W11] 1-@SUM(H87..H88)
I89: (P0) [W11] 1-@SUM(I87..I88)
J89: (P0) [W11] 1-@SUM(J87..J88)
K89: (P0) [W11] 1-@SUM(K87..K88)
L89: (P0) [W11] 1-@SUM(L87..L88)
M89: (P0) [W11] 1-@SUM(M87..M88)
N89: (P0) [W11] 1-@SUM(N87..N88)
O89: (P0) [W11] 1-@SUM(O87..O88)
P89: (P0) [W11] 1-@SUM(P87..P88)
Q89: (P0) [W11] 1-@SUM(Q87..Q88)
R89: (P0) [W11] 1-@SUM(R87..R88)
S89: (P0) [W11] 1-@SUM(S87..S88)
G90: [W11] ' --------
H90: [W11] ' --------
I90: [W11] ' --------
J90: [W11] ' --------
K90: [W11] ' --------
L90: [W11] ' --------
M90: [W11] ' --------
N90: [W11] ' --------
O90: [W11] ' --------
P90: [W11] ' --------
Q90: [W11] ' --------
R90: [W11] ' --------
S90: [W11] ' --------
T90: [W11] ' --------
A91: [W9] 'Total Payment for Expenses
G91: (C0) [W11] +E89*E85+F88*F85+G87*G85
H91: (C0) [W11] +F89*F85+G88*G85+H87*H85
I91: (C0) [W11] +G89*G85+H88*H85+I87*I85
J91: (C0) [W11] +H89*H85+I88*I85+J87*J85
K91: (C0) [W11] +I89*I85+J88*J85+K87*K85
L91: (C0) [W11] +J89*J85+K88*K85+L87*L85
M91: (C0) [W11] +K89*K85+L88*L85+M87*M85
N91: (C0) [W11] +L89*L85+M88*M85+N87*N85
O91: (C0) [W11] +M89*M85+N88*N85+O87*O85
P91: (C0) [W11] +N89*N85+O88*O85+P87*P85
Q91: (C0) [W11] +O89*O85+P88*P85+Q87*Q85
R91: (C0) [W11] +P89*P85+Q88*Q85+R87*R85
S91: (C0) [W11] +Q89*Q85+R88*R85+S87*S85
T91: (C0) [W11] @SUM(H91..S91)
G92: [W11] ' ========
H92: [W11] ' ========
I92: [W11] ' ========
J92: [W11] ' ========
K92: [W11] ' ========
L92: [W11] '. ========
M92: [W11] ' ========
N92: [W11] ' ========
O92: [W11] ' ========
P92: [W11] ' ========
Q92: [W11] ' ========
R92: [W11] ' ========
S92: [W11] ' ========
T92: [W11] ' ========
A94: [W9] \=
B94: [W9] \=
C94: [W9] \=
D94: [W9] \=
E94: [W11] \=
F94: [W11] \=
G94: [W11] \=
H94: [W11] \=
I94: [W11] \=
J94: [W11] \=
K94: [W11] \=
L94: [W11] \=
M94: [W11] \=
N94: [W11] \=
O94: [W11] \=
P94: [W11] \=
Q94: [W11] \=
R94: [W11] \=
S94: [W11] \=
T94: [W11] \=
A95: [W9] 'CASH FLOW SUMMARY
H95: [W11] ^Jan
I95: [W11] ^Feb
J95: [W11] ^Mar
K95: [W11] ^Apr
L95: [W11] ^May
M95: [W11] ^Jun
N95: [W11] ^Jul
O95: [W11] ^Aug
P95: [W11] ^Sep
Q95: [W11] ^Oct
R95: [W11] ^Nov
S95: [W11] ^Dec
T95: [W11] ^Total
A96: [W9] \=
B96: [W9] \=
C96: [W9] \=
D96: [W9] \=
E96: [W11] \=
F96: [W11] \=
G96: [W11] \=
H96: [W11] ' =========
I96: [W11] ' =========
J96: [W11] ' =========
K96: [W11] ' =========

```
L96: [W11] ' =========
M96: [W11] ' =========
N96: [W11] ' =========
O96: [W11] ' =========
P96: [W11] ' =========
Q96: [W11] ' =========
R96: [W11] ' =========
S96: [W11] ' =========
T96: [W11] ' =========
A97: [W9] 'Collection of Receivables
H97: (C0) [W11] +H38
I97: (C0) [W11] +I38
J97: (C0) [W11] +J38
K97: (C0) [W11] +K38
L97: (C0) [W11] +L38
M97: (C0) [W11] +M38
N97: (C0) [W11] +N38
O97: (C0) [W11] +O38
P97: (C0) [W11] +P38
Q97: (C0) [W11] +Q38
R97: (C0) [W11] +R38
S97: (C0) [W11] +S38
T97: (C0) [W11] @SUM(H97..S97)
A98: [W9] 'Other Cash Receipts
H98: (,0) [W11] 0
I98: (,0) [W11] 0
J98: (,0) [W11] 0
K98: (,0) [W11] 0
L98: (,0) [W11] 0
M98: (,0) [W11] 0
N98: (,0) [W11] 0
O98: (,0) [W11] 0
P98: (,0) [W11] 0
Q98: (,0) [W11] 0
R98: (,0) [W11] 0
S98: (,0) [W11] 50000
T98: (,0) [W11] 50000
A100: [W9] 'Cash Disbursements
A101: [W9] ' Payment for Purchases on Credit
H101: (,0) [W11] +H71
I101: (,0) [W11] +I71
J101: (,0) [W11] +J71
K101: (,0) [W11] +K71
L101: (,0) [W11] +L71
M101: (,0) [W11] +M71
N101: (,0) [W11] +N71
O101: (,0) [W11] +O71
P101: (,0) [W11] +P71
Q101: (,0) [W11] +Q71
R101: (,0) [W11] +R71
S101: (,0) [W11] +S71
T101: (,0) [W11] @SUM(H101..S101)

A102: [W9] ' Operating Expenses
H102: (,0) [W11] +H91
I102: (,0) [W11] +I91
J102: (,0) [W11] +J91
K102: (,0) [W11] +K91
L102: (,0) [W11] +L91
M102: (,0) [W11] +M91
N102: (,0) [W11] +N91
O102: (,0) [W11] +O91
P102: (,0) [W11] +P91
Q102: (,0) [W11] +Q91
R102: (,0) [W11] +R91
S102: (,0) [W11] +S91
T102: (,0) [W11] @SUM(H102..S102)
A103: [W9] ' Long-Term Debt Service
H103: (,0) [W11] 0
I103: (,0) [W11] 0
J103: (,0) [W11] 0
K103: (,0) [W11] 0
L103: (,0) [W11] 0
M103: (,0) [W11] 0
N103: (,0) [W11] 0
O103: (,0) [W11] 0
P103: (,0) [W11] 0
Q103: (,0) [W11] 0
R103: (,0) [W11] 0
S103: (,0) [W11] 0
T103: (,0) [W11] @SUM(H103..S103)
A104: [W9] ' Interest Payment on Line of Credit
A105: [W9] '  Interest Rate
G105: (P2) [W11] 0.135
H105: (P2) [W11] +G105
I105: (P2) [W11] +H105
J105: (P2) [W11] +I105
K105: (P2) [W11] +J105
L105: (P2) [W11] +K105
M105: (P2) [W11] +L105
N105: (P2) [W11] +M105
O105: (P2) [W11] +N105
P105: (P2) [W11] +O105
Q105: (P2) [W11] +P105
R105: (P2) [W11] +Q105
S105: (P2) [W11] +R105
A106: [W9] '  Payment
H106: (,0) [W11] +G105/12*G127
I106: (,0) [W11] +H105/12*H127
J106: (,0) [W11] +I105/12*I127
K106: (,0) [W11] +J105/12*J127
L106: (,0) [W11] +K105/12*K127
M106: (,0) [W11] +L105/12*L127
N106: (,0) [W11] +M105/12*M127
O106: (,0) [W11] +N105/12*N127
```

P106: (,0) [W11] +O105/12*O127
Q106: (,0) [W11] +P105/12*P127
R106: (,0) [W11] +Q105/12*Q127
S106: (,0) [W11] +R105/12*R127
T106: (,0) [W11] @SUM(H106..S106)
A107: [W9] ' Income Tax Payments
H107: (,0) [W11] 5340
I107: (,0) [W11] 5413
J107: (,0) [W11] 5677
K107: (,0) [W11] 5930
L107: (,0) [W11] 6179
M107: (,0) [W11] 6532
N107: (,0) [W11] 7109
O107: (,0) [W11] 7833
P107: (,0) [W11] 9315
Q107: (,0) [W11] 10681
R107: (,0) [W11] 11762
S107: (,0) [W11] 12767
T107: (,0) [W11] @SUM(H107..S107)
A108: [W9] ' Other
H108: (,0) [W11] 0
I108: (,0) [W11] 0
J108: (,0) [W11] 0
K108: (,0) [W11] 0
L108: (,0) [W11] 0
M108: (,0) [W11] 0
N108: (,0) [W11] 0
O108: (,0) [W11] 0
P108: (,0) [W11] 0
Q108: (,0) [W11] 0
R108: (,0) [W11] 0
S108: (,0) [W11] 0
T108: (,0) [W11] @SUM(H108..S108)
H109: [W11] ' --------
I109: [W11] ' --------
J109: [W11] ' --------
K109: [W11] ' --------
L109: [W11] ' --------
M109: [W11] ' --------
N109: [W11] ' --------
O109: [W11] ' --------
P109: [W11] ' --------
Q109: [W11] ' --------
R109: [W11] ' --------
S109: [W11] ' --------
T109: [W11] ' --------
A110: [W9] 'Total Cash Disbursements
H110: (,0) [W11] @SUM(H101..H104)+@SUM(H106..H109)
I110: (,0) [W11] @SUM(I101..I104)+@SUM(I106..I109)
J110: (,0) [W11] @SUM(J101..J104)+@SUM(J106..J109)
K110: (,0) [W11] @SUM(K101..K104)+@SUM(K106..K109)
L110: (,0) [W11] @SUM(L101..L104)+@SUM(L106..L109)
M110: (,0) [W11] @SUM(M101..M104)+@SUM(M106..M109)

N110: (,0) [W11] @SUM(N101..N104)+@SUM(N106..N109)
O110: (,0) [W11] @SUM(O101..O104)+@SUM(O106..O109)
P110: (,0) [W11] @SUM(P101..P104)+@SUM(P106..P109)
Q110: (,0) [W11] @SUM(Q101..Q104)+@SUM(Q106..Q109)
R110: (,0) [W11] @SUM(R101..R104)+@SUM(R106..R109)
S110: (,0) [W11] @SUM(S101..S104)+@SUM(S106..S109)
T110: (,0) [W11] @SUM(T101..T104)+@SUM(T106..T109)
H111: [W11] ' --------
I111: [W11] ' --------
J111: [W11] ' --------
K111: [W11] ' --------
L111: [W11] ' --------
M111: [W11] ' --------
N111: [W11] ' --------
O111: [W11] ' --------
P111: [W11] ' --------
Q111: [W11] ' --------
R111: [W11] ' --------
S111: [W11] ' --------
T111: [W11] ' --------
A112: [W9] 'Net Cash Generated This Period
H112: (C0) [W11] +H97+H98-H110
I112: (C0) [W11] +I97+I98-I110
J112: (C0) [W11] +J97+J98-J110
K112: (C0) [W11] +K97+K98-K110
L112: (C0) [W11] +L97+L98-L110
M112: (C0) [W11] +M97+M98-M110
N112: (C0) [W11] +N97+N98-N110
O112: (C0) [W11] +O97+O98-O110
P112: (C0) [W11] +P97+P98-P110
Q112: (C0) [W11] +Q97+Q98-Q110
R112: (C0) [W11] +R97+R98-R110
S112: (C0) [W11] +S97+S98-S110
T112: (C0) [W11] @SUM(H112..S112)
H113: [W11] ' ========
I113: [W11] ' ========
J113: [W11] ' ========
K113: [W11] ' ========
L113: [W11] ' ========
M113: [W11] ' ========
N113: [W11] ' ========
O113: [W11] ' ========
P113: [W11] ' ========
Q113: [W11] ' ========
R113: [W11] ' ========
S113: [W11] ' ========
T113: [W11] ' ========
A115: [W9] \=
B115: [W9] \=
C115: [W9] \=
D115: [W9] \=
E115: [W11] \=
F115: [W11] \=

```
G115: [W11] \=
H115: [W11] \=
I115: [W11] \=
J115: [W11] \=
K115: [W11] \=
L115: [W11] \=
M115: [W11] \=
N115: [W11] \=
O115: [W11] \=
P115: [W11] \=
Q115: [W11] \=
R115: [W11] \=
S115: [W11] \=
T115: [W11] \=
A116: [W9] 'ANALYSIS OF CASH REQUIREMENTS
G116: [W11] ^Dec
H116: [W11] ^Jan
I116: [W11] ^Feb
J116: [W11] ^Mar
K116: [W11] ^Apr
L116: [W11] ^May
M116: [W11] ^Jun
N116: [W11] ^Jul
O116: [W11] ^Aug
P116: [W11] ^Sep
Q116: [W11] ^Oct
R116: [W11] ^Nov
S116: [W11] ^Dec
A117: [W9] \=
B117: [W9] \=
C117: [W9] \=
D117: [W9] \=
E117: [W11] \=
F117: [W11] \=
G117: [W11] ' =========
H117: [W11] ' =========
I117: [W11] ' =========
J117: [W11] ' =========
K117: [W11] ' =========
L117: [W11] ' =========
M117: [W11] ' =========
N117: [W11] ' =========
O117: [W11] ' =========
P117: [W11] ' =========
Q117: [W11] ' =========
R117: [W11] ' =========
S117: [W11] ' =========
A118: [W9] 'Beginning Cash Balance
H118: (C0) [W11] +G9
I118: (C0) [W11] +H9
J118: (C0) [W11] +I9
K118: (C0) [W11] +J9
L118: (C0) [W11] +K9

M118: (C0) [W11] +L9
N118: (C0) [W11] +M9
O118: (C0) [W11] +N9
P118: (C0) [W11] +O9
Q118: (C0) [W11] +P9
R118: (C0) [W11] +Q9
S118: (C0) [W11] +R9
A119: [W9] 'Net Cash Generated This Period
H119: (,0) [W11] +H112
I119: (,0) [W11] +I112
J119: (,0) [W11] +J112
K119: (,0) [W11] +K112
L119: (,0) [W11] +L112
M119: (,0) [W11] +M112
N119: (,0) [W11] +N112
O119: (,0) [W11] +O112
P119: (,0) [W11] +P112
Q119: (,0) [W11] +Q112
R119: (,0) [W11] +R112
S119: (,0) [W11] +S112
H120: [W11] ' --------
I120: [W11] ' --------
J120: [W11] ' --------
K120: [W11] ' --------
L120: [W11] ' --------
M120: [W11] ' --------
N120: [W11] ' --------
O120: [W11] ' --------
P120: [W11] ' --------
Q120: [W11] ' --------
R120: [W11] ' --------
S120: [W11] ' --------
A121: [W9] 'Cash Balance before Borrowings
H121: (,0) [W11] +H118+H119
I121: (,0) [W11] +I118+I119
J121: (,0) [W11] +J118+J119
K121: (,0) [W11] +K118+K119
L121: (,0) [W11] +L118+L119
M121: (,0) [W11] +M118+M119
N121: (,0) [W11] +N118+N119
O121: (,0) [W11] +O118+O119
P121: (,0) [W11] +P118+P119
Q121: (,0) [W11] +Q118+Q119
R121: (,0) [W11] +R118+R119
S121: (,0) [W11] +S118+S119
A122: [W9] 'Minimum Acceptable Cash Balance
H122: (,0) [W11] 20000
I122: (,0) [W11] +H122
J122: (,0) [W11] +I122
K122: (,0) [W11] +J122
L122: (,0) [W11] +K122
M122: (,0) [W11] +L122
N122: (,0) [W11] +M122
```

```
O122: (,0) [W11] +N122
P122: (,0) [W11] +O122
Q122: (,0) [W11] +P122
R122: (,0) [W11] +Q122
S122: (,0) [W11] +R122
H123: [W11] ' --------
I123: [W11] ' --------
J123: [W11] ' --------
K123: [W11] ' --------
L123: [W11] ' --------
M123: [W11] ' --------
N123: [W11] ' --------
O123: [W11] ' --------
P123: [W11] ' --------
Q123: [W11] ' --------
R123: [W11] ' --------
S123: [W11] ' --------
A124: [W9] 'Amount above/(below) Minimum Acceptable Balance
H124: (,0) [W11] +H121-H122
I124: (,0) [W11] +I121-I122
J124: (,0) [W11] +J121-J122
K124: (,0) [W11] +K121-K122
L124: (,0) [W11] +L121-L122
M124: (,0) [W11] +M121-M122
N124: (,0) [W11] +N121-N122
O124: (,0) [W11] +O121-O122
P124: (,0) [W11] +P121-P122
Q124: (,0) [W11] +Q121-Q122
R124: (,0) [W11] +R121-R122
S124: (,0) [W11] +S121-S122
A126: [W9] 'Current Short-Term Borrowings
H126: (,0) [W11] @IF(H124<0,@ABS(H124),@IF(G127>0,@IF(G127>H124,-H124,-G127),0))
I126: (,0) [W11] @IF(I124<0,@ABS(I124),@IF(H127>0,@IF(H127>I124,-I124,-H127),0))
J126: (,0) [W11] @IF(J124<0,@ABS(J124),@IF(I127>0,@IF(I127>J124,-J124,-I127),0))
K126: (,0) [W11] @IF(K124<0,@ABS(K124),@IF(J127>0,@IF(J127>K124,-K124,-J127),0))
L126: (,0) [W11] @IF(L124<0,@ABS(L124),@IF(K127>0,@IF(K127>L124,-L124,-K127),0))
M126: (,0) [W11] @IF(M124<0,@ABS(M124),@IF(L127>0,@IF(L127>M124,-M124,-L127),0))
N126: (,0) [W11] @IF(N124<0,@ABS(N124),@IF(M127>0,@IF(M127>N124,-N124,-M127),0))
O126: (,0) [W11] @IF(O124<0,@ABS(O124),@IF(N127>0,@IF(N127>O124,-O124,-N127),0))
P126: (,0) [W11] @IF(P124<0,@ABS(P124),@IF(O127>0,@IF(O127>P124,-P124,-O127),0))
Q126: (,0) [W11] @IF(Q124<0,@ABS(Q124),@IF(P127>0,@IF(P127>Q124,-Q124,-P127),0))
R126: (,0) [W11] @IF(R124<0,@ABS(R124),@IF(Q127>0,@IF(Q127>R124,-R124,-Q127),0))
S126: (,0) [W11] @IF(S124<0,@ABS(S124),@IF(R127>0,@IF(R127>S124,-S124,-R127),0))
A127: [W9] 'Total Short-Term Borrowings
G127: (,0) [W11] +G15
H127: (,0) [W11] +G127+H126
I127: (,0) [W11] +H127+I126
J127: (,0) [W11] +I127+J126
K127: (,0) [W11] +J127+K126
L127: (,0) [W11] +K127+L126
M127: (,0) [W11] +L127+M126
N127: (,0) [W11] +M127+N126
```

```
O127: (,0) [W11] +N127+O126
P127: (,0) [W11] +O127+P126
Q127: (,0) [W11] +P127+Q126
R127: (,0) [W11] +Q127+R126
S127: (,0) [W11] +R127+S126
H128: [W11] ' --------
I128: [W11] ' --------
J128: [W11] ' --------
K128: [W11] ' --------
L128: [W11] ' --------
M128: [W11] ' --------
N128: [W11] ' --------
O128: [W11] ' --------
P128: [W11] ' --------
Q128: [W11] ' --------
R128: [W11] ' --------
S128: [W11] ' --------
A129: [W9] 'Ending Cash Balance
H129: (C0) [W11] +H121+H126
I129: (C0) [W11] +I121+I126
J129: (C0) [W11] +J121+J126
K129: (C0) [W11] +K121+K126
L129: (C0) [W11] +L121+L126
M129: (C0) [W11] +M121+M126
N129: (C0) [W11] +N121+N126
O129: (C0) [W11] +O121+O126
P129: (C0) [W11] +P121+P126
Q129: (C0) [W11] +Q121+Q126
R129: (C0) [W11] +R121+R126
S129: (C0) [W11] +S121+S126
H130: [W11] ' ========
I130: [W11] ' ========
J130: [W11] ' ========
K130: [W11] ' ========
L130: [W11] ' ========
M130: [W11] ' ========
N130: [W11] ' ========
O130: [W11] ' ========
P130: [W11] ' ========
Q130: [W11] ' ========
R130: [W11] ' ========
S130: [W11] ' ========
```

4

Managing Cash Flow

Introduction

Managing cash is one of the most important activities of financial management. The goal of cash management is to have enough money for day-to-day operations, a cushion for unexpected disbursements, and to invest excess reserves. The 1-2-3 Cash Flow Manager can help you with this task.

You can use the model in several ways. If you use it as a financial report, you can display all actual receipts and disbursements; or all year-to-date transactions (with projected receipts and disbursements for the balance of the year).

You can also use the Cash Flow Manager as a planning tool. You will be aware well in advance of potential cash shortfalls or excessively high cash balances. And you can use the model to do "what-if" analysis, such as the impact on cash flow of a week's delay of payments to your suppliers.

This chapter explains how to create, understand, and use the Cash Flow Manager. You also find tips on how to use 1-2-3 with your personal computer to create and modify the application.

This model has two sections: the Weekly Activity worksheet and, directly below it, the macro worksheet area. The model is straightforward and easy to understand. You need to do only a minimum of side-to-side scrolling because this application is exactly 70 spaces wide. Figure 4.1 shows the Cash Flow Manager model.

CASH FLOW MANAGER   Copyright (C) Que Corporation 1987

WEEKLY ACTIVITY

| | Receipts | | Disbursements | | |
Date	Description	Amount	Description	Amount	Balance
05-Jan-87	Opening Balance.....				$5,000
			Office Rent	$900	$4,100
			Payroll	$500	$3,600
			Phone	$100	$3,500
					$3,500
12-Jan-87	Sales	$1,000			$4,500
	Sale of Truck	$1,000			$5,500
					$5,500
19-Jan-87	Sales	$1,000			$5,500
			Office Supplies	$50	$6,450
			Payroll	$500	$5,950
					$5,950
26-Jan-87	Sales	$1,000			$5,950
			Truck Down Pymt	$1,000	$5,450
			Utilities	$500	$5,450
					$5,450
02-Feb-87	Beginning Balance.....				$5,450
	Sales	$1,000	Office Rent	$900	$5,550
			Payroll	$500	$5,050
			Phone	$100	$4,950
					$4,950
09-Feb-87	Sales	$1,000			$5,950
					$5,950
					$5,950
16-Feb-87	Sales	$1,000			$6,950
					$6,950
					$6,950
23-Feb-87	Sales	$1,000	Utilities	$500	$7,450
					$7,450
					$7,450
02-Mar-87	Beginning Balance.....				$7,450
	Sales	$1,000	Office Rent	$900	$7,550
			Payroll	$500	$7,050
			Phone	$100	$6,950
					$6,950
09-Mar-87	Sales	$1,000			$7,950
					$7,950
					$7,950
					$7,950
16-Mar-87	Sales	$1,000			$8,950
					$8,950
					$8,950
					$8,950
23-Mar-87	Sales	$1,000			$9,950
					$9,950
					$9,950
30-Mar-87	Sales	$1,000	Utilities	$500	$10,450
			Taxes	$4,000	$6,450
					$6,450
06-Apr-87	Beginning Balance.....				$6,450
	Sales	$1,000	Office Rent	$900	$6,550
			Payroll	$500	$6,050

Line	Date	Description	Deposit	Payment For	Payment	Balance
68				Phone	$100	$5,950
69	13-Apr-87	Sales				$5,950
70			$1,000			$6,950
71						$6,950
72						$6,950
73	20-Apr-87					$6,950
74		Sales	$1,000			$7,950
75						$7,950
76						$7,950
77	27-Apr-87					$7,950
78		Sales	$1,000	Utilities	$500	$8,450
79						$8,450
80						$8,450
81	04-May-87	Beginning Balance.....				$8,450
82		Sales	$1,000	Office Rent	$900	$8,550
83				Payroll	$500	$8,050
84				Phone	$100	$7,950
85	11-May-87					$7,950
86		Sales	$1,000			$8,950
87						$8,950
88						$8,950
89	18-May-87					$8,950
90		Sales	$1,000			$9,950
91						$9,950
92						$9,950
93	25-May-87					$9,950
94		Sales	$1,000	Utilities	$500	$10,450
95						$10,450
96						$10,450
97	01-Jun-87	Beginning Balance.....				$10,450
98		Sales	$1,000	Office Rent	$900	$10,550
99				Payroll	$500	$10,050
100				Phone	$100	$9,950
101	08-Jun-87					$9,950
102		Sales	$1,000	Insurance	$750	$10,200
103						$10,200
104						$10,200
105	15-Jun-87					$10,200
106		Sales	$1,000			$11,200
107						$11,200
108						$11,200
109	22-Jun-87					$11,200
110		Sales	$1,000	Owner's Draw	$5,000	$7,200
111						$7,200
112						$7,200
113	29-Jun-87					$7,200
114		Sales	$1,000	Utilities	$500	$7,700
115				Taxes	$4,000	$3,700
116						$3,700
117	06-Jul-87	Beginning Balance.....				$3,700
118		Sales	$1,000	Office Rent	$900	$3,800
119				Payroll	$500	$3,300
120				Phone	$100	$3,200
121	13-Jul-87					$3,200
122		Sales	$1,000			$4,200
123						$4,200
124						$4,200
125	20-Jul-87					$4,200
126		Sales	$1,000	Office Supplies	$75	$5,125
127						$5,125
128						$5,125
129	27-Jul-87					$5,125
130		Sales	$1,000	Utilities	$500	$5,625
131						$5,625
132						$5,625
133	03-Aug-87	Beginning Balance.....				$5,625
134		Sales	$1,000	Office Rent	$900	$5,725

Row	Date	Transaction	Amount	Balance
135				$5,225
136		Payroll	$500	$5,125
137	10-Aug-87	Phone	$100	$5,125
138		Sales	$1,000	$6,125
139				$6,125
140				$6,125
141	17-Aug-87			$7,125
142		Sales	$1,000	$7,125
143				$7,125
144				$7,125
145	24-Aug-87	Typewriter	$500	$7,625
146		Sales	$1,000	$7,625
147				$7,625
148				$7,625
149	31-Aug-87	Utilities	$500	$8,125
150		Sales	$1,000	$8,125
151				$8,125
152				$8,125
153	07-Sep-87	Beginning Balance.....		$8,225
154		Sales / Office Rent	$1,000 / $900	$8,225
155		Payroll	$500	$7,725
156		Phone	$100	$7,625
157	14-Sep-87			$7,625
158		Sales	$1,000	$8,625
159				$8,625
160				$8,625
161	21-Sep-87			$8,625
162		Sales	$1,000	$9,625
163				$9,625
164				$9,625
165	28-Sep-87	Utilities	$500	$9,625
166		Sales	$1,000	$10,125
167		Taxes	$4,000	$6,125
168				$6,125
169	05-Oct-87	Beginning Balance.....		$6,225
170		Sales / Office Rent	$1,000 / $900	$5,725
171		Payroll	$500	$5,625
172		Phone	$100	$5,625
173	12-Oct-87			$6,625
174		Sales	$1,000	$6,625
175				$6,625
176				$6,625
177	19-Oct-87			$7,625
178		Sales	$1,000	$7,625
179				$7,625
180				$8,125
181	26-Oct-87	Utilities	$500	$8,125
182		Sales	$1,000	$8,125
183				$8,125
184				$8,225
185	02-Nov-87	Beginning Balance.....		$7,725
186		Sales / Office Rent	$1,000 / $900	$7,625
187		Payroll	$500	$7,625
188		Phone	$100	$8,625
189	09-Nov-87			$8,625
190		Sales	$1,000	$8,625
191				$8,625
192				$9,625
193	16-Nov-87			$9,625
194		Sales	$1,000	$9,625
195				$9,625
196				$10,625
197	23-Nov-87			$10,625
198		Sales	$1,000	$10,625
199				$11,125
200	30-Nov-87			$11,125
201		Sales / Utilities	$1,000 / $500	
202				

```
203                                                               $11,125
204  07-Dec-87 Beginning Balance....                              $11,125
205            Sales         $1,000 Office Rent        $900       $11,225
206                                 Payroll            $500       $10,725
207                                 Phone              $100       $10,625
208  14-Dec-87                                                    $10,625
209            Sales         $1,000                               $11,625
210                                                               $11,625
211                                                               $11,625
212  21-Dec-87                                                    $11,625
213            Sales         $1,000 Bonus             $250        $12,375
214                                 Owner's Draw      $5,000       $7,375
215                                                                $7,375
216  28-Dec-87                                                     $7,375
217            Sales         $1,000 Insurance          $750        $7,625
218                                 Utilities          $500        $7,125
219                                 Taxes             $4,000       $3,125
220  04-Jan-88 Beginning Balance....                              $3,125
221            Sales         $1,000                               $4,125
222                                                               $4,125
223                                                               $4,125
224  ===========================================================
225  MONTH END BALANCE
226
227                    Month   Ending
228                    End     Balance
229                    Jan     $5,450
230                    Feb     $7,450
231                    Mar     $6,450
232                    Apr     $8,450
233                    May     $10,450
234                    Jun     $3,700
235                    Jul     $5,625
236                    Aug     $8,125
237                    Sep     $6,125
238                    Oct     $8,125
239                    Nov     $11,125
240                    Dec     $3,125
241
242  ===========================================================
243  MACROS
244  ===========================================================
245  Location UPDATE Macro  \0   (GOTO)UPDATE~            Go to range name Update
246
247  Row Insertion Macro    \1   (PANELOFF)(WINDOWSOFF)   Control panel and windows off
248                              /WIR~                    Insert row at location
249                              (GOTO)F13~               Move cursor to cell F13
250                              (END)(DOWN)              Move cursor to last cell in new row
251                              /C~(DOWN).(DOWN)~        Copy formula to new row and row below
252                              (END)(LEFT)              Return cursor to column A
253                              (PANELON)(WINDOWSON)     Control panel and windows on
```

Fig. 4.1. The Cash Flow Manager model.

The model's Weekly Activity section, located in cells A5 through H172, not only provides a data-entry area for cash receipts and disbursements but also keeps a running total (by transaction) of your firm's cash balance.

The macro worksheet area, which contains the \0 and \i macros, is located in cells A242 through I253.

Creating the Model

You need to build the template of the model before you add formulas and data. To perform this task, follow the instructions outlined in the following sections: Setting Column Widths, Naming Ranges, and Specifying Formats.

Setting Column Widths

The Cash Flow Manager is easy to create. Begin building the model by setting the column widths of a blank spreadsheet according to these specifications:

Column	Width
A, C, E, F	10
B, D	15

All other columns should remain at the default width of nine. As a timesaving trick, consider setting all columns at ten, using the /Worksheet Global Column-Width command, then resetting columns B and D to fifteen.

Naming Ranges

Then, using the /Range Name Create command, assign the name of the month to the cell that contains the first week of that month. Cell A14 has been named JAN, for example. By doing this for all twelve months, you will be able to move quickly around the model by pressing F5 (GOTO), entering the range name, and pressing Enter. Refer to table 4.1.

Table 4.1
Range Names

Name	Range
UPDATE	A13
JAN	A14
FEB	A30
MAR	A46
APR	A66
MAY	A82
JUN	A98
JUL	A118
AUG	A134
SEP	A154
OCT	A170
NOV	A186
DEC	A205
\0	D245
\i	D247

Specifying Cell Formats

Your next step is to enter the following cell formats for the Cash Flow Manager:

Column	Format
A	Date 1
C, E, F	Currency 0

You may select other formats, if you prefer.

First you type the row titles and column headings as shown in table 4.2.

Table 4.2
Row Titles and Column Headings

Enter into cell:	Original label:	Copy to:
A1:	\=	B1..H1, A5..H5, A7..H7, A224..I224, A226..I226, A242..I242, A244..I244
A3	'CASH FLOW MANAGER	
A6:	'WEEKLY ACTIVITY	
B9:	' Receipts	
D9:	' Disbursements	
B10:	' ---------------------	D10
A11:	' Date	
B11:	' Description	D11
C11:	' Amount	E11
F11:	' Balance	
A12:	'--------	
B12:	' -------------	D12
C12:	' -------	E12, F12
B13:	'Opening Balance	B13,B29,B45,B65,B81, B97,B117,B133,B153, B169,B185,B204,B220
A225:	'MONTH END BALANCE	
B227:	^Month	
C227:	^Ending	
B228:	^End	
C228:	^Balance	
B229:	^Jan	
B230:	^Feb	
B231:	^Mar	
B232:	^Apr	
B233:	^May	
B234:	^Jun	
B235:	^Jul	
B236:	^Aug	
B237:	^Sep	
B238:	^Oct	
B239:	^Nov	

Enter into cell:	Original label:	Copy to:
B240:	^Dec	
A243:	'MACROS	
A245:	'Location UPDATE Macro	
C245:	'\0	
D245:	'{GOTO}UPDATE~	
F245:	'Go to range name Update	
A247:	'Row Insertion Macro	
C247:	'\I	
D247:	'{PANELOFF}{WINDOWSOFF}	
F247:	'Control panel and windows off	
D248:	'/WIR~	
F248:	'Insert row at location	
D249:	'{GOTO}F13~	
F249:	'Move cursor to cell F13	
D250:	'{END}{DOWN}	
F250:	'Move cursor to last cell in new row	
D251:	'/C~{DOWN}.{DOWN}~	
F251:	'Copy formula to new row and row below	
D252:	'{END}{LEFT}	
F252:	'Return cursor to column A	
D253:	'{PANELON}{WINDOWSON}	
F253:	'Control panel and windows on	

Next, enter the formulas and functions according to table 4.3.

Consider using a variation on the **/C**opy command to enter the dates in column A. If you are using our example, enter the formula in cell A17. Then **/C**opy the formula from cell A17 to A21.

Now, use a slightly different technique—**/C**opy the formula from cell A17..A215 to cell A25. Notice that by using this variation you have copied the formula to all of the model's cells in which the date is needed. This trick can be used in 1-2-3 ONLY when the formulas are an even distance apart (in this case, four cells apart).

Table 4.3
Formulas and Functions

Enter into cell:	Original formula:	Copy to:
A13:	@DATE(87,1,5)	
F14:	+F13+C14-E14	F15..F223
A17:	+UPDATE+7	
A21:	+A17+7	
C229:	+F29	
C230:	+F45	
C231:	+F65	
C232:	+F81	
C233:	+F97	
C234:	+F117	
C235:	+F133	
C236:	+F153	
C237:	+F169	
C238:	+F185	
C239:	+F204	
C240:	+F220	

Cell	Copy From	Copy To
A25	A17..A215	A25

Creating the \0 and \i Macros

Two short macros are included in the model, beginning in cell A242 and ending in cell I253. The macros have been placed in the application for your convenience, but their use is optional.

The \i macro inserts additional rows into the model, thus providing you with two methods of adding rows to the model. You can type **/W**orksheet **I**nsert **R**ow and **/C**opy the formula in column F of the new cell; or you can press Alt and I simultaneously.

The \0 macro, as you may recall from previous 1-2-3 sessions, is the macro that executes automatically when a spreadsheet is loaded from your current drive to your computer's random access memory.

You can use the \0 macro to help you find a specific cell location. The \0 macro will bring up the model, and the cursor will be placed automatically on the cell named Update. If you use this macro, you won't need to scroll through many lines of data to update your planned or actual cash transactions.

The sample application has three rows per week. You can post three receipts and three disbursements weekly. When you modify the application to suit your own needs, however, you may need more space to accommodate your transactions.

Understanding the Model

This discussion begins with the Weekly Activity area first because it is the larger of the model's two main areas. To review the entire model, refer to figure 4.1.

Weekly Activity

The model's Weekly Activity section, located in cells A5 through F223, provides a data-entry area for cash receipts and disbursements. This section also keeps a running total by transaction of your firm's cash balance. A portion of the Weekly Activity section is shown in figure 4.2.

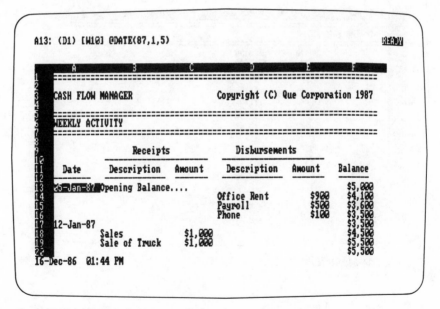

Fig. 4.2. The Weekly Activity section.

Basically, the model adds the cash receipts in column C and subtracts the cash disbursements in column E to (and from) your cash balance in column F. The application does so with the formula in cell F14

F14: +F13+C14-E14

This relationship is repeated in every cell in column F.

Month End Balance

The area of the worksheet from cell A224 through cell F241 displays the Ending Balances for all months. The balance at the end of each month is transferred from the running total in the Weekly Activity Section. For example, cell C229 (shown in fig. 4.3) contains the formula

C229: +F29

which retrieves and displays the cash balance at the end of January, 1987. Similarly, all other cells in column C will retrieve the appropriate end-of-month cash balances from column F.

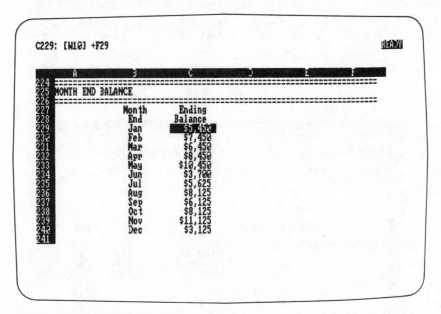

Fig. 4.3. The Month End Balance section.

\0 and \i Macros

Figure 4.4 shows the \0 and \i macros.

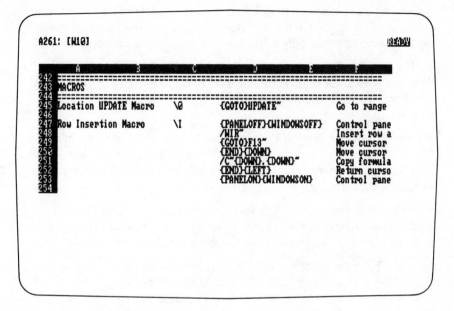

Fig. 4.4. The \0 and \i macros.

As mentioned earlier, the \0 macro will load the model so that your cursor is automatically positioned on the cell named Update. With \0, you can revise your Cash Manager immediately.

The Cash Flow Manager's second macro, \i, inserts a row, copies the running cash balance formula in column F, and then positions the cursor for your next entry.

Macro \i then moves the cursor to cell F13, the first cell in column F that calculates your running cash balance. The third line of the macro moves the cursor to the last cell in column F above the newly created row. The macro then copies the formula in this last cell to the new row and to the row immediately below it.

Finally, the macro moves the cursor to the new cell in column F and then to column A of the same row. In this fashion, you can continue to enter data immediately after the macro has finished working.

Using the Model

You will find the model as easy to use as it is to create. Simply move the cursor to cell A13 and enter your beginning date. Next, enter your beginning cash balance in cell F13. As the model builds on this value, it is important that your initial balance be correct. Always begin entering transactions *one row* below the current week's starting date.

Next, press F9 (CALC) to display the proper dates in column A. You are now ready to enter data. A description and the amount of your company's cash receipts should be placed in columns B and C, respectively.

Similar data for your cash disbursements should be entered in columns D and E. Press F9 once more to recalculate your cash balance for the data you have entered. You can now analyze, plan, or update your company's cash flow.

If you want to use macro \i, place your cursor in column F of the desired new row and then press Alt and I. A row will be inserted and the column F formula will be copied to the new cell location for you.

Macro \0, on the other hand, executes automatically when you retrieve the model. If you wish to use this macro, name the range UPDATE in a cell where you want to begin your next session with this application.

You may also want to try changing the name of the macro to one of the month range names so that the cursor will automatically be positioned in that cell location when the file is retrieved. For example, if you edit the macro from UPDATE to FEB, the cursor will be placed in cell F30 the next time the sample model is used. If you decline this option, use **/R**ange **E**rase to eliminate the macro.

You have probably noticed that the Cash Flow Manager is long—the example, not including the Month End Balances or the macros, contains more than 220 rows. Entering data in the proper column may be difficult as you work down the model.

Fortunately, you can overcome this handicap by freezing the column headings (**/W**orksheet **T**itles **H**orizontal) or creating a window (**/W**orksheet **W**indow **H**orizontal) at row 12. Then the column headings can serve as references for your data entry at any point during the year.

Finally, don't overlook the use of graphics with this model to analyze your monthly cash balances. Note that the bar graph in figure 4.5 provides you with your firm's projected annual cash flow on a monthly basis.

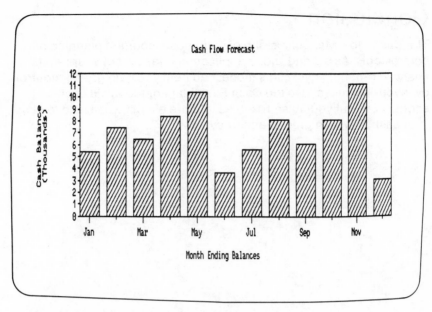

Fig. 4.5. Bar graph of projected cash flow.

To re-create this graph, select **/G**raph **T**ype **B**ar from the Graph menu. Specify the A range as C229..C240 and the X range as B229..B240. Select **O**ptions **T**itles **F**irst and enter *Cash Flow Forecast.* For the titles, enter the following information:

> **T**itles **X** Month (press Enter)
> **T**itles **Y** Cash Balance (press Enter)
> **S**cale **S**kip 2 (press Enter)
> **Q**uit
> **V**iew

After you've studied the graph, press Esc and then **Q**uit.

Pressing F10 (GRAPH) will display the graph with your current graph settings and will reflect any changes in the month end balances. First, however, be sure to press F9 (CALC) to calculate updated values.

If you plan to use your graph in future 1-2-3 sessions, don't forget to **/G**raph **N**ame your graph. In addition, you'll need to **/G**raph **S**ave your graph to print it out. Perform these two worksheet commands before you **/F**ile **S**ave your model.

Conclusion

The Cash Flow Manager is one of your most important planning and control tools. As a stand-alone application or as part of your regular financial reporting cycle, this model can help you gain greater control over your business. Use the Cash Flow Manager to avoid cash shortfalls, to put your cash reserves to more effective use, and to plan your cash flow with greater accuracy.

```
A1: [W10] \=
B1: [W15] \=
C1: (C0) [W10] \=
D1: [W15] \=
E1: (C0) [W10] \=
F1: [W10] \=
G1: \=
H1: \=
I1: \=
J1: \=
K1: \=
L1: \=
M1: \=
N1: \=
O1: 'UPDATE
P1: 'A13
O2: '\0
P2: 'D245
A3: [W10] 'CASH FLOW MANAGER
D3: [W15] 'Copyright (C) Que Corporation 1987
O3: '\I
P3: 'D247
A5: [W10] \=
B5: [W15] \=
C5: (C0) [W10] \=
D5: [W15] \=
E5: (C0) [W10] \=
F5: [W10] \=
G5: \=
H5: \=
I5: \=
J5: \=
K5: \=
L5: \=
M5: \=
N5: \=
A6: [W10] 'WEEKLY ACTIVITY
A7: [W10] \=
B7: [W15] \=
C7: [W10] \=
D7: [W15] \=
E7: [W10] \=
F7: [W10] \=
G7: \=
H7: \=
I7: \=
J7: \=
K7: \=
B9: [W15] '      Receipts
D9: [W15] '   Disbursements
B10: [W15] ' ----------------------
D10: [W15] ' ----------------------
A11: [W10] ' Date
B11: [W15] ' Description
```

```
C11: (C0) [W10] ' Amount
D11: [W15] ' Description
E11: (C0) [W10] ' Amount
F11: [W10] ' Balance
A12: [W10] '--------
B12: [W15] ' -------------
C12: (C0) [W10] ' -------
D12: [W15] ' -------------
E12: (C0) [W10] ' -------
F12: (C0) [W10] ' -------
A13: (D1) [W10] @DATE(87,1,5)
B13: [W15] 'Opening Balance....
F13: [W10] 5000
D14: [W15] 'Office Rent
E14: (C0) [W10] 900
F14: (C0) [W10] +F13+C14-E14
D15: [W15] 'Payroll
E15: [W10] 500
F15: (C0) [W10] +F14+C15-E15
D16: [W15] 'Phone
E16: (C0) [W10] 100
F16: (C0) [W10] +F15+C16-E16
A17: (D1) [W10] +UPDATE+7
F17: (C0) [W10] +F16+C17-E17
B18: [W15] 'Sales
C18: (C0) [W10] 1000
F18: (C0) [W10] +F17+C18-E18
B19: [W15] 'Sale of Truck
C19: [W10] 1000
F19: (C0) [W10] +F18+C19-E19
F20: (C0) [W10] +F19+C20-E20
A21: (D1) [W10] +A17+7
F21: (C0) [W10] +F20+C21-E21
B22: [W15] 'Sales
C22: (C0) [W10] 1000
D22: [W15] 'Office Supplies
E22: (C0) [W10] 50
F22: (C0) [W10] +F21+C22-E22
D23: [W15] 'Payroll
E23: [W10] 500
F23: (C0) [W10] +F22+C23-E23
F24: (C0) [W10] +F23+C24-E24
A25: (D1) [W10] +A21+7
F25: (C0) [W10] +F24+C25-E25
B26: [W15] 'Sales
C26: (C0) [W10] 1000
D26: [W15] 'Truck Down Pymt
E26: (C0) [W10] 1000
F26: (C0) [W10] +F25+C26-E26
D27: [W15] 'Utilities
E27: [W10] 500
F27: (C0) [W10] +F26+C27-E27
F28: (C0) [W10] +F27+C28-E28
A29: (D1) [W10] +A25+7
```

```
B29: [W15] 'Beginning Balance....
F29: (C0) [W10] +F28+C29-E29
B30: [W15] 'Sales
C30: (C0) [W10] 1000
D30: [W15] 'Office Rent
E30: (C0) [W10] 900
F30: (C0) [W10] +F29+C30-E30
D31: [W15] 'Payroll
E31: [W10] 500
F31: (C0) [W10] +F30+C31-E31
D32: [W15] 'Phone
E32: (C0) [W10] 100
F32: (C0) [W10] +F31+C32-E32
A33: (D1) [W10] +A29+7
F33: (C0) [W10] +F32+C33-E33
B34: [W15] 'Sales
C34: (C0) [W10] 1000
F34: (C0) [W10] +F33+C34-E34
F35: (C0) [W10] +F34+C35-E35
F36: (C0) [W10] +F35+C36-E36
A37: (D1) [W10] +A33+7
F37: (C0) [W10] +F36+C37-E37
B38: [W15] 'Sales
C38: (C0) [W10] 1000
F38: (C0) [W10] +F37+C38-E38
F39: (C0) [W10] +F38+C39-E39
F40: (C0) [W10] +F39+C40-E40
A41: (D1) [W10] +A37+7
F41: (C0) [W10] +F40+C41-E41
B42: [W15] 'Sales
C42: (C0) [W10] 1000
D42: [W15] 'Utilities
E42: (C0) [W10] 500
F42: (C0) [W10] +F41+C42-E42
F43: (C0) [W10] +F42+C43-E43
F44: (C0) [W10] +F43+C44-E44
A45: (D1) [W10] +A41+7
B45: [W15] 'Beginning Balance....
F45: (C0) [W10] +F44+C45-E45
B46: [W15] 'Sales
C46: (C0) [W10] 1000
D46: [W15] 'Office Rent
E46: (C0) [W10] 900
F46: (C0) [W10] +F45+C46-E46
D47: [W15] 'Payroll
E47: [W10] 500
F47: (C0) [W10] +F46+C47-E47
D48: [W15] 'Phone
E48: (C0) [W10] 100
F48: (C0) [W10] +F47+C48-E48
A49: (D1) [W10] +A45+7
F49: (C0) [W10] +F48+C49-E49
B50: [W15] 'Sales
C50: (C0) [W10] 1000

F50: (C0) [W10] +F49+C50-E50
F51: (C0) [W10] +F50+C51-E51
F52: (C0) [W10] +F51+C52-E52
A53: (D1) [W10] +A49+7
F53: (C0) [W10] +F52+C53-E53
B54: [W15] 'Sales
C54: (C0) [W10] 1000
F54: (C0) [W10] +F53+C54-E54
F55: (C0) [W10] +F54+C55-E55
F56: (C0) [W10] +F55+C56-E56
A57: (D1) [W10] +A53+7
F57: (C0) [W10] +F56+C57-E57
B58: [W15] 'Sales
C58: (C0) [W10] 1000
F58: (C0) [W10] +F57+C58-E58
F59: (C0) [W10] +F58+C59-E59
F60: (C0) [W10] +F59+C60-E60
A61: (D1) [W10] +A57+7
F61: (C0) [W10] +F60+C61-E61
B62: [W15] 'Sales
C62: (C0) [W10] 1000
D62: [W15] 'Utilities
E62: (C0) [W10] 500
F62: (C0) [W10] +F61+C62-E62
D63: [W15] 'Taxes
E63: [W10] 4000
F63: (C0) [W10] +F62+C63-E63
F64: (C0) [W10] +F63+C64-E64
A65: (D1) [W10] +A61+7
B65: [W15] 'Beginning Balance....
F65: (C0) [W10] +F64+C65-E65
B66: [W15] 'Sales
C66: (C0) [W10] 1000
D66: [W15] 'Office Rent
E66: (C0) [W10] 900
F66: (C0) [W10] +F65+C66-E66
D67: [W15] 'Payroll
E67: [W10] 500
F67: (C0) [W10] +F66+C67-E67
D68: [W15] 'Phone
E68: (C0) [W10] 100
F68: (C0) [W10] +F67+C68-E68
A69: (D1) [W10] +A65+7
F69: (C0) [W10] +F68+C69-E69
B70: [W15] 'Sales
C70: (C0) [W10] 1000
F70: (C0) [W10] +F69+C70-E70
F71: (C0) [W10] +F70+C71-E71
F72: (C0) [W10] +F71+C72-E72
A73: (D1) [W10] +A69+7
F73: (C0) [W10] +F72+C73-E73
B74: [W15] 'Sales
C74: (C0) [W10] 1000
F74: (C0) [W10] +F73+C74-E74
```

F75: (C0) [W10] +F74+C75-E75
F76: (C0) [W10] +F75+C76-E76
A77: (D1) [W10] +A73+7
F77: (C0) [W10] +F76+C77-E77
B78: [W15] 'Sales
C78: (C0) [W10] 1000
D78: [W15] 'Utilities
E78: (C0) [W10] 500
F78: (C0) [W10] +F77+C78-E78
F79: (C0) [W10] +F78+C79-E79
F80: (C0) [W10] +F79+C80-E80
A81: (D1) [W10] +A77+7
B81: [W15] 'Beginning Balance....
F81: (C0) [W10] +F80+C81-E81
B82: [W15] 'Sales
C82: (C0) [W10] 1000
D82: [W15] 'Office Rent
E82: (C0) [W10] 900
F82: (C0) [W10] +F81+C82-E82
D83: [W15] 'Payroll
E83: [W10] 500
F83: (C0) [W10] +F82+C83-E83
D84: [W15] 'Phone
E84: (C0) [W10] 100
F84: (C0) [W10] +F83+C84-E84
A85: (D1) [W10] +A81+7
F85: (C0) [W10] +F84+C85-E85
B86: [W15] 'Sales
C86: (C0) [W10] 1000
F86: (C0) [W10] +F85+C86-E86
F87: (C0) [W10] +F86+C87-E87
F88: (C0) [W10] +F87+C88-E88
A89: (D1) [W10] +A85+7
F89: (C0) [W10] +F88+C89-E89
B90: [W15] 'Sales
C90: (C0) [W10] 1000
F90: (C0) [W10] +F89+C90-E90
F91: (C0) [W10] +F90+C91-E91
F92: (C0) [W10] +F91+C92-E92
A93: (D1) [W10] +A89+7
F93: (C0) [W10] +F92+C93-E93
B94: [W15] 'Sales
C94: (C0) [W10] 1000
D94: [W15] 'Utilities
E94: (C0) [W10] 500
F94: (C0) [W10] +F93+C94-E94
F95: (C0) [W10] +F94+C95-E95
F96: (C0) [W10] +F95+C96-E96
A97: (D1) [W10] +A93+7
B97: [W15] 'Beginning Balance....
F97: (C0) [W10] +F96+C97-E97
B98: [W15] 'Sales
C98: (C0) [W10] 1000

D98: [W15] 'Office Rent
E98: (C0) [W10] 900
F98: (C0) [W10] +F97+C98-E98
D99: [W15] 'Payroll
E99: [W10] 500
F99: (C0) [W10] +F98+C99-E99
D100: [W15] 'Phone
E100: (C0) [W10] 100
F100: (C0) [W10] +F99+C100-E100
A101: (D1) [W10] +A97+7
F101: (C0) [W10] +F100+C101-E101
B102: [W15] 'Sales
C102: (C0) [W10] 1000
D102: [W15] 'Insurance
E102: (C0) [W10] 750
F102: (C0) [W10] +F101+C102-E102
F103: (C0) [W10] +F102+C103-E103
F104: (C0) [W10] +F103+C104-E104
A105: (D1) [W10] +A101+7
F105: (C0) [W10] +F104+C105-E105
B106: [W15] 'Sales
C106: (C0) [W10] 1000
F106: (C0) [W10] +F105+C106-E106
F107: (C0) [W10] +F106+C107-E107
F108: (C0) [W10] +F107+C108-E108
A109: (D1) [W10] +A105+7
F109: (C0) [W10] +F108+C109-E109
B110: [W15] 'Sales
C110: (C0) [W10] 1000
D110: [W15] 'Owner's Draw
E110: [W10] 5000
F110: (C0) [W10] +F109+C110-E110
F111: (C0) [W10] +F110+C111-E111
F112: (C0) [W10] +F111+C112-E112
A113: (D1) [W10] +A109+7
F113: (C0) [W10] +F112+C113-E113
B114: [W15] 'Sales
C114: (C0) [W10] 1000
D114: [W15] 'Utilities
E114: (C0) [W10] 500
F114: (C0) [W10] +F113+C114-E114
D115: [W15] 'Taxes
E115: [W10] 4000
F115: (C0) [W10] +F114+C115-E115
F116: (C0) [W10] +F115+C116-E116
A117: (D1) [W10] +A113+7
B117: [W15] 'Beginning Balance....
F117: (C0) [W10] +F116+C117-E117
B118: [W15] 'Sales
C118: (C0) [W10] 1000
D118: [W15] 'Office Rent
E118: (C0) [W10] 900
F118: (C0) [W10] +F117+C118-E118

D119: [W15] 'Payroll
E119: [W10] 500
F119: (C0) [W10] +F118+C119-E119
D120: [W15] 'Phone
E120: (C0) [W10] 100
F120: (C0) [W10] +F119+C120-E120
A121: (D1) [W10] +A117+7
F121: (C0) [W10] +F120+C121-E121
B122: [W15] 'Sales
C122: (C0) [W10] 1000
F122: (C0) [W10] +F121+C122-E122
F123: (C0) [W10] +F122+C123-E123
F124: (C0) [W10] +F123+C124-E124
A125: (D1) [W10] +A121+7
F125: (C0) [W10] +F124+C125-E125
B126: [W15] 'Sales
C126: (C0) [W10] 1000
D126: [W15] 'Office Supplies
E126: (C0) [W10] 75
F126: (C0) [W10] +F125+C126-E126
F127: (C0) [W10] +F126+C127-E127
F128: (C0) [W10] +F127+C128-E128
A129: (D1) [W10] +A125+7
F129: (C0) [W10] +F128+C129-E129
B130: [W15] 'Sales
C130: (C0) [W10] 1000
D130: [W15] 'Utilities
E130: [W10] 500
F130: (C0) [W10] +F129+C130-E130
F131: (C0) [W10] +F130+C131-E131
F132: (C0) [W10] +F131+C132-E132
A133: (D1) [W10] +A129+7
B133: [W15] 'Beginning Balance....
F133: (C0) [W10] +F132+C133-E133
B134: [W15] 'Sales
C134: (C0) [W10] 1000
D134: [W15] 'Office Rent
E134: (C0) [W10] 900
F134: (C0) [W10] +F133+C134-E134
D135: [W15] 'Payroll
E135: [W10] 500
F135: (C0) [W10] +F134+C135-E135
D136: [W15] 'Phone
E136: (C0) [W10] 100
F136: (C0) [W10] +F135+C136-E136
A137: (D1) [W10] +A133+7
F137: (C0) [W10] +F136+C137-E137
B138: [W15] 'Sales
C138: (C0) [W10] 1000
F138: (C0) [W10] +F137+C138-E138
F139: (C0) [W10] +F138+C139-E139
F140: (C0) [W10] +F139+C140-E140
A141: (D1) [W10] +A137+7
F141: (C0) [W10] +F140+C141-E141

B142: [W15] 'Sales
C142: (C0) [W10] 1000
F142: (C0) [W10] +F141+C142-E142
F143: (C0) [W10] +F142+C143-E143
F144: (C0) [W10] +F143+C144-E144
A145: (D1) [W10] +A141+7
F145: (C0) [W10] +F144+C145-E145
B146: [W15] 'Sales
C146: (C0) [W10] 1000
D146: [W15] 'Typewriter
E146: (C0) [W10] 500
F146: (C0) [W10] +F145+C146-E146
F147: (C0) [W10] +F146+C147-E147
F148: (C0) [W10] +F147+C148-E148
A149: (D1) [W10] +A145+7
F149: (C0) [W10] +F148+C149-E149
B150: [W15] 'Sales
C150: (C0) [W10] 1000
D150: [W15] 'Utilities
E150: [W10] 500
F150: (C0) [W10] +F149+C150-E150
F151: (C0) [W10] +F150+C151-E151
F152: (C0) [W10] +F151+C152-E152
A153: (D1) [W10] +A149+7
B153: [W15] 'Beginning Balance....
F153: (C0) [W10] +F152+C153-E153
B154: [W15] 'Sales
C154: (C0) [W10] 1000
D154: [W15] 'Office Rent
E154: (C0) [W10] 900
F154: (C0) [W10] +F153+C154-E154
D155: [W15] 'Payroll
E155: [W10] 500
F155: (C0) [W10] +F154+C155-E155
D156: [W15] 'Phone
E156: (C0) [W10] 100
F156: (C0) [W10] +F155+C156-E156
A157: (D1) [W10] +A153+7
F157: (C0) [W10] +F156+C157-E157
B158: [W15] 'Sales
C158: (C0) [W10] 1000
F158: (C0) [W10] +F157+C158-E158
F159: (C0) [W10] +F158+C159-E159
F160: (C0) [W10] +F159+C160-E160
A161: (D1) [W10] +A157+7
F161: (C0) [W10] +F160+C161-E161
B162: [W15] 'Sales
C162: (C0) [W10] 1000
F162: (C0) [W10] +F161+C162-E162
F163: (C0) [W10] +F162+C163-E163
F164: (C0) [W10] +F163+C164-E164
A165: (D1) [W10] +A161+7
F165: (C0) [W10] +F164+C165-E165
B166: [W15] 'Sales

C166: (C0) [W10] 1000
D166: [W15] 'Utilities
E166: (C0) [W10] 500
F166: (C0) [W10] +F165+C166-E166
D167: [W15] 'Taxes
E167: [W10] 4000
F167: (C0) [W10] +F166+C167-E167
F168: (C0) [W10] +F167+C168-E168
A169: (D1) [W10] +A165+7
B169: [W15] 'Beginning Balance....
F169: (C0) [W10] +F168+C169-E169
B170: [W15] 'Sales
C170: (C0) [W10] 1000
D170: [W15] 'Office Rent
E170: (C0) [W10] 900
F170: (C0) [W10] +F169+C170-E170
D171: [W15] 'Payroll
E171: [W10] 500
F171: (C0) [W10] +F170+C171-E171
D172: [W15] 'Phone
E172: (C0) [W10] 100
F172: (C0) [W10] +F171+C172-E172
A173: (D1) [W10] +A169+7
F173: (C0) [W10] +F172+C173-E173
B174: [W15] 'Sales
C174: (C0) [W10] 1000
F174: (C0) [W10] +F173+C174-E174
F175: (C0) [W10] +F174+C175-E175
F176: (C0) [W10] +F175+C176-E176
A177: (D1) [W10] +A173+7
F177: (C0) [W10] +F176+C177-E177
B178: [W15] 'Sales
C178: (C0) [W10] 1000
F178: (C0) [W10] +F177+C178-E178
F179: (C0) [W10] +F178+C179-E179
F180: (C0) [W10] +F179+C180-E180
A181: (D1) [W10] +A177+7
F181: (C0) [W10] +F180+C181-E181
B182: [W15] 'Sales
C182: (C0) [W10] 1000
D182: [W15] 'Utilities
E182: (C0) [W10] 500
F182: (C0) [W10] +F181+C182-E182
F183: (C0) [W10] +F182+C183-E183
F184: (C0) [W10] +F183+C184-E184
A185: (D1) [W10] +A181+7
B185: [W15] 'Beginning Balance....
F185: (C0) [W10] +F184+C185-E185
B186: [W15] 'Sales
C186: (C0) [W10] 1000
D186: [W15] 'Office Rent
E186: (C0) [W10] 900
F186: (C0) [W10] +F185+C186-E186

D187: [W15] 'Payroll
E187: [W10] 500
F187: (C0) [W10] +F186+C187-E187
D188: [W15] 'Phone
E188: (C0) [W10] 100
F188: (C0) [W10] +F187+C188-E188
A189: (D1) [W10] +A185+7
F189: (C0) [W10] +F188+C189-E189
B190: [W15] 'Sales
C190: (C0) [W10] 1000
F190: (C0) [W10] +F189+C190-E190
F191: (C0) [W10] +F190+C191-E191
F192: (C0) [W10] +F191+C192-E192
A193: (D1) [W10] +A189+7
F193: (C0) [W10] +F192+C193-E193
B194: [W15] 'Sales
C194: (C0) [W10] 1000
F194: (C0) [W10] +F193+C194-E194
F195: (C0) [W10] +F194+C195-E195
F196: (C0) [W10] +F195+C196-E196
A197: (D1) [W10] +A193+7
F197: (C0) [W10] +F196+C197-E197
B198: [W15] 'Sales
C198: (C0) [W10] 1000
F198: (C0) [W10] +F197+C198-E198
F199: (C0) [W10] +F198+C199-E199
A200: (D1) [W10] +A197+7
F200: (C0) [W10] +F199+C200-E200
B201: [W15] 'Sales
C201: (C0) [W10] 1000
D201: [W15] 'Utilities
E201: (C0) [W10] 500
F201: (C0) [W10] +F200+C201-E201
F202: (C0) [W10] +F201+C202-E202
F203: (C0) [W10] +F202+C203-E203
A204: (D1) [W10] +A200+7
B204: [W15] 'Beginning Balance....
F204: (C0) [W10] +F203+C204-E204
B205: [W15] 'Sales
C205: (C0) [W10] 1000
D205: [W15] 'Office Rent
E205: (C0) [W10] 900
F205: (C0) [W10] +F204+C205-E205
D206: [W15] 'Payroll
E206: [W10] 500
F206: (C0) [W10] +F205+C206-E206
D207: [W15] 'Phone
E207: (C0) [W10] 100
F207: (C0) [W10] +F206+C207-E207
A208: (D1) [W10] +A204+7
F208: (C0) [W10] +F207+C208-E208
B209: [W15] 'Sales
C209: (C0) [W10] 1000

F209: (CO) [W10] +F208+C209-E209
F210: (CO) [W10] +F209+C210-E210
F211: (CO) [W10] +F210+C211-E211
A212: (D1) [W10] +A208+7
F212: (CO) [W10] +F211+C212-E212
B213: [W15] 'Sales
C213: (CO) [W10] 1000
D213: [W15] 'Bonus
E213: [W10] 250
F213: (CO) [W10] +F212+C213-E213
D214: [W15] 'Owner's Draw
E214: [W10] 5000
F214: (CO) [W10] +F213+C214-E214
F215: (CO) [W10] +F214+C215-E215
A216: (D1) [W10] +A212+7
F216: (CO) [W10] +F215+C216-E216
B217: [W15] 'Sales
C217: (CO) [W10] 1000
D217: [W15] 'Insurance
E217: (CO) [W10] 750
F217: (CO) [W10] +F216+C217-E217
D218: [W15] 'Utilities
E218: (CO) [W10] 500
F218: (CO) [W10] +F217+C218-E218
D219: [W15] 'Taxes
E219: [W10] 4000
F219: (CO) [W10] +F218+C219-E219
A220: (D1) [W10] +A216+7
B220: [W15] 'Beginning Balance....
F220: (CO) [W10] +F219+C220-E220
B221: [W15] 'Sales
C221: (CO) [W10] 1000
F221: (CO) [W10] +F220+C221-E221
F222: (CO) [W10] +F221+C222-E222
F223: (CO) [W10] +F222+C223-E223
A224: [W10] \=
B224: [W15] \=
C224: [W10] \=
D224: [W15] \=
E224: [W10] \=
F224: [W10] \=
G224: \=
H224: \=
I224: \=
A225: [W10] 'MONTH END BALANCE
A226: [W10] \=
B226: [W15] \=
C226: (CO) [W10] \=
D226: [W15] \=
E226: [W10] \=
F226: [W10] \=
G226: \=
H226: \=
I226: \=

B227: [W15] ^Month
C227: [W10] ^Ending
B228: [W15] ^End
C228: [W10] +F11
B229: [W15] ^Jan
C229: [W10] +F29
B230: [W15] ^Feb
C230: [W10] +F45
B231: [W15] ^Mar
C231: [W10] +F65
B232: [W15] ^Apr
C232: [W10] +F81
B233: [W15] ^May
C233: [W10] +F97
B234: [W15] ^Jun
C234: [W10] +F117
B235: [W15] ^Jul
C235: [W10] +F133
B236: [W15] ^Aug
C236: [W10] +F153
B237: [W15] ^Sep
C237: [W10] +F169
B238: [W15] ^Oct
C238: [W10] +F185
B239: [W15] ^Nov
C239: [W10] +F204
B240: [W15] ^Dec
C240: [W10] +F220
A242: [W10] \=
B242: [W15] \=
C242: [W10] \=
D242: [W15] \=
E242: [W10] \=
F242: [W10] \=
G242: \=
H242: \=
I242: \=
A243: [W10] 'MACROS
A244: [W10] \=
B244: [W15] \=
C244: (CO) [W10] \=
D244: [W15] \=
E244: [W10] \=
F244: [W10] \=
G244: \=
H244: \=
I244: \=
A245: [W10] 'Location UPDATE Macro
C245: [W10] '\0
D245: [W15] '{GOTO}UPDATE~
F245: [W10] 'Go to range name Update
A247: [W10] 'Row Insertion Macro
C247: (CO) [W10] '\I
D247: [W15] '{PANELOFF}{WINDOWSOFF}

```
F247: [W10] 'Control panel and windows off
D248: [W15] '/WIR~
F248: [W10] 'Insert row at location
D249: [W15] '{GOTO}F13~
F249: [W10] 'Move cursor to cell F13
D250: [W15] '{END}{DOWN}
F250: [W10] 'Move cursor to last cell in new row
D251: [W15] '/C~{DOWN}.{DOWN}~
F251: [W10] 'Copy formula to new row and row below
D252: [W15] '{END}{LEFT}
F252: [W10] 'Return cursor to column A
D253: [W15] '{PANELON}{WINDOWSON}
F253: [W10] 'Control panel and windows on
```

5

Managing Accounts Receivable

Introduction

Accounts receivable is the one investment in current assets that you'd probably prefer not to make. Unfortunately, accounts receivable are inevitable if you extend credit to your customers.

One of the differences between successful and less successful firms, however, is the management of the accounts receivable asset. By helping you to understand your company's receivables so that you can take appropriate action, the 1-2-3 Accounts Receivable Tracker can minimize your accounts receivable and increase your cash flow.

This chapter explains how you can recreate the model, how the model operates, and how you can use the model in your business. But before you can put the Accounts Receivable Tracker to work, you should have a solid understanding of how the model functions.

The Accounts Receivable Tracker has seven sections: Invoice Register, Collections, Criterion Range, Analysis Area, Aging Report, Sales Summary Area, and Macros \i and \r.

Invoice Register and Collections are independent modules—reporting areas used to record your business's billing and collections activity. The four other sections (excluding the macros) are analysis and reporting modules. These modules depend on data you provide in the Invoice Register and Collections worksheet areas. Figure 5.1 shows the complete Accounts Receivable Tracker.

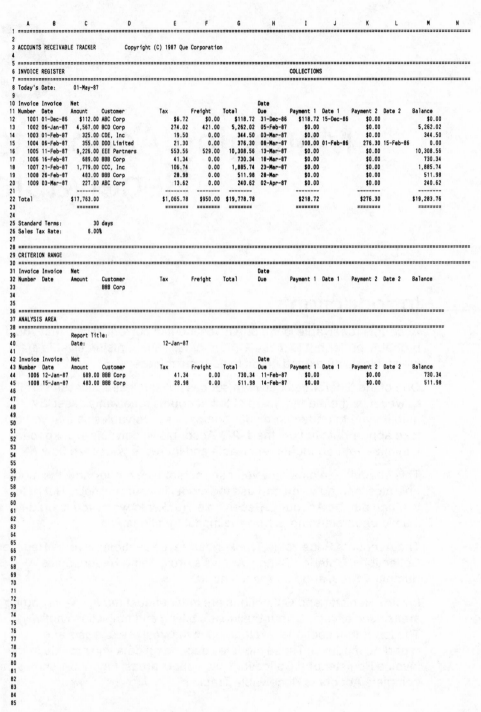

```
      A       B        C         D         E       F       G        H        I        J        K        L        M        N
 1 ==================================================================================================================================
 2
 3 ACCOUNTS RECEIVABLE TRACKER        Copyright (C) 1987 Que Corporation
 4
 5 ==================================================================================================================================
 6 INVOICE REGISTER                                                              COLLECTIONS
 7 ==================================================================================================================================
 8 Today's Date:     01-May-87
 9
10 Invoice Invoice   Net                                            Date
11 Number  Date      Amount    Customer     Tax     Freight  Total   Due      Payment 1 Date 1   Payment 2 Date 2   Balance
12   1001 01-Dec-86  $112.00 ABC Corp       $6.72    $0.00    $118.72 31-Dec-86  $118.72 15-Dec-86   $0.00            $0.00
13   1002 06-Jan-87 4,567.00 BCD Corp      274.02   421.00   5,262.02 05-Feb-87    $0.00             $0.00         5,262.02
14   1003 01-Feb-87  325.00 CDE, Inc        19.50     0.00    344.50 03-Mar-87    $0.00             $0.00          344.50
15   1004 06-Feb-87  355.00 DDD Limited     21.30     0.00    376.30 08-Mar-87   100.00 01-Feb-86  276.30 15-Feb-86     0.00
16   1005 11-Feb-87 9,226.00 EEE Partners  553.56   529.00  10,308.56 13-Mar-87    $0.00             $0.00        10,308.56
17   1006 16-Feb-87  689.00 BBB Corp        41.34     0.00    730.34 18-Mar-87    $0.00             $0.00          730.34
18   1007 21-Feb-87 1,779.00 CCC, Inc      106.74     0.00   1,885.74 23-Mar-87    $0.00             $0.00        1,885.74
19   1008 26-Feb-87  483.00 BBB Corp        28.98     0.00    511.98 28-Mar      $0.00             $0.00          511.98
20   1009 03-Mar-87  227.00 ABC Corp        13.62     0.00    240.62 02-Apr-87    $0.00             $0.00          240.62
21                   --------                       --------  --------  --------            --------           --------  --------
22 Total          $17,763.00                      $1,065.78 $950.00 $19,778.78             $218.72           $276.30  $19,283.76
23                   ========                       ======== ======== ========             ========           ========  ========
24
25 Standard Terms:        30 days
26 Sales Tax Rate:        6.00%
27
28 ==================================================================================================================================
29 CRITERION RANGE
30 ==================================================================================================================================
31 Invoice Invoice   Net                                            Date
32 Number  Date      Amount    Customer     Tax     Freight  Total   Due      Payment 1 Date 1   Payment 2 Date 2   Balance
33                             BBB Corp
34
35
36 ==================================================================================================================================
37 ANALYSIS AREA
38 ==================================================================================================================================
39                   Report Title:
40                   Date:             12-Jan-87
41
42 Invoice Invoice   Net                                            Date
43 Number  Date      Amount    Customer     Tax     Freight  Total   Due      Payment 1 Date 1   Payment 2 Date 2   Balance
44   1006 12-Jan-87  689.00 BBB Corp        41.34     0.00    730.34 11-Feb-87    $0.00             $0.00          730.34
45   1008 15-Jan-87  483.00 BBB Corp        28.98     0.00    511.98 14-Feb-87    $0.00             $0.00          511.98
46
47
48
49
50
51
52
53
54
55
56
57
58
59
60
61
62
63
64
65
66
67
68
69
70
71
72
73
74
75
76
77
78
79
80
81
82
83
84
85
```

Fig. 5.1. The Accounts Receivable Tracker.

```
          O         P         Q         R         S         T         U         V         W         X
========================================================================================

========================================================================================

========================================================================================
\I   {PANELOFF}{WINDOWSOFF}        Turn Control Panel & Windows Off
     {GOTO}BOTTOM~                 Go to range name Bottom
     /wir~                         Insert row
     {RIGHT 4}/C{ESC}{UP}~~        Move cursor 4 cells and copy formula
     {RIGHT 2}/C{ESC}{UP}~~        Move cursor 2 cell and copy formula
     {RIGHT 6}/C{ESC}{UP}~~        Move cursor 6 cell and copy formula
     {GOTO}BOTTOM~{UP}~            Go to range name Bottom then up one
     {PANELON}{WINDOWSON}          Turn Control Panel & Windows On

\R   {HOME}{MENUBRANCH MENU}       Goto A1, start MENU
MENU Aging Report    Sales Summary     Menu options Aging and Sales
     Data Table      Data Table        Description of options
     {BRANCH AGE}    {BRANCH SALES}    Action taken based on item chosen

AGE  {GOTO}AGING_TABLE~    SALES   {GOTO}SALES_TABLE~    Go to appropriate table
     /dtr/dt2                   /dtr/dt1              Reset data table, start data table
     AGING_TABLE~               SALES_TABLE~          Assign table to calculate
     IN1_1~IN2_1~               IN1_2~                Assign input cell(s)
     {BEEP 4}~                  {BEEP 4}              Beep when done

================================================================================
     AGING REPORT
================================================================================
                         Aged Amount
                                              120 days
               30 days   60 days   90 days   and over   Total
                    0        30        60        90
ABC Corp      $240.62     $0.00     $0.00     $0.00      $240.62
BCD Corp        0.00      0.00   5,262.02     0.00     5,262.02
CDE, Inc        0.00    344.50      0.00       0.00       344.50
DDD Limited     0.00      0.00      0.00       0.00         0.00
EEE Partners    0.00 10,308.56      0.00       0.00    10,308.56
BBB Corp        0.00  1,242.32      0.00       0.00     1,242.32
CCC, Inc        0.00  1,885.74      0.00       0.00     1,885.74
                                                           0.00
                                                           0.00
                                                           0.00
                                                           0.00
                                                           0.00
                                                           0.00
                                                           0.00
                                                           0.00
                                                           0.00
                                                           0.00
                                                           0.00
                                                           0.00
                                                           0.00
              --------  --------  --------   --------   ------------
              $240.62 $13,781.12 $5,262.02    $0.00   $19,283.76        0

     Customer      Date


                          30
================================================================================
     SALES SUMMARY REPORT
================================================================================
     For Period Beginning:        01-Jan-87
               Ending:            01-Feb-87


     Customer     Net Sales  Tax      Freight   Total

     ABC Corp        $0.00    $0.00    $0.00     $0.00
     BCD Corp     4,567.00   274.02   421.00   5,262.02
     CDE, Inc       325.00    19.50     0.00     344.50
     DDD Limited      0.00     0.00     0.00       0.00
     EEE Partners     0.00     0.00     0.00       0.00
     BBB Corp         0.00     0.00     0.00       0.00
     CCC, Inc         0.00     0.00     0.00       0.00
                                                  0.00
                                                  0.00
                                                  0.00
                                                  0.00
                                                  0.00
                                                  0.00
                                                  0.00
                                                  0.00
                                                  0.00
                                                  0.00
                                                  0.00
                                                  0.00
                 --------  --------  --------  --------
     Total       $4,892.00  $293.52  $421.00  $5,606.52
     Customer     Date
                  +C13>=$S$6
```

Creating the Model

Give some thought to the number of invoices your firm generates. If you have a high sales volume business, you may want to set up your Invoice Register and Collections database to be much larger than that shown in figure 5.1. Remember, however, that if you increase the size of the database, you must also adjust the four @DSUM functions and criteria ranges to reflect that increase. Doing so will reduce or eliminate any future need to add rows.

Setting Column Widths

As you can see from the example in figure 5.1, the model is not difficult to create. You begin creating the model by adjusting the column widths of a blank 1-2-3 spreadsheet according to these specifications:

Column	Width
A	8
B, J, L	10
C, E, F, H, I, K, M, Q, R, S, T	11
D	20
G, U	12
P	16
O	5

Leave all other columns set at 9, the default width. Also consider using the /Worksheet Global Column-width Set-width command and set your worksheet at eleven. Then adjust the remaining columns accordingly.

Specifying Cell Formats

Now you format the model's cells, according to table 5.1. Remember that these cell formats are suggestions. You can modify them where appropriate.

In general, following accounting conventions, the sample model has been formatted with a dollar sign in only the first and last rows of a report range. Again, feel free to format your model as you choose, referring to the cell listing as needed.

Table 5.1
Cell Formats

Format	*Cell/Range*
Invoice Register	
/rfd1	C8
/rfd1	Column B
/rfc2	C12, E12, F12, G12
/rf,2	C13..C20
/rf,2	E13..G20
/rfc2	C22, E22, F22, G22
/rfd1	Column H
/rfp2	C26
Collections	
/rfc2	I12, K12, L12
/rfd1	Columns J, L
/rfc2	I22, K22, M22
Aging Report	
/rfh	P34
/rff0	Q34..T34
/rfc2	Q35..U35
/rf,2	Q36..U54
/rfc2	Q56..U56
/rf,2	V56
Sales Summary	
/rfd1	R65..R66
/rfh	Q70..S70
/rfc2	Q71..T71
/rf,2	Q72..T88
/rfc2	Q90..T90
/rfh	Q93

Next, enter the column titles, row descriptions, and other labels listed in table 5.2. Use the \= trick to enter the separator lines if you plan to include them in your model. Don't forget to enter your customers' names in Column P of the Aging and Sales Summary Reports to enable the data table to calculate properly.

Table 5.2
Row Titles and Column Headings

Enter into cell:	Original label:	Copy to:
	Opening Headings	
A1:	\=	B1..U1, A5..U5, A7..U7, A28..U28, A30..U30, A36..M36, A38..M38, P62..U62, P64..U64
A3:	'ACCOUNTS RECEIVABLE TRACKER	
	Invoice Register	
A6:	'INVOICE REGISTER	
A8:	'Today's Date:	
A10:	'Invoice	B10
C10:	'Net	
H10:	'Date	B11
A11:	'Number	
C11:	'Amount	
D11:	'Customer	
E11:	'Tax	
F11:	'Freight	
G11:	'Total	
H11:	'Due	
C21:	' --------	E21..G21, I21, K21, M21
C23:	' ========	E23..G23, I23, K23, M23
A25:	'Standard Terms	
A26:	'Sales Tax Rate	
	Collections	
I6:	'COLLECTIONS	
I11:	'Payment 1	
J11:	'Date 1	
K11:	'Payment 2	
L11:	'Date 2	
M11:	'Balance	

Enter
into
cell: Original label: Copy to:

Criterion Range

A29:   'CRITERION RANGE

Cell	Copy From	Copy To
A31	A10..M11	A31

Analysis Area

A37:   'ANALYSIS RANGE
C39:   'Report Title:
C40:   'Date:

Cell	Copy From	Copy To
A42	A10..M11	A42

Macros

O8:   '\l
P8:   '{PANELOFF}{WINDOWSOFF}
P9:   '{GOTO}BOTTOM~
P10:   '/wir
P11:   '{RIGHT 4}/C{ESC}{UP}~~
P12:   '{RIGHT 2}/C{ESC}{UP}~~
P13:   '{RIGHT 6}/C{ESC}{UP}~~
P14:   '{GOTO}BOTTOM~{UP}~
P15:   '{PANELON}{WINDOWSON}~
O17:   '\R~
O18:   'MENU~
P17:   '{HOME}{MENUBRANCH MENU}~
P18:   'Aging report~
P19:   'Data Table~
P20:   '{BRANCH AGE}
Q18:   'Sales Summary~
Q19:   'Data Table~
Q20:   '{BRANCH SALES}
O22:   'AGE
P22:   '{GOTO}AGING_TABLE~
P23:   '/dtr/dt2
P24:   'AGING_TABLE~
P25:   'IN1_1~IN2_1~
P26:   '{BEEP 4}
R22:   'SALES
S22:   '{GOTO}SALES_TABLE~

Enter into cell:	Original label:	Copy to:
S23:	'/dtr/dt1	
S24:	'SALES_TABLE~	
S25:	'IN1_2~	
S26:	'{BEEP 4}	
R8:	'Turn Control Panel & Windows Off	
R9:	'Go to range name Bottom	
R10:	'Insert Row	
R11:	'Move cursor 4 cells and copy formula	
R12:	'Move cursor 2 cells and copy formula	
R13:	'Move cursor 6 cells and copy formula	
R14:	'Go to range name Bottom then up one	
R15:	'Turn Control Panel & Windows On	
S17:	'Goto A1, start MENU	
S18:	'Menu options Aging and Sales	
S19:	'Description of options	
S20:	'Action taken based on item chosen	
U22:	'Go to appropriate table	
U23:	'Reset data table, start data table	
U24:	'Assign table to calculate	
U25:	'Assign input cell(s)	
U26:	'Beep when done	

Aging Report

R31:	'Aged Amount	
Q33:	'30 Days	
R33:	'60 Days	
S33:	'90 Days	
T32:	'120 Days	
T33:	'and over	
U33:	'Total	
Q34:	'0	
R34:	'30	
S34:	'60	
T34:	'90	
Q55:	' --------	R55..U55
P58:	'Customer	
Q58:	'Date	

Enter into cell:	Original label:	Copy to:

Sales Summary Report

P65:	'For Period Beginning:	
P66:	' Ending:	
P69:	'Customer	
Q69:	'Net Sales	
R69:	'Tax	
S69:	'Freight	
T69:	'Total	
Q89:	' --------	R89..T89
P92	'Customer	
Q92:	'Date	

Naming Ranges

In this model, range names are used primarily for macro names and for the data tables discussed later in this chapter.

Remember, a macro name is nothing more than a range name. But there is a naming sequence that must be followed. A macro name is only two characters—the backslash (\) and one letter.

This model, however, uses range names as macro subroutines. The name that is used for a subroutine does not have to follow the naming convention. In the section on macros for this model, pay close attention to the usage of subroutines.

Now, using table 5.3, you enter the range names for the model. Be sure to type the macro names accurately and to assign the ranges properly.

Setting Up the Criterion Range

The Criterion Range and Analysis Area sections of the model perform database functions. The Criterion Range, located below the Invoice Register and Collections modules, occupies cells A28 through M35. The Analysis Area is located directly beneath the Criterion Range, in cells A36 through M43. To review these modules, refer to figure 5.1.

Table 5.3
Range Names

Range Name	Location
AGE	P22
AGE_TOT	U56
AGING_TABLE	P34..T41
COLL_BAL	M22
BOTTOM	A21
IN1_1	P59
IN1_2	P93
IN2_1	Q60
INV_REGISTER	A11..M21
MENU	P18
SALES	S22
SALES_TABLE	P70..S77
\I	P8
\R	P17

This is the time to set up the preliminary ranges needed for your database. To prepare the ranges, follow these steps:

1. Press **/D**ata **Q**uery **I**nput.

2. Type *INV_REGISTER*. Press Enter.

3. Press **C**riterion.

4. Type *A32..M33*. Press Enter.

5. Press **O**utput.

6. Type *A43..M43*. Press Enter.

7. Press **Q**uit.

These ranges will be used to **F**ind or **E**xtract records from the Invoice Register. Later, you will see how these ranges can be changed.

Next, you enter the model's formulas and functions. You can use table 5.4 as a guide to where the equations should be entered. Or you may prefer to use the model's complete cell listing, which appears at the end of this chapter.

Table 5.4
Formulas and Functions

Enter into cell:	Original formula:	Copy to:

Invoice Register

C8:	@DATE	
C22:	@SUM(C12..C21)	E22..G22, I22 K22, M22
E12:	+$C$26*C12	E13..E20
G12:	+C12+E12+F12	G13..G20
H12:	+C$25+B12	H13..H20

Collections

M12:	+G12-I12-K12	M13..M20

Aging Report

P34:	@DSUM(INV_REGISTER, 12,P58..Q59)	
Q56:	@SUM(Q35..Q55)	R56..U56
Q59:	+B12<=$C$8-$IN2_1#AND# B12>$C$8-$Q$61	
Q61:	@IF(IN2_1=90,IN2_1+365, IN2_1+30)	
Q70:	@DSUM(INV_REGISTER,2, P92..Q93)	
U35:	@SUM(Q35..T35)	U36..U54
V56:	+$COLL_BAL-$AGE_TOT	

Sales Summary Report

Q70:	@DSUM(INV_REGISTER,2, P92..Q93)	
Q90:	@SUM(Q71..Q89)	R90..T90
Q93:	+B12>=$R$65#AND# B12<=$R$66	

Enter into cell:	Original formula:	Copy to:
R65:	@DATE	
R66:	@DATE	
R70:	@DSUM(INV_REGISTER,4, P92..Q93)	
S70:	@DSUM(INV_REGISTER,5, P92..Q93)	
T71:	@SUM(Q71..S71)	T72..T88

You should be aware that you don't need to have the model calculate your state's sales tax. If you prefer to enter the tax yourself, do not enter the formulas in column E and cell C26. However, be sure to use the /Copy command for the @SUM functions, and to use your customer list for the Aging and Sales Summary Reports. Doing so will decrease setup time.

Understanding the Model

As you know, the model has seven distinct sections. An explanation of each section follows.

The Invoice Register

The Invoice Register is the first section of the model that requires data from your accounts receivable. The Invoice Register, a data-entry area, is located in cells A5 through H27 of the example. Figure 5.2 displays part of the specific range of this section.

As you can see, the Invoice Register is used to record all information about your invoices. Column A contains the invoice number, column B, the invoice date, and column C, the net amount of the invoice—the amount charged for your product or service.

Column D holds the customer names for each invoice. This information will be used extensively to prepare the Aging and Sales modules' statements. Column E shows the state sales tax that you pass along to

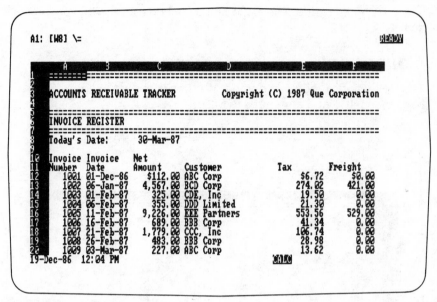

Fig. 5.2. The Invoice Register.

your clients. The value for the first invoice is calculated by the following formula:

E12: +$C$26*C12

Cell C26 is your state's sales tax rate and C12 is the net amount of your customer's invoice. A sales tax rate of six percent is assumed in the example.

Column F of the Invoice Register is used to record any freight charges. Column G computes the total amount of each invoice. For example, the first invoice total in figure 5.1 is calculated by the formula

G12: +C12+E12+F12

Cell C12 is the net amount of the invoice, E12 is the sales tax, and F12 is the charge for freight.

Column H displays the invoices' due dates, which are also computed for you. The due date for the first invoice is computed by the equation

H12: +C$25+B12

in which cell C25 contains the standard payment terms of thirty days. 1-2-3 will add thirty days to the invoice date to arrive at the date on which payment is due. The Collections section records this payment activity.

Collections

The Collections module, a portion of which is shown in figure 5.3, begins at cell I5 and continues to M27.

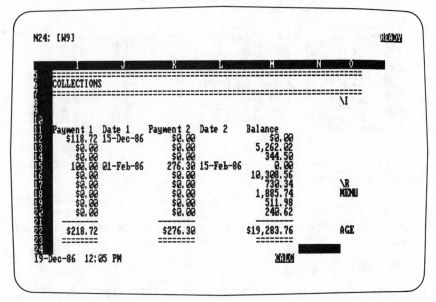

Fig. 5.3. Collections.

Using the model, you can record two payments on each invoice. Column I is used for the first, or total, payment received, and column J for the date of that payment. Columns K and L contain similar information about the second payment received.

Column M computes any outstanding balances. 1-2-3 calculates this value for the first invoice, using the formula

    M12: +G12-I12-K12

Cell G12 is the total amount of the invoice from the Invoice Register, I12 shows any initial payment, and K12 any subsequent payment.

Note that columns with dollar amounts in the Invoice Register and Collections sections are totaled in row 22 (refer to fig. 5.1). For instance, the total of the Net Amount of Invoices is computed by the formula in C22

    C22: @SUM(C12..C21)

The other columns in this section also are totaled by using the @SUM function.

Criterion Range and Analysis Area

The model's Criterion Range and Analysis Area sections perform database functions. The Criterion Range, which is located below the Invoice Register and Collections modules, occupies cells A28 through M35. The Analysis Area is located in cells A36 through M43, directly below the Criterion Range. Refer to figure 5.1 to review these modules.

Following 1-2-3 convention, the Criterion Range duplicates the Invoice Register and Collections headers, or column titles. Having a criterion range integrated into the model allows you to **D**elete, **F**ind, or **E**xtract records from the Invoice and Collections database.

Extracted records are written to the Analysis Area for your review. You can examine a specific invoice, review a particular client's payment behavior, or determine your amount of sales for the month. (The "Using the Model" section of this chapter explains how to do these operations.)

The Aging Report

The Aging Report, a data table constructed by 1-2-3, creates a statement of outstanding receivables by "age" category. The report shows you the amount of money owed you that is more than 30, 60, 90, and 120 days overdue. This module is located at cells P29 through U63. Figure 5.4 shows part of the module.

The Aging Report is more complex than the other sections of the Accounts Receivable model, but as a two-variable data table, the report's structure is similar to that of the Checkbook Manager (see Chapter 2).

In this model, the table range is P34 through T54; Input 1 is cell P59 and Input 2 is cell Q60. The table will be constructed with the @DSUM equation found in cell P34

    P34: @DSUM(INV_REGISTER,12,P58..Q59)

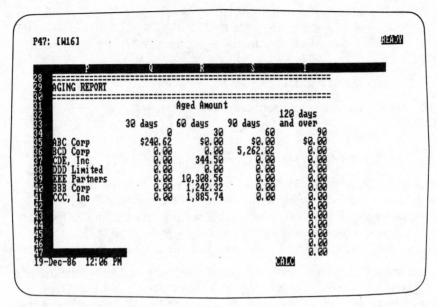

Fig. 5.4. Aging Report.

INV_REGISTER (A11 through M21) holds the Invoice Register and Collection databases, 12 is column M (your clients' outstanding balances), and P58 through Q59 is the criterion range.

When this table is run, each pair of customer names from column P and the date intervals from row 34 are entered in the criterion range (refer to fig. 5.1). The results generated by the @DSUM function using these inputs as criteria will be placed in the Aging Report.

The criterion range used in the @DSUM function will select records based on the Customer and Date fields. P58 is the "Customer" label. The following formula comprises cell Q59:

Q59:   +B12   <= $C$8 - $Q$60   #AND#   B12 > $C$8 - $Q61

Invoice   Curr   0   Invoice   Curr
Date   Date   Date   Date

@IF(Q60=90,Q60+365,Q60+30)

As you can see, this equation selects records for which your invoice date (B12) is less than or equal to the current date (C8) minus zero (Q60) AND for which your invoice date is greater than today's date minus 30 (Q61).

The data table automatically substitutes the label "ABC Corp" in cell P59 for the first criterion range (Customer), and the value zero into cell Q60 to complete the second criterion range (Date).

Thus, the second half of the criterion range will select only those invoices that are between zero and 30 days old. In the example, this criterion range will instruct 1-2-3 to select invoice 1009 to the ABC Company in the amount of $240.62 and place it in cell Q35. (Refer to fig. 5.1.)

The data table will continue to process in this manner until all customer names and remaining date intervals (60, 90, 120 days and over) are considered. Note that the @IF function in cell Q61 will cause the 90-day date selection interval to be widened when the final date interval of 90 is substituted into the input range. In this way, the last selection criteria will select records that are 120 days and over. Although these 1-2-3 database operations may appear complicated to you, they enable the model to build a customized Aging Report for your business.

Finally, the Aging Report relies on the @SUM function to total each time interval of receivables as well as the total amount due from each customer. For example, the 30-day receivable total is computed by the formula

Q56: @SUM(Q35..Q55)

The total outstanding from the customer is revealed by the formula

U35: @SUM(Q35..T35)

The Sales Summary Report

The Sales Summary Report, located below the Aging Report, occupies cells P62 through U93. A portion of this second data table is shown in figure 5.5.

The Sales Summary generates a report that displays net sales, tax, freight, and total invoice amounts for a specific time period. The report gives you the capability to determine your sales for a specific month, quarter, or year. This sales value can be used in other models, such as the 1-2-3 Cash Projector. Unlike the Aging Report, however, the Sales Summary Report is a one-variable data table.

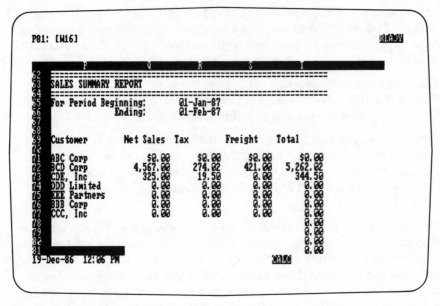

Fig. 5.5. Sales Summary.

The table range is the Sales Summary Report. In the example, the range is cells P70 through S77, with Input 1 being P93. When you invoke the **/D**ata **T**able command, the following @DSUM functions will compute the column totals based on the criteria in cell P92..Q93:

    Q70: @DSUM(A11..M21,2,P92..Q93) - Net Sales
    R70: @DSUM(A11..M21,4,P92..Q93) - Tax
    S70: @DSUM(A11..M21,5,P92..Q93) - Freight

For Net Sales, the range A11 through M21 is the Invoice Register and Collection database, column 2 is your net sales, and P92..Q93 is the criteria. Tax and Freight are calculated similarly, the only difference being the offset column to retrieve the appropriate amount.

Again, consider the criteria in these three equations. Cells P92 and Q92 contain the labels Customer and Date. Below Customer, cell P93 will become the input cell for the data table. Cell Q93 contains the formula

Q93: +B12 >= $R$65 #AND#   B12 <= $R$66
        | | | |
     Invoice   Beg   Invoice   End
      Date   Date   Date   Date

In this formula, records with an invoice date (B12) greater than or equal to the value in R65 AND an invoice date less than or equal to the value in cell R66 will be selected. The beginning and ending activity dates that you select become part of the criteria for the Sales Summary Report.

Total Sales, Net Sales, Tax, and Freight are computed by the @SUM function. In the example, cell T71 contains total sales for the ABC Corp:

   T71: @SUM(Q71..S71)

Similarly, Total Net Sales for the period you have selected is calculated by the formula in cell Q76:

   Q90: @SUM(Q71..Q89)

Finally, note the formula in cell V56:

   V56: +$COLL_BAL-$AGE_TOT

This formula serves as a check of whether your tables in the Collections and Aging Report agree. A zero indicates the two are equal; any amount other than zero is the difference between the two totals and informs you your Aging Report may be incomplete.

The \i and \r Macros

The model's macros and documentation are located in cells O8 through U13 and O15 through X26, in the area directly to the right of the Collection database (refer to fig. 5.1). Notice that directly below the \r macro there are three macros named MENU, AGE, and SALES. These are the macro *subroutines*.

When you invoke the \r macro, you will be given a choice of running either the Aging Report or the Sales Summary. After you select one of these alternatives (by pressing the appropriate letter or moving your cursor to your selection and pressing Enter, the model will execute the proper data table input, criteria, and ranges for the report you have selected. After the data table has executed, your personal computer will beep, indicating completion of the task.

The \r macro allows you to begin calculating either data table. Actually, \r starts the menu subroutine, MENU, which is called from the \r macro and allows you to choose the data table you wish to calculate. Your choice of *Aging Report* or *Sales Summary* will activate either the AGE or SALES subroutine.

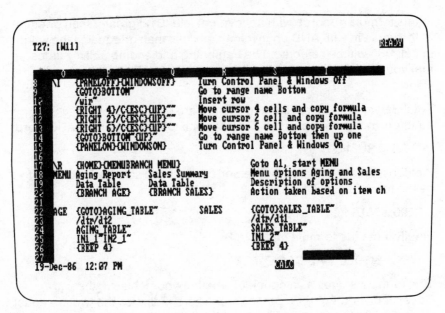

Fig. 5.6. \i Macro.

The \i macro, similar to others in this book, automatically inserts a row for you in the Invoice Register and Collections database.

The macro first turns off the control panel and windows. Next, 1-2-3 moves the cursor to the range name BOTTOM. If you have not used the macro before, BOTTOM is located at cell A21.

The macro then inserts a row with Insert Row and also moves the cursor and copies the formulas in columns E (Tax), G (Total Sales), and M (Balance) to the new cells in these columns. The operation ends when the cursor is returned to BOTTOM (now cell A22) and the control panel and windows are turned on.

Using the Model

When you understand the model, you are ready to put the Accounts Receivable Tracker to work in your business.

The Accounts Receivable Tracker may look intimidating, but it isn't difficult to use. To help you understand how to use the application, each module is discussed separately.

The Invoice Register and Collections

Think of the Invoice Register as your starting point. Enter your company's invoice data in the appropriate column: the invoice number in column A, the invoice date in column B, and the net amount of each invoice in column C. Consider using the /Data Fill command to enter your invoice numbers. In this manner, you are guaranteed they will be entered sequentially. Column D lists all your firm's customers, and column F contains the freight charges associated with your invoice.

Remember that column E (Sales Tax), column G (Total), and column H (Due Date), are computed for you. And keep in mind that you not only can enter the Sales Tax and Due Date manually but you also can modify them by adjusting the formula in a specific cell, depending on the financial arrangements with your customers.

Next, enter your clients' payment history in the Collections database. Columns I and J contain the amount and date, respectively, of a customer's first payment. Columns K and L contain similar data for the second payment, if there is one.

If you have not used the model previously, move the cursor to cell C25 and enter the number of days that comprise your standard payment terms. Your state sales tax rate should also be entered one cell below (in C26) if you want the model to compute the amount of sales tax included on your customers' invoices.

Finally, press F9 (CALC). The model will recalculate all your totals and invoice due dates. You then will be ready to manipulate the updated information.

The Criterion Range and Analysis Area

You have learned that you can use the Criterion Range and Analysis Area to Find, Delete, or Extract records (your company's invoices). To Extract all the records of a particular company, for example, you issue the /Range Erase command for the range A33..M35 to make sure that the criterion range is blank.

You then move the cursor to cell D33 and enter a client company's name. Now you issue the /Data Query Extract command to copy all records that meet the criteria to the Analysis Area. (If you remember, you previously set up the Input, Criterion, and Output ranges.)

If you had performed this operation on the BBB Corp in figure 5.1, invoices 1006 and 1008 would have been copied to the Analysis Area. You can perform all types of queries by experimenting with the criteria.

To delete records, such as paid invoices, from the database you will need to use the **/D**ata **Q**uery **D**elete command. First, reset the Criterion Range by entering **/R**ange **E**rase for the range A33..M34. Note the formula to type in cell M33

M33: +M12<0.005

The value 0.005 is used instead of zero to avoid potential problems that might be caused by 1-2-3's floating-point arithmetic. Fortunately, using this value will give you the same result that using zero would.

Now you issue the **/D**ata **Q**uery **D**elete command. All invoices with zero balances will be removed from the database. We do not recommend this operation because it will destroy your client's payment history, but you can use it to avoid overcrowding and to increase the number of rows in the Invoice Register and Collection database. Then you can delete these rows or use them to enter new invoices into the model.

The Criterion Range and Analysis Area take advantage of 1-2-3's database capability to give you a tool for analyzing your receivables. The Aging and Sales Summary Reports give you additional information to manage your receivables.

The Aging and Sales Summary Reports

Compared to the model's first four sections, the Aging and Sales Summary Reports are easy to generate and require very little input from you.

To run the Aging Report, you issue the **/D**ata **T**able **2** command. Input cell 1 will be cell P59 and Input cell 2 will be Q60. The number of rows in the data table range (which will be P34..T54) may increase or decrease according to the number of customers in your table. Based on this input, the model will construct the report and use the Invoice Register and Collection modules for data. After the Aging Report has run, press F9 (CALC) to have 1-2-3 calculate your client and time-interval totals.

The Sales Summary Report, a one-variable data table, is even easier to generate than the two-variable Aging Report. To produce the Sales Summary Report, you enter the beginning and ending dates of the period you wish to review in cells R65 and R66, respectively. If you do not specify a time period, the model will calculate totals for the entire database.

Always invoke the **/D**ata **T**able **R**eset command before you begin another **/D**ata **T**able operation. After resetting your **D**ata **T**ables, you issue the **/D**ata **T**able **1** command. Enter Input cell 1 as cell P93 and P70..S77 as the Table range.

After the model has built the table, press F9 (CALC) to calculate the client, net sales, tax, and freight amounts. Now you can see the similarity between the Aging and Sales Summary Reports and the Accounting Summary in the Checkbook Manager, all of which use 1-2-3's data-management functions to generate cash-management reports.

You may also want to sort your clients' names in ascending order for clearer understanding of the Aging and Sales Summary reports. To perform this, issue the **/D**ata **S**ort command. The data range will be your clients' names and payment information (columns P through T in these worksheet areas).

The **P**rimary **K**ey will be your customers' names. Then choose **A** for ascending order. Your customers and their account data will be sorted in alphabetical order.

This model is equipped with the \r macro which, as you have learned, takes the monotony out of issuing data table commands. This macro, however, *DOES NOT* change the size of the actual data tables. Therefore, you must manually change the ranges of the AGING_TABLE and SALES_TABLE to the appropriate size, based on the number of your customers in the table. You can do so by issuing the **/R**ange **N**ame **C**reate command, choosing the proper range to define, and typing in the new range setting.

Finally, if you find you need more room in your Aging and/or Sales Summary reports, use the **/W**orksheet **I**nsert **R**ow command.

Conclusion

The Accounts Receivable Tracker will help you manage and control your investment in accounts receivable. The model offers you (with no investment in additional software) most of the features of dedicated accounts-receivable systems: an invoice register, collections schedule, and aging and sales analysis reports. Furthermore, you can use 1-2-3 to tailor your accounts-receivable system to your business's specific needs. Using the Accounts Receivable Tracker will help you to better manage your company's finances.

A1: [W8] \=
B1: [W10] \=
C1: [W11] \=
D1: [W20] \=
E1: [W11] \=
F1: [W11] \=
G1: [W12] \=
H1: [W11] \=
I1: [W11] \=
J1: [W10] \=
K1: [W11] \=
L1: [W10] \=
M1: [W11] \=
N1: [W9] \=
O1: [W5] \=
P1: [W16] \=
Q1: [W11] \=
R1: [W11] \=
S1: [W11] \=
T1: [W11] \=
U1: [W14] \=
A3: [W8] 'ACCOUNTS RECEIVABLE TRACKER
D3: [W20] '   Copyright (C) 1987 Que Corporatio
A5: [W8] \=
B5: [W10] \=
C5: [W11] \=
D5: [W20] \=
E5: [W11] \=
F5: [W11] \=
G5: [W12] \=
H5: [W11] \=
I5: [W11] \=
J5: [W10] \=
K5: [W11] \=
L5: [W10] \=
M5: [W11] \=
N5: [W9] \=
O5: [W5] \=
P5: [W16] \=
Q5: [W11] \=
R5: [W11] \=
S5: [W11] \=
T5: [W11] \=
U5: [W14] \=
V5: \=
W5: \=
A6: [W8] 'INVOICE REGISTER
I6: [W11] 'COLLECTIONS
A7: [W8] \=
B7: [W10] \=
C7: [W11] \=
D7: [W20] \=
E7: [W11] \=
F7: [W11] \=

G7: [W12] \=
H7: [W11] \=
I7: [W11] \=
J7: [W10] \=
K7: [W11] \=
L7: [W10] \=
M7: [W11] \=
N7: [W9] \=
O7: [W5] \=
P7: [W16] \=
Q7: [W11] \=
R7: [W11] \=
S7: [W11] \=
T7: [W11] \=
U7: [W14] \=
V7: \=
W7: \=
A8: [W8] 'Today's Date:
C8: (D1) [W11] @INT(@NOW)+109
O8: [W5] '\I
P8: [W16] '{PANELOFF}{WINDOWSOFF}
R8: [W11] 'Turn Control Panel & Windows Off
P9: [W16] '{GOTO}BOTTOM~
R9: [W11] 'Go to range name Bottom
A10: [W8] 'Invoice
B10: [W10] 'Invoice
C10: [W11] 'Net
H10: [W11] 'Date
P10: [W16] '/wir~
R10: [W11] 'Insert row
A11: [W8] 'Number
B11: [W10] 'Date
C11: [W11] 'Amount
D11: [W20] 'Customer
E11: [W11] 'Tax
F11: [W11] 'Freight
G11: [W12] 'Total
H11: [W11] 'Due
I11: [W11] 'Payment 1
J11: [W10] 'Date 1
K11: [W11] 'Payment 2
L11: [W10] 'Date 2
M11: [W11] 'Balance
P11: [W16] '{RIGHT 4}/C{ESC}{UP}~~
R11: [W11] 'Move cursor 4 cells and copy formula
A12: [W8] 1001
B12: (D1) [W10] @DATE(86,12,1)
C12: (C2) [W11] 112
D12: [W20] 'ABC Corp
E12: (C2) [W11] +$C$26*C12
F12: (C2) [W11] 0
G12: (C2) [W12] +C12+E12+F12
H12: (D1) [W11] +C$25+B12
I12: (C2) [W11] 118.72

J12: (D1) [W10] @DATE(86,12,15)
K12: (C2) [W11] 0
M12: (C2) [W11] +G12-I12-K12
P12: [W16] '{RIGHT 2}/C{ESC}{UP}~~
R12: [W11] 'Move cursor 2 cell and copy formula
A13: [W8] +A12+1
B13: (D1) [W10] @DATE(87,1,6)
C13: (,2) [W11] 4567
D13: [W20] 'BCD Corp
E13: (,2) [W11] +$C$26*C13
F13: (,2) [W11] 421
G13: (,2) [W12] +C13+E13+F13
H13: (D1) [W11] +C$25+B13
I13: (C2) [W11] 0
K13: (C2) [W11] 0
M13: (,2) [W11] +G13-I13-K13
P13: [W16] '{RIGHT 6}/C{ESC}{UP}~~
R13: [W11] 'Move cursor 6 cell and copy formula
A14: [W8] +A13+1
B14: (D1) [W10] @DATE(87,2,1)
C14: (,2) [W11] 325
D14: [W20] 'CDE, Inc
E14: (,2) [W11] +$C$26*C14
F14: (,2) [W11] 0
G14: (,2) [W12] +C14+E14+F14
H14: (D1) [W11] +C$25+B14
I14: (C2) [W11] 0
K14: (C2) [W11] 0
M14: (,2) [W11] +G14-I14-K14
P14: [W16] '{GOTO}BOTTOM~{UP}~
R14: [W11] 'Go to range name Bottom then up one
A15: [W8] +A14+1
B15: (D1) [W10] @DATE(87,2,6)
C15: (,2) [W11] 355
D15: [W20] 'DDD Limited
E15: (,2) [W11] +$C$26*C15
F15: (,2) [W11] 0
G15: (,2) [W12] +C15+E15+F15
H15: (D1) [W11] +C$25+B15
I15: (,2) [W11] 100
J15: (D1) [W10] @DATE(86,2,1)
K15: (,2) [W11] 276.3
L15: (D1) [W10] @DATE(86,2,15)
M15: (,2) [W11] +G15-I15-K15
P15: [W16] '{PANELON}{WINDOWSON}
R15: [W11] 'Turn Control Panel & Windows On
A16: [W8] +A15+1
B16: (D1) [W10] @DATE(87,2,11)
C16: (,2) [W11] 9226
D16: [W20] 'EEE Partners
E16: (,2) [W11] +$C$26*C16
F16: (,2) [W11] 529
G16: (,2) [W12] +C16+E16+F16

H16: (D1) [W11] +C$25+B16
I16: (C2) [W11] 0
K16: (C2) [W11] 0
M16: (,2) [W11] +G16-I16-K16
A17: [W8] +A16+1
B17: (D1) [W10] @DATE(87,2,16)
C17: (,2) [W11] 689
D17: [W20] 'BBB Corp
E17: (,2) [W11] +$C$26*C17
F17: (,2) [W11] 0
G17: (,2) [W12] +C17+E17+F17
H17: (D1) [W11] +C$25+B17
I17: (C2) [W11] 0
K17: (C2) [W11] 0
M17: (,2) [W11] +G17-I17-K17
O17: [W5] '\R
P17: [W16] '{HOME}{MENUBRANCH MENU}
S17: [W11] 'Goto A1, start MENU
A18: [W8] +A17+1
B18: (D1) [W10] @DATE(87,2,21)
C18: (,2) [W11] 1779
D18: [W20] 'CCC, Inc
E18: (,2) [W11] +$C$26*C18
F18: (,2) [W11] 0
G18: (,2) [W12] +C18+E18+F18
H18: (D1) [W11] +C$25+B18
I18: (C2) [W11] 0
K18: (C2) [W11] 0
M18: (,2) [W11] +G18-I18-K18
O18: [W5] 'MENU
P18: [W16] 'Aging Report
Q18: [W11] 'Sales Summary
S18: [W11] 'Menu options Aging and Sales
A19: [W8] +A18+1
B19: (D1) [W10] @DATE(87,2,26)
C19: (,2) [W11] 483
D19: [W20] 'BBB Corp
E19: (,2) [W11] +$C$26*C19
F19: (,2) [W11] 0
G19: (,2) [W12] +C19+E19+F19
H19: (D1) [W11] +C$25+B19
I19: (C2) [W11] 0
K19: (C2) [W11] 0
M19: (,2) [W11] +G19-I19-K19
P19: [W16] 'Data Table
Q19: [W11] 'Data Table
S19: [W11] 'Description of options
A20: [W8] +A19+1
B20: (D1) [W10] @DATE(87,3,3)
C20: (,2) [W11] 227
D20: [W20] 'ABC Corp
E20: (,2) [W11] +$C$26*C20
F20: (,2) [W11] 0

```
G20: (,2) [W12] +C20+E20+F20          B28: [W10] \=
H20: (D1) [W11] +C$25+B20             C28: [W11] \=
I20: (C2) [W11] 0                     D28: [W20] \=
K20: (C2) [W11] 0                     E28: [W11] \=
M20: (,2) [W11] +G20-I20-K20          F28: [W11] \=
P20: [W16] '{BRANCH AGE}              G28: [W12] \=
Q20: [W11] '{BRANCH SALES}            H28: [W11] \=
S20: [W11] 'Action taken based on item chosen   I28: [W11] \=
C21: [W11] ' --------                 J28: [W10] \=
E21: [W11] ' --------                 K28: [W11] \=
F21: [W11] ' --------                 L28: [W10] \=
G21: [W12] ' --------                 M28: [W11] \=
I21: [W11] ' --------                 N28: [W9] \=
K21: [W11] ' --------                 O28: [W5] \=
M21: [W11] ' --------                 P28: [W16] \=
A22: [W8] 'Total                      Q28: [W11] \=
C22: (C2) [W11] @SUM(C12..C21)        R28: [W11] \=
E22: (C2) [W11] @SUM(E12..E21)        S28: [W11] \=
F22: (C2) [W11] @SUM(F12..F21)        T28: [W11] \=
G22: (C2) [W12] @SUM(G12..G21)        U28: [W14] \=
I22: (C2) [W11] @SUM(I12..I21)        A29: [W8] 'CRITERION RANGE
K22: (C2) [W11] @SUM(K12..K21)        P29: [W16] 'AGING REPORT
M22: (C2) [W11] @SUM(M12..M21)        A30: [W8] \=
O22: [W5] 'AGE                        B30: [W10] \=
P22: [W16] '{GOTO}AGING_TABLE~        C30: [W11] \=
R22: [W11] 'SALES                     D30: [W20] \=
S22: [W11] '{GOTO}SALES_TABLE~        E30: [W11] \=
U22: [W14] 'Go to appropriate table   F30: [W11] \=
C23: [W11] ' ========                 G30: [W12] \=
E23: [W11] ' ========                 H30: [W11] \=
F23: [W11] ' ========                 I30: [W11] \=
G23: [W12] ' ========                 J30: [W10] \=
I23: [W11] ' ========                 K30: [W11] \=
K23: [W11] ' ========                 L30: [W10] \=
M23: [W11] ' ========                 M30: [W11] \=
P23: [W16] '/dtr/dt2                  N30: [W9] \=
S23: [W11] '/dtr/dt1                  O30: [W5] \=
U23: [W14] 'Reset data table, start data table   P30: [W16] \=
P24: [W16] 'AGING_TABLE~              Q30: [W11] \=
                                      R30: [W11] \=
S24: [W11] 'SALES_TABLE~              S30: [W11] \=
U24: [W14] 'Assign table to calculate   T30: [W11] \=
A25: [W8] 'Standard Terms:            U30: [W14] \=
C25: [W11] 30                         A31: [W8] 'Invoice
D25: [W20] 'days                      B31: [W10] 'Invoice
P25: [W16] 'IN1_1~IN2_1~              C31: [W11] 'Net
S25: [W11] 'IN1_2~                    H31: [W11] 'Date
U25: [W14] 'Assign input cell(s)      R31: [W11] 'Aged Amount
A26: [W8] 'Sales Tax Rate:            A32: [W8] 'Number
C26: (P2) [W11] 0.06                  B32: [W10] 'Date
P26: [W16] '{BEEP 4}                  C32: [W11] 'Amount
S26: [W11] '{BEEP 4}                  D32: [W20] 'Customer
U26: [W14] 'Beep when done            E32: [W11] 'Tax
A28: [W8] \=
```

F32: [W11] 'Freight
G32: [W12] 'Total
H32: [W11] 'Due
I32: [W11] 'Payment 1
J32: [W10] 'Date 1
K32: [W11] 'Payment 2
L32: [W10] 'Date 2
M32: [W11] 'Balance
T32: [W11] '120 days
D33: [W20] 'BBB Corp
Q33: [W11] '30 days
R33: [W11] '60 days
S33: [W11] '90 days
T33: [W11] 'and over
U33: [W14] 'Total
P34: (H) [W16] @DSUM(INV_REGISTER,12,P58..Q59)
Q34: (F0) [W11] 0
R34: (F0) [W11] 30
S34: (F0) [W11] 60
T34: (F0) [W11] 90
P35: [W16] 'ABC Corp
Q35: (C2) [W11] 240.62
R35: (C2) [W11] 0
S35: (C2) [W11] 0
T35: (C2) [W11] 0
U35: (C2) [W14] @SUM(Q35..T35)
A36: [W8] \=
B36: [W10] \=
C36: [W11] \=
D36: [W20] \=
E36: [W11] \=
F36: [W11] \=
G36: [W12] \=
H36: [W11] \=
I36: [W11] \=
J36: [W10] \=
K36: [W11] \=
L36: [W10] \=
M36: [W11] \=
P36: [W16] 'BCD Corp
Q36: (,2) [W11] 0
R36: (,2) [W11] 0
S36: (,2) [W11] 5262.02
T36: (,2) [W11] 0
U36: (,2) [W14] @SUM(Q36..T36)
A37: [W8] 'ANALYSIS AREA
P37: [W16] 'CDE, Inc
Q37: (,2) [W11] 0
R37: (,2) [W11] 344.5
S37: (,2) [W11] 0
T37: (,2) [W11] 0
U37: (,2) [W14] @SUM(Q37..T37)
A38: [W8] \=

B38: [W10] \=
C38: [W11] \=
D38: [W20] \=
E38: [W11] \=
F38: [W11] \=
G38: [W12] \=
H38: [W11] \=
I38: [W11] \=
J38: [W10] \=
K38: [W11] \=
L38: [W10] \=
M38: [W11] \=
P38: [W16] 'DDD Limited
Q38: (,2) [W11] 0
R38: (,2) [W11] 0
S38: (,2) [W11] 0
T38: (,2) [W11] 0
U38: (,2) [W14] @SUM(Q38..T38)
C39: [W11] 'Report Title:
P39: [W16] 'EEE Partners
Q39: (,2) [W11] 0
R39: (,2) [W11] 10308.56
S39: (,2) [W11] 0
T39: (,2) [W11] 0
U39: (,2) [W14] @SUM(Q39..T39)
C40: [W11] 'Date:
E40: (D1) [W11] @INT(@NOW)
P40: [W16] 'BBB Corp
Q40: (,2) [W11] 0
R40: (,2) [W11] 1242.32
S40: (,2) [W11] 0
T40: (,2) [W11] 0
U40: (,2) [W14] @SUM(Q40..T40)
P41: [W16] 'CCC, Inc
Q41: (,2) [W11] 0
R41: (,2) [W11] 1885.74
S41: (,2) [W11] 0
T41: (,2) [W11] 0
U41: (,2) [W14] @SUM(Q41..T41)
A42: [W8] 'Invoice
B42: [W10] 'Invoice
C42: [W11] 'Net
H42: [W11] 'Date
T42: (,2) [W11] 0
U42: (,2) [W14] @SUM(Q42..T42)
A43: [W8] 'Number
B43: [W10] 'Date
C43: [W11] 'Amount
D43: [W20] 'Customer
E43: [W11] 'Tax
F43: [W11] 'Freight
G43: [W12] 'Total
H43: [W11] 'Due

I43: [W11] 'Payment 1
J43: [W10] 'Date 1
K43: [W11] 'Payment 2
L43: [W10] 'Date 2
M43: [W11] 'Balance
T43: (,2) [W11] 0
U43: (,2) [W14] @SUM(Q43..T43)
A44: [W8] 1006
B44: (D1) [W10] 31789
C44: (,2) [W11] 689
D44: [W20] 'BBB Corp
E44: (,2) [W11] 41.34
F44: (,2) [W11] 0
G44: (,2) [W12] 730.34
H44: (D1) [W11] 31819
I44: (C2) [W11] 0
K44: (C2) [W11] 0
M44: (,2) [W11] 730.34
T44: (,2) [W11] 0
U44: (,2) [W14] @SUM(Q44..T44)
A45: [W8] 1008
B45: (D1) [W10] 31792
C45: (,2) [W11] 483
D45: [W20] 'BBB Corp
E45: (,2) [W11] 28.98
F45: (,2) [W11] 0
G45: (,2) [W12] 511.98
H45: (D1) [W11] 31822
I45: (C2) [W11] 0
K45: (C2) [W11] 0
M45: (,2) [W11] 511.98
T45: (,2) [W11] 0
U45: (,2) [W14] @SUM(Q45..T45)
T46: (,2) [W11] 0
U46: (,2) [W14] @SUM(Q46..T46)
T47: (,2) [W11] 0
U47: (,2) [W14] @SUM(Q47..T47)
T48: (,2) [W11] 0
U48: (,2) [W14] @SUM(Q48..T48)
T49: (,2) [W11] 0
U49: (,2) [W14] @SUM(Q49..T49)
T50: (,2) [W11] 0
U50: (,2) [W14] @SUM(Q50..T50)
T51: (,2) [W11] 0
U51: (,2) [W14] @SUM(Q51..T51)
T52: (,2) [W11] 0
U52: (,2) [W14] @SUM(Q52..T52)
T53: (,2) [W11] 0
U53: (,2) [W14] @SUM(Q53..T53)
T54: (,2) [W11] 0
U54: (,2) [W14] @SUM(Q54..T54)
Q55: [W11] ' ---------
R55: [W11] ' ---------

S55: [W11] ' ---------
T55: [W11] ' ---------
U55: [W14] ' -------------
Q56: (C2) [W11] @SUM(Q35..Q55)
R56: (C2) [W11] @SUM(R35..R55)
S56: (C2) [W11] @SUM(S35..S55)
T56: (C2) [W11] @SUM(T35..T55)
U56: (C2) [W14] @SUM(U35..U55)
V56: +$COLL_BAL-$AGE_TOT
P58: [W16] 'Customer
Q58: [W11] 'Date
Q59: (H) [W11] +B12<=$C$8-$IN2_1#AND#B12>$C$8-$Q$61
Q61: [W11] @IF(IN2_1=90,IN2_1+365,IN2_1+30)
P62: [W16] \=
Q62: [W11] \=
R62: [W11] \=
S62: [W11] \=
T62: [W11] \=
U62: [W14] \=
P63: [W16] 'SALES SUMMARY REPORT
P64: [W16] \=
Q64: [W11] \=
R64: [W11] \=
S64: [W11] \=
T64: [W11] \=
U64: [W14] \=
P65: [W16] 'For Period Beginning:
R65: (D1) [W11] @DATE(87,1,1)
P66: [W16] '   Ending:
R66: (D1) [W11] @DATE(87,2,1)
P69: [W16] 'Customer
Q69: [W11] 'Net Sales
R69: [W11] 'Tax
S69: [W11] 'Freight
T69: [W11] 'Total
Q70: (H) [W11] @DSUM(INV_REGISTER,2,P92..Q93)
R70: (H) [W11] @DSUM(INV_REGISTER,4,P92..Q93)
S70: (H) [W11] @DSUM(INV_REGISTER,5,P92..Q93)
P71: [W16] 'ABC Corp
Q71: (C2) [W11] 0
R71: (C2) [W11] 0
S71: (C2) [W11] 0
T71: (C2) [W11] @SUM(Q71..S71)
P72: [W16] 'BCD Corp
Q72: (,2) [W11] 4567
R72: (,2) [W11] 274.02
S72: (,2) [W11] 421
T72: (,2) [W11] @SUM(Q72..S72)
P73: [W16] 'CDE, Inc
Q73: (,2) [W11] 325
R73: (,2) [W11] 19.5
S73: (,2) [W11] 0
T73: (,2) [W11] @SUM(Q73..S73)

P74: [W16] 'DDD Limited
Q74: (,2) [W11] 0
R74: (,2) [W11] 0
S74: (,2) [W11] 0
T74: (,2) [W11] @SUM(Q74..S74)
P75: [W16] 'EEE Partners
Q75: (,2) [W11] 0
R75: (,2) [W11] 0
S75: (,2) [W11] 0
T75: (,2) [W11] @SUM(Q75..S75)
P76: [W16] 'BBB Corp
Q76: (,2) [W11] 0
R76: (,2) [W11] 0
S76: (,2) [W11] 0
T76: (,2) [W11] @SUM(Q76..S76)
P77: [W16] 'CCC, Inc
Q77: (,2) [W11] 0
R77: (,2) [W11] 0
S77: (,2) [W11] 0
T77: (,2) [W11] @SUM(Q77..S77)
T78: (,2) [W11] @SUM(Q78..S78)
T79: (,2) [W11] @SUM(Q79..S79)
T80: (,2) [W11] @SUM(Q80..S80)
T81: (,2) [W11] @SUM(Q81..S81)
T82: (,2) [W11] @SUM(Q82..S82)
T83: (,2) [W11] @SUM(Q83..S83)
T84: (,2) [W11] @SUM(Q84..S84)
T85: (,2) [W11] @SUM(Q85..S85)
T86: (,2) [W11] @SUM(Q86..S86)
T87: (,2) [W11] @SUM(Q87..S87)
T88: (,2) [W11] @SUM(Q88..S88)
Q89: [W11] ' --------
R89: [W11] ' --------
S89: [W11] ' --------
T89: [W11] ' --------
P90: [W16] 'Total
Q90: (C2) [W11] @SUM(Q71..Q89)
R90: (C2) [W11] @SUM(R71..R89)
S90: (C2) [W11] @SUM(S71..S89)
T90: (C2) [W11] @SUM(T71..T89)
P92: [W16] 'Customer
Q92: [W11] 'Date
Q93: (T) [W11] +B12>=$R$65#AND#B12<=$R$66

III

Using Financial Statements

6

General Ledger Accounting

Introduction

If you have been shopping for accounting software to perform fundamental accounting and money management tasks, you know how expensive the software can be. Worse, many software packages do not have the flexibility to accommodate your firm's unique circumstances.

The good news is that the versatile 1-2-3 General Ledger can meet most accounting requirements of a small to medium-sized business without an additional investment in software. The ease and speed with which this model performs is an additional bonus.

This chapter explains how to create your own general ledger, how the model operates, and, step-by-step, how you or your accountant can use the model.

The General Ledger model consists of six sections: the Worksheet, Financial Statements, Transactions, Journal Entries, Names, and a macro. Figure 6.1 shows the sample General Ledger.

General Ledger   Copyright (C) Que Corporation 1987

			Trial Balance		Transactions		Adjustments		Adj Trial Balance		Income Statement		Balance Sheet		Com
ACCOUNT DESCRIPTION		Acct #	Debit	Credit	Debit	Credit	Debit	Credit	Debit	Credit	Debit	Credit	Debit	Credit	
Cash		100	9600.00		50.00	0.00	150.00	0.00	9800.00				9800.00		
Accounts Receivable		110	2330.00		50.00	50.00	0.00	150.00	2130.00				2130.00		
Office Equipment		150	1800.00		0.00	0.00	0.00	0.00	1800.00				1800.00		
Acc Depr - Office Equip		160		15.00	0.00	0.00	0.00	0.00		15.00				15.00	
Accounts Payable		200		7865.00	0.00	0.00	0.00	0.00		7865.00				7865.00	
Loan Payable		250		1000.00	0.00	0.00	0.00	0.00		1000.00				1000.00	
Capital Stock		275		3593.00	0.00	0.00	0.00	0.00		3593.00				3593.00	
Net Income/(Loss)		300		1257.00	0.00	0.00	0.00	0.00		1257.00				1257.00	
Sales		400		6347.00	0.00	0.00	0.00	0.00		6347.00		6347.00			
Salaries		600	1840.00		0.00	0.00	0.00	0.00	1840.00		1840.00				
Office Rent		606	550.00		0.00	0.00	0.00	0.00	550.00		550.00				
Postage		608	120.00		0.00	0.00	0.00	0.00	120.00		120.00				
Dues & Subscriptions		610	60.00		0.00	0.00	0.00	0.00	60.00		60.00				
Telephone		611	65.00		0.00	0.00	0.00	0.00	65.00		65.00				
Advertising		612	425.00		0.00	0.00	0.00	0.00	425.00		425.00				
Travel & Entertainment		618	500.00		0.00	0.00	0.00	0.00	500.00		500.00				
Miscellaneous		620	2787.00		0.00	0.00	0.00	0.00	2787.00		2787.00				
Total			$20,077.00	$20,077.00	$50.00	$50.00	$150.00	$150.00	$20,077.00	$20,077.00	$6,347.00	$6,347.00	$13,730.00	$13,730.00	

Balance Sheet
December 31, 1986

Current Assets		
Cash	9800.00	
Accounts receivable	2130.00	
Total Current Assets		11930.00
Fixed Assets		
Office Equipment	1800.00	
Less: Acc Depr	15.00	
Total Fixed Assets		1785.00
Total Assets		13715.00
Current Liabilities		
Accounts Payable	7865.00	
Total Current Liabilities		7865.00
Long-Term Liabilities		
Loan Payable		1000.00
Stockholders Equity		
Capital Stock	3593.00	
Curr Yr Net Income	1257.00	
Total Stockholder's Equity		4850.00

72 Total Liabilities & Stockholders Equity   13715.00

Income Statement
December 31, 1986

	Month		Year-to-Date		Prior Mo YTD
	Amount		Amount		
84 Sales	$6,347.00	100%	$6,347.00	100%	
85	0.00	0%	0.00	0%	
86	0.00	0%	0.00	0%	
87	0.00	0%	0.00	0%	
89 Total Sales	6,347.00	100%	6,347.00	100%	1
91 Operating Expenses					
93 Salaries	1,840.00	29%	1,840.00	29%	
94 Office Rent	550.00	9%	550.00	9%	
95 Postage	120.00	2%	120.00	2%	
96 Dues & Subscriptions	60.00	1%	60.00	1%	
97 Telephone	65.00	1%	65.00	1%	
98 Advertising	425.00	7%	425.00	7%	
99 Travel & Entertainment	500.00	8%	500.00	8%	
100 Miscellaneous	2,787.00	44%	2,787.00	44%	
101	0.00	0%	0.00	0%	
102	0.00	0%	0.00	0%	
103	0.00	0%	0.00	0%	
104	0.00	0%	0.00	0%	
106 Total Operating Expenses	6,347.00	100%	6,347.00	100%	
108 Net Income/(Loss)	$0.00	0%	$0.00	0%	

CHECKING ACCT TRANSACTIONS

Check #	Acct #	Amount	Clear
100		0	

BANK DEPOSIT TRANSACTIONS

Date	Acct #	Amount
30-Dec-86	110	50.00
100		50

SALES

Inv #	Date	Acct #	Amount
		110	0

```
  R    S     T     U     V     W     X     Y     Z            AA          AB    AC    AD    AE    AF    AG    AH    AI    AJ
=====================================================================================================================================

=====================================================================================================================================
                        \P      /ppagq~~
                        Printing                   JOURNAL ENTRIES
                        Macro                      -------------------
                                                   ACCOUNT DESCRIPTION            Acct #     Debit  Credit          Comments
                                                   -------------------            ------     -----  ------     -----------------
                                                   Cash                              100       150             Collected portion of receivable
                                                   Accounts Receivable               110               150     from ABC Corp





Acct #  Acct #  Acct #  Acct #  Acct #  Acct #  Acct #  Acct #  Acct #                                              Acct #  Acct #  Acct #
------  ------  ------  ------  ------  ------  ------  ------  ------                                              ------  ------  ------
   110     150     160     200     250     275     300     400     600                                                 606     608     610
```

Fig. 6.1. The General Ledger.

Before You Create the Model

This model requires that you plan before you create the application. Depending on the size of your business, you probably will have many more accounts than are shown in figure 6.1. After you have entered the model and are sure that it operates properly, you can include extra rows for future accounts as well as your regular chart of accounts.

Setting Column Widths

Start with a blank worksheet and change the column widths according to these settings:

Column	Width
A	30
C	6
D through P	13
AA	30

Next, enter the column headings and other labels from the list in table 6.1. As you create the application, keep in mind that this model lends itself well to the \- trick.

Table 6.1
Column Headings and Row Titles

Enter into cell:	Original label:	Copy to:
	Worksheet	
D5:	' Trial Balance	
F5:	' Transactions	
H5:	' Adjustments	
J5:	' Adj Trial Balance	
L5:	' Income Statement	
N5:	' Balance Sheet	
P5:	' Comments	
D6:	' -------------------	F6, H6, J6, L6, N6, P6
A7:	'ACCOUNT DESCRIPTION	
C7:	'Acct #	Q27..W27,

Enter into cell:	Original label:	Copy to:
D7:	'Debit	F7, H7, J7, L7, N7
E7:	'Credit	G7, I7, K7, M7, O7
A8:	'-------------------	
C8:	'------	D8..O8
A9:	'Cash	
A10:	'Accounts Receivable	
A11:	'Office Equipment	
A12:	'Acc Depr - Office Equip	
A13:	'Accounts Payable	
A14:	'Loan Payable	
A15:	'Capital Stock	
A16:	'Net Income/(Loss)	
A17:	'Sales	
A18:	'Salaries	
A19:	'Office Rent	
A20:	'Postage	
A21:	'Dues & Subscriptions	
A22:	'Telephone	
A23:	'Advertising	
A24:	'Travel & Entertainment	
A25:	'Miscellaneous	
D27:	'--------------	E27..O27
A28:	'Total	
D29:	'==============	E29..O29

Financial Statements

C33:	' Balance Sheet	
C34:	'December 31, 1986	
A36:	'Current Assets	
A37:	'-------------------	A44, A55, A61, A66, A92
A38:	'Cash	
A39:	'Accounts Receivable	
D40:	'--------------	D47, E50, D57, D69, E71
A41:	'Total Current Assets	
A43:	'Fixed Assets	
A45:	'Office Equipment	
A46:	'Less: Acc Depr	
A48:	'Total Fixed Assets	

Enter into cell:	Original label:	Copy to:
E52:	'===============	E73, D109, G109
A54:	'Current Liabilities	
A56:	'Accounts Payable	
A58:	'Total Current Liabilities	
A60:	'Long-Term Liabilities	
A62:	'Loan Payable	
A65:	'Stockholders Equity	
A67:	'Capital Stock	
A68:	'Curr Yr Net Income	
A70:	'Total Stockholders Equity	
A72:	'Total Liabilities & Stockholders Equity	
C77:	'Income Statement	
C78:	'December 31, 1986	
E81:	' Month	
G81:	' Year-to-Date	
J81:	'Prior Month YTD	
D82:	' -------	G82
E82:	'\-	H82, J82
D88:	'--------------	D105, D107, G88, G105, G107
E88:	''-----	H88, E105, E107, H105, H107
A89:	'Total Sales	
A91:	'Operating Expenses	
A93:	'Salaries	
A94:	'Payroll Taxes	
A95:	'Office Rent	
A96:	'Postage	
A97:	'Dues & Subscriptions	
A98:	'Telephone	
A99:	'Advertising	
A100:	'Travel & Entertainment	
A101:	'Miscellaneous	
A106:	'Total Operating Expenses	
A108:	'Net Income/(Loss)	
E109:	''=====	H109

Enter
into
cell: Original label: Copy to:

Macro

V4:   '\P
V5:   'Printing
V6:   'Macro
W4:   '/ppagq~~

Transactions

E120:   'CHECKING ACCOUNT TRANSACTIONS
I120:   'BANK ACCOUNT TRANSACTIONS
O120:   'SALES
D121:   '   ---------   I121, M121
E121:   '\-   F121..G121

D123:   "Check #
E123:   "Acct #   J123, O123
F123:   "Amount   K123, P123
G123:   "Clear
I123:   "Date   N123
M123:   "Inv #
D124:   "-------   E124..G124,
                                                       I124..K124,
                                                       M124..P124

F129:   "-------   K139, P139
E140:   100   J140
O140   110
F141:   "=======   K141, P141

Journal Entries

AA5:   'JOURNAL ENTRIES
AA6:   '------------------   AA8
AA7:   'ACCOUNT DESCRIPTION
AC7:   'Acct #
AC8:   "------   AD8..AE8
AD7:   "Debit
AE7:   "Credit
AH7:   'Comments
AG8:   '   ------------------

Enter into cell:	Original label:	Copy to:

Criterion Range

Q27:	'Acct #	R27..Z27, AH27..AN27
Q28:	'------	R28..Z28, AH28..AN28

Consider using the @VLOOKUP function to enter the row titles (account names) quickly and accurately. First, enter your chart of account numbers in an out-of-the-way area of the spreadsheet (column BA, in the example). Second, enter the corresponding account descriptions immediately to the right of your account numbers. Before continuing, check these entries to be sure they match exactly your chart of accounts.

If you are confident that your spreadsheet chart of accounts reflects your firm's accounts, **/C**opy the account numbers to column C in the Worksheet area. Now enter the appropriate @VLOOKUP equation for your first account description. **/C**opy this equation down column A as many times as your firm has accounts and then press F9 (CALC). The model has entered your account descriptions for you.

Specifying Cell Formats

Finally, you format the General Ledger by using the **/R**ange **F**ormat **F**ixed **2** command, except in the Financial Statements area, where you follow accounting convention. Be sure to perform this last step before using your model.

Naming Ranges

As you know, the application relies extensively on range names. Refer to table 6.2, which lists the model's range names and cell locations, and enter these names next.

Table 6.2
Range Names

Name	Location
ATB	J9..K26
CHECKS	D123..G223
DEPOSITS	I123..K223
JES	AC7..AE8192
NAMES	BA1..BD18
SALES	M123..P223
YTD	G84..G109
\P	W4

The \p Macro

This simple macro is located at cell W4 (see fig. 6.2). After you set your print formats, you can use the \p macro to print your financial statements or any range you want to print. You just type Alt-P. You may want to include this macro in your other 1-2-3 applications.

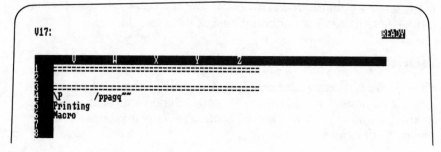

Fig. 6.2. The \p macro.

At this point, you should create the print range. Type **/P**rint **P**rinter **R**ange **A32..M109** and press Enter. Then type **Q**uit to finish the range. After you have created the print range and saved the model, 1-2-3 will always remember the print range.

Enter the formulas and functions into the model. Table 6.3 contains the information needed for the example, but you probably will need to build on this list when you create your own General Ledger.

Table 6.3
Formulas and Functions

Enter into cell:	Original formula:	Copy to:
	Worksheet	
A9:	@VLOOKUP(C9,$NAMES,1)	A10..A25
F9:	@DSUM($DEPOSITS,2, $Q$27..$Q$29)	
G9:	@DSUM($CHECKS,2,$Q$27..$Q$29)	
H9:	@DSUM($JES,1,$Q$27..$Q$29)	
I9:	@DSUM($JES,2,$Q$27..$Q$29)	
J9:	+D9+F9+H9-E9-I9-G9	J10..J11
N9:	+J9	N10..N11, O12..O16
F10:	@DSUM($CHECKS,2,$R$27..$R$29)+ @DSUM($SALES,3,$R$27..$R$29)	
G10:	@DSUM($DEPOSITS,2,$R$27..$R$29)	
H10:	@DSUM($JES,1,$R$27..$R$29)	
I10:	@DSUM($JES,2,$R$27..$R$29)	
F11:	@DSUM($CHECKS,2,$S$27..$S$29)	
H11:	@DSUM($JES,1,$S$27..$S$29)	
I11:	@DSUM($JES,2,$S$27..$S$29)	
F12:	@DSUM($CHECKS,2,$T$27..$T$29)	
H12:	@DSUM($JES,1,$T$27..$T$29)	
I12:	@DSUM($JES,2,$T$27..$T$29)	
K12:	+E12+G12+I12	K13..K15
F13:	@DSUM($CHECKS,2,$U$27..$U$29)	
G13:	@DSUM($CHECKS,2,$U$27..$U$29)	
H13:	@DSUM($JES,1,$U$27..$U$29)	
I13:	@DSUM($JES,2,$U$27..$U$29)	
F14:	@DSUM($CHECKS,2,$V$27..$V$29)	
H14:	@DSUM($JES,1,$V$27..$V$29)	
I14:	@DSUM($JES,2,$V$27..$V$29)	
F15:	@DSUM($CHECKS,2,$W$27..$W$29)	
H15:	@DSUM($JES,1,$W$27..$W$29)	
I15:	@DSUM($JES,2,$W$27..$W$29)	
F16:	@DSUM($CHECKS,2,$X$27..$X$29)	

Enter into cell:	Original formula:	Copy to:
H16:	@DSUM($JES,1,$X$27..$X$29)	
I16:	@DSUM($JES,2,$X$27..$X$29)	
K16:	+E16+G16+I16-D16-F16-H16	
F17:	@DSUM($CHECKS,2,$Y$27..$Y$29)	
G17:	@DSUM($SALES,3,$Y$27..$Y$29)	
H17:	@DSUM($JES,1,$Y$27..$Y$29)	
I17:	@DSUM($JES,2,$Y$27..$Y$29)	
K17:	+E17+G17+I17-F17-H17	
M17:	+K17	
F18:	@DSUM($CHECKS,2,$Z$27..$Z$29)	
H18:	@DSUM($JES,1,$Z$27..$Z$29)	
I18:	@DSUM($JES,2,$Z$27..$Z$29)	
J18:	(D18+F18+H18)-(E18+G18+I18)	J19..J25
L18:	+J18	L19..L25
F19:	@DSUM($CHECKS,2,$AH$27..$AH$29)	
H19:	@DSUM($JES,1,$AH$27..$AH$29)	
I19:	@DSUM($JES,2,$AH$27..$AH$29)	
F20:	@DSUM($CHECKS,2,$AI$27..$AI$29)	
H20:	@DSUM($JES,1,$AI$27..$AI$29)	
I20:	@DSUM($JES,2,$AI$27..$AI$29)	
F21:	@DSUM($CHECKS,2,$AJ$27..$AJ$29)	
H21:	@DSUM($JES,1,$AJ$27..$AJ$29)	
I21:	@DSUM($JES,2,$AJ$27..$AJ$29)	
F22:	@DSUM($CHECKS,2,$AK$27..$AK$29)	
H22:	@DSUM($JES,1,$AK$27..$AK$29)	
I22:	@DSUM($JES,2,$AK$27..$AK$29)	
F23:	@DSUM($CHECKS,2,$AL$27..$AL$29)	
H23:	@DSUM($JES,1,$AL$27..$AL$29)	
I23:	@DSUM($JES,2,$AL$27..$AL$29)	
F24:	@DSUM($CHECKS,2,$AM$27..$AM$29)	
H24:	@DSUM($JES,1,$AM$27..$AM$29)	
I24:	@DSUM($JES,2,$AM$27..$AM$29)	
F25:	@DSUM($CHECKS,2,$AN$27..$AN$29)	
H25:	@DSUM($JES,1,$AN$27..$AN$29)	
I25:	@DSUM($JES,2,$AN$27..$AN$29)	
D28:	@SUM(D9..D25)	E28..O28

Enter
into
cell: Original formula: Copy to:

Financial Statements

Enter into cell:	Original formula:	Copy to:
D38:	+N9	
D39:	+N10	
D45:	+N11	
D46:	+O12	
E41:	@SUM(D38..D39)	
E48:	+D45-D46	
E51:	+E41+E48	
D56:	+O13	
E58:	+D56	
E62:	+O14	
D67:	+O15	
D68:	+O16	
E70:	+D67+D68	
E72:	+E58+E62+E70	
D84:	+M17	
E84:	+D84/D$89	E85..E87, E89
G84:	+D84+J84	G85..G87, G93..G101
H84:	+G84/G$89	H85..H87, H89
D89:	@SUM(D84..D87)	G89
D93:	+L18	D94..D101
E93:	+D93/D$106	E94..E104, E106
H93:	+G93/G$106	H94..H104, H106
D106:	@SUM(D93..D104)	G106
D108:	+D89-D106	G108
E108:	+D108/D89	
H108:	+G108/G89	

Transactions

F140:	@SUM(F125..F139)	K140, P140

Understanding the Model

Like an accountant's worksheet, this General Ledger model captures
your business's financial activity for a specified time period. However,
the model goes far beyond a basic paper worksheet. The 1-2-3 General

Ledger not only totals your accounts but also generates your financial statements. To do so, the model draws on accounting information from the Worksheet area.

The Worksheet

The model's Worksheet area is located at cells C4 through P29. A portion of this section is shown in figure 6.3.

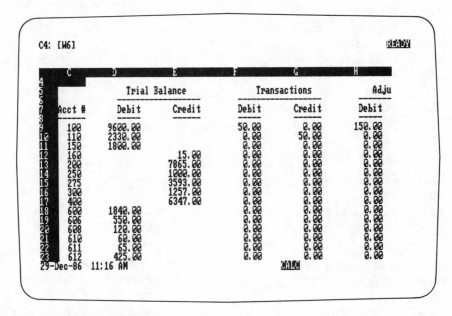

Fig. 6.3. The Worksheet Area.

The Worksheet's layout should resemble the paper ledger that accountants use. In fact, this is an application of 1-2-3's basic purpose—an electronic spreadsheet.

In the example, column A contains your account descriptions and column C, the corresponding account numbers. Columns D through O consist of debit and credit entries for your Trial Balance, Transactions, Adjustments, Adjusted Trial Balance, Income Statement, Balance Sheet, and Comments. Because the Trial Balance is a data-entry area, the operation of the Transactions section is discussed first.

The Transactions columns, F and G, account for all your firm's business-generated activity. This activity is represented in the model as inflows (bank deposits and sales) and outflows (checks). Generally, the model uses 1-2-3's @DSUM function to add and post your transactions to the proper account number. For example, the debit to Accounts Receivable transactions in figure 6.1 is calculated with the formula

F10: @DSUM($CHECKS,2,$R$27..$R$29)+@DSUM
($SALES,3,$R$27..$R$29)

The first phrase of this formula totals checks written for the time period; the second phrase adds this amount to your sales for the same period. Similarly, the credit to Accounts Receivable is calculated with the formula

G10: @DSUM($DEPOSITS,2,$R$27..$R$29)

which is your total bank deposits applied against Accounts Receivable.

Most of your debit and credit Transactions will be checking account transactions that use the general formula

@DSUM($CHECKS,2,xx..yy)

The phrase xx..yy is the appropriate criterion range or account number.

Columns H and I comprise your Adjustments. Adjustments are Journal Entries or bookkeeping transactions. For example, the debit in cell H10 is calculated by the formula

H10: @DSUM($JES,1,$R$27..$R$29)

In this formula, JES is the Journal Entries range name, 1 is the offset number (the debit), and $R$27..$R$29 is the criterion range (or account number). The transaction's credit counterpart (in cell I10) is calculated by the equation

I10: @DSUM($JES,2,$R$27..$R$29)

This formula is the same as that found in H10, except that the offset number (2) represents a credit in the Journal Entries range.

Generally, Adjustments are calculated by the formula

@DSUM($JES,z,xx..yy)

in which z is 1 for the account's debit balance, 2 for the credit balance, and $xx..yy$ is the criterion range, or account number.

Columns J and K contain the debits and credits to calculate the Adjusted Trial Balance. Generally, this balance will be the sum of all the debits and credits for each income and balance-sheet account in the Worksheet. For instance, Salaries expense is calculated by the formula in cell J18:

J18: (D18+F18+H18)–(E18+G18+I18)

| Tr Bal | Trans | Adj | Tr Bal | Trans | Adj |
| Debit | Debit | Debit | Credit | Credit | Credit |

The first phrase of this formula is the sum of your Trial Balance debit (D18), Transactions debit (F18), and Adjustments debit (H18), from which is subtracted the second phrase—the sum of your Trial Balance credit (E18), Transactions credit (G18), and Adjustments credit (I18). Your other income and balance-sheet accounts are computed in the same way.

Columns L and M, your worksheet's Income Statement columns, will be used to generate your Income Statement in the model's Financial Statements section. The formulas in these columns reference the appropriate column in the Adjusted Trial Balance. For example, your Sales balance is computed by the formula

M17: +K17

K17 is your total Sales from your Adjusted Trial Balance.

Columns N and O are your Balance Sheet debit and credit summaries. The logic contained in these columns is similar to that used in the Income Statement's columns L and M.

Column P (an explanatory note area) is included in the model for your convenience. It does not affect the model's calculations.

Finally, columns D through O are totaled using 1-2-3's @SUM function to ensure balancing.

The next section, Financial Statements, will use your Income Statement and Balance Sheet data to generate your reports.

Financial Statements

Directly below the Worksheet area, the Financial Statements module occupies cells A33 through I109. Figure 6.4 shows a portion of the Balance Sheet.

Operating this section is quite simple. Each line item references the appropriate cell location in the Worksheet area. For example, the Balance Sheet Asset, Cash, is calculated by the formula

D38: +N9

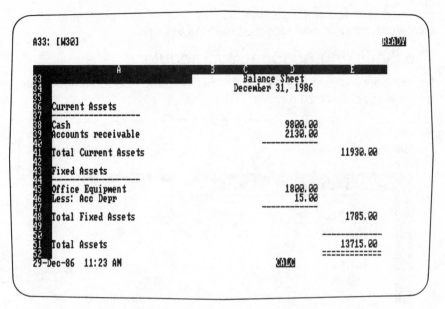

Fig. 6.4. The Balance Sheet.

N9 is the Cash balance from the Worksheet's Balance Sheet.

The Financial Statements section also calculates totals by using @SUM functions.

The only deviation from this simplicity is when the model computes your year-to-date Income Statement by copying the previous period's income statement to the current income statement area in column J.

In this manner, the current month's income statement accounts are added to the previous period's account totals. For example, your year-to-date sales are computed by the formula in cell G84:

   G84: +D84+J84

Cell D84 is the current month's sales and cell J84 is the year-to-date sales, copied from the previous period's General Ledger.

The remaining line items in the year-to-date section are computed in the same way.

Transactions

The Transactions section is the core of this model. Located in cells D120 through P141, directly below the Financial Statements module, this important part of the application comprises three subsections, or databases, that account for your business activity.

The Checking Account Submodule

The leftmost transactions database, the Checking Account submodule, is located at cells D120 through G141 (see fig. 6.5).

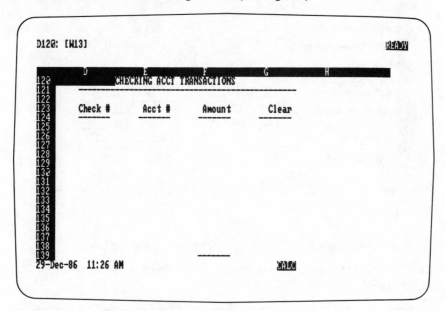

Fig. 6.5. The Checking Account Database.

This database, like the others, is a data-entry area. The Checking Account database records your business's checking account activity. The model will sum and post data in columns E and F of the database to the proper Transactions account in the Worksheet area. For this reason, it is important that the correct account number be entered to the corresponding check number in column D.

The corresponding debit to cash for these transactions is calculated by the formula

   F140: @SUM(F125..F139)

Note that the account number for cash, 100, has been placed in cell E140, so that 1-2-3 will post this credit in the proper account.

Column G is another reference area provided to help you balance your checking account. By placing an "x" in the appropriate cell, you can indicate that one of your checks has cleared. (Using column G is optional. The model does not use this data.)

Bank Deposit Transactions

The model includes your checking account's deposit activity in the Bank Deposit Transactions subsection. This database occupies cells I120 through K141, between the Checking Account and Sales submodules. Figure 6.6 shows a portion of this database.

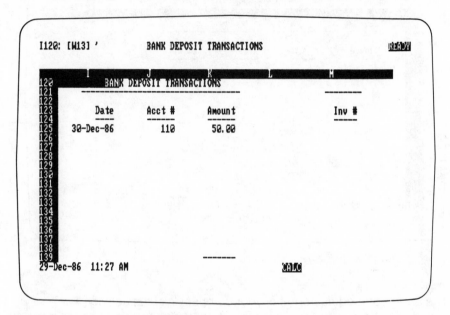

Fig. 6.6. The Bank Deposit Database.

As it does in the Checking Account database, the model totals and posts your bank deposit data in columns J and K to the appropriate Transactions account in your Worksheet. For example, many of your bank deposits will be posted as a credit to Accounts Receivable. It is important, therefore, that the correct account number be entered in column K.

An @SUM function will total your bank deposits:

K140: @SUM(K125..K139)

This will also be the total debit to cash.

Like column G in the previous section, column I (the date of deposit) is an optional reference in the Bank Deposit Transactions submodule.

The Sales Database

In the example, the Sales database is located to the right of the Bank Deposit subsection, in cells M120 through P141. Figure 6.7 shows this part of the model.

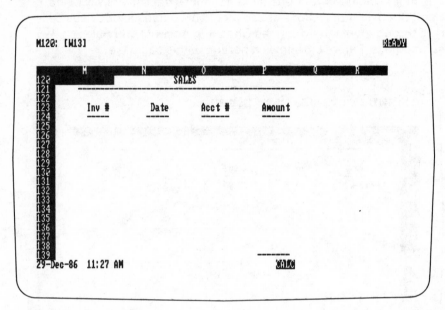

Fig. 6.7. The Sales Database.

The Sales submodule contains your company's sales activity. The model will total and post your sales activity to the proper account in the Worksheet's Transactions columns. Much of this activity will be part of the credit to Sales. Therefore, the critical columns in this database are O and P, your account number and amount of sale. Column M can be used as a reference to record your invoice on the sale; and column N, the date of the sale.

Like the two other databases, your sales are totaled and then posted as a credit to Accounts Receivable with the formula

P140: @SUM(P125..P139)

These three databases capture your business activity for the Transactions section of the Worksheet. The next segment, Journal Entries, adjusts these transactions.

Journal Entries

The Journal Entries area is located in cells AA4 through AI20, to the right of the macro. Figure 6.8 shows you the structure of this module.

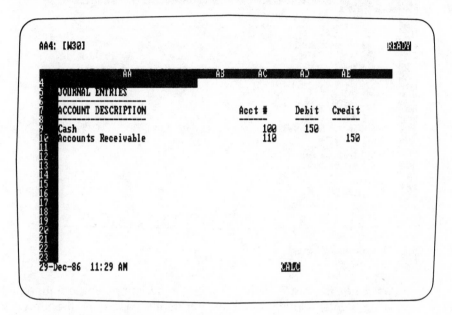

Fig. 6.8. Journal Entries.

The Journal Entries section provides you or your accountant with an area in which to make adjustments, additions, or subtractions to your business transactions. This section functions in the same way that paper and pencil general ledger journal entries do. By now, this module should look familiar to you; it is a database. Using the @DSUM function, the model will total and post these entries to the Adjustments columns in the Worksheet (see the Worksheet discussion). Therefore, be sure to code the correct account number to your entry.

The Names section contains a list of the account numbers used in figure 6.1.

The Names Range

The Names range is located to the extreme right of the model, in cells BA1 and BD11 (see fig. 6.9).

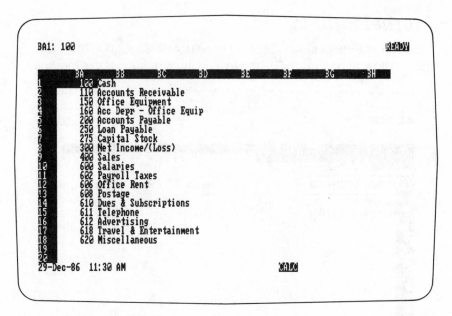

Fig. 6.9. The Names Range.

The Names range is a copy of your account descriptions and numbers, or chart of accounts. You can enter this information once and then rely on the Names range to accurately enter your Account Descriptions in column A and your debit and credit Adjustments in columns F and G, respectively. The purpose of including this Release 2 feature is to reduce manual entry as much as possible, thereby decreasing errors.

For example, consider the formula in cell A9, your account description for Cash. This formula contains the function

    A9: @VLOOKUP(C9,$NAMES,1)

By entering this formula and then copying it down column A, you ensure that all your account descriptions will be included correctly in the model.

Likewise, instead of entering account descriptions for your journal entries, the @VLOOKUP function can be used as a substitute method for entering your account descriptions. In the general formula for Journal Entries

    @VLOOKUP(xx,$NAMES,1)

xx is the cell location (test variable), $NAMES is the range, and 1 is the offset number. The model will operate normally if you choose to enter your account descriptions manually rather than use the formula.

Using the Model

Despite its intimidating size, the 1-2-3 General Ledger is easy to use. Use it carefully for the first few reporting periods. Soon using the General Ledger (like most 1-2-3 applications) will become second nature.

The first time you use the General Ledger, enter your beginning trial balance in columns D and E. Before continuing, press F9 (CALC) to make sure that the debits and credits balance.

Then move the cursor to the Transactions area and enter your Checking, Bank Deposits, and Sales activity. Be sure that these transactions are properly coded with the correct account numbers.

For another timesaving, error-reducing trick, you can use 1-2-3's /Data Fill capability to enter your check numbers. Move the cursor to the Check Number column in your Checking database and then issue the /Data Fill command. The range should be large enough to accommodate all of your checks for the current reporting period.

The Start Value will be your first check number (101, for instance), the Step number will be 1, and press [Enter] for the Stop number (when you specify a range, 1-2-3 will take care of the Stop number). In this fashion, the model will perform yet another routine but important task for you.

Next, enter your accruals and other adjustments in the Journal Entries section, as you would with a paper ledger. You may want to save time and reduce the possibility of error by using the @VLOOKUP function to enter your account name.

Finally, press F9 (CALC) to recalculate the General Ledger. The size of your firm will dictate how patient you may have to be; the model needs time to process all your entries. However, after those entries have been processed, your company's financial statements will be prepared, ready to print, and waiting for your review.

After you have set the print attributes you want, you can use the /Print Printer Align Go command or the \p macro to print the statements. Whichever method you choose, you have harnessed 1-2-3's power to do your business's accounting.

To use the General Ledger for subsequent periods, you will need to perform two **/F**ile **C**ombine **C**opy **N**amed/**S**pecified **R**ange operations. This is necessary for your beginning Trial Balance and Year-to-Date Income Statement calculations.

First, **/F**ile **R**etrieve your blank General Ledger. Next, issue the **/F**ile **C**ombine **C**opy **N**amed/**S**pecified **R**ange command. The range will be the named range ATB (Adjusted Trial Balance) from your last reporting cycle, and should be copied to the upper-left cell in your Trial Balance. (In the example, this would be the debit Cash in cell D10.) After you have completed this step, you are ready to begin using your General Ledger for the next reporting cycle.

After you have finished entering your transactions and journal entries and have recalculated the model, you should again issue the **/F**ile **C**ombine **C**opy **N**amed/**S**pecified **R**ange command, this time to allow the model to compute your year-to-date income statement.

In this case, the named/range will be YTD from your previous reporting period's file. (In figure 6.1 this would be copied to cell J84.) For your model, be sure that this range lands in the proper cell so that your General Ledger will calculate properly. Press F9 (CALC) to update the model for this operation and review your financial statements. Follow this procedure whenever you use the model.

The General Ledger is easy to modify. If you need to add more accounts, simply use the **/W**orksheet **I**nsert **R**ow command and adjust the formulas accordingly. Don't forget to include new accounts in the Names range and the Account Description column. (Of course, the best way to do this is to plan the number of accounts you need and include extra rows for expansion.)

Consider using the General Ledger model with some of the other applications in this book. The General Ledger lends itself well, for example, to Chapter 8's Ratio Analyzer. You can build the Ratio Analyzer into this model or **/F**ile **C**ombine **C**opy **N**amed/**S**pecified **R**ange the financial statements into the Ratio Analyzer. Feel free to experiment with the applications, tailoring them to your business.

Conclusion

The 1-2-3 General Ledger is the most useful application in this book. By making your accounting more accurate and by generating timely financial reports, the General Ledger model can streamline your company's accounting system.

A1: [W30] \=
B1: \=
C1: [W6] \=
D1: [W13] \=
E1: [W13] \=
F1: [W13] \=
G1: [W13] \=
H1: [W13] \=
I1: [W13] \=
J1: [W13] \=
K1: [W13] \=
L1: [W13] \=
M1: [W13] \=
N1: [W13] \=
O1: [W13] \=
P1: [W13] \=
Q1: \=
R1: \=
S1: \=
T1: \=
U1: \=
V1: \=
W1: \=
X1: \=
Y1: \=
Z1: \=
AA1: [W30] \=
AB1: \=
AC1: \=
AD1: \=
AE1: \=
AF1: \=
AG1: \=
AH1: \=
AI1: \=
BA1: 100
BB1: 'Cash
A2: [W30] 'General Ledger
B2: '   Copyright (C) Que Corporation 1987
BA2: 110
BB2: 'Accounts Receivable
A3: [W30] \=
B3: \=
C3: [W6] \=
D3: [W13] \=
E3: [W13] \=
F3: [W13] \=
G3: [W13] \=
H3: [W13] \=
I3: [W13] \=
J3: [W13] \=
K3: [W13] \=
L3: [W13] \=

M3: [W13] \=
N3: [W13] \=
O3: [W13] \=
P3: [W13] \=
Q3: \=
R3: \=
S3: \=
T3: \=
U3: \=
V3: \=
W3: \=
X3: \=
Y3: \=
Z3: \=
AA3: [W30] \=
AB3: \=
AC3: \=
AD3: \=
AE3: \=
AF3: \=
AG3: \=
AH3: \=
AI3: \=
BA3: 150
BB3: 'Office Equipment
V4: '\P
W4: '/ppagq~~
BA4: 160
BB4: 'Acc Depr - Office Equip
D5: [W13] '   Trial Balance
F5: [W13] '   Transactions
H5: [W13] '   Adjustments
J5: [W13] '   Adj Trial Balance
L5: [W13] '   Income Statement
N5: [W13] '   Balance Sheet
P5: [W13] '   Comments
V5: 'Printing
AA5: [W30] 'JOURNAL ENTRIES
BA5: 200
BB5: 'Accounts Payable
D6: [W13] '   -------------------
F6: [W13] '   -------------------
H6: [W13] '   -------------------
J6: [W13] '   -------------------
L6: [W13] '   -------------------
N6: [W13] '   -------------------
P6: [W13] '   -------------------
V6: 'Macro
AA6: [W30] '--------------------
BA6: 250
BB6: 'Loan Payable
A7: [W30] 'ACCOUNT DESCRIPTION
C7: [W6] 'Acct #
D7: [W13] "Debit

E7: [W13] "Credit
F7: [W13] "Debit
G7: [W13] "Credit
H7: [W13] "Debit
I7: [W13] "Credit
J7: [W13] "Debit
K7: [W13] "Credit
L7: [W13] "Debit
M7: [W13] "Credit
N7: [W13] "Debit
O7: [W13] "Credit
AA7: [W30] 'ACCOUNT DESCRIPTION
AC7: 'Acct #
AD7: "Debit
AE7: "Credit
AG7: '   Comments
BA7: 275
BB7: 'Capital Stock
A8: [W30] '--------------------
C8: [W6] '------
D8: [W13] "-----
E8: [W13] "------
F8: [W13] "-----
G8: [W13] "------
H8: [W13] "-----
I8: [W13] "------
J8: [W13] "-----
K8: [W13] "------
L8: [W13] "-----
M8: [W13] "------
N8: [W13] "-----
O8: [W13] "------
AA8: [W30] '--------------------
AC8: '------
AD8: "-----
AE8: "------
AG8: '   ------------------
BA8: 300
BB8: 'Net Income/(Loss)
A9: [W30] @VLOOKUP(C9,$NAMES,1)
C9: [W6] 100
D9: (F2) [W13] 9600
F9: (F2) [W13] @DSUM($DEPOSITS,2,$Q$27..$Q$29)
G9: (F2) [W13] @DSUM($CHECKS,2,$Q$27..$Q$29)
H9: (F2) [W13] @DSUM($JES,1,$Q$27..$Q$29)
I9: (F2) [W13] @DSUM($JES,2,$Q$27..$Q$29)
J9: (F2) [W13] +D9+F9+H9-E9-I9-G9
N9: (F2) [W13] +J9
AA9: [W30] @VLOOKUP(AC9,$NAMES,1)
AC9: 100
AD9: 150
AG9: '   Collected portion of receivable
BA9: 400
BB9: 'Sales

A10: [W30] @VLOOKUP(C10,$NAMES,1)
C10: [W6] 110
D10: (F2) [W13] 2330
F10: (F2) [W13] @DSUM($CHECKS,2,$R$27..$R$29)+@DSUM($SALES,3,$R$27..$R$29)
G10: (F2) [W13] @DSUM($DEPOSITS,2,$R$27..$R$29)
H10: (F2) [W13] @DSUM($JES,1,$R$27..$R$29)
I10: (F2) [W13] @DSUM($JES,2,$R$27..$R$29)
J10: (F2) [W13] +D10+F10+H10-E10-I10-G10
N10: (F2) [W13] +J10
AA10: [W30] @VLOOKUP(AC10,$NAMES,1)
AC10: 110
AE10: 150
AG10: '   from ABC Corp
BA10: 600
BB10: 'Salaries
A11: [W30] @VLOOKUP(C11,$NAMES,1)
C11: [W6] 150
D11: (F2) [W13] 1800
F11: (F2) [W13] @DSUM($CHECKS,2,$S$27..$S$29)
G11: (F2) [W13] 0
H11: (F2) [W13] @DSUM($JES,1,$S$27..$S$29)
I11: (F2) [W13] @DSUM($JES,2,$S$27..$S$29)
J11: (F2) [W13] +D11+F11+H11-E11-I11-G11
N11: (F2) [W13] +J11
BA11: 602
BB11: 'Payroll Taxes
A12: [W30] @VLOOKUP(C12,$NAMES,1)
C12: [W6] 160
E12: (F2) [W13] 15
F12: (F2) [W13] @DSUM($CHECKS,2,$T$27..$T$29)
G12: (F2) [W13] 0
H12: (F2) [W13] @DSUM($JES,1,$T$27..$T$29)
I12: (F2) [W13] @DSUM($JES,2,$T$27..$T$29)
K12: (F2) [W13] +E12+G12+I12
O12: (F2) [W13] +K12
BA12: 606
BB12: 'Office Rent
A13: [W30] @VLOOKUP(C13,$NAMES,1)
C13: [W6] 200
E13: (F2) [W13] 7865
F13: (F2) [W13] @DSUM($CHECKS,2,$U$27..$U$29)
G13: (F2) [W13] @DSUM($CHECKS,2,$U$27..$U$29)
H13: (F2) [W13] @DSUM($JES,1,$U$27..$U$29)
I13: (F2) [W13] @DSUM($JES,2,$U$27..$U$29)
K13: (F2) [W13] +E13+G13+I13
O13: (F2) [W13] +K13
BA13: 608
BB13: 'Postage
A14: [W30] @VLOOKUP(C14,$NAMES,1)
C14: [W6] 250
E14: (F2) [W13] 1000
F14: (F2) [W13] @DSUM($CHECKS,2,$V$27..$V$29)
G14: (F2) [W13] 0
H14: (F2) [W13] @DSUM($JES,1,$V$27..$V$29)

I14: (F2) [W13] @DSUM($JES,2,$V$27..$V$29)
K14: (F2) [W13] +E14+G14+I14
O14: (F2) [W13] +K14
BA14: 610
BB14: 'Dues & Subscriptions
A15: [W30] @VLOOKUP(C15,$NAMES,1)
C15: [W6] 275
E15: (F2) [W13] 3593
F15: (F2) [W13] @DSUM($CHECKS,2,$W$27..$W$29)
G15: (F2) [W13] 0
H15: (F2) [W13] @DSUM($JES,1,$W$27..$W$29)
I15: (F2) [W13] @DSUM($JES,2,$W$27..$W$29)
K15: (F2) [W13] +E15+G15+I15
O15: (F2) [W13] +K15
BA15: 611
BB15: 'Telephone
A16: [W30] @VLOOKUP(C16,$NAMES,1)
C16: [W6] 300
E16: (F2) [W13] 1257
F16: (F2) [W13] @DSUM($CHECKS,2,$X$27..$X$29)
G16: (F2) [W13] 0
H16: (F2) [W13] @DSUM($JES,1,$X$27..$X$29)
I16: (F2) [W13] @DSUM($JES,2,$X$27..$X$29)
K16: (F2) [W13] +E16+G16+I16-D16-F16-H16
O16: (F2) [W13] +K16
BA16: 612
BB16: 'Advertising
A17: [W30] 'Sales
C17: [W6] 400
E17: (F2) [W13] 6347
F17: (F2) [W13] @DSUM($CHECKS,2,$Y$27..$Y$29)
G17: (F2) [W13] @DSUM($SALES,3,$Y$27..$Y$29)
H17: (F2) [W13] @DSUM($JES,1,$Y$27..$Y$29)
I17: (F2) [W13] @DSUM($JES,2,$Y$27..$Y$29)
K17: (F2) [W13] +E17+G17+I17-F17-H17
M17: (F2) [W13] +K17
BA17: 618
BB17: 'Travel & Entertainment
A18: [W30] @VLOOKUP(C18,$NAMES,1)
C18: [W6] 600
D18: (F2) [W13] 1840
F18: (F2) [W13] @DSUM($CHECKS,2,$Z$27..$Z$29)
G18: (F2) [W13] 0
H18: (F2) [W13] @DSUM($JES,1,$Z$27..$Z$29)
I18: (F2) [W13] @DSUM($JES,2,$Z$27..$Z$29)
J18: (F2) [W13] (D18+F18+H18)-(E18+G18+I18)
L18: (F2) [W13] +J18
BA18: 620
BB18: 'Miscellaneous
A19: [W30] @VLOOKUP(C19,$NAMES,1)
C19: [W6] 606
D19: (F2) [W13] 550
F19: (F2) [W13] @DSUM($CHECKS,2,$AH$27..$AH$29)
G19: (F2) [W13] 0

H19: (F2) [W13] @DSUM($JES,1,$AH$27..$AH$29)
I19: (F2) [W13] @DSUM($JES,2,$AH$27..$AH$29)
J19: (F2) [W13] (D19+F19+H19)-(E19+G19+I19)
L19: (F2) [W13] +J19
A20: [W30] @VLOOKUP(C20,$NAMES,1)
C20: [W6] 608
D20: (F2) [W13] 120
F20: (F2) [W13] @DSUM($CHECKS,2,$AI$27..$AI$29)
G20: (F2) [W13] 0
H20: (F2) [W13] @DSUM($JES,1,$AI$27..$AI$29)
I20: (F2) [W13] @DSUM($JES,2,$AI$27..$AI$29)
J20: (F2) [W13] (D20+F20+H20)-(E20+G20+I20)
L20: (F2) [W13] +J20
A21: [W30] @VLOOKUP(C21,$NAMES,1)
C21: [W6] 610
D21: (F2) [W13] 60
F21: (F2) [W13] @DSUM($CHECKS,2,$AJ$27..$AJ$29)
G21: (F2) [W13] 0
H21: (F2) [W13] @DSUM($JES,1,$AJ$27..$AJ$29)
I21: (F2) [W13] @DSUM($JES,2,$AJ$27..$AJ$29)
J21: (F2) [W13] (D21+F21+H21)-(E21+G21+I21)
L21: (F2) [W13] +J21
A22: [W30] @VLOOKUP(C22,$NAMES,1)
C22: [W6] 611
D22: (F2) [W13] 65
F22: (F2) [W13] @DSUM($CHECKS,2,$AK$27..$AK$29)
G22: (F2) [W13] 0
H22: (F2) [W13] @DSUM($JES,1,$AK$27..$AK$29)
I22: (F2) [W13] @DSUM($JES,2,$AK$27..$AK$29)
J22: (F2) [W13] (D22+F22+H22)-(E22+G22+I22)
L22: (F2) [W13] +J22
A23: [W30] @VLOOKUP(C23,$NAMES,1)
C23: [W6] 612
D23: (F2) [W13] 425
F23: (F2) [W13] @DSUM($CHECKS,2,$AL$27..$AL$29)
G23: (F2) [W13] 0
H23: (F2) [W13] @DSUM($JES,1,$AL$27..$AL$29)
I23: (F2) [W13] @DSUM($JES,2,$AL$27..$AL$29)
J23: (F2) [W13] (D23+F23+H23)-(E23+G23+I23)
L23: (F2) [W13] +J23
A24: [W30] @VLOOKUP(C24,$NAMES,1)
C24: [W6] 618
D24: (F2) [W13] 500
F24: (F2) [W13] @DSUM($CHECKS,2,$AM$27..$AM$29)
G24: (F2) [W13] 0
H24: (F2) [W13] @DSUM($JES,1,$AM$27..$AM$29)
I24: (F2) [W13] @DSUM($JES,2,$AM$27..$AM$29)
J24: (F2) [W13] (D24+F24+H24)-(E24+G24+I24)
L24: (F2) [W13] +J24
A25: [W30] @VLOOKUP(C25,$NAMES,1)
C25: [W6] 620
D25: (F2) [W13] 2787
F25: (F2) [W13] @DSUM($CHECKS,2,$AN$27..$AN$29)
G25: (F2) [W13] 0

H25: (F2) [W13] @DSUM($JES,1,$AN$27..$AN$29)
I25: (F2) [W13] @DSUM($JES,2,$AN$27..$AN$29)
J25: (F2) [W13] (D25+F25+H25)-(E25+G25+I25)
L25: (F2) [W13] +J25
A27: [W30] 'Total
D27: [W13] '------------
E27: [W13] '------------
F27: [W13] '------------
G27: [W13] '------------
H27: [W13] '------------
I27: [W13] '------------
J27: [W13] '------------
K27: [W13] '------------
L27: [W13] '------------
M27: [W13] '------------
N27: [W13] '------------
O27: [W13] '------------
Q27: 'Acct #
R27: 'Acct #
S27: 'Acct #
T27: 'Acct #
U27: 'Acct #
V27: 'Acct #
W27: 'Acct #
X27: 'Acct #
Y27: 'Acct #
Z27: 'Acct #
AH27: 'Acct #
AI27: 'Acct #
AJ27: 'Acct #
AK27: 'Acct #
AL27: 'Acct #
AM27: 'Acct #
AN27: 'Acct #
D28: (C2) [W13] @SUM(D9..D25)
E28: (C2) [W13] @SUM(E9..E25)
F28: (C2) [W13] @SUM(F9..F25)
G28: (C2) [W13] @SUM(G9..G25)
H28: (C2) [W13] @SUM(H9..H25)
I28: (C2) [W13] @SUM(I9..I25)
J28: (C2) [W13] @SUM(J9..J25)
K28: (C2) [W13] @SUM(K9..K25)
L28: (C2) [W13] @SUM(L9..L25)
M28: (C2) [W13] @SUM(M9..M25)
N28: (C2) [W13] @SUM(N9..N25)
O28: (C2) [W13] @SUM(O9..O25)
Q28: '------
R28: '------
S28: '------
T28: '------
U28: '------
V28: '------
W28: '------

X28: '------
Y28: '------
Z28: '------
AH28: '------
AI28: '------
AJ28: '------
AK28: '------
AL28: '------
AM28: '------
AN28: '------
D29: [W13] '============
E29: [W13] '============
F29: [W13] '============
G29: [W13] '============
H29: [W13] '============
I29: [W13] '============
J29: [W13] '============
K29: [W13] '============
L29: [W13] '============
M29: [W13] '============
N29: [W13] '============
O29: [W13] '============
Q29: 100
R29: 110
S29: 150
T29: 160
U29: 200
V29: 250
W29: 275
X29: 300
Y29: 400
Z29: 600
AH29: 606
AI29: 608
AJ29: 610
AK29: 611
AL29: 612
AM29: 618
AN29: 620
C33: [W6] ' Balance Sheet
C34: (D1) [W6] 'December 31, 1986
A36: [W30] 'Current Assets
A37: [W30] '------------------
A38: [W30] 'Cash
D38: (F2) [W13] +N9
A39: [W30] 'Accounts receivable
D39: (F2) [W13] +N10
D40: [W13] '------------
A41: [W30] 'Total Current Assets
E41: (F2) [W13] @SUM(D38..D39)
A43: [W30] 'Fixed Assets
A44: [W30] '------------------
A45: [W30] 'Office Equipment

```
D45: (F2) [W13] +N11
A46: [W30] 'Less: Acc Depr
D46: (F2) [W13] +O12
D47: [W13] '------------
A48: [W30] 'Total Fixed Assets
E48: (F2) [W13] +D45-D46
E50: [W13] '-------------
A51: [W30] 'Total Assets
E51: (F2) [W13] +E41+E48
E52: [W13] '============
A54: [W30] 'Current Liabilities
A55: [W30] '-------------------
A56: [W30] 'Accounts Payable
D56: (F2) [W13] +O13
D57: [W13] '------------
A58: [W30] 'Total Current Liabilities
E58: (F2) [W13] +D56
A60: [W30] 'Long-Term Liabilities
A61: [W30] '----------------------
A62: [W30] 'Loan Payable
E62: (F2) [W13] +O14
A65: [W30] 'Stockholders Equity
A66: [W30] '----------------------
A67: [W30] 'Capital Stock
D67: (F2) [W13] +O15
A68: [W30] 'Curr Yr Net Income
D68: (F2) [W13] +O16
D69: [W13] '-------------
A70: [W30] 'Total Stockholder's Equity
E70: (F2) [W13] +D67+D68
E71: [W13] '-------------
A72: [W30] 'Total Liabilities & Stockholders Equity
E72: (F2) [W13] +E58+E62+E70
E73: [W13] '============
C77: [W6] 'Income Statement
C78: (D1) [W6] 'December 31, 1986
D81: [W13] '          Month
G81: [W13] '       Year-to-Date
J81: [W13] 'Prior Mo YTD
D82: [W13] '       -------
E82: [W13] \-
G82: [W13] '       -------
H82: [W13] \-
J82: [W13] \-
A84: [W30] 'Sales
D84: (C2) [W13] +M17
E84: (P0) [W13] +D84/D$89
G84: (C2) [W13] +D84+J84
H84: (P0) [W13] +G84/G$89
D85: (,2) [W13] 0
E85: (P0) [W13] +D85/D$89
G85: (,2) [W13] 0
H85: (P0) [W13] +G85/G$89
D86: (,2) [W13] 0
```

```
E86: (P0) [W13] +D86/D$89
G86: (,2) [W13] 0
H86: (P0) [W13] +G86/G$89
D87: (,2) [W13] 0
E87: (P0) [W13] +D87/D$89
G87: (,2) [W13] 0
H87: (P0) [W13] +G87/G$89
D88: [W13] '-------------
E88: [W13] "-----
G88: [W13] '-------------
H88: [W13] "-----
A89: [W30] 'Total Sales
D89: (,2) [W13] @SUM(D84..D87)
E89: (P0) [W13] +D89/D$89
G89: (,2) [W13] @SUM(G84..G87)
H89: [W13] +G89/G$89
A91: [W30] 'Operating Expenses
A92: [W30] '--------------------
A93: [W30] 'Salaries
D93: (,2) [W13] +L18
E93: (P0) [W13] +D93/D$106
G93: (,2) [W13] +D93+J93
H93: (P0) [W13] +G93/G$106
A94: [W30] 'Office Rent
D94: (,2) [W13] +L19
E94: (P0) [W13] +D94/D$106
G94: (,2) [W13] +D94+J94
H94: (P0) [W13] +G94/G$106
A95: [W30] 'Postage
D95: (,2) [W13] +L20
E95: (P0) [W13] +D95/D$106
G95: (,2) [W13] +D95+J95
H95: (P0) [W13] +G95/G$106
A96: [W30] 'Dues & Subscriptions
D96: (,2) [W13] +L21
E96: (P0) [W13] +D96/D$106
G96: (,2) [W13] +D96+J96
H96: (P0) [W13] +G96/G$106
A97: [W30] 'Telephone
D97: (,2) [W13] +L22
E97: (P0) [W13] +D97/D$106
G97: (,2) [W13] +D97+J97
H97: (P0) [W13] +G97/G$106
A98: [W30] 'Advertising
D98: (,2) [W13] +L23
E98: (P0) [W13] +D98/D$106
G98: (,2) [W13] +D98+J98
H98: (P0) [W13] +G98/G$106
A99: [W30] 'Travel & Entertainment
D99: (,2) [W13] +L24
E99: (P0) [W13] +D99/D$106
G99: (,2) [W13] +D99+J99
H99: (P0) [W13] +G99/G$106
A100: [W30] 'Miscellaneous
```

D100: (,2) [W13] +L25
E100: (P0) [W13] +D100/D$106
G100: (,2) [W13] +D100+J100
H100: (P0) [W13] +G100/G$106
D101: (,2) [W13] +L26
E101: (P0) [W13] +D101/D$106
G101: (,2) [W13] +D101+J101
H101: (P0) [W13] +G101/G$106
D102: (,2) [W13] 0
E102: (P0) [W13] +D102/D$106
G102: (,2) [W13] +D102+J102
H102: (P0) [W13] +G102/G$106
D103: (,2) [W13] 0
E103: (P0) [W13] +D103/D$106
G103: (,2) [W13] +D103+J103
H103: (P0) [W13] +G103/G$106
D104: (,2) [W13] 0
E104: (P0) [W13] +D104/D$106
G104: (,2) [W13] +D104+J104
H104: (P0) [W13] +G104/G$106
D105: [W13] '-------------
E105: [W13] "-----
G105: [W13] '-------------
H105: [W13] "-----
A106: [W30] 'Total Operating Expenses
D106: (,2) [W13] @SUM(D93..D104)
E106: (P0) [W13] +D106/D$106
G106: (,2) [W13] @SUM(G93..G104)
H106: (P0) [W13] +G106/G$106
D107: [W13] '-------------
E107: [W13] "-----
G107: [W13] '-------------
H107: [W13] "-----
A108: [W30] 'Net Income/(Loss)
D108: (C2) [W13] +D89-D106
E108: (P0) [W13] +D108/D89
G108: (C2) [W13] +G89-G106
H108: (P0) [W13] +G108/G89
D109: [W13] '=============
E109: [W13] "=====
G109: [W13] '=============
H109: [W13] "=====
E120: [W13] 'CHECKING ACCT TRANSACTIONS
I120: [W13] '   BANK DEPOSIT TRANSACTIONS
O120: [W13] 'SALES
D121: [W13] '   --------
E121: [W13] \-
F121: [W13] \-
G121: [W13] \-
I121: [W13] '   --------
J121: [W13] \-
K121: [W13] \-
M121: [W13] '   --------

N121: [W13] \-
O121: [W13] \-
P121: [W13] \-
D123: [W13] "Check #
E123: [W13] "Acct #
F123: [W13] "Amount
G123: [W13] "Clear
I123: [W13] "Date
J123: [W13] "Acct #
K123: [W13] "Amount
M123: [W13] "Inv #
N123: [W13] "Date
O123: [W13] "Acct #
P123: [W13] "Amount
D124: [W13] "-------
E124: [W13] "-------
F124: [W13] "-------
G124: [W13] "-------
I124: [W13] "----
J124: [W13] "------
K124: [W13] "------
M124: [W13] "-----
N124: [W13] "-----
O124: [W13] "------
P124: [W13] "------
I125: (D1) [W13] @DATE(86,12,30)
J125: [W13] 110
K125: (F2) [W13] 50
F139: [W13] "-------
K139: [W13] "-------
P139: [W13] "-------
E140: [W13] 100
F140: [W13] @SUM(F125..F139)
J140: [W13] 100
K140: [W13] @SUM(K125..K139)
O140: [W13] 110
P140: [W13] @SUM(P125..P139)
F141: [W13] "=======
K141: [W13] "=======
P141: [W13] "=======

7

Interactive Financial Statements

Introduction

To make sound business decisions, you need accurate financial reporting and analysis systems. This model, the Interactive Financial Statement, should be one of your business tools. By using 1-2-3 to perform routine business tasks quickly and easily, you'll have time for the more demanding aspects of your work.

The model is both an income statement and balance sheet for a typical business. It is interactive in the sense that the modules or sections share data (interact) with each other. 1-2-3 lends itself especially to this type of application. You can do "what-if" analysis of your business's financial performance over a number of time periods or just quickly assimilate a correction in your data.

This chapter describes how to create the Interactive Financial Statements model, how the model operates, and how you can use the application in your business.

The Interactive Financial Statement, shown in figure 7.1, is made up of four major modules: Fixed Assumptions, Variable Assumptions, Income Statement, and Balance Sheet. The Fixed Assumptions section is located in cells A6 through F16; Variable Assumptions in cells A21 through P34; Income Statement in cells A36 through Q76; and Balance Sheet in cells A81 through P128.

	A	B	C	D	E	F	G	H	I	J	K	L	M	N	O	P	Q

INTERACTIVE INCOME STATEMENT AND BALANCE SHEET   (C) Que Corp 1987

FIXED ASSUMPTIONS

Depreciable Life of Assets	60 months
Beginning Accumulated Depreciation	$50,000
Beginning Retained Earnings Balance	$200,000
Payroll Data	
Payroll Taxes as a % of Salaries	11%
Benefits as a % of Salaries	10%

VARIABLE ASSUMPTIONS

	Jan	Feb	Mar	Apr	May	Jun	Jul	Aug	Sep	Oct	Nov	Dec
Interest Income Data												
Rate	8.00%	8.00%	8.00%	8.00%	8.00%	8.00%	8.00%	8.00%	8.00%	8.00%	8.00%	8.00%
Earned on Cash Balance Over	$10,000	$10,000	$10,000	$10,000	$10,000	$10,000	$10,000	$10,000	$10,000	$10,000	$10,000	$10,000
Interest Expense Data												
Short-Term Rate	12.00%	12.00%	12.00%	12.00%	12.00%	12.00%	12.00%	12.00%	12.00%	12.00%	12.00%	12.00%
Long-Term Rate	13.50%	13.50%	13.50%	13.50%	13.50%	13.50%	13.50%	13.50%	13.50%	13.50%	13.50%	13.50%
Average Cost of Goods Sold Percentage	40%	40%	40%	40%	40%	40%	40%	40%	40%	40%	40%	40%
Days Sales in Receivables	30	30	30	30	30	30	30	30	30	30	30	30
Days Cost of Goods Sold in Inventory	40	40	40	40	40	40	40	40	40	40	40	40
Days Cost of Goods Sold in Payables	50	50	50	50	50	50	50	50	50	50	50	50

INCOME STATEMENT

	Growth	Jan	Feb	Mar	Apr	May	Jun	Jul	Aug	Sep	Oct	Nov	Dec	Total
Gross Income														
Product Sales	1%	$125,000	$126,250	$127,513	$128,788	$130,076	$131,376	$132,690	$134,017	$135,357	$136,711	$138,078	$139,459	$1,585,313
Income from Service	0%	25,000	25,000	25,000	25,000	25,000	25,000	25,000	25,000	25,000	25,000	25,000	25,000	300,000
Other Sales		0	0	0	0	0	0	0	0	0	0	0	0	0
Interest Income		236	447	599	801	1,000	1,197	1,391	1,583	1,785	1,984	2,179	2,370	15,572
Total Gross Income		150,236	151,697	153,112	154,589	156,076	157,573	159,081	160,600	162,142	163,695	165,257	166,829	1,900,885
Cost of Goods Sold		50,000	50,500	51,005	51,515	52,030	52,551	53,076	53,607	54,143	54,684	55,231	55,783	634,125
Gross Margin		100,236	101,197	102,107	103,074	104,045	105,023	106,005	106,993	107,999	109,010	110,026	111,045	1,266,760
Operating Expenses	3%													
Salaries and Wages		36,000	37,080	38,192	39,338	40,518	41,734	42,986	44,275	45,604	46,972	48,381	49,832	510,913
Benefits	0%	3,600	3,708	3,819	3,934	4,052	4,173	4,299	4,428	4,560	4,697	4,838	4,983	51,091
Payroll Taxes	0%	3,960	4,079	4,201	4,327	4,457	4,591	4,728	4,870	5,016	5,167	5,322	5,482	56,200
Office Rent	0%	2,000	2,000	2,000	2,000	2,000	2,000	2,000	2,000	2,000	2,000	2,000	2,000	24,000
Supplies	0%	500	500	500	500	500	500	500	500	500	500	500	500	6,000
Postage	0%	100	100	100	100	100	100	100	100	100	100	100	100	1,200
Telephone	0%	200	200	200	200	200	200	200	200	200	200	200	200	2,400
Insurance	0%	200	200	200	200	200	200	200	200	200	200	200	200	2,400
Dues and Subscriptions	0%	50	50	50	50	50	50	50	50	50	50	50	50	600
Advertising and Promotion	0%	1,000	1,000	1,000	1,000	1,000	1,000	1,000	1,000	1,000	1,000	1,000	1,000	12,000
Travel and Entertainment	0%	500	500	500	500	500	500	500	500	500	500	500	500	6,000
Professional Fees	0%	250	250	250	250	250	250	250	250	250	250	250	250	3,000
Depreciation		4,726	4,726	4,726	4,726	4,726	4,726	4,726	4,726	4,726	4,726	4,726	4,726	56,712

#	Item	%	Jan	Feb	Mar	Apr	May	Jun	Jul	Aug	Sep	Oct	Nov	Dec	Total
65	Maintenance	5%	200	210	221	232	243	255	268	281	295	310	326	342	3,183
66	Interest	0%	818	718	618	618	618	618	618	618	618	618	618	618	7,716
67	Equipment Rental	5%	0	0	0	0	0	0	0	0	0	0	0	0	0
68	Other		1,000	1,050	1,103	1,158	1,216	1,276	1,340	1,407	1,477	1,551	1,629	1,710	15,917
69															
70	Total Operating Expenses		55,104	56,371	57,680	59,132	60,630	62,174	63,765	65,406	67,097	68,842	70,640	72,494	759,333
71															
72	Gross Profit/(Loss) before Tax		45,132	44,826	44,427	43,941	43,416	42,849	42,240	41,587	40,902	40,169	39,386	38,551	507,426
73															
74	Federal Income Tax		6,770	15,241	17,326	17,137	16,932	16,711	16,474	14,140	13,907	13,657	13,391	13,108	174,794
75															
76	Net Income/(Loss)		$38,362	$29,585	$27,100	$26,804	$26,483	$26,138	$25,766	$27,448	$26,995	$26,511	$25,995	$25,444	$332,633
77															
78															
79															
80															
81	BALANCE SHEET		Jan	Feb	Mar	Apr	May	Jun	Jul	Aug	Sep	Oct	Nov	Dec	
82															
83															
84	Current Assets														
85	Cash		$45,406	$77,120	$99,952	$130,203	$160,107	$189,638	$218,770	$247,475	$277,818	$307,649	$336,935	$365,640	
86	Accounts Receivable		123,287	124,520	125,765	127,023	128,293	129,576	130,872	132,181	133,502	134,837	136,186	137,548	
87	Inventory		65,753	66,410	67,075	67,745	68,423	69,107	69,798	70,496	71,201	71,913	72,632	73,359	
88															
89	Total Current Assets		234,446	268,050	292,792	324,971	356,823	388,321	419,440	450,152	482,521	514,399	545,753	576,547	
90															
91	Fixed Assets														
92	Plant, Property, and Equipment														
93	Leasehold Improvements		5,689	5,689	5,689	5,689	5,689	5,689	5,689	5,689	5,689	5,689	5,689	5,689	
94	Furniture and Fixtures		27,388	27,388	27,388	27,388	27,388	27,388	27,388	27,388	27,388	27,388	27,388	27,388	
95	Equipment		235,890	235,890	235,890	235,890	235,890	235,890	235,890	235,890	235,890	235,890	235,890	235,890	
96	Office Equipment		14,637	14,637	14,637	14,637	14,637	14,637	14,637	14,637	14,637	14,637	14,637	14,637	
97															
98	Gross PP&E		283,604	283,604	283,604	283,604	283,604	283,604	283,604	283,604	283,604	283,604	283,604	283,604	
99	Accumulated Depreciation		54,726	59,452	64,178	68,904	73,630	78,356	83,082	87,808	92,534	97,260	101,986	106,712	
100															
101	Net PP&E		228,878	224,152	219,426	214,700	209,974	205,248	200,522	195,796	191,070	186,344	181,618	176,892	
102															
103	Deposits		1,000	1,000	1,000	1,000	1,000	1,000	1,000	1,000	1,000	1,000	1,000	1,000	
104	Other		0	0	0	0	0	0	0	0	0	0	0	0	
105															
106	Total Fixed Assets		229,878	225,152	220,426	215,700	210,974	206,248	201,522	196,796	192,070	187,344	182,618	177,892	
107															
108	Total Assets		464,324	493,202	513,218	540,671	567,797	594,569	620,962	646,948	674,591	701,743	728,371	754,439	
109															
110															
111															
112	Current Liabilities														
113	Accounts Payable		82,192	83,014	83,844	84,682	85,529	86,384	87,248	88,121	89,002	89,892	90,791	91,699	
114	Short-Term Debt		20,000	10,000	0	0	0	0	0	0	0	0	0	0	
115	Income Taxes Payable		6,770	15,241	17,326	17,137	16,932	16,711	16,474	14,140	13,907	13,657	13,391	13,108	
116															
117	Total Current Liabilities		108,962	108,255	101,170	101,819	102,461	103,096	103,722	102,260	102,909	103,549	104,182	104,806	
118															
119	Noncurrent Liabilities														
120	Long-Term Debt		55,000	55,000	55,000	55,000	55,000	55,000	55,000	55,000	55,000	55,000	55,000	55,000	
121															
122	Total Liabilities		163,962	163,255	156,170	156,819	157,461	158,096	158,722	157,260	157,909	158,549	159,182	159,806	
123															
124	Common Stock		62,000	62,000	62,000	62,000	62,000	62,000	62,000	62,000	62,000	62,000	62,000	62,000	
125															
126	Retained Earnings		238,362	267,947	295,048	321,852	348,335	374,473	400,240	427,687	454,683	481,194	507,189	532,633	
127															
128	Total Liabilities and Equity		$464,324	$493,202	$513,218	$540,671	$567,797	$594,569	$620,962	$646,948	$674,591	$701,743	$728,371	$754,439	
129															

Fig. 7.1. The Interactive Financial Statement.

Creating the Model

You will find that creating the application is easy; but the process may be lengthy, depending on how detailed your income statement and balance sheet are. Start with a blank 1-2-3 spreadsheet.

Setting Column Widths

Change the width of column D to seven, and column Q to 11. All other columns should remain at the default width of nine.

Specifying Cell Formats

Format the cells according to table 7.1. Remember that you can modify the cell formats if you wish. Table 7.1 is simply a list of suggested formats.

Table 7.1
Cell Formats

Format	Location
Fixed Assumptions	
/rff0	E9
/rfc0	E10
/rfco	E12
/rfp0	E15..E16
Variable Assumptions	
/rfp2	E24..P24
/rfc0	E25..P25
/rfp2	E27..P27
/rfp2	E28..P28
/rfp2	E30..P30
/rff0	E32..P34
Income Statement	
/rfp0	D40..D43
/rfp0	D52..D68
/rfc0	E40..Q40
/rf,0	E41..Q74
/rfc0	E76..Q76
Balance Sheet	
/rfc0	E85..P85
/rf,0	E86..P126
/rfc	0E128..P128

Next, enter the column headings and row titles from table 7.2. When you enter separator lines, don't forget to use the backslash trick (\-).

Table 7.2
Row Titles and Column Headings

Enter into cell:	Original label:	Copy to:
	Opening Headings	
A1:	\=	B1..Q1, A5..Q5, A7..Q7, A22..D22, A37..D37, A82..D82
A3:	'INTERACTIVE INCOME STATEMENT & BALANCE SHEET	
	Fixed Assumptions	
A6:	'FIXED ASSUMPTIONS	
A9:	'Depreciable Life of Assets	
F9:	'Months	
F10:	'Beginning Depreciation	
F12:	'Beginning Retained Earnings Balance	
A14:	'Payroll Data	
A15:	' Payroll Taxes as a % of Salaries	
A16:	' Benefits as a % of Salaries	
	Variable Assumptions	
A21:	'VARIABLE ASSUMPTIONS	
E21:	^Jan	
F21:	^Feb	
G21:	^Mar	
H21:	^Apr	
I21:	^May	
J21:	^Jun	
K21:	^Jul	
L21:	^Aug	
M21:	^Sep	
N21:	^Oct	
O21:	^Nov	
P21:	^Dec	
E22:	' =======	F22..P22, D37..Q37, E77..Q77, E82..P82, E109..P109, E129..P129

Enter into cell:	Original label:	Copy to:
A23:	'Interest Income Data	
A24:	' Rate	
A25:	' Earned on Cash Over	
A26:	'Interest Expense Data	
A27:	' Short-Term Rate	
A28:	' Long-Term Rate	
A30:	'Average Cost of Goods Sold Percentage	
A32:	'Days Sales in Receivables	
A33:	'Days Cost of Goods Sold in Inventory	
A34:	'Days Cost of Goods Sold in Payables	

Income Statement

Enter into cell:	Original label:	Copy to:
D36:	'Growth	
Q36:	'Total	
A39:	'Gross Income	
A40:	' Product Sales	
A41:	' Income from Service	
A42:	' Other Sales	
A43:	' Interest Income	
E44:	'-------	F44..Q44, E48..Q48, E69..Q69, E71..Q71, E75..Q75, E88..P88, E97..P97, E100..P100, E105..P105, E107..P107, E116..P116, E121..P121, E127..P127
A45:	'Total Gross Income	
A47:	'Cost of Goods Sold	
A49:	'Gross Margin	
A51:	'Operating Expenses	
A52:	' Salaries and Wages	
A53:	' Benefits	
A54:	' Payroll Taxes	
A55:	' Office Rent	
A56:	' Supplies	
A57:	' Postage	
A58:	' Telephone	
A59:	' Insurance	

Enter into cell:	Original label:	Copy to:
A60:	' Dues and Subscriptions	
A61:	' Advertising and Promotion	
A62:	' Travel and Entertainment	
A63:	' Professional Fees	
A64:	' Depreciation	
A65:	' Maintenance	
A66:	' Interest	
A67:	' Equipment Rental	
A68:	' Other	
A70:	'Total Operating Expenses	
A72:	'Gross Profit/(Loss) before Tax	
A74:	'Federal Income Tax	
A76:	'Net Income/(Loss)	

Balance Sheet

Enter into cell:	Original label:	Copy to:
A81:	'BALANCE SHEET	
A84:	'Current Assets	
A85:	' Cash	
A86:	' Accounts Receivable	
A87:	' Inventory	
A89:	'Total Current Assets	
A91:	'Fixed Assets	
A92:	' Plant, Property and Equipment	
A93:	' Leasehold Improvements	
A94:	' Furniture and Fixtures	
A95:	' Equipment	
A96:	' Office Equipment	
A98:	'Gross PP&E	
A99:	'Accumulated Depreciation	
A101:	'Net PP&E	
A103:	'Deposits	
A104:	'Other	
A106:	'Total Fixed Assets	
A108:	'Total Assets	
A112:	'Current Liabilities	
A113:	' Accounts Payable	
A114:	' Short-Term Debt	
A115:	' Income Taxes Payable	
A117:	'Total Current Liabilities	
A119:	'Non-Current Liabilities	

Enter into cell:	Original label:	Copy to:
A120:	' Long-Term Debt	
A122:	'Total Liabilites	
A124:	'Common Stock	
A126:	'Retained Earnings	
A128:	'Total Liabilites and Equity	

Copy From:	Copy To:
E21..P21	E36..P36, E81..P81

Now enter the equations listed in table 7.3. Although you have a number of formulas to enter for this model, the task is manageable if you work in one section at a time.

By using the /Copy command liberally, particularly for Interest Income (F43..P43) and Federal Income Taxes (F74..P74), then using the F2 (EDIT) key, you will greatly reduce setup time.

Table 7.3

Formulas and Functions

Enter into cell:	Original formula:	Copy to:
	Variable Assumptions	
F24	+E24	G24..P24
F25:	+E25	G25..P25
F27:	+E27	G27..P27
F28:	+E28	G28..P28
F30:	+E30	G30..P30
F32:	+E32	G32..P32
F33:	+E33	G33..P33
F34:	+F33	G34..P34

Enter into cell:	Original formula:	Copy to:

Income Statement

F40:	(1+$D40)*E40	F40..P41
Q40:	@SUM(E40..P40)	Q41..Q43, Q45, Q47, Q49, Q52..Q68, Q70, Q72, Q74, Q76
E43:	@IF(@ISERR(E85),0, @IF(E85>E25,@INT (E24/12*(E85-E25)),0))	F43..P43
E45:	@SUM(E40..E44)	F45..P45
E47:	+E30*E40	F47..P47
E49:	+E45-E47	F49..P49
F52:	(1+$D52)*E52	G52..P52, F55..P63, F65..P65, F67..P68
E53:	+$E$16*E52	F53..P53
E54:	+$E$15*E52	F54..P54
E64:	@INT(E98/$E9)	F64..P64
E66:	@INT(E28/12*E120)+ @INT(E27/12*E114)	F66..P66
E70:	@SUM(E52..E69)	F70..P70
E72:	(E49-E70)	F72..P72
E74:	+E72*@IF(@SUM($E$72..E72)> 335000, 0.34,@IF(@SUM($E$72..E72)> 100000, 0.39,@IF(@SUM($E$72..E72)> 75000, 0.34,@IF(@SUM($E$72..E72)> 50000, 0.25,0.15))))	F74..P74
E76:	(E72-E74)	F76..P76

Enter into cell:	Original formula:	Copy to:

Balance Sheet

E85:	+E128-E106-E87-E86	
E86:	@INT((E32/365)*(E40+E42)*12)	
E87:	@INT((E33/365)*E47*12)	
E89:	@SUM(E85..E88)	F89..P89
E98:	@SUM(E93..E97)	
E99:	+E10+E64	
E106:	+E101+E103+E104	F106..P106
E108:	+E89+E106	F108..P108
E101:	+E98-E99	F101..P101
E113:	(E34/365)*E47*12	F113..P113
E115:	+E74	F115..P115
E117:	@SUM(E113..E116)	F117..P117
E122:	(E117+E120)	F122..P122
E126:	+E12+E76	F126..P126
E128:	+E122+E124+E126	F128..P128

Copy From:	Copy To:
E85..E87	F85..P85
E98..E99	F98..P98

Remember that the Income Statement and Balance Sheet are interrelated; thus, the contents of one cell may influence the formula in another. To guard against circular references, you activate 1-2-3's iterative recalculation feature.

Select **/W**orksheet **G**lobal **R**ecalculation Iterative **10**. The worksheet will calculate ten times when the F9 (CALC) key is pressed, which should eliminate the circular reference problem. Although the CIRC message at the bottom of the screen *will not* disappear, you can set iterations in the calculation to ensure that the CIRC message does not cause incorrect results.

Understanding the Model

Although the application is quite large, you will find that it is straightforward and does not use many complicated or lengthy formulas. Modifying the model to suit your specific needs should not be difficult.

The first two sections of this application, Fixed and Variable
Assumptions, are data-entry worksheets for the financial statements.

Fixed Assumptions

The Fixed Assumptions worksheet, located in cells A5 through E16,
contains three categories of assumptions that are not likely to change
during the year: long-term assets, retained earnings, and manpower-
related expenses. Figure 7.2 shows the layout of the Fixed Assumptions
worksheet area.

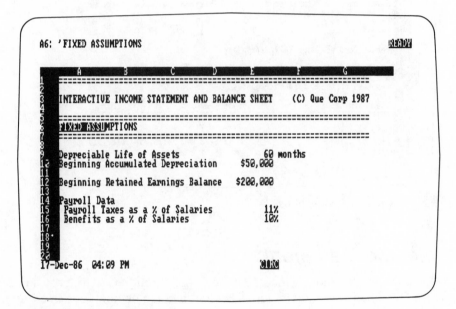

Fig. 7.2. Fixed Assumptions.

Variable Assumptions

The Variable Assumptions worksheet is located in cells A21 through
P34, directly below Fixed Assumptions. Like the previous section, this
worksheet holds three categories of assumptions: interest income,
interest expense, and sales-related information. Specific line items are
shown in figure 7.3.

Variable Assumptions may change during a reporting period. Therefore, these assumptions have been extended on a monthly basis to accommodate any changes in your forecast or in business conditions.

```
A21: 'VARIABLE ASSUMPTIONS                                         READY

        A        B          C        D        E        F        G
21  VARIABLE ASSUMPTIONS                         Jan      Feb      Mar
22  =================================         =======  =======  =======
23  Interest Income Data
24    Rate                                     8.00%    8.00%    8.00%
25    Earned on Cash Balance Over            $10,000  $10,000  $10,000
26  Interest Expense Data
27    Short-Term Rate                         12.00%   12.00%   12.00%
28    Long-Term Rate                          13.50%   13.50%   13.50%
29
30  Average Cost of Goods Sold Percentage      40%      40%      40%
31
32  Days Sales in Receivables                   30       30       30
33  Days Cost of Goods Sold in Inventory        40       40       40
34  Days Cost of Goods Sold in Payables         50       50       50
35
36  INCOME STATEMENT                  Growth   Jan      Feb      Mar
37  ================================  ======  =======  =======  =======
38
39  Gross Income
40    Product Sales                     1%  $125,000 $126,250 $127,513
17-Dec-86  04:10 PM                               CALC
```

Fig. 7.3. Variable Assumptions.

Income Statement

The Income Statement is located in cells A36 through Q76 (refer to fig. 7.1). This financial report includes two extra columns not found in other areas of the model. Column Q displays the results of all account categories for the entire year. Column D gives you the option of entering a monthly percentage growth rate for most Income Statement categories.

To understand what happens in column D, look at the formula in cell F40: (1+$D40)*E40. This formula adds one to the monthly growth rate in cell D40 and multiplies that figure by the beginning amount in cell E40. You can use this capability to forecast, for example, the effect on net income of a 3% monthly growth rate in salaries and wages.

The model also can accommodate zero growth in expenses. If you enter an amount in cell E40 and enter zero in cell D40, the model will simply multiply the January amount (E40) by one. This may be appropriate, for example, for an office lease with fixed monthly payments that begin in January. This method is appropriate also if you periodically need to change expense amounts manually. In either case, the model will carry your values forward to each subsequent reporting period in the Income Statement.

In general, the model relies on the @SUM function and growth rate formulas to compute the Income Statement. There are, however, several categories of expenses that use lengthier formulas and deserve further attention.

Interest Income, beginning in cell E43, is calculated by the following formula:

E43: @IF(@ISERR(E85),0,@IF(E85>E25,@INT(E24/12*(E85-E25)),0))

First, the formula tells 1-2-3 to determine whether the cash balance in cell E85 contains an @ERR message. If so, a zero is returned in cell E43 so that the model will calculate properly.

If not, the formula continues, determining whether the cash balance in cell E85 is larger than the amount in cell E25. If so, a monthly interest income rate is calculated (E24/12) and then multiplied by the excess cash amount (E85-E25). This calculation yields the interest income amount for the month.

If the cash balance in E85 is smaller than the amount in E25, zero is returned in cell E43.

Employee Benefits for January are calculated in cell E53, using the formula:

E53: +$E$16*E52

In this formula, E16 is the "employee benefits as a percent of salaries" estimate from the Fixed Assumptions worksheet.

Similarly, payroll taxes are computed using the formula:

E54: +$E$15*E52

In this case, E15 is your estimate of payroll taxes as a percentage of salaries and wages expense.

Depreciation expense, which begins in cell E64, is based on a straight-line schedule and the depreciable life forecast in cell E9. The formula

E64: @INT(E98/$E9)

divides gross property, plant, and equipment by cell E9's life of the assets (in months).

Interest expense is based on the annual interest rates (in cells E28 and E27) on any outstanding long- and short-term debt (in cells E120 and E114, respectively). The formula is

E66: @INT(E28/12*E120)+@INT(E27/12*E114)

The interest rates in cells E28 and E27 are divided by twelve to convert the annual rates to monthly rates.

The Federal Income Tax calculation is the final Income Statement formula that needs to be explained. Although the equation is longer than others in this section, you shouldn't have any trouble understanding its concept.

Income taxes in cell E74 are computed by the formula:

E74: +E72*@IF(@SUM($E$72..E72)>335000,0.34
          @IF(@SUM($E$72..E72)>100000,0.39,
          @IF(@SUM($E$72..E72)>75000,0.34,
          @IF(@SUM($E$72..E72)>50000,0.25,
          0.15))))

In this formula, your Gross Profit (cell E72) is multiplied by a tax rate selected by the @IF statements. If the sum of the range ($E$72..E72) is greater than 335,000, the rate is 0.34; if the sum is greater than 100,000 but less than 335,000 the rate is 0.39, and so on. The tax rates shown in table 7.4 are the corporate federal tax rates enacted by Congress in 1986.

Table 7.4
Corporate Federal Income Tax Rates

Taxable Income	Rate
0 - 50,000	15%
50,001 - 75,000	25%
75,001 - 100,000	34%
100,001 - 335,000	39%
335,001 - and above	34%

Keep in mind that these rates are based on the cumulative income for your company. You will need to compute that cumulative (year-to-date) income before you calculate your federal income tax expense for each month.

You can easily compute cumulative income by using anchored sum ranges. An *anchored sum range* has a fixed (anchored) beginning range and a *free* ending range, which allows the equation to include subsequent periods. For example, the phrase

@SUM($E$72..E72)

is an anchored sum range.

Compare the equation in cell F74 to the one in cell E74:

F74: +F72*@IF(@SUM($E$72..F72)>335000,0.34
            @IF(@SUM($E$72..F72)>100000,0.39,
            @IF(@SUM($E$72..F72)>75000,0.34,
            @IF(@SUM($E$72..F72)>50000,0.25,
            0.15))))

The first term in each sum range, $E$72, remains constant but the second term changes as the formula is /Copied across the model. As each month's formula is copied, 1-2-3 will calculate a close approximation of your federal income tax liability for you. The model will also reference these income tax amounts in the Balance Sheet worksheet.

The Balance Sheet

The final section of the model, the Balance Sheet, is located in cells A81 to P128 (refer to fig. 7.1). Because it is a "snapshot" of your company's financial performance, the Balance Sheet is a cumulative, or year-to-date, report. Like the Income Statement, the Balance Sheet relies on simple addition, subtraction, and @SUM relationships. Several Balance Sheet equations need further explanation.

The first account, Cash, (in cell E85) is defined by referencing other cells in the Balance Sheet

E85: +E128-E106-E87-E86

Cash is computed by a formula that subtracts accounts receivable, inventory, and total fixed assets (uses of cash) from total liabilities and equity (sources of cash). The cash balance for the month is the difference between the sources and uses.

Accounts receivable is based on your (variable) assumption made in cell E32 about days sales outstanding and your monthly sales amount (E40+E42). The formula is

E86: @INT((E32/365)*(E40+E42)*12)

This formula converts the number of days in cell E32 into a fraction of a year by dividing by 365; then the formula multiplies this result by an annualized sales estimate based on your monthly sales. In figure 7.1, accounts receivable is 30/365ths of $150,000 times 12 (the annualized sales number), or $148,014.

The balance in the inventory account is calculated by a similar formula:

E87: @INT((E33/365)*E47*12)

This formula uses the variable assumption in cell E33 and the cost of goods sold number in cell E47 to compute the inventory balance. Notice that this formula is based on your annualized cost of goods sold.

Similarly, the first liability account, accounts payable, is determined by your assumption (in cell E34) regarding days cost of goods sold in payables, and the current period's cost of goods sold (in cell E47). The equation is

E113: (E34/365)*E47*12

You should have no problem understanding the rest of the Balance Sheet, which is made up of simple addition relationships. You will find the model easy to use.

Using the Model

Before you calculate the the model, you need to enter two assumptions that are related to long-term assets. Enter the average depreciable life, in months, in cell E9, and the beginning accumulated depreciation, in cell E10. This is your accumulated depreciation to date. Then, in cell E12, enter your firm's retained earnings balance (the balance from the previous reporting period).

Finally, enter assumptions about your company's payroll taxes and employee benefits, as a percent of total salaries, in cells E15 and E16, respectively. In summary, the Fixed Assumptions worksheet requires five key pieces of data.

You are now ready to enter Variable Assumptions. Variable Assumptions provide data the model can use to compute interest income. The interest rate you will earn on excess cash is entered in cell E24; the amount of cash that will not be invested, in cell E25. In our example, any amount over $10,000 will be invested at an eight-percent return.

The third and fourth variable assumptions address interest expense. The rate of interest paid on your company's short-term debt should be entered in cell E27; on long-term debt, in cell E28.

The final four assumptions supply the model with sales-related data needed for Balance Sheet calculations. The first of these, Cost of Goods Sold, is the approximate cost of your company's product sales, expressed as a percentage. Enter this value in cell E30.

Days Sales in Receivables is represented in cell E32; Days Cost of Goods Sold in Inventory and Days Cost of Goods Sold in Accounts Payable are displayed in cells E33 and E34, respectively. (See Chapter 8, "Performing Ratio Analysis," for a discussion of these statistics. You may want to use the Ratio Analyzer or its formulas to calculate the values for these assumptions.)

Finally, remember that variable assumptions need to be entered only once in column E. The model will carry forward any data that you input for the remaining reporting periods. However, at any time, you can modify the assumptions to reflect changes in internal or external business conditions. You can update the model by entering data according to table 7.5 and then pressing F9 (CALC).

You may want to study the equations in Chapter 8 to see how the values in the Variable Assumptions section are calculated, or you may prefer to use Variable Assumption values from your own experience.

Table 7.5
Data Entry

Description	Location
Fixed Assumptions	
Depreciable Life of Asset	E9
Beginning Accumulated Depreciation	E10
Beginning Retained Earnings Balance	E12
Payroll Taxes as a % of Salary	E15
Benefits as a % of Salary	E16

Description	Location
Variable Assumptions	
Interest Rate on Income	E24
Earned on Cash Balance Over ___	E25
Interest Expense-Short Term Debt	E27
Interest Expense-Long Term Debt	E28
Avg Cost of Goods Sold Percentage	E30
Days Sales in Receivables	E32
Days Cost of Goods Sold in Inventory	E33
Days Cost of Goods Sold in Payables	E34
Income Statement	
Product Sales	E40
Income from Service	E41
Other Sales	E42
Salaries & Wages	E52
Office Rent	E55
Supplies	E56
Postage	E57
Telephone	E58
Insurance	E59
Dues & Subscriptions	E60
Advertising & Promotion	E61
Travel & Entertainment	E62
Professional Fees	E63
Maintenance	E65
Equipment Rental	E67
Other	E68

*Note: The model allows you to specify a monthly growth rate for these account categories. Other Sales is not included. If you wish to use this option, enter the rate in the appropriate cell in Column D.

You can use this model for planning and budgeting, "what-if" analysis, and monthly financial reporting. Consider also using two sets of financial statements—one for actual results, the other for planned performance. You can use the **/F**ile **C**ombine **S**ubtract command to determine the amount your company is over (negative) or under (positive) budget by account. Make the incoming worksheet the actual values; save this worksheet under a separate file name, for further analysis and review. You will discover many ways to improve your operating results with this application's powerful modeling capability.

Conclusion

The Interactive Financial Statements model, one of 1-2-3's most versatile applications, fully utilizes the power of the electronic spreadsheet. To improve planning and control, and for timely results, include this application in your financial reporting.

A1: \=
B1: \=
C1: \=
D1: [W7] \=
E1: \=
F1: \=
G1: \=
H1: \=
I1: \=
J1: \=
K1: \=
L1: \=
M1: \=
N1: \=
O1: \=
P1: \=
Q1: [W11] \=
A3: 'INTERACTIVE INCOME STATEMENT AND BALANCE SHEET
F3: '   (C) Que Corp 1987
A5: \=
B5: \=
C5: \=
D5: [W7] \=
E5: \=
F5: \=
G5: \=
H5: \=
I5: \=
J5: \=
K5: \=
L5: \=
M5: \=
N5: \=
O5: \=
P5: \=
Q5: [W11] \=
A6: 'FIXED ASSUMPTIONS
A7: \=
B7: \=
C7: \=
D7: [W7] \=
E7: \=
F7: \=
G7: \=
H7: \=
I7: \=
J7: \=
K7: \=
L7: \=
M7: \=
N7: \=
O7: \=
P7: \=
Q7: [W11] \=
A9: 'Depreciable Life of Assets

E9: (F0) 60
F9: 'months
A10: 'Beginning Accumulated Depreciation
E10: (C0) 50000
A12: 'Beginning Retained Earnings Balance
E12: (C0) 200000
A14: 'Payroll Data
A15: ' Payroll Taxes as a % of Salaries
E15: (P0) 0.11
A16: ' Benefits as a % of Salaries
E16: (P0) 0.1
A21: 'VARIABLE ASSUMPTIONS
E21: ^Jan
F21: ^Feb
G21: ^Mar
H21: ^Apr
I21: ^May
J21: ^Jun
K21: ^Jul
L21: ^Aug
M21: ^Sep
N21: ^Oct
O21: ^Nov
P21: ^Dec
A22: \=
B22: \=
C22: \=
D22: [W7] \=
E22: ' =======
F22: ' =======
G22: ' =======
H22: ' =======
I22: ' =======
J22: ' =======
K22: ' =======
L22: ' =======
M22: ' =======
N22: ' =======
O22: ' =======
P22: ' =======
A23: 'Interest Income Data
A24: ' Rate
E24: (P2) 0.08
F24: (P2) +E24
G24: (P2) +F24
H24: (P2) +G24
I24: (P2) +H24
J24: (P2) +I24
K24: (P2) +J24
L24: (P2) +K24
M24: (P2) +L24
N24: (P2) +M24
O24: (P2) +N24
P24: (P2) +O24
A25: ' Earned on Cash Balance Over

E25: (C0) 10000
F25: +E25
G25: +F25
H25: +G25
I25: +H25
J25: +I25
K25: +J25
L25: +K25
M25: +L25
N25: +M25
O25: +N25
P25: +O25
A26: 'Interest Expense Data
A27: ' Short-Term Rate
E27: (P2) 0.12
F27: (P2) +E27
G27: (P2) +F27
H27: (P2) +G27
I27: (P2) +H27
J27: (P2) +I27
K27: (P2) +J27
L27: (P2) +K27
M27: (P2) +L27
N27: (P2) +M27
O27: (P2) +N27
P27: (P2) +O27
A28: ' Long-Term Rate
E28: (P2) 0.135
F28: (P2) +E28
G28: (P2) +F28
H28: (P2) +G28
I28: (P2) +H28
J28: (P2) +I28
K28: (P2) +J28
L28: (P2) +K28
M28: (P2) +L28
N28: (P2) +M28
O28: (P2) +N28
P28: (P2) +O28
A30: 'Average Cost of Goods Sold Percentage
E30: (P0) 0.4
F30: (P0) +E30
G30: (P0) +F30
H30: (P0) +G30
I30: (P0) +H30
J30: (P0) +I30
K30: (P0) +J30
L30: (P0) +K30
M30: (P0) +L30
N30: (P0) +M30
O30: (P0) +N30
P30: (P0) +O30
A32: 'Days Sales in Receivables

E32: (F0) 30
F32: (F0) +E32
G32: (F0) +F32
H32: (F0) +G32
I32: (F0) +H32
J32: (F0) +I32
K32: (F0) +J32
L32: (F0) +K32
M32: (F0) +L32
N32: (F0) +M32
O32: (F0) +N32
P32: (F0) +O32
A33: 'Days Cost of Goods Sold in Inventory
E33: (F0) 40
F33: (F0) +E33
G33: (F0) +F33
H33: (F0) +G33
I33: (F0) +H33
J33: (F0) +I33
K33: (F0) +J33
L33: (F0) +K33
M33: (F0) +L33
N33: (F0) +M33
O33: (F0) +N33
P33: (F0) +O33
A34: 'Days Cost of Goods Sold in Payables
E34: (F0) 50
F34: (F0) +E34
G34: (F0) +F34
H34: (F0) +G34
I34: (F0) +H34
J34: (F0) +I34
K34: (F0) +J34
L34: (F0) +K34
M34: (F0) +L34
N34: (F0) +M34
O34: (F0) +N34
P34: (F0) +O34
A36: 'INCOME STATEMENT
D36: [W7] ' Growth
E36: ^Jan
F36: ^Feb
G36: ^Mar
H36: ^Apr
I36: ^May
J36: ^Jun
K36: ^Jul
L36: ^Aug
M36: ^Sep
N36: ^Oct
O36: ^Nov
P36: ^Dec
Q36: [W11] ^Total

A37: \=
B37: \=
C37: \=
D37: [W7] ' ======
E37: ' =======
F37: ' =======
G37: ' =======
H37: ' =======
I37: ' =======
J37: ' =======
K37: ' =======
L37: ' =======
M37: ' =======
N37: ' =======
O37: ' =======
P37: ' =======
Q37: [W11] ' =======
A39: 'Gross Income
A40: ' Product Sales
D40: (P0) [W7] 0.01
E40: 125000
F40: (1+$D40)*E40
G40: (1+$D40)*F40
H40: (1+$D40)*G40
I40: (1+$D40)*H40
J40: (1+$D40)*I40
K40: (1+$D40)*J40
L40: (1+$D40)*K40
M40: (1+$D40)*L40
N40: (1+$D40)*N40
O40: (1+$D40)*O40
P40: (1+$D40)*O40
Q40: [W11] @SUM(E40..P40)
A41: ' Income from Service
D41: (P0) [W7] 0
E41: (,0) 25000
F41: (,0) (1+$D41)*E41
G41: (,0) (1+$D41)*F41
H41: (,0) (1+$D41)*G41
I41: (,0) (1+$D41)*H41
J41: (,0) (1+$D41)*I41
K41: (,0) (1+$D41)*J41
L41: (,0) (1+$D41)*K41
M41: (,0) (1+$D41)*L41
N41: (,0) (1+$D41)*M41
O41: (,0) (1+$D41)*N41
P41: (,0) (1+$D41)*O41
Q41: (,0) [W11] @SUM(E41..P41)
A42: ' Other Sales
E42: (,0) 0
F42: (,0) 0
G42: (,0) 0
H42: (,0) 0
I42: (,0) 0
J42: (,0) 0

K42: (,0) 0
L42: (,0) 0
M42: (,0) 0
N42: (,0) 0
O42: (,0) 0
P42: (,0) 0
Q42: (,0) [W11] @SUM(E42..P42)
A43: ' Interest Income
E43: (,0) @IF(@ISERR(E85),0,@IF(E85>E25,@INT(E24/12*(E85-E25)),0))
F43: (,0) @IF(@ISERR(F85),0,@IF(F85>F25,@INT(F24/12*(F85-F25)),0))
G43: (,0) @IF(@ISERR(G85),0,@IF(G85>G25,@INT(G24/12*(G85-G25)),0))
H43: (,0) @IF(@ISERR(H85),0,@IF(H85>H25,@INT(H24/12*(H85-H25)),0))
I43: (,0) @IF(@ISERR(I85),0,@IF(I85>I25,@INT(I24/12*(I85-I25)),0))
J43: (,0) @IF(@ISERR(J85),0,@IF(J85>J25,@INT(J24/12*(J85-J25)),0))
K43: (,0) @IF(@ISERR(K85),0,@IF(K85>K25,@INT(K24/12*(K85-K25)),0))
L43: (,0) @IF(@ISERR(L85),0,@IF(L85>L25,@INT(L24/12*(L85-L25)),0))
M43: (,0) @IF(@ISERR(M85),0,@IF(M85>M25,@INT(M24/12*(M85-M25)),0))
N43: (,0) @IF(@ISERR(N85),0,@IF(N85>N25,@INT(N24/12*(N85-N25)),0))
O43: (,0) @IF(@ISERR(O85),0,@IF(O85>O25,@INT(O24/12*(O85-O25)),0))
P43: (,0) @IF(@ISERR(P85),0,@IF(P85>P25,@INT(P24/12*(P85-P25)),0))
Q43: (,0) [W11] @SUM(E43..P43)
E44: (,0) ' -------
F44: (,0) ' -------
G44: (,0) ' -------
H44: (,0) ' -------
I44: (,0) ' -------
J44: (,0) ' -------
K44: (,0) ' -------
L44: (,0) ' -------
M44: (,0) ' -------
N44: (,0) ' -------
O44: (,0) ' -------
P44: (,0) ' -------
Q44: (,0) [W11] ' --------
A45: 'Total Gross Income
E45: (,0) @SUM(E40..E44)
F45: (,0) @SUM(F40..F44)
G45: (,0) @SUM(G40..G44)
H45: (,0) @SUM(H40..H44)
I45: (,0) @SUM(I40..I44)
J45: (,0) @SUM(J40..J44)
K45: (,0) @SUM(K40..K44)
L45: (,0) @SUM(L40..L44)
M45: (,0) @SUM(M40..M44)
N45: (,0) @SUM(N40..N44)
O45: (,0) @SUM(O40..O44)
P45: (,0) @SUM(P40..P44)
Q45: (,0) [W11] @SUM(E45..P45)
A47: 'Cost of Goods Sold
E47: (,0) +E30*E40
F47: (,0) +F30*F40
G47: (,0) +G30*G40
H47: (,0) +H30*H40
I47: (,0) +I30*I40
J47: (,0) +J30*J40

K47: (,0) +K30*K40
L47: (,0) +L30*L40
M47: (,0) +M30*M40
N47: (,0) +N30*N40
O47: (,0) +O30*O40
P47: (,0) +P30*P40
Q47: (,0) [W11] @SUM(E47..P47)
E48: (,0) ' -------
F48: (,0) ' -------
G48: (,0) ' -------
H48: (,0) ' -------
I48: (,0) ' -------
J48: (,0) ' -------
K48: (,0) ' -------
L48: (,0) ' -------
M48: (,0) ' -------
N48: (,0) ' -------
O48: (,0) ' -------
P48: (,0) ' -------
Q48: (,0) [W11] ' --------
A49: 'Gross Margin
E49: (,0) +E45-E47
F49: (,0) +F45-F47
G49: (,0) +G45-G47
H49: (,0) +H45-H47
I49: (,0) +I45-I47
J49: (,0) +J45-J47
K49: (,0) +K45-K47
L49: (,0) +L45-L47
M49: (,0) +M45-M47
N49: (,0) +N45-N47
O49: (,0) +O45-O47
P49: (,0) +P45-P47
Q49: (,0) [W11] @SUM(E49..P49)
A51: 'Operating Expenses
A52: ' Salaries and Wages
D52: (P0) [W7] 0.03
E52: (,0) 36000
F52: (,0) (1+$D52)*E52
G52: (,0) (1+$D52)*F52
H52: (,0) (1+$D52)*G52
I52: (,0) (1+$D52)*H52
J52: (,0) (1+$D52)*I52
K52: (,0) (1+$D52)*J52
L52: (,0) (1+$D52)*K52
M52: (,0) (1+$D52)*L52
N52: (,0) (1+$D52)*M52
O52: (,0) (1+$D52)*N52
P52: (,0) (1+$D52)*O52
Q52: (,0) [W11] @SUM(E52..P52)
A53: ' Benefits
E53: (,0) +$E$16*E52
F53: (,0) +$E$16*F52
G53: (,0) +$E$16*G52
H53: (,0) +$E$16*H52

I53: (,0) +$E$16*I52
J53: (,0) +$E$16*J52
K53: (,0) +$E$16*K52
L53: (,0) +$E$16*L52
M53: (,0) +$E$16*M52
N53: (,0) +$E$16*N52
O53: (,0) +$E$16*O52
P53: (,0) +$E$16*P52
Q53: (,0) [W11] @SUM(E53..P53)
A54: ' Payroll Taxes
E54: (,0) +$E$15*E52
F54: (,0) +$E$15*F52
G54: (,0) +$E$15*G52
H54: (,0) +$E$15*H52
I54: (,0) +$E$15*I52
J54: (,0) +$E$15*J52
K54: (,0) +$E$15*K52
L54: (,0) +$E$15*L52
M54: (,0) +$E$15*M52
N54: (,0) +$E$15*N52
O54: (,0) +$E$15*O52
P54: (,0) +$E$15*P52
Q54: (,0) [W11] @SUM(E54..P54)
A55: ' Office Rent
D55: (P0) [W7] 0
E55: (,0) 2000
F55: (,0) (1+$D55)*E55
G55: (,0) (1+$D55)*F55
H55: (,0) (1+$D55)*G55
I55: (,0) (1+$D55)*H55
J55: (,0) (1+$D55)*I55
K55: (,0) (1+$D55)*J55
L55: (,0) (1+$D55)*K55
M55: (,0) (1+$D55)*L55
N55: (,0) (1+$D55)*M55
O55: (,0) (1+$D55)*N55
P55: (,0) (1+$D55)*O55
Q55: (,0) [W11] @SUM(E55..P55)
A56: ' Supplies
D56: (P0) [W7] 0
E56: (,0) 500
F56: (,0) (1+$D56)*E56
G56: (,0) (1+$D56)*F56
H56: (,0) (1+$D56)*G56
I56: (,0) (1+$D56)*H56
J56: (,0) (1+$D56)*I56
K56: (,0) (1+$D56)*J56
L56: (,0) (1+$D56)*K56
M56: (,0) (1+$D56)*L56
N56: (,0) (1+$D56)*M56
O56: (,0) (1+$D56)*N56
P56: (,0) (1+$D56)*O56
Q56: (,0) [W11] @SUM(E56..P56)
A57: ' Postage
D57: (P0) [W7] 0

E57: (,0) 100
F57: (,0) (1+$D57)*E57
G57: (,0) (1+$D57)*F57
H57: (,0) (1+$D57)*G57
I57: (,0) (1+$D57)*H57
J57: (,0) (1+$D57)*I57
K57: (,0) (1+$D57)*J57
L57: (,0) (1+$D57)*K57
M57: (,0) (1+$D57)*L57
N57: (,0) (1+$D57)*M57
O57: (,0) (1+$D57)*N57
P57: (,0) (1+$D57)*O57
Q57: (,0) [W11] @SUM(E57..P57)
A58: ' Telephone
D58: (P0) [W7] 0
E58: (,0) 200
F58: (,0) (1+$D58)*E58
G58: (,0) (1+$D58)*F58
H58: (,0) (1+$D58)*G58
I58: (,0) (1+$D58)*H58
J58: (,0) (1+$D58)*I58
K58: (,0) (1+$D58)*J58
L58: (,0) (1+$D58)*K58
M58: (,0) (1+$D58)*L58
N58: (,0) (1+$D58)*M58
O58: (,0) (1+$D58)*N58
P58: (,0) (1+$D58)*O58
Q58: (,0) [W11] @SUM(E58..P58)
A59: ' Insurance
D59: (P0) [W7] 0
E59: (,0) 200
F59: (,0) (1+$D59)*E59
G59: (,0) (1+$D59)*F59
H59: (,0) (1+$D59)*G59
I59: (,0) (1+$D59)*H59
J59: (,0) (1+$D59)*I59
K59: (,0) (1+$D59)*J59
L59: (,0) (1+$D59)*K59
M59: (,0) (1+$D59)*L59
N59: (,0) (1+$D59)*M59
O59: (,0) (1+$D59)*N59
P59: (,0) (1+$D59)*O59
Q59: (,0) [W11] @SUM(E59..P59)
A60: ' Dues and Subscriptions
D60: (P0) [W7] 0
E60: (,0) 50
F60: (,0) (1+$D60)*E60
G60: (,0) (1+$D60)*F60
H60: (,0) (1+$D60)*G60
I60: (,0) (1+$D60)*H60
J60: (,0) (1+$D60)*I60
K60: (,0) (1+$D60)*J60
L60: (,0) (1+$D60)*K60
M60: (,0) (1+$D60)*L60

N60: (,0) (1+$D60)*M60
O60: (,0) (1+$D60)*N60
P60: (,0) (1+$D60)*O60
Q60: (,0) [W11] @SUM(E60..P60)
A61: ' Advertising and Promotion
D61: (P0) [W7] 0
E61: (,0) 1000
F61: (,0) (1+$D61)*E61
G61: (,0) (1+$D61)*F61
H61: (,0) (1+$D61)*G61
I61: (,0) (1+$D61)*H61
J61: (,0) (1+$D61)*I61
K61: (,0) (1+$D61)*J61
L61: (,0) (1+$D61)*K61
M61: (,0) (1+$D61)*L61
N61: (,0) (1+$D61)*M61
O61: (,0) (1+$D61)*N61
P61: (,0) (1+$D61)*O61
Q61: (,0) [W11] @SUM(E61..P61)
A62: ' Travel and Entertainment
D62: (P0) [W7] 0
E62: (,0) 500
F62: (,0) (1+$D62)*E62
G62: (,0) (1+$D62)*F62
H62: (,0) (1+$D62)*G62
I62: (,0) (1+$D62)*H62
J62: (,0) (1+$D62)*I62
K62: (,0) (1+$D62)*J62
L62: (,0) (1+$D62)*K62
M62: (,0) (1+$D62)*L62
N62: (,0) (1+$D62)*M62
O62: (,0) (1+$D62)*N62
P62: (,0) (1+$D62)*O62
Q62: (,0) [W11] @SUM(E62..P62)
A63: ' Professional Fees
D63: (P0) [W7] 0
E63: (,0) 250
F63: (,0) (1+$D63)*E63
G63: (,0) (1+$D63)*F63
H63: (,0) (1+$D63)*G63
I63: (,0) (1+$D63)*H63
J63: (,0) (1+$D63)*I63
K63: (,0) (1+$D63)*J63
L63: (,0) (1+$D63)*K63
M63: (,0) (1+$D63)*L63
N63: (,0) (1+$D63)*M63
O63: (,0) (1+$D63)*N63
P63: (,0) (1+$D63)*O63
Q63: (,0) [W11] @SUM(E63..P63)
A64: ' Depreciation
E64: (,0) @INT(E98/$E9)
F64: (,0) @INT(F98/$E9)
G64: (,0) @INT(G98/$E9)
H64: (,0) @INT(H98/$E9)

I64: (,0) @INT(I98/$E9)
J64: (,0) @INT(J98/$E9)
K64: (,0) @INT(K98/$E9)
L64: (,0) @INT(L98/$E9)
M64: (,0) @INT(M98/$E9)
N64: (,0) @INT(N98/$E9)
O64: (,0) @INT(O98/$E9)
P64: (,0) @INT(P98/$E9)
Q64: (,0) [W11] @SUM(E64..P64)
A65: ' Maintenance
D65: (P0) [W7] 0.05
E65: (,0) 200
F65: (,0) (1+$D65)*E65
G65: (,0) (1+$D65)*F65
H65: (,0) (1+$D65)*G65
I65: (,0) (1+$D65)*H65
J65: (,0) (1+$D65)*I65
K65: (,0) (1+$D65)*J65
L65: (,0) (1+$D65)*K65
M65: (,0) (1+$D65)*L65
N65: (,0) (1+$D65)*M65
O65: (,0) (1+$D65)*N65
P65: (,0) (1+$D65)*O65
Q65: (,0) [W11] @SUM(E65..P65)
A66: ' Interest
E66: (,0) @INT(E28/12*E120)+@INT(E27/12*E114)
F66: (,0) @INT(F28/12*F120)+@INT(F27/12*F114)
G66: (,0) @INT(G28/12*G120)+@INT(G27/12*G114)
H66: (,0) @INT(H28/12*H120)+@INT(H27/12*H114)
I66: (,0) @INT(I28/12*I120)+@INT(I27/12*I114)
J66: (,0) @INT(J28/12*J120)+@INT(J27/12*J114)
K66: (,0) @INT(K28/12*K120)+@INT(K27/12*K114)
L66: (,0) @INT(L28/12*L120)+@INT(L27/12*L114)
M66: (,0) @INT(M28/12*M120)+@INT(M27/12*M114)
N66: (,0) @INT(N28/12*N120)+@INT(N27/12*N114)
O66: (,0) @INT(O28/12*O120)+@INT(O27/12*O114)
P66: (,0) @INT(P28/12*P120)+@INT(P27/12*P114)
Q66: (,0) [W11] @SUM(E66..P66)
A67: ' Equipment Rental
D67: (P0) [W7] 0
E67: (,0) 0
F67: (,0) (1+$D67)*E67
G67: (,0) (1+$D67)*F67
H67: (,0) (1+$D67)*G67
I67: (,0) (1+$D67)*H67
J67: (,0) (1+$D67)*I67
K67: (,0) (1+$D67)*J67
L67: (,0) (1+$D67)*K67
M67: (,0) (1+$D67)*L67
N67: (,0) (1+$D67)*M67
O67: (,0) (1+$D67)*N67
P67: (,0) (1+$D67)*O67
Q67: (,0) [W11] @SUM(E67..P67)

A68: ' Other
D68: (P0) [W7] 0.05
E68: (,0) 1000
F68: (,0) (1+$D68)*E68
G68: (,0) (1+$D68)*F68
H68: (,0) (1+$D68)*G68
I68: (,0) (1+$D68)*H68
J68: (,0) (1+$D68)*I68
K68: (,0) (1+$D68)*J68
L68: (,0) (1+$D68)*K68
M68: (,0) (1+$D68)*L68
N68: (,0) (1+$D68)*M68
O68: (,0) (1+$D68)*N68
P68: (,0) (1+$D68)*O68
Q68: (,0) [W11] @SUM(E68..P68)
E69: (,0) ' -------
F69: (,0) ' -------
G69: (,0) ' -------
H69: (,0) ' -------
I69: (,0) ' -------
J69: (,0) ' -------
K69: (,0) ' -------
L69: (,0) ' -------
M69: (,0) ' -------
N69: (,0) ' -------
O69: (,0) ' -------
P69: (,0) ' -------
Q69: (,0) [W11] ' ----- ---
A70: 'Total Operating Expenses
E70: (,0) @SUM(E52..E69)
F70: (,0) @SUM(F52..F69)
G70: (,0) @SUM(G52..G69)
H70: (,0) @SUM(H52..H69)
I70: (,0) @SUM(I52..I69)
J70: (,0) @SUM(J52..J69)
K70: (,0) @SUM(K52..K69)
L70: (,0) @SUM(L52..L69)
M70: (,0) @SUM(M52..M69)
N70: (,0) @SUM(N52..N69)
O70: (,0) @SUM(O52..O69)
P70: (,0) @SUM(P52..P69)
Q70: (,0) [W11] @SUM(E70..P70)
E71: (,0) ' -------
F71: (,0) ' -------
G71: (,0) ' -------
H71: (,0) ' -------
I71: (,0) ' -------
J71: (,0) ' -------
K71: (,0) ' -------
L71: (,0) ' -------
M71: (,0) ' -------
N71: (,0) ' -------
O71: (,0) ' -------

```
P71: (,0) '  -------
Q71: (,0) [W11] '  --------
A72: 'Gross Profit/(Loss) before Tax
E72: (,0) (E49-E70)
F72: (,0) (F49-F70)
G72: (,0) (G49-G70)
H72: (,0) (H49-H70)
I72: (,0) (I49-I70)
J72: (,0) (J49-J70)
K72: (,0) (K49-K70)
L72: (,0) (L49-L70)
M72: (,0) (M49-M70)
N72: (,0) (N49-N70)
O72: (,0) (O49-O70)
P72: (,0) (P49-P70)
Q72: (,0) [W11] @SUM(E72..P72)
A74: 'Federal Income Tax
E74: (,0) +E72*@IF(@SUM($E$72..E72)>335000,0.34,
               @IF(@SUM($E$72..E72)>100000,0.39,
               @IF(@SUM($E$72..E72)>75000,0.34,
               @IF(@SUM($E$72..E72)>50000,0.25,0.15))))
F74: (,0) +F72*@IF(@SUM($E$72..F72)>335000,0.34,
               @IF(@SUM($E$72..F72)>100000,0.39,
               @IF(@SUM($E$72..F72)>75000,0.34,
               @IF(@SUM($E$72..F72)>50000,0.25,0.15))))
G74: (,0) +G72*@IF(@SUM($E$72..G72)>335000,0.34,
               @IF(@SUM($E$72..G72)>100000,0.39,
               @IF(@SUM($E$72..G72)>75000,0.34,
               @IF(@SUM($E$72..G72)>50000,0.25,0.15))))
H74: (,0) +H72*@IF(@SUM($E$72..H72)>335000,0.34,
               @IF(@SUM($E$72..H72)>100000,0.39,
               @IF(@SUM($E$72..H72)>75000,0.34,
               @IF(@SUM($E$72..H72)>50000,0.25,0.15))))
I74: (,0) +I72*@IF(@SUM($E$72..I72)>335000,0.34,
               @IF(@SUM($E$72..I72)>100000,0.39,
               @IF(@SUM($E$72..I72)>75000,0.34,
               @IF(@SUM($E$72..I72)>50000,0.25,0.15))))
J74: (,0) +J72*@IF(@SUM($E$72...J72)>335000,0.34,
               @IF(@SUM($E$72...J72)>100000,0.39,
               @IF(@SUM($E$72...J72)>75000,0.34,
               @IF(@SUM($E$72...J72)>50000,0.25,0.15))))
K74: (,0) +K72*@IF(@SUM($E$72..K72)>335000,0.34,
               @IF(@SUM($E$72..K72)>100000,0.39,
               @IF(@SUM($E$72..K72)>75000,0.34,
               @IF(@SUM($E$72..K72)>50000,0.25,0.15))))
L74: (,0) +L72*@IF(@SUM($E$72..L72)>335000,0.34,
               @IF(@SUM($E$72..L72)>100000,0.39,
               @IF(@SUM($E$72..L72)>75000,0.34,
               @IF(@SUM($E$72..L72)>50000,0.25,0.15))))
M74: (,0) +M72*@IF(@SUM($E$72..M72)>335000,0.34,
               @IF(@SUM($E$72..M72)>100000,0.39,
               @IF(@SUM($E$72..M72)>75000,0.34,
               @IF(@SUM($E$72..M72)>50000,0.25,0.15))))
```

N74: (,0) +N72*@IF(@SUM($E$72..N72)>335000,0.34,
          @IF(@SUM($E$72..N72)>100000,0.39,
          @IF(@SUM($E$72..N72)>75000,0.34,
          @IF(@SUM($E$72..N72)>50000,0.25,0.15))))
O74: (,0) +O72*@IF(@SUM($E$72..O72)>335000,0.34,
          @IF(@SUM($E$72..O72)>100000,0.39,
          @IF(@SUM($E$72..O72)>75000,0.34,
          @IF(@SUM($E$72..O72)>50000,0.25,0.15))))

P74: (,0) +P72*@IF(@SUM($E$72..P72)>335000,0.34,
          @IF(@SUM($E$72..P72)>100000,0.39,
          @IF(@SUM($E$72..P72)>75000,0.34,
          @IF(@SUM($E$72..P72)>50000,0.25,0.15))))
Q74: (,0) [W11] @SUM(E74..P74)
E75: ' -------
F75: ' -------
G75: ' -------
H75: ' -------
I75: ' -------
J75: ' -------
K75: ' -------
L75: ' -------
M75: ' -------
N75: ' -------
O75: ' -------
P75: ' -------
Q75: [W11] ' --------
A76: 'Net Income/(Loss)
E76: (E72-E74)
F76: (F72-F74)
G76: (G72-G74)
H76: (H72-H74)
I76: (I72-I74)
J76: (J72-J74)
K76: (K72-K74)
L76: (L72-L74)
M76: (M72-M74)
N76: (N72-N74)
O76: (O72-O74)
P76: (P72-P74)
Q76: [W11] @SUM(E76..P76)
E77: ' =======
F77: ' =======
G77: ' =======
H77: ' =======
I77: ' =======
J77: ' =======
K77: ' =======
L77: ' =======
M77: ' =======
N77: ' =======
O77: ' =======
P77: ' =======
Q77: [W11] ' ========

A81: 'BALANCE SHEET
E81: ^Jan
F81: ^Feb
G81: ^Mar
H81: ^Apr
I81: ^May
J81: ^Jun
K81: ^Jul
L81: ^Aug
M81: ^Sep
N81: ^Oct
O81: ^Nov
P81: ^Dec
A82: \=
B82: \=
C82: \=
D82: [W7] \=
E82: ' =======
F82: ' =======
G82: ' =======
H82: ' =======
I82: ' =======
J82: ' =======
K82: ' =======
L82: ' =======
M82: ' =======
N82: ' =======
O82: ' =======
P82: ' =======
A84: 'Current Assets
A85: ' Cash
E85: (C0) +E128-E106-E87-E86
F85: (C0) +F128-F106-F87-F86
G85: (C0) +G128-G106-G87-G86
H85: (C0) +H128-H106-H87-H86
I85: (C0) +I128-I106-I87-I86
J85: (C0) +J128-J106-J87-J86
K85: (C0) +K128-K106-K87-K86
L85: (C0) +L128-L106-L87-L86
M85: (C0) +M128-M106-M87-M86
N85: (C0) +N128-N106-N87-N86
O85: (C0) +O128-O106-O87-O86
P85: (C0) +P128-P106-P87-P86
A86: ' Accounts Receivable
E86: (,0) @INT((E32/365)*(E40+E42)*12)
F86: (,0) @INT((F32/365)*(F40+F42)*12)
G86: (,0) @INT((G32/365)*(G40+G42)*12)
H86: (,0) @INT((H32/365)*(H40+H42)*12)
I86: (,0) @INT((I32/365)*(I40+I42)*12)
J86: (,0) @INT((J32/365)*(J40+J42)*12)
K86: (,0) @INT((K32/365)*(K40+K42)*12)
L86: (,0) @INT((L32/365)*(L40+L42)*12)
M86: (,0) @INT((M32/365)*(M40+M42)*12)
N86: (,0) @INT((N32/365)*(N40+N42)*12)

O86: (,0) @INT((O32/365)*(O40+O42)*12)
P86: (,0) @INT((P32/365)*(P40+P42)*12)
A87: ' Inventory
E87: (,0) @INT((E33/365)*E47*12)
F87: (,0) @INT((F33/365)*F47*12)
G87: (,0) @INT((G33/365)*G47*12)
H87: (,0) @INT((H33/365)*H47*12)
I87: (,0) @INT((I33/365)*I47*12)
J87: (,0) @INT((J33/365)*J47*12)
K87: (,0) @INT((K33/365)*K47*12)
L87: (,0) @INT((L33/365)*L47*12)
M87: (,0) @INT((M33/365)*M47*12)
N87: (,0) @INT((N33/365)*N47*12)
O87: (,0) @INT((O33/365)*O47*12)
P87: (,0) @INT((P33/365)*P47*12)
E88: (,0) ' -------
F88: (,0) ' -------
G88: (,0) ' -------
H88: (,0) ' -------
I88: (,0) ' -------
J88: (,0) ' -------
K88: (,0) ' -------
L88: (,0) ' -------
M88: (,0) ' -------
N88: (,0) ' -------
O88: (,0) ' -------
P88: (,0) ' -------
A89: 'Total Current Assets
E89: (,0) @SUM(E85..E88)
F89: (,0) @SUM(F85..F88)
G89: (,0) @SUM(G85..G88)
H89: (,0) @SUM(H85..H88)
I89: (,0) @SUM(I85..I88)
J89: (,0) @SUM(J85..J88)
K89: (,0) @SUM(K85..K88)
L89: (,0) @SUM(L85..L88)
M89: (,0) @SUM(M85..M88)
N89: (,0) @SUM(N85..N88)
O89: (,0) @SUM(O85..O88)
P89: (,0) @SUM(P85..P88)
A91: 'Fixed Assets
A92: ' Plant, Property, and Equipment
A93: ' Leasehold Improvements
E93: (,0) 5689
F93: (,0) 5689
G93: (,0) 5689
H93: (,0) 5689
I93: (,0) 5689
J93: (,0) 5689
K93: (,0) 5689
L93: (,0) 5689
M93: (,0) 5689
N93: (,0) 5689
O93: (,0) 5689
P93: (,0) 5689

A94: ' Furniture and Fixtures
E94: (,0) 27388
F94: (,0) 27388
G94: (,0) 27388
H94: (,0) 27388
I94: (,0) 27388
J94: (,0) 27388
K94: (,0) 27388
L94: (,0) 27388
M94: (,0) 27388
N94: (,0) 27388
O94: (,0) 27388
P94: (,0) 27388
A95: ' Equipment
E95: (,0) 235890
F95: (,0) 235890
G95: (,0) 235890
H95: (,0) 235890
I95: (,0) 235890
J95: (,0) 235890
K95: (,0) 235890
L95: (,0) 235890
M95: (,0) 235890
N95: (,0) 235890
O95: (,0) 235890
P95: (,0) 235890
A96: ' Office Equipment
E96: (,0) 14637
F96: (,0) 14637
G96: (,0) 14637
H96: (,0) 14637
I96: (,0) 14637
J96: (,0) 14637
K96: (,0) 14637
L96: (,0) 14637
M96: (,0) 14637
N96: (,0) 14637
O96: (,0) 14637
P96: (,0) 14637
E97: (,0) ' -------
F97: (,0) ' -------
G97: (,0) ' -------
H97: (,0) ' -------
I97: (,0) ' -------
J97: (,0) ' -------
K97: (,0) ' -------
L97: (,0) ' -------
M97: (,0) ' -------
N97: (,0) ' -------
O97: (,0) ' -------
P97: (,0) ' -------
A98: ' Gross PP&E
E98: (,0) @SUM(E93..E97)
F98: (,0) @SUM(F93..F97)
G98: (,0) @SUM(G93..G97)

```
H98: (,0) @SUM(H93..H97)
I98: (,0) @SUM(I93..I97)
J98: (,0) @SUM(J93..J97)
K98: (,0) @SUM(K93..K97)
L98: (,0) @SUM(L93..L97)
M98: (,0) @SUM(M93..M97)
N98: (,0) @SUM(N93..N97)
O98: (,0) @SUM(O93..O97)
P98: (,0) @SUM(P93..P97)
A99: ' Accumululated Depreciation
E99: (,0) +E10+E64
F99: (,0) +E99+F64
G99: (,0) +F99+G64
H99: (,0) +G99+H64
I99: (,0) +H99+I64
J99: (,0) +I99+J64
K99: (,0) +J99+K64
L99: (,0) +K99+L64
M99: (,0) +L99+M64
N99: (,0) +M99+N64
O99: (,0) +N99+O64
P99: (,0) +O99+P64
E100: (,0) ' -------
F100: (,0) ' -------
G100: (,0) ' -------
H100: (,0) ' -------
I100: (,0) ' -------
J100: (,0) ' -------
K100: (,0) ' -------
L100: (,0) ' -------
M100: (,0) ' -------
N100: (,0) ' -------
O100: (,0) ' -------
P100: (,0) ' -------
A101: ' Net PP&E
E101: (,0) +E98-E99
F101: (,0) +F98-F99
G101: (,0) +G98-G99
H101: (,0) +H98-H99
I101: (,0) +I98-I99
J101: (,0) +J98-J99
K101: (,0) +K98-K99
L101: (,0) +L98-L99
M101: (,0) +M98-M99
N101: (,0) +N98-N99
O101: (,0) +O98-O99
P101: (,0) +P98-P99
A103: ' Deposits
E103: (,0) 1000
F103: (,0) 1000
G103: (,0) 1000
H103: (,0) 1000
I103: (,0) 1000
J103: (,0) 1000
K103: (,0) 1000
L103: (,0) 1000
M103: (,0) 1000
N103: (,0) 1000
O103: (,0) 1000
P103: (,0) 1000
A104: ' Other
E104: (,0) 0
F104: (,0) 0
G104: (,0) 0
H104: (,0) 0
I104: (,0) 0
J104: (,0) 0
K104: (,0) 0
L104: (,0) 0
M104: (,0) 0
N104: (,0) 0
O104: (,0) 0
P104: (,0) 0
E105: (,0) ' -------
F105: (,0) ' -------
G105: (,0) ' -------
H105: (,0) ' -------
I105: (,0) ' -------
J105: (,0) ' -------
K105: (,0) ' -------
L105: (,0) ' -------
M105: (,0) ' -------
N105: (,0) ' -------
O105: (,0) ' -------
P105: (,0) ' -------
A106: 'Total Fixed Assets
E106: (,0) +E101+E103+E104
F106: (,0) +F101+F103+F104
G106: (,0) +G101+G103+G104
H106: (,0) +H101+H103+H104
I106: (,0) +I101+I103+I104
J106: (,0) +J101+J103+J104
K106: (,0) +K101+K103+K104
L106: (,0) +L101+L103+L104
M106: (,0) +M101+M103+M104
N106: (,0) +N101+N103+N104
O106: (,0) +O101+O103+O104
P106: (,0) +P101+P103+P104
E107: (,0) ' -------
F107: (,0) ' -------
G107: (,0) ' -------
H107: (,0) ' -------
I107: (,0) ' -------
J107: (,0) ' -------
K107: (,0) ' -------
L107: (,0) ' -------
```

M107: (,0) ' -------
N107: (,0) ' -------
O107: (,0) ' -------
P107: (,0) ' -------
A108: 'Total Asssets
E108: (,0) +E89+E106
F108: (,0) +F89+F106
G108: (,0) +G89+G106
H108: (,0) +H89+H106
I108: (,0) +I89+I106
J108: (,0) +J89+J106
K108: (,0) +K89+K106
L108: (,0) +L89+L106
M108: (,0) +M89+M106
N108: (,0) +N89+N106
O108: (,0) +O89+O106
P108: (,0) +P89+P106
E109: (,0) ' =======
F109: (,0) ' =======
G109: (,0) ' =======
H109: (,0) ' =======
I109: (,0) ' =======
J109: (,0) ' =======
K109: (,0) ' =======
L109: (,0) ' =======
M109: (,0) ' =======
N109: (,0) ' =======
O109: (,0) ' =======
P109: (,0) ' =======
A112: 'Current Liabilities
A113: ' Accounts Payable
E113: (,0) (E34/365)*E47*12
F113: (,0) (F34/365)*F47*12
G113: (,0) (G34/365)*G47*12
H113: (,0) (H34/365)*H47*12
I113: (,0) (I34/365)*I47*12
J113: (,0) (J34/365)*J47*12
K113: (,0) (K34/365)*K47*12
L113: (,0) (L34/365)*L47*12
M113: (,0) (M34/365)*M47*12
N113: (,0) (N34/365)*N47*12
O113: (,0) (O34/365)*O47*12
P113: (,0) (P34/365)*P47*12
A114: ' Short-Term Debt
E114: (,0) 20000
F114: (,0) 10000
G114: (,0) 0
H114: (,0) 0
I114: (,0) 0
J114: (,0) 0
K114: (,0) 0
L114: (,0) 0
M114: (,0) 0

N114: (,0) 0
O114: (,0) 0
P114: (,0) 0
A115: ' Income Taxes Payable
E115: (,0) +E74
F115: (,0) +F74
G115: (,0) +G74
H115: (,0) +H74
I115: (,0) +I74
J115: (,0) +J74
K115: (,0) +K74
L115: (,0) +L74
M115: (,0) +M74
N115: (,0) +N74
O115: (,0) +O74
P115: (,0) +P74
A116: '
E116: (,0) ' -------
F116: (,0) ' -------
G116: (,0) ' -------
H116: (,0) ' -------
I116: (,0) ' -------
J116: (,0) ' -------
K116: (,0) ' -------
L116: (,0) ' -------
M116: (,0) ' -------
N116: (,0) ' -------
O116: (,0) ' -------
P116: (,0) ' -------
A117: 'Total Current Liabilities
E117: (,0) @SUM(E113..E116)
F117: (,0) @SUM(F113..F116)
G117: (,0) @SUM(G113..G116)
H117: (,0) @SUM(H113..H116)
I117: (,0) @SUM(I113..I116)
J117: (,0) @SUM(J113..J116)
K117: (,0) @SUM(K113..K116)
L117: (,0) @SUM(L113..L116)
M117: (,0) @SUM(M113..M116)
N117: (,0) @SUM(N113..N116)
O117: (,0) @SUM(O113..O116)
P117: (,0) @SUM(P113..P116)
A119: 'Noncurrent Liabilities
A120: ' Long-Term Debt
E120: (,0) 55000
F120: (,0) 55000
G120: (,0) 55000
H120: (,0) 55000
I120: (,0) 55000
J120: (,0) 55000
K120: (,0) 55000
L120: (,0) 55000
M120: (,0) 55000

```
N120: (,0) 55000                          E127: '  -------
O120: (,0) 55000                          F127: '  -------
P120: (,0) 55000                          G127: '  -------
E121: (,0) '  -------                      H127: '  -------
F121: (,0) '  -------                      I127: '  -------
G121: (,0) '  -------                      J127: '  -------
H121: (,0) '  -------                      K127: '  -------
I121: (,0) '  -------                      L127: '  -------
J121: (,0) '  -------                      M127: '  -------
K121: (,0) '  -------                      N127: '  -------
L121: (,0) '  -------                      O127: '  -------
M121: (,0) '  -------                      P127: '  -------
N121: (,0) '  -------                      A128: 'Total Liabilities and Equity
O121: (,0) '  -------                      E128: (CO) +E122+E124+E126
P121: (,0) '  -------                      F128: (CO) +F122+F124+F126
A122: 'Total Liabilities                   G128: (CO) +G122+G124+G126
E122: (,0) (E117+E120)                     H128: (CO) +H122+H124+H126
F122: (,0) (F117+F120)                     I128: (CO) +I122+I124+I126
G122: (,0) (G117+G120)                     J128: (CO) +J122+J124+J126
H122: (,0) (H117+H120)                     K128: (CO) +K122+K124+K126
I122: (,0) (I117+I120)                     L128: (CO) +L122+L124+L126
J122: (,0) (J117+J120)                     M128: (CO) +M122+M124+M126
K122: (,0) (K117+K120)                     N128: (CO) +N122+N124+N126
L122: (,0) (L117+L120)                     O128: (CO) +O122+O124+O126
M122: (,0) (M117+M120)                     P128: (CO) +P122+P124+P126
N122: (,0) (N117+N120)                     E129: '  =======
O122: (,0) (O117+O120)                     F129: '  =======
P122: (,0) (P117+P120)                     G129: '  =======
A124: 'Common Stock                        H129: '  =======
E124: (,0) 62000                           I129: '  =======
F124: (,0) 62000                           J129: '  =======
G124: (,0) 62000                           K129: '  =======
H124: (,0) 62000                           L129: '  =======
I124: (,0) 62000                           M129: '  =======
J124: (,0) 62000                           N129: '  =======
K124: (,0) 62000                           O129: '  =======
L124: (,0) 62000                           P129: '  =======
M124: (,0) 62000
N124: (,0) 62000
O124: (,0) 62000
P124: (,0) 62000
A126: 'Retained Earnings
E126: (,0) +E12+E76
F126: (,0) +E126+F76
G126: (,0) +F126+G76
H126: (,0) +G126+H76
I126: (,0) +H126+I76
J126: (,0) +I126+J76
K126: (,0) +J126+K76
L126: (,0) +K126+L76
M126: (,0) +L126+M76
N126: (,0) +M126+N76
O126: (,0) +N126+O76
P126: (,0) +O126+P76
```

8

Performing Ratio Analysis

Introduction

Financial ratios are used by investors, bankers, and managers to evaluate the financial soundness and performance of businesses. Although not a substitute for sound business judgement, ratios give you another information resource for decision-making.

You can use ratios to make two types of comparisons: historical and competitor. Analyzing your firm's past performance can give you insight into trends and the future financial health of your firm. Evaluating your company's key ratios against industry competitors gives you a relative measure of financial performance.

The Ratio Analyzer is a powerful management tool that can be used in a number of ways: as a stand-alone application, using data from your financial statements; as a part of your current financial statements; or incorporated into the Interactive Financial Statements application described in Chapter 7.

This chapter tells you how to create the model and explains the financial ratios and aids that you will need to use the model.

The Ratio Analyzer, shown in figure 8.1, consists of eight worksheet areas: Assets, Liabilities and Stockholder's Equity, Income Statement, Ratios, Historical Data, Criterion Range, Output Range, and a macro.

		E	F	G
RATIO ANALYZER		Copyright (C) Que Corp. 1987		
ASSETS				
				Percent
			31-Jul-86	of Total
Current Assets				
Cash			$75,000	2%
Marketable Securities			35,000	1%
Accounts Receivable		1,256,000		42%
Less: Allowance for Doubtful Accounts		8,000		0%
Net Accounts Receivable			1,248,000	41%
Inventory			359,000	12%
Prepaid Expenses			70,000	2%
Other			23,000	1%
Total Current Assets			1,810,000	60%
Noncurrent Assets				
Property, Plant, and Equipment		1,156,700		38%
Less: Accumulated Depreciation		346,788		11%
Net Property, Plant, and Equipment			809,912	27%
Investment in Subsidiary			396,000	13%
Total Noncurrent Assets			1,205,912	40%
Total Assets			$3,015,912	100%
LIABILITIES				
				Percent
			31-Jul-86	of Total
Current Liabilities				
Notes Payable			$52,912	2%
Accounts Payable			678,000	22%
Accrued Expenses			98,000	3%
Other Current Liabilities			25,000	1%
Total Current Liabilities			853,912	28%
Long-Term Debt			533,000	18%
Stockholder's Equity				
Common Stock, $1.00 Par Value			301,000	10%
Retained Earnings			1,328,000	44%
Total Stockholders' Equity			1,629,000	54%
Total Liabilities and Equity			$3,015,912	100%

Macro (columns J–M):

{PANELOFF}{WINDOWSOFF}~	Turn Control Panel and Windows Off
{GOTO}BOTTOM~	Position to dbase area
/win~	Insert a row
/rfd3~	Format cell to date
+DATE~	Date
/rv~{RIGHT}~	Convert from formula
/rfco~	Format cell for currency
+TA~	Total Assets
/rv~{RIGHT}~	Convert from formula
/rfco~	Format cell for currency
+CA~	Current Assets
/rv~{RIGHT}~	Convert from formula
/rfco~	Format cell for currency
+CA-CL~	Working Capital
/rv~{RIGHT}~	Convert from formula
/rfco~	Format cell for currency
+SALES~	Monthly Gross Sales
/rv~{RIGHT}~	Convert from formula
/rfco~	Format cell for currency
+EAT~	Monthly Earn After Taxes
/rv~{RIGHT}~	Convert from formula
/rff2~	Format cell to fixed
+CA/CL~	Current Ratio
/rv~{RIGHT}~	Convert from formula
/rff0~	Format cell to fixed
+DAYSALES~	Days Sales in Receivables
/rv~{RIGHT}~	Convert from formula
/rff0~	Format cell to fixed
+DAYSPAY~	Pays Purchases in Payables
/rv~{RIGHT}~	Convert from formula
/rff2~	Format cell to fixed
+(CL+LTD)/EQUITY~	Debt to Equity Ratio
/rv~{RIGHT}~	Convert from formula
/rff2~	Format cell to fixed
(EAT*12)/EQUITY~	Return On Equity Ratio
/rv~	Convert from formula
{HOME}{PANELON}{WINDOWSON}'Move Cursor to Home/Turn Control Panel and Windows On	

66 INCOME STATEMENT

		Percent
	Jul-86	of Sales
71 Gross Sales	$732,730	100%
72 Cost of Goods Sold	338,947	46%
74 Gross Margin	393,783	54%
76 Operating Expenses	201,042	27%
77 Depreciation	23,112	3%
79 Earnings before Interest and Taxes	169,629	23%
80 Interest Expense	7,043	1%
82 Earnings before Taxes	162,586	22%
83 Income Taxes	83,888	11%
85 Earnings after Taxes	78,698	11%
86 Cash Dividends	0	0%
88 Earnings after Dividends	$78,698	11%

96 RATIOS

	Current Month
100 INDICATORS OF SOLVENCY	
101 Debt/Equity Ratio	0.85
102 Times Interest Earned	24.08
104 INDICATORS OF LIQUIDITY	
105 Net Working Capital	$956,088
106 Net Working Capital/Assets	0.32
107 Current Ratio	2.12
108 Quick Ratio	1.70
109 Cash Ratio	0.13
111 FUNDS MANAGEMENT RATIOS	
112 Receivables/Sales (Annualized)	0.14
113 Days Sales in Receivables	52
114 Payables/Cost of Goods Sold (Annualized)	0.17
115 Days Cost of Goods Sold in Payables	61
116 Inventory Turnover (Annualized)	11.33
117 Days Cost of Goods Sold in Inventory	32
118 Sales/Fixed Assets (Annualized)	10.86
120 PROFITABILITY RATIOS (Annualized)	
121 Return on Sales	0.11
122 Return on Total Assets	0.31
123 Return on Stockholders' Equity	0.58

125
126 HISTORICAL DATA
127

	Assets		Net Working	Month Gross	Month	Current	Days Sales in	Days CGS in	Debt to	Annualized Return	
Date	Total	Current	Capital	Sales	EAT	Ratio	Receivables	Payables	Equity	on Equity	
131 Jan-84	$1,479,030	$1,112,391	$264,174	$405,488	$1,110	1.31	42	48	1.75	0.19	1654.703
132 Feb-84	$1,525,879	$1,113,539	$280,609	$428,390	$5,882	1.31	40	49	1.75	0.19	6365.139
133 Mar-84	$1,557,329	$1,122,411	$271,498	$434,066	$10,613	1.32	40	49	1.74	0.19	7532.567
134 Apr-84	$1,604,414	$1,148,291	$302,883	$452,928	$10,798	1.36	40	50	1.73	0.19	11412.06
135 May-84	$1,654,074	$1,179,906	$334,289	$473,490	$13,048	1.40	40	50	1.72	0.19	15641.21
136 Jun-84	$1,693,968	$1,244,671	$395,640	$473,685	$15,748	1.47	45	50	1.70	0.19	15681.32
137 Jul-84	$1,710,837	$1,277,567	$426,916	$478,030	$18,430	1.50	46	50	1.69	0.19	20689.57
138 Aug-84	$1,744,472	$1,315,120	$462,735	$498,035	$22,559	1.54	46	50	1.67	0.19	22139.19
139 Sep-84	$1,747,042	$1,343,389	$492,632	$505,083	$24,372	1.58	47	51	1.64	0.19	22557.97
140 Oct-84	$1,783,579	$1,351,523	$507,061	$521,705	$29,003	1.60	46	51	1.62	0.18	27231.57
141 Nov-84	$1,802,591	$1,370,643	$517,344	$529,842	$29,985	1.61	47	51	1.59	0.18	31730.78
142 Dec-84	$1,823,069	$1,374,177	$525,516	$551,717	$34,606	1.62	45	52	1.56	0.18	32692.53
143 Jan-85	$1,859,853	$1,410,243	$557,583	$556,393	$35,779	1.65	47	52	1.53	0.18	37127.97
144 Feb-85	$1,870,213	$1,446,516	$602,287	$577,958	$36,325	1.71	47	53	1.49	0.18	40402.98
145 Mar-85	$1,917,012	$1,465,815	$613,368	$593,881	$38,427	1.72	47	54	1.46	0.18	42426.23
146 Apr-85	$1,938,934	$1,506,298	$658,325	$603,718	$38,672	1.78	48	55	1.43	0.18	44976.23
147 May-85	$2,455,065	$1,075,325	$225,373	$616,116	$41,911	1.27	26	55	1.39	0.18	50034.67
148 Jun-85	$2,464,279	$1,117,617	$266,576	$640,710	$42,292	1.31	27	56	1.36	0.17	51284.99
149 Jul-85	$2,468,198	$1,162,811	$316,541	$646,789	$45,193	1.37	29	56	1.32	0.17	51442.74
150 Aug-85	$2,459,628	$1,209,561	$363,768	$647,556	$46,751	1.43	31	57	1.29	0.17	54352.67
151 Sep-85	$2,478,815	$1,257,593	$404,600	$661,704	$48,031	1.47	32	57	1.25	0.17	56110.60
152 Oct-85	$2,482,507	$1,309,485	$461,463	$670,251	$51,892	1.54	34	58	1.21	0.17	56462.93
153 Nov-85	$2,493,223	$1,364,449	$512,698	$671,954	$54,964	1.60	37	58	1.17	0.17	60310.13
154 Dec-85	$2,984,698	$1,181,446	$334,457	$690,669	$59,325	1.39	27	59	1.13	0.17	60782.16
155 Jan-86	$2,985,456	$1,240,938	$390,396	$692,964	$59,492	1.46	30	59	1.09	0.17	62519.73
156 Feb-86	$2,990,930	$1,003,022	$451,185	$701,412	$62,084	1.53	32	59	1.05	0.17	63264.08
157 Mar-86	$2,996,175	$1,366,767	$516,699	$705,031	$63,745	1.61	35	60	1.01	0.17	63865.28
158 Apr-86	$2,907,620	$1,433,977	$589,385	$707,954	$67,210	1.70	38	60	0.97	0.17	64559.23
159 May-86	$3,000,449	$1,567,038	$718,443	$711,328	$69,939	1.85	43	60	0.93	0.17	67857.49
160 Jun-86	$3,007,287	$1,648,990	$804,337	$727,364	$74,761	1.95	46	60	0.89	0.17	68961.15
161 Jul-86	$3,015,912	$1,810,000	$956,088	$732,730	$78,698	2.12	52	61	0.85	0.58	

Regression Output:

Constant	-81745.2
Std Err of Y Est	3978.646
R Squared	0.968402
No. of Observations	31
Degrees of Freedom	29
X Coefficient(s)	0.205677
Std Err of Coef.	0.007121

162
163
164
165
166 CRITERION RANGE
167

	Assets		Net Working	Month Gross	Month	Current	Days Sales in	Days CGS in	Debt to	Annualized Return	
Date	Total	Current	Capital	Sales	EAT	Ratio	Receivables	Payables	Equity	on Equity	
170	0										

174
175
176 OUTPUT RANGE
177

	Assets		Net Working	Month Gross	Month	Current	Days Sales in	Days CGS in	Debt to	Annualized Return	
Date	Total	Current	Capital	Sales	EAT	Ratio	Receivables	Payables	Equity	on Equity	
181 Jul-86	$3,015,912	$1,810,000	$956,088	$732,730	$78,698	2.12	52	61	0.85	0.58	
182 Jul-85	$2,468,198	$1,162,811	$316,541	$646,789	$45,193	1.37	29	56	1.32	0.17	

Fig. 8.1. The Ratio Analyzer Model.

Creating the Model

To create the Ratio Analyzer, start with a blank 1-2-3 worksheet on your screen and then follow the steps outlined in the following sections: Setting Column Widths, Specifying Cell Formats, Naming Ranges, The \d Macro, and Defining **/D**ata **Q**uery.

Setting Column Widths

Select **/W**orksheet **C**olumn **S**et-Width and specify the column widths as listed:

Column	Width
A	8
B, C, D, E, F, H	11
I	10

All other columns should remain set at the default width.

Specifying Cell Formats

Table 8.1 lists cell formats suggested for the Ratio Analyzer. Enter these formats or use your own cell formats where appropriate.

Table 8.1
Cell Formats

Assets

Format	Cell/Range
/rfd1	F9
/rfc0	F12
/rf,0	F13
/rf,0	E14..E15
/rf,0	F17..F20
/rf,0	F22
/rf,0	E25..E26
/rf,0	F28..F29
/rf,0	F31
/rfc0	F33
/rfp0	Column G

Format	Cell/Range
Format	*Cell/Range*

Liabilities

Format	Cell/Range
/rfd1	F39
/rfc0	F42
/rf,0	F43..F45
/rf,0	F47
/rf,0	F49
/rf,0	F52..F53
/rf,0	F55
/rfc0	F57
/rfp0	Column G

Income Statement

Format	Cell/Range
/rfd3	F69
/rfc0	F71
/rf,0	F72
/rf,0	F74
/rf,0	F76..F77
/rf,0	F79..F80
/rf,0	F82..F83
/rf,0	F85..F86
/rfc0	F88
/rfp0	Column G

Ratios

Format	Cell/Range
/rff2	G101..G102
/rfc0	G105
/rff2	G106..G109
/rff2	G112
/rff0	G113
/rff2	G114
/rff0	G115
/rff2	G116
/rff0	G117
/rff2	G118
/rff2	G121..G123

This list formats the columns according to standard accounting convention, using the **/W**orksheet **R**ange **F**ormat **C**omma command.

Naming Ranges

To compute the Ratio Analyzer's values, the model uses range names extensively. Table 8.2 lists all range names used in the model.

Table 8.2
Range Names

Cell	Name
A131	BOTTOM
F22	CA
F47	CL
F9	DATE
G113	DAYSALES
G115	DAYSPAY
F88	EAT
F55	EQUITY
F49	LTD
F71	SALES
F33	TA
J1	\D

Remember to name the macro (\d in our example) if you use this spreadsheet aid to move data from the financial statements to the Historical Data.

The \d Macro

The \d macro, shown in figure 8.1, extracts data from the financial statements to the Historical Data area. Enter the macro as shown in figure 8.1 or table 8.3. A full explanation of how the macro operates is given later in this chapter.

Defining /Data Query

The model's Criterion Range (A166..K171) and Output Range (A176..K180) worksheet areas are directly below the Historical Data section (refer to fig. 8.1). Records from your Historical Data area will be copied to the Output Range based on the Criterion Range and when the /Data Query Extract command is issued. Figure 8.2 shows portions of these worksheet areas.

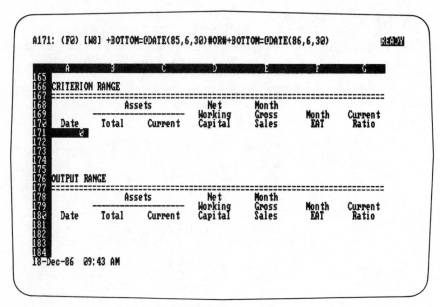

Fig. 8.2. The Criterion and Output Ranges.

At this point, you should designate the ranges that will be needed for extracting or finding information. The following steps should be used to create the model's Input, Criterion, and Output Ranges.

1. Press Input

2. Type *A130..K162* and press Enter

3. Press Criterion

4. Type *A170..K171* and press Enter

5. Press Output

6. Type *A180..K180* and press Enter

7. Press Quit to exit the /Data menu.

Next, enter the column headings, row titles, and labels listed in table 8.3.

Table 8.3
Row Titles and Column Headings

Enter into cell:	Original label:	Copy to:
	Opening Headings	
A1:	\=	B1..G1, A5..G5, A7..G7, A37..G37, A67..G67, A97..G97, A127..R127, A167..R167, A177..R177
A3:	'RATIO ANALYZER	
	Assets	
A6:	'ASSETS	
A8:	^Percent	G38, P68
A9:	^of Total	
F10:	'---------	E16, F21, E27, F30, F32
G10:	'-------	
A11:	'Current Assets	
A12:	' Cash	
A13:	' Marketable Securities	
A14:	' Accounts Receivable	
A15:	' Less: Allowance for Doubtful Accounts	
A17:	' Net Accounts Receivable	
A18:	' Inventory	
A19:	' Prepaid Expenses	
A20:	' Other	
G21:	' -----	G30, G32
A22:	'Total Current Assets	
A24:	'Noncurrent Assets	
A25:	' Property, Plant, and Equipment	
A26:	' Less: Accumulated Depreciation	
A28:	' Net Property, Plant, and Equipment	
A29:	' Investment in Subsidiary	
A31:	'Total Noncurrent Assets	
A33:	'Total Assets	

Enter into cell:	Original label:	Copy to:
F34:	'========	
G34:	' =====	

Liabilities

A36:	'LIABILITIES	
G39:	^of Total	
F40:	' ---------	F46, F54, F56
G40:	' -------	G46, G54, H56
A41:	'Current Liabilities	
A42:	' Notes Payable	
A43:	' Accounts Payable	
A44:	' Accrued Expenses	
A45:	' Other Current Liabilities	
A47:	'Total Current Liabilites	
A49:	'Long-Term Debt	
A51:	'Stockholder's Equity	
A52:	' Common Stock, $1.00 Par Value	
A53:	' Retained Earnings	
A55:	'Total Stockholder's Equity	
A57:	'Total Liabilities and Equity	
F58:	' =========	
G58:	' =====	

Income Statement

A66:	'INCOME STATEMENT	
G69:	^of Sales	
F70:	'---------	F73, F78, F81, F84, F87
G70:	' ------	G73, G78, G81, G84, G87
A71:	'Gross Sales	
A72:	'Cost of Goods Sold	
A74:	'Gross Margin	
A76:	'Operating Expenses	
A77:	'Depreciation	
A79:	'Earnings before Interest and Taxes	
A80:	'Interest Expense	
A82:	'Earnings before Taxes	
A83:	'Income Taxes	
A85:	'Earnings after Taxes	
A86:	'Cash Dividends	
A88:	'Earnings after Dividends	

Enter
into
cell: Original label: Copy to:

F89:   ' =========
G89:   ' =====

Ratios

A96:   'RATIOS
G98:   ^Current
G99:   ^Month
A100:   'INDICATORS OF SOLVENCY
A101:   ' Debt/Equity Ratio
A102:   ' Times Interest Earned
A104:   'INDICATORS of LIQUIDITY
A105:   ' Net Working Capital
A106:   ' Net Working Capital/Assets
A107:   ' Current Ratio
A108:   ' Quick Ratio
A109:   ' Cash Ratio
A111:   'FUNDS MANAGEMENT RATIOS
A112:   ' Receivables/Sales (Annualized)
A113:   ' Days Sales in Receivables
A114:   ' Payables/Cost of Goods Sold
                (Annualized)
A115:   ' Days Cost of Goods Sold in Payables
A116:   ' Inventory Turnover (Annualized)
A117:   ' Days Cost of Goods Sold in Inventory
A118:   ' Sales/Fixed Assets (Annualized)
A120:   'PROFITABILITY RATIOS (Annualized)
A121:   ' Return on Sales
A122:   ' Return of Total Assets
A123:   ' Return on Stockholder's Equity

Historical Data

A126:   'HISTORICAL DATA
B128:   '   Assets
D128:   ^Net
E128:   ^Month
H128:   'Days Sales
I128:   'Days CGS
K128:   'Annualized
B129:   ' --------------------
D129:   ^Working

Enter into cell:	Original label:	Copy to:
E129:	^Gross	
F129:	^Month	
G129:	^Current	
H129:	^in	I129
J129:	^Debt to	
K129:	^Return	
A130:	^Date	
B130:	^Total	
C130:	^Current	
D130:	^Capital	
E130:	^Sales	
F130:	^EAT	
G130:	^Ratio	
H130:	^Receivables	
I130:	' Payables	
J130:	^Equity	
K130:	^on Equity	

Criterion Range

A166:	'CRITERION RANGE

Copy From	Copy To
A128..K130	A168

Output Range

A176:	'OUTPUT RANGE

Copy From	Copy To
A128..K130	A178

Macros

I1:	'\D
J1:	'{PANELOFF}{WINDOWSOFF}~
M1:	'Turn Control Panel and Windows Off
J2:	'{GOTO}BOTTOM~
M2:	'Position to dbase area
J3:	'/wir~
M3:	'Insert a row
J4:	'/rfd3~
M4:	'Format cell to date
J5:	'+DATE~~

Enter into cell:	Original label:	Copy to:
M5:	'Date	
J6:	'/rv~~{RIGHT}~	
M6:	'Convert from formula	
J7:	'/rfco~~	
M7:	'Format cell for currency	
J8:	'+TA~~	
M8:	'Total Assets	
J9:	'/rv~~{RIGHT}~	
M9:	'Convert from formula	
J10:	'/rfco~~	
M10:	'Format cell for currency	
J11:	'+CA~~	
M11:	'Current Assets	
J12:	'/rv~~{RIGHT}~	
M12:	'Convert from formula	
J13:	'/rfco~~	
M13:	'Format cell for currency	
J14:	'+CA-CL~	
M14:	'Working Capital	
J15:	'/rv~~{RIGHT}~	
M15:	'Convert from formula	
J16:	'/rfco~~	
M16:	'Format cell for currency	
J17:	'+SALES~~	
M17:	'Monthly Gross Sales	
J18:	'/rv~~{RIGHT}~	
M18:	'Convert from formula	
J19:	'/rfco~~	
M19:	'Format cell for currency	
J20:	'+EAT~~	
M20:	'Monthly Earn After Taxes	
J21:	'/rv~~{RIGHT}~	
M21:	'Convert from formula	
J22:	'/rff2~~	
M22:	'Format cell to fixed	
J23:	'+CA/CL~	
M23:	'Current Ratio	
J24:	'/rv~~{RIGHT}~	
M24:	'Convert from formula	

Enter into cell:	Original label:	Copy to:
J25:	'/rff0~~	
M25:	'Format cell to fixed	
J26:	'+DAYSALES~~	
M26:	'Days Sales in Receivables	
J27:	'/rv~~{RIGHT}~	
M27:	'Convert from formula	
J28:	'/rff0~~	
M28:	'Format cell to fixed	
J29:	'+DAYSPAY~~	
M29:	'Pays Purchases in Payables	
J30:	'/rv~~{RIGHT}~	
M30:	'Convert from formula	
J31:	'/rff2~~	
M31:	'Format cell to fixed	
J32:	'+(CL+LTD)/EQUITY~	
M32:	'Debt to Equity Ratio	
J33:	'/rv~~{RIGHT}~	
M33:	'Convert from formula	
J34:	'/rff2~~	
M34:	'Format cell to fixed	
J35:	'(EAT*12)/EQUITY~	
M35:	'Return On Equity Ratio	
J36:	'/rv~~	
M36:	'Convert from formula	
J37:	'{HOME}{PANELON}{WINDOWSON}~	
M37:	'Move Cursor to Home/Turn Control Panel and Windows On	

Now enter the formulas and functions shown in table 8.4.

Table 8.4
Formulas and Functions

Enter into cell:	Original formula:	Copy to:
	Assets	
F9:	@DATE	
G12:	+F12/$TA	G13, G17..G20, G22, G28..G29, G31, G33
G14:	+E15/$TA	G15, G25..G26
F17:	$E$14-$E$15	
F22:	@SUM(F12..F13)+@SUM(F17..F21)	
F28:	$E$25-$E$26	
F31:	@SUM(F28..F29)	
F33:	+$CA+$F$31	
	Liabilities	
G42:	+F42/$F$57	G43..G45, G47, G49, G52..G53, G55, G57
F47:	@SUM(F42..F46)	
F55:	@SUM(F52..F53)	
F57:	+CL+LTD+EQUITY	
	Income Statement	
G71:	+F71/$SALES	G72, G74, G76..G77, G79..G80, G82..G83, G85..G86, G88
F74:	+SALES-F72	
F79:	+F74-F76-F77	
F82:	+F79-F80	
F85:	+F82-F83	
F88:	+F85-F86	
	Ratios	
G101:	(LTD+CL)/EQUITY	
G102:	+F79/F80	
G105:	+CA-CL	
G106:	+G105/TA	
G107:	+CA/CL	
G108:	(F12+F13+F17)/CL	
G109:	(F12+F13)/CL	
G112:	+F17/(SALES*12)	

Enter into cell:	Original formula:	Copy to:
G113:	+G112*365	
G114:	+F43/(F72*12)	
G115:	+G114*365	
G116:	+F72*12/F18	
G117:	365/G116	
G118:	(SALES*12)/F28	
G121:	+F85/SALES	
G122:	(F85/TA)*12	
G123:	(F85/EQUITY)*12	

Most of the Income Statement and Balance Sheet formulas are simple addition and @SUM functions, but proceed with caution when you enter the ratio formulas. The model assumes that you generate monthly financial reports. If your reporting cycle is something other than monthly, be sure to adjust the ratio formulas accordingly.

Understanding the Model

The model's Assets, Liabilities and Stockholder's Equity, and Income Statement sections, found in cells A5..G89, will hold your firm's data. Column G displays the proportion of each account as a percent of a total. A portion of the Balance Sheet section is shown in figure 8.3.

Each of the balance sheet's asset and liability accounts is compared to its respective total. On the other hand, each income statement line item is a percentage of Gross Sales.

These statistics can help you as you plan and manage your company's finances. If you refer to figure 8.1, for instance, you'll see that current assets comprise sixty-percent of the sample company's total assets for the month. Or you can think of assets as a pie, with current assets a large slice—more than half the pie.

Understanding Financial Ratios

Ratios can be divided into four major categories:

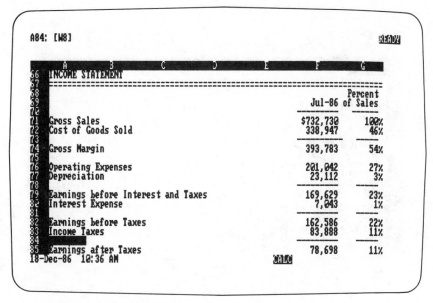

Fig. 8.3. A portion of the Income Statement.

- Indicators of Solvency
- Indicators of Liquidity
- Funds Management Ratios
- Profitability Ratios

The model's Ratios section (cells A96..G123) is an area of the worksheet that calculates financial ratios based upon data in the balance sheet and income statement. Figure 8.4 shows a portion of the Ratios module.

Indicators of Solvency

Indicators of Solvency Ratios, which provide information about the company's capital structure and the management of its current debt burden, measure the long-term financial health of a company. These ratios indicate the degree to which the firm is leveraged.

The Debt/Equity Ratio is calculated by dividing total debt (current and long-term) by stockholder's equity (capital stock plus retained earnings). A result greater than 1 indicates that more long-term financing is being provided by outside creditors than by the stockholders. Because high levels of debt are common in certain

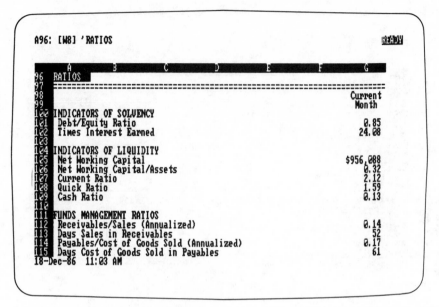

A96: [W8] 'RATIOS   READY

```
      A          B          C          D       E       F          G
96  RATIOS
97  =================================================================
98
99                                                             Current
                                                               Month
100 INDICATORS OF SOLVENCY
101   Debt/Equity Ratio                                          0.85
102   Times Interest Earned                                     24.08
103
104 INDICATORS OF LIQUIDITY
105   Net Working Capital                                    $956,088
106   Net Working Capital/Assets                                 0.32
107   Current Ratio                                              2.12
108   Quick Ratio                                                1.59
109   Cash Ratio                                                 0.13
110
111 FUNDS MANAGEMENT RATIOS
112   Receivables/Sales (Annualized)                             0.14
113   Days Sales in Receivables                                    52
114   Payables/Cost of Goods Sold (Annualized)                   0.17
115   Days Cost of Goods Sold in Payables                          61
18-Dec-86  11:03 AM
```

Fig. 8.4. A portion of the Ratios section.

industries, this situation is not necessarily cause for alarm, but the ratio does have implications for future financing. A company with a high Debt/Equity Ratio may not be able to obtain more outside financing to take advantage of business opportunities or to weather a downturn in sales or profits.

For example, the Debt/Equity Ratio in figure 8.1 is calculated by the formula in G101:

G101: (F49+F47)/F55

or

G101: (LTD+CL)/EQUITY

in which the sum of your long-term debt (F49) and current liabilities (F47) is divided by your total stockholder equity.

Times Interest Earned indicates how well a company's interest obligations are met by its earnings. If a firm's interest payments can be covered several times by its earnings, there is little risk of that firm defaulting on a loan even if earnings drop. If interest payments are being barely met, however, the chance of default is greater. Times

Interest Earned is computed by dividing earnings before interest and taxes (F79) by interest expense

F80: G102: +F79/F80

Indicators of Liquidity

Indicators of Liquidity Ratios provide signals of a firm's short-term financial health. They show how well a company is able to meet such immediate financial obligations as accounts payable or loan repayments due.

Net Working Capital is not a ratio but a dollar amount that is determined by subtracting current liabilities from current assets. Or, to put it another way, Net Working Capital represents your company's liquid, unencumbered resources.

A *liquid* asset is one that can easily be converted into cash and spent. Cash, which requires no conversion, is the most liquid asset. On the other hand, fixed assets such as buildings and heavy machinery, cannot be converted quickly. These assets are *illiquid*.

Unencumbered assets are not offset by current liabilities. The company in the example has current assets of $1,810,000 and current liabilities of $853,912. The company's net working capital, therefore, is $956,088. This sum is unencumbered; that is, it can be invested or spent at the discretion of the company's management.

Because current liabilities are obligations due for payment within a year, current assets (cash and items, such as accounts receivable, that soon will be converted into cash) should be greater than current liabilities. Net Working Capital, therefore, should be positive. Cell G105 contains the formula

G105: +F22-F47

or

G105: +CA-CL

in which current liabilities are subtracted from current assets.

Net Working Capital/Assets equals Net Working Capital divided by total assets. This ratio indicates the percentage of a firm's assets that are liquid and unencumbered. Figure 8.1 shows Net Working Capital/Assets calculated by the formula

G106: +G105/F33

or

    G106: +G105/TA

in which G105 represents Net Working Capital and F33 represents Total Assets.

The Current Ratio is determined by dividing current assets by current liabilities. Like Net Working Capital, the Current Ratio is an indicator of a firm's ability to meet its short-term obligations with its current assets. In an ideal situation, current assets exceed current liabilities, and the Current Ratio is greater than 1. In our example, the Current Ratio is calculated by the equation in cell G107

    G107: +F22/F47

or

    G107: +CA/CL

which divides your current assets in cell F22 by your current liabilities in cell F47.

The Quick Ratio, also known as the Acid Test Ratio, is calculated by subtracting inventories (the least-liquid current asset) from total current assets and dividing the result by current liabilities. The Quick Ratio is a good indicator of how well current obligations can be met without liquidating inventories. Cell G108 contains the formula

    G108: (F22-F18)/F47

or

    G108: (CA-F18)/CL

which divides the difference between your current assets (F22) and inventory (F18) by your current liabilities (F47).

A firm's Cash Ratio, computed by dividing cash and near-cash items (marketable securities) by current liabilities, indicates the firm's capacity to meet its current obligations with its current cash and investments. This ratio shows what percentage of current liabilities could be paid if all short-term creditors were to demand immediate payment. In the example, cash and marketable securities total $110,000; current liabilities are $853,912; the cash ratio is 0.13. This ratio indicates that 13 percent of all current obligations can be met with cash and marketable securities that the firm presently holds. The Cash Ratio is computed by the formula

    G109: (F12+F13)/F47

or

    G109: (F12+F13)/CL

in which the sum of your cash (F12) and marketable securities (F13) is divided by your current liabilities (F47).

Funds Management Ratios

Funds Management Ratios, which measure the amount of cash that is tied up in the business as a result of operations, indicate the firm's efficiency.

The Receivables/Sales Ratio is calculated by dividing accounts receivable by total sales for the reporting period. The resulting value shows what percentage of sales has not been paid.

For example, if accounts receivable are $1,248,000 and annualized sales are $8,792,760, the Receivables/Sales Ratio is 0.14; that is, the dollar amount in accounts receivable is approximately 14 percent of the year's sales.

This ratio is one indication of how extensively a company is lending money to its customers by extending trade credit. The equation in cell G112

    G112: +F17/(F71*12)

or

    G112: +F17/(SALES*12)

computes your Receivables/Sales ratio by dividing net accounts receivable by your annualized sales value.

Because the income statement in the example is a monthly statement, you must annualize the numbers in the statement before using them to compute ratios. To annualize the numbers, you would multiply by 12 the monthly sales total in cell F71.

If, on the other hand, you use the model on year-to-date financial statements, annualization of the ratios (a seven month year-to-date reporting period) would be computed as follows:

    G112: +F17/((F71/7)*12)

or

    G112: +F17/((SALES/7)*12)

Days Sales in Receivables is another way of expressing the percentage of sales in accounts receivable. This ratio is computed by dividing accounts receivable by sales and multiplying the result by the number of days in the reporting period. Like the Receivables/Sales example, dividing receivables by sales gives the percentage of sales for which payments have not been collected.

In the example, the Receivables/Sales Ratio is 0.14 and the reporting period is one year; therefore 0.14 × 365 or 52 days worth of sales are in receivables. If customer payments are due in 30 days, this result indicates collection problems. Cell G113 contains

   G113: +G112*365

which is your annualized Receivables/Sales Ratio (G112) multiplied by the number of days in the year, 365. Payables/Cost of Goods Sold is calculated by dividing accounts payable by the cost of goods sold for the reporting period. This ratio indicates the percentage of the current period's cost of goods sold that has not been paid. The example assumes that all accounts payable represent purchases of items eventually included in cost of goods to be sold. Cell G114 contains the formula

   G114: +F43/(F72*12)

in which F43 represents your accounts payable divided by your annualized cost of goods sold value, which is located in F72.

Note that this ratio also is computed using an annualized cost of goods sold value. Keep your reporting time frame in mind when you work with this model. Days Cost of Goods Sold in Payables is calculated by dividing accounts payable by the Cost of Goods Sold for the reporting period and multiplying the result by the number of days in the period.

For example, if the Accounts Payable/Cost of Goods Sold Ratio is 0.17 and the reporting period is one year, 61 days of cost of goods sold have not been paid (0.17 × 365 = 61 days). If standard payment terms are 30 days, the company is delinquent in paying its suppliers.

The formula in cell G1154

   G115: +G114*365

multiplies your annualized Payables/Cost of Goods Ratio (G114) by the number of days in the year (365) to arrive at your Days Cost of Goods Sold in Payables value.

You can see that the Days Cost of Goods Sold in Payables Ratio provides you wih information that is the converse of the Days Sales in Receivables Ratio.

Inventory Turnover measures the average number of times that inventories were replenished during the reporting period. This ratio is calculated by dividing cost of goods sold by inventory. High inventory turnover indicates a relatively low level of inventory at any given time. Because stocking inventory ties up funds, most managers prefer having minimal inventory on hand.

Inventory is computed by the formula

    G116: +F72*12/F18

in which your cost of goods sold (F72) is annualized by multiplying by 12, the number of months in the year, then dividing the result by your inventory (F18).

The Days Cost of Goods Sold in Inventory Ratio is calculated by dividing inventory by cost of goods sold and multiplying the result by the number of days in the reporting period. In the example, inventory is \$359,000; annualized cost of goods sold is \$388,947 × 12, or \$4,067,364. The firm in our example has 32 days of inventory on hand or [(\$359,000/\$4,067,364) × 365] = 32 days.

The target number of Days Cost of Goods Sold in Inventory Ratio varies widely from industry to industry. If a fairly low level of inventory is preferred, 32 days of sales in inventory can be a sign of good inventory management. On the other hand, certain seasonal businesses require much higher inventory levels at certain times of the year. In these businesses, such as retail snow ski equipment sales, having only 32 days in sales in inventory could be a disaster.

In our example, cell G117 computes the Days Cost of Goods Sold in Inventory with the formula

    G117: 365/G116

in which the number of days in the year (365) is divided by your annualized inventory turnover ratio (GII6).

The Sales/Fixed Assets Ratio is calculated by dividing sales by net fixed assets. Think of fixed assets as the long-term investment in your business. The Sales/Fixed Assets Ratio measures the revenue generated by this investment. A low ratio indicates a capital-intensive business, such as the manufacture of steel, where large investments in plant and equipment are needed to generate sales. A higher ratio suggests a business with low capital requirements, such as an accounting service. This ratio, like all others, is significant only when compared to a budget or to the ratios generated by competitors.

The formula

G118: (F71*12)/F28

or

G118: (SALES*12)/F28

multiplies your monthly sales (F71) by 12 to arrive at your annualized sales value, then divides this result by your net property, plant, and equipment (F28) to calculate your Sales/Fixed Asset Ratio.

Profitability Ratios

Profitability Ratios measure the dollar return (profit) generated by the resources invested in a business. This return is expressed in relation to sales, assets, and stockholder's equity. These important indicators of business performance provide more useful information than dollar values alone.

Return on Sales compares a business's profit to the sales required to generate that profit. Return on Sales equals earnings after taxes divided by sales. A ratio lower than the industry average may indicate poor expense management or operational inefficiency. Cell G121 contains the formula

G121: +F85/F71

or

G121: +F85/SALES

in which earnings after taxes (F85) are divided by your sales (F71).

The Return on Total Assets is calculated by dividing earnings after taxes by total assets. Because assets represent the amount invested in a business, it is important to determine the return realized on them. If a business's returns on assets are consistently below what could be earned if the assets were used elsewhere, management may want to consider shifting to a different product or service. Thus, the formula in cell G122

G122: (F85/F33)*12

or

G122: (F85/TA)*12

divides your earnings after taxes (F85) by your total assets. The result of this operation is multiplied by the number of months in the year, 12, to arrive at your Return on Total Assets Ratio.

Return on Stockholder's Equity equals earnings after taxes divided by total stockholder's equity. This ratio is perhaps the most important profitability ratio because it measures the return the owners of the company are earning on their investment. They may compare this return to other potential investments—real estate, mutual funds, stock in other companies—to determine whether their investment in the company is worthwhile.

If the return on equity is below the rate that can be earned on similar investments, the stockholders of a publicly traded company may bid down the price of the company's stock. In the same situation, the owners of a small business may consider closing their doors.

The Return on Stockholder's Equity is calculated by the formula

G123: (F85/F55)*12

or

G123: (F85/EQUITY)*12

in which your earnings after taxes (F85) are divided by your total stockholder's equity (F55), then annualized by mutiplying by 12.

Historical Data

The model's Historical Data section (A126..K131) contains monthly financial ratios and data (see fig. 8.5).

The Historical Data section gives you a standard with which to measure your business on a monthly basis. This database stores by month your total assets, current assets, net working capital, gross sales, earnings after taxes (EAT), current ratio, days sales in receivables, days cost of goods sold in payables, debt-to-equity ratio, and annualized return on equity. The data can be posted manually from the balance sheet and income statement, or copied from these statements by invoking the \d macro.

The \d Macro

The \d macro shown in figure 8.6 is similar to the posting macro found in Chapter 13, "Fixed Asset Management." The \d macro, located in cells I1..J37, will copy the data from the three financial statements to the

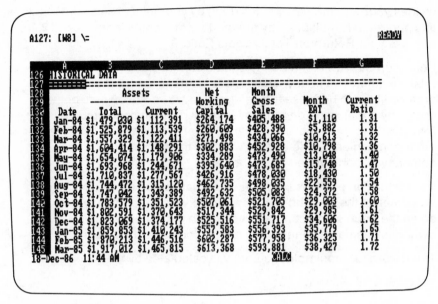

Fig. 8.5. The Historical Data section.

Historical Data area. Basically, the second line of the macro moves the cursor to the range named BOTTOM, which is always the bottom cell in the database. In an unused model (a model with no historical data) BOTTOM is located at cell A131. In the example, BOTTOM is cell A162.

After moving the cursor to BOTTOM, the macro inserts a row using the /Worksheet Insert Row command. At this point, the macro begins copying data from the application. The date is copied, formatted as MMM-YY, and the cellpointer moved one space to the right. Next, the values of TA and CA are copied, and both are formatted as Currency with 0 decimals.

Note that the /Range Value command is used extensively in this macro. The /Range Value command, which works very much like the /Copy command, copies only the *value* of a formula, not the formula itself.

For example, notice what happens in cells J13..J15. First, the cell is formatted. Then the formula +CA-CL computes your Working Capital Value. Next, the /Range Value command is used in the same cell location. The value is extracted from the formula, the formula itself is removed, and ONLY the value remains in this location.

The macro continues, moving the cellpointer to the right and filling the cells with information as it goes. At the end of the macro, the panel and

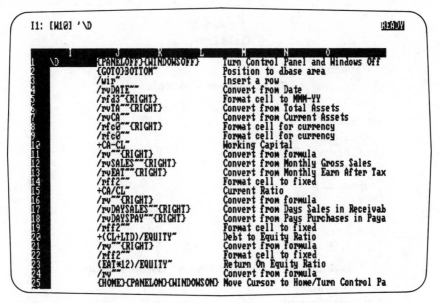

```
I1: [W10] '\D                                                    READY

      I    J         K         L         M         N         O
 1    \D        {PANELOFF}{WINDOWSOFF}    Turn Control Panel and Windows Off
 2              {GOTO}BOTTOM~             Position to dbase area
 3              /wir~                     Insert a row
 4              /rvDATE~~                 Convert from Date
 5              /rfd3~{RIGHT}             Format cell to MMM-YY
 6              /rvTA~~{RIGHT}            Convert from Total Assets
 7              /rvCA~~                   Convert from Current Assets
 8              /rfc0~~{RIGHT}            Format cell for currency
 9              /rfc0~~                   Format cell for currency
10              +CA-CL~                   Working Capital
11              /rv~~{RIGHT}              Convert from formula
12              /rvSALES~~{RIGHT}         Convert from Monthly Gross Sales
13              /rvEAT~~{RIGHT}           Convert from Monthly Earn After Tax
14              /rff2~~                   Format cell to fixed
15              +CA/CL~                   Current Ratio
16              /rv~~{RIGHT}              Convert from formula
17              /rvDAYSALES~~{RIGHT}      Convert from Days Sales in Receivab
18              /rvDAYSPAY~~{RIGHT}       Convert from Pays Purchases in Paya
19              /rff2~~                   Format cell to fixed
20              +(CL+LTD)/EQUITY~         Debt to Equity Ratio
21              /rv~~{RIGHT}              Convert from formula
22              /rff2~~                   Format cell to fixed
23              (EAT*12)/EQUITY~          Return On Equity Ratio
24              /rv~                      Convert from formula
25              {HOME}{PANELON}{WINDOWSON} Move Cursor to Home/Turn Control Pa
```

Fig. 8.6. The \d macro.

windows are turned on, and the cellpointer is returned to the home position (cell A1).

Using the Model

Begin using the model by entering your data according to table 8.5. Change the date in cell F9 to reflect the current month reporting period. Using F2 (Edit) is one easy way to do this. When you finish entering data (or incorporating the model into your reports), press F9 (CALC).

Next, invoke the macro by pressing Alt and d or, if you prefer, enter the data directly from the Balance Sheet and Income Statement to the Historical Data section.

The model has calculated and stored the statistics for the current month and is ready for the next month's transactions.

But there are other ways to use the Ratio Analyzer (particularly the Historical Data area) to better manage your business.

Suppose, for example, that you want to know the gross sales and earnings for January 31, 1984. You use the **/D**ata **Q**uery **F**ind command to locate this information. First, enter the formula

    A171: +A131=@DATE(84,1,31)

Table 8.5
Data Entry

Description	*Location*
Balance Sheet—Assets	
Cash	F12
Mkt Securities	F13
Accts Rec	E14
Less: Allow	E15
Inventory	F18
Prepaid Exp	F19
Other	F20
P,P,&E	E25
Less: Acc Dep	E26
Inv in Sub	F29
Balance Sheet—Liabilities and Owners Equity	
Notes Payable	F42
Accounts Payable	F43
Accrued Expenses	F44
Other Curr Liab	F45
Long-Term Debt	F49
Common Stock	F52
Retained Earnings	F53
Income Statement	
Gross Sales	F71
COGS	F72
Operating Exp	F76
Depreciation	F77
Interest Exp	F80
Income Taxes	F83
Cash Dividends	F86

---

in cell A171; this becomes the criterion for the search. (If you have executed the macro or inserted rows in the model, the cell address will continue to be in column A, but with different row numbers.) The equation causes the **/D**ata **Q**uery **F**ind command to select only those records for which the date field equals the date January 31, 1984.

The Input Range for this search is the entire database, cells A130..K162. The Criterion Range is A170..K171. (Recall that these ranges were set up earlier.) When you issue the **F**ind command, the cursor moves to cell A144 because row 144 contains the records for January 31, 1984.

Or suppose that you want to analyze the changes in working capital during the first six months of 1984. You can do so by using the **/D**ata **Q**uery **E**xtract command. First, enter the following new criterion in cell A171:

$$+A131>@DATE(83,12,31)\#AND\#+A131<@DATE(84,7,1)$$

This criterion selects all records with dates between January 1, 1984, and June 30, 1984. The Criterion and Input Ranges for this operation are the same as they were before, but you must designate an Output Range.

In the sample model, the Output Range is A180..K180. Issuing the **E**xtract command causes 1-2-3 to retrieve the records for the first six months of 1984 and display them in the Output Range. Then the working capital values for those months can be reviewed easily.

Or suppose that you want to use the operation shown in the example to display the results on June 30, 1984, and June 30, 1985, so that they can easily be compared. Again, the **E**xtract command is used. The Criterion for this search is expressed by the equation

$$+A132=@DATE(84,6,30)\#OR\#+A132=@DATE(85,6,30)$$

This formula should be stored in cell A171. Because the ranges for this operation are the same as for the last **Q**uery, all you need to do is issue the **E**xtract command. The Output Range will now display the records for June, 1984, and June, 1985, for your analysis and comparison.

These are only a few of the many ways you can use 1-2-3's data commands on this database. When you use this model, consider other uses for the **/D**ata **Q**uery **F**ind and **E**xtract commands.

The Ratio Analyzer also lends itself to 1-2-3's **/G**raph command. Suppose, for example, that you want to graph the trend in earnings after taxes over the last two years. Before you begin, make sure that the database has been sorted into ascending order. If it has not, rearrange the table by using the **/D**ata **S**ort command as shown in the following steps:

1. Press **/D**ata **S**ort **D**ata-Range

2. Type *A131..K161* and press Enter

3. Press **P**rimary-Key

4. Type *A131*, press Enter, and then press **A**(scending) and press Enter

5. Press **G**o **Q**uit

The database is now in the proper order

Next, issue the **/G**raph **T**ype command and select the **L**ine option. The **A** Range for this graph is G132..G162. If you now select the **V**iew command, the graph shown in figure 8.7 will result.

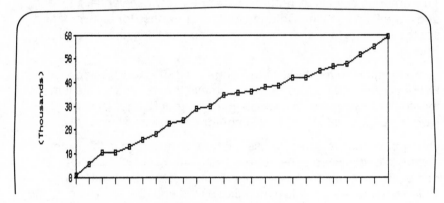

Fig. 8.7. A graph of Trend in Earnings.

To dress up the graph, you can choose such graph options as adding titles or imposing a grid. These options can be invoked by the **/G**raph **O**ptions command. The graph in figure 8.8 is a polished version of the graph in figure 8.7.

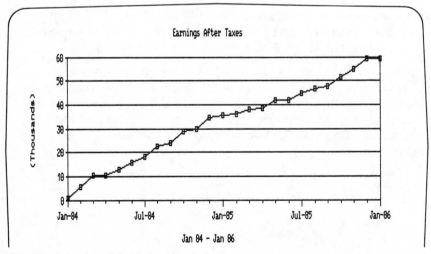

Fig. 8.8. A more polished graph.

Many other graphs can be constructed from your data. Be sure to consider other ways to analyze and review your data through graphics.

Finally, advanced users can take advantage of the **/D**ata **R**egression feature that Lotus has included with 1-2-3 Release 2. With this statistic, you can determine the relationship between a dependent variable and one or more independent variables.

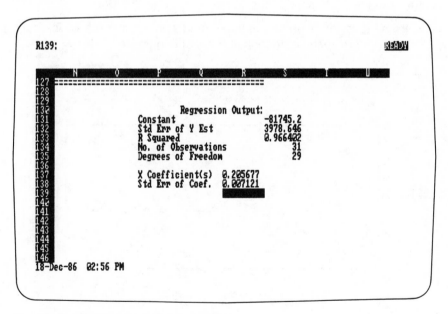

In the sample model, you can determine how earnings after taxes relates to gross sales. The independent variable will be sales, thus the range E131..E161 will be the **X** Range. Because Earnings After Taxes is dependent on Sales, the **Y** Range will be G131..G162.

The Output Range should be placed in an unused section of the model because the regression statistics will write over any existing cell entries. You may want to consider cell P130, which is located in an unused area of the model near the Historical Data section. When you are ready to run the regression analysis, select **O**utput Range, enter P130, then press **G**o. Your regression analysis should look like figure 8.9.

```
R139:                                                    READY

       N     O     P       Q       R       S     T     U
127  ========================================================
128
129
130                        Regression Output:
131          Constant                      -81745.2
132          Std Err of Y Est              3978.646
133          R Squared                     0.966402
134          No. of Observations                 31
135          Degrees of Freedom                  29
136
137          X Coefficient(s)  0.205677
138          Std Err of Coef.  0.007121
139
140
141
142
143
144
145
146
18-Dec-86  02:56 PM
```

Fig. 8.9. Regression Analysis information.

As you can see, particularly from the R-squared statistic, there is a strong (almost 100 percent) relationship between sales and earnings after taxes. This relationship can be seen and clearly understood if you graph these results.

To begin the graphing process, the regression line requires that you add the constant to the X coefficient and multiply this sum by each sales value for the range that begins, for example, in N131, as in the formula:

M131: $S$131+$R$137*E131

/Copy this formula down column M for each sales value in your Historical Data section.

Select /Graph from the main menu options, and then Select the option for the XY Type of graph. Because the X Range will be sales, you highlight the range E131..E161. The A Range will be Earnings After Taxes, F131..F161. The range M131..M161 will be both the regression line and the B Range for your graph.

Next, you need to format the A and B Ranges. To format the A Range, use the /Graph Options Format A Symbols command. Format the B Range similarly, but use the Line option instead of Symbols.

Now, from the graph main menu, View the graph. After some additional polishing, your graph should look like the one in figure 8.10.

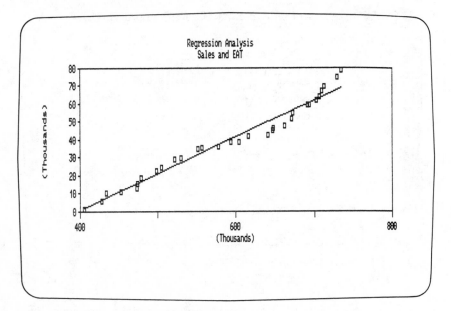

Fig. 8.10. A Regression Analysis graph.

Notice how well the regression line "fits" the sales and earnings after taxes values. This indicates very little variance between the relationship of gross sales and earnings after taxes.

With some experimentation, you will discover many other ways to use 1-2-3 and the Ratio Analyzer as you manage your firm.

Modifying the Model

Modifying the Ratio Analyzer is relatively simple. If you need to add or subtract account descriptions from the Income Statement or the Balance Sheet, use the /Worksheet Insert Row or /Worksheet Delete Row command. Be sure to adjust any of the affected formulas accordingly.

NOTE: Handle this operation with care! Deleting rows can destroy macros or other data that does not appear on the screen.

If you want ratios other than those shown in the example, include them in the ratios worksheet. If you want your ratios to be included in the Historical Data section, change the column headings in the database and Criterion and Output Ranges. Then, after they have been computed from the Ratios section, copy them manually to the Historical Data section. Or press F2 (Edit) and change the macro so that it will retrieve this information and automatically place it in the database.

Conclusion

The Ratio Analyzer is an analytical tool that can help you make better, more informed business decisions. The model enables you to compare key indicators of your firm's performance, to manipulate data for further analysis, and to produce graphs that display the results.

Reviewing your results over time will give you insight into your company's profitability and overall financial condition and may help you to compete more successfully.

```
A1: [W8] \=
B1: [W11] \=
C1: [W11] \=
D1: [W11] \=
E1: [W11] \=
F1: [W11] \=
G1: [W9] \=
I1: '\D
J1: '{PANELOFF}{WINDOWSOFF}~
M1: 'Turn Control Panel and Windows Off
J2: '{GOTO}BOTTOM~
M2: 'Position to dbase area
A3: [W8] 'RATIO ANALYZER
E3: [W11] ' Copyright (C) Que Corp. 1987
J3: '/wir~
M3: 'Insert a row
J4: '/rfd3~
M4: 'Format cell to date
A5: [W8] \=
B5: [W11] \=
C5: [W11] \=
D5: [W11] \=
E5: [W11] \=
F5: [W11] \=
G5: [W9] \=
J5: '+DATE~~
M5: 'Date
A6: [W8] 'ASSETS
J6: '/rv~~{RIGHT}~
M6: 'Convert from formula
A7: [W8] \=
B7: [W11] \=
C7: [W11] \=
D7: [W11] \=
E7: [W11] \=
F7: [W11] \=
G7: [W9] \=
J7: '/rfco~~
M7: 'Format cell for currency
G8: [W9] ^Percent
J8: '+TA~~
M8: 'Total Assets
F9: (D1) [W11] @DATE(86,7,31)
G9: [W9] ^of Total
J9: '/rv~~{RIGHT}~
M9: 'Convert from formula
F10: (C0) [W11] ' ---------
G10: (C0) [W9] ' -------
J10: '/rfco~~
M10: 'Format cell for currency
A11: [W8] 'Current Assets
J11: '+CA~~
M11: 'Current Assets
A12: [W8] ' Cash
```

```
F12: (C0) [W11] 75000
G12: (P0) [W9] +F12/$TA
J12: '/rv~~{RIGHT}~
M12: 'Convert from formula
A13: [W8] ' Marketable Securities
F13: (,0) [W11] 35000
G13: (P0) [W9] +F13/$TA
J13: '/rfco~~
M13: 'Format cell for currency
A14: [W8] ' Accounts Receivable
E14: (,0) [W11] 1256000
G14: (P0) [W9] +E14/$TA
J14: '+CA-CL~
M14: 'Working Capital
A15: [W8] '   Less: Allowance for Doubtful Accounts
E15: (,0) [W11] 8000
G15: (P0) [W9] +E15/$TA
J15: '/rv~~{RIGHT}~
M15: 'Convert from formula
E16: (,0) [W11] ' ---------
J16: '/rfco~~
M16: 'Format cell for currency
A17: [W8] ' Net Accounts Receivable
F17: (,0) [W11] +$E$14-$E$15
G17: (P0) [W9] +F17/$TA
J17: '+SALES~~
M17: 'Monthly Gross Sales
A18: [W8] ' Inventory
F18: (,0) [W11] 359000
G18: (P0) [W9] +F18/$TA
J18: '/rv~~{RIGHT}~
M18: 'Convert from formula
A19: [W8] ' Prepaid Expenses
F19: (,0) [W11] 70000
G19: (P0) [W9] +F19/$TA
J19: '/rfco~~
M19: 'Format cell for currency
A20: [W8] ' Other
F20: (,0) [W11] 23000
G20: (P0) [W9] +F20/$TA
J20: '+EAT~~
M20: 'Monthly Earn After Taxes
A21: [W8] '
F21: (,0) [W11] ' ---------
G21: [W9] '   -----
J21: '/rv~~{RIGHT}~
M21: 'Convert from formula
A22: [W8] 'Total Current Assets
F22: (,0) [W11] @SUM(F12..F13)+@SUM(F17..F21)
G22: (P0) [W9] +CA/$TA
J22: '/rff2~~
M22: 'Format cell to fixed
A23: [W8] '
J23: '+CA/CL~
```

M23: 'Current Ratio
A24: [W8] 'Noncurrent Assets
J24: '/rv~~{RIGHT}~
M24: 'Convert from formula
A25: [W8] ' Property, Plant, and Equipment
E25: (,0) [W11] 1156700
G25: (P0) [W9] +E25/$TA
J25: '/rff0~~
M25: 'Format cell to fixed
A26: [W8] '   Less: Accumulated Depreciation
E26: (,0) [W11] 346788
G26: (P0) [W9] +E26/$TA
J26: '+DAYSALES~~
M26: 'Days Sales in Receivables
E27: (,0) [W11] ' ---------
J27: '/rv~~{RIGHT}~
M27: 'Convert from formula
A28: [W8] ' Net Property, Plant, and Equipment
F28: (,0) [W11] +E25-E26
G28: (P0) [W9] +F28/$TA
J28: '/rff0~~
M28: 'Format cell to fixed
A29: [W8] ' Investment in Subsidiary
F29: (,0) [W11] 396000
G29: (P0) [W9] +F29/$TA
J29: '+DAYSPAY~~
M29: 'Pays Purchases in Payables
A30: [W8] '
F30: (,0) [W11] ' ---------
G30: [W9] '   -----
J30: '/rv~~{RIGHT}~
M30: 'Convert from formula
A31: [W8] 'Total Noncurrent Assets
F31: (,0) [W11] @SUM(F28..F29)
G31: (P0) [W9] +F31/$TA
J31: '/rff2~~
M31: 'Format cell to fixed
A32: [W8] '
F32: [W11] ' ----------
G32: [W9] '   -----
J32: '+(CL+LTD)/EQUITY~
M32: 'Debt to Equity Ratio
A33: [W8] 'Total Assets
F33: (C0) [W11] +$CA+$F$31
G33: (P0) [W9] +TA/$TA
J33: '/rv~~{RIGHT}~
M33: 'Convert from formula
F34: (C0) [W11] ' =========
G34: [W9] '   =====
J34: '/rff2~~
M34: 'Format cell to fixed
J35: '(EAT*12)/EQUITY~
M35: 'Return On Equity Ratio

A36: [W8] 'LIABILITIES
J36: '/rv~~
M36: 'Convert from formula
A37: [W8] \=
B37: [W11] \=
C37: [W11] \=
D37: [W11] \=
E37: [W11] \=
F37: [W11] \=
G37: [W9] \=
J37: '{HOME}{PANELON}{WINDOWSON}~
M37: 'Move Cursor to Home/Turn Control Panel and Windows On
G38: [W9] ^Percent
F39: (D1) [W11] +DATE
G39: [W9] ^of Total
F40: (C0) [W11] ' ---------
G40: (C0) [W9] ' -------
A41: [W8] 'Current Liabilities
A42: [W8] ' Notes Payable
F42: (C0) [W11] 52912
G42: (P0) [W9] +F42/$F$57
A43: [W8] ' Accounts Payable
F43: (,0) [W11] 678000
G43: (P0) [W9] +F43/$F$57
A44: [W8] ' Accrued Expenses
F44: (,0) [W11] 98000
G44: (P0) [W9] +F44/$F$57
A45: [W8] ' Other Current Liabilities
F45: (,0) [W11] 25000
G45: (P0) [W9] +F45/$F$57
A46: [W8] '
F46: [W11] ' ---------
G46: [W9] '   -----
A47: [W8] 'Total Current Liabilities
F47: (,0) [W11] @SUM(F42..F46)
G47: (P0) [W9] +CL/$F$57
A49: [W8] 'Long-Term Debt
F49: (,0) [W11] 533000
G49: (P0) [W9] +LTD/$F$57
A50: [W8] '
A51: [W8] 'Stockholder's Equity
A52: [W8] ' Common Stock, $1.00 Par Value
F52: (,0) [W11] 301000
G52: (P0) [W9] +F52/$F$57
A53: [W8] ' Retained Earnings
F53: (,0) [W11] 1328000
G53: (P0) [W9] +F53/$F$57
F54: (,0) [W11] ' ---------
G54: [W9] '   -----
A55: [W8] 'Total Stockholders' Equity
F55: (,0) [W11] @SUM(F52..F53)
G55: (P0) [W9] +EQUITY/$F$57
F56: (,0) [W11] ' ---------
G56: [W9] '   -----

A57: [W8] 'Total Liabilities and Equity
F57: (C0) [W11] +CL+LTD+EQUITY
G57: (P0) [W9] +F57/$F$57
F58: (C0) [W11] ' =========
G58: (C0) [W9] ' =====
A66: [W8] 'INCOME STATEMENT
A67: [W8] \=
B67: [W11] \=
C67: [W11] \=
D67: [W11] \=
E67: [W11] \=
F67: [W11] \=
G67: [W9] \=
G68: [W9] ^Percent
F69: (D3) [W11] +DATE
G69: [W9] ^of Sales
F70: (C0) [W11] ' ---------
G70: (C0) [W9] ' ------
A71: [W8] 'Gross Sales
F71: (C0) [W11] 732730
G71: (P0) [W9] +SALES/$SALES
A72: [W8] 'Cost of Goods Sold
F72: (,0) [W11] 338947
G72: (P0) [W9] +F72/$SALES
F73: (,0) [W11] ' ---------
G73: [W9] ' -----
A74: [W8] 'Gross Margin
F74: (,0) [W11] +SALES-F72
G74: (P0) [W9] +F74/$SALES
A76: [W8] 'Operating Expenses
F76: (,0) [W11] 201042
G76: (P0) [W9] +F76/$SALES
A77: [W8] 'Depreciation
F77: (,0) [W11] 23112
G77: (P0) [W9] +F77/$SALES
F78: (,0) [W11] ' ---------
G78: [W9] ' -----
A79: [W8] 'Earnings before Interest and Taxes
F79: (,0) [W11] +F74-F76-F77
G79: (P0) [W9] +F79/$SALES
A80: [W8] 'Interest Expense
F80: (,0) [W11] 7043
G80: (P0) [W9] +F80/$SALES
F81: (,0) [W11] ' ---------
G81: [W9] ' -----
A82: [W8] 'Earnings before Taxes
F82: (,0) [W11] +F79-F80
G82: (P0) [W9] +F82/$SALES
A83: [W8] 'Income Taxes
F83: (,0) [W11] 83888
G83: (P0) [W9] +F83/$SALES
F84: (,0) [W11] ' ---------
G84: [W9] ' -----

A85: [W8] 'Earnings after Taxes
F85: (,0) [W11] +F82-F83
G85: (P0) [W9] +F85/$SALES
A86: [W8] 'Cash Dividends
G86: (P0) [W9] +F86/$SALES
F87: (,0) [W11] ' ---------
G87: [W9] ' -----
A88: [W8] 'Earnings after Dividends
F88: (C0) [W11] +F85-F86
G88: (P0) [W9] +EAT/$SALES
F89: (C0) [W11] ' =========
G89: (C0) [W9] ' =====
A96: [W8] 'RATIOS
A97: [W8] \=
B97: [W11] \=
C97: [W11] \=
D97: [W11] \=
E97: [W11] \=
F97: [W11] \=
G97: [W9] \=
G98: [W9] ^Current
G99: [W9] ^Month
A100: [W8] 'INDICATORS OF SOLVENCY
A101: [W8] ' Debt/Equity Ratio
G101: (F2) [W9] (LTD+CL)/EQUITY
A102: [W8] ' Times Interest Earned
G102: (F2) [W9] +F79/F80
A104: [W8] 'INDICATORS OF LIQUIDITY
A105: [W8] ' Net Working Capital
G105: (C0) [W9] +CA-CL
A106: [W8] ' Net Working Capital/Assets
G106: (F2) [W9] +G105/TA
A107: [W8] ' Current Ratio
G107: (F2) [W9] +CA/CL
A108: [W8] ' Quick Ratio
G108: (F2) [W9] (CA-F18)/CL
A109: [W8] ' Cash Ratio
G109: (F2) [W9] (F12+F13)/CL
A111: [W8] 'FUNDS MANAGEMENT RATIOS
A112: [W8] ' Receivables/Sales (Annualized)
G112: (F2) [W9] +F17/(SALES*12)
A113: [W8] ' Days Sales in Receivables
G113: (F0) [W9] +G112*365
A114: [W8] ' Payables/Cost of Goods Sold (Annualized)
G114: (F2) [W9] +F43/(F72*12)
A115: [W8] ' Days Cost of Goods Sold in Payables
G115: (F0) [W9] +G114*365
A116: [W8] ' Inventory Turnover (Annualized)
G116: (F2) [W9] +F72*12/F18
A117: [W8] ' Days Cost of Goods Sold in Inventory
G117: (F0) [W9] 365/G116
A118: [W8] ' Sales/Fixed Assets (Annualized)
G118: (F2) [W9] (SALES*12)/F28

A120: [W8] 'PROFITABILITY RATIOS (Annualized)
A121: [W8] ' Return on Sales
G121: (F2) [W9] (F85/SALES)
A122: [W8] ' Return on Total Assets
G122: (F2) [W9] (F85/TA)*12
A123: [W8] ' Return on Stockholders' Equity
G123: (F2) [W9] (F85/EQUITY)*12
A126: [W8] 'HISTORICAL DATA
A127: [W8] \=
B127: [W11] \=
C127: [W11] \=
D127: [W11] \=
E127: [W11] \=
F127: [W11] \=
G127: [W9] \=
H127: [W11] \=
I127: \=
J127: \=
K127: \=
L127: \=
M127: \=
N127: \=
O127: \=
P127: \=
Q127: \=
R127: \=
B128: [W11] '   Assets
D128: [W11] ^Net
E128: [W11] ^Month
H128: [W11] 'Days Sales
I128: 'Days CGS
K128: 'Annualized
B129: [W11] ' --------------------
D129: [W11] ^Working
E129: [W11] ^Gross
F129: [W11] ^Month
G129: (F1) [W9] ^Current
H129: [W11] ^in
I129: ^in
J129: ^Debt to
K129: (F1) ^Return
A130: (D3) [W8] ^Date
B130: [W11] ^Total
C130: [W11] ^Current
D130: (C0) [W11] ^Capital
E130: (C0) [W11] ^Sales
F130: (C0) [W11] ^EAT
G130: [W9] ^Ratio
H130: [W11] 'Receivables
I130: ' Payables
J130: (F1) ^Equity
K130: (F1) ^on Equity
Q130: 'Regression Output:
A131: (D3) [W8] @DATE(84,1,30)

B131: (C0) [W11] 1479030
C131: (C0) [W11] 1112391
D131: (C0) [W11] 264174
E131: (C0) [W11] 405488
F131: (C0) [W11] 1110
G131: (F2) [W9] 1.31
H131: [W11] 42
I131: 48
J131: (F2) 1.75
K131: 0.19
M131: +$S$131+$R$137*E131
P131: 'Constant
S131: -81745.22632
A132: (D3) [W8] @DATE(84,2,28)
B132: (C0) [W11] 1525879
C132: (C0) [W11] 1113539
D132: (C0) [W11] 260609
E132: (C0) [W11] 428390
F132: (C0) [W11] 5882
G132: (F2) [W9] 1.31
H132: [W11] 40
I132: 49
J132: (F2) 1.75
K132: 0.19
M132: +$S$131+$R$137*E132
P132: 'Std Err of Y Est
S132: 3978.6467393
A133: (D3) [W8] @DATE(84,3,30)
B133: (C0) [W11] 1557329
C133: (C0) [W11] 1122411
D133: (C0) [W11] 271498
E133: (C0) [W11] 434066
F133: (C0) [W11] 10613
G133: (F2) [W9] 1.32
H133: [W11] 40
I133: 49
J133: (F2) 1.74
K133: 0.19
M133: +$S$131+$R$137*E133
P133: 'R Squared
S133: 0.9664025533
A134: (D3) [W8] @DATE(84,4,30)
B134: (C0) [W11] 1604414
C134: (C0) [W11] 1148291
D134: (C0) [W11] 302883
E134: (C0) [W11] 452928
F134: (C0) [W11] 10798
G134: (F2) [W9] 1.36
H134: [W11] 40
I134: 50
J134: (F2) 1.73
K134: 0.19
M134: +$S$131+$R$137*E134
P134: 'No. of Observations

S134: 31
A135: (D3) [W8] @DATE(84,5,30)
B135: (C0) [W11] 1654074
C135: (C0) [W11] 1179906
D135: (C0) [W11] 334289
E135: (C0) [W11] 473490
F135: (C0) [W11] 13048
G135: (F2) [W9] 1.4
H135: [W11] 40
I135: 50
J135: (F2) 1.72
K135: 0.19
M135: +$S$131+$R$137*E135
P135: 'Degrees of Freedom
S135: 29
A136: (D3) [W8] @DATE(84,6,30)
B136: (C0) [W11] 1693968
C136: (C0) [W11] 1244671
D136: (C0) [W11] 395640
E136: (C0) [W11] 473685
F136: (C0) [W11] 15748
G136: (F2) [W9] 1.47
H136: [W11] 45
I136: 50
J136: (F2) 1.7
K136: 0.19
M136: +$S$131+$R$137*E136
A137: (D3) [W8] @DATE(84,7,30)
B137: (C0) [W11] 1710837
C137: (C0) [W11] 1277567
D137: (C0) [W11] 426916
E137: (C0) [W11] 478030
F137: (C0) [W11] 18430
G137: (F2) [W9] 1.5
H137: [W11] 46
I137: 50
J137: (F2) 1.69
K137: 0.19
M137: +$S$131+$R$137*E137
P137: 'X Coefficient(s)
R137: 0.2056779231
A138: (D3) [W8] @DATE(84,8,30)
B138: (C0) [W11] 1744472
C138: (C0) [W11] 1315120
D138: (C0) [W11] 462735
E138: (C0) [W11] 498035
F138: (C0) [W11] 22559
G138: (F2) [W9] 1.54
H138: [W11] 46
I138: 50
J138: (F2) 1.67
K138: 0.19
M138: +$S$131+$R$137*E138

P138: 'Std Err of Coef.
R138: 0.0071213574
A139: (D3) [W8] @DATE(84,9,30)
B139: (C0) [W11] 1747042
C139: (C0) [W11] 1343389
D139: (C0) [W11] 492632
E139: (C0) [W11] 505083
F139: (C0) [W11] 24372
G139: (F2) [W9] 1.58
H139: [W11] 47
I139: 51
J139: (F2) 1.64
K139: 0.19
M139: +$S$131+$R$137*E139
A140: (D3) [W8] @DATE(84,10,30)
B140: (C0) [W11] 1783579
C140: (C0) [W11] 1351523
D140: (C0) [W11] 507061
E140: (C0) [W11] 521705
F140: (C0) [W11] 29003
G140: (F2) [W9] 1.6
H140: [W11] 46
I140: 51
J140: (F2) 1.62
K140: 0.18
M140: +$S$131+$R$137*E140
A141: (D3) [W8] @DATE(84,11,30)
B141: (C0) [W11] 1802591
C141: (C0) [W11] 1370643
D141: (C0) [W11] 517344
E141: (C0) [W11] 529842
F141: (C0) [W11] 29985
G141: (F2) [W9] 1.61
H141: [W11] 47
I141: 51
J141: (F2) 1.59
K141: 0.18
M141: +$S$131+$R$137*E141
A142: (D3) [W8] @DATE(84,12,30)
B142: (C0) [W11] 1823069
C142: (C0) [W11] 1374177
D142: (C0) [W11] 525516
E142: (C0) [W11] 551717
F142: (C0) [W11] 34606
G142: (F2) [W9] 1.62
H142: [W11] 45
I142: 52
J142: (F2) 1.56
K142: 0.18
M142: +$S$131+$R$137*E142
A143: (D3) [W8] @DATE(85,1,30)
B143: (C0) [W11] 1859853
C143: (C0) [W11] 1410243

D143: (C0) [W11] 557583
E143: (C0) [W11] 556393
F143: (C0) [W11] 35779
G143: (F2) [W9] 1.65
H143: [W11] 47
I143: 52
J143: (F2) 1.53
K143: 0.18
M143: +$S$131+$R$137*E143
A144: (D3) [W8] @DATE(85,2,28)
B144: (C0) [W11] 1870213
C144: (C0) [W11] 1446516
D144: (C0) [W11] 602287
E144: (C0) [W11] 577958
F144: (C0) [W11] 36325
G144: (F2) [W9] 1.71
H144: [W11] 47
I144: 53
J144: (F2) 1.49
K144: 0.18
M144: +$S$131+$R$137*E144
A145: (D3) [W8] @DATE(85,3,30)
B145: (C0) [W11] 1917012
C145: (C0) [W11] 1465815
D145: (C0) [W11] 613368
E145: (C0) [W11] 593881
F145: (C0) [W11] 38427
G145: (F2) [W9] 1.72
H145: [W11] 47
I145: 54
J145: (F2) 1.46
K145: 0.18
M145: +$S$131+$R$137*E145
A146: (D3) [W8] @DATE(85,4,30)
B146: (C0) [W11] 1938934
C146: (C0) [W11] 1506298
D146: (C0) [W11] 658325
E146: (C0) [W11] 603718
F146: (C0) [W11] 38672
G146: (F2) [W9] 1.78
H146: [W11] 48
I146: 55
J146: (F2) 1.43
K146: 0.18
M146: +$S$131+$R$137*E146
A147: (D3) [W8] @DATE(85,5,30)
B147: (C0) [W11] 2455065
C147: (C0) [W11] 1075325
D147: (C0) [W11] 225373
E147: (C0) [W11] 616116
F147: (C0) [W11] 41911
G147: (F2) [W9] 1.27
H147: [W11] 26

I147: 55
J147: (F2) 1.39
K147: 0.18
M147: +$S$131+$R$137*E147
A148: (D3) [W8] @DATE(85,6,30)
B148: (C0) [W11] 2464279
C148: (C0) [W11] 1117617
D148: (C0) [W11] 266576
E148: (C0) [W11] 640710
F148: (C0) [W11] 42292
G148: (F2) [W9] 1.31
H148: [W11] 27
I148: 56
J148: (F2) 1.36
K148: 0.17
M148: +$S$131+$R$137*E148
A149: (D3) [W8] @DATE(85,7,30)
B149: (C0) [W11] 2468198
C149: (C0) [W11] 1162811
D149: (C0) [W11] 316541
E149: (C0) [W11] 646789
F149: (C0) [W11] 45193
G149: (F2) [W9] 1.37
H149: [W11] 29
I149: 56
J149: (F2) `1.32
K149: 0.17
M149: +$S$131+$R$137*E149
A150: (D3) [W8] @DATE(85,8,30)
B150: (C0) [W11] 2469628
C150: (C0) [W11] 1209561
D150: (C0) [W11] 363768
E150: (C0) [W11] 647556
F150: (C0) [W11] 46751
G150: (F2) [W9] 1.43
H150: [W11] 31
I150: 57
J150: (F2) 1.29
K150: 0.17
M150: +$S$131+$R$137*E150
A151: (D3) [W8] @DATE(85,9,30)
B151: (C0) [W11] 2478815
C151: (C0) [W11] 1257593
D151: (C0) [W11] 404600
E151: (C0) [W11] 661704
F151: (C0) [W11] 48031
G151: (F2) [W9] 1.47
H151: [W11] 32
I151: 57
J151: (F2) 1.25
K151: 0.17
M151: +$S$131+$R$137*E151
A152: (D3) [W8] @DATE(85,10,30)

B152: (C0) [W11] 2482507
C152: (C0) [W11] 1309485
D152: (C0) [W11] 461463
E152: (C0) [W11] 670251
F152: (C0) [W11] 51892
G152: (F2) [W9] 1.54
H152: [W11] 34
I152: 58
J152: (F2) 1.21
K152: 0.17
M152: +$S$131+$R$137*E152
A153: (D3) [W8] @DATE(85,11,30)
B153: (C0) [W11] 2483223
C153: (C0) [W11] 1364449
D153: (C0) [W11] 512698
E153: (C0) [W11] 671964
F153: (C0) [W11] 54964
G153: (F2) [W9] 1.6
H153: [W11] 37
I153: (F0) 58
J153: (F2) 1.17
K153: (F2) 0.17
M153: +$S$131+$R$137*E153
A154: (D3) [W8] @DATE(85,12,30)
B154: (C0) [W11] 2984698
C154: (C0) [W11] 1181446
D154: (C0) [W11] 334457
E154: (C0) [W11] 690669
F154: (C0) [W11] 59325
G154: (F2) [W9] 1.39
H154: (F0) [W11] 27
I154: (F0) 59
J154: (F2) 1.13
K154: (F2) 0.17
M154: +$S$131+$R$137*E154
A155: (D3) [W8] @DATE(86,1,30)
B155: (C0) [W11] 2985456
C155: (C0) [W11] 1240938
D155: (C0) [W11] 390396
E155: (C0) [W11] 692964
F155: (C0) [W11] 59492
G155: (F2) [W9] 1.46
H155: [W11] 30
I155: 59
J155: (F2) 1.09
K155: 0.17
M155: +$S$131+$R$137*E155
A156: (D3) [W8] @DATE(86,2,28)
B156: (C0) [W11] 2990930
C156: (C0) [W11] 1303022
D156: (C0) [W11] 451185
E156: (C0) [W11] 701412
F156: (C0) [W11] 62084
G156: (F2) [W9] 1.53

H156: [W11] 32
I156: 59
J156: (F2) 1.05
K156: 0.17
M156: +$S$131+$R$137*E156
A157: (D3) [W8] @DATE(86,3,30)
B157: (C0) [W11] 2996175
C157: (C0) [W11] 1366767
D157: (C0) [W11] 516699
E157: (C0) [W11] 705031
F157: (C0) [W11] 63745
G157: (F2) [W9] 1.61
H157: [W11] 35
I157: 60
J157: (F2) 1.01
K157: 0.17
M157: +$S$131+$R$137*E157
A158: (D3) [W8] @DATE(86,4,30)
B158: (C0) [W11] 2997620
C158: (C0) [W11] 1433977
D158: (C0) [W11] 589365
E158: (C0) [W11] 707954
F158: (C0) [W11] 67210
G158: (F2) [W9] 1.7
H158: [W11] 38
I158: 60
J158: (F2) 0.97
K158: 0.17
M158: +$S$131+$R$137*E158
A159: (D3) [W8] @DATE(86,5,30)
B159: (C0) [W11] 3000449
C159: (C0) [W11] 1567038
D159: (C0) [W11] 718443
E159: (C0) [W11] 711328
F159: (C0) [W11] 69939
G159: (F2) [W9] 1.85
H159: [W11] 43
I159: 60
J159: (F2) 0.93
K159: 0.17
M159: +$S$131+$R$137*E159
A160: (D3) [W8] @DATE(86,6,30)
B160: (C0) [W11] 3007287
C160: (C0) [W11] 1648990
D160: (C0) [W11] 804337
E160: (C0) [W11] 727364
F160: (C0) [W11] 74761
G160: (F2) [W9] 1.95
H160: [W11] 46
I160: 60
J160: (F2) 0.89
K160: 0.17
M160: +$S$131+$R$137*E160
A161: (D3) [W8] @DATE(86,7,30)

B161: (C0) [W11] 3015912
C161: (C0) [W11] 1810000
D161: (C0) [W11] 956088
E161: (C0) [W11] 732730
F161: (C0) [W11] 78698
G161: (F2) [W9] 2.12
H161: [W11] 52
I161: 61
J161: (F2) 0.85
K161: 0.58
M161: +$S$131+$R$137*E161
A166: [W8] 'CRITERION RANGE
A167: [W8] \=
B167: [W11] \=
C167: [W11] \=
D167: [W11] \=
E167: [W11] \=
F167: [W11] \=
G167: [W9] \=
H167: [W11] \=
I167: \=
J167: \=
K167: \=
L167: \=
M167: \=
N167: \=
B168: [W11] '   Assets
D168: [W11] ^Net
E168: [W11] ^Month
H168: [W11] 'Days Sales
I168: 'Days CGS
K168: 'Annualized
B169: [W11] ' ----------------------
D169: [W11] ^Working
E169: [W11] ^Gross
F169: [W11] ^Month
G169: (F1) [W9] ^Current
H169: [W11] ^in
I169: ^in
J169: ^Debt to
K169: (F1) ^Return
A170: (D3) [W8] ^Date
B170: [W11] ^Total
C170: [W11] ^Current
D170: (C0) [W11] ^Capital
E170: (C0) [W11] ^Sales
F170: (C0) [W11] ^EAT
G170: [W9] ^Ratio
H170: [W11] 'Receivables
I170: ' Payables
J170: (F1) ^Equity
K170: (F1) ^on Equity
A171: (F0) [W8] +A131=@DATE(85,6,30)#OR#+A131=@DATE(86,6,30)
A176: [W8] 'OUTPUT RANGE

A177: [W8] \=
B177: [W11] \=
C177: [W11] \=
D177: [W11] \=
E177: [W11] \=
F177: [W11] \=
G177: [W9] \=
H177: [W11] \=
I177: \=
J177: \=
K177: \=
L177: \=
M177: \=
N177: \=
B178: [W11] '   Assets
D178: [W11] ^Net
E178: [W11] ^Month
H178: [W11] 'Days Sales
I178: 'Days CGS
K178: 'Annualized
B179: [W11] ' --------------------
D179: [W11] ^Working
E179: [W11] ^Gross
F179: [W11] ^Month
G179: (F1) [W9] ^Current
H179: [W11] ^in
I179: ^in
J179: ^Debt to
K179: (F1) ^Return
A180: (D3) [W8] ^Date
B180: [W11] ^Total
C180: [W11] ^Current
D180: (C0) [W11] ^Capital
E180: (C0) [W11] ^Sales
F180: (C0) [W11] ^EAT
G180: [W9] ^Ratio
H180: [W11] 'Receivables
I180: ' Payables
J180: (F1) ^Equity
K180: (F1) ^on Equity
A181: (D3) [W8] @DATE(86,7,30)
B181: (C0) [W11] 3015912
C181: (C0) [W11] 1810000
D181: (C0) [W11] 956088
E181: (C0) [W11] 732730
F181: (C0) [W11] 78698
G181: (F2) [W9] 2.12
H181: [W11] 52
I181: 61
J181: (F2) 0.85
K181: 0.58
A182: (D3) [W8] @DATE(85,7,30)
B182: (C0) [W11] 2468198
C182: (C0) [W11] 1162811

D182: (C0) [W11] 316541
E182: (C0) [W11] 646789
F182: (C0) [W11] 45193
G182: (F2) [W9] 1.37
H182: [W11] 29
I182: 56
J182: (F2) 1.32
K182: 0.17

9

Calculating Growth Capacity

Introduction

The growth potential of your business depends on many factors—1) the condition of the economy, 2) competition (domestic and international), 3) the availability of qualified employees, 4) your product or service, 5) management, and 6) financing.

If you use 1-2-3 and the Financial Growth Capacity Calculator to analyze the financial factors that impact your company's capacity for growth, you'll be better informed about this important component of your business.

This chapter not only explains how financing influences growth potential but also discusses how to create the model, how the model functions, and how to use the application in your business.

As you probably know, your firm's growth potential is related to your financial resources. To increase sales, you need working capital with which to hire employees, purchase raw materials, invest in new equipment, and increase advertising. Increased sales will lead to higher accounts receivable that you may need to finance. Three financing alternatives are available to you: issuing common stock, borrowed funds, or retained earnings.

The advantages and disadvantages of each of these sources are summarized in table 9.1.

Table 9.1
Financing Sources

Method	Advantage	Disadvantage
Common Stock	Interest & dividend pymts not required	Lessening or loss of control over firm
Debt or Other Loan	Leverage	Interest Expense
Retained Earnings	Least expensive method of financing	Requires profitability and an adequate amount to finance growth

By borrowing funds you create or increase a business expense (interest) that will affect your firm's profitability. Common stock dividends and taxes also affect profitability and the amount of earnings you can retain. By addressing these factors, the model arrives at your firm's *sustainable growth rate*, which is the rate at which a company can grow without additional outside financing.

To calculate your firm's growth rate, the Financial Growth Capacity Calculator relies on two modules: Capitalization (cells A5 through I26) and Profitability (cells A27 through H51). Figure 9.1 shows the Financial Growth Capacity Calculator.

Creating the Model

The Financial Growth Capacity Calculator is easy to create. Begin by issuing the /**W**orksheet **G**lobal **C**olumn-Width command and setting all columns at 12. Then enter the column headings, row titles, and other labels according to table 9.2.

```
        A       B       C       D       E       F       G       H
 1 ================================================================================
 2
 3 FINANCIAL GROWTH CAPACITY CALCULATOR        (C) 1987 Que Corporation
 4
 5 ================================================================================
 6 CAPITALIZATION                      Year 1    Year 2    Year 3    Year 4    Year 5
 7 ================================================= ========= ========= ========= =========
 8 Equity
 9  New Equity                                  $106,990  $127,550  $152,061  $181,283
10 Total Equity             $625,000  $731,990  $859,540 $1,011,601 $1,192,884
11
12 Affordable New Debt                $138,488  $165,101  $196,828  $234,652
13
14 Debt
15  Current Liabilities     $525,000  $663,488  $828,589 $1,025,417 $1,260,069
16  Short term Debt         $130,000  $130,000  $130,000  $130,000  $130,000
17   ST Interest Rate             7%        7%        7%        7%        7%
18  Long Term Debt          $154,000  $154,000  $154,000  $154,000  $154,000
19   LT Interest Rate          6.5%        7%        7%        7%        7%
20
21 Total Debt               $809,000  $947,488 $1,112,589 $1,309,417 $1,544,069
22
23 Debt Equity Ratio            1.29      1.29      1.29      1.29      1.29
24
25 Total Assets           $1,434,000 $1,679,478 $1,972,129 $2,321,018 $2,736,954
26
27 ================================================================================
28 PROFITABILITY                       Year 1    Year 2    Year 3    Year 4    Year 5
29 ================================================= ========= ========= ========= =========
30 Profit before Interest and Taxes  $175,000  $204,957  $240,671  $283,248  $334,008
31 Return on Assets           12.20%    12.20%    12.20%    12.20%    12.20%
32
33 Interest Expense          $19,110   $19,110   $19,110   $19,110   $19,110
34                          --------  --------  --------  --------  --------
35 Profit before Tax         $155,890  $185,847  $221,561  $264,138  $314,898
36 Tax Rate                     31%       31%       31%       31%       31%
37                          --------  --------  --------  --------  --------
38 Tax Expense               $48,900   $58,297   $69,500   $82,856   $98,778
39                          --------  --------  --------  --------  --------
40 Profit after Tax          $106,990  $127,550  $152,061  $181,283  $216,120
41
42 Dividend payout percentage  0.00%     0.00%     0.00%     0.00%     0.00%
43 Dividends paid                 $0        $0        $0        $0        $0
44                          --------  --------  --------  --------  --------
45 Earnings Reinvested       $106,990  $127,550  $152,061  $181,283  $216,120
46                          ========  ========  ========  ========  ========
47
48 Net Return on Equity         17%       17%       18%       18%       18%
49
50
51 Sustainable Growth Rate      17%       17%       18%       18%       18%
```

Fig. 9.1. The Financial Growth Capacity Calculator.

Now, format the entire worksheet area by using **/W**orksheet **G**lobal **F**ormat **C**urrency **0** and then individually format the following rows:

Row	Format
17, 19	Percent 2
23	Fixed 2
31, 36, 42, 48, 51	Percent 2

After you have entered the column headings and row titles, and have formatted the cells, enter the formulas listed in table 9.3.

Table 9.2
Row Titles and Column Headings

Enter into cell:	Original label:	Copy to:
	Opening Headings	
A1:	\=	B1..H1, A5..H5, A7..C7, A27..H27
A3:	'FINANCIAL GROWTH CAPACITY CALCULATOR	
	Capitalization	
A6:	'CAPITALIZATION	
D6:	^Year 1	
E6:	^Year 2	
F6:	^Year 3	
G6:	^Year 4	
H6:	^Year 5	
D7:	' ==========	E7..H7, D29..H29, D46..H46
A8:	'Equity	
A9:	' New Equity	
A10:	'Total Equity	
A12:	'Affordable New Debt	
A14:	'Debt	
A15:	' Current Liabilities	
A16:	' Short term Debt	
A17:	' ST Interest Rate	
A18:	' Long Term Debt	
A19:	' LT Interest Rate	
A21:	'Total Debt	
A23:	'Debt Equity Ratio	
A25:	'Total Assets	
	Profitability	
A28:	'PROFITABILITY	
A30:	'Profit before Interest and Taxes	
A31:	'Return on Assets	
A33:	'Interest Expense	
D34:	' --------	D34..H34, D37..H37, D39..H39, D44..H44

Enter into cell:	Original label:	Copy to:
A35:	'Profit before Tax	
A36:	'Tax Rate	
A38:	'Tax Expense	
A40:	'Profit after Tax	
A42:	'Dividend payout percentage	
A43:	'Dividends paid	
A45:	'Earnings Reinvested	
A48:	'Net Return on Equity	
A51:	'Sustainable Growth Rate	

Table 9.3
Formulas and Functions

Enter into cell:	Original formula:	Copy to:
	Capitalization	
E9:	+D45	F9..H9
E10:	+D10+E9	F10..H10
E12:	+D23*E10-D21	F12..H12
E15:	+D15+(E12-(E16-D16) -(E18-D18))	F15..H15
E16:	+D16	F16..H16
E17:	+D17	F17..H17
E18:	+D18	F18..H18
E19:	+D19	F19..H19
D21:	+D15+D16+D18	E21..H21
D23:	+D21/D10	E23..H23
D25:	+D10+D21	E25..H25

Enter
into
cell: Original formula: Copy to:

Profitability

Enter into cell:	Original formula:	Copy to:
E30:	+E31*E25	F30..H30
D31:	+D30/D25	
E31:	+D31	F31..H31
D33:	+D19*D18+D17*D16	E33..H33
D35:	+D30-D33	E35..H35
D36:	+D38/D35	
E36:	+D36	F36..H36
E38:	+E35*E36	F38..H38
D40:	+D35-D38	E40..H40
D42:	+D43/D40	
E42:	+D42	F42..H42
E43:	+E42*E40	F43..H43
D45:	+D40-D43	E45..H45
D48:	+D40/D10	E48..H48
D51:	(1-D42)*D48	E51..H51

Understanding the Model

Unlike many models in this book, this application does not use a dedicated data-entry worksheet area. Most of the data is entered in the Capitalization section.

The Capitalization Module

The Capitalization module, a portion of which is shown in figure 9.2, is located in cells A5 through H26. Information about your company's capital structure is entered here. To compute growth capacity, the model specifically requires data about your firm's equity, debt, and assets.

Line 9, New Equity, is the previous year's Earnings Reinvested. This amount is calculated for you in year two by the formula

   E9: +D45

which references cell D45, Earnings Reinvested for year one. Line 10, Total Equity, which is calculated similarly, shows an amount that is the

```
A6: 'CAPITALIZATION                                                    READY

          A           B           C           D           E           F
5  ═══════════════════════════════════════════════════════════════════════
6  CAPITALIZATION                              Year 1      Year 2      Year 3
7  ═══════════════════════════════════════════════════════════════════════
8  Equity
9    New Equity                                            $106,990    $127,550
10 Total Equity                                $625,000    $731,990    $859,540
11
12 Affordable New Debt                                     $138,488    $165,101
13
14 Debt
15   Current Liabilities                       $525,000    $663,488    $828,589
16   Short term Debt                           $130,000    $130,000    $130,000
17     ST Interest Rate                              7%          7%          7%
18   Long Term Debt                            $154,000    $154,000    $154,000
19     LT Interest Rate                            6.5%          7%          7%
20
21 Total Debt                                  $809,000    $947,488  $1,112,589
22
23 Debt Equity Ratio                               1.29        1.29        1.29
24
17-Dec-86   04:38 PM
```

Fig. 9.2. The Capitalization module.

sum of the previous year's equity and new equity. In cell E10, this would be

E10: +D10+E9

Line 12, Affordable New Debt, is the additional amount your firm can borrow without exceeding the debt-to-equity ratio shown in line 23. For year two, affordable new debt is calculated by the formula

E12: +D23*E10-D21

In this formula, D23 is your previous year's debt-to-equity ratio, E10 is your current year's total equity, and D21 is your previous year's total debt.

Line 15 computes your Current Liabilities. The model assumes that 1) you will use your entire debt capacity, and (2) the new debt is in the form of current liabilities. However, a portion of the new debt can be added as short- or long-term debt. For example, the formula in cell E15 is

E15: +D15+(E12-(E16-D16)-(E18-D18))

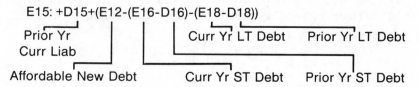

This equation reads: The total current liabilities (E15) equals the prior period current liabilities plus the difference between the affordable new debt (E12) and the amount of new short- (E16-D16) and long-term debt (E18-D18).

The cells in lines 16 (Short-term Debt), 17 (ST Interest Rate), 18 (Long-term Debt), and 19 (LT Interest Rate) all contain formulas that refer to the prior year's respective cell addresses.

Line 21 calculates your firm's Total Debt, which is the sum of current liabilities, short-term debt, and long-term debt. In cell E21, for example, this would be

    E21: +E15+E16+E18

Line 23 contains your business's Debt-to-Equity ratio. Logically, this is your debt divided by your equity which, for year 2 (cell E23) will be

    E23: +E21/E10

Line 25, Total Assets, is derived from the balance sheet equation:

    ASSETS = LIABILITIES + EQUITY

Before the model can project Profit before Interest and Taxes (in the Profitability section), it needs to know your total assets. The formula in cell E25:

    E25: +E10+E21

adds cell E10, your Total Equity, and cell E21, your Total Debt, for year 2.

The Profitability Module

The model's Profitability module is located in cells A27 through H51. Figure 9.3 shows a portion of this module.

Line 30 calculates your Profit before Interest and Taxes, based on your Return on Assets. In the formula which calculates this profit for year 2,

    E30: +E31*E25

cell E31 is your Return on Assets (as a percent) and cell E25 is your business's Total Assets.

The value in line 31 is carried forward from year 1 for years 2 through 5. To compute Return on Assets, the model uses the equation in cell D31:

    D31: +D30/D25

```
A28: 'PROFITABILITY                                          READY

           A        B         C        D         E         F
27 =========================================================
28 PROFITABILITY                        Year 1    Year 2    Year 3
29 =========================================================
30 Profit before Interest and Taxes    $175,000  $204,957  $240,671
31 Return on Assets                      12.20%    12.20%    12.20%
32
33 Interest Expense                     $19,110   $19,110   $19,110
34                                     --------  --------  --------
35 Profit before Tax                   $155,890  $185,847  $221,561
36 Tax Rate                                31%       31%       31%
37
38 Tax Expense                          $48,900   $58,297   $69,500
39                                     --------  --------  --------
40 Profit after Tax                    $106,990  $127,550  $152,061
41
42 Dividend payout percentage            0.00%     0.00%     0.00%
43 Dividends paid                          $0        $0        $0
44                                     --------  --------  --------
45 Earnings Reinvested                 $106,990  $127,550  $152,061
46                                     ========  ========  ========
17-Dec-86  04:39 PM
```

Fig. 9.3. The Profitability module.

In this formula, cell D30 is your Profit before Interest and Taxes (for year 1) and cell D25 is your Total Assets, also for year 1.

Line 33, Interest Expense, is calculated in year 1 and carried forward for subsequent years. The model uses the equation

D33: +D19*D18+D17*D16

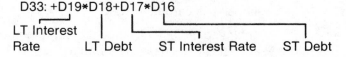

LT Interest
Rate   LT Debt   ST Interest Rate   ST Debt

which multiplies long-term debt (D18) by long-term interest rate (D19); multiplies short-term debt (D16) by short-term interest rate (D17); and adds the two products to compute your interest cost for year 1.

Line 35, Profit before Tax, is simply your profit less interest cost before taxes. In cell E35, for example, the formula to compute Profit before Tax is

E35: +E30-E33

Line 36 displays your Tax Rate. As it does in lines 31 and 33, the model calculates your tax rate in year 1 and carries that rate forward. Thus, the equation in cell D36 is

D36: +D38/D35

which is the amount of tax for year 1 (D38) divided by the Profit before Tax for year 1 (D35).

Line 38 is your company's annual Tax Expense. The model calculates this value with the formula

E38: +E35*E36

Your Profit before Tax (E35) is multiplied by your Tax Rate (E36) to arrive at your Tax Expense.

Line 40 contains your Profit after Tax. As the name implies, this is simply your firm's profit after income taxes. In year 2, this will be

E40: +E35-E38

Cell E35 is your second year Profit before Tax; E38, your second year Tax Expense.

Lines 42 and 43 address your company's dividend policy. You can see that instead of paying dividends, this sample firm retains its earnings. If your company pays a dividend, however, the payout percentage is calculated by the formula in cell D42:

D42: +D43/D40

In this formula, your firm's total dividend (D43) is divided by its total after-tax profit (D40). The relationship is carried forward.

Line 43 uses the payout percentage to project the amount of dividends your firm will pay in future years. The model uses the formula

E43: +E42*E40

in which E42, the Dividend Payout Percentage, is multiplied by E40, Profit after Tax (both for year 2).

Line 45 computes the amount of earnings you retain, or reinvest, in your business. This is the amount of after-tax profit less any dividends paid. In year 2, for example, the amount is calculated by the formula

E45: +E40-E43

Line 48 computes your Net Return on Equity as a percentage. For year 2, the computation is performed by the equation

   E48: +E40/E10

Your Profit after Tax (E40) is divided by your Total Equity (E10).

Finally, row 51 computes your Sustainable Growth Rate as a percentage. This value is calculated by the formula

   E51: (1-E42)*E48

Percent Earnings Retained   Return on Equity

The phrase (1-E42) is the Percent Earnings Retained (1 minus the Dividend Payout Percentage) multiplied by your Return on Equity for year 2. This value will indicate how much growth you can expect from year to year, without additional financing from new debt or equity.

In figure 9.1, the sample firm can grow 17 percent in year 2 without additional financing from external sources. This value equals your Net Return on Equity because the sample company does not pay a dividend. However, if you wanted or were experiencing sales growth of more than 17 percent, you would need to issue additional stock or increase your level of debt to accommodate this growth rate.

In summary, your Sustainable Growth Rate will be higher if you can keep asset growth lower than sales growth, or if you can increase the percentage of after-tax profit. On the other hand, if asset growth exceeds sales growth or if the percentage of after-tax profit decreases, your Sustainable Growth Rate will be lower.

You are now ready to calculate your firm's growth capacity.

Using the Model

The Financial Growth Capacity Calculator is easy to use. You begin by entering financial information about your business, according to table 9.4.

Now press F9 (CALC) and examine the values for years 2 through 5. Is this where you want your business to be in five years?

Consider displaying your results graphically. Figure 9.4 shows one of several ways to graph the information provided by your Financial Growth Capacity Calculator.

Table 9.4
Data Entry

Capitalization

Description	*Cell*
Total Equity	D10
Current Liabilities	D15
Short-term Debt	D16
ST Interest Rate	D17
Long-term Debt	D18
LT Interest Rate	D19

Profitability

Profit Before Interest and Taxes	D30
Tax Expense	D38
Dividends Paid	D43

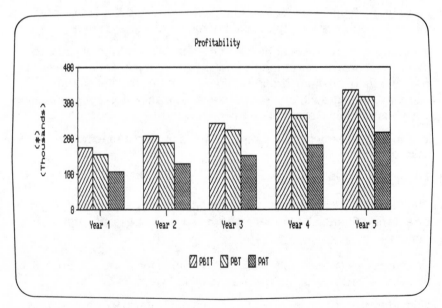

Fig. 9.4. The Profitability graph.

This graph shows Profit before Interest and Taxes (PBIT), Profit before Tax (PBT), and Profit after Tax (PAT) for years 1 through 5.

To create this graph, you first type **/G**raph **T**ype **B**ar. Then enter the specifics by following these steps:

1. Type **X** and then *D28..H28* and press Enter.

2. Type **A** and then *D30..H30* and press Enter.

3. Type **B** and then *D35..H35* and press Enter.

4. Type **C** and then *D40..H40* and press Enter.

Type **V**iew, to see your graph and, to enhance it, add **T**itles and **L**egends.

You also can perform "what-if" scenarios and see their impact on your company's profit and growth rate by changing your first year assumptions and any of the model's constants: the amount of new debt or equity, the composition of debt, interest rates, profitability, tax rate, or your dividend payout percentage. Simply move the cursor to the appropriate cell and enter a new number, press F9 (CALC) and then F10 (GRAPH). In this manner, you can take charge of your business and shape its future.

Conclusion

The Financial Growth Capacity Calculator is a useful forecasting application. You can use the model to see your company's limitations and growth potential in relation to its financial situation. To better manage and understand your business, make the Financial Growth Capacity Calculator part of your planning and reporting system.

```
A1: \=
B1: \=
C1: \=
D1: \=
E1: \=
F1: \=
G1: \=
H1: \=
A3: 'FINANCIAL GROWTH CAPACITY CALCULATOR
E3: '(C) 1987 Que Corporation
A5: \=
B5: \=
C5: \=
D5: \=
E5: \=
F5: \=
G5: \=
H5: \=
A6: 'CAPITALIZATION
D6: ^Year 1
E6: ^Year 2
F6: ^Year 3
G6: ^Year 4
H6: ^Year 5
A7: \=
B7: \=
C7: \=
D7: ' ==========
E7: ' ==========
F7: ' ==========
G7: ' ==========
H7: ' ==========
A8: 'Equity
A9: ' New Equity
E9: +D45
F9: +E45
G9: +F45
H9: +G45
A10: 'Total Equity
D10: 625000
E10: +D10+E9
F10: +E10+F9
G10: +F10+G9
H10: +G10+H9
A12: 'Affordable New Debt
E12: +D23*E10-D21
F12: +E23*F10-E21
G12: +F23*G10-F21
H12: +G23*H10-G21
A14: 'Debt
A15: ' Current Liabilities
D15: 525000
E15: +D15+(E12-(E16-D16)-(E18-D18))
```

```
F15: +E15+(F12-(F16-E16)-(F18-E18))
G15: +F15+(G12-(G16-F16)-(G18-F18))
H15: +G15+(H12-(H16-G16)-(H18-G18))
A16: ' Short term Debt
D16: 130000
E16: +D16
F16: +E16
G16: +F16
H16: +G16
A17: '  ST Interest Rate
D17: (P0) 0.07
E17: (P0) +D17
F17: (P0) +E17
G17: (P0) +F17
H17: (P0) +G17
A18: ' Long Term Debt
D18: 154000
E18: +D18
F18: +E18
G18: +F18
H18: +G18
A19: '  LT Interest Rate
D19: (P1) 0.065
E19: (P0) +D19
F19: (P0) +E19
G19: (P0) +F19
H19: (P0) +G19
A21: 'Total Debt
D21: +D15+D16+D18
E21: +E15+E16+E18
F21: +F15+F16+F18
G21: +G15+G16+G18
H21: +H15+H16+H18
A23: 'Debt Equity Ratio
D23: (F2) +D21/D10
E23: (F2) +E21/E10
F23: (F2) +F21/F10
G23: (F2) +G21/G10
H23: (F2) +H21/H10
A25: 'Total Assets
D25: +D10+D21
E25: +E10+E21
F25: +F10+F21
G25: +G10+G21
H25: +H10+H21
A27: \=
B27: \=
C27: \=
D27: \=
E27: \=
F27: \=
G27: \=
H27: \=
```

A28: 'PROFITABILITY
D28: ^Year 1
E28: ^Year 2
F28: ^Year 3
G28: ^Year 4
H28: ^Year 5
A29: \=
B29: \=
C29: \=
D29: ' ==========
E29: ' ==========
F29: ' ==========
G29: ' ==========
H29: ' ==========
A30: 'Profit before Interest and Taxes
D30: 175000
E30: +E31*E25
F30: +F31*F25
G30: +G31*G25
H30: +H31*H25
A31: 'Return on Assets
D31: (P2) +D30/D25
E31: (P2) +D31
F31: (P2) +E31
G31: (P2) +F31
H31: (P2) +G31
A33: 'Interest Expense
D33: +D19*D18+D17*D16
E33: +E19*E18+E17*E16
F33: +F19*F18+F17*F16
G33: +G19*G18+G17*G16
H33: +H19*H18+H17*H16
D34: ' --------
E34: ' --------
F34: ' --------
G34: ' --------
H34: ' --------
A35: 'Profit before Tax
D35: +D30-D33
E35: +E30-E33
F35: +F30-F33
G35: +G30-G33
H35: +H30-H33
A36: 'Tax Rate
D36: (P0) +D38/D35
E36: (P0) +D36
F36: (P0) +E36
G36: (P0) +F36
H36: (P0) +G36
D37: ' --------
E37: ' --------
F37: ' --------
G37: ' --------
H37: ' --------
A38: 'Tax Expense

D38: 48900
E38: +E35*E36
F38: +F35*F36
G38: +G35*G36
H38: +H35*H36
D39: ' --------
E39: ' --------
F39: ' --------
G39: ' --------
H39: ' --------
A40: 'Profit after Tax
D40: +D35-D38
E40: +E35-E38
F40: +F35-F38
G40: +G35-G38
H40: +H35-H38
A42: 'Dividend payout percentage
D42: (P2) +D43/D40
E42: (P2) +D42
F42: (P2) +E42
G42: (P2) +F42
H42: (P2) +G42
A43: 'Dividends paid
D43: 0
E43: +E42*E40
F43: +F42*F40
G43: +G42*G40
H43: +H42*H40
D44: ' --------
E44: ' --------
F44: ' --------
G44: ' --------
H44: ' --------
A45: 'Earnings Reinvested
D45: +D40-D43
E45: +E40-E43
F45: +F40-F43
G45: +G40-G43
H45: +H40-H43
D46: ' ========
E46: ' ========
F46: ' ========
G46: ' ========
H46: ' ========
A48: 'Net Return on Equity
D48: (P0) +D40/D10
E48: (P0) +E40/E10
F48: (P0) +F40/F10
G48: (P0) +G40/G10
H48: (P0) +H40/H10
A51: 'Sustainable Growth Rate
D51: (P0) (1-D42)*D48
E51: (P0) (1-E42)*E48
F51: (P0) (1-F42)*F48
G51: (P0) (1-G42)*G48
H51: (P0) (1-H42)*H48

IV
Managing Debt

10

Tracking a Line
of Credit

Introduction

If you need short-term financing to be in business, you know the importance of accurately managing this source of financing. You need to know the cost of your line of credit, when your bank requires repayment, and when your current line is no longer adequate. The 1-2-3 Line-of-Credit Tracker can monitor your line of credit daily and furnish you with important statistical information to help you use these funds wisely.

This chapter explores how this valuable application operates. The chapter also explains how to create the model and suggests ways of adapting the Line-of-Credit Tracker to your business.

The Line-of-Credit Tracker comprises two sections—Daily Activity and Statistics (see fig. 10.1).

Creating the Model

To create this simple model, you must start with a blank 1-2-3 spreadsheet. First change the column widths, then enter the the row titles and column headings. Next, format the worksheet and enter the formulas and functions. The following steps will guide you through the process, which is quick and easy.

```
        A       B       C       D       E       F       G       H
1  ==========================================================================
2
3  LINE OF CREDIT TRACKER            Copyright (C) 1987 Que Corporation
4
5  ==========================================================================
6  DAILY ACTIVITY
7  ==========================================================================
8
9        Beginning Balance:                            $25,000
10       Credit Limit:                                 $100,000
11
12                              Annual
13            New             Interest Interest            Available
14  Date   Borrowings Repayments Rate   Expense   Balance   Credit
15  ------ ---------- ---------- -------- --------- ---------- --------
16  01-Jan                       7.50%    $5.14    $25,005   $74,995
17  02-Jan  $25,000              7.50%   $10.28    $25,015   $74,985
18  03-Jan                       7.50%    $5.14    $50,021   $49,979
19  04-Jan                       7.50%   $10.28    $50,031   $49,969
20  05-Jan                       7.50%   $10.28    $50,041   $49,959
21  06-Jan                       7.50%   $10.28    $50,051   $49,949
22  07-Jan                       7.00%    $9.60    $50,061   $49,939
23  08-Jan                       7.00%    $9.60    $50,071   $49,929
24  09-Jan                       7.00%    $9.60    $50,080   $49,920
25  10-Jan            $10,000    7.00%    $7.69    $50,088   $49,912
26  11-Jan                       7.00%    $9.61    $40,097   $59,903
27  12-Jan                       7.00%    $7.69    $40,105   $59,895
28  13-Jan                       7.00%    $7.69    $40,113   $59,887
29  14-Jan                       7.00%    $7.69    $40,121   $59,879
30  15-Jan  $25,000              7.00%   $12.49    $40,133   $59,867
31  16-Jan                       7.00%    $7.70    $65,141   $34,859
32  17-Jan                       7.00%   $12.49    $65,153   $34,847
33  18-Jan                       7.00%   $12.50    $65,166   $34,834
34  19-Jan                       7.00%   $12.50    $65,178   $34,822
35  20-Jan            $10,000    7.00%   $10.58    $65,189   $34,811
36  21-Jan                       7.00%   $12.50    $55,201   $44,799
37  22-Jan                       7.00%   $10.59    $55,212   $44,788
38  23-Jan                       7.00%   $10.59    $55,222   $44,778
39  24-Jan                       7.00%   $10.59    $55,233   $44,767
40  25-Jan                       7.00%   $10.59    $55,244   $44,756
41  26-Jan                       7.00%   $10.59    $55,254   $44,746
42  27-Jan                       7.00%   $10.60    $55,265   $44,735
43  28-Jan                       7.50%   $11.36    $55,276   $44,724
44  29-Jan                       7.50%   $11.36    $55,288   $44,712
45  30-Jan            $10,000    7.50%    $9.31    $55,297   $44,703
46  31-Jan                       7.50%   $11.36    $45,308   $54,692
47
48
49
50  ==========================================================================
51  STATISTICS
52  ==========================================================================
53
54       Average Interest Rate            7.16%
55       Total Interest Expense          $308.25
56       Annualized Interest Expense   $3,698.99
57
58       Average Outstanding Balance   $50,796
59       Maximum Balance               $65,189
60       Minimum Balance               $25,005
61       Ending Balance                $45,308
```

Fig. 10.1. The Line-of-Credit Tracker.

First, change the column widths to match this listing:

Column	Width
A	8
B, C, F, G	11
D	9
E	10

You can use the **/W**orksheet **G**lobal **C**olumn-Width command and change the widths of all columns to eleven. Then adjust the widths of columns A, D, and E accordingly.

Next, enter the row titles and column headings, according to table 10.1 or to one of your own design. For additional information, refer to the complete cell listing at the end of this chapter.

Table 10.1
Row Titles and Column Headings

Enter into cell:	Original label:	Copy to:
	Opening Headings	
A1:	\=	B1..H1, A5..H5, A7..H7, A50..G50, A52..G52
A3:	'LINE OF CREDIT TRACKER	
	Daily Activity	
A6:	'DAILY ACTIVITY	
B9:	'Beginning Balance:	
B10:	'Credit Limit:	
D12:	' Annual	
B13:	^New	
D13:	' Interest	
E13:	' Interest	
G13:	' Available	
A14:	' Date	
B14:	'Borrowings	
C14:	'Repayments	
D14:	' Rate	
E14:	' Expense	
F14:	' Balance	
G14:	' Credit	
A15:	'------	
B15:	'----------	C15, F15, G15
D15:	'--------	
E15:	'---------	

Enter
into
cell: Original label: Copy to:

Statistics

A51:   'STATISTICS
B54:   'Average Interest Rate
B55:   'Total Interest Expense
B56:   'Annualized Interest Expense
B58:   'Average Outstanding Balance
B59:   'Maximum Balance
B60:   'Minimum Balance
B61:   'Ending Balance

You can now format your worksheet to match the list in table 10.2 (or use your own formats).

Table 10.2
Cell Formats

Format	Column or Cell
Daily Activity	
/rfd2	Column A
/rfc0	Column B,C
/rfp0	Column D
/rfc2	Column E
/rfc0	Column F,G
Statistics	
/rfp2	E54
/rfc2	E55, E56
/rfc0	E58, E59, E60, E61

Now enter the model's formulas according to table 10.3. Don't forget to leave the worksheet in automatic recalculation mode.

Table 10.3
Formulas and Functions

Enter into cell:	Original formula:	Copy to:
	Daily Activity	
A16:	@DATE	
E16:	+D16/365*(G9+B16-C16)	
F16:	+G9+B16-C16+E16	
G16:	+$G$10-F16	G17..G46
A17:	+A16+1	A18..A46
D17:	+D16	D18..D46
E17:	+D17/365*(F16+B16-C17)	E18..E46
F17:	+F16+B16-C16+E17	F18..F46
	Statistics	
E54:	@AVG(D16..D46)	
E55:	@SUM(E16..E46)	
E56:	+E55*12	
E58:	@AVG(F16..F46)	
E59:	@MAX(F16..F46)	
E60:	@MIN(F16..F46)	
E61:	+F46	

Understanding the Model

Discussion of the first module, Daily Activity, is followed by an explanation of the Statistics section.

The Daily Activity Module

Figure 10.2 displays the important elements of the Daily Activity module, which is located in cells A5 through G46.

This section of the application calculates your daily interest cost, outstanding balance, and available credit based on your arrangements with your bank and any repayments or new borrowings you may make during the month.

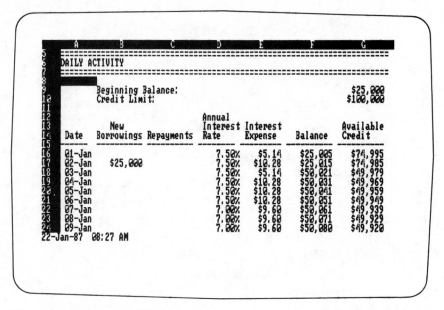

Fig. 10.2. The Daily Activity module.

To perform these operations, the model relies on columns A through D as data-entry areas for Date, New Borrowings, Repayments, and Annual Interest Rate information, respectively. The remaining columns, E through G, will be calculated for you. The Statistics section uses the columns to summarize your line of credit activity for the month.

To help you understand how the module operates, each column's function is addressed separately. Column E, for example, calculates your Daily Interest expense. In the formula in cell E17:

E17: +D17/365*(F16+B16-C16)

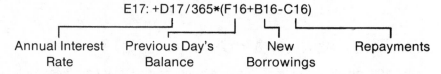

| Annual Interest Rate | Previous Day's Balance | New Borrowings | Repayments |

D17 (your annual interest rate) is divided by 365 days to arrive at a daily interest rate. The daily interest rate is multiplied by the previous day's balance plus any new borrowings less any repayments you may have made. This calculation gives you your interest expense for the day.

Subsequent days are computed in the same way, the only difference being the first day of the month. For the first day's interest expense, your interest expense is based on your beginning line of credit balance (G9) plus any new borrowings (B16), less any repayments (C16), both on the first day of the month.

Column F displays your daily outstanding balance, which is calculated, for example, by the formula in cell F17:

F17: +F16+B16-C16+E17

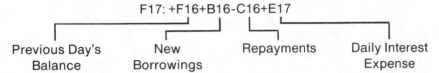

| Previous Day's Balance | New Borrowings | Repayments | Daily Interest Expense |

This formula adds your previous day's outstanding loan balance to any new borrowings, less any repayments, plus your daily interest expense. Like column E, this equation is repeated on a relative basis for each subsequent day. Again, the only difference is the first day of the month, where the previous day's balance (F16) is replaced by your Beginning Balance (G9).

Column G calculates your remaining available credit balance. In cell G17, for example, this is simply

G17: +$G$10-F17

G10 is your previous day's available credit balance less today's outstanding balance. The following days are calculated similarly.

At this point, the model has performed all your short-term credit line calculations, which will be summarized in the Statistics module.

The Statistics Module

The Statistics module, located directly below the Daily Activity module in cells A50 through E61, is shown in figure 10.3.

This section provides you with summary information about your line of credit activity for the month. To accomplish this, the model uses several 1-2-3 @Functions.

For example, cell E54 calculates your Average Interest Rate with the formula

E54: @AVG(D16..D46)

Your Total Interest Expense is computed next in cell E55. This is simply

E55: @SUM(E16..E46)

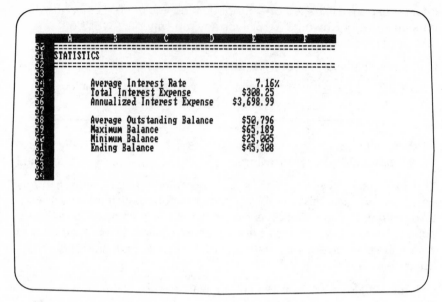

Fig. 10.3. The Statistics module.

This amount is then annualized to give you an estimate of your interest cost for one year. Your Annualized Interest Cost, in cell E56, is

E56: +E55*12

Your Average Outstanding Balance indicates the extent of reliance on your company's line of credit. In cell E58, this is calculated by the function

E58: @AVG(F16..F46)

Cells E59 and E60 calculate your Maximum and Minimum Balances, respectively. Cell E59 contains the function

E59: @MAX(F16..F46)

and cell E60 utilizes the function

E60: @MIN(F16..F46)

Finally, your Ending Balance in cell E61 is calculated by referencing cell F46:

E61: +F46

As you can see, the Line-of-Credit Tracker is straight-forward and easy to understand.

Using the Model

The Line-of-Credit Tracker is easy to use. Each month, enter your company's outstanding line-of-credit balance in cell G9 and your beginning interest rate in cell D16. You enter your Credit Limit only once (in cell G10) unless you receive an increase or decrease in the amount of money you can borrow on a short-term basis.

Enter any new borrowings in column B, and any repayments in column C. If the interest rate on your line of credit changes, update your model by entering the new rate (as a decimal) in column D. Because the application is in automatic recalculation, these changes will be reflected immediately in the model.

Instead of using the @DATE function to enter the new day in the date column, simply add 1 to the previous day. If the interest rate remains the same, place your cursor in the cell displaying the interest rate. Type +, move the cursor up one cell, and press {ENTER}. This will carry the previous interest rate down, and you can then /Copy the interest rate to any remaining cells in column D. (Refer to table 10.3.)

Consider some of the following modifications to the Line-of- Credit Tracker. Many businesses have their line of credit interest rate tied to the Prime Interest Rate. If yours is one of these companies, column D can be modified to reflect the linked rates. For example, if your short-term interest rate is "prime plus two," and the prime rate is 7.5%, enter .075 in cell G11 and label cell B11 as the "prime rate." Next, enter the following formula in cell D16:

D16: $G$11+0.02

All you have to do to reflect an increase or decrease in your interest rate is press F2 (EDIT) and change the prime rate or the number of points that you are being charged in cell D16.

You can keep a history of several months' short-term credit experience, calculating monthly, quarterly, and annual averages on your outstanding principal. Consider using a separate 1-2-3 spreadsheet to record your totals and averages, or creating at the bottom of this model a History Table similar to that in Chapter 7's Ratio Analyzer.

If you have several lines of credit with more than one lender, consider creating one generic Line-of-Credit Tracker, customizing one for each financial institution and then using /File Combine Add Named/ Specified-Range on a separate spreadsheet as a summary.

Conclusion

The Line-of-Credit Tracker is a simple but useful model that you can apply almost immediately to your business. Use the application to monitor your short-term credit usage and as an audit mechanism for your bank-generated statements.

```
A1: [W8] \=
B1: [W11] \=
C1: [W11] \=
D1: [W9] \=
E1: [W10] \=
F1: [W11] \=
G1: [W11] \=
H1: \=
A3: [W8] 'LINE OF CREDIT TRACKER
D3: [W9] '        Copyright (C) 1987 Que Corporation
A5: [W8] \=
B5: [W11] \=
C5: [W11] \=
D5: [W9] \=
E5: [W10] \=
F5: [W11] \=
G5: [W11] \=
H5: \=
A6: [W8] 'DAILY ACTIVITY
A7: [W8] \=
B7: [W11] \=
C7: [W11] \=
D7: [W9] \=
E7: [W10] \=
F7: [W11] \=
G7: [W11] \=
H7: \=
B9: [W11] 'Beginning Balance:
G9: [W11] 25000
B10: [W11] 'Credit Limit:
G10: [W11] 100000
D12: [W9] ' Annual
B13: [W11] ^New
D13: [W9] ' Interest
E13: [W10] ' Interest
G13: [W11] ' Available
A14: [W8] ' Date
B14: [W11] 'Borrowings
C14: [W11] 'Repayments
D14: [W9] ' Rate
E14: [W10] ' Expense
F14: [W11] '  Balance
G14: [W11] ' Credit
A15: [W8] '------
B15: [W11] '----------
C15: [W11] '----------
D15: [W9] '--------
E15: [W10] '---------
F15: [W11] '----------
G15: [W11] '----------
A16: (D2) [W8] @DATE(87,1,1)
D16: (P2) [W9] 0.075
E16: (C2) [W10] +D16/365*(G9+B16-C16)
F16: [W11] +G9+B16-C16+E16
G16: [W11] +$G$10-F16
A17: (D2) [W8] +A16+1
B17: [W11] 25000
D17: (P2) [W9] +D16
E17: (C2) [W10] +D17/365*(F16+B17-C17)
F17: [W11] +F16+B16-C16+E17
G17: [W11] +$G$10-F17
A18: (D2) [W8] +A17+1
D18: (P2) [W9] +D17
E18: (C2) [W10] +D18/365*(F17+B18-C18)
F18: [W11] +F17+B17-C17+E18
G18: [W11] +$G$10-F18
A19: (D2) [W8] +A18+1
D19: (P2) [W9] +D18
E19: (C2) [W10] +D19/365*(F18+B19-C19)
F19: [W11] +F18+B18-C18+E19
G19: [W11] +$G$10-F19
A20: (D2) [W8] +A19+1
D20: (P2) [W9] +D19
E20: (C2) [W10] +D20/365*(F19+B20-C20)
F20: [W11] +F19+B19-C19+E20
G20: [W11] +$G$10-F20
A21: (D2) [W8] +A20+1
D21: (P2) [W9] +D20
E21: (C2) [W10] +D21/365*(F20+B21-C21)
F21: [W11] +F20+B20-C20+E21
G21: [W11] +$G$10-F21
A22: (D2) [W8] +A21+1
D22: (P2) [W9] 0.07
E22: (C2) [W10] +D22/365*(F21+B22-C22)
F22: [W11] +F21+B21-C21+E22
G22: [W11] +$G$10-F22
A23: (D2) [W8] +A22+1
D23: (P2) [W9] +D22
E23: (C2) [W10] +D23/365*(F22+B23-C23)
F23: [W11] +F22+B22-C22+E23
G23: [W11] +$G$10-F23
A24: (D2) [W8] +A23+1
D24: (P2) [W9] +D23
E24: (C2) [W10] +D24/365*(F23+B24-C24)
F24: [W11] +F23+B23-C23+E24
G24: [W11] +$G$10-F24
A25: (D2) [W8] +A24+1
C25: [W11] 10000
D25: (P2) [W9] +D24
E25: (C2) [W10] +D25/365*(F24+B25-C25)
F25: [W11] +F24+B24-C24+E25
G25: [W11] +$G$10-F25
A26: (D2) [W8] +A25+1
D26: (P2) [W9] +D25
E26: (C2) [W10] +D26/365*(F25+B26-C26)
F26: [W11] +F25+B25-C25+E26
```

```
G26: [W11] +$G$10-F26
A27: (D2) [W8] +A26+1
D27: (P2) [W9] +D26
E27: (C2) [W10] +D27/365*(F26+B27-C27)
F27: [W11] +F26+B26-C26+E27
G27: [W11] +$G$10-F27
A28: (D2) [W8] +A27+1
D28: (P2) [W9] 0.07
E28: (C2) [W10] +D28/365*(F27+B28-C28)
F28: [W11] +F27+B27-C27+E28
G28: [W11] +$G$10-F28
A29: (D2) [W8] +A28+1
D29: (P2) [W9] +D28
E29: (C2) [W10] +D29/365*(F28+B29-C29)
F29: [W11] +F28+B28-C28+E29
G29: [W11] +$G$10-F29
A30: (D2) [W8] +A29+1
B30: [W11] 25000
D30: (P2) [W9] +D29
E30: (C2) [W10] +D30/365*(F29+B30-C30)
F30: [W11] +F29+B29-C29+E30
G30: [W11] +$G$10-F30
A31: (D2) [W8] +A30+1
D31: (P2) [W9] +D30
E31: (C2) [W10] +D31/365*(F30+B31-C31)
F31: [W11] +F30+B30-C30+E31
G31: [W11] +$G$10-F31
A32: (D2) [W8] +A31+1
D32: (P2) [W9] +D31
E32: (C2) [W10] +D32/365*(F31+B32-C32)
F32: [W11] +F31+B31-C31+E32
G32: [W11] +$G$10-F32
A33: (D2) [W8] +A32+1
D33: (P2) [W9] +D32
E33: (C2) [W10] +D33/365*(F32+B33-C33)
F33: [W11] +F32+B32-C32+E33
G33: [W11] +$G$10-F33
A34: (D2) [W8] +A33+1
D34: (P2) [W9] +D33
E34: (C2) [W10] +D34/365*(F33+B34-C34)
F34: [W11] +F33+B33-C33+E34
G34: [W11] +$G$10-F34
A35: (D2) [W8] +A34+1
C35: [W11] 10000
D35: (P2) [W9] +D34
E35: (C2) [W10] +D35/365*(F34+B35-C35)
F35: [W11] +F34+B34-C34+E35
G35: [W11] +$G$10-F35
A36: (D2) [W8] +A35+1
D36: (P2) [W9] +D35
E36: (C2) [W10] +D36/365*(F35+B36-C36)
F36: [W11] +F35+B35-C35+E36
G36: [W11] +$G$10-F36
```

```
A37: (D2) [W8] +A36+1
D37: (P2) [W9] +D36
E37: (C2) [W10] +D37/365*(F36+B37-C37)
F37: [W11] +F36+B36-C36+E37
G37: [W11] +$G$10-F37
A38: (D2) [W8] +A37+1
D38: (P2) [W9] +D37
E38: (C2) [W10] +D38/365*(F37+B38-C38)
F38: [W11] +F37+B37-C37+E38
G38: [W11] +$G$10-F38
A39: (D2) [W8] +A38+1
D39: (P2) [W9] +D38
E39: (C2) [W10] +D39/365*(F38+B39-C39)
F39: [W11] +F38+B38-C38+E39
G39: [W11] +$G$10-F39
A40: (D2) [W8] +A39+1
D40: (P2) [W9] +D39
E40: (C2) [W10] +D40/365*(F39+B40-C40)
F40: [W11] +F39+B39-C39+E40
G40: [W11] +$G$10-F40
A41: (D2) [W8] +A40+1
D41: (P2) [W9] +D40
E41: (C2) [W10] +D41/365*(F40+B41-C41)
F41: [W11] +F40+B40-C40+E41
G41: [W11] +$G$10-F41
A42: (D2) [W8] +A41+1
D42: (P2) [W9] +D41
E42: (C2) [W10] +D42/365*(F41+B42-C42)
F42: [W11] +F41+B41-C41+E42
G42: [W11] +$G$10-F42
A43: (D2) [W8] +A42+1
D43: (P2) [W9] 0.075
E43: (C2) [W10] +D43/365*(F42+B43-C43)
F43: [W11] +F42+B42-C42+E43
G43: [W11] +$G$10-F43
A44: (D2) [W8] +A43+1
D44: (P2) [W9] +D43
E44: (C2) [W10] +D44/365*(F43+B44-C44)
F44: [W11] +F43+B43-C43+E44
G44: [W11] +$G$10-F44
A45: (D2) [W8] +A44+1
C45: [W11] 10000
D45: (P2) [W9] +D44
E45: (C2) [W10] +D45/365*(F44+B45-C45)
F45: [W11] +F44+B44-C44+E45
G45: [W11] +$G$10-F45
A46: (D2) [W8] +A45+1
D46: (P2) [W9] +D45
E46: (C2) [W10] +D46/365*(F45+B46-C46)
F46: [W11] +F45+B45-C45+E46
G46: [W11] +$G$10-F46
A50: (D2) [W8] \=
B50: (D2) [W11] \=
```

C50: (D2) [W11] \=
D50: (D2) [W9] \=
E50: (D2) [W10] \=
F50: (D2) [W11] \=
G50: (D2) [W11] \=
A51: (D2) [W8] 'STATISTICS
A52: (D2) [W8] \=
B52: (D2) [W11] \=
C52: (D2) [W11] \=
D52: (D2) [W9] \=
E52: (D2) [W10] \=
F52: (D2) [W11] \=
G52: (D2) [W11] \=
B54: [W11] 'Average Interest Rate
E54: (P2) [W10] @AVG(D16..D46)
B55: [W11] 'Total Interest Expense
E55: (C2) [W10] @SUM(E16..E46)
B56: [W11] 'Annualized Interest Expense
E56: (C2) [W10] +E55*12
B58: [W11] 'Average Outstanding Balance
E58: [W10] @AVG(F16..F46)
B59: [W11] 'Maximum Balance
E59: [W10] @MAX(F16..F46)
B60: [W11] 'Minimum Balance
E60: [W10] @MIN(F16..F46)
B61: [W11] 'Ending Balance
E61: [W10] +F46

11

Amortizing a Loan

Introduction

One common use of 1-2-3 is to calculate loan amortization schedules. In the blink of an eye, you can obtain a schedule of loan payments and determine what effect overpaying would have on your loan. Although you may be using your own model, the application in this chapter has certain special attributes that you may want to incorporate into your loan amortization spreadsheet.

The 1-2-3 Loan Amortization Calculator is composed of four sections: Terms of Loan, Amortization Schedule, the Criterion, Statistics, and Output Ranges, and a macro (see fig. 11.1).

The model requires the first two sections (your loan and amortization schedule) to calculate and amortize your loan properly. The Criterion, Statistics, and Output Ranges are for data-management functions; you will not need this section if you don't plan to perform data-management analysis. Finally, the \a macro will adjust the amortization table to the number of months your loan is to be amortized.

Creating the Model

You should find the Loan Amortization Calculator, which is relatively small, easy to create. Using a blank 1-2-3 spreadsheet, change your column widths according to this table:

Column	Width
A, C, J	7
B, K, L, N	12
D, E, F, G	11
H	8

```
      A        B        C        D        E        F        G        H        I        J        K        L        M        N
 1 ====================================================================================================================
 2
 3 LOAN AMORTIZATION CALCULATOR      Copyright (C) Que Corporation 1987
 4
 5 ====================================================================================================================
 6 TERMS OF LOAN                                          CRITERION RANGE
 7 ====================================================================================================================
 8     First Payment Date              28-Jan-87      Payment   Payment   Current            Interest Principal Principal
 9     Principal Borrowed              $10,000        Number    Date      Rate    Payment    Portion  Portion   Balance
10     Term in Months                  36
11     Beginning Interest Rate         9.75%
12     Payment                         $321.50
13
14 ====================================================================================================================
15 AMORTIZATION SCHEDULE                                  STATISTICS RANGE
16 ====================================================================================================================
17
18 Payment  Payment   Current          Interest Principal Principal Beginning Balance      $9,759.75 Interest Paid       $842.61
19 Number   Date      Rate    Payment  Portion  Portion   Balance   Ending Balance         $6,984.62 Principal Paid    $3,015.38
20    1     28-Jan-87 9.75%   $321.50  $81.25   $240.25   $9,759.75 =========================================================
21    2     28-Feb-87 9.75%   $321.50  $79.30   $242.20   $9,517.55 OUTPUT RANGE
22    3     28-Mar-87 9.75%   $321.50  $77.33   $244.17   $9,273.38
23    4     28-Apr-87 9.75%   $321.50  $75.35   $246.15   $9,027.23 Payment   Payment   Current            Interest Principal Principal
24    5     28-May-87 9.75%   $321.50  $73.35   $248.15   $8,779.07 Number    Date      Rate    Payment    Portion  Portion   Balance
25    6     28-Jun-87 9.75%   $321.50  $71.33   $250.17   $8,528.90    1 28-Jan-87  9.75%  $321.50    $81.25   $240.25  $9,759.75
26    7     28-Jul-87 9.75%   $321.50  $69.30   $252.20   $8,276.70    2 28-Feb-87  9.75%  $321.50    $79.30   $242.20  $9,517.55
27    8     28-Aug-87 9.75%   $321.50  $67.25   $254.25   $8,022.45    3 28-Mar-87  9.75%  $321.50    $77.33   $244.17  $9,273.38
28    9     28-Sep-87 9.75%   $321.50  $65.18   $256.32   $7,766.13    4 28-Apr-87  9.75%  $321.50    $75.35   $246.15  $9,027.23
29   10     28-Oct-87 9.75%   $321.50  $63.10   $258.40   $7,507.73    5 28-May-87  9.75%  $321.50    $73.35   $248.15  $8,779.07
30   11     28-Nov-87 9.75%   $321.50  $61.00   $260.50   $7,247.24    6 28-Jun-87  9.75%  $321.50    $71.33   $250.17  $8,528.90
31   12     28-Dec-87 9.75%   $321.50  $58.88   $262.62   $6,984.62    7 28-Jul-87  9.75%  $321.50    $69.30   $252.20  $8,276.70
32   13     28-Jan-88 9.75%   $321.50  $56.75   $264.75   $6,719.87    8 28-Aug-87  9.75%  $321.50    $67.25   $254.25  $8,022.45
33   14     28-Feb-88 9.75%   $321.50  $54.60   $266.90   $6,452.97    9 28-Sep-87  9.75%  $321.50    $65.18   $256.32  $7,766.13
34   15     28-Mar-88 9.75%   $321.50  $52.43   $269.07   $6,183.90   10 28-Oct-87  9.75%  $321.50    $63.10   $258.40  $7,507.73
35   16     28-Apr-88 9.75%   $321.50  $50.24   $271.26   $5,912.65   11 28-Nov-87  9.75%  $321.50    $61.00   $260.50  $7,247.24
36   17     28-May-88 9.75%   $321.50  $48.04   $273.46   $5,639.19   12 28-Dec-87  9.75%  $321.50    $58.88   $262.62  $6,984.62
37   18     28-Jun-88 9.75%   $321.50  $45.82   $275.68   $5,363.51
38   19     28-Jul-88 9.75%   $321.50  $43.58   $277.92   $5,085.58
39   20     28-Aug-88 9.75%   $321.50  $41.32   $280.18   $4,805.41
40   21     28-Sep-88 9.75%   $321.50  $39.04   $282.46   $4,522.95
41   22     28-Oct-88 9.75%   $321.50  $36.75   $284.75   $4,238.20
42   23     28-Nov-88 9.75%   $321.50  $34.44   $287.06   $3,951.14
43   24     28-Dec-88 9.75%   $321.50  $32.10   $289.40   $3,661.74
44   25     28-Jan-89 9.75%   $321.50  $29.75   $291.75   $3,369.99
45   26     28-Feb-89 9.75%   $321.50  $27.38   $294.12   $3,075.87
46   27     28-Mar-89 9.75%   $321.50  $24.99   $296.51   $2,779.36
47   28     28-Apr-89 9.75%   $321.50  $22.58   $298.92   $2,480.45
48   29     28-May-89 9.75%   $321.50  $20.15   $301.35   $2,179.10
49   30     28-Jun-89 9.75%   $321.50  $17.71   $303.79   $1,875.31
50   31     28-Jul-89 9.75%   $321.50  $15.24   $306.26   $1,569.05
51   32     28-Aug-89 9.75%   $321.50  $12.75   $308.75   $1,260.29
52   33     28-Sep-89 9.75%   $321.50  $10.24   $311.26     $949.03
53   34     28-Oct-89 9.75%   $321.50  $7.71    $313.79     $635.25
54   35     28-Nov-89 9.75%   $321.50  $5.16    $316.34     $318.91
55   36     28-Dec-89 9.75%   $321.50  $2.59    $318.91       $0.00
56
57 ==========================================================
58 MACRO
59 ==========================================================
60
61 \a      {RECALC COUNT_ROWS}                      Calculate Count_rows
62         {GETNUMBER "How many rows do you need (greater than 35)? ",NEW_ROWS}
63         {PANELOFF}{WINDOWSOFF}                   Total Length;off screen
64         {IF NEW_ROWS<36}{HOME}{QUIT}             Must be > 35; Go to Home and Quit
65         {IF COUNT_ROWS=NEW_ROWS}{HOME}{QUIT}     Quit if rows exist
66         {IF NEW_ROWS<COUNT_ROWS}{BRANCH DEL_ROW} Decide to add or del
67         {GOTO}TOTAL_ROWS~                        Move to Total_rows
68         +NEW_ROWS-COUNT_ROWS-1~                  Formula for Total_rows
69         {RECALC ADD}                             Calulate ADD
70         {GOTO}AMORT_TABLE~                       Move to Amort. Table
71         {END}{DOWN}                              End of Amort. Table
72         /wir                                     Insert Row
73 ADD     {DOWN -1}                                Number of rows to insert
74         ~{UP}/c.{END}{RIGHT}~                    Copy the formulas
75         {DOWN}.{END}{DOWN}~{HOME}                Area to copy to
76         {PANELON}{WINDOWSON}{BEEP 4}             Panel & Windows on; Beep when finished
77
78 DEL_ROW {GOTO}TOTAL_ROWS~                        Move to Total_rows
79         {RECALC DEL}                             Calculate Del
80         {GOTO}AMORT_TABLE~                       Move to Amort. Table
81 DEL     {DOWN 36}                                Move down rows
82         /wdr                                     Delete rows
83         {END}{DOWN}{UP}~                         All but last row
84         {UP}/c{END}{RIGHT}~                      Copy Formulas
85         {DOWN}~{HOME}                            Area to copy to
86         {PANELON}{WINDOWSON}{BEEP 4}             Panel & Windows on; Beep when finished
87
88         COUNT_ROWS      NEW_ROWS  TOTAL_ROWS
89         36              36        -1
```

Fig. 11.1. The Loan Amortization Calculator.

Next, enter the model's row titles, column headings, and other labels according to table 11.1 or to your own business's format.

Table 11.1
Row Titles and Column Headings

Enter into cell:	Original label:	Copy to:
	Opening Headings	
A1:	\=	B1..N1, A5..N5, A7..N7, A14..N14, A16..N16, A57..F57, A59..F59, H20..N20, H22..N22
A3:	'LOAN AMORTIZATION CALCULATOR	
	Terms of Loan	
A6:	'TERMS OF LOAN	
B8:	'First Payment Date	
B9:	'Principal Borrowed	
B10:	'Term in Months	
B11:	'Beginning Interest Rate	
B12:	'Payment	
	Amortization Schedule	
A18:	'Payment	
B18:	' Payment	
C18:	' Current	
E18:	^Interest	
F18:	^Principal	G18
A19:	'Number	
B19:	' Date	
C19:	' Rate	
D19:	^ Payment	
E19:	^Portion	F19

Enter
into
cell: Original label:

Macro

A61:   '\a
B61:   '{RECALC COUNT_ROWS}
F61:   'Calculate Count_rows
B62:   '{GETNUMBER "How many rows do
        you need (greater than 35)? ",NEW_ROWS}
B63:   '{PANELOFF}{WINDOWSOFF}
F63:   'Total Length;off screen
B64:   '{IF NEW_ROWS<36}{HOME}{QUIT}
F64:   'Must be > 35; Go to Home and Quit
B65:   '{IF COUNT_ROWS=NEW_ROWS}{HOME}{QUIT}
F65:   'Quit if rows exist
B66:   '{IF NEW_ROWS<COUNT_ROWS}{BRANCH DEL_ROW}
F66:   'Decide to add or del
B67:   '{GOTO}TOTAL_ROWS~
F67:   'Move to Total_rows
B68:   '+NEW_ROWS-COUNT_ROWS-1~
F68:   'Formula for Total_rows
B69:   '{RECALC ADD}
F69:   'Calculate ADD
B70:   '{GOTO}AMORT_TABLE~
F70:   'Move to Amort. Table
B71:   '{END}{DOWN}
F71:   'End of Amort. Table
B72:   '/wir
F72:   'Insert Row
A73:   'ADD
F73:   'Number of rows to insert
B74:   '~{UP}/c.{END}{RIGHT}~
F74:   'Copy the formulas
B75:   '{DOWN}.{END}{DOWN}~{HOME}
F75:   'Area to copy to
B76:   '{PANELON}{WINDOWSON}{BEEP 4}
F76:   'Panel & Windows on; Beep when finished
A78:   'DEL_ROW
B78:   '{GOTO}TOTAL_ROWS~
F78:   'Move to Total_rows
B79:   '{RECALC DEL}

Enter
into
cell: Original label:

Cell	Original label
F79:	'Calculate Del
B80:	'{GOTO}AMORT_TABLE~
F80:	'Move to Amort. Table
A81:	'DEL
F81:	'Move down rows
B82:	'/wdr
F82:	'Delete rows
B83:	'{END}{DOWN}{UP}~
F83:	'All but last row
B84:	'{UP}/c{END}{RIGHT}~
F84:	'Copy Formulas
B85:	'{DOWN}~{HOME}
F85:	'Area to copy to
B86:	'{PANELON}{WINDOWSON}{BEEP 4}
F86:	'Panel & Windows on; Beep when finished
B88:	'COUNT_ROWS
D88:	'NEW_ROWS
E88:	'TOTAL_ROWS

Criterion Range

H6:   'CRITERION RANGE

Cell	Copy From	Copy To
H8	A18..G19	H8

Statistics Range

H15:	'STATISTICS RANGE
H18:	'Beginning Balance
L18:	'Interest Paid
H19:	'Ending Balance
L19:	'Principal Paid

Output Range

H21:   'OUTPUT RANGE

Cell	Copy From	Copy To
H23:	A18..G19	H23

Specifying Cell Formats

Next, format the model, following the suggested list of formats in
table 11.2.

Table 11.2
Cell Formats

Format	Cell/Column
Terms of Loan	
/rfd1	F8
/rfc2	F9
/rfp2	F11
/rfc2	F12
Amortization Schedule	
/rfd1	Column B
/rfp2	Column C
/rfc2	Column D, E, F, G
Statistics Range	
/rfc2	K18, K19, N18, N19

Range Names

The Amortization model uses a total of nine range names (see table
11.3). Although these range names are used primarily with the \a
macro, the model uses AMORT_TABLE with other formulas and
operations.

To create the range names, press **/R**ange **N**ame **C**reate, type the range
name, and press Enter. Then type the range address and press Enter.

The Criterion, Statistics, and Output Ranges

The optional Criterion, Statistics, and Output Ranges are located in
cells H5 through N24 (see fig. 11.2). These ranges can be accessed
easily from cell A1 {HOME} by pressing the Tab key.

Table 11.3
Range Names

Name	Range
ADD	B73
AMORT_TABLE	A19..G55
COUNT_ROWS	B89
DEL	B81
DEL_ROW	B78
NEW _ROWS	D89
TOTAL_ROWS	E89
UP	B81
\A	B61

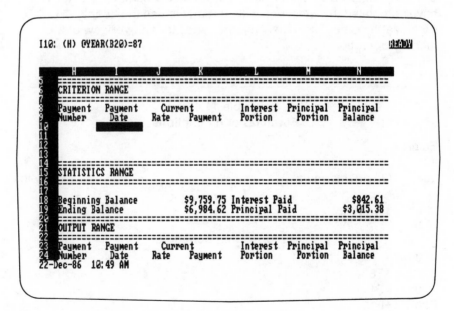

Fig. 11.2. The Criterion, Statistics, and Output Ranges.

To create the ranges needed for extracting data from your amortization table, follow these steps:

1. Press **/D**ata **Q**uery **I**nput.

2. Type *Amort_Table* and press Enter.

3. Press **C**riterion.

4. Type *H9..N10* and press Enter.

5. Press **O**utput.

6. Type *H24..N24* and press Enter.

7. Press **E**xtract **Q**uit.

You now have set up the essential ranges to extract data from your amortization table. After you have completed the amortization table, simply press F7 (QUERY) to extract records.

Now enter the formulas and functions according to table 11.4. For your payment numbers, consider using the **/D**ata **F**ill command. After you have completed this step, you will be ready to use the Loan Amortization Calculator. Now you are ready for an overview of the model's operation.

Table 11.4
Formulas and Functions

Enter into cell:	Original formula:	Copy to:
	Terms of Loan	
F12:	@PMT(F9,F11/12,F10)	
	Amortization Schedule	
A20:	1	
B20:	+F8	
C20:	+F11	
D20:	+F12	
E20:	+C20/12*F9	
F20:	+D20-E20	
G20:	+F9-F20	
A21:	+A20+1	A22..A55

Enter into cell:	Original formula:	Copy to:
B21:	+B20+@CHOOSE(@MONTH(B20) -1,31,@IF(@MOD(@YEAR(B20), 4)=0,29,28),31,30,31,30, 31,31,30,31,30,31)	B22..B55
C21:	+C20	C22..C55
D21:	@IF(C21=C20,@IF(G20 <D20,G20∗(1+C21/12), D20),@PMT(G20,C21/12, $F$10-A21+1))	D22..D55
E21:	+C21/12∗G20	E22..E55
F21:	@IF(G20<0.005,0,D21-E21)	F22..F55
G21:	+G20-F21	5G22..G55

Macro

B73:	+"{DOWN "&@STRING(TOTAL_ROWS,0)&"}"
B81:	+"{DOWN "&@STRING(NEW_ROWS,0)&"}"
B89:	@COUNT(AMORT_TABLE)/7-1
E89:	+NEW_ROWS-COUNT_ROWS-1

Criterion Range

I10:	@YEAR(B20)=87

Statistics

K18:	@DMAX(AMORT_TABLE,6,I9..I10)
N18:	@DSUM(AMORT_TABLE,4,I9..I10)
K19:	@DMIN(AMORT_TABLE,6,I9..I10)
N19:	@DSUM(AMORT_TABLE,5,I9..I10)

Understanding the Model

The Terms of Loan module, which begins at cell A5 and ends at cell F13, is a data-entry worksheet area (see fig. 11.3).

As you can see from figure 11.3, key data about your loan is included here. Your monthly loan payment is computed in cell F12 with the formula

F12: @PMT(F9,F11/12,F10)

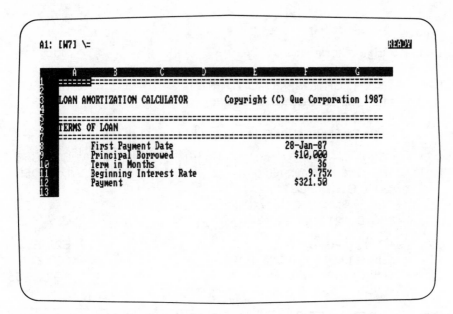

Fig. 11.3. The Terms of Loan Module.

in which F9 is the amount of your loan, the phrase F11/12 represents your monthly interest rate, and F10 is the term (in months) of your loan. The model uses this important information in the next section to build your Amortization Schedule.

The Amortization Schedule

Directly below the Terms of Loan section, the Amortization Schedule module begins at cell A14 and ends, in our example, at cell G56. Figure 11.4 shows the essential elements of this section.

Column A of this module contains your Payment Number. Column B contains the monthly date of your loan payment, as calculated by the model. The first payment date in cell B20 is computed using the formula

   B20: +F8

(Cell F8 contains your First Payment Date from the Terms of Loan section.)

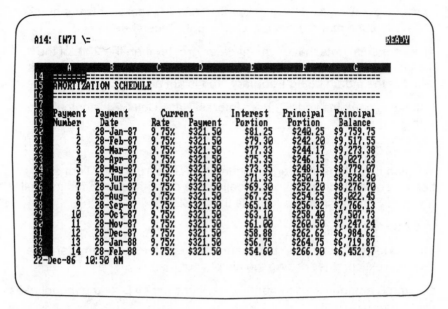

Fig. 11.4. The Amortization Schedule.

Your second payment date, in cell B21, contains the formula

    B21: +B20+@CHOOSE(@MONTH(B20)-1,31,
          @IF(@MOD(@YEAR(B20),4)=0,29,28),
          31,30,31,30,31,31,30,31,30,31)

This lengthy formula computes your payment date in cell B21 by adding
the correct number of days, based on the @CHOOSE function and the
date in cell B20. The @CHOOSE function will select the correct number
of days for the second month, based on the date in cell B20 and the
following 1-2-3 phrases.

The equation's first phrase, *(@MONTH(B20)-1,31,* represents the month
of January, which accommodates 1-2-3's @CHOOSE rules.

The second phrase, *@IF(@MOD(@YEAR(B20),4)=0,29,28),* instructs the
model to determine the number of days in February of the current year,
using the @MOD function. This operation divides the year in cell B20
by four and, depending on the result, selects 29 days for February if the
remainder is zero, or 28 days if there is a remainder. (For example, 28
days will be returned for 1987, because 87/4=21.3.)

The final phrase, *31,30,31,30,31,31,30,31,30,31)*, represents the number of days in each month from March through December.

Make a mental note that payment dates greater than the 28th of the month may change as the amortization schedule continues. This is a result of the month being February, and is not an error.

Column C contains your Current Interest Rate. Cell C20 is calculated with the formula

    C20: +F11

in which cell F11 is the Beginning Interest Rate from your Terms of Loan module. Each subsequent cell in this column references the cell above it. For example, the formula in cell C21 is

    C21: +C20

The model is structured in this manner to accommodate any variable-rate interest changes during the life of your loan.

Column D computes your monthly Payment. In cell D20, the model uses the formula

    D20: +F12

which is, again, a reference to your Payment from the Terms of Loan worksheet area. As in column B, your second payment is computed with a slightly more complex equation. The formula in cell D21 is

    D21: @IF(C21=C20,@IF(G20<D20,G20*(1+C21/12),D20),
         @PMT(G20,C21/12,$F$10-A21+1))

The formula is designed to accommodate any changes in your payment amount or interest rate.

The first phrase, *@IF(C21=C20,@IF(G20<D20,G20*(1+C21/12),D20)*, uses an @IF statement to determine whether the interest rate has changed since the previous month. If not, and if the remaining balance in cell G20 is less than your normal monthly payment (cell D20), your payment will be computed based on the remaining principal balance (G20) and one month's interest (1+C21/12) on this balance.

If the balance in cell D20 is larger than that in cell G20, cell D20's value will be returned. Thus, the possibility of overamortizing your loan is eliminated.

The equation's second phrase, *@PMT(G20,C21/12,$F$10-A21+1))*, addresses the impact of interest rate changes on your loan payment. If you experience such an adjustment, your new payment amount will be calculated by 1-2-3's @PMT function, which multiplies the ending principal balance (G20) by the new monthly interest rate (C21/12) for the new term ($F$10-A21+1) of your loan.

This equation, although somewhat more complicated than other loan-payment formulas, gives you a great deal of flexibility to meet your business needs. You need to enter the equation only once and then copy it.

Column E calculates the Interest Portion of your loan payment. In the formula in cell E20:

   E20: +C20/12*F9

the phrase +C20/12 is your calculated monthly interest rate. Cell F9 contains your beginning principal balance from the Terms of Loan module. This formula is repeated down the column, with cell F9 replaced by the corresponding cell in column G. For example, the equation in cell E21 is

   E21: +C21/12*G20

Column F calculates the principal amount of your loan payment. In cell F20, this amount is

   F20: +D20-E20

which is your loan payment (D20) less the interest portion (E20). The remaining equations in column F enhance the formula in cell F20. For example, in the formula in cell F21:

   F21: @IF(G20<0.005,0,D21-E21)

the addition of the @IF(G20<0.005,0 phrase acts as an electronic brake to stop the amortization process. In this case, if your remaining loan balance is less than 0.005 (this value is used as a substitute for zero, because of 1-2-3's floating-point arithmetic), the principal portion of your payment will be returned as zero. Otherwise, the model subtracts the interest portion (E21) from your total payment (D21).

Finally, column G computes the remaining Principal Balance, which is simply the previous month's principal balance less your principal amount paid. In the formula in cell G20,

   G20: +F9-F20

cell F9 is your initial loan amount and cell F20 is the principal portion of your first loan payment. To calculate your new Principal Balance, subsequent cells in column G reference the appropriate cell in column F (the Principal Portion) and column G (the ending Principal Balance). For example, the formula for cell G21 is

G21: +G20-F21

The remaining cells in column G are computed using formulas that are relative to the one contained in cell G21.

The Criterion, Statistics, and Output Ranges

The Criterion and Output headings follow 1-2-3's data-management protocol and are identical to the Amortization Table's column headings in row 19. Therefore, you can perform data query operations from the Amortization Table to the Output Range. In our example, the /Data Query Extract is executed by placing the following equation in cell I10:

I10: @YEAR(B20)=87

In this equation, the @YEAR phrase selects the year portion of the loan payment from column B of the Amortization Schedule and will obtain all information about 1987 loan payments.

The Statistics subsection provides you with additional information about your loan, based on the criteria in cell I10 of the Criterion Range. For example, the formula in cell K18

K18: @DMAX(AMORT_TABLE,6,I9..I10)

calculates the beginning principal balance for the selected period. Conversely, the equation in cell K19

K19: @DMIN(AMORT_TABLE,6,I9..I10)

computes your ending principal balance for the period.

Cell N18 calculates the total interest paid for this period. The formula is

N18: @DSUM(AMORT_TABLE,4,I9..I10)

Finally, your total principal is calculated in cell N19 with the formula

N19: @DSUM(AMORT_TABLE,5,I9..I10)

Note the similarity among these four formulas, all of which contain the same Input and Criterion Ranges. The formulas differ only in 1) the database function in the first set of equations, and 2) the column offset number in the second set of database functions. These database functions provide you with more useful information than a simple amortization schedule only.

The \a Macro

The \a macro, shown in figure 11.5, can be used to adjust the
Amortization Schedule loans with terms longer than 36 months.

```
        A       B        C        D       E        F         G
61  \a      {RECALC COUNT_ROWS}                    Calculate Count_rows
62          {GETNUMBER "How many rows do you need (greater than 35)? ",NEW_RO
63          {PANELOFF}{WINDOWSOFF}                 Total Length;off screen
64          {IF NEW_ROWS<36}{HOME}{QUIT}           Must be > 35; Go to Home
65          {IF COUNT_ROWS=NEW_ROWS}{HOME}{QUIT}   Quit if rows exist
66          {IF NEW_ROWS<COUNT_ROWS}{BRANCH DEL_ROW} Decide to add or del
67          {GOTO}TOTAL_ROWS~                      Move to Total_rows
68          +NEW_ROWS-COUNT_ROWS-1~                Formula for Total_rows
69          {RECALC ADD}                           Calulate ADD
70          {GOTO}AMORT_TABLE~                     Move to Amort. Table
71          {END}{DOWN}                            End of Amort. Table
72          /wir                                   Insert Row
73  ADD     {DOWN -1}                              Number of rows to insert
74          ~{UP}/c.{END}{RIGHT}~                  Copy the formulas
75          {DOWN},{END}{DOWN}~{HOME}              Area to copy to
76          {PANELON}{WINDOWSON}{BEEP 4}           Panel & Windows on; Beep
77
78  DEL_ROW {GOTO}TOTAL_ROWS~                      Move to Total_rows
79          {RECALC DEL}                           Calculate Del
80          {GOTO}AMORT_TABLE~                     Move to Amort. Table
81  DEL     {DOWN 36}                              Move down rows
82          /wdr                                   Delete rows
83          {END}{DOWN}{UP}~                       All but last row
84          {UP}/c{END}{RIGHT}~                    Copy Formulas
85          {DOWN}~{HOME}                          Area to copy to
86          {PANELON}{WINDOWSON}{BEEP 4}           Panel & Windows on; Beep
87
88          COUNT_ROWS        NEW_ROWS    TOTAL_ROWS
89              36                36          -1
90
91
```

Fig. 11.5. The \a Macro.

The \a macro, located at cells A57..H89, automatically inserts the
proper number of rows you need for the length of your loan. The macro
also will copy the formulas from the last original row to the new rows in
the Amortization Schedule.

When you press Alt-A, the macro begins by calculating the number of
rows in your current Amortization Schedule. The formula to determine
the number of rows, found in cell B92, or range name COUNT_ROWS

R2

B92: @COUNT(AMORT_TABLE)/7-1

computes the number of cell entries using 1-2-3's @COUNT function, then divides this result by seven and subtracts one to determine the number of rows in the range.

Using a string function, the macro places your choice of number of rows in cell D89, then turns your control panel and windows off. Lines 64 through 66 instruct the macro to take appropriate action based on your response to the question:

How many rows do you need (greater than 35)?

If you have requested fewer than 36 rows, or the number that already exists in your Amortization Schedule, your cursor will be moved to cell A1 and the macro will stop.

However, if you request fewer rows than are currently contained in your Amortization Schedule (for example, you have just amortized a 30-year loan and would like to amortize a 4-year loan), the macro will branch to the subroutine DEL_ROW.

The first line of the DEL_ROW subroutine instructs the macro to go to the range name TOTAL_ROWS, cell E89. Next, macro \a recalculates the formula contained in cell E89

E89: +NEW_ROWS-COUNT_ROWS-1

which computes the difference between the number of requested rows and current rows in your current Amortization Schedule to determine the number of rows to delete.

Next, your cursor is moved to row 20 of the Amortization Schedule, moves down 36 rows, and deletes all unneeded rows, except the last row. The subroutine continues by copying the Amortization Schedule's formulas and placing them in the new Amortization Schedule range. Finally, your control panel and windows are turned back on, and the macro will cause your computer to beep, indicating macro \a is finished.

The macro performs in a manner similar to that of the DEL_ROW subroutine if you have indicated you need more rows than are currently contained in your Amortization Schedule. The only difference between the \a macro and its DEL_ROW subroutine is that the \a macro will add the proper number of rows instead of deleting rows.

Using the Model

This model is as easy to use as it is to create. In the Terms of Loan worksheet, simply enter your data according to table 11.5. Then press F9 (CALC). Within seconds, 1-2-3 will amortize your loan for you.

Table 11.5
Data Entry

Description	Cell
First Payment Date	F8
Amount of Loan	F9
Term of Loan in Months	F10
Beginning Interest Rate	F11
Monthly Payment	F12

Remember that the model is designed for a 36-month loan. If you need to amortize a loan that is longer than 36 months, use the /Worksheet Insert Row command, or macro \a, to insert the appropriate number of rows.

If you decide to use the macro, press Alt-A, enter the number of rows you need, and press Enter. The macro will insert the selected number of rows and copy the formulas for your new Amortization Schedule. Table 11.6 shows the number of rows needed for each term of loan.

Remember that if you do not use the \a macro, you also will need to /Copy the formulas for the Amortization Schedule.

Should the interest rate change during the life of your loan, enter the new rate in the month the rate takes effect. Then press F9 (CALC) to update the model and reflect this change.

Table 11.6
Terms of Loan and Required Rows

Number of Rows	Last Row in Amortization Schedule	Years
1	12	31
2	24	43
3	36	55
4	48	67
5	60	79
10	120	139
15	180	199
20	240	259
25	300	319
30	360	379

Also, if you decide to pay more than your monthly minimum required payment, the application can accommodate this change. For example, suppose that beginning in January, 1988, you want to pay an extra $100 (over and above your minimum payment). Move the cursor to cell D13, the payment amount for January, 1988, and issue the Release 2 /**R**ange **V**alue command for this cell location

D13: +100

and press F9 (CALC). The new payment amount will be repeated in each subsequent cell of column D, and the updated model will reflect this change.

If you want to use the application's database capability, place an appropriate criterion in cell I10. For example, the formula

I10: @YEAR(B20)=87

will extract all 1987 payment records from the Amortization Schedule in figure 11.1. Then, provided that you set up the data query ranges correctly, pressing F7 (QUERY) will result in the twelve-record database in the Output Range (see fig. 11.1). This is but one of many data queries you can perform with this application.

Conclusion

The Loan Amortization Calculator is a practical template for your business. If you already use another amortization model, consider applying some of this application's features to your own. The model is an effective money-management tool.

A1: [W7] \=
B1: [W12] \=
C1: [W7] \=
D1: [W11] \=
E1: [W11] \=
F1: [W11] \=
G1: [W11] \=
H1: [W8] \=
I1: \=
J1: [W7] \=
K1: [W12] \=
L1: [W12] \=
M1: \=
N1: [W12] \=
A3: [W7] 'LOAN AMORTIZATION CALCULATOR   Copyright (C) Que
                Corporation 1987
A5: [W7] \=
B5: [W12] \=
C5: [W7] \=
D5: [W11] \=
E5: [W11] \=
F5: [W11] \=
G5: [W11] \=
H5: [W8] \=
I5: \=
J5: [W7] \=
K5: [W12] \=
L5: [W12] \=
M5: \=
N5: [W12] \=
A6: [W7] 'TERMS OF LOAN
H6: [W8] 'CRITERION RANGE
A7: [W7] \=
B7: [W12] \=
C7: [W7] \=
D7: [W11] \=
E7: [W11] \=
F7: [W11] \=
G7: [W11] \=
H7: [W8] \=
I7: \=
J7: [W7] \=
K7: [W12] \=
L7: [W12] \=
M7: \=
N7: [W12] \=
B8: [W12] 'First Payment Date
F8: (D1) [W11] @DATE(87,1,28)
H8: [W8] 'Payment
I8: ' Payment
J8: [W7] '   Current
L8: [W12] ^Interest
M8: ^Principal
N8: [W12] ^Principal

B9: [W12] 'Principal Borrowed
F9: (C0) [W11] 10000
H9: [W8] 'Number
I9: '   Date
J9: [W7] ' Rate
K9: [W12] ^ Payment
L9: [W12] ^Portion
M9: ^ Portion
N9: [W12] ^Balance
B10: [W12] 'Term in Months
F10: [W11] 36
I10: (H) @YEAR(B20)=87
B11: [W12] 'Beginning Interest Rate
F11: (P2) [W11] 0.0975
B12: [W12] 'Payment
F12: (C2) [W11] @PMT(F9,F11/12,F10)
A14: [W7] \=
B14: [W12] \=
C14: [W7] \=
D14: [W11] \=
E14: [W11] \=
F14: [W11] \=
G14: [W11] \=
H14: [W8] \=
I14: \=
J14: [W7] \=
K14: [W12] \=
L14: [W12] \=
M14: \=
N14: [W12] \=
A15: [W7] 'AMORTIZATION SCHEDULE
H15: [W8] 'STATISTICS RANGE
A16: [W7] \=
B16: [W12] \=
C16: [W7] \=
D16: [W11] \=
E16: [W11] \=
F16: [W11] \=
G16: [W11] \=
H16: [W8] \=
I16: \=
J16: [W7] \=
K16: [W12] \=
L16: [W12] \=
M16: \=
N16: [W12] \=
A18: [W7] 'Payment
B18: [W12] ' Payment
C18: [W7] '   Current
E18: [W11] ^Interest
F18: [W11] ^Principal
G18: [W11] ^Principal
H18: [W8] 'Beginning Balance

```
K18: (C2) [W12] @DMAX(AMORT_TABLE,6,I9..I10)
L18: [W12] 'Interest Paid
N18: (C2) [W12] @DSUM(AMORT_TABLE,4,I9..I10)
A19: [W7] 'Number
B19: [W12] '  Date
C19: [W7] ' Rate
D19: [W11] ^  Payment
E19: [W11] ^Portion
F19: [W11] ^ Portion
G19: [W11] ^Balance
H19: [W8] 'Ending Balance
K19: (C2) [W12] @DMIN(AMORT_TABLE,6,I9..I10)
L19: [W12] 'Principal Paid
N19: (C2) [W12] @DSUM(AMORT_TABLE,5,I9..I10)
A20: [W7] 1
B20: (D1) [W12] +F8
C20: (P2) [W7] +F11
D20: (C2) [W11] +F12
E20: (C2) [W11] +C20/12*F9
F20: (C2) [W11] +D20-E20
G20: (C2) [W11] +F9-F20
H20: [W8] \=
I20: \=
J20: [W7] \=
K20: [W12] \=
L20: [W12] \=
M20: \=
N20: [W12] \=
A21: [W7] +A20+1
B21: (D1) [W12] +B20+@CHOOSE(@MONTH(B20)-1,31,@IF(@MOD(@YEAR(B20),4)=0,29,
                            28),31,30,31,30,31,31,30,31,30,31)
C21: (P2) [W7] +C20
D21: (C2) [W11] @IF(C21=C20,@IF(G20<D20,G20*(1+C21/12),D20),
                    @PMT(G20,C21/12,$F$10-A21+1))
E21: (C2) [W11] +C21/12*G20
F21: (C2) [W11] @IF(G20<0.005,0,D21-E21)
G21: (C2) [W11] +G20-F21
H21: [W8] 'OUTPUT RANGE
A22: [W7] +A21+1
B22: (D1) [W12] +B21+@CHOOSE(@MONTH(B21)-1,31,@IF(@MOD(@YEAR(B21),4)=0,29,
                            28),31,30,31,30,31,31,30,31,30,31)
C22: (P2) [W7] +C21
D22: (C2) [W11] @IF(C22=C21,@IF(G21<D21,G21*(1+C22/12),D21),
                  @PMT(G21,C22/12,$F$10-A22+1))
E22: (C2) [W11] +C22/12*G21
F22: (C2) [W11] @IF(G21<0.005,0,D22-E22)
G22: (C2) [W11] +G21-F22
H22: [W8] \=
I22: \=
J22: [W7] \=
K22: [W12] \=
L22: [W12] \=
M22: \=
N22: [W12] \=
```

A23: [W7] +A22+1
B23: (D1) [W12] +B22+@CHOOSE(@MONTH(B22)-1,31,@IF(@MOD(@YEAR(B22),4)=0,29,
                        28),31,30,31,30,31,31,30,31,30,31)
C23: (P2) [W7] +C22
D23: (C2) [W11] @IF(C23=C22,@IF(G22<D22,G22*(1+C23/12),D22),
                        @PMT(G22,C23/12,$F$10-A23+1))
E23: (C2) [W11] +C23/12*G22
F23: (C2) [W11] @IF(G22<0.005,0,D23-E23)
G23: (C2) [W11] +G22-F23
H23: [W8] 'Payment
I23: ' Payment
J23: [W7] '   Current
L23: [W12] ^Interest
M23: ^Principal
N23: [W12] ^Principal
A24: [W7] +A23+1
B24: (D1) [W12] +B23+@CHOOSE(@MONTH(B23)-1,31,@IF(@MOD(@YEAR(B23),4)=0,29,
                            28),31,30,31,30,31,31,30,31,30,31)
C24: (P2) [W7] +C23
D24: (C2) [W11] @IF(C24=C23,@IF(G23<D23,G23*(1+C24/12),D23),
                        @PMT(G23,C24/12,$F$10-A24+1))
E24: (C2) [W11] +C24/12*G23
F24: (C2) [W11] @IF(G23<0.005,0,D24-E24)
G24: (C2) [W11] +G23-F24
H24: [W8] 'Number
I24: '   Date
J24: [W7] ' Rate
K24: [W12] ^ Payment
L24: [W12] ^Portion
M24: ^ Portion
N24: [W12] ^Balance
A25: [W7] +A24+1
B25: (D1) [W12] +B24+@CHOOSE(@MONTH(B24)-1,31,@IF(@MOD(@YEAR(B24),4)=0,29,
                            28),31,30,31,30,31,31,30,31,30,31)
C25: (P2) [W7] +C24
D25: (C2) [W11] @IF(C25=C24,@IF(G24<D24,G24*(1+C25/12),D24),
                        @PMT(G24,C25/12,$F$10-A25+1))
E25: (C2) [W11] +C25/12*G24
F25: (C2) [W11] @IF(G24<0.005,0,D25-E25)
G25: (C2) [W11] +G24-F25
H25: [W8] 1
I25: (D1) 31805
J25: (P2) [W7] 0.0975
K25: (C2) [W12] 321.49941014
L25: (C2) [W12] 81.25
M25: (C2) 240.24941014
N25: (C2) [W12] 9759.7505899
A26: [W7] +A25+1
B26: (D1) [W12] +B25+@CHOOSE(@MONTH(B25)-1,31,@IF(@MOD(@YEAR(B25),4)=0,29,
                            28),31,30,31,30,31,31,30,31,30,31)
C26: (P2) [W7] +C25
D26: (C2) [W11] @IF(C26=C25,@IF(G25<D25,G25*(1+C26/12),D25),
                        @PMT(G25,C26/12,$F$10-A26+1))

E26: (C2) [W11] +C26/12*G25
F26: (C2) [W11] @IF(G25<0.005,0,D26-E26)
G26: (C2) [W11] +G25-F26
H26: [W8] 2
I26: (D1) 31836
J26: (P2) [W7] 0.0975
K26: (C2) [W12] 321.49941014
L26: (C2) [W12] 79.297973543
M26: (C2) 242.2014366
N26: (C2) [W12] 9517.5491533
A27: [W7] +A26+1
B27: (D1) [W12] +B26+@CHOOSE(@MONTH(B26)-1,31,@IF(@MOD(@YEAR(B26),4)=0,29,
                         28),31,30,31,30,31,31,30,31,30,31)
C27: (P2) [W7] +C26
D27: (C2) [W11] @IF(C27=C26,@IF(G26<D26,G26*(1+C27/12),D26),
                   @PMT(G26,C27/12,$F$10-A27+1))
E27: (C2) [W11] +C27/12*G26
F27: (C2) [W11] @IF(G26<0.005,0,D27-E27)
G27: (C2) [W11] +G26-F27
H27: [W8] 3
I27: (D1) 31864
J27: (P2) [W7] 0.0975
K27: (C2) [W12] 321.49941014
L27: (C2) [W12] 77.33008687
M27: (C2) 244.16932327
N27: (C2) [W12] 9273.37983
A28: [W7] +A27+1
B28: (D1) [W12] +B27+@CHOOSE(@MONTH(B27)-1,31,@IF(@MOD(@YEAR(B27),4)=0,29,
                         28),31,30,31,30,31,31,30,31,30,31)
C28: (P2) [W7] +C27
D28: (C2) [W11] @IF(C28=C27,@IF(G27<D27,G27*(1+C28/12),D27),
                   @PMT(G27,C28/12,$F$10-A28+1))
E28: (C2) [W11] +C28/12*G27
F28: (C2) [W11] @IF(G27<0.005,0,D28-E28)
G28: (C2) [W11] +G27-F28
H28: [W8] 4
I28: (D1) 31895
J28: (P2) [W7] 0.0975
K28: (C2) [W12] 321.49941014
L28: (C2) [W12] 75.346211119
M28: (C2) 246.15319903
N28: (C2) [W12] 9027.226631
A29: [W7] +A28+1
B29: (D1) [W12] +B28+@CHOOSE(@MONTH(B28)-1,31,@IF(@MOD(@YEAR(B28),4)=0,29,
                         28),31,30,31,30,31,31,30,31,30,31)
C29: (P2) [W7] +C28
D29: (C2) [W11] @IF(C29=C28,@IF(G28<D28,G28*(1+C29/12),D28),
                   @PMT(G28,C29/12,$F$10-A29+1))
E29: (C2) [W11] +C29/12*G28
F29: (C2) [W11] @IF(G28<0.005,0,D29-E29)
G29: (C2) [W11] +G28-F29
H29: [W8] 5
I29: (D1) 31925

J29: (P2) [W7] 0.0975
K29: (C2) [W12] 321.49941014
L29: (C2) [W12] 73.346216376
M29: (C2) 248.15319377
N29: (C2) [W12] 8779.0734372
A30: [W7] +A29+1
B30: (D1) [W12] +B29+@CHOOSE(@MONTH(B29)-1,31,@IF(@MOD(@YEAR(B29),4)=0,29,
                           28),31,30,31,30,31,31,30,31,30,31)
C30: (P2) [W7] +C29
D30: (C2) [W11] @IF(C30=C29,@IF(G29<D29,G29*(1+C30/12),D29),
                    @PMT(G29,C30/12,$F$10-A30+1))
E30: (C2) [W11] +C30/12*G29
F30: (C2) [W11] @IF(G29<0.005,0,D30-E30)
G30: (C2) [W11] +G29-F30
H30: [W8] 6
I30: (D1) 31956
J30: (P2) [W7] 0.0975
K30: (C2) [W12] 321.49941014
L30: (C2) [W12] 71.329971677
M30: (C2) 250.16943847
N30: (C2) [W12] 8528.9039987
A31: [W7] +A30+1
B31: (D1) [W12] +B30+@CHOOSE(@MONTH(B30)-1,31,@IF(@MOD(@YEAR(B30),4)=0,29,
                           28),31,30,31,30,31,31,30,31,30,31)
C31: (P2) [W7] +C30
D31: (C2) [W11] @IF(C31=C30,@IF(G30<D30,G30*(1+C31/12),D30),
                    @PMT(G30,C31/12,$F$10-A31+1))
E31: (C2) [W11] +C31/12*G30
F31: (C2) [W11] @IF(G30<0.005,0,D31-E31)
G31: (C2) [W11] +G30-F31
H31: [W8] 7
I31: (D1) 31986
J31: (P2) [W7] 0.0975
K31: (C2) [W12] 321.49941014
L31: (C2) [W12] 69.29734499
M31: (C2) 252.20206515
N31: (C2) [W12] 8276.7019336
A32: [W7] +A31+1
B32: (D1) [W12] +B31+@CHOOSE(@MONTH(B31)-1,31,@IF(@MOD(@YEAR(B31),4)=0,29,
                           28),31,30,31,30,31,31,30,31,30,31)
C32: (P2) [W7] +C31
D32: (C2) [W11] @IF(C32=C31,@IF(G31<D31,G31*(1+C32/12),D31),
                    @PMT(G31,C32/12,$F$10-A32+1))
E32: (C2) [W11] +C32/12*G31
F32: (C2) [W11] @IF(G31<0.005,0,D32-E32)
G32: (C2) [W11] +G31-F32
H32: [W8] 8
I32: (D1) 32017
J32: (P2) [W7] 0.0975
K32: (C2) [W12] 321.49941014
L32: (C2) [W12] 67.24820321
M32: (C2) 254.25120693
N32: (C2) [W12] 8022.4507266

A33: [W7] +A32+1
B33: (D1) [W12] +B32+@CHOOSE(@MONTH(B32)-1,31,@IF(@MOD(@YEAR(B32),4)=0,29,
                        28),31,30,31,30,31,31,30,31,30,31)
C33: (P2) [W7] +C32
D33: (C2) [W11] @IF(C33=C32,@IF(G32<D32,G32*(1+C33/12),D32),
                        @PMT(G32,C33/12,$F$10-A33+1))
E33: (C2) [W11] +C33/12*G32
F33: (C2) [W11] @IF(G32<0.005,0,D33-E33)
G33: (C2) [W11] +G32-F33
H33: [W8] 9
I33: (D1) 32048
J33: (P2) [W7] 0.0975
K33: (C2) [W12] 321.49941014
L33: (C2) [W12] 65.182412154
M33: (C2) 256.31699799
N33: (C2) [W12] 7766.1337286
A34: [W7] +A33+1
B34: (D1) [W12] +B33+@CHOOSE(@MONTH(B33)-1,31,@IF(@MOD(@YEAR(B33),4)=0,29,
                        28),31,30,31,30,31,31,30,31,30,31)
C34: (P2) [W7] +C33
D34: (C2) [W11] @IF(C34=C33,@IF(G33<D33,G33*(1+C34/12),D33),
                        @PMT(G33,C34/12,$F$10-A34+1))
E34: (C2) [W11] +C34/12*G33
F34: (C2) [W11] @IF(G33<0.005,0,D34-E34)
G34: (C2) [W11] +G33-F34
H34: [W8] 10
I34: (D1) 32078
J34: (P2) [W7] 0.0975
K34: (C2) [W12] 321.49941014
L34: (C2) [W12] 63.099836545
M34: (C2) 258.3995736
N34: (C2) [W12] 7507.734155
A35: [W7] +A34+1
B35: (D1) [W12] +B34+@CHOOSE(@MONTH(B34)-1,31,@IF(@MOD(@YEAR(B34),4)=0,29,
                        28),31,30,31,30,31,31,30,31,30,31)
C35: (P2) [W7] +C34
D35: (C2) [W11] @IF(C35=C34,@IF(G34<D34,G34*(1+C35/12),D34),
                        @PMT(G34,C35/12,$F$10-A35+1))
E35: (C2) [W11] +C35/12*G34
F35: (C2) [W11] @IF(G34<0.005,0,D35-E35)
G35: (C2) [W11] +G34-F35
H35: [W8] 11
I35: (D1) 32109
J35: (P2) [W7] 0.0975
K35: (C2) [W12] 321.49941014
L35: (C2) [W12] 61.00034001
M35: (C2) 260.49907013
N35: (C2) [W12] 7247.2350849
A36: [W7] +A35+1
B36: (D1) [W12] +B35+@CHOOSE(@MONTH(B35)-1,31,@IF(@MOD(@YEAR(B35),4)=0,29,
                        28),31,30,31,30,31,31,30,31,30,31)
C36: (P2) [W7] +C35
D36: (C2) [W11] @IF(C36=C35,@IF(G35<D35,G35*(1+C36/12),D35),
                        @PMT(G35,C36/12,$F$10-A36+1))

E36: (C2) [W11] +C36/12*G35
F36: (C2) [W11] @IF(G35<0.005,0,D36-E36)
G36: (C2) [W11] +G35-F36
H36: [W8] 12
I36: (D1) 32139
J36: (P2) [W7] 0.0975
K36: (C2) [W12] 321.49941014
L36: (C2) [W12] 58.883785065
M36: (C2) 262.61562508
N36: (C2) [W12] 6984.6194598
A37: [W7] +A36+1
B37: (D1) [W12] +B36+@CHOOSE(@MONTH(B36)-1,31,@IF(@MOD(@YEAR(B36),4)=0,29,
                          28),31,30,31,30,31,31,30,31,30,31)
C37: (P2) [W7] +C36
D37: (C2) [W11] @IF(C37=C36,@IF(G36<D36,G36*(1+C37/12),D36),
                    @PMT(G36,C37/12,$F$10-A37+1))
E37: (C2) [W11] +C37/12*G36
F37: (C2) [W11] @IF(G36<0.005,0,D37-E37)
G37: (C2) [W11] +G36-F37
A38: [W7] +A37+1
B38: (D1) [W12] +B37+@CHOOSE(@MONTH(B37)-1,31,@IF(@MOD(@YEAR(B37),4)=0,29,
                          28),31,30,31,30,31,31,30,31,30,31)
C38: (P2) [W7] +C37
D38: (C2) [W11] @IF(C38=C37,@IF(G37<D37,G37*(1+C38/12),D37),
                    @PMT(G37,C38/12,$F$10-A38+1))
E38: (C2) [W11] +C38/12*G37
F38: (C2) [W11] @IF(G37<0.005,0,D38-E38)
G38: (C2) [W11] +G37-F38
A39: [W7] +A38+1
B39: (D1) [W12] +B38+@CHOOSE(@MONTH(B38)-1,31,@IF(@MOD(@YEAR(B38),4)=0,29,
                          28),31,30,31,30,31,31,30,31,30,31)
C39: (P2) [W7] +C38
D39: (C2) [W11] @IF(C39=C38,@IF(G38<D38,G38*(1+C39/12),D38),
                    @PMT(G38,C39/12,$F$10-A39+1))
E39: (C2) [W11] +C39/12*G38
F39: (C2) [W11] @IF(G38<0.005,0,D39-E39)
G39: (C2) [W11] +G38-F39
A40: [W7] +A39+1
B40: (D1) [W12] +B39+@CHOOSE(@MONTH(B39)-1,31,@IF(@MOD(@YEAR(B39),4)=0,29,
                          28),31,30,31,30,31,31,30,31,30,31)
C40: (P2) [W7] +C39
D40: (C2) [W11] @IF(C40=C39,@IF(G39<D39,G39*(1+C40/12),D39),
                    @PMT(G39,C40/12,$F$10-A40+1))
E40: (C2) [W11] +C40/12*G39
F40: (C2) [W11] @IF(G39<0.005,0,D40-E40)
G40: (C2) [W11] +G39-F40
A41: [W7] +A40+1
B41: (D1) [W12] +B40+@CHOOSE(@MONTH(B40)-1,31,@IF(@MOD(@YEAR(B40),4)=0,29,
                          28),31,30,31,30,31,31,30,31,30,31)
C41: (P2) [W7] +C40
D41: (C2) [W11] @IF(C41=C40,@IF(G40<D40,G40*(1+C41/12),D40),
                    @PMT(G40,C41/12,$F$10-A41+1))
E41: (C2) [W11] +C41/12*G40
F41: (C2) [W11] @IF(G40<0.005,0,D41-E41)

```
G41: (C2) [W11] +G40-F41
A42: [W7] +A41+1
B42: (D1) [W12] +B41+@CHOOSE(@MONTH(B41)-1,31,@IF(@MOD(@YEAR(B41),4)=0,29,
                        28),31,30,31,30,31,31,30,31,30,31)
C42: (P2) [W7] +C41
D42: (C2) [W11] @IF(C42=C41,@IF(G41<D41,G41*(1+C42/12),D41),
                    @PMT(G41,C42/12,$F$10-A42+1))
E42: (C2) [W11] +C42/12*G41
F42: (C2) [W11] @IF(G41<0.005,0,D42-E42)
G42: (C2) [W11] +G41-F42
A43: [W7] +A42+1
B43: (D1) [W12] +B42+@CHOOSE(@MONTH(B42)-1,31,@IF(@MOD(@YEAR(B42),4)=0,29,
                        28),31,30,31,30,31,31,30,31,30,31)
C43: (P2) [W7] +C42
D43: (C2) [W11] @IF(C43=C42,@IF(G42<D42,G42*(1+C43/12),D42),
                    @PMT(G42,C43/12,$F$10-A43+1))
E43: (C2) [W11] +C43/12*G42
F43: (C2) [W11] @IF(G42<0.005,0,D43-E43)
G43: (C2) [W11] +G42-F43
A44: [W7] +A43+1
B44: (D1) [W12] +B43+@CHOOSE(@MONTH(B43)-1,31,@IF(@MOD(@YEAR(B43),4)=0,29,
                        28),31,30,31,30,31,31,30,31,30,31)
C44: (P2) [W7] +C43
D44: (C2) [W11] @IF(C44=C43,@IF(G43<D43,G43*(1+C44/12),D43),
                    @PMT(G43,C44/12,$F$10-A44+1))
E44: (C2) [W11] +C44/12*G43
F44: (C2) [W11] @IF(G43<0.005,0,D44-E44)
G44: (C2) [W11] +G43-F44
A45: [W7] +A44+1
B45: (D1) [W12] +B44+@CHOOSE(@MONTH(B44)-1,31,@IF(@MOD(@YEAR(B44),4)=0,29,
                        28),31,30,31,30,31,31,30,31,30,31)
C45: (P2) [W7] +C44
D45: (C2) [W11] @IF(C45=C44,@IF(G44<D44,G44*(1+C45/12),D44),
                    @PMT(G44,C45/12,$F$10-A45+1))
E45: (C2) [W11] +C45/12*G44
F45: (C2) [W11] @IF(G44<0.005,0,D45-E45)
G45: (C2) [W11] +G44-F45
A46: [W7] +A45+1
B46: (D1) [W12] +B45+@CHOOSE(@MONTH(B45)-1,31,@IF(@MOD(@YEAR(B45),4)=0,29,
                        28),31,30,31,30,31,31,30,31,30,31)
C46: (P2) [W7] +C45
D46: (C2) [W11] @IF(C46=C45,@IF(G45<D45,G45*(1+C46/12),D45),
                    @PMT(G45,C46/12,$F$10-A46+1))
E46: (C2) [W11] +C46/12*G45
F46: (C2) [W11] @IF(G45<0.005,0,D46-E46)
G46: (C2) [W11] +G45-F46
A47: [W7] +A46+1
B47: (D1) [W12] +B46+@CHOOSE(@MONTH(B46)-1,31,@IF(@MOD(@YEAR(B46),4)=0,29,
                        28),31,30,31,30,31,31,30,31,30,31)
C47: (P2) [W7] +C46
D47: (C2) [W11] @IF(C47=C46,@IF(G46<D46,G46*(1+C47/12),D46),
                    @PMT(G46,C47/12,$F$10-A47+1))
E47: (C2) [W11] +C47/12*G46
```

F47: (C2) [W11] @IF(G46<0.005,0,D47-E47)
G47: (C2) [W11] +G46-F47
A48: [W7] +A47+1
B48: (D1) [W12] +B47+@CHOOSE(@MONTH(B47)-1,31,@IF(@MOD(@YEAR(B47),4)=0,29,
                          28),31,30,31,30,31,31,30,31,30,31)
C48: (P2) [W7] +C47
D48: (C2) [W11] @IF(C48=C47,@IF(G47<D47,G47*(1+C48/12),D47),
                     @PMT(G47,C48/12,$F$10-A48+1))
E48: (C2) [W11] +C48/12*G47
F48: (C2) [W11] @IF(G47<0.005,0,D48-E48)
G48: (C2) [W11] +G47-F48
A49: [W7] +A48+1
B49: (D1) [W12] +B48+@CHOOSE(@MONTH(B48)-1,31,@IF(@MOD(@YEAR(B48),4)=0,29,
                          28),31,30,31,30,31,31,30,31,30,31)
C49: (P2) [W7] +C48
D49: (C2) [W11] @IF(C49=C48,@IF(G48<D48,G48*(1+C49/12),D48),
                     @PMT(G48,C49/12,$F$10-A49+1))
E49: (C2) [W11] +C49/12*G48
F49: (C2) [W11] @IF(G48<0.005,0,D49-E49)
G49: (C2) [W11] +G48-F49
A50: [W7] +A49+1
B50: (D1) [W12] +B49+@CHOOSE(@MONTH(B49)-1,31,@IF(@MOD(@YEAR(B49),4)=0,29,
                          28),31,30,31,30,31,31,30,31,30,31)
C50: (P2) [W7] +C49
D50: (C2) [W11] @IF(C50-C49,@IF(G49<D49,G49*(1+C50/12),D49),
                     @PMT(G49,C50/12,$F$10-A50+1))
E50: (C2) [W11] +C50/12*G49
F50: (C2) [W11] @IF(G49<0.005,0,D50-E50)
G50: (C2) [W11] +G49-F50
A51: [W7] +A50+1
B51: (D1) [W12] +B50+@CHOOSE(@MONTH(B50)-1,31,@IF(@MOD(@YEAR(B50),4)=0,29,
                          28),31,30,31,30,31,31,30,31,30,31)
C51: (P2) [W7] +C50
D51: (C2) [W11] @IF(C51=C50,@IF(G50<D50,G50*(1+C51/12),D50),
                     @PMT(G50,C51/12,$F$10-A51+1))
E51: (C2) [W11] +C51/12*G50
F51: (C2) [W11] @IF(G50<0.005,0,D51-E51)
G51: (C2) [W11] +G50-F51
A52: [W7] +A51+1
B52: (D1) [W12] +B51+@CHOOSE(@MONTH(B51)-1,31,@IF(@MOD(@YEAR(B51),4)=0,29,
                          28),31,30,31,30,31,31,30,31,30,31)
C52: (P2) [W7] +C51
D52: (C2) [W11] @IF(C52=C51,@IF(G51<D51,G51*(1+C52/12),D51),
                     @PMT(G51,C52/12,$F$10-A52+1))
E52: (C2) [W11] +C52/12*G51
F52: (C2) [W11] @IF(G51<0.005,0,D52-E52)
G52: (C2) [W11] +G51-F52
A53: [W7] +A52+1
B53: (D1) [W12] +B52+@CHOOSE(@MONTH(B52)-1,31,@IF(@MOD(@YEAR(B52),4)=0,29,
                          28),31,30,31,30,31,31,30,31,30,31)
C53: (P2) [W7] +C52
D53: (C2) [W11] @IF(C53=C52,@IF(G52<D52,G52*(1+C53/12),D52),
                     @PMT(G52,C53/12,$F$10-A53+1))

```
E53: (C2) [W11] +C53/12*G52
F53: (C2) [W11] @IF(G52<0.005,0,D53-E53)
G53: (C2) [W11] +G52-F53
A54: [W7] +A53+1
B54: (D1) [W12] +B53+@CHOOSE(@MONTH(B53)-1,31,@IF(@MOD(@YEAR(B53),4)=0,29,
                            28),31,30,31,30,31,31,30,31,30,31)
C54: (P2) [W7] +C53
D54: (C2) [W11] @IF(C54=C53,@IF(G53<D53,G53*(1+C54/12),D53),
                    @PMT(G53,C54/12,$F$10-A54+1))
E54: (C2) [W11] +C54/12*G53
F54: (C2) [W11] @IF(G53<0.005,0,D54-E54)
G54: (C2) [W11] +G53-F54
A55: [W7] +A54+1

B55: (D1) [W12] +B54+@CHOOSE(@MONTH(B54)-1,31,@IF(@MOD(@YEAR(B54),4)=0,29,
                            28),31,30,31,30,31,31,30,31,30,31)
C55: (P2) [W7] +C54
D55: (C2) [W11] @IF(C55=C54,@IF(G54<D54,G54*(1+C55/12),D54),
                    @PMT(G54,C55/12,$F$10-A55+1))
E55: (C2) [W11] +C55/12*G54
F55: (C2) [W11] @IF(G54<0.005,0,D55-E55)
G55: (C2) [W11] +G54-F55
A57: [W7] \=
B57: [W12] \=
C57: [W7] \=
D57: [W11] \=
E57: [W11] \=
F57: [W11] \=
G57: [W11] \=
A58: [W7] 'MACRO
A59: [W7] \=
B59: [W12] \=
C59: [W7] \=
D59: [W11] \=
E59: [W11] \=
F59: [W11] \=
G59: [W11] \=
A61: [W7] '\a
B61: [W12] '{RECALC COUNT_ROWS}
F61: [W11] 'Calculate Count_rows
B62: [W12] '{GETNUMBER "How many rows do you need (greater than 35)? ",
                NEW_ROWS}
B63: [W12] '{PANELOFF}{WINDOWSOFF}
F63: [W11] 'Total Length;off screen
B64: [W12] '{IF NEW_ROWS<36}{HOME}{QUIT}
F64: [W11] 'Must be > 35; Go to Home and Quit
B65: [W12] '{IF COUNT_ROWS=NEW_ROWS}{HOME}{QUIT}
F65: [W11] 'Quit if rows exist
B66: [W12] '{IF NEW_ROWS<COUNT_ROWS}{BRANCH DEL_ROW}
F66: [W11] 'Decide to add or del
B67: [W12] '{GOTO}TOTAL_ROWS~
F67: [W11] 'Move to Total_rows
B68: [W12] '+NEW_ROWS-COUNT_ROWS-1~
```

```
F68: [W11] 'Formula for Total_rows
B69: [W12] '{RECALC ADD}
F69: [W11] 'Calulate ADD
B70: [W12] '{GOTO}AMORT_TABLE~
F70: [W11] 'Move to Amort. Table
B71: [W12] '{END}{DOWN}
F71: [W11] 'End of Amort. Table
B72: [W12] '/wir
F72: [W11] 'Insert Row
A73: [W7] 'ADD
B73: [W12] +"{DOWN "&@STRING(TOTAL_ROWS,0)&"}"
F73: [W11] 'Number of rows to insert
B74: [W12] '~{UP}/c.{END}{RIGHT}~
F74: [W11] 'Copy the formulas
B75: [W12] '{DOWN}.{END}{DOWN}~{HOME}
F75: [W11] 'Area to copy to
B76: [W12] '{PANELON}{WINDOWSON}{BEEP 4}
F76: [W11] 'Panel & Windows on; Beep when finished
A78: [W7] 'DEL_ROW
B78: [W12] '{GOTO}TOTAL_ROWS~
F78: [W11] 'Move to Total_rows
B79: [W12] '{RECALC DEL}
F79: [W11] 'Calculate Del
B80: [W12] '{GOTO}AMORT_TABLE~
F80: [W11] 'Move to Amort. Table
A81: [W7] 'DEL
B81: [W12] +"{DOWN "&@STRING(NEW_ROWS,0)&"}"
F81: [W11] 'Move down rows
B82: [W12] '/wdr
F82: [W11] 'Delete rows
B83: [W12] '{END}{DOWN}{UP}~
F83: [W11] 'All but last row
B84: [W12] '{UP}/c{END}{RIGHT}~
F84: [W11] 'Copy Formulas
B85: [W12] '{DOWN}~{HOME}
F85: [W11] 'Area to copy to
B86: [W12] '{PANELON}{WINDOWSON}{BEEP 4}
F86: [W11] 'Panel & Windows on; Beep when finished
B88: [W12] 'COUNT_ROWS
D88: [W11] 'NEW_ROWS
E88: [W11] 'TOTAL_ROWS
B89: [W12] @COUNT(AMORT_TABLE)/7-1
D89: [W11] 36
E89: [W11] +NEW_ROWS-COUNT_ROWS-1
```

12

Lease versus Debt

Introduction

Few decisions have as great an impact on cash flow and profitability as the decision to lease or purchase assets. Thus, for your firm to stay competitive, you must choose the financing alternative that is less expensive.

The 1-2-3 Lease versus Debt Evaluator can help you choose the proper alternative for your firm. This chapter explains how to construct the model, how the model works, and how you can use the Lease versus Debt Evaluator in your business.

The Lease versus Debt Evaluator has eight modules: Assumptions, Implicit Rate Calculator, Lease Alternative, Debt Alternative, Salvage Value of Equipment, Depreciation Table, Results, and Macro \d. This model resembles others in the book: the first section, Assumptions, is a data-entry worksheet; the next five sections are computational areas; and the final spreadsheet, Results, summarizes these calculations. Figure 12.1 shows the entire model.

Creating the Model

The Lease versus Debt Evaluator is easy to create. You begin by bringing up a blank 1-2-3 spreadsheet on your computer's screen.

In this model, only column A's width needs to be changed—to 20.

Then, using 1-2-3's /Copy command and, wherever possible, the backslash copying trick, enter the column headings, row titles, and labels, according to table 12.1 or your own personal preference. As

```
        A      B     C      D      E       F       G      H      I      J       K      L      M    N    O   P   Q
1  ===============================================================================================\d  {PANELOFF}{WINDOWSOFF}~
2                                                                                            Depr   {IF (E14=3)}{GOTO}ACRS3~
3  LEASE VS. DEBT EVALUATOR        Copyright (C) 1987 Que Corporation                        Macro  {IF (E14=5)}{GOTO}ACRS5~
4                                                                                                   {IF (E14=7)}{GOTO}ACRS7~
5  =================================================================================================  {CALC}
6  ASSUMPTIONS                                    IMPLICIT RATE CALCULATOR                            {DOWN 2}
7  =================================================================================================  /rv{END}{DOWN}~H60~
8                                                        Implied  Actual                             {GOTO}H60~
9  Corporate Tax Rate                 34%                Payment  Payment Difference                 /rt{END}{DOWN}~C46~~
10                                                                                                   {CALC}~
11 Interest Rate on Loan             7.50%               $35,714                                     /reH60..H67~~
12                                              4%  $41,652  $48,018  ($6,366)    4%                 {GOTO}RESULTS~
13 Annual Lease Payment            $48,018       5%  $43,205  $48,018  ($4,813)    5%                 {PANELON}{WINDOWSON}{BEEP 4}
14 Term of Lease                   7 years       6%  $44,784  $48,018  ($3,234)    6%
15 Implicit Interest Rate of Lease    8%         7%  $46,388  $48,018  ($1,630)    7%
16                                              8%  $48,018  $48,018       $0     8%
17 Cost of Equipment              $250,000       9%  $49,673  $48,018   $1,655     9%
18                                             10%  $51,351  $48,018   $3,333    10%
19 Salvage Value of Equipment      $25,000
20 =================================================================================================
21 LEASE ALTERNATIVE
22 =================================================================================================
23
24 Year          0      1      2      3      4      5      6      7      8     9    10    11   12   13   14   15
25             ----   ----   ----   ----   ----   ----   ----   ----
26 Lease Payments $0 ($48,018)($48,018)($48,018)($48,018)($48,018)($48,018)($48,018)  $0   $0   $0   $0   $0   $0   $0   $0
27 Tax Savings      (16,326)(16,326)(16,326)(16,326)(16,326)(16,326)(16,326)   0    0    0    0    0    0    0    0
28             ----   ----   ----   ----   ----   ----   ----   ----
29 Payment after Tax $0 ($31,692)($31,692)($31,692)($31,692)($31,692)($31,692)($31,692)  $0   $0   $0   $0   $0   $0   $0   $0
30
31 Present Value  ($183,714)
32
33
34
35 =================================================================================================
36 DEBT ALTERNATIVE
37 =================================================================================================
38 Year          0      1      2      3      4      5      6      7      8     9    10    11   12   13   14   15
39             ----   ----   ----   ----   ----   ----   ----   ----
40 Beginning Balance 250,000 250,000 214,286 178,571 142,857 107,143 71,429 35,714  0   0    0    0    0    0    0    0
41 Principal Payment   (35,714)(35,714)(35,714)(35,714)(35,714)(35,714)(35,714)  0   0    0    0    0    0    0    0
42             ----   ----   ----   ----   ----   ----   ----   ----
43 Ending Balance 250,000 214,286 178,571 142,857 107,143 71,429 35,714   0    0   0    0    0    0    0    0    0
44
45 Interest Expense  (18,750)(16,071)(13,393)(10,714)(8,036)(5,357)(2,679)  (0)  (0)  (0)  (0)  (0)  (0)  (0)  (0)
46 Depreciation      (35,714)(61,225)(43,732)(31,237)(22,312)(22,312)(22,312)(11,156)  0    0    0    0    0    0    0
47             ----   ----   ----   ----   ----   ----   ----   ----
48 Tax Shield         18,518  26,281  19,422  14,263  10,318   9,408   8,497   3,793   0    0    0    0    0    0    0
49             ----   ----   ----   ----   ----   ----   ----   ----
50 Salvage Value       0      0      0      0      0      0    9,137     0    0    0    0    0    0    0    0
51             -----  -----  -----  -----  -----  -----  -----  -----
52 Cash Flow    ($250,000)($35,947)($25,505)($29,685)($32,165)($33,432)($31,664)($20,759) $3,793 ($0)($0)($0)($0)($0)($0)($0)
53             =====  =====  =====  =====  =====  =====  =====  =====
54
55 Present Value  ($174,354)
56
57 =================================================================================================
58 SALVAGE VALUE OF EQUIPMENT              DEPRECIATION TABLE   YEAR   3    5     7
59 =================================================================================================
60                                                             1     0    0   (35,714)
61 Salvage Value at End of Loan      $25,000                    2     0    0   (61,225)
62 Book Value at End of Loan          11,156                    3     0    0   (43,732)
63                                 ----------                   4     0    0   (31,237)
64 Gain on Sale of Asset              13,844                    5          0   (22,312)
65 Tax on Sale of Asset                4,707                    6          0   (22,312)
66                                 ----------                   7              (22,312)
67 Net Cash Flow from Disposal        $9,137                    8              (11,156)
68                                 ==========
69
70                                                             0    0   (250,000)
71                                                            ==============================
72
73
74
75 =================================================================================================
76 RESULTS
77 =================================================================================================
78
79
80 Present Value of Lease    ($183,714)
81
82 Present Value of Loan     ($174,354)
```

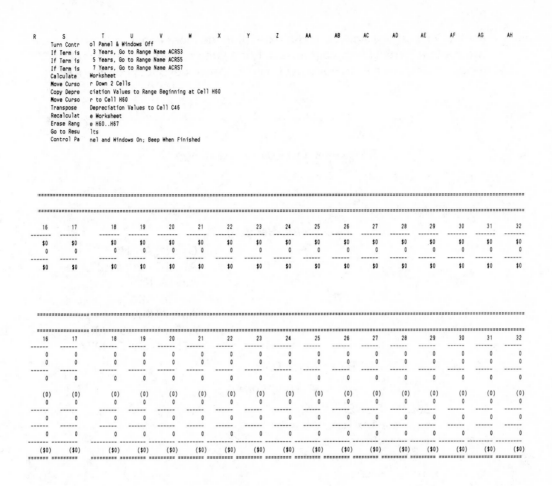

R	S	T	U	V	W	X	Y	Z	AA	AB	AC	AD	AE	AF	AG	AH
	Turn Contr	ol Panel & Windows Off														
	If Term is	3 Years, Go to Range Name ACRS3														
	If Term is	5 Years, Go to Range Name ACRS5														
	If Term is	7 Years, Go to Range Name ACRS7														
	Calculate	Worksheet														
	Move Curso	r Down 2 Cells														
	Copy Depre	ciation Values to Range Beginning at Cell H60														
	Move Curso	r to Cell H60														
	Transpose	Depreciation Values to Cell C46														
	Recalculat	e Worksheet														
	Erase Rang	e H60..H67														
	Go to Resu	lts														
	Control Pa	nel and Windows On; Beep When Finished														

16	17	18	19	20	21	22	23	24	25	26	27	28	29	30	31	32
$0	$0	$0	$0	$0	$0	$0	$0	$0	$0	$0	$0	$0	$0	$0	$0	$0
0	0	0	0	0	0	0	0	0	0	0	0	0	0	0	0	0
$0	$0	$0	$0	$0	$0	$0	$0	$0	$0	$0	$0	$0	$0	$0	$0	$0

16	17	18	19	20	21	22	23	24	25	26	27	28	29	30	31	32
0	0	0	0	0	0	0	0	0	0	0	0	0	0	0	0	0
0	0	0	0	0	0	0	0	0	0	0	0	0	0	0	0	0
0	0	0	0	0	0	0	0	0	0	0	0	0	0	0	0	0
(0)	(0)	(0)	(0)	(0)	(0)	(0)	(0)	(0)	(0)	(0)	(0)	(0)	(0)	(0)	(0)	(0)
0	0	0	0	0	0	0	0	0	0	0	0	0	0	0	0	0
0	0	0	0	0	0	0	0	0	0	0	0	0	0	0	0	0
0	0	0	0	0	0	0	0	0	0	0	0	0	0	0	0	0
($0)	($0)	($0)	($0)	($0)	($0)	($0)	($0)	($0)	($0)	($0)	($0)	($0)	($0)	($0)	($0)	($0)

Fig. 12.1. The Lease versus Debt Evaluator.

another timesaving step, consider extending the model only a year or two past the useful life of your assets. For example, if you have no real estate assets, there is no need to construct the model out to column AH.

Table 12.1

Row Titles and Column Headings

Enter into cell:	Original label:	Copy to:
	Opening Headings	
A1:	\=	B1..N1, A5..N5, A7..N7, A20..AH20, A22..AH22, A35..AH35, A37..AH37, A57..M57, A59..M59, A75..M75, A77..M77
A3:	'LEASE VS. DEBT EVALUATOR	
	Assumptions	
A6:	'ASSUMPTIONS	
A9:	'Corporate Tax Rate	
A11:	'Interest Rate on Loan	
A13:	'Annual Lease Payment	
A14:	'Term of Lease	
F14:	'years	
A15:	'Implicit Interest Rate of Lease	
A17:	'Cost of Equipment	
A19:	'Salvage Value of Equipment	
	Implicit Rate Calculator	
G6:	'IMPLICIT RATE CALCULATOR	
I8:	' Implied	
J8:	' Actual	
I9:	' Payment	
J9:	' Payment	
K9:	'Difference	

Enter into cell:	Original label:	Copy to:

Lease Alternative

A21:	'LEASE ALTERNATIVE	
A24:	'Year	A38
B25:	'-------	C28..AH28
A26:	'Lease Payments	
A27:	'Tax Savings	
A29:	'Payment after Tax	
A31:	'Present Value	A55

Debt Alternative

A36:	'DEBT ALTERNATIVE	
A39:	'------	B39..AH39, C42..AH42, C47..AH47, C49..AH49
A40:	'Beginning Balance	
A41:	'Principal Payment	
A43:	'Ending Balance	
A45:	'Interest Expense	
A46:	'Depreciation	
A48:	'Tax Shield	
A50:	'Salvage Value	
B51:	'--------	C51..AH51
A52:	'Cash Flow	
B53:	'========	C53..AH53

Salvage Value of Equipment

A58:	'SALVAGE VALUE OF EQUIPMENT	
A61:	'Salvage Value at End of Loan	
A62:	'Book Value at End of Loan	
D63:	'--------	D66
A64:	'Gain on Sale of Asset	
A67:	'Net Cash Flow from Disposal	
D68:	'========	

Depreciation Table

G58:	'DEPRECIATION TABLE	
I58:	"YEAR	
J69:	\-	K69..L69
J71:	\=	K71..L71

Enter
into
cell: Original label: Copy to:

Results

A76:   'RESULTS
A80:   'Present Value of Lease
A82:   'Present Value of Loan

Macro

N1:   '\d
O1:   '{PANELOFF}{WINDOWSOFF}~
S1:   'Turn Control Panel & Windows Off
N2:   'Depr
O2:   '{IF (E14=3)}{GOTO}ACRS3~
S2:   'If Term is 3 Years, Go to Range Name ACRS3
N3:   'Macro
O3:   '{IF (E14=5)}{GOTO}ACRS5~
S3:   'If Term is 5 Years, Go to Range Name ACRS5
O4:   '{IF (E14=7)}{GOTO}ACRS7~
S4:   'If Term is 7 Years, Go to Range Name ACRS7
O5:   '{CALC}
S5:   'Calculate Worksheet
O6:   '{DOWN 2}
S6:   'Move Cursor Down 2 Cells
O7:   '/rv{END}{DOWN}~H60~
S7:   'Copy Depreciation Values to Range Beginning at Cell H60
O8:   '{GOTO}H60~
S8:   'Move Cursor to Cell H60
O9:   '/rt{END}{DOWN}~C46~~
S9:   'Transpose Depreciation Values to Cell C46
O10:   '{CALC}~
S10:   'Recalculate Worksheet
O11:   '/reH60..H67~~
S11:   'Erase Range H60..H67
O12:   '{GOTO}RESULTS~
S12:   'Go to Results
O13:   '{PANELON}{WINDOWSON}{BEEP 4}
S13:   'Control Panel and Windows On; Beep When Finished

Naming Ranges

After you have entered the labels, and if you intend to use the macro, name the ranges according to table 12.2.

Table 12.2
Range Names

Name	Location
ACRS	G58
ACRS3	J58
ACRS5	K58
ACRS7	L58
RESULTS	A76
\D	O1

Specifying Cell Formats

You format the model according to your own personal preference or by following the schedule of formats in table 12.3.

Table 12.3
Cell Formats

Format	Range
Assumptions	
/rfp0	E9, E15
/rfp2	E11
/rfc0	E13, E17, E19
Implicit Rate Calculator	
/rfp0	Column H, L
/rfc0	Column I, J, K
Lease Alternative	
/rfc0	Row 26, 29; Cell C31
/rf,0	Row 27

	Format	*Range*

Debt Alternative

	/rfc0	Row 40, 52; Cell C55
	/rf,0	Row 41,43,45,46,48,50

Salvage Value of Equipment

	/rfc0	E61, E67
	/rf,0	E62, E64, E65
	/rfc0	E67

Depreciation Table

	/rf,0	H60..H67, J60..L70

Results

	/rfc0	E80, E81

Formulas should be entered next. Use the list of formulas and their cell locations found in table 12.4. Although the model contains many lengthy formulas, most of them can be entered once, copied, and then edited using the F2 (EDIT) key.

Table 12.4
Formulas and Functions

Enter into cell:	Original formula:	Copy to:
	Assumptions	
E15:	@VLOOKUP(1,K12..L18,1)	
	Implicit Rate Calculator	
I11:	@PMT(E17,H11,E14)	
J12:	+E13	
K12:	+I12-J12	K13..K18
L12:	+H12	L13..L18
J13:	+J12	J14..J18
	Lease Alternative	
D24:	+C24+1	D24..AH24
		D38..AH38
C26:	@IF($E$14>=C24,-$E$13,0)	D26..AH26
C27:	+$E$9*C26	D27..AH27
B29:	+B26*(1-$E$9)	
C29:	+C26-C27	D29..AH29
C31:	@NPV($E$11*(1-$E$9), C29..AH29)	

Enter
into
cell: Original formula: Copy to:

Debt Alternative

B40:   +E17
C40:   +B43   D40..AH40
C41:   @IF(C38<=$E14,-$B40/$E14,0)   D41..AH41
B43:   +B40+B41   C43..AH43
C45:   -$E$11*C40   D45..AH45
C48:   (C45+C46)*-$E$9   D48..AH48
C50:   @IF($E$14=C38,$E$67,0)   D50..AH50
B52:   -B43
C52:   +C41+C45+C48+C50   D52..AH52
C55:   @IF(E14=3,@NPV($E$11*(1-$E$9),C52..E52),
        @IF(E14=5,@NPV($E$11*(1-$E$9),C52..G52),
        @IF(E14=7,@NPV($E$11*(1-$E$9),C52..I52),0)))

Salvage Value of Equipment

E61:   +$E$19
E62:   +B40+@IF(E14=3,@SUM(C46..E46),@IF(E14=5,@SUM(C46..G46),
        @IF(E14=7,@SUM(C46..I46),@IF(E14=10,@SUM(C46..L46),
        @IF(E14=15,@SUM(C46..Q46),@IF(E14=20,@SUM(C46..V46),
        @IF(E14=27.5,@SUM(C46..AE46),
        @IF(E14=31.5,@SUM(C46..AH46),0))))))))
E64:   +E61-E62
E65:   +E64*E9
E67:   +E64-E65

Depreciation Table

J60:   @ROUND(@IF($E$14=3,@CHOOSE
        (+$E$14,0,0,0,2/3,0,2/5,0,2/7)*-$E$17*0.5,0),0)
K60:   @ROUND(@IF($E$14=5,@CHOOSE
        (+$E$14,0,0,0,2/3,0,2/5,0,2/7)*-$E$17*0.5,0),0)
L60:   @ROUND(@IF($E$14=7,@CHOOSE
        (+$E$14,0,0,0,2/3,0,2/5,0,2/7)*-$E$17*0.5,0),0)
J61:   @ROUND(@IF($E$14=3,@CHOOSE(+$E$14,0,0,0,2/3,0,2/5,0,2/7)*
        (-$E$17-@SUM($J$60..J60)),0),0)
K61:   @ROUND(@IF($E$14=5,@CHOOSE(+$E$14,0,0,0,2/3,0,2/5,0,2/7)*
        (-$E$17-@SUM($K$60..K60)),0),0)
L61:   @ROUND(@IF($E$14=7,@CHOOSE(+$E$14,0,0,0,2/3,0,2/5,0,2/7)*
        (-$E$17-@SUM($L$60..L60)),0),0)
J62:   @ROUND(@IF($E$14=3,(-$E$17-$J$60-$J$61)/($E$14/2),0),0)

K62:   @ROUND(@IF($E$14=5,@CHOOSE(+$E$14,0,0,0,2/3,0,2/5,0,2/7)*
        (-$E$17-@SUM($K$60..K61)),0),0)
L62:   @ROUND(@IF($E$14=7,@CHOOSE(+$E$14,0,0,0,2/3,0,2/5,0,2/7)*
        (-$E$17-@SUM($L$60..L61)),0),0)
J63:   @ROUND(@IF($E$14=3,-$E$17-@SUM($J$60..$J$62),0),0)
K63:   @ROUND(@IF($E$14=5,(-$E$17-$K$60-$K$61-$K$62)/($E$14/2),0),0)
L63:   @ROUND(@IF($E$14=7,@CHOOSE(+$E$14,0,0,0,2/3,0,2/5,0,2/7)*
        (-$E$17-@SUM($L$60..L62)),0),0)
K64:   @ROUND(@IF($E$14=5,(-$E$17-$K$60-$K$61-$K$62)/($E$14/2),0),0)
L64:   @ROUND(@IF($E$14=7,(-$E$17-$L$60-$L$61-$L$62-$L$63)/
        ($E$14/2),0),0)
K65:   @ROUND(@IF($E$14=5,-$E$17-@SUM(K$60..K64),0),0)
L65:   @ROUND(@IF($E$14=7,(-$E$17-$L$60-$L$61-$L$62-$L$63)/
        ($E$14/2),0),0)
L66:   @ROUND(@IF($E$14=7,(-$E$17-$L$60-$L$61-$L$62-$L$63)/
        ($E$14/2),0),0)
L67:   @ROUND(@IF($E$14=7,-$E$17-@SUM(L$59..L66),0),0)
J70:   @SUM(J60..J63)
K70:   @SUM(K60..K65)
L70:   @SUM(L60..L67)

Results

E80:   +C31
E82:   +C55

Understanding the Model

As you can see, the Lease versus Debt Evaluator is an application that relies on interdependent worksheet areas. Before discussing the individual modules, it is important that you understand the concept of the time value of money. This concept is an integral part of the model.

The Time Value of Money

The cornerstone of financial theory states that, because of the interest you could be earning on the dollar today, your money is more valuable to you at the present rather than in the future. In other words, a dollar today is worth more to you than a dollar a year from now. Hence, you should choose the investment with the highest "present value" of future cash flows.

We use this generally accepted theory in the Lease versus Debt Evaluator to determine the best, or least expensive, financing alternative for your firm. You will want to choose the financing option with the highest present value. But because the lease and debt payments represent cash outflows to your business, you need to choose the alternative with the lowest negative value. In the example in figure 12.1, the choice would be the Loan Alternative.

Now that you have been introduced to the concept behind the model, the assumptions about your business's financing alternatives will be addressed.

The Assumptions Module

The Assumptions module begins at cell A5 and continues to cell G20 (see fig. 12.2). In this module, you provide data about your financing alternatives. The model then can indicate the most cost-effective method for your business.

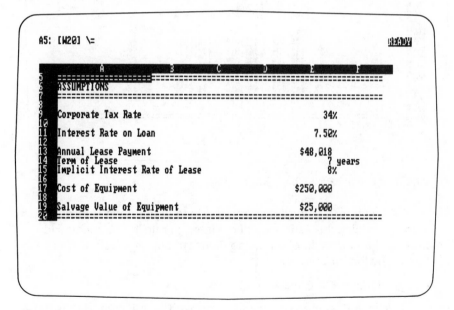

Fig. 12.2. The Assumptions module.

With the exception of the implicit interest rate of your lease, the information required in this model is self-explanatory. You can enter your lease's implicit interest rate manually from information provided by

your lessor, or you can use the model's Implicit Rate Calculator to
calculate the rate for you.

The Implicit Rate Calculator

The Implicit Rate Calculator module is located in cells I1 through M20,
directly to the right of the Assumptions section (see fig. 12.3). If you do
not know the implicit interest rate of your lease, the model uses a one-
variable data table to compute the rate for you.

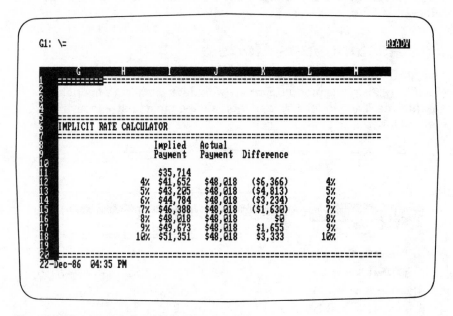

Fig. 12.3. The Implicit Rate Calculator module.

To understand how this module operates, look at columns H through L.
Column H contains the estimates of the interest rate 1-2-3 will use to
calculate column I, the Implied Lease Payment column. Column I is
calculated by the formula in cell I11:

I11: @PMT(E17,H11,E14)

In this formula, E17 is the cost of your proposed acquisition, H11 is the
interest rate, and E14 is the term of your lease. When you activate the
data table, each rate from the range H12..H18 is substituted into cell
H11. After each substitution, the function in cell I11 is recomputed by
the rate that has been substituted into cell H11. The results of the
computation are placed in the range I12..I18.

To understand these calculations, refer to figure 12.3. Column I displays the Implied Payment amounts as a result of the formula in cell I11 and the data table operation. Column J contains the actual lease payment from your data in the Assumptions module. Specifically, the amount in cell J12 uses the formula

J12: +E13

to retrieve this value. The remaining cells in column J, which reference cell J12, also contain your lease payment.

By subtracting column J from column I, column K computes the difference between the Implied Payment and the Actual Payment. For example, in the formula in cell K12:

K12: +I12-J12

I12 is the Implied Payment, J12 is the Actual Payment, and K12 is the difference between the two cells.

Finally, column L forms a lookup table by referencing the cells in column H. For example, cell L12 contains the formula

L12: +H12

The column L cells allow cell E15, the Implicit Interest Rate from the Assumptions module, to read the correct interest rate from the Implicit Rate Calculator. The formula contained in cell E15 is

E15: @VLOOKUP(1,K12..L18,1)

In this formula, the first 1 is the test variable, K12..L18 is the range, and the final 1 is the column offset number. In this scenario, 1-2-3 will search column K for 1. However, because 1 is not in column K, and 1655 is too large a number, zero is the next logical choice. The corresponding value in column L (8%) is returned to cell E15. After the model computes the Implicit Interest Rate, this interest rate will be used to calculate the present value of your total lease expense.

The Lease Alternative Module

The Lease Alternative module is located in cells A21 through AH31, below the Assumptions and Implicit Rate Calculator modules. Figure 12.4 displays a portion of this module. The module uses the data in the Assumptions section to calculate your annual after-tax cost and its present value.

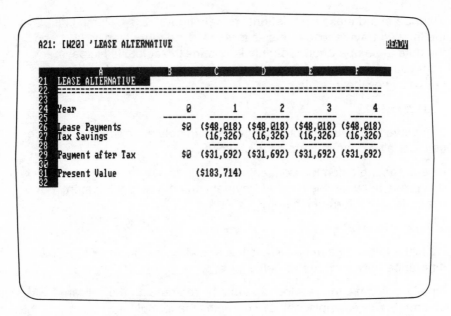

Fig. 12.4. A portion of the Lease Alternative module.

Row 24 displays the time frame (as many as 15 years) of this financing alternative. The columns are numbered by the formula, for example, in cell D24

D24: +C24+1

The remaining column headings are numbered similarly. Row 26 contains your annual lease payment, which is entered for you by the equation

C26: @IF($E$14>=C24,-$E$13,0)

This formula states that if the term of the lease in cell E14 is greater than or equal to the number of the current year, then enter the negative payment amount from cell E13 into cell C26; otherwise, enter a zero into cell C26. In other words, the formula tells 1-2-3 to stop entering lease payments when the number of the current year exceeds the term of the lease. The other cells in row 26 contain relative versions of this equation.

The next row, 27, calculates the amount of tax savings you realize because lease payments are tax deductible. For example, cell C27 contains the formula

C27: +$E9*C26

which retrieves the corporate tax rate of your business and multiplies it by your annual lease payment to arrive at the amount of tax savings to your firm.

Row 28 computes your annual after-tax lease payments, which are used by the model to calculate the present value of your lease. The difference between your lease payment (row 26) and the tax savings (row 27) is your annual after-tax lease payment. In year 1, cell C29, this is calculated by the formula

C29: +C26-C27

Row 31 holds the final calculation, the Present Value of the Lease. Cell C31 contains the 1-2-3 @NPV function to perform this calculation:

C31: @NPV($E$11*(1-$E$9),C29..AH29)

The expression $E$11*(1-$E$9) is the discount rate and C29..AH29 is the range of cash flows.

Current thinking is that the appropriate discount rate is the after-tax cost of debt. This is represented in the equation by cell E11, the interest rate of your loan alternative, multiplied by the cost of borrowing, which is calculated by subtracting 1 from your corporate tax rate (in cell E9). This equation computes your proper discount rate and will be used to calculate the present value of your loan alternative.

The Debt Alternative Module

The Debt Alternative is located in cells A35 through AH55, directly below the Lease Alternative. Figure 12.5 shows the components of the Debt Alternative module.

Except for the addition of several line items to accommodate the financial advantages of debt financing, the structure of this section is similar to that of the Lease Alternative. To number years, for example, row 38 uses the same arithmetic used by row 24 in the Lease Alternative.

Row 40, however, displays your declining loan balance by year, as opposed to your proposed fixed-lease payment amount. 1-2-3 uses references to other cells in the model to accomplish this. For example, your beginning loan amount in cell B40 contains the formula

B40: +E17

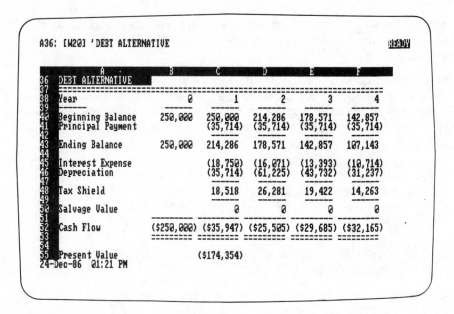

Fig. 12.5. The Debt Alternative module.

from the Assumptions section, and your first year loan balance is calculated by the formula

C40: +B43

All subsequent years refer to the previous year's ending balance to compute your beginning loan balances.

Row 41 calculates your annual principal payment. The formula in cell C41,

C41: @IF(C38<=$E14,-$B40/$E14,0)

instructs 1-2-3 to test whether the year value in C38 is less than or equal to the financing term. If so, the model will divide the loan amount by the number of years in the term (7, in our example) and place this amount in the cell. If not, a zero will be returned. In this manner, the first phrase in the equation stops the model from making principal payments when the term of the loan expires.

Row 43 calculates the end-of-year loan balances by subtracting your principal payment from the beginning year balance. For example, cell C43 holds the equation

C43: +C40+C41

Next, row 45 computes your annual interest expense. The equation in C45, for instance, contains the formula

C45: -$E$11*C40

which simply multiplies the interest rate of the loan found in the Assumptions section by the current year's beginning loan balance.

Row 46 contains your annual depreciation expense. These values, which are calculated by the Depreciation Table, can be placed in row 46 by the \d macro or entered manually. (The operation of the Depreciation Table and of the macro is discussed later in the chapter.)

Row 48 calculates the tax shield that the Loan Alternative generates from the tax-deductibility of your interest and depreciation expenses. (Note that, because of changes in the tax law, figure 12.4 does not include Investment Tax Credit (ITC). Repeal of the ITC reduces the tax shield and makes the alternative less financially attractive to your firm.) Cell C48 calculates the tax-shield for year 1 with the formula

C48: (C45+C46)*-$E$9

which multiplies the sum of your first year interest and depreciation expenses by your corporate tax rate.

Row 50 includes the salvage value in the Debt Alternative worksheet area of your proposed asset acquisition. (Those of you who are familiar with the first edition of this book will recall that the present value of the salvage value of your proposed equipment purchase was addressed only in the book's "Salvage Value of Equipment" section.) In this edition, any after-tax gain on the sale of the asset is still calculated in the "Salvage Value of Equipment" section. However, the formula in C50, for example, is used to place this amount in the proper year in the Debt Alternative:

C50: @IF($E$14=C38,$E$67,0)

This formula states that if the number of financing years equals the Debt Alternative year, place the salvage value in cell E67 into cell C50. If not, place a zero in the cell.

Row 52 calculates the annual cash flows to be used in computing your loan alternative's present value. The sum of your loan payments, interest expense, tax shield, and salvage value of the equipment equals your company's cash flow for your debt alternative. Cell C52, for instance, calculates the debt alternative's cash flows with the formula

C52: +C41+C45+C48+C50

The final row in this section, row 55, contains the equation to calculate the present value for your debt alternative. Cell C55 contains the formula

C55: @IF(E14=3,@NPV($E$11*(1-$E$9),C52..E52),
        @IF(E14=5,@NPV($E$11*(1-$E$9),C52..G52),
        @IF(E14=7,@NPV($E$11*(1-$E$9),C52..I52),0)))

In this formula, the three @IF statements determine (from cell E14) which @NPV statement to use. Choosing the proper @IF statement is necessary because you want to include in the calculation only those cash flows that are appropriate for the useful life of the asset. The phrase $E$11*(1-$E$9) is your discount rate (discussed in the Lease Alternative section) and the range C52 to E, G, or I52 is the proper cash flow for your loan alternative.

The Salvage-Value-of-Equipment Module

The Salvage-Value-of-Equipment module begins at cell A58 and continues to E68 (see fig. 12.6). Located directly below the Loan Alternative module, this worksheet area calculates the after-tax cash flow from your asset disposal.

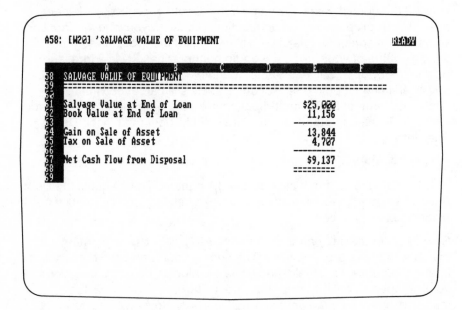

Fig. 12.6. The Salvage-Value-of-Equipment module.

Salvage Value is calculated by referencing your salvage value estimate from the Assumptions module. The formula for this computation is

E61: +$E$19

Next, the book value of your equipment proposal is calculated at cell E62, which uses the formula

```
E62: +B40+@IF(E14=3,@SUM(C46..E46),
            @IF(E14=5,@SUM(C46..G46),
            @IF(E14=7,@SUM(C46..I46),
            @IF(E14=10,@SUM(C46..L46),
            @IF(E14=15,@SUM(C46..Q46),
            @IF(E14=20,@SUM(C46..V46),
            @IF(E14=27.5,@SUM(C46..AE46),
            @IF(E14=31.5,@SUM(C46..AH46),0))))))))
```

This formula is similar to that in cell C55, which computes the present value of your loan alternative. Cell B40, your loan amount, is added to the sum of the appropriate annual depreciation amounts. 1-2-3 uses the @IF statements to determine the proper number of years of depreciation to sum, based on the useful life of the asset from cell E14 in the Assumptions worksheet.

Your Gain on Sale of the Asset, which is the difference between the Salvage and Book Values of the proposed equipment, is calculated in cell E64 by the formula

E64: +E61-E62

Next, the amount of federal income tax is computed in cell E65. To arrive at the amount of tax on any gain on the sale of the asset, the formula in this cell references your federal corporate tax rate in the Assumptions section. The equation is

E65: +E64*E9

which multiplies the amount of the gain (E64) by your tax rate (E9).

Finally, the Net Cash Flow from the asset's disposal is computed in cell E67. This amount will be the difference between your gain on the sale and the tax liability it generates. The formula is simply

E67: +E64-E65

This is the same value that will be used by the model to compute the present value of your Debt Alternative. Another factor that influences cash flow is your depreciation expense, which is calculated in the Depreciation Table module.

The Depreciation Table

New with this edition of the book, the modified ACRS Depreciation Table is located in cells G58 through L71, directly to the left of the Salvage Value worksheet (see fig. 12.7).

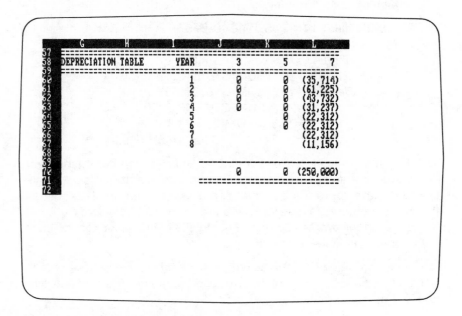

Fig. 12.7. The modified ACRS Depreciation Table.

In the first edition, you had to enter the appropriate ACRS depreciation rate for the appropriate asset class and year for the Debt Alternative, so that the model could calculate depreciation for this option.

In this edition, however, the model performs the depreciation calculation for you, using a series of @CHOOSE functions and the new depreciation rules. The new depreciation rules are, in effect, the double-declining balance method, switching to straight-line depreciation at the asset's midlife, with a midyear convention. (See Chapter 13 for a more thorough discussion of the Tax Reform Act of 1986, as it relates to cost recovery.)

Consider the following formula in cell J60, which is the first year depreciation formula for the three-year ACRS asset classification:

```
J60: @ROUND(@IF($E$14=3,
     @CHOOSE(+$E$14,0,0,0,2/3,0,2/5,0,2/7)*$E$17*0.5,0),0)
```

This formula tells 1-2-3 to determine (by examining cell E14) whether the asset is in the three-year category. If so, the @CHOOSE function uses the key cell (E14) to select 2/3, multiply it by cell E17 (cost of asset), and multiply it again by 0.5 (mid-year convention). If not, zero is returned in cell J60. Both results are rounded by 1-2-3's @ROUND function.

Subsequently, the model will examine the contents of cells K60 and L60 and then place the first year depreciation, or zero, in the correct depreciation column. Using the @CHOOSE function in this manner, 1-2-3 will select the correct asset classification and year, based on the year value in cell E14.

Your total depreciation expense is totaled by using the @SUM function. For three-year assets, this formula is

J60: @SUM(J60..J63)

You can transfer this depreciation data manually or use the \d macro to transfer it automatically. If you intend to use the macro, study the following section. If you're not going to use the macro, you can move on to the Results section.

Using the \d Macro

The \d macro shown in figure 12.8 helps you to transfer the annual depreciation values from the Depreciation Table to the proper cell locations in the Debt Alternative module.

This macro, like the others in this book, begins with Release 2's Paneloff and Windowsoff feature. The next three lines of the macro instruct 1-2-3 to examine the contents of cell E14 to determine the useful life of the asset. Based on this information, the cursor will be moved to the proper depreciation column.

The worksheet is then calculated to compute your annual depreciation values. After the worksheet has been calculated, the cursor is moved down two cell locations from the proper depreciation range name.

The macro's sixth through eleventh lines address copying of the annual depreciation values. Using Release 2's /Range Value command, these amounts are copied from the appropriate column in the Depreciation Table to cell H60. Then the /Range Transpose command is used to copy these values horizontally to cell C46, the first cell in the depreciation row.

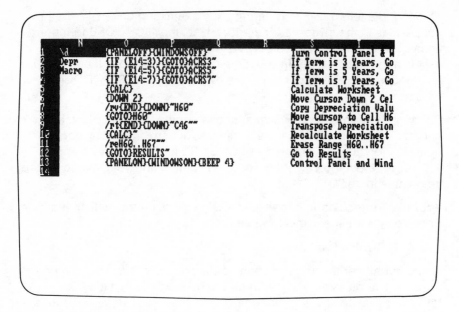

Fig. 12.8. The \d macro.

Next, the model is again recalculated to determine the present value of both alternatives, after which the macro erases the range H60..H67.

Finally, the cursor is moved to the range name RESULTS in the Results module so that you can see the outcome of the model's operations. The control panel and windows are turned on and the computer will beep, indicating that the macro has ended.

The Results Module

Located directly below the Salvage Value section, the model's Results section appears in cells A76 through E82 (see fig. 12.9). This section serves as a summary area and a convenience to you. You can use Results instead of paging up or down to compare the two present values.

Cell E80 contains the present value of your lease, a value calculated by referencing cell C31 in the Lease Alternative module:

E80: +C31

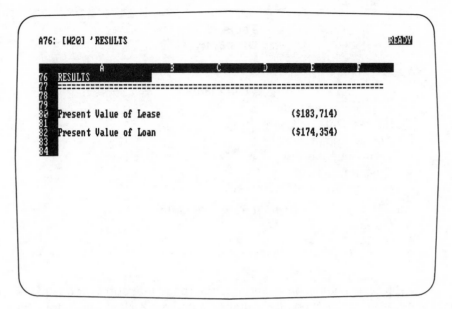

A76: [W20] 'RESULTS   READY

```
          A          B        C        D        E        F
76  RESULTS
77  ============================================================
78
79
80  Present Value of Lease                      ($183,714)
81
82  Present Value of Loan                       ($174,354)
83
84
```

Fig. 12.9. The Results module.

The present value of your debt alternative is calculated by referencing cell C55 in the Debt Alternative:

   E82: +C55

If you understand this practical application and how it can assist you in selecting the best financing arrangement for your firm, you are ready to use the model.

Using the Model

The Lease versus Debt Evaluator is straightforward and easy to use. Because the model's data-entry requirements are confined, for the most part, to the Assumptions section, begin using the model by entering your data according to table 12.5.

Next, issue the **/D**ata **T**able **1** command. Remember that the Implicit Rate Calculator is a one-variable data table. The range will be H11..I18, with H11 as the input cell.

After performing the **D**ata **T**able operation, if you do not have a zero value in column K, you'll need to repeat the **/D**ata **T**able **1** command. First, issue the **/D**ata **T**able **R**eset command and then change your

Table 12.5
Data Entry

Description	Cell Location
Assumptions	
Corporate Tax Rate	E9
Interest Rate on Loan	E11
Annual Lease Pymt	E13
Term of Lease	E14
Cost of Equipment	E17
Salvage Value of Equipment	E19
Implicit Rate Calculator	
Interest Rates	H12..H18

interest rate estimates in column H to the range that corresponds to the first negative and first positive number in column K. (In fig. 12.1, for example, this would be .08 and .09, and values between these numbers.)

If you reissue the /Data Table 1 command, you get an exact interest rate of 0.825. After 1-2-3 has performed the Data Table routine, the next step is to have the model calculate your depreciation values.

At this point, you can use the \d macro or manually calculate the depreciation. If you decide to use the macro, press the Alt key and then hold it down while you press also the d key. The model will calculate depreciation, transfer the values to the Debt Alternative, and calculate the present values of your two financing alternatives.

If, on the other hand, you prefer to perform the depreciation calculation manually, press F9 (CALC). 1-2-3 will compute your annual depreciation. Enter these amounts in the appropriate cell in row 46 of the Debt Alternative. Finally, press F9 (CALC) again for the present value calculations. The lower amount in the Results section will be the less expensive financing option for your business. In the sample model, this would be the Debt Alternative, despite the loss of the Investment Tax Credit and lengthened depreciation life.

The Lease versus Debt Evaluator is also easy to modify. Use the /Worksheet Insert Row command if you need to tailor the model to your business or want to consider "what-if" scenarios. You may need to do this, because the sample model assumes, for example, that maintenance and insurance are the responsibility of the lessee and that these costs are the same for both leased and purchased assets. The example also assumes that your lease payments occur once a year, at the end of the year. Fortunately, 1-2-3 and the model can accommodate your firm's unique needs.

Conclusion

The Lease versus Debt Evaluator can help you decide the best, least expensive financing arrangements for your firm's asset acquisitions. You have learned that, although the Investment Tax Credit has been eliminated and depreciation lives have been lengthened, comparing the cost of your financing alternatives is still worthwhile. Let 1-2-3 and the Lease versus Debt Evaluator perform this analysis quickly and easily for you.

A1: [W20] \=
B1: \=
C1: \=
D1: \=
E1: \=
F1: \=
G1: \=
H1: \=
I1: \=
J1: \=
K1: \=
L1: \=
M1: \=
N1: '\d
O1: '{PANELOFF}{WINDOWSOFF}~
S1: 'Turn Control Panel & Windows Off
N2: 'Depr
O2: '{IF (E14=3)}{GOTO}ACRS3~
S2: 'If Term is 3 Years, Go to Range Name ACRS3
A3: [W20] 'LEASE VS. DEBT EVALUATOR
C3: '   Copyright (C) 1987 Que Corporation
N3: 'Macro
O3: '{IF (E14=5)}{GOTO}ACRS5~
S3: 'If Term is 5 Years, Go to Range Name ACRS5
O4: '{IF (E14=7)}{GOTO}ACRS7~
S4: 'If Term is 7 Years, Go to Range Name ACRS7
A5: [W20] \=
B5: \=
C5: \=
D5: \=
E5: \=
F5: \=
G5: \=
H5: \=
I5: \=
J5: \=
K5: \=
L5: \=
M5: \=
O5: '{CALC}
S5: 'Calculate Worksheet
A6: [W20] 'ASSUMPTIONS
G6: 'IMPLICIT RATE CALCULATOR
O6: '{DOWN 2}
S6: 'Move Cursor Down 2 Cells
A7: [W20] \=
B7: \=
C7: \=
D7: \=
E7: \=
F7: \=
G7: \=
H7: \=
I7: \=

J7: \=
K7: \=
L7: \=
M7: \=
O7: '/rv{END}{DOWN}~H60~
S7: 'Copy Depreciation Values to Range Beginning at Cell H60
I8: ' Implied
J8: ' Actual
O8: '{GOTO}H60~
S8: 'Move Cursor to Cell H60
A9: [W20] 'Corporate Tax Rate
E9: (P0) 0.34
I9: ' Payment
J9: ' Payment
K9: 'Difference
O9: '/rt{END}{DOWN}~C46~~
S9: 'Transpose Depreciation Values to Cell C46
O10: '{CALC}~
S10: 'Recalculate Worksheet
A11: [W20] 'Interest Rate on Loan
E11: (P2) 0.075
I11: (C0) @PMT(E17,H11,E14)
O11: '/reH60..H67~~
S11: 'Erase Range H60..H67
H12: (P0) 0.04
I12: (C0) 41652.40301
J12: (C0) +E13
K12: (C0) +I12-J12
L12: (P0) +H12
O12: '{GOTO}RESULTS~
S12: 'Go to Results
A13: [W20] 'Annual Lease Payment
E13: (C0) 48018
H13: (P0) 0.05
I13: (C0) 43204.954612
J13: (C0) +J12
K13: (C0) +I13-J13
L13: (P0) +H13
O13: '{PANELON}{WINDOWSON}{BEEP 4}
S13: 'Control Panel and Windows On; Beep When Finished
A14: [W20] 'Term of Lease
E14: 7
F14: 'years
H14: (P0) 0.06
I14: (C0) 44783.754515
J14: (C0) +J13
K14: (C0) +I14-J14
L14: (P0) +H14
A15: [W20] 'Implicit Interest Rate of Lease
E15: (P0) @VLOOKUP(1,K12..L18,1)
H15: (P0) 0.07
I15: (C0) 46388.304908
J15: (C0) +J14
K15: (C0) +I15-J15

L15: (P0) +H15
H16: (P0) 0.08
I16: (C0) 48018.100357
J16: (C0) +J15
K16: (C0) +I16−J16
L16: (P0) +H16
A17: [W20] 'Cost of Equipment
E17: (C0) 250000
H17: (P0) 0.09
I17: (C0) 49672.629208
J17: (C0) +J16
K17: (C0) +I17−J17
L17: (P0) +H17
H18: (P0) 0.1
I18: (C0) 51351.374925
J18: (C0) +J17
K18: (C0) +I18−J18
L18: (P0) +H18
A19: [W20] 'Salvage Value of Equipment
E19: (C0) 25000
A20: [W20] \=
B20: \=
C20: \=
D20: \=
E20: \=
F20: \=
G20: \=
H20: \=
I20: \=
J20: \=
K20: \=
L20: \=
M20: \=
N20: \=
O20: \=
P20: \=
Q20: \=
R20: \=
S20: \=
T20: \=
U20: \=
V20: \=
W20: \=
X20: \=
Y20: \=
Z20: \=
AA20: \=
AB20: \=
AC20: \=
AD20: \=
AE20: \=
AF20: \=
AG20: \=
AH20: \=

A21: [W20] 'LEASE ALTERNATIVE
A22: [W20] \=
B22: \=
C22: \=
D22: \=
E22: \=
F22: \=
G22: \=
H22: \=
I22: \=
J22: \=
K22: \=
L22: \=
M22: \=
N22: \=
O22: \=
P22: \=
Q22: \=
R22: \=
S22: \=
T22: \=
U22: \=
V22: \=
W22: \=
X22: \=
Y22: \=
Z22: \=
AA22: \=
AB22: \=
AC22: \=
AD22: \=
AE22: \=
AF22: \=
AG22: \=
AH22: \=
A24: [W20] 'Year
B24: 0
C24: 1
D24: +C24+1
E24: +D24+1
F24: +E24+1
G24: +F24+1
H24: +G24+1
I24: +H24+1
J24: +I24+1
K24: +J24+1
L24: +K24+1
M24: +L24+1
N24: +M24+1
O24: +N24+1
P24: +O24+1
Q24: +P24+1
R24: +Q24+1
S24: +R24+1

```
T24: +S24+1                          G26: (C0) @IF($E$14>=G24,-$E$13,0)
U24: +T24+1                          H26: (C0) @IF($E$14>=H24,-$E$13,0)
V24: +U24+1                          I26: (C0) @IF($E$14>=I24,-$E$13,0)
W24: +V24+1                          J26: (C0) @IF($E$14>=J24,-$E$13,0)
X24: +W24+1                          K26: (C0) @IF($E$14>=K24,-$E$13,0)
Y24: +X24+1                          L26: (C0) @IF($E$14>=L24,-$E$13,0)
Z24: +Y24+1                          M26: (C0) @IF($E$14>=M24,-$E$13,0)
AA24: +Z24+1                         N26: (C0) @IF($E$14>=N24,-$E$13,0)
AB24: +AA24+1                        O26: (C0) @IF($E$14>=O24,-$E$13,0)
AC24: +AB24+1                        P26: (C0) @IF($E$14>=P24,-$E$13,0)
AD24: +AC24+1                        Q26: (C0) @IF($E$14>=Q24,-$E$13,0)
AE24: +AD24+1                        R26: (C0) @IF($E$14>=R24,-$E$13,0)
AF24: +AE24+1                        S26: (C0) @IF($E$14>=S24,-$E$13,0)
AG24: +AF24+1                        T26: (C0) @IF($E$14>=T24,-$E$13,0)
AH24: +AG24+1                        U26: (C0) @IF($E$14>=U24,-$E$13,0)
B25: ' -------                       V26: (C0) @IF($E$14>=V24,-$E$13,0)
C25: ' -------                       W26: (C0) @IF($E$14>=W24,-$E$13,0)
D25: ' -------                       X26: (C0) @IF($E$14>=X24,-$E$13,0)
E25: ' -------                       Y26: (C0) @IF($E$14>=Y24,-$E$13,0)
F25: ' -------                       Z26: (C0) @IF($E$14>=Z24,-$E$13,0)
G25: ' -------                       AA26: (C0) @IF($E$14>=AA24,-$E$13,0)
H25: ' -------                       AB26: (C0) @IF($E$14>=AB24,-$E$13,0)
I25: ' -------                       AC26: (C0) @IF($E$14>=AC24,-$E$13,0)
J25: ' -------                       AD26: (C0) @IF($E$14>=AD24,-$E$13,0)
K25: ' -------                       AE26: (C0) @IF($E$14>=AE24,-$E$13,0)
L25: ' -------                       AF26: (C0) @IF($E$14>=AF24,-$E$13,0)
M25: ' -------                       AG26: (C0) @IF($E$14>=AG24,-$E$13,0)
N25: ' -------                       AH26: (C0) @IF($E$14>=AH24,-$E$13,0)
O25: ' -------                       A27: [W20] 'Tax Savings
P25: ' -------                       C27: (,0) +$E9*C26
Q25: ' -------                       D27: (,0) +$E9*D26
R25: ' -------                       E27: (,0) +$E9*E26
S25: ' -------                       F27: (,0) +$E9*F26
T25: ' -------                       G27: (,0) +$E9*G26
U25: ' -------                       H27: (,0) +$E9*H26
V25: ' -------                       I27: (,0) +$E9*I26
W25: ' -------                       J27: (,0) +$E9*J26
X25: ' -------                       K27: (,0) +$E9*K26
Y25: ' -------                       L27: (,0) +$E9*L26
Z25: ' -------                       M27: (,0) +$E9*M26
AA25: ' -------                      N27: (,0) +$E9*N26
AB25: ' -------                      O27: (,0) +$E9*O26
AC25: ' -------                      P27: (,0) +$E9*P26
AD25: ' -------                      Q27: (,0) +$E9*Q26
AE25: ' -------                      R27: (,0) +$E9*R26
AF25: ' -------                      S27: (,0) +$E9*S26
AG25: ' -------                      T27: (,0) +$E9*T26
AH25: ' -------                      U27: (,0) +$E9*U26
A26: [W20] 'Lease Payments           V27: (,0) +$E9*V26
B26: (C0) 0                          W27: (,0) +$E9*W26
C26: (C0) @IF($E$14>=C24,-$E$13,0)   X27: (,0) +$E9*X26
D26: (C0) @IF($E$14>=D24,-$E$13,0)   Y27: (,0) +$E9*Y26
E26: (C0) @IF($E$14>=E24,-$E$13,0)   Z27: (,0) +$E9*Z26
F26: (C0) @IF($E$14>=F24,-$E$13,0)   AA27: (,0) +$E9*AA26
```

```
AB27: (,0) +$E9*AB26          P29: (C0) +P26-P27
AC27: (,0) +$E9*AC26          Q29: (C0) +Q26-Q27
AD27: (,0) +$E9*AD26          R29: (C0) +R26-R27
AE27: (,0) +$E9*AE26           S29: (C0) +S26-S27
AF27: (,0) +$E9*AF26          T29: (C0) +T26-T27
AG27: (,0) +$E9*AG26          U29: (C0) +U26-U27
AH27: (,0) +$E9*AH26          V29: (C0) +V26-V27
C28: '   ------              W29: (C0) +W26-W27
D28: '   ------              X29: (C0) +X26-X27
E28: '   ------              Y29: (C0) +Y26-Y27
F28: '   ------              Z29: (C0) +Z26-Z27
G28: '   ------              AA29: (C0) +AA26-AA27
H28: '   ------              AB29: (C0) +AB26-AB27
I28: '   ------              AC29: (C0) +AC26-AC27
J28: '   ------              AD29: (C0) +AD26-AD27
K28: '   ------              AE29: (C0) +AE26-AE27
L28: '   ------              AF29: (C0) +AF26-AF27
M28: '   ------              AG29: (C0) +AG26-AG27
N28: '   ------              AH29: (C0) +AH26-AH27
O28: '   ------              A31: [W20] 'Present Value
P28: '   ------              C31: (C0) @NPV($E$11*(1-$E$9),C29..AH29)
Q28: '   ------              A35: [W20] \=
R28: '   ------              B35: \=
S28: '   ------              C35: \=
T28: '   ------              D35: \=
U28: '   ------              E35: \=
V28: '   ------              F35: \=
W28: '   ------              G35: \=
X28: '   ------              H35: \=
Y28: '   ------              I35: \=
Z28: '   ------              J35: \=
AA28: '   ------             K35: \=
AB28: '   ------             L35: \=
AC28: '   ------             M35: \=
AD28: '   ------             N35: \=
AE28: '   ------             O35: \=
AF28: '   ------             P35: \=
AG28: '   ------             Q35: \=
AH28: '   ------             R35: \=
A29: [W20] 'Payment after Tax S35: \=
B29: (C0) +B26*(1-$E$9)      T35: \=
C29: (C0) +C26-C27           U35: \=
D29: (C0) +D26-D27           V35: \=
E29: (C0) +E26-E27           W35: \=
F29: (C0) +F26-F27           X35: \=
G29: (C0) +G26-G27           Y35: \=
H29: (C0) +H26-H27           Z35: \=
I29: (C0) +I26-I27           AA35: \=
J29: (C0) +J26-J27           AB35: \=
K29: (C0) +K26-K27           AC35: \=
L29: (C0) +L26-L27           AD35: \=
M29: (C0) +M26-M27           AE35: \=
N29: (C0) +N26-N27           AF35: \=
O29: (C0) +O26-O27           AG35: \=
```

AH35: \=
A36: [W20] 'DEBT ALTERNATIVE
A37: [W20] \=
B37: \=
C37: \=
D37: \=
E37: \=
F37: \=
G37: \=
H37: \=
I37: \=
J37: \=
K37: \=
L37: \=
M37: \=
N37: \=
O37: \=
P37: \=
Q37: \=
R37: \=
S37: \=
T37: \=
U37: \=
V37: \=
W37: \=
X37: \=
Y37: \=
Z37: \=
AA37: \=
AB37: \=
AC37: \=
AD37: \=
AE37: \=
AF37: \=
AG37: \=
AH37: \=
A38: [W20] 'Year
B38: 0
C38: 1
D38: +C38+1
E38: +D38+1
F38: +E38+1
G38: +F38+1
H38: +G38+1
I38: +H38+1
J38: +I38+1
K38: +J38+1
L38: +K38+1
M38: +L38+1
N38: +M38+1
O38: +N38+1
P38: +O38+1
Q38: +P38+1
R38: +Q38+1

S38: +R38+1
T38: +S38+1
U38: +T38+1
V38: +U38+1
W38: +V38+1
X38: +W38+1
Y38: +X38+1
Z38: +Y38+1
AA38: +Z38+1
AB38: +AA38+1
AC38: +AB38+1
AD38: +AC38+1
AE38: +AD38+1
AF38: +AE38+1
AG38: +AF38+1
AH38: +AG38+1
A39: [W20] '------
B39: ' ------
C39: ' ------
D39: ' ------
E39: ' ------
F39: ' ------
G39: ' ------
H39: ' ------
I39: ' ------
J39: ' ------
K39: ' ------
L39: ' ------
M39: ' ------
N39: ' ------
O39: ' ------
P39: ' ------
Q39: ' ------
R39: ' ------
S39: ' ------
T39: ' ------
U39: ' ------
V39: ' ------
W39: ' ------
X39: ' ------
Y39: ' ------
Z39: ' ------
AA39: ' ------
AB39: ' ------
AC39: ' ------
AD39: ' ------
AE39: ' ------
AF39: ' ------
AG39: ' ------
AH39: ' ------
A40: [W20] 'Beginning Balance
B40: (,0) +E17
C40: (,0) +B43
D40: (,0) +C43

```
E40: (,0) +D43                          Z41: (,0) @IF(Z38<=$E14,-$B40/$E14,0)
F40: (,0) +E43                          AA41: (,0) @IF(AA38<=$E14,-$B40/$E14,0)
G40: (,0) +F43                          AB41: (,0) @IF(AB38<=$E14,-$B40/$E14,0)
H40: (,0) +G43                          AC41: (,0) @IF(AC38<=$E14,-$B40/$E14,0)
I40: (,0) +H43                          AD41: (,0) @IF(AD38<=$E14,-$B40/$E14,0)
J40: (,0) +I43                          AE41: (,0) @IF(AE38<=$E14,-$B40/$E14,0)
K40: (,0) +J43                          AF41: (,0) @IF(AF38<=$E14,-$B40/$E14,0)
L40: (,0) +K43                          AG41: (,0) @IF(AG38<=$E14,-$B40/$E14,0)
M40: (,0) +L43                          AH41: (,0) @IF(AH38<=$E14,-$B40/$E14,0)
N40: (,0) +M43                          C42: '  ------
O40: (,0) +N43                          D42: '  ------
P40: (,0) +O43                          E42: '  ------
Q40: (,0) +P43                          F42: '  ------
R40: (,0) +Q43                          G42: '  ------
S40: (,0) +R43                          H42: '  ------
T40: (,0) +S43                          I42: '  ------
U40: (,0) +T43                          J42: '  ------
V40: (,0) +U43                          K42: '  ------
W40: (,0) +V43                          L42: '  ------
X40: (,0) +W43                          M42: '  ------
Y40: (,0) +X43                          N42: '  ------
Z40: (,0) +Y43                          O42: '  ------
AA40: (,0) +Z43                         P42: '  ------
AB40: (,0) +AA43                        Q42: '  ------
AC40: (,0) +AB43                        R42: '  ------
AD40: (,0) +AC43                        S42: '  ------
AE40: (,0) +AD43                        T42: '  ------
AF40: (,0) +AE43                        U42: '  ------
AG40: (,0) +AF43                        V42: '  ------
AH40: (,0) +AG43                        W42: '  ------
A41: [W20] 'Principal Payment           X42: '  ------
C41: (,0) @IF(C38<=$E14,-$B40/$E14,0)    Y42: '  ------
D41: (,0) @IF(D38<=$E14,-$B40/$E14,0)    Z42: '  ------
                                        AA42: '  ------
E41: (,0) @IF(E38<=$E14,-$B40/$E14,0)    AB42: '  ------
F41: (,0) @IF(F38<=$E14,-$B40/$E14,0)    AC42: '  ------
G41: (,0) @IF(G38<=$E14,-$B40/$E14,0)    AD42: '  ------
H41: (,0) @IF(H38<=$E14,-$B40/$E14,0)    AE42: '  ------
I41: (,0) @IF(I38<=$E14,-$B40/$E14,0)    AF42: '  ------
J41: (,0) @IF(J38<=$E14,-$B40/$E14,0)    AG42: '  ------
K41: (,0) @IF(K38<=$E14,-$B40/$E14,0)    AH42: '  ------
L41: (,0) @IF(L38<=$E14,-$B40/$E14,0)    A43: [W20] 'Ending Balance
M41: (,0) @IF(M38<=$E14,-$B40/$E14,0)    B43: (,0) +B40+B41
N41: (,0) @IF(N38<=$E14,-$B40/$E14,0)    C43: (,0) +C40+C41
O41: (,0) @IF(O38<=$E14,-$B40/$E14,0)    D43: (,0) +D40+D41
P41: (,0) @IF(P38<=$E14,-$B40/$E14,0)    E43: (,0) +E40+E41
Q41: (,0) @IF(Q38<=$E14,-$B40/$E14,0)    F43: (,0) +F40+F41
R41: (,0) @IF(R38<=$E14,-$B40/$E14,0)    G43: (,0) +G40+G41
S41: (,0) @IF(S38<=$E14,-$B40/$E14,0)    H43: (,0) +H40+H41
T41: (,0) @IF(T38<=$E14,-$B40/$E14,0)    I43: (,0) +I40+I41
U41: (,0) @IF(U38<=$E14,-$B40/$E14,0)    J43: (,0) +J40+J41
V41: (,0) @IF(V38<=$E14,-$B40/$E14,0)    K43: (,0) +K40+K41
W41: (,0) @IF(W38<=$E14,-$B40/$E14,0)    L43: (,0) +L40+L41
X41: (,0) @IF(X38<=$E14,-$B40/$E14,0)    M43: (,0) +M40+M41
Y41: (,0) @IF(Y38<=$E14,-$B40/$E14,0)
```

N43: (,0) +N40+N41
O43: (,0) +O40+O41
P43: (,0) +P40+P41
Q43: (,0) +Q40+Q41
R43: (,0) +R40+R41
S43: (,0) +S40+S41
T43: (,0) +T40+T41
U43: (,0) +U40+U41
V43: (,0) +V40+V41
W43: (,0) +W40+W41
X43: (,0) +X40+X41
Y43: (,0) +Y40+Y41
Z43: (,0) +Z40+Z41
AA43: (,0) +AA40+AA41
AB43: (,0) +AB40+AB41
AC43: (,0) +AC40+AC41
AD43: (,0) +AD40+AD41
AE43: (,0) +AE40+AE41
AF43: (,0) +AF40+AF41
AG43: (,0) +AG40+AG41
AH43: (,0) +AH40+AH41
A45: [W20] 'Interest Expense
B45: (,0) '
C45: (,0) -$E$11*C40
D45: (,0) -$E$11*D40
E45: (,0) -$E$11*E40
F45: (,0) -$E$11*F40
G45: (,0) -$E$11*G40
H45: (,0) -$E$11*H40
I45: (,0) -$E$11*I40
J45: (,0) -$E$11*J40
K45: (,0) -$E$11*K40
L45: (,0) -$E$11*L40
M45: (,0) -$E$11*M40
N45: (,0) -$E$11*N40
O45: (,0) -$E$11*O40
P45: (,0) -$E$11*P40
Q45: (,0) -$E$11*Q40
R45: (,0) -$E$11*R40
S45: (,0) -$E$11*S40
T45: (,0) -$E$11*T40
U45: (,0) -$E$11*U40
V45: (,0) -$E$11*V40
W45: (,0) -$E$11*W40
X45: (,0) -$E$11*X40
Y45: (,0) -$E$11*Y40
Z45: (,0) -$E$11*Z40
AA45: (,0) -$E$11*AA40
AB45: (,0) -$E$11*AB40
AC45: (,0) -$E$11*AC40
AD45: (,0) -$E$11*AD40
AE45: (,0) -$E$11*AE40
AF45: (,0) -$E$11*AF40

AG45: (,0) -$E$11*AG40
AH45: (,0) -$E$11*AH40
A46: [W20] 'Depreciation
C46: (,0) -35714
D46: (,0) -61225
E46: (,0) -43732
F46: (,0) -31237
G46: (,0) -22312
H46: (,0) -22312
I46: (,0) -22312
J46: (,0) -11156
K46: (,0) 0
L46: (,0) 0
M46: (,0) 0
N46: (,0) 0
O46: (,0) 0
P46: (,0) 0
Q46: (,0) 0
R46: (,0) 0
S46: (,0) 0
T46: (,0) 0
U46: (,0) 0
V46: (,0) 0
W46: (,0) 0
X46: (,0) 0
Y46: (,0) 0
Z46: (,0) 0
AA46: (,0) 0
AB46: (,0) 0
AC46: (,0) 0
AD46: (,0) 0
AE46: (,0) 0
AF46: (,0) 0
AG46: (,0) 0
AH46: (,0) 0
C47: ' ------
D47: ' ------
E47: ' ------
F47: ' ------
G47: ' ------
H47: ' ------
I47: ' ------
J47: ' ------
K47: ' ------
L47: ' ------
M47: ' ------
N47: ' ------
O47: ' ------
P47: ' ------
Q47: ' ------
R47: ' ------
S47: ' ------
T47: ' ------

```
U47: '  ------              J49: '  ------
V47: '  ------              K49: '  ------
W47: '  ------              L49: '  ------
X47: '  ------              M49: '  ------
Y47: '  ------              N49: '  ------
Z47: '  ------              O49: '  ------
AA47: '  ------             P49: '  ------
AB47: '  ------             Q49: '  ------
AC47: '  ------             R49: '  ------
AD47: '  ------             S49: '  ------
AE47: '  ------             T49: '  ------
AF47: '  ------             U49: '  ------
AG47: '  ------             V49: '  ------
AH47: '  ------             W49: '  ------
A48: [W20] 'Tax Shield      X49: '  ------
C48: (,0) (C45+C46)*-$E$9    Y49: '  ------
D48: (,0) (D45+D46)*-$E$9    Z49: '  ------
E48: (,0) (E45+E46)*-$E$9    AA49: '  ------
F48: (,0) (F45+F46)*-$E$9    AB49: '  ------
G48: (,0) (G45+G46)*-$E$9    AC49: '  ------
H48: (,0) (H45+H46)*-$E$9    AD49: '  ------
I48: (,0) (I45+I46)*-$E$9    AE49: '  ------
J48: (,0) (J45+J46)*-$E$9    AF49: '  ------
K48: (,0) (K45+K46)*-$E$9    AG49: '  ------
L48: (,0) (L45+L46)*-$E$9    AH49: '  ------
M48: (,0) (M45+M46)*-$E$9    A50: [W20] 'Salvage Value
N48: (,0) (N45+N46)*-$E$9    C50: (,0) @IF($E$14=C38,$E$67,0)
O48: (,0) (O45+O46)*-$E$9    D50: (,0) @IF($E$14=D38,$E$67,0)
P48: (,0) (P45+P46)*-$E$9    E50: (,0) @IF($E$14=E38,$E$67,0)
Q48: (,0) (Q45+Q46)*-$E$9    F50: (,0) @IF($E$14=F38,$E$67,0)
R48: (,0) (R45+R46)*-$E$9    G50: (,0) @IF($E$14=G38,$E$67,0)
S48: (,0) (S45+S46)*-$E$9    H50: (,0) @IF($E$14=H38,$E$67,0)
T48: (,0) (T45+T46)*-$E$9    I50: (,0) @IF($E$14=I38,$E$67,0)
U48: (,0) (U45+U46)*-$E$9    J50: (,0) @IF($E$14=J38,$E$67,0)
V48: (,0) (V45+V46)*-$E$9    K50: (,0) @IF($E$14=K38,$E$67,0)
W48: (,0) (W45+W46)*-$E$9    L50: (,0) @IF($E$14=L38,$E$67,0)
X48: (,0) (X45+X46)*-$E$9    M50: (,0) @IF($E$14=M38,$E$67,0)
Y48: (,0) (Y45+Y46)*-$E$9    N50: (,0) @IF($E$14=N38,$E$67,0)
Z48: (,0) (Z45+Z46)*-$E$9    O50: (,0) @IF($E$14=O38,$E$67,0)
AA48: (,0) (AA45+AA46)*-$E$9 P50: (,0) @IF($E$14=P38,$E$67,0)
AB48: (,0) (AB45+AB46)*-$E$9 Q50: (,0) @IF($E$14=Q38,$E$67,0)
AC48: (,0) (AC45+AC46)*-$E$9 R50: (,0) @IF($E$14=R38,$E$67,0)
AD48: (,0) (AD45+AD46)*-$E$9 S50: (,0) @IF($E$14=S38,$E$67,0)
AE48: (,0) (AE45+AE46)*-$E$9 T50: (,0) @IF($E$14=T38,$E$67,0)
AF48: (,0) (AF45+AF46)*-$E$9 U50: (,0) @IF($E$14=U38,$E$67,0)
AG48: (,0) (AG45+AG46)*-$E$9 V50: (,0) @IF($E$14=V38,$E$67,0)
AH48: (,0) (AH45+AH46)*-$E$9 W50: (,0) @IF($E$14=W38,$E$67,0)
C49: '  ------             X50: (,0) @IF($E$14=X38,$E$67,0)
D49: '  ------             Y50: (,0) @IF($E$14=Y38,$E$67,0)
E49: '  ------             Z50: (,0) @IF($E$14=Z38,$E$67,0)
F49: '  ------             AA50: (,0) @IF($E$14=AA38,$E$67,0)
G49: '  ------             AB50: (,0) @IF($E$14=AB38,$E$67,0)
H49: '  ------             AC50: (,0) @IF($E$14=AC38,$E$67,0)
I49: '  ------             AD50: (,0) @IF($E$14=AD38,$E$67,0)
```

AE50: (,0) @IF($E$14=AE38,$E$67,0)
AF50: (,0) @IF($E$14=AF38,$E$67,0)
AG50: (,0) @IF($E$14=AG38,$E$67,0)
AH50: (,0) @IF($E$14=AH38,$E$67,0)
B51: '---------
C51: '---------
D51: '---------
E51: '---------
F51: '---------
G51: '---------
H51: '---------
I51: '---------
J51: '---------
K51: '---------
L51: '---------
M51: '---------
N51: '---------
O51: '---------
P51: '---------
Q51: '---------
R51: '---------
S51: '---------
T51: '---------
U51: '---------
V51: '---------
W51: '---------
X51: '---------
Y51: '---------
Z51: '---------
AA51: '---------
AB51: '---------
Z53: "=========
AA53: "=========
AB53: "=========
AC53: "=========
AD53: "=========
AE53: "=========
AF53: "=========
AG53: "=========
AH53: "=========
A55: [W20] 'Present Value
C55: (C0) @IF(E14=3,@NPV($E$11*(1-$E$9),C52..E52),
            @IF(E14=5,@NPV($E$11*(1-$E$9),C52..G52),
            @IF(E14=7,@NPV($E$11*(1-$E$9),C52..I52),0)))
A57: [W20] \=
B57: \=
C57: \=
D57: \=
E57: \=
F57: \=
G57: \=
H57: \=
I57: \=

J57: \=
K57: \=
L57: \=
A58: [W20] 'SALVAGE VALUE OF EQUIPMENT
G58: 'DEPRECIATION TABLE
I58: "YEAR
J58: 3
K58: 5
L58: 7
A59: [W20] \=
B59: \=
C59: \=
D59: \=
E59: \=
F59: \=
G59: \=
H59: \=
I59: \=
J59: \=
K59: \=
L59: \=
I60: 1
J60: (,0) @ROUND(@IF($E$14=3,@CHOOSE(+$E$14,0,0,0,2/3,0,2/5,0,2/7)*
             -$E$17*0.5,0),0)
K60: (,0) @ROUND(@IF($E$14=5,@CHOOSE(+$E$14,0,0,0,2/3,0,2/5,0,2/7)*
             -$E$17*0.5,0),0)
L60: (,0) @ROUND(@IF($E$14=7,@CHOOSE(+$E$14,0,0,0,2/3,0,2/5,0,2/7)*
             -$E$17*0.5,0),0)
A61: [W20] 'Salvage Value at End of Loan
E61: (C0) +$E$19
I61: 2
J61: (,0) @ROUND(@IF($E$14=3,@CHOOSE(+$E$14,0,0,0,2/3,0,2/5,0,2/7)*
             (-$E$17-@SUM($J$60..J60)),0),0)
K61: (,0) @ROUND(@IF($E$14=5,@CHOOSE(+$E$14,0,0,0,2/3,0,2/5,0,2/7)*
             (-$E$17-@SUM($K$60..K60)),0),0)
L61: (,0) @ROUND(@IF($E$14=7,@CHOOSE(+$E$14,0,0,0,2/3,0,2/5,0,2/7)*
             (-$E$17-@SUM($L$60..L60)),0),0)
A62: [W20] 'Book Value at End of Loan
E62: (,0) +B40+@IF(E14=3,@SUM(C46..E46),@IF(E14=5,@SUM(C46..G46),
                @IF(E14=7,@SUM(C46..I46),@IF(E14=10,@SUM(C46..L46),
                @IF(E14=15,@SUM(C46..Q46),@IF(E14=20,@SUM(C46..V46),
                @IF(E14=27.5,@SUM(C46..AE46),@IF(E14=31.5,@SUM(C46..AH46),
AC51: '---------
AD51: '---------
AE51: '---------
AF51: '---------
AG51: '---------
AH51: '---------
A52: [W20] 'Cash Flow
B52: (C0) -B43
C52: (C0) +C41+C45+C48+C50
D52: (C0) +D41+D45+D48+D50
E52: (C0) +E41+E45+E48+E50
F52: (C0) +F41+F45+F48+F50

```
G52: (C0) +G41+G45+G48+G50
H52: (C0) +H41+H45+H48+H50
I52: (C0) +I41+I45+I48+I50
J52: (C0) +J41+J45+J48+J50
K52: (C0) +K41+K45+K48+K50
L52: (C0) +L41+L45+L48+L50
M52: (C0) +M41+M45+M48+M50
N52: (C0) +N41+N45+N48+N50
O52: (C0) +O41+O45+O48+O50
P52: (C0) +P41+P45+P48+P50
Q52: (C0) +Q41+Q45+Q48+Q50
R52: (C0) +R41+R45+R48+R50
S52: (C0) +S41+S45+S48+S50
T52: (C0) +T41+T45+T48+T50
U52: (C0) +U41+U45+U48+U50
V52: (C0) +V41+V45+V48+V50
W52: (C0) +W41+W45+W48+W50
X52: (C0) +X41+X45+X48+X50
Y52: (C0) +Y41+Y45+Y48+Y50
Z52: (C0) +Z41+Z45+Z48+Z50
AA52: (C0) +AA41+AA45+AA48+AA50
AB52: (C0) +AB41+AB45+AB48+AB50
AC52: (C0) +AC41+AC45+AC48+AC50
AD52: (C0) +AD41+AD45+AD48+AD50
AE52: (C0) +AE41+AE45+AE48+AE50
AF52: (C0) +AF41+AF45+AF48+AF50
AG52: (C0) +AG41+AG45+AG48+AG50
AH52: (C0) +AH41+AH45+AH48+AH50
B53: "=========
C53: "=========
D53: "=========
E53: "=========
F53: "=========
G53: "=========
H53: "=========
I53: "=========
J53: "=========
K53: "=========
L53: "=========
M53: "=========
N53: "=========
O53: "=========
P53: "=========
Q53: "=========
R53: "=========
S53: "=========
T53: "=========
U53: "=========
V53: "=========
W53: "=========
X53: "=========
Y53: "=========
```

```
I62: 3
J62: (,0) @ROUND(@IF($E$14=3,(-$E$17-$J$60-$J$61)/($E$14/2),0),0)
K62: (,0) @ROUND(@IF($E$14=5,@CHOOSE(+$E$14,0,0,0,2/3,0,2/5,0,2/7)*
              (-$E$17-@SUM($K$60..K61)),0),0)
L62: (,0) @ROUND(@IF($E$14=7,@CHOOSE(+$E$14,0,0,0,2/3,0,2/5,0,2/7)*
              (-$E$17-@SUM($L$60..L61)),0),0)
E63: (C0) '---------
I63: 4
J63: (,0) @ROUND(@IF($E$14=3,-$E$17-@SUM($J$60..$J$62),0),0)
K63: (,0) @ROUND(@IF($E$14=5,(-$E$17-$K$60-$K$61-$K$62)/($E$14/2),0),0)
L63: (,0) @ROUND(@IF($E$14=7,@CHOOSE(+$E$14,0,0,0,0,2/3,0,2/5,0,2/7)*
              (-$E$17-@SUM($L$60..L62)),0),0)
A64: [W20] 'Gain on Sale of Asset
E64: (,0) +E61-E62
I64: 5
K64: (,0) @ROUND(@IF($E$14=5,(-$E$17-$K$60-$K$61-$K$62)/($E$14/2),0),0)
L64: (,0) @ROUND(@IF($E$14=7,(-$E$17-$L$60-$L$61-$L$62-$L$63)/($E$14/2),0),0)
A65: [W20] 'Tax on Sale of Asset
E65: (,0) +E64*E9
I65: 6
J65: (,0) "
K65: (,0) @ROUND(@IF($E$14=5,-$E$17-@SUM(K60..K64),0),0)
L65: (,0) @ROUND(@IF($E$14=7,(-$E$17-$L$60-$L$61-$L$62-$L$63)/($E$14/2),0),0)
E66: (C0) '---------
I66: 7
L66: (,0) @ROUND(@IF($E$14=7,(-$E$17-$L$60-$L$61-$L$62-$L$63)/($E$14/2),0),0)
A67: [W20] 'Net Cash Flow from Disposal
E67: (C0) +E64-E65
I67: 8
L67: (,0) @ROUND(@IF($E$14=7,-$E$17-@SUM(L$59..L66),0),0)
E68: '=========
J69: \-
K69: \-
L69: \-
J70: (,0) @SUM(J60..J63)
K70: (,0) @SUM(K60..K65)
L70: (,0) @SUM(L60..L67)
J71: \=
K71: \=
L71: \=
A75: [W20] \=
B75: \=
C75: \=
D75: \=
E75: \=
F75: \=
G75: \=
H75: \=
I75: \=
J75: \=
K75: \=
L75: \=
M75: \=
```

A76: [W20] 'RESULTS
A77: [W20] \=
B77: \=
C77: \=
D77: \=
E77: \=
F77: \=
G77: \=
H77: \=
I77: \=
J77: \=
K77: \=
L77: \=
M77: \=
A80: [W20] 'Present Value of Lease
E80: (C0) +C31
A82: [W20] 'Present Value of Loan
E82: (C0) +C55

13

Fixed Asset Management

Introduction

Whatever the size of your investment in fixed assets, you need an accurate, reliable system to manage and control your long-term assets (property, plant, and equipment).

By recording acquisitions and disposals, calculating annual depreciation for tax purposes, and maintaining a summary of current capital assets, the 1-2-3 Fixed Asset Manager can help you manage your capital assets. This chapter, which begins with an overview of the Tax Reform Act of 1986 and includes tips on creating the application, explains how the model operates and how to use it.

The Tax Reform Act of 1986

The passage of the Tax Reform Act of 1986 brought sweeping changes to the federal income tax system. Individual and corporate tax rates have been lowered, and the tax base broadened, through the elimination of many tax deductions and credits. However, these changes have been achieved at the expense of simplicity.

As the tax legislation relates to asset-cost recovery, the new depreciation system returns to the method used before 1981 and is also a modification of the Accelerated Cost Recovery System (ACRS). For personal property, you use the 200 percent declining-balance method, switching to straight-line depreciation to maximize the deduction, with a half-year convention.

A midquarter convention applies when more than 40 percent of your personal property is placed in service during the last three months of a tax year. For real property, you use the straight-line depreciation method with a midmonth convention. See table 13.1 for an overview of the asset classes and their depreciation methods.

Table 13.1

1987 Asset Depreciation Classes and Methods

Class Year	Asset	Method
3	Property with ADR midpoints of 4 years or less, except autos and light trucks, and certain horses.	200% DB
5	Property with ADR midpoints of more than 4 and less than 10 years. Includes autos and light trucks, certain technological equipment, semiconductor manufacturing equipment, computer-based central office switching equipment, renewable energy and biomass properties that are small power production facilities, and R&D property.	200% DB
7	Property with ADR midpoint of at least 10 and less than 16 years. Includes railroad track, single-purpose agricultural or horticultural structures, and property having no ADR midpoint classified elsewhere.	200% DB
10	Property with ADR midpoint of at least 16 and less than 20 years.	200% DB
15	Property with ADR midpoint of at least 20 and less than 25 years. Includes municipal wastewater treatment plants, and telephone distribution plants and comparable equipment used for the two-way exchange of voice and data communications.	150% DB

20	Property with ADR midpoint of 25 years or more, other than real property with ADR midpoint of 27.5 years or more. Includes municipal sewers.	150% DB
27.5	Residential rental property.	Straight-line
31.5	Nonresidential and other real property with ADR midpoints of 27.5 years or more.	Straight-line

The $10,000 expensing in lieu of cost recovery has been retained, but the Investment Tax Credit has been repealed. As a result of these changes, the simple ACRS tables have been replaced by complicated formulas to compute depreciation.

Those of you who are experienced *1-2-3 for Business* users will notice that the new tax law has had a substantial impact on Chapters 12 and 13. For example, the @VLOOKUP function in the Fixed Asset Management application has been replaced by @CHOOSE functions. Computing depreciation by multiplying the cost of the asset by an appropriate percentage rate is no longer possible. Nevertheless, you will find that these modifications are satisfactory and do not in any way detract from the model's performance.

Creating the Model

Think of the Fixed Asset System as seven individual worksheet areas: Acquisition Worksheet, Asset Depreciation, Capital Asset Summary, Disposal Worksheet, Disposal Summary, Depreciation Table, and the macros (see fig. 13.1).

FIXED ASSET SYSTEM

Copyright (C) Que Corporation 1987

ACQUISITION WORKSHEET

Description of Asset	Personal Computer
Asset ID Number	1006
Net Purchase Cost of Asset	$9,000
Depreciation Life of Asset	5 years
Date Placed in Service	01-Sep-88
Current Depreciation Allowance	$0

ASSET DEPRECIATION

Year	Period	Deprec Allow	Beg Basis	Dep Expense	Remain Basis
1988	1	$0	$9,000	$1,800	$7,200
1989	2			$2,880	$4,320
1990	3			$1,728	$2,592
1991	4			$1,037	$1,555
1992	5			$518	$518
1993	6				$0
1994	7				$0
1995	8				$0

DISPOSAL WORKSHEET

ID	1003
Number	3
Asset	Personal Computer
Purchase ID	1003
Purchase Date	01-Sep-87
Dep Life	5
Sale Date	31-Oct-88
Sale Price	$3,500
Basis	6,000
Gain (Loss) on Sale	($2,500)

DISPOSALS

ID	Disposal Date	Asset	Sale Price	Gain (Loss) on Sale
1001	31-Dec-89	Automobile	$5,000	$4,424

DEPRECIATION TABLE

	YEAR						
	1	2	3	4	5	6	7
1			0		1,800		0
2			0		2,880		0
3			0		1,728		0
4					1,037		0
5					518		0
6							
7							
8							
			0		9,000		0

CAPITAL ASSET SUMMARY

Number	Asset	ID	Net Purchase Cost	Asset Life	Purchase Date	First Year Expense	Annual Depreciation												
							1987	1988	1989	1990	1991	1992	1993	1994	1995	1996	1997	1998	1999
2	Office Furniture	1002	$15,000	7	01-Jun-87	$0	$2,143	$3,673	$2,624	$1,874	$1,339	$1,339	$1,339	$669					
3	Personal Computer	1003	$7,500	5	01-Sep-87	$0	$1,500	$2,400	$1,440	$864	$864	$432							
4	R&D Equipment	1004	$20,000	5	01-Jan-88	$10,000		$2,000	$3,200	$1,920	$1,152	$1,152	$576						
5	Truck	1005	$15,000	5	01-Mar-88	$0		$3,000	$4,800	$2,880	$1,728	$1,728	$864						
6	Personal Computer	1006	$9,000	5	01-Sep-88	$0		$1,800	$2,880	$1,728	$1,037	$1,037	$518						
						$3,643	$12,873	$14,944	$9,266	$6,120	$5,688	$3,297	$669	$0	$0	$0	$0	$0

Posting Macro

```
\p  {PANELOFF}{WINDOWSOFF}~                    Control Panel & Windows Off
    {GOTO}BOTTOM~/win~                         To dbase area/insert row
    +(UP)+1~/rv~                               Number row 1
    {RIGHT}/c99~                               Copy cell G9
    {RIGHT 2}+G10~/rv~~/rfc0~~                 Copy cell G10
    {RIGHT}+G11/rv~~/rfd1~~                    Copy cell G11
    {RIGHT}+G12/rv~~                           Copy cell G12
    {RIGHT}+G13+G14~/rv~~/rfc0~~               Copy cell G13
    {CALC}~                                    Copy cell G14
                                               Recalculate worksheet
    {IF @YEAR(G13)=87}{RIGHT}/mcDEP~~          Create range name DEP if 1987 Asset
    {IF @YEAR(G13)=88}{RIGHT 2}/mcDEP~~        Create range name DEP if 1988 Asset
    /rvP25..F32 E25~~                          Copy values to cell E25
    /rtE25..E32 DEP~~                          Transpose values to range name DEP
    /reE25..E32~                               Erase range
    /mcDEP~~                                   Delete range name DEP
    {RIGHT 18}~/mcREMAIN~                      Create range name REMAIN
    /rvH25..H32 G25~~                          Copy values
    /rtG25..G32 REMAIN~~                       Transpose values to range name REMAIN
    /reG25..G32~                               Erase range
    /mcREMAIN~~                                Delete range name REMAIN
    {CALC}~                                    Recalculate worksheet
    {GOTO}G9~/reG9..G14~~                      Go to cell G9 and erase range
    {HOME}~{PANELON}{WINDOWSON}{BEEP 4}        To Home/Control Panel & Windows On/Beep When Finished
```

Disposal Macro

```
\D  {PANELOFF}{WINDOWSOFF}~                    Control Panel & Windows Off
    {GOTO}BOTTOM2~/mdBOTTOM2~                  To dbase area/Delete range name Bottom2
    {CALC}~                                    Recalculate worksheet
    /cJ12~                                     Copy J12
    {RIGHT 2}+L12~/rv~~                        Copy L12/Convert to value
    {RIGHT}+M14~/rv~~/rfd1~~                   Copy M14/Convert to Value/Format for Date 1
    {RIGHT}+M15~/rv~~/rfc0~~                   Copy M15/Convert to value/Format for currency
    {RIGHT 2}+M18~/rv~~/rfc0~~                 Copy M18/Convert to value/Format for currency
    {DOWN}{LEFT 6}/mcBOTTOM2~~                 Move cursor/Create range name Bottom2
    /dqdq                                      Delete data query
    /reJ12..O12~~                              Erase range
    /reM14..M15~~                              Erase range
    /reJ19~~                                   Erase cell
    {CALC}~                                    Recalculate worksheet
    {HOME}~{PANELON}{WINDOWSON}{BEEP 4}        To Home/Control Panel & Windows On/Beep When Finished
```

	1987	1988	1989	1990	1991	1992	1993	1994	1995	2000	2001	2002	2003	2004
						Remaining Assets								
	$12,857	$9,184	$6,560	$4,686	$3,347	$2,008	$669	$0	$0					
	$6,000	$3,600	$2,160	$1,296	$432	$0	$0	$0	$0					
		$8,000	$4,800	$2,880	$1,728	$576	$0	$0						
		$7,200	$4,320	$2,592	$864	$0	$0							
			$4,320	$2,592	$1,555	$518								
	$18,857	$39,384	$25,040	$15,774	$9,654	$3,966	$669	$0	$0	$0	$0	$0	$0	$0

Fig. 13.1. The Fixed Asset System.

Setting Column Widths

With a blank 1-2-3 worksheet, begin creating the model and setting column widths, according to the following table:

Column	Width
B, D, H, J, P	8
E, F, G, L, M	10

Next, enter the column headings, row titles, and labels according to table 13.2 or your firm's reporting formats. Remember that you can include separator lines by typing \=.

Table 13.2
Row Titles and Column Headings

Enter into cell:	Original label:	Copy to:
	Opening Headings	
A1:	\=	B1..V1, A5..V5, A7..V7, A20..P20, A22..P22, S22..V22, A50..AS50, A52..AS52
A3:	'FIXED ASSET SYSTEM	
	Acquisition Worksheet	
A6:	'ACQUISITION WORKSHEET	
A9:	'Description of Asset	
A10:	'Asset ID Number	
A11:	'Net Purchase Cost of Asset	
A12:	'Depreciation Life of Asset	
H12:	'years	
A13:	'Date Placed in Service	
A14:	'Current Depreciation Allowance	
	Asset Depreciation	
A21:	'ASSET DEPRECIATION	
C23:	^Deprec	
D23:	^Beg	
F23:	^Dep	
H23:	^Remain	
A24:	'Year	
B24:	'Period	

Enter into cell:	Original label:	Copy to:
C24:	^Allow	
D24:	^Basis	
F24:	^Expense	
H24:	^Basis	

Capital Asset Summary

A51:	'CAPITAL ASSET SUMMARY	
E54:	^Net	
I54:	^First	
J54:	' ----	
K54:	\-	L54..N54, S54..AF54, AK54..AS54
P54:	'Annual Depreciation	
AH54:	'Remaining Assets	
E55:	^Purchase	
F55:	^Asset	
G55:	^Purchase	
I55:	^Year	
A56:	'Number	
B56:	'Asset	
D56:	'ID	
E56:	' Cost	
F56:	' Life	
G56:	' Date	
I56:	'Expense	
J62:	"-------	K62..AS62
J64:	'=======	K64..AS64

Disposal Worksheet

I6:	'DISPOSAL WORKSHEET
I8:	'ID
I11:	'Number
J11:	'Asset
L11:	^ID
M11:	' Date
N11:	' Life
J14:	'Sale Date
J15:	'Sale Price
J16:	'Basis
M17:	' -------
J18:	'Gain (Loss) on Sale

Enter into cell:	Original label:	Copy to:

Disposals

I21:	'DISPOSALS	
O24:	' Gain	
L25:	'Disposal	
M25:	'Sale	
O25:	' (Loss)	
I26:	'Asset	
K26:	'ID	
L26:	'Date	
M26:	'Price	
O26:	' on Sale	

Depreciation Table

Q6:	'DEPRECIATION TABLE	
S6:	"YEAR	
T18:	\-	U18..V18
T20:	\=	U20..V20

Macros

X1:	'\P	
Y1:	'{PANELOFF}{WINDOWSOFF}~	
AD1:	'Control Panel & Windows Off	
AJ1:	'\D	
AK1:	'{PANELOFF}{WINDOWSOFF}~	
AQ1:	'Control Panel & Windows Off	
X2:	'Posting	
Y2:	'{GOTO}BOTTOM~/wir~	
AD2:	'To dbase area/insert row	
AJ2:	'Disposal	
AK2:	'{GOTO}BOTTOM2~/rndBOTTOM2~	
AQ2:	'To dbase area/Delete range name Bottom2	
X3:	'Macro	
Y3:	'+{UP}+1~/rv~~	
AD3:	'Number row 1	
AJ3:	'Macro	
AK3:	'{CALC}~	
AQ3:	'Recalculate worksheet	
Y4:	'{RIGHT}/cG9~~	
AD4:	'Copy cell G9	
AK4:	'/cJ12~~	

Enter
into
cell: Original label:

AQ4:   'Copy J12
Y5:   '{RIGHT 2}+G10~/rv~~
AD5:   'Copy cell G10
AK5:   '{RIGHT 2}+L12~/rv~~
AQ5:   'Copy L12/Convert to value
Y6:   '{RIGHT}+G11~/rv~~/rfc0~~
AD6:   'Copy cell G11
AK6:   '{RIGHT}+M14~/rv~~/rfd1~
AQ6:   'Copy M14/Convert to Value/Format for Date 1
Y7:   '{RIGHT}+G12~/rv~~
AD7:   'Copy cell G12
AK7:   '{RIGHT}+M15~/rv~~/rfc0~~
AQ7:   'Copy M15/Convert to value/Format for currency
Y8:   '{RIGHT}+G13~/rv~~/rfd1~
AD8:   'Copy cell G13
AK8:   '{RIGHT 2}+M18~/rv~~/rfc0~~
AQ8:   'Copy M18/Convert to value/Format for currency
Y9:   '{RIGHT 2}+G14~/rv~~/rfc0~~
AD9:   'Copy cell G14
AK9:   '{DOWN}{LEFT 6}/rncBOTTOM2~~
AQ9:   'Move cursor/Create range name Bottom2
Y10:   '{CALC}~
AD10:   'Recalculate worksheet
AK10:   '/dqddq~
AQ10:   'Delete data query
Y11:   '{IF @YEAR(G13)=87}{RIGHT}~/rncDEP~~
AD11:   'Create range name DEP if 1987 Asset
AK11:   '/rel12..O12~~
AQ11:   'Erase range
Y12:   '{IF @YEAR(G13)=88}{RIGHT 2}~/rncDEP~~
AD12:   'Create range name DEP if 1988 Asset
AK12:   '/reM14..M15~~
AQ12:   'Erase range
Y13:   '/rvF25..F32~E25~~
AD13:   'Copy values to cell E25
AK13:   '/rel9~~
AQ13:   'Erase cell
Y14:   '/rtE25..E32~DEP~~
AD14:   'Transpose values to range name DEP
AK14:   '{CALC}~

Enter
into
cell: Original label:

AQ14:   'Recalculate worksheet
Y15:   '/reE25..E32~~
AD15:   'Erase range
AK15:   '{HOME}{PANELON}{WINDOWSON}{BEEP 4}
AQ15:   'To Home/Control Panel & Windows On/Beep When Finished
Y16:   '/rndDEP~~
AD16:   'Delete range name DEP
Y17:   '{RIGHT 18}~/rncREMAIN~~
AD17:   'Create range name REMAIN
Y18:   '/rvH25..H32~G25~~
AD18:   'Copy values
Y19:   '/rtG25..G32~REMAIN~~
AD19:   'Transpose values to range name REMAIN
Y20:   '/reG25..G32~~
AD20:   'Erase range
Y21:   '/rndREMAIN~~
AD21:   'Delete range name REMAIN
Y22:   '{CALC}~
AD22:   'Recalculate worksheet
Y23:   '{GOTO}G9~/reG9..G14~~
AD23:   'Go to cell G9 and erase range
Y24:   '{HOME}~{PANELON}{WINDOWSON}{BEEP 4}
AD24:   'To Home/Control Panel & Windows On/Beep When Finished

Naming Ranges

If you intend to use the model's macros, you will need to enter the range names. Name the following ranges according to table 13.3 (feel free to include additional ranges to help you move around the application).

The \p Macro

The \p (posting) macro begins at cell X1 and ends at cell AB24. Directly to the macro's right, its explanation occupies the area AD1..AI24 (see fig. 13.2).

Table 13.3
Range Names

Name	Cell
BOTTOM	A58
BOTTOM2	I28
\D	AJ1
\P	X1

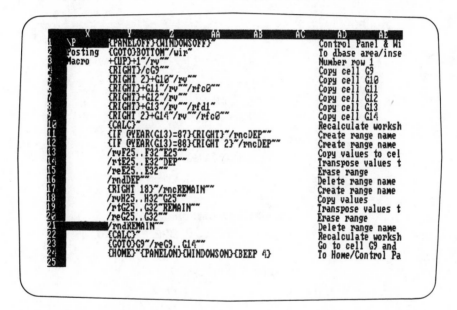

Fig. 13.2. The \p macro.

The \d Macro

The \d (disposal) macro begins at cell AJ1 and ends at cell AN15. Its explanation, directly to the macro's right, occupies the area AQ1..AV15. Figure 13.3 shows the macro commands.

Specifying Cell Formats

Next, format the cells of the worksheet. Table 13.4 contains a list of suggested formats, or follow your own reporting policy.

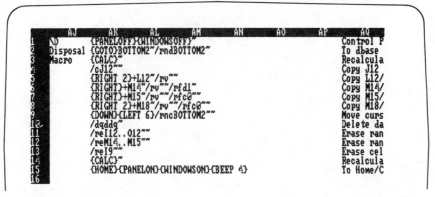

Fig. 13.3. The \d macro.

Table 13.4
Cell Formats

Acquisition Worksheet

Format	Cell/Range
/rfc0	G11, G15
/rfd1	G13

Asset Depreciation

/rfc0	C25, D25, F25..F40, H25..H40

Disposal Worksheet

/rfd1	M12, M14
/rfc0	M15..M16, M18

Disposal Summary

/rfd1	L27
/rfc0	M27, O27

After you have formatted the model, enter the model's formulas and functions as outlined in table 13.5.

Table 13.5
Formulas and Functions

Enter into cell:	Original formula:	Copy to:
	Acquisition Worksheet	
G13:	@DATE(YY,MM,DD)	
	Asset Depreciation	
A25:	@YEAR(G13)+1900	
A26:	+A25+1	A27..A32
B26:	+B25+1	B27..B32
C25:	@IF($G$14>$G$11, $G$11,$G$14)	
D25:	+$G$11-$C$25	
F25:	@IF($G$12=3,$T9, @IF($G$12=5,$U9, @IF($G$12=7,$V9,0)))	F26..F32
H25:	+$D$25-F25	
H26:	+$D$25-F25-F26	
H27:	$D$25-@SUM($F$25..$F$27)	
H28:	$D$25-@SUM($F$25..$F$28)	
H29:	$D$25-@SUM($F$25..$F$29)	
H30:	$D$25-@SUM($F$25..$F$30)	
H31:	$D$25-@SUM($F$25..$F$31)	
H32:	$D$25-@SUM($F$25..$F$32)	
	Disposal Worksheet	
M14:	@DATE(YY,MM,DD)	
M16:	@VLOOKUP(I9,D57..AS63,@YEAR(M14)-64)	
	Capital Asset Summary	
L56:	+K56+1	M56..AS56
J63:	@SUM(J57..J62)	K63..AS63
	Depreciation Table	
T9:	@ROUND(@IF($G$12=3,@CHOOSE(+$G$12,0,0,0,2/3,0,2/5,0,2/7)* $D$25*0.5,0),0)	
U9:	@ROUND(@IF($G$12=5,@CHOOSE(+$G$12,0,0,0,2/3,0,2/5,0,2/7)* $D$25*0.5,0),0)	
V9:	@ROUND(@IF($G$12=7,@CHOOSE(+$G$12,0,0,0,2/3,0,2/5,0,2/7)* $D$25*0.5,0),0)	
T10:	@ROUND(@IF($G$12=3,@CHOOSE(+$G$12,0,0,0,2/3,0,2/5,0,2/7)* ($D$25-@SUM($T$9..T9)),0),0)	
U10:	@ROUND(@IF($G$12=5,@CHOOSE(+$G$12,0,0,0,2/3,0,2/5,0,2/7)* ($D$25-$U9),0),0)	

Enter
into
cell: Original formula:

V10:   @ROUND(@IF($G$12=7,@CHOOSE(+$G$12,0,0,0,2/3,0,2/5,0,2/7)∗
         ($D$25-V9),0),0)
T11:   @ROUND(@IF($G$12=3,($D$25-$T$9-$T$10)/($G$12/2),0),0)
U11:   @ROUND(@IF($G$12=5,@CHOOSE(+$G$12,0,0,0,2/3,0,2/5,0,2/7)∗
         ($D$25-U9-U10),0),0)
V11:   @ROUND(@IF($G$12=7,@CHOOSE(+$G$12,0,0,0,2/3,0,2/5,0,2/7)∗
         ($D$25-@SUM($V$9..V10)),0),0)
T12:   @ROUND(@IF($G$12=3,+$D$25-@SUM($T$9..$T$11),0),0)
U12:   @ROUND(@IF($G$12=5,($D$25-U9-U10-U11)/($G$12/2),0),0)
V12:   @ROUND(@IF($G$12=7,@CHOOSE(+$G$12,0,0,0,2/3,0,2/5,0,2/7)∗
         ($D$25-@SUM(V9..V11)),0),0)
U13:   @ROUND(@IF($G$12=5,($D$25-U9-U10-U11)/($G$12/2),0),0)
V13:   @ROUND(@IF($G$12=7,($D$25-V9-V10-V11-V12)/($G$12/2),0),0)
U14:   @ROUND(@IF($G$12=5,+$D$25-@SUM(U9..U13),0),0)
V14:   @ROUND(@IF($G$12=7,($D$25-V9-V10-V11-V12)/($G$12/2),0),0)
V15:   @ROUND(@IF($G$12=7,($D$25-V9-V10-V11-V12)/($G$12/2),0),0)
V16:   @ROUND(@IF($G$12=7,+$D$25-@SUM(V9..V15),0),0)
T19:   @SUM(T9..T12)
U19:   @SUM(U9..U14)
V19:   @SUM(V9..V16)

Understanding the Model

The Acquisition Worksheet, the data-entry area for new assets, is the
worksheet area that you probably will use most often. The Acquisition
Worksheet occupies the area A5 through H19 in the model (see
fig. 13.4).

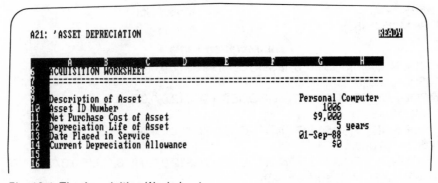

Fig. 13.4. The Acquisition Worksheet.

In this area, you will need to enter six items of data about your new asset. This data will be used extensively in the other worksheet areas of the model. For example, the Asset Depreciation module uses several of your data entries for its calculations.

Asset Depreciation

Asset Depreciation, cells A21 through H32, is located directly below the Acquisition Worksheet (see fig. 13.5).

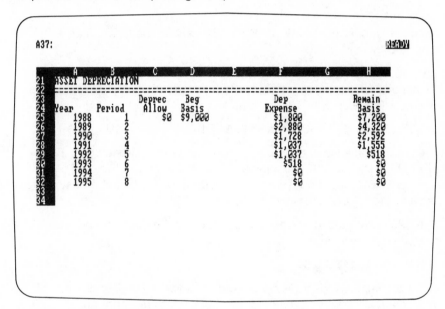

Fig. 13.5. Asset Depreciation.

This worksheet calculates your annual depreciation and remaining asset basis, taking into account any first year depreciation expense. Column A of the Depreciation Table, the first column with formulas, defines the depreciable life of the asset. Cell A25 contains the formula:

   A25: @YEAR(G13)+1900

This formula adds 1900 to the year portion of the date that was entered in cell G13 in the Acquisition Worksheet. Because the @YEAR function returns only a two-digit number, only the last two digits of the acquisition year will be returned. 1900 is included in the formula to restore the date to a full four digits. The following year, cell A26, is calculated as follows:

A26: +A25+1

All subsequent years (A27..A32) use similar 1-2-3 logic.

Column B of the Asset Depreciation module numbers the asset's depreciation years. Cell B25 will always be period one, the year of acquisition. Cell B26, which is similar to cell A26, contains the formula:

B26: +B25+1

Again, all subsequent periods (B27..B32) rely on the formula on a relative basis.

Column C, first-year depreciation expense, is computed by comparing the asset's total cost (in cell G11) with the amount of first-year expense available (in cell G16). The formula is

C25: @IF($G$14>$G$11,$G$11,$G$14)

The model will always post the appropriate amount to cell C25. For example, if the full $10,000 allowance is available and the cost of the asset is $9,000, the model will post $9,000 to cell C25. If the cost of the asset is $11,000, $10,000 will be posted to C25.

Cell D25 computes your beginning amount to be depreciated. The model uses the formula

D25: +$G$11-$C$25

In this formula, G11 is your net asset cost and C25 is your current depreciation allowance. The model will take into account any remaining depreciation allowance so that the correct asset value will be depreciated.

Column F retrieves from the Depreciation Table the modified ACRS depreciation for each year in the asset's recovery life. For example, the formula in cell F25:

F25: @IF($G$12=3,$T9,@IF($G$12=5,$U9,@IF($G$12=7,$V9,0)))

instructs 1-2-3 to select the proper first-year depreciation expense from the Depreciation Table, based on a series of @IF statements, and to put that expense into cell F25. Your subsequent year's depreciation will be retrieved in this way.

Column H of the Depreciation Table calculates your asset's remaining basis, which will be used as the beginning basis in the following year. Cell H25 contains the formula:

H25: $D$25-F25

This formula subtracts your beginning depreciation basis (cell D25) from your first-year depreciation expense (cell F25) to arrive at the basis for year 1. Successive years use a similar logical relationship.

The Depreciation Table

The Depreciation Table is located in cells Q1 through V20, between the Disposal Worksheet and the posting macro (see fig. 13.6). This module computes depreciation values for three classes of assets. Most of your assets will fall in the five- and seven-year categories.

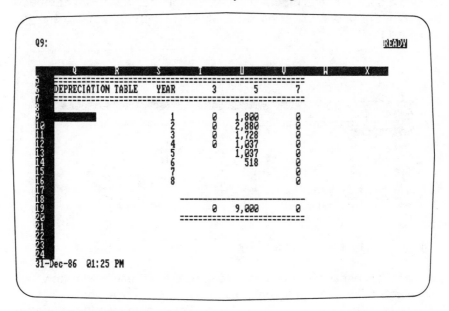

Fig. 13.6. The Depreciation Table.

The Depreciation Table (which is basically a duplication of Chapter 12's Depreciation Table in the Lease versus Debt Evaluator model) computes your depreciation expense for the proper asset class and year from a series of @CHOOSE statements. As an example of computing depreciation, consider the formula in cell T9:

T9: @ROUND(@IF($G$12=3,@CHOOSE(+$G$12,0,0,0,2/3,0,2/5,0,2/7)
*$D$25*0.5,0),0)

This formula begins by determining (from cell G12) whether your asset is in the three-year class. If so, the @CHOOSE phrase selects the fraction *2/3* and multiplies it by your beginning depreciation, then multiplies it again by 0.5 to accommodate the half-year convention. If it is not a three-year asset, zero is returned so that the correct depreciation expense will always be placed in the correct year. The @ROUND function will round off either value to zero decimal places.

The next module summarizes your current assets, depreciation, and remaining assets' basis.

Capital Asset Summary

The Capital Asset Summary, a listing of your firm's current capital assets, begins at cell A51 and continues to cell AS58. Figure 13.7 shows a portion of this module. Depending on the nature and number of your firm's assets, your list will probably look different from that shown in figure 13.7.

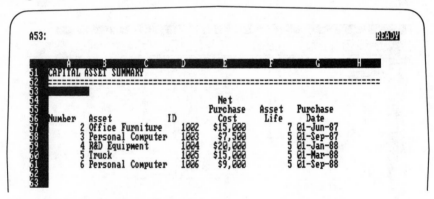

Fig. 13.7. The Capital Asset Summary.

You can use either of two methods to update the Summary for new asset acquisitions. You can enter the data manually from the Acquisition Worksheet and Depreciation Table, or invoke the \p macro to perform the task automatically.

The \p Macro

For a close look at the \p macro, refer to figure 13.2. The macro first turns off the control panel and windows. Next, the cursor is moved to the range name BOTTOM, which is cell A57 if the model has not been previously used.

A row is inserted at the current cursor location, pushing the cell named BOTTOM down one row. The third line of the macro numbers the new record by referring to the record immediately above it. For example, if the last record in the database is number 7, the new record will be number 8. Lines 4 through 9 of this posting macro retrieve data from the Acquisition Worksheet and place that data in the appropriate cells in the Capital Asset Summary. Line 10 recalculates the worksheet to compute your depreciation amounts.

Using Release 2's {IF} command, lines 11 and 12 determine whether the asset was acquired in 1987 or 1988. Depending on the year, the macro will place the cursor in the appropriate cell (in the Capital Asset Summary) for the first-year depreciation and create the name "Dep" (Depreciation) for that cell location. Next, in lines 13 through 17, the macro translates the formulas into values from range F25..F32 to E25, transposes these values to "Dep", and erases the values from E25..E32 and the range name "Dep".

Line 17 moves the cursor to the first year of the asset's remaining basis, again depending on the year of acquisition, and creates the range name REMAIN (Remaining Asset Value). Like lines 13 through 16, lines 18 through 21 translate the formulas into values from range H25..H32 to G25, transpose these values to REMAIN, and erase the values G25..G32 and the range name REMAIN. In this way, the macro's lines 13 and 18 take advantage of the new **/R**ange **V**alue command, eliminating the need for the {EDIT}{CALC} trick.

This model has been enhanced by the addition of annual depreciation and remaining asset totals. Line 22 of the macro recalculates the worksheet to total your annual depreciation and remaining assets.

Refer to figure 13.1 and note the formulas (in row 63) that are used to calculate these values. The model uses @SUM functions that include the dashed line (row 62 of the Capital Asset Summary) in the equation to accommodate any additional assets your firm may acquire. The annual totals enable you to plan your tax-depreciation expense and capital-asset amounts by year.

The cursor is moved to cell G9 in the Acquisition Worksheet by line 23 of the macro. The data that was entered earlier is erased from rows G9..G14. Finally, the cursor is returned to Home (cell A8), the control panel and windows are turned on, and your computer beeps to let you know that the macro has finished. The model is now ready for the next new asset or asset disposal.

The Disposal Worksheet

Like the Acquisition Worksheet, the Disposal Worksheet is used as a data-entry area for assets that your firm sells or otherwise disposes of. The Disposal Worksheet is a vehicle for updating your Capital Asset Summary and creating a list of Disposed Assets. This worksheet occupies cells I6..P20 (see fig. 13.8).

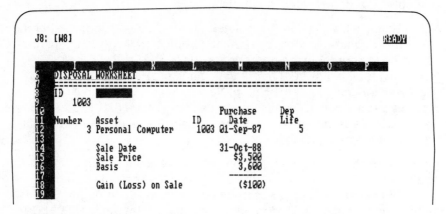

Fig. 13.8. The Disposal Worksheet.

To record an asset disposal, you provide your asset's identification number, the sale date, and the price. The model automates several additional Asset Disposal operations.

First, the model will use the **/D**ata **Q**uery **E**xtract command to obtain the rest of the data required for the Disposal Summary. When you issue this command, the model will use your asset's identification number to search for the proper asset in the Capital Asset Summary. Information associated with your asset will be placed in cells I11..O12.

When you recalculate the worksheet, the current basis of the asset to be disposed of and the gain or loss on the sale is calculated. 1-2-3's @VLOOKUP function is used to compute the current basis in cell M16, which contains the formula:

M16: @VLOOKUP(I9,D57..AS63,@YEAR(M14)-64)

This formula searches the basis of the asset from the remaining basis in columns AB through AS in the Capital Asset Summary. Cell I9, your asset identification number, is used as the lookup key. The offset cell is determined by the year portion of your disposal date, less 64. This value is used so that 1-2-3 will look across (horizontally) to the correct year in the Remaining Assets section of the database. Remember that, under present depreciation rules, you cannot take depreciation on an asset in the year it is sold. Thus, the formula in cell M16 will instruct the model to use the previous year's remaining basis.

Beginning from cell D56, the ID column in the Capital Asset Summary, there are exactly 23 cells to 1987 in the Remaining Assets section (1987 - 23 = 64). The lookup range, A57..AS64, includes an extra row for expansion.

Cell M18 calculates the gain or loss on the sale by subtracting cell M15 from M16. A negative balance indicates a loss; a positive balance, a gain on the sale.

The Disposal Summary Module

Your disposed assets are posted to the Disposal Summary in cells I21..O30. This module, directly below the Disposal Worksheet, can be seen in figure 13.9.

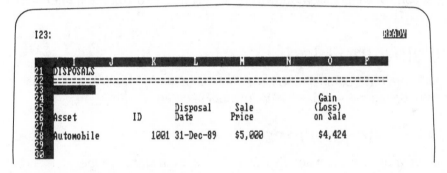

Fig. 13.9. The Disposal Summary.

You will need to update the Disposal Summary to maintain your lists of current and disposed capital assets and to accurately report, for tax purposes, any gains on sales of assets. To do this manually, you simply copy the disposal data from the Disposal Worksheet to the Disposal Summary.

The Capital Asset Summary also will need to be updated. To do this, find your disposed asset by its ID number and use the **/W**orksheet **D**elete **R**ow command to erase all data associated with this asset. Don't forget to recalculate the annual depreciation and remaining asset values in the Capital Asset Summary.

You may prefer to use the \d macro for these operations.

The \d Macro

Refer to figure 13.3 to see how the \d macro works. The macro begins by turning off the control panel and windows. Line 2 moves the cursor to the cell named BOTTOM2 (if you have not used the \d macro previously, BOTTOM2 is cell I28) and temporarily deletes this range name. Then line 3 recalculates the worksheet to compute your gain or loss on the sale of your asset.

The next five lines of the macro copy the data from the Disposal Worksheet to the Disposal Summary. Line 9 returns the cursor to the cell in column I, one row below the last entry in the Disposal Summary, and names it BOTTOM2 for the next disposed asset. The macro then uses 1-2-3's **/D**ata **Q**uery **D**elete command to remove the disposed asset from the Capital Asset Summary.

The last five lines of the \d macro are similar to those in the \p macro. Yearly depreciation and remaining asset values are updated for removal of the disposed asset, the Disposal Worksheet data is erased, the control panel and windows are reactivated, and your computer will beep. The model is now ready for the next transaction.

Using the Model

After you have planned and constructed the model, you'll be ready to enter data into the individual worksheet sections.

Asset Acquisitions

Enter your new asset acquisitions into the model through the Acquisition Worksheet. Enter information about the asset according to table 13.6. Don't forget to use the @DATE function when you enter the purchase date of your asset in cell G13.

For your Current Depreciation Allowance, enter *10000* if you have not previously purchased assets; otherwise, type the amount of current year depreciation allowance that has not been used on other current year assets. This will complete the data-entry requirement for your new asset.

Next, press F9 (CALC). 1-2-3 will compute the annual depreciation and remaining assets by year. You can post these manually to the Capital Asset Summary, or press Alt-P for the Posting macro to do the job for you. The Capital Asset Summary is updated for your new acquisition, and you can review your firm's current asset composition.

Table 13.6
Data Entry

Description	Cell
Acquisition Worksheet	
Description of Asset	G9
Asset ID Number	G10
Net Purchase Cost of Asset	G11
Depreciation Life of Asset	G12
Date Placed in Service	G13
Current Depreciation Allowance	G14
Disposal Worksheet	
Asset ID Number	I9
Date of Disposal	M14
Sale Price	M15

Asset Disposals

You update the Capital Asset Summary for sales and other disposals through the Disposal Worksheet. Because the asset is already incorporated into the Capital Asset Summary, there will be less data to enter into the Disposal Worksheet relative to the Acquisition Worksheet.

Begin by using the cursor keys or F5 (GOTO) to place the cursor at cell I9. (If the cursor is at the Home position, you can move quickly to the Disposal Worksheet by pressing the Tab key.) Next, enter the required data according to table 13.6. Now press F9 (CALC). The model will compute your gain or loss on the asset's sale.

Next, use the **/D**ata **Q**uery **E**xtract command to obtain the rest of the needed asset information for the Disposal Worksheet. If the model has never been used, enter the following commands:

1. Type **/D**ata **Q**uery **I**nput.

2. Enter *A56..I64* and press Enter.

3. Press **C**riterion, enter *I8..I9*, and press Enter.

4. Press **O**utput, enter *I11..O12*, and press Enter.

5. Press **E**xtract.

Your disposed asset will be retrieved from the Capital Asset Summary and placed in the Disposal Worksheet for you.

As with the Acquisition Worksheet, asset disposal information can be entered into the Disposal Summary manually or by using a macro (in this case, the \d macro). To do the job manually, enter the following Disposal Worksheet data to the Disposal Summary: the Asset Description and Asset ID, the Disposal Date, Sale Price, and the Gain (or Loss) on Sale. You may want to /Range Erase this data in the Disposal Worksheet in preparation for your next asset disposal.

If you prefer to use the macro, press Alt-D to invoke the Disposal macro. The posting procedure will be done automatically.

In summary, four operations are required to update the model for asset disposals: data entry, (CALC), the /Data Query Extract operation, and updating your Disposal Summary manually or with the \d macro.

Conclusion

The Fixed Asset Management model provides you with a basic capital asset system and a useful framework that can be used in small and medium-sized businesses. Because of the new tax laws, however, be careful when you use the model. Note also that the model does not accommodate assets purchased before 1987; thus, ITC recapture is not addressed for assets purchased in prior periods but disposed during or after 1987. Consult your accountant, tax professional, or the IRS if you are unsure about current regulations.

A1: \=
B1: [W8] \=
C1: \=
D1: [W8] \=
E1: [W10] \=
F1: [W10] \=
G1: [W10] \=
H1: [W8] \=
I1: \=
J1: [W8] \=
K1: \=
L1: [W10] \=
M1: [W10] \=
N1: \=
O1: \=
P1: [W8] \=
Q1: \=
R1: \=
S1: \=
T1: \=
U1: \=
V1: \=
X1: '\P
Y1: '{PANELOFF}{WINDOWSOFF}~
AD1: 'Control Panel & Windows Off
AJ1: '\D
AK1: '{PANELOFF}{WINDOWSOFF}~
AQ1: 'Control Panel & Windows Off
X2: 'Posting
Y2: '{GOTO}BOTTOM~/wir~
AD2: 'To dbase area/insert row
AJ2: 'Disposal
AK2: '{GOTO}BOTTOM2~/rndBOTTOM2~
AQ2: 'To dbase area/Delete range name Bottom2
A3: 'FIXED ASSET SYSTEM
E3: [W10] '   Copyright (C) Que Corporation 1987
X3: 'Macro
Y3: '+{UP}+1~/rv~~
AD3: 'Number row 1
AJ3: 'Macro
AK3: '{CALC}~
AQ3: 'Recalculate worksheet
Y4: '{RIGHT}/cG9~~
AD4: 'Copy cell G9
AK4: '/cJ12~~
AQ4: 'Copy J12
A5: \=
B5: [W8] \=
C5: \=
D5: [W8] \=
E5: [W10] \=
F5: [W10] \=
G5: [W10] \=
H5: [W8] \=

I5: \=
J5: [W8] \=
K5: \=
L5: [W10] \=
M5: [W10] \=
N5: \=
O5: \=
P5: [W8] \=
Q5: \=
R5: \=
S5: \=
T5: \=
U5: \=
V5: \=
Y5: '{RIGHT 2}+G10~/rv~~
AD5: 'Copy cell G10
AK5: '{RIGHT 2}+L12~/rv~~
AQ5: 'Copy L12/Convert to value
A6: 'ACQUISITION WORKSHEET
I6: 'DISPOSAL WORKSHEET
Q6: 'DEPRECIATION TABLE
S6: "YEAR
T6: 3
U6: 5
V6: 7
Y6: '{RIGHT}+G11~/rv~~/rfc0~~
AD6: 'Copy cell G11
AK6: '{RIGHT}+M14~/rv~~/rfd1~
AQ6: 'Copy M14/Convert to Value/Format for Date 1
A7: \=
B7: [W8] \=
C7: \=
D7: [W8] \=
E7: [W10] \=
F7: [W10] \=
G7: [W10] \=
H7: [W8] \=
I7: \=
J7: [W8] \=
K7: \=
L7: [W10] \=
M7: [W10] \=
N7: \=
O7: \=
P7: [W8] \=
Q7: \=
R7: \=
S7: \=
T7: \=
U7: \=
V7: \=
Y7: '{RIGHT}+G12~/rv~~
AD7: 'Copy cell G12
AK7: '{RIGHT}+M15~/rv~~/rfc0~~

AQ7: 'Copy M15/Convert to value/Format for currency
I8: 'ID
Y8: '{RIGHT}+G13~/rv~~/rfd1~
AD8: 'Copy cell G13
AK8: '{RIGHT 2}+M18~/rv~~/rfc0~~
AQ8: 'Copy M18/Convert to value/Format for currency
A9: 'Description of Asset
G9: [W10] 'Personal Computer
I9: 1003
S9: 1
T9: (,0) @ROUND(@IF($G$12=3,@CHOOSE(+$G$12,0,0,0,2/3,0,2/5,0,2/7)*
          $D$25*0.5,0),0)
U9: (,0) @ROUND(@IF($G$12=5,@CHOOSE(+$G$12,0,0,0,2/3,0,2/5,0,2/7)*
          $D$25*0.5,0),0)
V9: (,0) @ROUND(@IF($G$12=7,@CHOOSE(+$G$12,0,0,0,2/3,0,2/5,0,2/7)*
          $D$25*0.5,0),0)
Y9: '{RIGHT 2}+G14~/rv~~/rfc0~~
AD9: 'Copy cell G14
AK9: '{DOWN}{LEFT 6}/rncBOTTOM2~~
AQ9: 'Move cursor/Create range name Bottom2
A10: 'Asset ID Number
G10: [W10] 1006
M10: [W10] 'Purchase
N10: ' Dep
S10: 2
T10: (,0) @ROUND(@IF($G$12=3,@CHOOSE(+$G$12,0,0,0,2/3,0,2/5,0,2/7)*
          ($D$25-@SUM($T$9..T9)),0),0)
U10: (,0) @ROUND(@IF($G$12=5,@CHOOSE(+$G$12,0,0,0,2/3,0,2/5,0,2/7)*
          ($D$25-$U$9),0),0)
V10: (,0) @ROUND(@IF($G$12=7,@CHOOSE(+$G$12,0,0,0,2/3,0,2/5,0,2/7)*
          ($D$25-V9),0),0)
Y10: '{CALC}~
AD10: 'Recalculate worksheet
AK10: '/dqddq~
AQ10: 'Delete data query
A11: 'Net Purchase Cost of Asset
G11: (C0) [W10] 9000
I11: 'Number
J11: [W8] 'Asset
L11: [W10] ^ID
M11: [W10] ' Date
N11: ' Life
S11: 3
T11: (,0) @ROUND(@IF($G$12=3,($D$25-$T$9-$T$10)/($G$12/2),0),0)
U11: (,0) @ROUND(@IF($G$12=5,@CHOOSE(+$G$12,0,0,0,2/3,0,2/5,0,2/7)*
          ($D$25-U9-U10),0),0)
V11: (,0) @ROUND(@IF($G$12=7,@CHOOSE(+$G$12,0,0,0,2/3,0,2/5,0,2/7)*
          ($D$25-@SUM($V$9..V10)),0),0)
Y11: '{IF @YEAR(G13)=87}{RIGHT}~/rncDEP~~
AD11: 'Create range name DEP if 1987 Asset
AK11: '/reI12..O12~~
AQ11: 'Erase range
A12: 'Depreciation Life of Asset
G12: [W10] 5

H12: [W8] 'years
I12: 3
J12: [W8] 'Personal Computer
L12: [W10] 1003
M12: (D1) [W10] 32021
N12: 5
S12: 4
T12: (,0) @ROUND(@IF($G$12=3,+$D$25-@SUM($T$9..$T$11),0),0)
U12: (,0) @ROUND(@IF($G$12=5,($D$25-U9-U10-U11)/($G$12/2),0),0)
V12: (,0) @ROUND(@IF($G$12=7,@CHOOSE(+$G$12,0,0,0,2/3,0,2/5,0,2/7)*
                ($D$25-@SUM(V9..V11)),0),0)
Y12: '{IF @YEAR(G13)=88}{RIGHT 2}~/rncDEP~~
AD12: 'Create range name DEP if 1988 Asset
AK12: '/reM14..M15~~
AQ12: 'Erase range
A13: 'Date Placed in Service
G13: (D1) [W10] @DATE(88,9,1)
S13: 5
U13: (,0) @ROUND(@IF($G$12=5,($D$25-U9-U10-U11)/($G$12/2),0),0)
V13: (,0) @ROUND(@IF($G$12=7,($D$25-V9-V10-V11-V12)/($G$12/2),0),0)
Y13: '/rvF25..F32~E25~~
AD13: 'Copy values to cell E25
AK13: '/reI9~~
AQ13: 'Erase cell
A14: 'Current Depreciation Allowance
G14: (C0) [W10] 0
J14: [W8] 'Sale Date
M14: (D1) [W10] @DATE(88,10,31)
S14: 6
T14: (,0) "
U14: (,0) @ROUND(@IF($G$12=5,+$D$25-@SUM(U9..U13),0),0)
V14: (,0) @ROUND(@IF($G$12=7,($D$25-V9-V10-V11-V12)/($G$12/2),0),0)
Y14: '/rtE25..E32~DEP~~
AD14: 'Transpose values to range name DEP
AK14: '{CALC}~
AQ14: 'Recalculate worksheet
J15: [W8] 'Sale Price
M15: (C0) [W10] 3500
S15: 7
V15: (,0) @ROUND(@IF($G$12=7,($D$25-V9-V10-V11-V12)/($G$12/2),0),0)
Y15: '/reE25..E32~~
AD15: 'Erase range
AK15: '{HOME}{PANELON}{WINDOWSON}{BEEP 4}
AQ15: 'To Home/Control Panel & Windows On/Beep When Finished
J16: [W8] 'Basis
M16: (,0) [W10] @VLOOKUP(I9,D57..AS63,@YEAR(M14)-64)
S16: 8
V16: (,0) @ROUND(@IF($G$12=7,+$D$25-@SUM(V9..V15),0),0)
Y16: '/rndDEP~~
AD16: 'Delete range name DEP
M17: [W10] ' -------
Y17: '{RIGHT 18}~/rncREMAIN~~
AD17: 'Create range name REMAIN
J18: [W8] 'Gain (Loss) on Sale

M18: (CO) [W10] +M15-M16
T18: \-
U18: \-
V18: \-
Y18: '/rvH25..H32~G25~~
AD18: 'Copy values
T19: (,0) @SUM(T9..T12)
U19: (,0) @SUM(U9..U14)
V19: (,0) @SUM(V9..V16)
Y19: '/rtG25..G32~REMAIN~~
AD19: 'Transpose values to range name REMAIN
A20: \=
B20: [W8] \=
C20: \=
D20: [W8] \=
E20: [W10] \=
F20: [W10] \=
G20: [W10] \=
H20: [W8] \=
I20: \=
J20: [W8] \=
K20: \=
L20: [W10] \=
M20: [W10] \=
N20: \=
O20: \=
P20: [W8] \=
T20: \=
U20: \=
V20: \=
Y20: '/reG25..G32~~
AD20: 'Erase range
A21: 'ASSET DEPRECIATION
I21: 'DISPOSALS
Y21: '/rndREMAIN~~
AD21: 'Delete range name REMAIN
A22: \=
B22: [W8] \=
C22: \=
D22: [W8] \=
E22: [W10] \=
F22: [W10] \=
G22: [W10] \=
H22: [W8] \=
I22: \=
J22: [W8] \=
K22: \=
L22: [W10] \=
M22: [W10] \=
N22: \=
O22: \=
P22: [W8] \=
Y22: '{CALC}~
AD22: 'Recalculate worksheet

C23: ^Deprec
D23: [W8] ^Beg
F23: [W10] ^Dep
H23: [W8] ^Remain
Y23: '{GOTO}G9~/reG9..G14~~
AD23: 'Go to cell G9 and erase range
A24: 'Year
B24: [W8] 'Period
C24: ^Allow
D24: [W8] ^Basis
F24: [W10] ^Expense
H24: [W8] ^Basis
O24: ^Gain
Y24: '{HOME}~{PANELON}{WINDOWSON}{BEEP 4}
AD24: 'To Home/Control Panel & Windows On/Beep When Finished
A25: @YEAR(G13)+1900
B25: [W8] 1
C25: (C0) @IF($G$14>$G$11,$G$11,$G$14)
D25: (C0) [W8] +$G$11-$C$25
F25: (C0) [W10] @IF($G$12=3,$T9,@IF($G$12=5,$U9,@IF($G$12=7,$V9,0)))
H25: (C0) [W8] +$D$25-F25
L25: [W10] 'Disposal
M25: [W10] ^Sale
O25: ^(Loss)
A26: +A25+1
B26: [W8] +B25+1
F26: (C0) [W10] @IF($G$12=3,$T10,@IF($G$12=5,$U10,@IF($G$12=7,$V10,0)))
H26: (C0) [W8] +$D$25-F25-F26
I26: 'Asset
K26: 'ID
L26: [W10] 'Date
M26: [W10] ^Price
O26: ^on Sale
A27: +A26+1
B27: [W8] +B26+1
F27: (C0) [W10] @IF($G$12=3,$T11,@IF($G$12=5,$U11,@IF($G$12=7,$V11,0)))
H27: (C0) [W8] +$D$25-@SUM($F$25..$F$27)
A28: +A27+1
B28: [W8] +B27+1
F28: (C0) [W10] @IF($G$12=3,$T12,@IF($G$12=5,$U12,@IF($G$12=7,$V12,0)))
H28: (C0) [W8] +$D$25-@SUM($F$25..$F$28)
I28: 'Automobile
K28: 1001
L28: (D1) [W10] 32873
M28: (C0) [W10] 5000
O28: (C0) 4424
A29: +A28+1
B29: [W8] +B28+1
F29: (C0) [W10] @IF($G$12=3,$T13,@IF($G$12=5,$U13,@IF($G$12=7,$V13,0)))
H29: (C0) [W8] +$D$25-@SUM($F$25..$F$29)
A30: +A29+1
B30: [W8] +B29+1
F30: (C0) [W10] @IF($G$12=3,$T14,@IF($G$12=5,$U14,@IF($G$12=7,$V14,0)))
H30: (C0) [W8] +$D$25-@SUM($F$25..$F$30)

A31: +A30+1
B31: [W8] +B30+1
F31: (C0) [W10] @IF($G$12=3,$T15,@IF($G$12=5,$U15,@IF($G$12=7,$V15,0)))
H31: (C0) [W8] +$D$25-@SUM($F$25..$F$31)
A32: +A31+1
B32: [W8] +B31+1
F32: (C0) [W10] @IF($G$12=3,$T16,@IF($G$12=5,$U16,@IF($G$12=7,$V16,0)))
H32: (C0) [W8] +$D$25-@SUM($F$25..$F$32)
A50: \=
B50: [W8] \=
C50: \=
D50: [W8] \=
E50: [W10] \=
F50: [W10] \=
G50: [W10] \=
H50: [W8] \=
I50: \=
J50: [W8] \=
K50: \=
L50: [W10] \=
M50: [W10] \=
N50: \=
O50: \=
P50: [W8] \=
Q50: \=
R50: \=
S50: \=
T50: \=
U50: \=
V50: \=
W50: \=
X50: \=
Y50: \=
Z50: \=
AA50: \=
AB50: \=
AC50: \=
AD50: \=
AE50: \=
AF50: \=
AG50: \=
AH50: \=
AI50: \=
AJ50: \=
AK50: \=
AL50: \=
AM50: \=
AN50: \=
AO50: \=
AP50: \=
AQ50: \=
AR50: \=
AS50: \=
A51: 'CAPITAL ASSET SUMMARY

A52: \=
B52: [W8] \=
C52: \=
D52: [W8] \=
E52: [W10] \=
F52: [W10] \=
G52: [W10] \=
H52: [W8] \=
I52: \=
J52: [W8] \=
K52: \=
L52: [W10] \=
M52: [W10] \=
N52: \=
O52: \=
P52: [W8] \=
Q52: \=
R52: \=
S52: \=
T52: \=
U52: \=
V52: \=
W52: \=
X52: \=
Y52: \=
Z52: \=
AA52: \=
AB52: \=
AC52: \=
AD52: \=
AE52: \=
AF52: \=
AG52: \=
AH52: \=
AI52: \=
AJ52: \=
AK52: \=
AL52: \=
AM52: \=
AN52: \=
AO52: \=
AP52: \=
AQ52: \=
AR52: \=
AS52: \=
E54: [W10] ^Net
I54: ^First
J54: [W8] '   ----
K54: \-
L54: [W10] \-
M54: [W10] \-
N54: \-
P54: [W8] 'Annual Depreciation
S54: \-

T54: \-
U54: \-
V54: \-
W54: \-
X54: \-
Y54: \-
Z54: \-
AA54: \-
AB54: '   ------
AC54: \-
AD54: \-
AE54: \-
AF54: \-
AH54: 'Remaining Assets
AK54: \-
AL54: \-
AM54: \-
AN54: \-
AO54: \-
AP54: \-
AQ54: \-
AR54: \-
AS54: \-
E55: [W10] ^Purchase
F55: [W10] ^Asset
G55: [W10] ^Purchase
I55: ^Year
A56: 'Number
B56: [W8] 'Asset
D56: [W8] 'ID
E56: [W10] '   Cost
F56: [W10] '   Life
G56: [W10] ' Date
I56: 'Expense
J56: [W8] 1987
K56: +J56+1
L56: [W10] +K56+1
M56: [W10] +L56+1
N56: +M56+1
O56: +N56+1
P56: [W8] +O56+1
Q56: +P56+1
R56: +Q56+1
S56: +R56+1
T56: +S56+1
U56: +T56+1
V56: +U56+1
W56: +V56+1
X56: +W56+1
Y56: +X56+1
Z56: +Y56+1
AA56: +Z56+1
AB56: 1987
AC56: +AB56+1

AD56: +AC56+1
AE56: +AD56+1
AF56: +AE56+1
AG56: +AF56+1
AH56: +AG56+1
AI56: +AH56+1
AJ56: +AI56+1
AK56: +AJ56+1
AL56: +AK56+1
AM56: +AL56+1
AN56: +AM56+1
AO56: +AN56+1
AP56: +AO56+1
AQ56: +AP56+1
AR56: +AQ56+1
AS56: +AR56+1
A58: 2
B58: [W8] 'Office Furniture
D58: [W8] 1002
E58: (C0) [W10] 15000
F58: [W10] 7
G58: (D1) [W10] 31929
I58: (C0) 0
J58: (C0) [W8] 2143
K58: (C0) 3673
L58: (C0) [W10] 2624
M58: (C0) [W10] 1874
N58: (C0) 1339
O58: (C0) 1339
P58: (C0) [W8] 1339
Q58: (C0) 669
AB58: (C0) 12857
AC58: (C0) 9184
AD58: (C0) 6560
AE58: (C0) 4686
AF58: (C0) 3347
AG58: (C0) 2008
AH58: (C0) 669
AI58: (C0) 0
A59: 3
B59: [W8] 'Personal Computer
D59: [W8] 1003
E59: (C0) [W10] 7500
F59: [W10] 5
G59: (D1) [W10] 32021
I59: (C0) 0
J59: (C0) [W8] 1500
K59: (C0) 2400
L59: (C0) [W10] 1440
M59: (C0) [W10] 864
N59: (C0) 864
O59: (C0) 432
P59: (C0) [W8] 0
Q59: (C0) 0

AB59: (C0) 6000
AC59: (C0) 3600
AD59: (C0) 2160
AE59: (C0) 1296
AF59: (C0) 432
AG59: (C0) 0
AH59: (C0) 0
AI59: (C0) 0
A60: 4
B60: [W8] 'R&D Equipment
D60: [W8] 1004
E60: (C0) [W10] 20000
F60: [W10] 5
G60: (D1) [W10] 32143
I60: (C0) 10000
K60: (C0) 2000
L60: (C0) [W10] 3200
M60: (C0) [W10] 1920
N60: (C0) 1152
O60: (C0) 1152
P60: (C0) [W8] 576
Q60: (C0) 0
R60: (C0) 0
AC60: (C0) 8000
AD60: (C0) 4800
AE60: (C0) 2880
AF60: (C0) 1728
AG60: (C0) 576
AH60: (C0) 0
AI60: (C0) 0
AJ60: (C0) 0
A61: 5
B61: [W8] 'Truck
D61: [W8] 1005
E61: (C0) [W10] 15000
F61: [W10] 5
G61: (D1) [W10] 32203
I61: (C0) 0
K61: (C0) 3000
L61: (C0) [W10] 4800
M61: (C0) [W10] 2880
N61: (C0) 1728
O61: (C0) 1728
P61: (C0) [W8] 864
Q61: (C0) 0
R61: (C0) 0
AC61: (C0) 12000
AD61: (C0) 7200
AE61: (C0) 4320
AF61: (C0) 2592
AG61: (C0) 864
AH61: (C0) 0
AI61: (C0) 0
AJ61: (C0) 0

A62: 6
B62: [W8] 'Personal Computer
D62: [W8] 1006
E62: (C0) [W10] 9000
F62: [W10] 5
G62: (D1) [W10] @DATE(88,9,1)
I62: (C0) 0
K62: (C0) 1800
L62: (C0) [W10] 2880
M62: (C0) [W10] 1728
N62: (C0) 1037
O62: (C0) 1037
P62: (C0) [W8] 518
Q62: (C0) 0
R62: (C0) 0
AC62: (C0) 7200
AD62: (C0) 4320
AE62: (C0) 2592
AF62: (C0) 1555
AG62: (C0) 518
J63: (C0) [W8] "-------
K63: (C0) "-------
L63: (C0) [W10] "-------
M63: (C0) [W10] "-------
N63: (C0) "-------
O63: (C0) "-------
P63: (C0) [W8] "-------
Q63: (C0) "-------
R63: (C0) "-------
S63: (C0) "-------
T63: (C0) "-------
U63: (C0) "-------
V63: (C0) "-------
W63: (C0) "-------
X63: (C0) "-------
Y63: (C0) "-------
Z63: (C0) "-------
AA63: (C0) "-------
AB63: (C0) "-------
AC63: (C0) "-------
AD63: (C0) "-------
AE63: (C0) "-------
AF63: (C0) "-------
AG63: (C0) "-------
AH63: (C0) "-------
AI63: (C0) "-------
AJ63: (C0) "-------
AK63: (C0) "-------
AL63: (C0) "-------
AM63: (C0) "-------
AN63: (C0) "-------
AO63: (C0) "-------
AP63: (C0) "-------

AQ63: (C0) "-------
AR63: (C0) "-------
AS63: (C0) "-------
J64: (C0) [W8] @SUM(J58..J63)
K64: (C0) @SUM(K58..K63)
L64: (C0) [W10] @SUM(L58..L63)
M64: (C0) [W10] @SUM(M58..M63)
N64: (C0) @SUM(N58..N63)
O64: (C0) @SUM(O58..O63)
P64: (C0) [W8] @SUM(P58..P63)
Q64: (C0) @SUM(Q58..Q63)
R64: (C0) @SUM(R58..R63)
S64: (C0) @SUM(S58..S63)
T64: (C0) @SUM(T58..T63)
U64: (C0) @SUM(U58..U63)
V64: (C0) @SUM(V58..V63)
W64: (C0) @SUM(W58..W63)
X64: (C0) @SUM(X58..X63)
Y64: (C0) @SUM(Y58..Y63)
Z64: (C0) @SUM(Z58..Z63)
AA64: (C0) @SUM(AA58..AA63)
AB64: (C0) @SUM(AB58..AB63)
AC64: (C0) @SUM(AC58..AC63)
AD64: (C0) @SUM(AD58..AD63)
AE64: (C0) @SUM(AE58..AE63)
AF64: (C0) @SUM(AF58..AF63)
AG64: (C0) @SUM(AG58..AG63)
AH64: (C0) @SUM(AH58..AH63)
AI64: (C0) @SUM(AI58..AI63)
AJ64: (C0) @SUM(AJ58..AJ63)
AK64: (C0) @SUM(AK58..AK63)
AL64: (C0) @SUM(AL58..AL63)
AM64: (C0) @SUM(AM58..AM63)
AN64: (C0) @SUM(AN58..AN63)
AO64: (C0) @SUM(AO58..AO63)
AP64: (C0) @SUM(AP58..AP63)
AQ64: (C0) @SUM(AQ58..AQ63)
AR64: (C0) @SUM(AR58..AR63)
AS64: (C0) @SUM(AS58..AS63)
J65: (C0) [W8] "=======
K65: (C0) "=======
L65: (C0) [W10] "=======
M65: (C0) [W10] "=======
N65: (C0) "=======
O65: (C0) "=======
P65: (C0) [W8] "=======
Q65: (C0) "=======
R65: (C0) "=======
S65: (C0) "=======
T65: (C0) "=======
U65: (C0) "=======
V65: (C0) "=======
W65: (C0) "=======

```
X65: (C0) "=======
Y65: (C0) "=======
Z65: (C0) "=======
AA65: (C0) "=======
AB65: (C0) "=======
AC65: (C0) "=======
AD65: (C0) "=======
AE65: (C0) "=======
AF65: (C0) "=======
AG65: (C0) "=======
AH65: (C0) "=======
AI65: (C0) "=======
AJ65: (C0) "=======
AK65: (C0) "=======
AL65: (C0) "=======
AM65: (C0) "=======
AN65: (C0) "=======
AO65: (C0) "=======
AP65: (C0) "=======
AQ65: (C0) "=======
AR65: (C0) "=======
AS65: (C0) "=======
```

V

General Management
Applications

14

Managing Time

Introduction

If you are a manager or a professional in a consulting capacity, you know the importance of time. At one time or another, we all have been asked, " . . . can I have a moment of your time?" Time is probably the most difficult resource to measure.

The Time Manager application can help you to analyze and review the use of your company's time. The model makes extensive use of 1-2-3's data-management capabilities, primarily the **/D**ata **Q**uery and **/D**ata **T**able commands, to help you track and report the use of your time.

Even if you do not need the model at the moment, understanding the application and how it operates will greatly increase your understanding of 1-2-3's often overlooked but powerful database capability. The model also may provide you with ideas on how to put 1-2-3's data-management functions to work in your business.

The Time Manager is divided into eight sections: the Time Accounting Worksheet, Employee Rate Table, Client History, Criterion and Analysis Area, Client Summary, Time Utilization Reports, and a macro (see fig. 14.1).

As in other models in this book, the first and second sections are data-entry areas. The Client History, Client Summary, and Time Utilization Reports are 1-2-3 data tables. As you will see, the model functions in much the same way as Chapter 1's Checkbook Manager.

===

TIME MANAGER   Copyright (C) Que Corp 1987

===

TIME ACCOUNTING WORKSHEET

Date	Staff Member	Client	Task	Rate	Hours	Charges
15-Dec-86	1	101	102	1	1.0	$50
15-Jan-87	3	101	101	2	3.0	$270
20-Jan-87	3	101	104	1	2.0	$150
25-Jan-87	3	101	102	1	1.5	$113
06-Feb-87	1	101	103	1	2.0	$100
02-Jan-87	2	102	103	3	0.5	$50
				Total	10.0	$733

EMPLOYEE RATE TABLE

Name	Number	Rate 1	2	3	4	5
Smith	1	$50	$60	$75	$120	$200
Jones	2	$55	$80	$100		
Webster	3	$75	$90	$100		

===

CLIENT HISTORY

Client: 101

Task Description	Number	Dec-86	Jan-87	Feb-87	Mar-87	Apr-87	May-87	Jun-87	Jul-87	Aug-87	Sep-87	Oct-87	Nov-87	Total
Planning	101	0.0	3.0	0.0	0.0	0.0	0.0	0.0	0.0	0.0	0.0	0.0	0.0	3.0
Client Conference	102	1.0	1.5	0.0	0.0	0.0	0.0	0.0	0.0	0.0	0.0	0.0	0.0	2.5
Research	103	0.0	0.0	2.0	0.0	0.0	0.0	0.0	0.0	0.0	0.0	0.0	0.0	2.0
Review	104	0.0	2.0	0.0	0.0	0.0	0.0	0.0	0.0	0.0	0.0	0.0	0.0	2.0
	105	0.0	0.0	0.0	0.0	0.0	0.0	0.0	0.0	0.0	0.0	0.0	0.0	0.0
	106	0.0	0.0	0.0	0.0	0.0	0.0	0.0	0.0	0.0	0.0	0.0	0.0	0.0
	107	0.0	0.0	0.0	0.0	0.0	0.0	0.0	0.0	0.0	0.0	0.0	0.0	0.0
	108	0.0	0.0	0.0	0.0	0.0	0.0	0.0	0.0	0.0	0.0	0.0	0.0	0.0
	109	0.0	0.0	0.0	0.0	0.0	0.0	0.0	0.0	0.0	0.0	0.0	0.0	0.0
	110	0.0	0.0	0.0	0.0	0.0	0.0	0.0	0.0	0.0	0.0	0.0	0.0	0.0
	111	0.0	0.0	0.0	0.0	0.0	0.0	0.0	0.0	0.0	0.0	0.0	0.0	0.0
	112	0.0	0.0	0.0	0.0	0.0	0.0	0.0	0.0	0.0	0.0	0.0	0.0	0.0
	113	0.0	0.0	0.0	0.0	0.0	0.0	0.0	0.0	0.0	0.0	0.0	0.0	0.0
	114	0.0	0.0	0.0	0.0	0.0	0.0	0.0	0.0	0.0	0.0	0.0	0.0	0.0
	115	0.0	0.0	0.0	0.0	0.0	0.0	0.0	0.0	0.0	0.0	0.0	0.0	0.0
	116	0.0	0.0	0.0	0.0	0.0	0.0	0.0	0.0	0.0	0.0	0.0	0.0	0.0
	117	0.0	0.0	0.0	0.0	0.0	0.0	0.0	0.0	0.0	0.0	0.0	0.0	0.0
	118	0.0	0.0	0.0	0.0	0.0	0.0	0.0	0.0	0.0	0.0	0.0	0.0	0.0
	119	0.0	0.0	0.0	0.0	0.0	0.0	0.0	0.0	0.0	0.0	0.0	0.0	0.0
	120	0.0	0.0	0.0	0.0	0.0	0.0	0.0	0.0	0.0	0.0	0.0	0.0	0.0
Total		1.0	6.5	2.0	0.0	0.0	0.0	0.0	0.0	0.0	0.0	0.0	0.0	9.5

===

CLIENT SUMMARY

Client: 101
For Period from: 31-Dec-86
to: 01-Feb-87

Task Description	Number	Hours
Planning	101	3.0
Client Conference	102	1.5
Research	103	2.0
Review	104	0.0
	105	0.0
	106	0.0
	107	0.0
	108	0.0
	109	0.0
	110	0.0
	111	0.0
	112	0.0
	113	0.0
	114	0.0
	115	0.0
	116	0.0
	117	0.0
	118	0.0
	119	0.0
	120	0.0
Totals		6.5

Criterion Range
Client	Task	Date
1		0

UTILIZATION REPORT

Period Beginning: 01-Jan-87
Ending: 31-Jan-87

Task Description	Number	
Planning	101	1
Client Conference	102	0.0
Research	103	0.0
Review	104	0.0
	105	0.0
	106	0.0
	107	0.0
	108	0.0
	109	0.0
	110	0.0
	111	0.0
	112	0.0
	113	0.0
	114	0.0
	115	0.0
	116	0.0
	117	0.0
	118	0.0
	119	0.0
	120	0.0
Total		0.0

Client		
ABC Corp	101	1
BCD Corp	102	0.0
EFG Partners	103	0.0
Smith Bros	104	0.0
	105	0.0
	106	0.0
	107	0.0
	108	0.0
	109	0.0
	110	0.0
	111	0.0
	112	0.0
	113	0.0
	114	0.0
	115	0.0
	116	0.0
	117	0.0
	118	0.0
	119	0.0
	120	0.0
Total		0.0

Criterion Range
Task	Member	Date	Client
			0

		Dec-86	Jan-87	Feb-87	Mar-87	Apr-87	May-87	Jun-87	Jul-87	Aug-87	Sep-87	Oct-87	Nov-87	Total
Planning	101	$0	$270	$0	$0	$0	0	0	0	0	0	0	0	$270
Client Conference	102	$50	$113	$0	$0	$0	0	0	0	0	0	0	0	$163
Research	103	$0	$0	$100	$0	$0	0	0	0	0	0	0	0	$100
Review	104	$0	$150	$0	$0	$0	0	0	0	0	0	0	0	$150
	105	0	0	0	0	0	0	0	0	0	0	0	0	$0
	106	0	0	0	0	0	0	0	0	0	0	0	0	$0
	107	0	0	0	0	0	0	0	0	0	0	0	0	$0
	108	0	0	0	0	0	0	0	0	0	0	0	0	$0
	109	0	0	0	0	0	0	0	0	0	0	0	0	$0
	110	0	0	0	0	0	0	0	0	0	0	0	0	$0
	111	0	0	0	0	0	0	0	0	0	0	0	0	$0
	112	0	0	0	0	0	0	0	0	0	0	0	0	$0
	113	0	0	0	0	0	0	0	0	0	0	0	0	$0
	114	0	0	0	0	0	0	0	0	0	0	0	0	$0
	115	0	0	0	0	0	0	0	0	0	0	0	0	$0
	116	0	0	0	0	0	0	0	0	0	0	0	0	$0
	117	0	0	0	0	0	0	0	0	0	0	0	0	$0
	118	0	0	0	0	0	0	0	0	0	0	0	0	$0
	119	0	0	0	0	0	0	0	0	0	0	0	0	$0
	120	0	0	0	0	0	0	0	0	0	0	0	0	$0
Total		$50	$533	$100	$0	$0	$0	$0	$0	$0	$0	$0	$0	$683

Criterion Range
Client	Task	Date
1		0

CRITERION RANGE

Date	Staff Member	Client	Task	Rate	Hours	Charges
		101	102			

ANALYSIS AREA

Date	Staff Member	Client	Task	Rate	Hours	Charges
15-Dec-86	1	101	102	1	1.0	$50
25-Jan-87	3	101	102	1	1.5	$113

Criterion Range
Task	Member	Date	Client
			0

```
        V   W   X   Y   Z   AA      AB          AC      AD      AE      AF      AG      AH

                            \t      {MENUBRANCH}Execute Time Manager Data Table Menu

                            T MENU  A           B       C       D       E       QUIT
                                    Client HiClient HiClient SuTime UtilTime UtilExit from Macro
                                    {BRANCH T(BRANCH T(BRANCH T(BRANCH T6 MC)

                            T1 MC   {PANELOFF}{WINDOWSOFF}`
                                    /dt2c44..o64~d108~e109~~
                                    /dtr~~
                                    {PANELON}{WINDOWSON}{BEEP 4}~
                                    {BRANCH \t}

                            T2 MC   {PANELOFF}{WINDOWSOFF}~
                                    /dt2c81..o101~d108~e109~~
                                    /dtr~
                                    {PANELON}{WINDOWSON}{BEEP 4}~
                                    {BRANCH \t}

                            T3 MC   {PANELOFF}{WINDOWSOFF}~
                                    /dt1t44..u64~s71~~
                                    /dtr~
                                    /dt1t44..v64~s71~~
                                    /dtr~~
                                    {PANELON}{WINDOWSON}{BEEP 4}~
                                    {BRANCH \t}

                            T4 MC   {PANELOFF}{WINDOWSOFF}~
                                    /dt2t81..ad101~r134~s134~~
                                    /dtr~~
                                    {PANELON}{WINDOWSON}{BEEP 4}~
                                    {BRANCH \t}

                            T5 MC   {PANELOFF}{WINDOWSOFF}~
                                    /dt2t107..ad127~u134~s134~~
                                    /dtr~
                                    {PANELON}{WINDOWSON}{BEEP 4}~
                                    {BRANCH \t}

                            T6 MC   {QUIT}
```

Total Billings	Average Rate
$270.00	$90.00
$112.50	$75.00
$0.00	$0.00
$150.00	$75.00
$0.00	$0.00
$0.00	$0.00
$0.00	$0.00
$0.00	$0.00
$0.00	$0.00
$0.00	$0.00
$0.00	$0.00
$0.00	$0.00
$0.00	$0.00
$0.00	$0.00
$0.00	$0.00
$532.50	$81.92

Staff Member

	2	3	4	5	6	7	8	9	10	Total
	0.0	3.0	0.0	0.0	0.0	0.0	0.0	0.0	0.0	3.0
	0.0	1.5	0.0	0.0	0.0	0.0	0.0	0.0	0.0	1.5
	0.5	0.0	0.0	0.0	0.0	0.0	0.0	0.0	0.0	0.5
	0.0	2.0	0.0	0.0	0.0	0.0	0.0	0.0	0.0	2.0
	0.0	0.0	0.0	0.0	0.0	0.0	0.0	0.0	0.0	0.0
	0.0	0.0	0.0	0.0	0.0	0.0	0.0	0.0	0.0	0.0
	0.0	0.0	0.0	0.0	0.0	0.0	0.0	0.0	0.0	0.0
	0.0	0.0	0.0	0.0	0.0	0.0	0.0	0.0	0.0	0.0
	0.0	0.0	0.0	0.0	0.0	0.0	0.0	0.0	0.0	0.0
	0.0	0.0	0.0	0.0	0.0	0.0	0.0	0.0	0.0	0.0
	0.0	0.0	0.0	0.0	0.0	0.0	0.0	0.0	0.0	0.0
	0.0	0.0	0.0	0.0	0.0	0.0	0.0	0.0	0.0	0.0
	0.0	0.0	0.0	0.0	0.0	0.0	0.0	0.0	0.0	0.0
	0.0	0.0	0.0	0.0	0.0	0.0	0.0	0.0	0.0	0.0
	0.0	0.0	0.0	0.0	0.0	0.0	0.0	0.0	0.0	0.0
	0.0	0.0	0.0	0.0	0.0	0.0	0.0	0.0	0.0	0.0
	0.0	0.0	0.0	0.0	0.0	0.0	0.1	0.0	0.0	0.0
	0.5	6.5	0.0	0.0	0.0	0.0	0.0	0.0	0.0	7.0

Staff Member

	2	3	4	5	6	7	8	9	10	Total
	0.0	6.5	0.0	0.0	0.0	0.0	0.0	0.0	0.0	6.5
	0.5	0.0	0.0	0.0	0.0	0.0	0.0	0.0	0.0	0.5
	0.0	0.0	0.0	0.0	0.0	0.0	0.0	0.0	0.0	0.0
	0.0	0.0	0.0	0.0	0.0	0.0	0.0	0.0	0.0	0.0
	0.0	0.0	0.0	0.0	0.0	0.0	0.0	0.0	0.0	0.0
	0.0	0.0	0.0	0.0	0.0	0.0	0.0	0.0	0.0	0.0
	0.0	0.0	0.0	0.0	0.0	0.0	0.0	0.0	0.0	0.0
	0.0	0.0	0.0	0.0	0.0	0.0	0.0	0.0	0.0	0.0
	0.0	0.0	0.0	0.0	0.0	0.0	0.0	0.0	0.0	0.0
	0.0	0.0	0.0	0.0	0.0	0.0	0.0	0.0	0.0	0.0
	0.0	0.0	0.0	0.0	0.0	0.0	0.0	0.0	0.0	0.0
	0.0	0.0	0.0	0.0	0.0	0.0	0.0	0.0	0.0	0.0
	0.0	0.0	0.0	0.0	0.0	0.0	0.0	0.0	0.0	0.0
	0.0	0.0	0.0	0.0	0.0	0.0	0.0	0.0	0.0	0.0
	0.0	0.0	0.0	0.0	0.0	0.0	0.0	0.0	0.0	0.0
	0.0	0.0	0.0	0.0	0.0	0.0	0.0	0.0	0.0	0.0
	0.0	0.0	0.0	0.0	0.0	0.0	0.0	0.0	0.0	0.0
	0.5	6.5	0.0	0.0	0.0	0.0	0.0	0.0	0.0	7.0

Fig. 14.1. The Time Manager model.

This chapter guides you in creating the Time Manager, discusses how the application operates, and shows you how to use the model in your business.

Creating the Model

Although relatively large, the Time Manager is not difficult to create. Before you begin, make sure that you have a good idea of the number of your clients, tasks, rates, and employees. Because your firm probably has more business than we have displayed in figure 14.1, you'll want to be sure that your model includes all of your business activity.

Setting Column Widths

Using a blank 1-2-3 spreadsheet, change the widths of the columns according to the following list:

Column	Width
A, C, Q, T	10

All other columns should be left at the default width.

Specifying Cell Formats

Now, format the cells of your 1-2-3 Time Manager. A list of the formats used in the example is shown in table 14.1.

Table 14.1
Cell Formats

Format	Cell/Range
Time Accounting Worksheet	
/rfd1	Column A
/rff1	Column F
/rfc0	Column G
Employee Rate Table	
/rfc0	J11..N13
Client History 1	
/rfh	C44
/rfd3	D44..O44
/rff1	D45..P64, D66..P66

Format	Cell/Range

Client History 2

/rfh	C81
/rfd3	D81..O81
/rfc0	D82..P102, D104..P104

Client Summary

/rfd1	T38, T39
/rfh	U44, V44
/rff1	Column U
/rfc2	Column V, Column W

Utilization Report 1

/rfd1	T75, T76
/rfh	T81
/rff1	U82..AE101, U103..AE103
Format	Cell/Range

Utilization Report 2

| /rfh | T107 |
| /rff1 | U109..AE127, U129..AE129 |

Range Names

The Time Manager requires the use of range names only if you plan to use the optional macro. To name the macro and its subroutines quickly, issue the /Range Name Label Right command from cells AA1..AA39.

Next, enter the row titles, column headings, and labels according to the format in table 14.2 or to one of your own design.

Table 14.2
Row Titles and Column Headings

Enter into cell:	Original label:	Copy to:

Opening Headings

| A1: | \= | B1..U1, A5..U5, A7..U7, A37..U37, A112..G112, A117..G117, A119..G119, R74..X74 |

Enter
into
cell: Original label: Copy to:

A3:   'TIME MANAGER

Time Accounting Worksheet

A6:   'TIME ACCOUNTING WORKSHEET
B8:   "Staff
A9:   'Date
B9:   "Member
C9:   "Client
D9:   "Task
E9:   "Rate
F9:   "Hours
G9:   "Charges
F32:   '   ------   G32
E33:   ^Total
F34:   '   ======   G34

Employee Rate Table

H6:   'EMPLOYEE RATE TABLE
H10:   'Name
I10:   'Number

Client History

A36:   'CLIENT HISTORY
A38:   'Client:
B42:   '   Task
A43:   'Description
C43:   'Number
P44:   '   Total   AE81
D65:   '   ------   E65..P65, U65..W65
D67:   '   ======   E67..P67, U67..W67
C106:   'Criterion Range
C107:   "Client
D107:   "Task
E107:   'Date

Criterion Range and Analysis Area

A111:   'CRITERION RANGE
B113:   "Staff   B120
A114:   'Date   A121
B114:   "Member   B121

Enter
into
cell: Original label: Copy to:

C114:   "Client   C121
D114:   "Task   D121
E114:   "Rate   E121
F114:   "Hours   F121
G114:   "Charges   G121
A118:   'ANALYSIS AREA

Client Summary

R36:   'CLIENT SUMMARY
R38:   'Client:
R39:   'For Period from
S40:   '   to:
S42:   '   Task
V42:   ' Total
W42:   'Average
R43:   '   Description
T43:   'Number
U43:   ^Hours
V43:   'Billings
W43:   ' Rate
S66:   'Totals
R69:   'Criterion Range
R70:   "Client
S70:   "Task
T70:   'Date

Utilization Report

R73:   'UTILIZATION REPORT
R75:   'Period Beginning
R76:   '   Ending:
S79:   '   Task
R80:   '   Description
T80:   'Number
V80:   'Staff Member   V106
AE81:   'Total   AE107
D102:   ' ------   E102..P102,
                                                         U102..AE102,
                                                         U128..AE128

D104:   ' ======   E104..P104,
                                                         U104..AE104,
                                                         U130..AE130

Enter into cell:	Original label:	Copy to:
T103:	^Total	T129
R106:	' Client	
R132:	'Criterion Range	
R133:	"Task	
S133:	"Member	
T133:	"Date	
U133:	'Client	

Macro

AA1:	'\t
AB1:	'{MENUBRANCH T MENU}
AC1:	'Execute Time Manager Data Table Menu
AA3:	'T MENU
AB3:	'A
AC3:	'B
AD3:	'C
AE3:	'D
AF3:	'E
AG3:	'QUIT
AB4:	'Client History 1
AC4:	'Client History 2
AD4:	'Client Summary
AE4:	'Time Utilization 1
AF4:	'Time Utilization 2
AG4:	'Exit from Macro
AB5:	'{BRANCH T1 MC}
AC5:	'{BRANCH T2 MC}
AD5:	'{BRANCH T3 MC}
AE5:	'{BRANCH T4 MC}
AF5:	'{BRANCH T5 MC}
AG5:	'{BRANCH T6 MC}
AA7:	'T1 MC
AB7:	'{PANELOFF}{WINDOWSOFF}~
AB8:	'/dt2c44..o64~d108~e109~~
AB9:	'/dtr~~
AB10:	'{PANELON}{WINDOWSON}{BEEP 4}~
AB11:	'{BRANCH \t}
AA13:	'T2 MC
AB13:	'{PANELOFF}{WINDOWSOFF}~
AB14:	'/dt2c81..o101~d108~e109~~

Enter into cell:	Original label:	Copy to:
AB15	'/dtr~~	
AB16:	'{PANELON}{WINDOWSON}{BEEP 4}~	
AB17:	'{BRANCH \t}	
AA19:	'T3 MC	
AB19:	'{PANELOFF}{WINDOWSOFF}~	
AB20:	'/dt1t44..u64~s71~~	
AB21:	'/dtr~~	
AB22:	'/dt1t44..v64~s71~~	
AB23:	'/dtr~~	
AB24:	'{PANELON}{WINDOWSON}{BEEP 4}~	
AB25:	'{BRANCH \t}	
AA27:	'T4 MC	
AB27:	'{PANELOFF}{WINDOWSOFF}~	
AB28:	'/dt2t81..ad101~r134~s134~~	
AB29:	'/dtr~~	
AB30:	'{PANELON}{WINDOWSON}{BEEP 4}~	
AB31:	'{BRANCH \t}~	
AA33:	'T5 MC	
AB33:	'{PANELOFF}{WINDOWSOFF}~	
AB34:	'/dt2t107..ad127~u134~s134~~	
AB35:	'/dtr~~	
AB36:	'{PANELON}{WINDOWSON}{BEEP 4}~	
AB37:	'{BRANCH \t}	
AA39:	'T6 MC	
AB39:	'{QUIT}	

Setting Up /Data Query

To Query your Time Manager, you will need to establish /Data Query parameters. Enter the following Input, Criterion, and Output Ranges:

1. Press /Data Query Input.

2. Type *A9..G32* and press Enter.

3. Press Criterion.

4. Type *A114..G115* and press Enter.

5. Press **O**utput.

6. Type *A121..G121* and press Enter.

7. Press **Q**uit.

Now you need to press only the F7 (QUERY) key to **Q**uery the Time Manager's database.

Next, you enter the model's formulas. Table 14.3 lists the formulas and their locations.

Table 14.3
Formulas and Functions

Enter into cell:	Original formula:	Copy to:
	Time Accounting Worksheet	
Column A	@DATE	
G10:	+F10*@VLOOKUP(B10,I$11..N$30, E10)	G11..G15
F33:	@SUM(F10..F32)	G33
	Client History 1	
C44:	@DSUM($A$9..$G$32,5,C107..E108)	
D44:	@DATE	
E44:	+D44+31	F44..Q44
P45:	@SUM(D45..O45)	P46..P64
D66:	@SUM(D45..D65)	E66..P66
	Client History 2	
C81:	@DSUM($A$9..$G$32,6,C107..E108)	
D82:	+D44	E82..O82
P83:	@SUM(D83..O83)	P84..P102
D104:	@SUM(D83..D103)	E104..P104
E108:	@MONTH(A10)=@MONTH($E$109)	
C108:	+C10=$C$38	
	Client Summary	
T39:	@DATE	
T40:	@DATE	
U44:	@DSUM($A$9..$G$32,5,R70..T71)	
V44:	@DSUM($A$9..$G$32,6,R71..T72)	
W45:	@IF(V45=0,0,V45/U45)	W46..W63, W66

Enter into cell:	Original formula:	Copy to:
U66:	@SUM(U45..U65)	V66
R71:	+C10=$T$38	
T71:	+A10>=$T$39#AND#+A10<=$T$40	

Utilization Report 1

T75:	@DATE	
T76:	@DATE	
T81:	@DSUM($A$9..$G$32,5,R134..T135)	
AE82:	@SUM(U82..AD82)	AE83..AE101
U103:	@SUM(U82..U102)	V103..AE103

Utilization Report 2

T107:	@DSUM($A$9..$G$32,5,S134..U135)	
AE108:	@SUM(U108..AD108)	AE109..AE127
U129:	@SUM(U108..U128)	V129..AE129
T134:	+A10>=$T$75#AND#+A10<=$T$76	

Understanding the Model

You will be able to use the application effectively if you understand how each module operates.

The Time Accounting Worksheet

The first of two data-entry areas in the model, the Time Accounting Worksheet is located at cells A5 through G15 (refer to fig. 14.1). Figure 14.2 shows the critical elements of this module.

	A	B	C	D	E	F	G
6	TIME ACCOUNTING WORKSHEET						
7	===						
8		Staff					
9	Date	Member	Client	Task	Rate	Hours	Charges
10	15-Dec-86	1	101	102	1	1.0	$50
11	15-Jan-87	3	101	101	2	3.0	$270
12	20-Jan-87	3	101	104	1	2.0	$150
13	25-Jan-87	3	101	102	1	1.5	$113
14	06-Feb-87	1	101	103	1	2.0	$100
15	02-Jan-87	2	102	103	3	0.5	$50
16							
17							

Fig. 14.2. The Time Accounting Worksheet.

Key data about your business activity is entered in this module. The date of the service performed, and your employee, client, task, rate, and hours are recorded in columns A, B, C, D, E, and F, respectively. All of this data will be used in the model's data tables.

Your charge for the service performed is calculated in column G of this module. For example, the formula in cell G10

G10: +F10*@VLOOKUP(B10,I$11..H$30,E10)

multiplies the number of hours in cell F10 by the result of the @VLOOKUP function, in which *B10* is a specific employee, the range *I11..H30* is the Employee Rate Table, and *E10* is the hourly rate for that particular task. This @VLOOKUP equation will select the proper hourly rate for the employee assigned to the task. The formula is repeated on a relative basis for subsequent cells in column G.

Columns F and G, Hours and Charges, are totaled using @SUM functions. In the example, the formula in cell F33 is

F33: @SUM(F10..F32)

and cell G33 is

G33: @SUM(G10..G32)

As you can see, the successful completion of this section depends on the next module, the Employee Rate Table.

The Employee Rate Table

The Employee Rate Table is located directly to the right of the Time Accounting Worksheet (at cells H5 through N13 in the example). Figure 14.3 outlines the structure of this section.

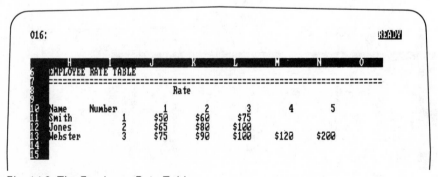

Fig. 14.3. The Employee Rate Table.

This module forms a data table that contains your hourly salary rates, which are the rates that you eventually pass on to your customers. Column H of this section contains your employees' names; column I holds their numbers, values that you assign for purposes of this analysis. To make sure that the equations incorporating @VLOOKUP functions (column G of the Time Accounting Worksheet) operate properly, it is crucial that the numbers be in ascending order.

The remaining columns, J, K, L, M, and N, display the hourly billing rates for each of your employees. For example, employee 1, Smith, has rates of $50, $60, and $75.

As you can see, the Time Accounting Worksheet and the Employee Rate Table provide the information needed for the model to generate management reports about your business. The first of these reports is the Client History.

The Client History

The Client History is actually two reports. The first of these reports shows you the amount of time charged monthly to an activity (Planning, for example); the second displays this same information as a dollar amount, for a specific client. Figures 14.4 and 14.5 show you this section of the model.

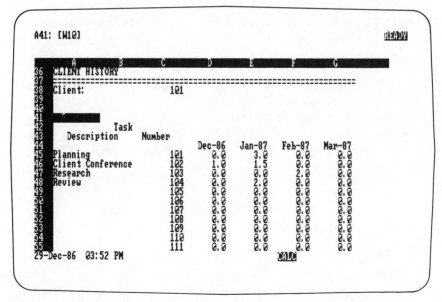

Fig. 14.4. The Client History: Time Charged.

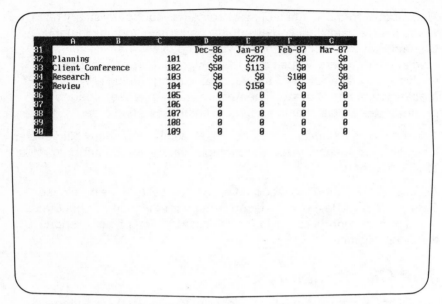

	A	B	C	D	E	F	G
81				Dec-86	Jan-87	Feb-87	Mar-87
82	Planning		101	$0	$270	$0	$0
83	Client Conference		102	$50	$113	$0	$0
84	Research		103	$0	$0	$100	$0
85	Review		104	$0	$150	$0	$0
86			105	0	0	0	0
87			106	0	0	0	0
88			107	0	0	0	0
89			108	0	0	0	0
90			109	0	0	0	0

Fig. 14.5. The Client History: Dollar Amounts.

To generate the Client History reports, the module is structured as a two-variable data table. The module closely follows the same logic and design as the Accounting Summary in Chapter 1's Checkbook Manager. To generate the first table, the model uses the formula in cell C44:

C44: @DSUM($A$9..$G$32,5,C107..E108)

The range *A9..G32* is the Time Accounting Worksheet data, the general area where you will retrieve the necessary data. The number *5* represents column F, the number of hours in the Time Accounting Worksheet, which is the specific location of the information you need. The Criterion Range, *C107..E108*, is illustrated in table 14.4.

Table 14.4
The Search Criteria for Client History

Row		*Column*	
	C	*D*	*E*
107	Client	Task	Date
108	+C10=$C$38		@MONTH(A10)=@MONTH($E$109)

As you can see, the range *C107..E108* matches the column headings found in the Time Accounting Worksheet, as defined in cell C44's @DSUM function. The formula in cell C108:

C108: +C10=$C$38

instructs the model to select from the list in column C of the Time Accounting Worksheet, only the client whose number is found in cell C38.

Cell D108, the Task Number, is blank because it is the first input cell for this data table. When you issue the **/D**ata **T**able **2** command, each Task Number in the range *C45..C64* (column C of the first Client History Report) will be substituted into this cell for you. (This is similar to what happens with the Checkbook Manager's Accounting Summary.)

Cell E108, the date the service was performed, contains the formula:

E108: @MONTH(A10)=@MONTH($E$109)

which compares the value of the date's month portion (in cell A10, the first cell in the Date column of the Time Accounting Worksheet) to the value of the month portion of the date stored in cell E109 (the second input cell for this data table). When you activate this data table, each date in the range *D44..O44* (the column headings for this report) is substituted in cell E109.

Finally, the client hours are totaled with 1-2-3's @SUM function. For example, the equation in cell D66

D66: @SUM(D45..D65)

totals the hours for client 101 for the month of December, 1986.

To generate the first Client History Report in figure 14.1, we placed the client number 101 in cell C38. Next, we issued the **/D**ata **T**able **R**eset command, followed by the **/D**ata **T**able **2** command. The Table Range for this report is C44..O64, Input 1 is cell D108, and Input 2 is cell E109. When completed, this report tells you the number of hours your employees have spent per task on a monthly basis for a specific client.

Conversely, the second Client History data table generates similar information for the same client, tasks, and time frame, but on a dollar-amount basis. To accomplish this, the model uses the formula:

C81: @DSUM($A$9..$G$32,6,C107..E108)

If you compare this formula with the one in cell C44, you'll see that they are identical except for the offset number, 6. Thus, charges, rather than hours, will be retrieved from your Time Accounting Worksheet.

To build this table, you issue the /Data Table Reset and /Data Table 2 commands. This time, the Table Range is *C81..O101*, Input 1 is cell D108, and Input 2 is cell E109. This report will tell you the amount of charges per task for a specific client on a monthly basis.

Table 14.5 summarizes the major similarities and differences between the two Client History data tables.

Table 14.5
Client History Data Table Summary

	Client History 1	*Client History 2*
Purpose	Summarizes tasks on a monthly basis for a single client in hours	Summarizes tasks on a monthly basis for a single client in dollars
@DSUM function	@DSUM($A$9..$G$32,5, C107..E108)	@DSUM($A$9..$G$32,6, C107..E108)
Task (E109)	Range C45..C64	Range C82..C106
Table Range	Range C44..O64	Range C81..O101
Criteria	See Table 14.4	See Table 14.4

The Analysis Area and Criterion Range

In the example, this area is located at cells A111 through G123, directly below the second Client History data table (see fig. 14.6).

The Criterion Range, which follows 1-2-3 protocol and is a copy of the Time Accounting Worksheet column headings, gives you the opportunity to perform special analyses through /Data Query Find and /Data Query Extract operations. For an Extract operation, this information will be placed in the Analysis subsection, which uses column headings identical to those in the Time Accounting Worksheet and Criterion Range.

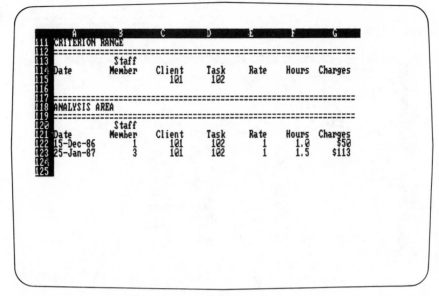

Fig. 14.6. The Analysis and Criterion Range.

In the sample model in figure 14.1, we used the **/D**ata **Q**uery **E**xtract command to select all records for client 101 and task 102. To do this, you place the client number in cell C115 and the task number in cell D115 of the Criterion Range. Then you issue the **/D**ata **Q**uery **E**xtract command with the Input Range as *A9..G32* (the Time Accounting Worksheet), the Criterion Range as *A114..G115* (this section's Criterion Range), and the Output Range as *A121..G121* (the Analysis Area). The two records copied to the Analysis Area result from this operation.

You can use this module in a number of ways, some of which will be discussed in this chapter's "Using the Model" section.

The Client Summary

The Client Summary is the model's second data table. This module, a one-variable data table, is located at cells Q35 through W72 in the example (see fig. 14.7).

As its name implies, the Client Summary recaps the information found in your Client History—the total hours and charges for a particular client. For example, if you specify the time frame of the Client History shown in figure 14.1 (December 1986 through February 1987), this data will be summarized in the Client Summary's Hours and Total Billings columns by Task.

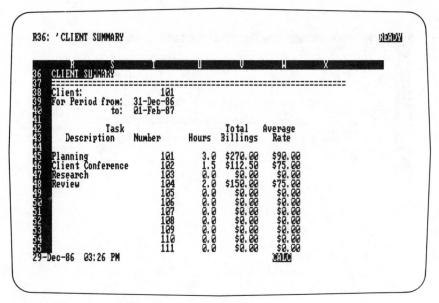

Fig. 14.7. The Client Summary.

To compute the number of hours per task for client 101, the following function is placed (in Hidden format) in cell U44:

    U44: @DSUM($A$9..$G$32,5,R70..T71)

In this function, the range *A9..G32* and the offset of *5* are from the Time Accounting Worksheet, and the range *R70..T71* defines the Criterion Range. Note that row 32 in the Time Accounting Worksheet (the dashed line) is included to accommodate additional rows in this database.

The Client Summary's Criterion Range will select records based on the client number, task number, and date. This range is similar to the Client History's Criterion Range, but the formulas contained in the Client Summary's Criterion Range are slightly different. For example, the formula in cell R71

    R71: +C10=$T$38

varies slightly from its counterpart in cell C108. In this case, the model will select only records for which the client number in cell C10 matches the client number in cell T38.

Cell S71 (which is similar to cell S108) is blank because, for this @DSUM equation, 1-2-3 will substitute the Task Numbers in the range T44..T64 for the values.

The formula in cell T71 contains the date criteria

T71: +A10>=$T$39#AND#+A10<=$T$40

This formula uses the dates entered in cells T39 (31-Dec-86) and T40 (01-Feb-87) to determine which records to select. This equation instructs the model to choose records that have dates that equal or fall between those in cells T39 and T40.

Table 14.6 shows the primary characteristics of the Client Summary's Criterion Range.

Table 14.6
The Search Criteria for Client Summary

Row	Column		
	R	**S**	**T**
70	Client	Task	Date
71	+C10=$T$38		+A10>=$T$39#AND# +A10<=$T$40

To calculate the Hours column, you issue the **/D**ata **T**able **1** command. In the example, the Table Range is *T44..U64* and the Input cell is *S71*. Each value in the range T44..U64 is substituted into this cell, then the model calculates the @DSUM formula for each value and enters the result of this calculation into the Hours column, next to its corresponding input value. For instance, the first value in the range T44..T64 is (Task) 101. When you issue the **Data T**able command, this value is copied into cell S71 to complete the Criterion Range.

Next, the command recalculates the @DSUM function in cell U44; the function computes the total of the Hours fields for all records that meet the criteria: Client (101), Task (101), and Date greater than or equal to 31-Dec-86 and less than or equal to 01-Feb-87. The model enters this total, 3, in cell U45, next to Task number 101. After the first Task has been substituted into cell S71, the model substitutes the second Task Number into that cell. This process continues until all of the Task Numbers have been used.

A similar Data Table operation calculates column V, Total Billings, using the formula in cell V44:

V44: @DSUM($A$9..$G$32,6,R70..T71)

This @DSUM function is similar to the formula in cell U44. The only difference is the column offset number, 6. In this case, you want the model to retrieve the Charges data from the Time Accounting Worksheet. To have Client 101's Total Billings calculated, you issue the /**D**ata **T**able **1** command, with the same Input Range, Criterion Range, and Input cell as before. The Table Range will be *T44..V64*. When you issue the command, /**D**ata **T**able, 1-2-3 will calculate the Total Billings for each task.

Table 14.7 highlights several functions of the Hours and Total Billings columns.

Table 14.7
Client Summary Data Table Summary

Column	*Hours* **U**	*Total Billings* **V**
Purpose	Summarizes total hours per task for a single client	Summarizes total billings per task for a single client
@DSUM function	@DSUM($A$9..$G$32,5, R70..T71)	@DSUM($A$9..$G$32,6, R70..T71)
Task (S71)	Range T44..U64	Range T44..V64
Table Range	Range T44..U64	Range T44..V64
Criteria	See Table 14.6	See Table 14.6

Finally, the Client Summary provides you with two statistics about your client. First, your Average Billing Rate is calculated in column W. In cell W45, this rate is computed by the formula

W45: @IF(V45=0,0,V45/U45)

which uses an @IF statement to determine whether the value in cell V45 (Total Billings for Task 101) is zero. If so, zero is returned in cell W45. If not, the value in cell V45 is divided by the value in cell U45 (Hours for Task 101) to arrive at your Average Rate. In the example, the Average Rate for Task 101 (W45) is $90.00.

As you might expect, @SUM functions are used to total Hours and Total Billings. For example, Total Hours are calculated by the formula

U66: @SUM(U44..U64)

Total Billings uses the equation

V66: @SUM(V44..V64)

to sum the cells in column V.

The Time Utilization Reports

The example's Time Utilization Reports begin at cell R73 and continue to AE134. These two-variable data tables, which are based on @DSUM functions, are similar to the Client History Reports. Figures 14.8 and 14.9 show portions of this section.

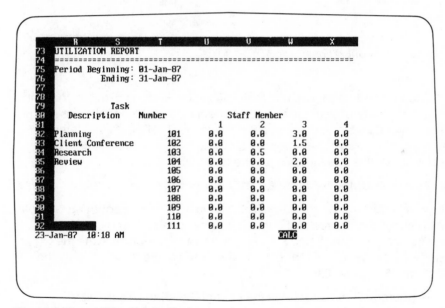

Fig. 14.8. Time Utilization by Task.

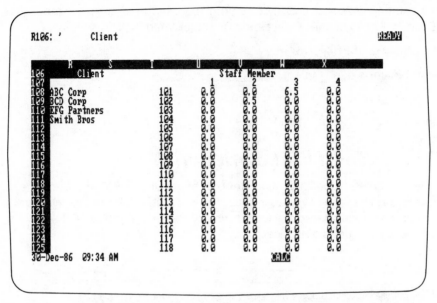

Fig. 14.9. Time Utilization by Client.

Unlike the other modules, the Time Utilization Reports provide you with information about your employees—specifically, about their time usage. The first data table, located at cells T81 through AE104, calculates the number of hours your employees charged to a particular Task. To accomplish this, the model uses the formula:

    T81: @DSUM($A$9..$G$32,5,R133..T134)

As you know by now, the range A9..G32 is the Time Accounting Worksheet, the source of the information; 5 is the offset (column F, Hours); and the range R133..T134 is the Criterion Range. Note the similarity between this formula and the formula in cell C44— only the Criterion Range is different.

This Criterion Range contains the column headings *Task, (Staff) Member,* and *Date,* in cells R133 through T133, respectively. Cells R134 and S134 will be the Input cells for this Data Table. Cell T134 contains the formula

    T134: +A10>=$T$75#AND#+A10<=$T$76

which instructs the model to select only those records that have dates that are less than or equal to the dates you have placed in cells T75 and

T76. In the example, records with dates that fall between January 1, 1987, and January 31, 1987, will be retrieved by 1-2-3.

The **/D**ata **T**able **R**eset command, followed by the **/D**ata **T**able **2** command, was used to create the first Time Utilization Report. In our example, the Table Range is T81..AD101 (the range of the data table), Input 1 is cell R134, and Input 2 is cell S134. The model will go through the same substitution and calculation process as the Client History reports (refer to that discussion if you are unsure about how the data tables operate).

After the model has finished calculating, this table shows you the amount of time that was spent on each task by each of your staff members. The cells in column AE and row 103 compute totals on the results of this table. Column AE computes the total time spent on each task by all employees. For example, cell AE82 contains the formula

AE82: @SUM(U82..U102)

Row 103 calculates each employee's total time during the defined time period. Cell U103 contains the equation

U103: @SUM(U82..U102)

which is the total time for Staff Member 1 for the month of January, 1987.

The second Time Utilization Report begins at cell T107 and continues to cell AE130. This table uses the formula

T107: @DSUM($A$9..$G$32,5,S133..U134)

to compute the total hours spent by each employee for each client during the time period defined in cells T75 and T76. Again, notice the similarity between this equation and the one in cell T134. Only the Criterion Range is different, because in this table you want to retrieve client data rather then task data.

For this table, you issue the **/D**ata **T**able **R**eset and then the **/D**ata **T**able **2** command. The Table Range for this table is T107..AE130, with Input 1 as cell U134 and Input 2 as cell S134. The completed table will show you the amount of time each of your staff members worked for each client during the time period. As in the first Time Utilization Report, column AE and row 129 total this data. For example, in cell AE107, the equation

AE107: @SUM(U107..AD107)

computes the total time spent on Client 101. On the other hand, the formula in cell U130

U130: @SUM(U107..U128)

calculates the total time of Staff Member 1 for January 1987. Because the two Time Utilization Reports display the same data, rows 103 and 130, the Total rows, will be equal upon completion of the two data table operations. Table 14.8 summarizes the Time Utilization Reports, and table 14.9 displays the Criterion Ranges for these reports.

Table 14.8
Time Utilization Data Tables Summary

	Utilization Report 1	*Utilization Report 2*
Purpose	Summarizes staff member time by task	Summarizes staff member time by client
@DSUM function	@DSUM($A$9..$G$32,5, R133..T134)	@DSUM($A$9..$G$32,5, S133..U134)
Criteria	See Table 14.9	See Table 14.9
Table Range	Range T81..AD101	Range T107..AE130

Table 14.9
The Time Utilization Report Criterion Ranges

Row   *Column*

	R	S	T	U
133	Task	Member	Date	Client
134			+A10>= $T$39#AND# +A10<=$T$76	

| Criterion Range for Time Utilization Report One
: Criterion Range for Time Utilization Report Two

The \t Macro

The \t macro, which is located at cells AA1..AI39 in figure 14.1, will enter your data table commands and ranges and build your data tables. To accomplish these tasks, the macro relies on several Release 2 features.

The macro uses the {MENUBRANCH} command to offer you a series of choices about the data table you want to have run. Your selection will cause the macro to branch to the proper subroutine to perform the requested task. When the macro has finished its work, your computer will beep and the model will wait for your next choice.

After you finish building your data tables, you can exit the macro by typing *Q* or selecting **Q**uit and pressing Enter. If you use the \t macro, you do not need to enter **/D**ata **T**able commands or reset your data tables. The macro will do the job for you.

If you understand how the model operates, you are ready to use the Time Manager in your business.

Using the Model

First you need to decide which report or reports you want to review and analyze. Do you need information about your clients' charges, or staff time? Table 14.10 outlines the purpose and use of the Time Manager's modules. Remember, the model is capable of many more data-management functions than are listed here.

After you have decided what information you need, you can go directly to that module for the report. (Be sure to read the "Time Accounting Worksheet" and "Employee Rate Table" section before you do so.)

Don't forget to use the **/D**ata **T**able **R**eset command if you plan to perform more than one data-table operation.

The Time Accounting Worksheet and Employee Rate Table

These sections contain the data that the model will use to generate your reports. Before you perform any calculations, enter the required data according to table 14.11.

Table 14.10
The Time Manager Modules

Report	*Purpose/Use*
Client History 1	Summarizes tasks on a monthly basis for a single client in hours
Client History 2	Summarizes tasks on a monthly basis for a single client in dollars
Analysis Area/ Criterion Range	Analyzes and reviews time and charges for a particular client and task; Prepares monthly billing
Client Summary	Totals Hours and Billings by Task for a single client
Utilization Report 1	Summarizes staff member time by task
Utilization Report 2	Summarizes staff member time by client

Table 14.11
Data Entry

Description	*Location*
Time Accounting Worksheet	
Date of Service	Column A
Staff Member	Column B
Client	Column C
Task	Column D
Rate	Column E
Hours	Column F
Employee Rate Table	
Employee Name	Column H
Employee Number	Column I
Rates	J11..N13
Client History 1	
Task Description	Column A
Task Number	Column C

Description	Location
Client History 2	
Task Description	Column A
Task Number	Column C
Client Summary	
Task Description	Column R
Task Number	Column T
Utilization Report 1	
Staff Member ID Number	Row 81
Task Description	Column R
Task Number	Column T
Utilization Report 2	
Staff Member ID Number	Row 107
Client Name	Column R
Client ID Number	Column T

After you have entered the information in the Time Accounting Worksheet, you can sort it in any order you choose. For instance, the data in the example was sorted in ascending date order by issuing the command **/D**ata **S**ort **D**ata-range **A10..G15 P**rimary **C10 S**econdary **A10 A**scending **G**o.

Other possibilities include: Client and Date; Staff Member and Client; and Staff Member and Task.

If you already have an identification system for your client companies and staff members, you may want to consider using those identifying numbers. In this manner, you won't have to create and maintain a second set of identification numbers. However, if you plan to enter the Rate and Staff Member numbers sequentially, try using the **/D**ata **F**ill command. This will ensure accuracy and accelerate completion of the task.

Now press F9 (CALC) to instruct the model to compute the Client Charges in column G of the Time Accounting Worksheet. As you know, these values will be used extensively throughout the model.

One final reminder—be sure that the staff member identification numbers are in ascending order in your Employee Rate Table. The model will not function properly if these numbers are not in ascending order.

The Client History Reports

As with all data tables, the Client History Reports are not difficult to generate. But you do need to be careful. Begin by selecting the client number. (In the example, this number is entered in cell C38.)

Next, enter your search criteria in this section's Criterion Range. We used the formula

+C10=$C$38

in cell C108 and

@MONTH(A10)= @MONTH($E$109)

in cell E108.

If you have already performed a **D**ata **T**able operation in this 1-2-3 session, enter the **/D**ata **T**able **R**eset command. You are now ready to build the Client History Report 1 table.

Issue the **/D**ata **T**able **2** command. If your table ranges are the same as those in the example, Input **1** should be cell *D108*, Input 2 should be cell *E109*, and the Table Range should be *C44..O64*. After a few moments, the model will generate this first report. Then, to ensure that the data tables run properly, enter the **/D**ata **T**able **R**eset command again. This is a good habit to adopt after each data table operation.

The second Client History report is even simpler to run, because you have already reset the data table and established the criteria. To generate this report, simply issue the **/D**ata **T**able **2** command. Input 1 will be cell *D108*, Input 2 will be cell *E109* (both the same as last time), but the Table Range will be *C81..O101*. The model will complete the second report in moments. Be sure to use **/D**ata **T**able **R**eset after this operation.

The Analysis Area and Criterion Range

As you are probably aware, this section of the model functions differently from the other report modules. Although this section requires you to use a little imagination, it can be quite useful.

There are many ways to use this section. Two common methods use 1-2-3's **/D**ata **Q**uery **F**ind and **E**xtract operations. Before beginning either operation, place the Client and Task Number in the appropriate cell location in your Criterion Range.

To perform a **F**ind operation, issue the **/D**ata **Q**uery **F**ind command. The Input Range will be your Time Accounting Worksheet, range A9..G32, and the Criterion Range will be A114..G115. After you press Enter, the cursor will move to the first record that meets the criteria in the Time Accounting Worksheet.

To review any other records that meet your criteria, press the {UP} or {DOWN} cursor keys. Release 2 gives you the ability to edit these records with the ← and → cursor keys, which is useful if one of your records needs to be corrected.

The **E**xtract operation is similar to the **F**ind process. The Input and Criterion Ranges are the same, but you will need to specify an Output Range. In the example, this is the Analysis Area, *A121..G121*. When you press **E**xtract, the model will copy the records shown in figure 14.1 from the Time Accounting Worksheet to the Analysis Area. You can save this information by using **/P**rint **F**ile and then, to generate client billings, reformat the information with your word-processing system.

Use your creativity to realize the full potential of the Analysis Area.

The Client Summary

The Client Summary is the model's only one-variable, two-equation data table. Because this module relies on two @DSUM functions, you will need to perform two Data Table operations.

Begin by making sure that you have reset the data tables by typing */dtr*. Next, enter your client number in cell T38, and the beginning and ending dates that you want summarized in cells T39 and T40, respectively. Now move to this section's Criterion Range and enter an appropriate criterion for your client in cell R71 and a date in cell T71. (In the example, we used +C10=$T$38 for the client criteria and +A10>=$T$39#AND#+A10<=$T$40 for the date criteria.)

Next, issue the **/D**ata **T**able **1** command. Input 1 will be cell S71, and the Table Range, *T44..U64*. Based on these instructions, the model will complete column U (Hours) of this module.

After you have reset the data tables, you are ready to complete column V (Total Billings) of the Client Summary. Simply reissue the **/D**ata **T**able **1** command, with Input 1 as *T44..V64*. This will generate the values displayed in figure 14.1 and will calculate your Average Billing Rates in column W and the totals in row 66.

The Time Utilization Reports

Your Time Utilization Reports are the last set of (two-variable) data tables. Although you probably have enough experience to *operate* them successfully, this section explains how to *generate* them. (With a little practice, they'll become second nature to you.)

It is vital that you always remember to reset your data tables after you use them. If you haven't done so, type */dtr*. Next, place the beginning and ending time period that you want reviewed in cells T75 and T76, respectively. These tables require you to enter one formula in the Criterion Range for this section, in cell T134. The equation *+A10>=$T$75#AND#+A10<=$T$76* is entered in T134 so that the model would process all records between the dates referenced in the formula.

For the first Time Utilization Report (Tasks), issue the **/D**ata **T**able **2** command. Input 1 will be cell R134 (Task), Input 2 will be cell S134 (Date), and the Table Range will be T81..AD101 (Time Utilization Report 1) from our example. With these instructions, the model will build this data table and calculate the totals in column AE and row 103.

Your second Time Utilization Report (Client) is created similarly. After you have reset your data table, reissue the **/D**ata **T**able **2** command. Input 1 will now be U134 (Client), Input 2 remains cell S134 (Date), and the Table Range will be T107..AD127 (Time Utilization Report 2) in figure 14.1. This series of commands constructed the data table and computed the totals in column AE and row 129 in this example. You should get the same results with your Time Manager.

The \t Macro

The macro is simple to operate. When you press Alt-T, a menu of data-table choices will appear in the 1-2-3 control-panel area. Using the space bar or the → or ← cursor keys to move the cursor, choose the data table that you want to generate. Next, press Enter or the letter of your data-table choice to begin the operation. The model will process the data for that particular table, reset the table, and cause your computer to beep upon completion.

To make the report meaningful, the macro will run both Client Summary data tables (Hours and Total Billings). Because we did not use range names for the data table ranges, you can use the F2 (EDIT) key to review the values and edit these ranges.

Modifying the Model

The example is structured in such a way that adding rows to the model without damaging any of the modules is simple. As presented, the Time Manager can accommodate 20 clients, tasks, and employees. Your business will probably need more.

To add rows to the Time Accounting Worksheet and Employee Rate Table, simply use the **/W**orksheet **I**nsert **R**ow command above the Time Accounting Worksheet's dashed line. Then adjust your model's @DSUM functions to accommodate this change.

To add new tasks to the application, move the cursor to cell A65 (in the example), and enter **/W**orksheet **I**nsert **R**ow. Enter the new Task number in column C and repeat this process in cell A102.

If you need to add clients, move the cursor to cell T128 and type */wir*. Enter the new client name and number in columns R and T, respectively.

When you issue the **/D**ata **T**able commands, be sure to include the new rows that you have entered in the Table Range.

Consider naming the ranges in the \t macro, and developing a similar menu-driven macro for printing your reports. If you are uncomfortable with menu-driven macros, you may want to consolidate the \t macro into one macro that processes all the data tables when you type Alt-T.

R2

You may have several different jobs for one client going at one time if, for example, your firm contracts with the government. In this case, consider creating for each client a range of numbers (such as client numbers 101 through 109) representing all jobs for client 100. Remember, however, that the Client History and Client Summary reports can report on only one client number at a time. If you have 10 different numbers, representing 10 different jobs for one client, you will need to create 10 separate tables to examine all the activity for that particular client.

On the other hand, you can modify the data tables to report on a range of client numbers rather than on just one number. In this case, use the tables that report on a range of dates as models for tables that report on a range of client numbers. Remember, 1-2-3 is limited only by your imagination and ingenuity.

Conclusion

The Time Manager demonstrates the power of 1-2-3's data-management capability. The model can accommodate a large number of clients, tasks, and staff members, and more than 1,000 individual task records. As you have seen, the application can produce important reports, such as Client Histories and Staff Utilization. Use the power of 1-2-3 to manage and control your company's time.

A1: [W10] \=
B1: [W9] \=
C1: [W10] \=
D1: \=
E1: \=
F1: \=
G1: \=
H1: \=
I1: \=
J1: \=
K1: \=
L1: \=
M1: \=
N1: \=
O1: \=
P1: \=
Q1: [W10] \=
R1: \=
S1: \=
T1: [W10] \=
U1: \=
AA1: '\t
AB1: '{MENUBRANCH T MENU}
AC1: 'Execute Time Manager Data Table Menu
A3: [W10] 'TIME MANAGER
E3: 'Copyright (C) Que Corp 1987
AA3: 'T MENU
AB3: 'A
AC3: 'B
AD3: 'C
AE3: 'D
AF3: 'E
AG3: 'QUIT
AB4: 'Client History 1
AC4: 'Client History 2
AD4: 'Client Summary
AE4: 'Time Utilization 1
AF4: 'Time Utilization 2
AG4: 'Exit from Macro
A5: [W10] \=
B5: [W9] \=
C5: [W10] \=
D5: \=
E5: \=
F5: \=
G5: \=
H5: \=
I5: \=
J5: \=
K5: \=
L5: \=
M5: \=
N5: \=

O5: \=
P5: \=
Q5: [W10] \=
R5: \=
S5: \=
T5: [W10] \=
U5: \=
AB5: '{BRANCH T1 MC}
AC5: '{BRANCH T2 MC}
AD5: '{BRANCH T3 MC}
AE5: '{BRANCH T4 MC}
AF5: '{BRANCH T5 MC}
AG5: '{BRANCH T6 MC}
A6: [W10] 'TIME ACCOUNTING WORKSHEET
H6: 'EMPLOYEE RATE TABLE
A7: [W10] \=
B7: [W9] \=
C7: [W10] \=
D7: \=
E7: \=
F7: \=
G7: \=
H7: \=
I7: \=
J7: \=
K7: \=
L7: \=
M7: \=
N7: \=
O7: \=
P7: \=
Q7: [W10] \=
R7: \=
S7: \=
T7: [W10] \=
U7: \=
AA7: 'T1 MC
AB7: '{PANELOFF}{WINDOWSOFF}~
B8: [W9] "Staff
K8: 'Rate
AB8: '/dt2c44..o64~d108~e109~~
A9: [W10] 'Date
B9: [W9] "Member
C9: [W10] "Client
D9: "Task
E9: "Rate
F9: "Hours
G9: "Charges
AB9: '/dtr~~
A10: (D1) [W10] @DATE(86,12,15)
B10: [W9] 1
C10: [W10] 101
D10: 102

E10: 1
F10: (F1) 1
G10: (C0) +F10*@VLOOKUP(B10,I$11..N$30,E10)
H10: 'Name
I10: 'Number
J10: 1
K10: 2
L10: 3
M10: 4
N10: 5
AB10: '{PANELON}{WINDOWSON}{BEEP 4}~
A11: (D1) [W10] @DATE(87,1,15)
B11: [W9] 3
C11: [W10] 101
D11: 101
E11: 2
F11: (F1) 3
G11: (C0) +F11*@VLOOKUP(B11,I$11..N$30,E11)
H11: 'Smith
I11: 1
J11: (C0) 50
K11: (C0) 60
L11: (C0) 75
AB11: '{BRANCH \t}
A12: (D1) [W10] @DATE(87,1,20)
B12: [W9] 3
C12: [W10] 101
D12: 104
E12: 1
F12: (F1) 2
G12: (C0) +F12*@VLOOKUP(B12,I$11..N$30,E12)
H12: 'Jones
I12: 2
J12: (C0) 65
K12: (C0) 80
L12: (C0) 100
A13: (D1) [W10] @DATE(87,1,25)
B13: [W9] 3
C13: [W10] 101
D13: 102
E13: 1
F13: (F1) 1.5
G13: (C0) +F13*@VLOOKUP(B13,I$11..N$30,E13)
H13: 'Webster
I13: 3
J13: (C0) 75
K13: (C0) 90
L13: (C0) 100
M13: (C0) 120
N13: (C0) 200
AA13: 'T2 MC
AB13: '{PANELOFF}{WINDOWSOFF}~
A14: (D1) [W10] @DATE(87,2,6)

B14: [W9] 1
C14: [W10] 101
D14: 103
E14: 1
F14: (F1) 2
G14: (C0) +F14*@VLOOKUP(B14,I$11..N$30,E14)
AB14: '/dt2c81..o101~d108~e109~~
A15: (D1) [W10] @DATE(87,1,2)
B15: [W9] 2
C15: [W10] 102
D15: 103
E15: 3
F15: (F1) 0.5
G15: (C0) +F15*@VLOOKUP(B15,I$11..N$30,E15)
AB15: '/dtr~~
AB16: '{PANELON}{WINDOWSON}{BEEP 4}~
AB17: '{BRANCH \t}
AA19: 'T3 MC
AB19: '{PANELOFF}{WINDOWSOFF}~
AB20: '/dt1t44..u64~s71~~
AB21: '/dtr~~
AB22: '/dt1t44..v64~s71~~
AB23: '/dtr~~
AB24: '{PANELON}{WINDOWSON}{BEEP 4}~
AB25: '{BRANCH \t}
AA27: 'T4 MC
AB27: '{PANELOFF}{WINDOWSOFF}~
AB28: '/dt2t81..ad101~r134~s134~~
AB29: '/dtr~~
AB30: '{PANELON}{WINDOWSON}{BEEP 4}~
AB31: '{BRANCH \t}~
F32: ' ------
G32: ' ------
E33: ^Total
F33: (F1) @SUM(F10..F32)
G33: (C0) @SUM(G10..G32)
AA33: 'T5 MC
AB33: '{PANELOFF}{WINDOWSOFF}~
F34: ' ======
G34: ' ======
AB34: '/dt2t107..ad127~u134~s134~~
AB35: '/dtr~~
A36: [W10] 'CLIENT HISTORY
R36: 'CLIENT SUMMARY
AB36: '{PANELON}{WINDOWSON}{BEEP 4}~
A37: [W10] \=
B37: [W9] \=
C37: [W10] \=
D37: \=
E37: \=
F37: \=
G37: \=
H37: \=

```
I37: \=
J37: \=
K37: \=
L37: \=
M37: \=
N37: \=
O37: \=
P37: \=
Q37: [W10] \=
R37: \=
S37: \=
T37: [W10] \=
U37: \=
V37: \=
W37: \=
X37: \=
AB37: '{BRANCH \t}
A38: [W10] 'Client:
C38: [W10] 101
R38: 'Client:
T38: [W10] 101
R39: 'For Period from:
T39: (D1) [W10] @DATE(86,12,31)
AA39: 'T6 MC
AB39: '{QUIT}
S40: '   to:
T40: (D1) [W10] @DATE(87,2,1)
B42: [W9] '   Task
S42: '   Task
V42: ' Total
W42: 'Average
A43: [W10] '   Description
C43: [W10] 'Number
R43: '   Description
T43: [W10] 'Number
U43: ^Hours
V43: 'Billings
W43: ' Rate
C44: (H) [W10] @DSUM($A$9..$G$32,5,C107..E108)
D44: (D3) @DATE(86,12,1)
E44: (D3) +D44+31
F44: (D3) +E44+31
G44: (D3) +F44+31
H44: (D3) +G44+31
I44: (D3) +H44+31
J44: (D3) +I44+31
K44: (D3) +J44+31
L44: (D3) +K44+31
M44: (D3) +L44+31
N44: (D3) +M44+31
O44: (D3) +N44+31
P44: '  Total
U44: (H) @DSUM($A$9..$G$32,5,R70..T71)
```

```
V44: (H) @DSUM($A$9..$G$32,6,R70..T71)
A45: [W10] 'Planning
C45: [W10] 101
D45: (F1) 0
E45: (F1) 3
F45: (F1) 0
G45: (F1) 0
H45: (F1) 0
I45: (F1) 0
J45: (F1) 0
K45: (F1) 0
L45: (F1) 0
M45: (F1) 0
N45: (F1) 0
O45: (F1) 0
P45: (F1) @SUM(D45..O45)
R45: 'Planning
T45: [W10] 101
U45: (F1) 3
V45: (C2) 270
W45: (C2) @IF(V45=0,0,V45/U45)
A46: [W10] 'Client Conference
C46: [W10] 102
D46: (F1) 1
E46: (F1) 1.5
F46: (F1) 0
G46: (F1) 0
H46: (F1) 0
I46: (F1) 0
J46: (F1) 0
K46: (F1) 0
L46: (F1) 0
M46: (F1) 0
N46: (F1) 0
O46: (F1) 0
P46: (F1) @SUM(D46..O46)
R46: 'Client Conference
T46: [W10] 102
U46: (F1) 1.5
V46: (C2) 112.5
W46: (C2) @IF(V46=0,0,V46/U46)
A47: [W10] 'Research
C47: [W10] 103
D47: (F1) 0
E47: (F1) 0
F47: (F1) 2
G47: (F1) 0
H47: (F1) 0
I47: (F1) 0
J47: (F1) 0
K47: (F1) 0
L47: (F1) 0
M47: (F1) 0
```

N47: (F1) 0
O47: (F1) 0
P47: (F1) @SUM(D47..O47)
R47: 'Research
T47: [W10] 103
U47: (F1) 0
V47: (C2) 0
W47: (C2) @IF(V47=0,0,V47/U47)
A48: [W10] 'Review
C48: [W10] 104
D48: (F1) 0
E48: (F1) 2
F48: (F1) 0
G48: (F1) 0
H48: (F1) 0
I48: (F1) 0
J48: (F1) 0
K48: (F1) 0
L48: (F1) 0
M48: (F1) 0
N48: (F1) 0
O48: (F1) 0
P48: (F1) @SUM(D48..O48)
R48: 'Review
T48: [W10] 104
U48: (F1) 2
V48: (C2) 150
W48: (C2) @IF(V48=0,0,V48/U48)
C49: [W10] 105
D49: (F1) 0
E49: (F1) 0
F49: (F1) 0
G49: (F1) 0
H49: (F1) 0
I49: (F1) 0
J49: (F1) 0
K49: (F1) 0
L49: (F1) 0
M49: (F1) 0
N49: (F1) 0
O49: (F1) 0
P49: (F1) @SUM(D49..O49)
T49: [W10] 105
U49: (F1) 0
V49: (C2) 0
W49: (C2) @IF(V49=0,0,V49/U49)
C50: [W10] 106
D50: (F1) 0
E50: (F1) 0
F50: (F1) 0
G50: (F1) 0
H50: (F1) 0
I50: (F1) 0

J50: (F1) 0
K50: (F1) 0
L50: (F1) 0
M50: (F1) 0
N50: (F1) 0
O50: (F1) 0
P50: (F1) @SUM(D50..O50)
T50: [W10] 106
U50: (F1) 0
V50: (C2) 0
W50: (C2) @IF(V50=0,0,V50/U50)
C51: [W10] 107
D51: (F1) 0
E51: (F1) 0
F51: (F1) 0
G51: (F1) 0
H51: (F1) 0
I51: (F1) 0
J51: (F1) 0
K51: (F1) 0
L51: (F1) 0
M51: (F1) 0
N51: (F1) 0
O51: (F1) 0
P51: (F1) @SUM(D51..O51)
T51: [W10] 107
U51: (F1) 0
V51: (C2) 0
W51: (C2) @IF(V51=0,0,V51/U51)
C52: [W10] 108
D52: (F1) 0
E52: (F1) 0
F52: (F1) 0
G52: (F1) 0
H52: (F1) 0
I52: (F1) 0
J52: (F1) 0
K52: (F1) 0
L52: (F1) 0
M52: (F1) 0
N52: (F1) 0
O52: (F1) 0
P52: (F1) @SUM(D52..O52)
T52: [W10] 108
U52: (F1) 0
V52: (C2) 0
W52: (C2) @IF(V52=0,0,V52/U52)
C53: [W10] 109
D53: (F1) 0
E53: (F1) 0
F53: (F1) 0
G53: (F1) 0
H53: (F1) 0

I53: (F1) 0
J53: (F1) 0
K53: (F1) 0
L53: (F1) 0
M53: (F1) 0
N53: (F1) 0
O53: (F1) 0
P53: (F1) @SUM(D53..O53)
T53: [W10] 109
U53: (F1) 0
V53: (C2) 0
W53: (C2) @IF(V53=0,0,V53/U53)
C54: [W10] 110
D54: (F1) 0
E54: (F1) 0
F54: (F1) 0
G54: (F1) 0
H54: (F1) 0
I54: (F1) 0
J54: (F1) 0
K54: (F1) 0
L54: (F1) 0
M54: (F1) 0
N54: (F1) 0
O54: (F1) 0
P54: (F1) @SUM(D54..O54)
T54: [W10] 110
U54: (F1) 0
V54: (C2) 0
W54: (C2) @IF(V54=0,0,V54/U54)
C55: [W10] 111
D55: (F1) 0
E55: (F1) 0
F55: (F1) 0
G55: (F1) 0
H55: (F1) 0
I55: (F1) 0
J55: (F1) 0
K55: (F1) 0
L55: (F1) 0
M55: (F1) 0
N55: (F1) 0
O55: (F1) 0
P55: (F1) @SUM(D55..O55)
T55: [W10] 111
U55: (F1) 0
V55: (C2) 0
W55: (C2) @IF(V55=0,0,V55/U55)
C56: [W10] 112
D56: (F1) 0
E56: (F1) 0
F56: (F1) 0
G56: (F1) 0

H56: (F1) 0
I56: (F1) 0
J56: (F1) 0
K56: (F1) 0
L56: (F1) 0
M56: (F1) 0
N56: (F1) 0
O56: (F1) 0
P56: (F1) @SUM(D56..O56)
T56: [W10] 112
U56: (F1) 0
V56: (C2) 0
W56: (C2) @IF(V56=0,0,V56/U56)
C57: [W10] 113
D57: (F1) 0
E57: (F1) 0
F57: (F1) 0
G57: (F1) 0
H57: (F1) 0
I57: (F1) 0
J57: (F1) 0
K57: (F1) 0
L57: (F1) 0
M57: (F1) 0
N57: (F1) 0
O57: (F1) 0
P57: (F1) @SUM(D57..O57)
T57: [W10] 113
U57: (F1) 0
V57: (C2) 0
W57: (C2) @IF(V57=0,0,V57/U57)
C58: [W10] 114
D58: (F1) 0
E58: (F1) 0
F58: (F1) 0
G58: (F1) 0
H58: (F1) 0
I58: (F1) 0
J58: (F1) 0
K58: (F1) 0
L58: (F1) 0
M58: (F1) 0
N58: (F1) 0
O58: (F1) 0
P58: (F1) @SUM(D58..O58)
T58: [W10] 114
U58: (F1) 0
V58: (C2) 0
W58: (C2) @IF(V58=0,0,V58/U58)
C59: [W10] 115
D59: (F1) 0
E59: (F1) 0
F59: (F1) 0

```
G59: (F1) 0                                  F62: (F1) 0
H59: (F1) 0                                  G62: (F1) 0
I59: (F1) 0                                  H62: (F1) 0
J59: (F1) 0                                  I62: (F1) 0
K59: (F1) 0                                  J62: (F1) 0
L59: (F1) 0                                  K62: (F1) 0
M59: (F1) 0                                  L62: (F1) 0
N59: (F1) 0                                  M62: (F1) 0
O59: (F1) 0                                  N62: (F1) 0
P59: (F1) @SUM(D59..O59)                      O62: (F1) 0
T59: [W10] 115                               P62: (F1) @SUM(D62..O62)
U59: (F1) 0                                  T62: [W10] 118
V59: (C2) 0                                  U62: (F1) 0
W59: (C2) @IF(V59=0,0,V59/U59)                V62: (C2) 0
C60: [W10] 116                               W62: (C2) @IF(V62=0,0,V62/U62)
D60: (F1) 0                                  C63: [W10] 119
E60: (F1) 0                                  D63: (F1) 0
F60: (F1) 0                                  E63: (F1) 0
G60: (F1) 0                                  F63: (F1) 0
H60: (F1) 0                                  G63: (F1) 0
I60: (F1) 0                                  H63: (F1) 0
J60: (F1) 0                                  I63: (F1) 0
K60: (F1) 0                                  J63: (F1) 0
L60: (F1) 0                                  K63: (F1) 0
M60: (F1) 0                                  L63: (F1) 0
N60: (F1) 0                                  M63: (F1) 0
O60: (F1) 0                                  N63: (F1) 0
P60: (F1) @SUM(D60..O60)                      O63: (F1) 0
T60: [W10] 116                               P63: (F1) @SUM(D63..O63)
U60: (F1) 0                                  T63: [W10] 119
V60: (C2) 0                                  U63: (F1) 0
W60: (C2) @IF(V60=0,0,V60/U60)                V63: (C2) 0
C61: [W10] 117                               W63: (C2) @IF(V63=0,0,V63/U63)
D61: (F1) 0                                  C64: [W10] 120
E61: (F1) 0                                  D64: (F1) 0
F61: (F1) 0                                  E64: (F1) 0
G61: (F1) 0                                  F64: (F1) 0
H61: (F1) 0                                  G64: (F1) 0
I61: (F1) 0                                  H64: (F1) 0
J61: (F1) 0                                  I64: (F1) 0
K61: (F1) 0                                  J64: (F1) 0
L61: (F1) 0                                  K64: (F1) 0
M61: (F1) 0                                  L64: (F1) 0
N61: (F1) 0                                  M64: (F1) 0
O61: (F1) 0                                  N64: (F1) 0
P61: (F1) @SUM(D61..O61)                      O64: (F1) 0
T61: [W10] 117                               P64: (F1) @SUM(D64..O64)
U61: (F1) 0                                  T64: [W10] 120
V61: (C2) 0                                  U64: (F1) 0
W61: (C2) @IF(V61=0,0,V61/U61)                V64: (C2) 0
C62: [W10] 118                               W64: (C2) @IF(V64=0,0,V64/U64)
D62: (F1) 0                                  D65: (F1) '  ------
E62: (F1) 0                                  E65: (F1) '  ------
```

F65: (F1) ' ------
G65: (F1) ' ------
H65: (F1) ' ------
I65: (F1) ' ------
J65: (F1) ' ------
K65: (F1) ' ------
L65: (F1) ' ------
M65: (F1) ' ------
N65: (F1) ' ------
O65: (F1) ' ------
P65: (F1) ' ------
U65: (F1) ' ------
V65: (C2) ' ------
W65: ' ------
C66: [W10] ^Total
D66: (F1) @SUM(D45..D65)
E66: (F1) @SUM(E45..E65)
F66: (F1) @SUM(F45..F65)
G66: (F1) @SUM(G45..G65)
H66: (F1) @SUM(H45..H65)
I66: (F1) @SUM(I45..I65)
J66: (F1) @SUM(J45..J65)
K66: (F1) @SUM(K45..K65)
L66: (F1) @SUM(L45..L65)
M66: (F1) @SUM(M45..M65)
N66: (F1) @SUM(N45..N65)
O66: (F1) @SUM(O45..O65)
P66: (F1) @SUM(P45..P65)
S66: 'Totals
U66: (F1) @SUM(U45..U65)
V66: (C2) @SUM(V45..V65)
W66: (C2) @IF(V66=0,0,V66/U66)
D67: (F1) ' ======
E67: (F1) ' ======
F67: (F1) ' ======
G67: (F1) ' ======
H67: (F1) ' ======
I67: (F1) ' ======
J67: (F1) ' ======
K67: (F1) ' ======
L67: (F1) ' ======
M67: (F1) ' ======
N67: (F1) ' ======
O67: (F1) ' ======
P67: (F1) ' ======
U67: ' ======
V67: (C2) ' ======
W67: ' ======
R69: 'Criterion Range
R70: "Client
S70: "Task
T70: [W10] 'Date
R71: +C10=$T$38

T71: [W10] +A10>=$T$39#AND#+A10<=$T$40
R73: 'UTILIZATION REPORT
R74: \=
S74: \=
T74: [W10] \=
U74: \=
V74: \=
W74: \=
X74: \=
R75: 'Period Beginning:
T75: (D1) [W10] @DATE(87,1,1)
R76: ' Ending:
T76: (D1) [W10] @DATE(87,1,31)
S79: ' Task
R80: ' Description
T80: [W10] 'Number
V80: 'Staff Member
C81: (H) [W10] @DSUM($A$9..$G$32,6,C107..E108)
D81: (D3) +D44
E81: (D3) +D81+31
F81: (D3) +E81+31
G81: (D3) +F81+31
H81: (D3) +G81+31
I81: (D3) +H81+31
J81: (D3) +I81+31
K81: (D3) +J81+31
L81: (D3) +K81+31
M81: (D3) +L81+31
N81: (D3) +M81+31
O81: (D3) +N81+31
P81: ' Total
T81: (H) [W10] @DSUM($A$9..$G$32,5,R133..T134)
U81: 1
V81: 2
W81: 3
X81: 4
Y81: 5
Z81: 6
AA81: 7
AB81: 8
AC81: 9
AD81: 10
AE81: ' Total
A82: [W10] 'Planning
C82: [W10] 101
D82: (C0) 0
E82: (C0) 270
F82: (C0) 0
G82: (C0) 0
H82: (C0) 0
I82: 0
J82: 0
K82: 0

L82: 0
M82: 0
N82: 0
O82: 0
P82: (C0) @SUM(D82..O82)
R82: 'Planning
T82: [W10] 101
U82: (F1) 0
V82: (F1) 0
W82: (F1) 3
X82: (F1) 0
Y82: (F1) 0
Z82: (F1) 0
AA82: (F1) 0
AB82: (F1) 0
AC82: (F1) 0
AD82: (F1) 0
AE82: (F1) @SUM(U82..AD82)
A83: [W10] 'Client Conference
C83: [W10] 102
D83: (C0) 50
E83: (C0) 112.5
F83: (C0) 0
G83: (C0) 0
H83: (C0) 0
I83: 0
J83: 0
K83: 0
L83: 0
M83: 0
N83: 0
O83: 0
P83: (C0) @SUM(D83..O83)
R83: 'Client Conference
T83: [W10] 102
U83: (F1) 0
V83: (F1) 0
W83: (F1) 1.5
X83: (F1) 0
Y83: (F1) 0
Z83: (F1) 0
AA83: (F1) 0
AB83: (F1) 0
AC83: (F1) 0
AD83: (F1) 0
AE83: (F1) @SUM(U83..AD83)
A84: [W10] 'Research
C84: [W10] 103
D84: (C0) 0
E84: (C0) 0
F84: (C0) 100
G84: (C0) 0
H84: (C0) 0

I84: 0
J84: 0
K84: 0
L84: 0
M84: 0
N84: 0
O84: 0
P84: (C0) @SUM(D84..O84)
R84: 'Research
T84: [W10] 103
U84: (F1) 0
V84: (F1) 0.5
W84: (F1) 0
X84: (F1) 0
Y84: (F1) 0
Z84: (F1) 0
AA84: (F1) 0
AB84: (F1) 0
AC84: (F1) 0
AD84: (F1) 0
AE84: (F1) @SUM(U84..AD84)
A85: [W10] 'Review
C85: [W10] 104
D85: (C0) 0
E85: (C0) 150
F85: (C0) 0
G85: (C0) 0
H85: (C0) 0
I85: 0
J85: 0
K85: 0
L85: 0
M85: 0
N85: 0
O85: 0
P85: (C0) @SUM(D85..O85)
R85: 'Review
T85: [W10] 104
U85: (F1) 0
V85: (F1) 0
W85: (F1) 2
X85: (F1) 0
Y85: (F1) 0
Z85: (F1) 0
AA85: (F1) 0
AB85: (F1) 0
AC85: (F1) 0
AD85: (F1) 0
AE85: (F1) @SUM(U85..AD85)
C86: [W10] 105
D86: 0
E86: 0
F86: 0

G86: 0
H86: 0
I86: 0
J86: 0
K86: 0
L86: 0
M86: 0
N86: 0
O86: 0
P86: (C0) @SUM(D86..O86)
T86: [W10] 105
U86: (F1) 0
V86: (F1) 0
W86: (F1) 0
X86: (F1) 0
Y86: (F1) 0
Z86: (F1) 0
AA86: (F1) 0
AB86: (F1) 0
AC86: (F1) 0
AD86: (F1) 0
AE86: (F1) @SUM(U86..AD86)
C87: [W10] 106
D87: 0
E87: 0
F87: 0
G87: 0
H87: 0
I87: 0
J87: 0
K87: 0
L87: 0
M87: 0
N87: 0
O87: 0
P87: (C0) @SUM(D87..O87)
T87: [W10] 106
U87: (F1) 0
V87: (F1) 0
W87: (F1) 0
X87: (F1) 0
Y87: (F1) 0
Z87: (F1) 0
AA87: (F1) 0
AB87: (F1) 0
AC87: (F1) 0
AD87: (F1) 0
AE87: (F1) @SUM(U87..AD87)
C88: [W10] 107
D88: 0
E88: 0
F88: 0
G88: 0

H88: 0
I88: 0
J88: 0
K88: 0
L88: 0
M88: 0
N88: 0
O88: 0
P88: (C0) @SUM(D88..O88)
T88: [W10] 107
U88: (F1) 0
V88: (F1) 0
W88: (F1) 0
X88: (F1) 0
Y88: (F1) 0
Z88: (F1) 0
AA88: (F1) 0
AB88: (F1) 0
AC88: (F1) 0
AD88: (F1) 0
AE88: (F1) @SUM(U88..AD88)
C89: [W10] 108
D89: 0
E89: 0
F89: 0
G89: 0
H89: 0
I89: 0
J89: 0
K89: 0
L89: 0
M89: 0
N89: 0
O89: 0
P89: (C0) @SUM(D89..O89)
T89: [W10] 108
U89: (F1) 0
V89: (F1) 0
W89: (F1) 0
X89: (F1) 0
Y89: (F1) 0
Z89: (F1) 0
AA89: (F1) 0
AB89: (F1) 0
AC89: (F1) 0
AD89: (F1) 0
AE89: (F1) @SUM(U89..AD89)
C90: [W10] 109
D90: 0
E90: 0
F90: 0
G90: 0
H90: 0

```
I90: 0
J90: 0
K90: 0
L90: 0
M90: 0
N90: 0
O90: 0
P90: (CO) @SUM(D90..O90)
T90: [W10] 109
U90: (F1) 0
V90: (F1) 0
W90: (F1) 0
X90: (F1) 0
Y90: (F1) 0
Z90: (F1) 0
AA90: (F1) 0
AB90: (F1) 0
AC90: (F1) 0
AD90: (F1) 0
AE90: (F1) @SUM(U90..AD90)
C91: [W10] 110
D91: 0
E91: 0
F91: 0
G91: 0
H91: 0
I91: 0
J91: 0
K91: 0
L91: 0
M91: 0
N91: 0
O91: 0
P91: (CO) @SUM(D91..O91)
T91: [W10] 110
U91: (F1) 0
V91: (F1) 0
W91: (F1) 0
X91: (F1) 0
Y91: (F1) 0
Z91: (F1) 0
AA91: (F1) 0
AB91: (F1) 0
AC91: (F1) 0
AD91: (F1) 0
AE91: (F1) @SUM(U91..AD91)
C92: [W10] 111
D92: 0
E92: 0
F92: 0
G92: 0
H92: 0
I92: 0
```

```
J92: 0
K92: 0
L92: 0
M92: 0
N92: 0
O92: 0
P92: (CO) @SUM(D92..O92)
T92: [W10] 111
U92: (F1) 0
V92: (F1) 0
W92: (F1) 0
X92: (F1) 0
Y92: (F1) 0
Z92: (F1) 0
AA92: (F1) 0
AB92: (F1) 0
AC92: (F1) 0
AD92: (F1) 0
AE92: (F1) @SUM(U92..AD92)
C93: [W10] 112
D93: 0
E93: 0
F93: 0
G93: 0
H93: 0
I93: 0
J93: 0
K93: 0
L93: 0
M93: 0
N93: 0
O93: 0
P93: (CO) @SUM(D93..O93)
T93: [W10] 112
U93: (F1) 0
V93: (F1) 0
W93: (F1) 0
X93: (F1) 0
Y93: (F1) 0
Z93: (F1) 0
AA93: (F1) 0
AB93: (F1) 0
AC93: (F1) 0
AD93: (F1) 0
AE93: (F1) @SUM(U93..AD93)
C94: [W10] 113
D94: 0
E94: 0
F94: 0
G94: 0
H94: 0
I94: 0
J94: 0
```

K94: 0
L94: 0
M94: 0
N94: 0
O94: 0
P94: (C0) @SUM(D94..O94)
T94: [W10] 113
U94: (F1) 0
V94: (F1) 0
W94: (F1) 0
X94: (F1) 0
Y94: (F1) 0
Z94: (F1) 0
AA94: (F1) 0
AB94: (F1) 0
AC94: (F1) 0
AD94: (F1) 0
AE94: (F1) @SUM(U94..AD94)
C95: [W10] 114
D95: 0
E95: 0
F95: 0
G95: 0
H95: 0
I95: 0
J95: 0
K95: 0
L95: 0
M95: 0
N95: 0
O95: 0
P95: (C0) @SUM(D95..O95)
T95: [W10] 114
U95: (F1) 0
V95: (F1) 0
W95: (F1) 0
X95: (F1) 0
Y95: (F1) 0
Z95: (F1) 0
AA95: (F1) 0
AB95: (F1) 0
AC95: (F1) 0
AD95: (F1) 0
AE95: (F1) @SUM(U95..AD95)
C96: [W10] 115
D96: 0
E96: 0
F96: 0
G96: 0
H96: 0
I96: 0
J96: 0
K96: 0

L96: 0
M96: 0
N96: 0
O96: 0
P96: (C0) @SUM(D96..O96)
T96: [W10] 115
U96: (F1) 0
V96: (F1) 0
W96: (F1) 0
X96: (F1) 0
Y96: (F1) 0
Z96: (F1) 0
AA96: (F1) 0
AB96: (F1) 0
AC96: (F1) 0
AD96: (F1) 0
AE96: (F1) @SUM(U96..AD96)
C97: [W10] 116
D97: 0
E97: 0
F97: 0
G97: 0
H97: 0
I97: 0
J97: 0
K97: 0
L97: 0
M97: 0
N97: 0
O97: 0
P97: (C0) @SUM(D97..O97)
T97: [W10] 116
U97: (F1) 0
V97: (F1) 0
W97: (F1) 0
X97: (F1) 0
Y97: (F1) 0
Z97: (F1) 0
AA97: (F1) 0
AB97: (F1) 0
AC97: (F1) 0
AD97: (F1) 0
AE97: (F1) @SUM(U97..AD97)
C98: [W10] 117
D98: 0
E98: 0
F98: 0
G98: 0
H98: 0
I98: 0
J98: 0
K98: 0
L98: 0

M98: 0
N98: 0
O98: 0
P98: (C0) @SUM(D98..O98)
T98: [W10] 117
U98: (F1) 0
V98: (F1) 0
W98: (F1) 0
X98: (F1) 0
Y98: (F1) 0
Z98: (F1) 0
AA98: (F1) 0
AB98: (F1) 0
AC98: (F1) 0
AD98: (F1) 0
AE98: (F1) @SUM(U98..AD98)
C99: [W10] 118
D99: 0
E99: 0
F99: 0
G99: 0
H99: 0
I99: 0
J99: 0
K99: 0
L99: 0
M99: 0
N99: 0
O99: 0
P99: (C0) @SUM(D99..O99)
T99: [W10] 118
U99: (F1) 0
V99: (F1) 0
W99: (F1) 0
X99: (F1) 0
Y99: (F1) 0
Z99: (F1) 0
AA99: (F1) 0
AB99: (F1) 0
AC99: (F1) 0
AD99: (F1) 0
AE99: (F1) @SUM(U99..AD99)
C100: [W10] 119
D100: 0
E100: 0
F100: 0
G100: 0
H100: 0
I100: 0
J100: 0
K100: 0
L100: 0
M100: 0

N100: 0
O100: 0
P100: (C0) @SUM(D100..O100)
T100: [W10] 119
U100: (F1) 0
V100: (F1) 0
W100: (F1) 0
X100: (F1) 0
Y100: (F1) 0
Z100: (F1) 0
AA100: (F1) 0
AB100: (F1) 0
AC100: (F1) 0
AD100: (F1) 0
AE100: (F1) @SUM(U100..AD100)
C101: [W10] 120
D101: 0
E101: 0
F101: 0
G101: 0
H101: 0
I101: 0
J101: 0
K101: 0
L101: 0
M101: 0
N101: 0
O101: 0
P101: (C0) @SUM(D101..O101)
T101: [W10] 120
U101: (F1) 0
V101: (F1) 0
W101: (F1) 0
X101: (F1) 0
Y101: (F1) 0
Z101: (F1) 0
AA101: (F1) 0
AB101: (F1) 0
AC101: (F1) 0
AD101: (F1) 0
AE101: (F1) @SUM(U101..AD101)
D102: (C0) ' ------
E102: (C0) ' ------
F102: (C0) ' ------
G102: (C0) ' ------
H102: (C0) ' ------
I102: ' ------
J102: ' ------
K102: ' ------
L102: ' ------
M102: ' ------
N102: ' ------
O102: ' ------

P102: ' ------
U102: (F1) ' ------
V102: (F1) ' ------
W102: (F1) ' ------
X102: (F1) ' ------
Y102: (F1) ' ------
Z102: (F1) ' ------
AA102: (F1) ' ------
AB102: (F1) ' ------
AC102: (F1) ' ------
AD102: (F1) ' ------
AE102: (F1) ' ------
C103: [W10] ^Total
D103: (C0) @SUM(D82..D102)
E103: (C0) @SUM(E82..E102)
F103: (C0) @SUM(F82..F102)
G103: (C0) @SUM(G82..G102)
H103: (C0) @SUM(H82..H102)
I103: (C0) @SUM(I82..I102)
J103: (C0) @SUM(J82..J102)
K103: (C0) @SUM(K82..K102)
L103: (C0) @SUM(L82..L102)
M103: (C0) @SUM(M82..M102)
N103: (C0) @SUM(N82..N102)
O103: (C0) @SUM(O82..O102)
P103: (C0) @SUM(P82..P102)
T103: [W10] ^Total
U103: (F1) @SUM(U82..U102)
V103: (F1) @SUM(V82..V102)
W103: (F1) @SUM(W82..W102)
X103: (F1) @SUM(X82..X102)
Y103: (F1) @SUM(Y82..Y102)
Z103: (F1) @SUM(Z82..Z102)
AA103: (F1) @SUM(AA82..AA102)
AB103: (F1) @SUM(AB82..AB102)
AC103: (F1) @SUM(AC82..AC102)
AD103: (F1) @SUM(AD82..AD102)
AE103: (F1) @SUM(AE82..AE102)
D104: ' ======
E104: ' ======
F104: ' ======
G104: ' ======
H104: ' ======
I104: ' ======
J104: ' ======
K104: ' ======
L104: ' ======
M104: ' ======
N104: ' ======
O104: ' ======
P104: (C0) ' ======
U104: ' ======
V104: ' ======

W104: ' ======
X104: ' ======
Y104: ' ======
Z104: ' ======
AA104: ' ======
AB104: ' ======
AC104: ' ======
AD104: ' ======
AE104: ' ======
C106: [W10] 'Criterion Range
R106: '   Client
V106: 'Staff Member
C107: [W10] "Client
D107: "Task
E107: 'Date
T107: (H) [W10] @DSUM($A$9..$G$32,5,S133..U134)
U107: 1
V107: 2
W107: ·3
X107: 4
Y107: 5
Z107: 6
AA107: 7
AB107: 8
AC107: 9
AD107: 10
AE107: ' Total
C108: [W10] +C10=$C$38
E108: @MONTH(A10)=@MONTH($E$109)
R108: 'ABC Corp
T108: [W10] 101
U108: (F1) 0
V108: (F1) 0
W108: (F1) 6.5
X108: (F1) 0
Y108: (F1) 0
Z108: (F1) 0
AA108: (F1) 0
AB108: (F1) 0
AC108: (F1) 0
AD108: (F1) 0
AE108: (F1) @SUM(U108..AD108)
R109: 'BCD Corp
T109: [W10] 102
U109: (F1) 0
V109: (F1) 0.5
W109: (F1) 0
X109: (F1) 0
Y109: (F1) 0
Z109: (F1) 0
AA109: (F1) 0
AB109: (F1) 0
AC109: (F1) 0

AD109: (F1) 0
AE109: (F1) @SUM(U109..AD109)
R110: 'EFG Partners
T110: [W10] 103
U110: (F1) 0
V110: (F1) 0
W110: (F1) 0
X110: (F1) 0
Y110: (F1) 0
Z110: (F1) 0
AA110: (F1) 0
AB110: (F1) 0
AC110: (F1) 0
AD110: (F1) 0
AE110: (F1) @SUM(U110..AD110)
A111: [W10] 'CRITERION RANGE
R111: 'Smith Bros
T111: [W10] 104
U111: (F1) 0
V111: (F1) 0
W111: (F1) 0
X111: (F1) 0
Y111: (F1) 0
Z111: (F1) 0
AA111: (F1) 0
AB111: (F1) 0
AC111: (F1) 0
AD111: (F1) 0
AE111: (F1) @SUM(U111..AD111)
A112: [W10] \=
B112: [W9] \=
C112: [W10] \=
D112: \=
E112: \=
F112: \=
G112: \=
T112: [W10] 105
U112: (F1) 0
V112: (F1) 0
W112: (F1) 0
X112: (F1) 0
Y112: (F1) 0
Z112: (F1) 0
AA112: (F1) 0
AB112: (F1) 0
AC112: (F1) 0
AD112: (F1) 0
AE112: (F1) @SUM(U112..AD112)
B113: [W9] "Staff
T113: [W10] 106
U113: (F1) 0
V113: (F1) 0
W113: (F1) 0

X113: (F1) 0
Y113: (F1) 0
Z113: (F1) 0
AA113: (F1) 0
AB113: (F1) 0
AC113: (F1) 0
AD113: (F1) 0
AE113: (F1) @SUM(U113..AD113)
A114: [W10] 'Date
B114: [W9] "Member
C114: [W10] "Client
D114: "Task
E114: "Rate
F114: "Hours
G114: "Charges
T114: [W10] 107
U114: (F1) 0
V114: (F1) 0
W114: (F1) 0
X114: (F1) 0
Y114: (F1) 0
Z114: (F1) 0
AA114: (F1) 0
AB114: (F1) 0
AC114: (F1) 0
AD114: (F1) 0
AE114: (F1) @SUM(U114..AD114)
C115: [W10] 101
D115: 102
T115: [W10] 108
U115: (F1) 0
V115: (F1) 0
W115: (F1) 0
X115: (F1) 0
Y115: (F1) 0
Z115: (F1) 0
AA115: (F1) 0
AB115: (F1) 0
AC115: (F1) 0
AD115: (F1) 0
AE115: (F1) @SUM(U115..AD115)
T116: [W10] 109
U116: (F1) 0
V116: (F1) 0
W116: (F1) 0
X116: (F1) 0
Y116: (F1) 0
Z116: (F1) 0
AA116: (F1) 0
AB116: (F1) 0
AC116: (F1) 0
AD116: (F1) 0
AE116: (F1) @SUM(U116..AD116)

A117: [W10] \=
B117: [W9] \=
C117: [W10] \=
D117: \=
E117: \=
F117: \=
G117: \=
T117: [W10] 110
U117: (F1) 0
V117: (F1) 0
W117: (F1) 0
X117: (F1) 0
Y117: (F1) 0
Z117: (F1) 0
AA117: (F1) 0
AB117: (F1) 0
AC117: (F1) 0
AD117: (F1) 0
AE117: (F1) @SUM(U117..AD117)
A118: [W10] 'ANALYSIS AREA
T118: [W10] 111
U118: (F1) 0
V118: (F1) 0
W118: (F1) 0
X118: (F1) 0
Y118: (F1) 0
Z118: (F1) 0
AA118: (F1) 0
AB118: (F1) 0
AC118: (F1) 0
AD118: (F1) 0
AE118: (F1) @SUM(U118..AD118)
A119: [W10] \=
B119: [W9] \=
C119: [W10] \=
D119: \=
E119: \=
F119: \=
G119: \=
T119: [W10] 112
U119: (F1) 0
V119: (F1) 0
W119: (F1) 0
X119: (F1) 0
Y119: (F1) 0
Z119: (F1) 0
AA119: (F1) 0
AB119: (F1) 0
AC119: (F1) 0
AD119: (F1) 0
AE119: (F1) @SUM(U119..AD119)
B120: [W9] "Staff
T120: [W10] 113
U120: (F1) 0
V120: (F1) 0
W120: (F1) 0
X120: (F1) 0
Y120: (F1) 0
Z120: (F1) 0
AA120: (F1) 0
AB120: (F1) 0
AC120: (F1) 0
AD120: (F1) 0
AE120: (F1) @SUM(U120..AD120)
A121: [W10] 'Date
B121: [W9] "Member
C121: [W10] "Client
D121: "Task
E121: "Rate
F121: "Hours
G121: "Charges
T121: [W10] 114
U121: (F1) 0
V121: (F1) 0
W121: (F1) 0
X121: (F1) 0
Y121: (F1) 0
Z121: (F1) 0
AA121: (F1) 0
AB121: (F1) 0
AC121: (F1) 0
AD121: (F1) 0
AE121: (F1) @SUM(U121..AD121)
A122: (D1) [W10] 31761
B122: [W9] 1
C122: [W10] 101
D122: 102
E122: 1
F122: (F1) 1
G122: (C0) 50
T122: [W10] 115
U122: (F1) 0
V122: (F1) 0
W122: (F1) 0
X122: (F1) 0
Y122: (F1) 0
Z122: (F1) 0
AA122: (F1) 0
AB122: (F1) 0
AC122: (F1) 0
AD122: (F1) 0
AE122: (F1) @SUM(U122..AD122)
A123: (D1) [W10] 31802
B123: [W9] 3
C123: [W10] 101
D123: 102

E123: 1
F123: (F1) 1.5
G123: (C0) 112.5
T123: [W10] 116
U123: (F1) 0
V123: (F1) 0
W123: (F1) 0
X123: (F1) 0
Y123: (F1) 0
Z123: (F1) 0
AA123: (F1) 0
AB123: (F1) 0
AC123: (F1) 0
AD123: (F1) 0
AE123: (F1) @SUM(U123..AD123)
T124: [W10] 117
U124: (F1) 0
V124: (F1) 0
W124: (F1) 0
X124: (F1) 0
Y124: (F1) 0
Z124: (F1) 0
AA124: (F1) 0
AB124: (F1) 0
AC124: (F1) 0
AD124: (F1) 0
AE124: (F1) @SUM(U124..AD124)
T125: [W10] 118
U125: (F1) 0
V125: (F1) 0
W125: (F1) 0
X125: (F1) 0
Y125: (F1) 0
Z125: (F1) 0
AA125: (F1) 0
AB125: (F1) 0
AC125: (F1) 0
AD125: (F1) 0
AE125: (F1) @SUM(U125..AD125)
T126: [W10] 119
U126: (F1) 0
V126: (F1) 0
W126: (F1) 0
X126: (F1) 0
Y126: (F1) 0
Z126: (F1) 0
AA126: (F1) 0
AB126: (F1) 0
AC126: (F1) 0
AD126: (F1) 0
AE126: (F1) @SUM(U126..AD126)
T127: [W10] 120
U127: (F1) 0

V127: (F1) 0
W127: (F1) 0
X127: (F1) 0
Y127: (F1) 0
Z127: (F1) 0
AA127: (F1) 0
AB127: (F1) 0
AC127: (F1) 0
AD127: (F1) 0
AE127: (F1) @SUM(U127..AD127)
U128: (F1) ' ------
V128: (F1) ' ------
W128: (F1) ' ------
X128: (F1) ' ------
Y128: (F1) ' ------
Z128: (F1) ' ------
AA128: (F1) ' ------
AB128: (F1) ' ------
AC128: (F1) ' ------
AD128: (F1) ' ------
AE128: (F1) ' ------
T129: [W10] ^Total
U129: (F1) @SUM(U108..U127)
V129: (F1) @SUM(V108..V127)
W129: (F1) @SUM(W108..W127)
X129: (F1) @SUM(X108..X127)
Y129: (F1) @SUM(Y108..Y127)
Z129: (F1) @SUM(Z108..Z127)
AA129: (F1) @SUM(AA108..AA127)
AB129: (F1) @SUM(AB108..AB127)
AC129: (F1) @SUM(AC108..AC127)
AD129: (F1) @SUM(AD108..AD127)
AE129: (F1) @SUM(AE108..AE128)
U130: ' ======
V130: ' ======
W130: ' ======
X130: ' ======
Y130: ' ======
Z130: ' ======
AA130: ' ======
AB130: ' ======
AC130: ' ======
AD130: ' ======
AE130: ' ======
R132: 'Criterion Range
R133: "Task
S133: "Member
T133: [W10] "Date
U133: 'Client
T134: [W10] +A10>=$T$75#AND#+A10<=$T$76

15

Project Management

Introduction

Businesses increasingly are turning to project management and goal-oriented activity to provide a guide for the company's direction. This approach gives your firm a purpose or corporate mission which can lead to increased efficiency and an advantage over your competitors. Fortunately, you have a 1-2-3 tool that you can use for this purpose.

You can implement a project-management system with the 1-2-3 Project Manager. The model tells you the completion date of your project, its duration and cost, and any overruns of these two factors. In addition, the application can produce striking graphs that will help you understand your firm's resource commitments to a particular project.

To accomplish these tasks, the model, shown in figure 15.1, is divided into three sections—the Project Calculation Schedule, the Cost Summary, and the \d macro. The first module functions as a data-entry and calculation worksheet; the second summarizes these results for your analysis and review. The third module can help you enter dates.

This final chapter shows you how to create the 1-2-3 Project Manager, discusses how the model operates, and helps you use the application in your company.

Creating the Model

The 1-2-3 Project Manager is another application that requires some thought before you create the model. You will need to identify the logic of interrelated activities: for example, Activity B not starting until A has started (a Start-Start (S-S) tie); Activity B not starting until A has finished

```
     A         B            C         D       E       F      G       H        I       J    K    L    M    N        O         P            Q        R       S       T       U
 1 ================================================================================================================================================
 2 PROJECT MANAGER            Copyright (C) Que Corporation 1987
 3 ================================================================================================================================================
 4                                                                                                                                          \d       @DATE(87,{?},{?})¯
 5 PROJECT ENGINEERING IMPACT CALCULATION SCHEDULE                                                                                          Date
 6                                                                                                                                          Macro
 7 TOTAL PROJECT DURATION =        76              DURATION OVERRUN          0 DAYS
 8
 9 TOTAL PROJECT COST =          $740              COST OVERRUN             $0 MANHOURS                          COST SUMMARY
10                                                                                                       ------------------------------------
11 ACTIVITY                    START DATE     DAYS    FINISH DATE     DAYS      LAG        TOTAL          GROUP      DEFINE  ASSESS  REVISE   TOT
12 NO.  DESCRIPTION    GROUP  DUR  TARGET   CURRENT LATE TARGET    CURRENT LATE S-S  F-S  F-F  COST       -----      ------  ------  ------  ---
13 --------------------------------------------------------------------------------------------------------
14    1 DEFINE IMPACT    MECH   3  02-Jan-87 02-Jan-87  0  06-Jan-87 06-Jan-87  0   0    0    0   $36      Mechanical    $36    $70    $100   $206
15    2 EVALUATE IMPACT  MECH   6  07-Jan-87 07-Jan-87  0  15-Jan-87 15-Jan-87  0   0    0    0    70      Civil                 24    200    224
16    3 EVALUATE IMPACT  CIVIL  4  07-Jan-87 07-Jan-87  0  12-Jan-87 12-Jan-87  0   0    0    0    24      Electrical            16     50     66
17    4 EVALUATE IMPACT  ELEC   3  07-Jan-87 07-Jan-87  0  11-Jan-87 11-Jan-87  0   0    0    0    16      Controls              16    100    116
18    5 EVALUATE IMPACT  CONT   3  07-Jan-87 07-Jan-87  0  11-Jan-87 11-Jan-87  0   0    0    0    16      Environmental  32      8     80    120
19    6 ASSESS IMPACTS   ENV    5  16-Jan-87 16-Jan-87  0  23-Jan-87 23-Jan-87  0   0    0    0    32      Management             8              8
20    7 ISSUE ASSESSMENT ENV    2  24-Jan-87 24-Jan-87  0  27-Jan-87 27-Jan-87  0   0    0    0     8                 ------  ------  ------  ------
21    8 REVISE DESIGN    MECH  10  28-Jan-87 28-Jan-87  0  11-Feb-87 11-Feb-87  0   0    0    0   100      Total        $68    $142    $530   $740
22    9 REVISE DESIGN    CIVIL 15  28-Jan-87 28-Jan-87  0  18-Feb-87 18-Feb-87  0   0    0    0   200                 ======  ======  ======  ======
23   10 REVISE DESIGN    ELEC   8  28-Jan-87 28-Jan-87  0  08-Feb-87 08-Feb-87  0   0    0    0    50
24   11 REVISE DESIGN    CONT  10  28-Jan-87 28-Jan-87  0  11-Feb-87 11-Feb-87  0   0    0    0   100
25   12 ASSESS REVISIONS ENV    5  09-Feb-87 09-Feb-87  0  22-Feb-87 22-Feb-87  0   0    0    3    80
26   13 APPROVE REVISIONS ENV   2  23-Feb-87 23-Feb-87  0  26-Feb-87 26-Feb-87  0   0    0    0     8
27                                                                                            ----------
28                                                                                               $740
29                                                                                            =========
```

Fig. 15.1. The Project Manager.

(a Finish-Start (F-S) tie); or Activity B not finishing until Activity A has finished (a Finish-Finish (F-F) tie). All of these ties can have a lag value of plus or minus *n* days. In other words, Activity B cannot start until 10 days after Activity A finishes (F-S + 10). The activity interties in our example are listed in table 15.1.

Table 15.1
Logic Interties

Activity	*Intertie*
2 through 5	Cannot start until 1 is finished
6	Cannot start until 2 through 5 are finished
7	Cannot start until 6 is finished
8 through 11	Cannot start until 7 is finished
12	Cannot start until at least one of activities 8 through 11 is finished
12	Cannot finish until three days after the last of activities 8 through 11 is finished
13	Cannot start until 12 is finished

Once you have completed your preliminary planning, creating the model should be relatively easy.

Setting Column Widths

To begin the formal construction process, change the column widths of one of your blank 1-2-3 spreadsheets according to the following list:

Column	Width
A, D, J	6
B	18
C	9
E, F, H, I, Q	12
G	3
K, L, M	7
N	4

Next, enter the row titles, column headings, and labels listed in table 15.2. You may use variations of these items to suit your application. (The sample application shown in figure 15.1 is for an engineering concern.)

Table 15.2
Row Titles and Column Headings

Enter into cell:	Original label:	Copy to:
	Opening Headings	
A1:	\=	B1..V1, A3..V3, O29
A2:	'PROJECT MANAGER	
	Project Calculation Schedule	
A5:	'PROJECT CALCULATION SCHEDULE	
A7:	'TOTAL PROJECT DURATION =	
G7:	'DURATION OVERRUN =	
K7:	'DAYS	
A9:	'TOTAL PROJECT COST =	
G9:	'COST OVERRUN =	
K9:	'MANHOURS	
A11:	'ACTIVITY	
E11:	' START	
F11:	'DATE	I11
G11:	'DAYS	J11

Enter into cell:	Original label:	Copy to:
H11:	' FINISH	
L11:	^LAG	
O11:	' TOTAL	
A12:	'NO.	
B12:	'DESCRIPTION	
C12:	'GROUP	Q12
D12:	'DUR	
E12:	^TARGET	H12
F12:	^CURRENT	I12
G12:	'LATE	J12
K12:	"S-S	
L12:	"F-S	
M12:	"F-F	
O12:	"COST	
A13:	\-	B13..O13, O27, T11..V11

Cost Summary

T10:	"COST	
U10:	'SUMMARY	
V12:	'TOT	
Q13:	'-----	
S13:	"------	T13..V13, S20..V20
S22:	"======	T22..V22

Macro

V4:	'\d
U4:	'@DATE(87,{?},{?})~
V5:	'Date
V6:	'Macro

Enter the formulas next. The formulas used in the sample application are listed in table 15.3 but again, yours may be different because of your activity interties. Use table 15.3 as a guide only.

Table 15.3
Formulas and Functions

Enter into cell:	Original formula:	Copy to:

Project Calculation Schedule

D7:	@SUM(D14..D26)	
J7:	+H26-@DATE(87,2,26)	
D9:	+O28	
J9:	+O28-740	
G14:	+F14-E14	G15..G26, J14..J26
E15:	@IF($K$15>$L$15,$E$14+1.4*$K$15,1+$H$14+1.4*$L$15)	E16..E18
E19:	@IF(K19>L19,@MAX(E15..E18)+1.4*K19,1+@MAX(H15..H18)+1.4*L19)	E20..E21
E22:	@IF($K$22>$L$22,$E$21+1.4*$K$22,1+$H$20+1.4*$L$22)	E23..E24
E25:	@IF(K25>L25,H23+1.4*K25,1+H23+1.4*L25)	
E26:	@IF(K26>L26,H25+1.4*K26,1+H25+1.4*L26)	
H15:	@IF($H$14+1.4*M15>E15+1.4*(D15+K15),$H$14+1.4*M15,E15+1.4*(D15+K15))	H16..H18
H19:	@IF(@MAX(H15..H18)+1.4*M19>E19+1.4*(D19+K19),@MAX(H15..H18)+1.4*M19,E19+1.4*(D19+K19))	H20..H22
H23:	@IF(@MAX(H19..H20)+1.4*M23>E23+1.4*(D23+K23),@MAX(H19..H20)+1.4*M23,E23+1.4*(D23+K23))	H24
H25:	@IF(@MAX(H21..H24)+1.4*M25>E25+1.4*(D25+K25),@MAX(H21..H24)+1.4*M25,E25+1.4*(D25+K25))	
H26:	@IF(H25+1.4*M26>E26+1.4*(D26+K26),H25+1.4*M26,E26+1.4*(D26+K26))	
O28:	@SUM(O14..O26)	

Cost Summary

S14:	+O14	
S18:	+O19	
S21:	@SUM(S14..S19)	T21..V21
T14:	+O15	T15..T17
T18:	+O20	
T19:	+O26	
U14:	+O21	U15..U18
V14:	@SUM(S14..U14)	V15..V19

Specifying Cell Formats

Now, format the cells of your model. Table 15.4 summarizes the formats used in figure 15.1.

Table 15.4
Cell Formats

Format	Cell/Range
Project Calculation Schedule	
/rfc0	D9, J9, O28
/rfd1	Columns E, F, H, I
Cost Summary	
/rfc0	S14..V14,
	S21..V21

If you plan to use the macro, be sure to name it by using the **/R**ange **N**ame **L**abel **R**ight command.

Now that you have created the model, you'll need to know how the Project Manager functions.

Understanding the Model

If you look at the sample Project Manager in figure 15.1, you'll see that the Project Calculation Schedule is the application's major module. The Cost Summary is a dependent module which references your total project costs. The model's graphics, in turn, are generated from the Cost Summary totals. Thus, like the other models in this book, this application comprises interrelated sections and functions.

The Project Calculation Schedule

This important module, located in cells A4 through O29, contains key information about your project's activity, group, start and finish dates, number of days late for both, lags, duration, and costs (refer to fig. 15.1).

Columns A and B of this module contain the activity's number and description, respectively. Column C displays the name of the group assigned to your activity, and column D is the planned duration, in days, of this activity.

Column E holds the Target, or planned, Start Date of each activity. Initially, the Start Date for Activity 1 is the only "fixed" date; all other dates derive logically from the Start Date. The formula for Activity 2's Start Date, in cell E15, is

E15: @IF($K$15>$L$15,$E$14+1.4*$K$15,1+$H$14+1.4*$L$15)

Is S-S Lag > F-S Lag?

Yes	No
Activity 1 Start Date	1 + Act 1 Target Finish Date
+	+
(1.4 * Activity 1 S-S Lag)	(1.4 * Activity 1 F-S Lag)

This equation reads: Is the Start-Start (S-S) Lag greater than the Finish-Start (F-S) Lag? If so, cell E15's date will be cell E14's date plus the product of the Start-Start Lag times 1.4.

If not, the date in cell E15 is the previous activity's Finish Date plus one day plus the product of Activity 1's Finish-Start Lag times 1.4. The factor of 1.4 converts durations in working days into calendar days to account for weekends (7 divided by 5 = 1.4). This equation is the general formula for your Start-Date logic.

Conversely, your Target Finish Date formula for Activity 2 is

H15: @IF(H14+1.4*M15>E15+1.4*(D15+K15),
          H14+1.4*M15,E15+1.4*(D15+K15))

which can be separated into

H15: @IF(H14+1.4*M15>E15+1.4*(D15+K15),

Previous Finish Date+(1.4*F-F Lag)>Start Date+(1.4*(Dur+S-S Lag)?

Yes	No
H14+1.4*M15,	E15+1.4*(D15+K15))
Previous Target Fin Date	Target Start Date
+	+
(1.4 * F-F Lag)	(1.4*(Duration + S-S Lag))

This formula translates: Is the previous activity's Finish Date plus the product of 1.4 times the F-F Lag greater than the Target Start Date plus the product of 1.4 times the sum of this activity's duration and the S-S Lag? If so, cell H15's date will be the previous Target Finish Date plus the product of 1.4 times the F-F Lag.

If not, cell H15's date will be the Target Start Date plus the product of 1.4 times the sum of the activity's duration and S-S Lag. This equation is the general formula for your Finish-Date logic.

As you know, identifying interrelated activities before you construct the spreadsheet is important. You will not be able to use /Copy to enter your remaining Start and Finish equations because not all of the statements contain simple Finish-Start logic from the previous line. Consider, for example, the formula in cell E19:

E19: @IF(K19>L19,@MAX(E15..E18)+1.4*K19,
          1+@MAX(H15..H18)+1.4*L19)

which can be separated into

E19: @IF(K19>L19, ---> Is S-S Lag > F-S Lag?

Yes	No
@MAX(E15..E18)+1.4*K19	1+@MAX(H15..H18)+1.4*L19)
The latest of the four previous start dates plus the product of 1.4 and the S-S Lag	1 day plus the latest of four previous finish dates plus the product of 1.4 and the F-S Lag

In other words: Is the S-S Lag greater than the F-S Lag? If so, the date in cell E19 will be the latest of the four previous start dates plus the product of 1.4 times the activity's S-S Lag. If not, cell E19's date will be one day plus the latest of the four previous days' finish dates plus the product of 1.4 times the F-S Lag.

Similarly, this activity's finish logic is

H19: @IF(@MAX(H15..H18)+1.4*M19>E19+1.4*(D19+K19),
          @MAX(H15..H18)+1.4*M19,
          E19+1.4*(D19+K19))

which can be separated into

H19: @IF(@MAX(H15..H18)+1.4*M19>E19+1.4*(D19+K19),

Yes	No
@MAX(H15..H18)+1.4*M19	E19+1.4*(D19+K19))
The latest of the four previous start dates plus the product of 1.4 and the F-F Lag	Target Start Date plus the product of 1.4 and the sum of the duration and the S-S Lag

which reads: Is the latest of the four previous finish dates plus the product of 1.4 times the F-F Lag greater than the Start Date plus the product of 1.4 times the sum of the duration and the S-S Lag? If so, the Finish Date in cell H19 is the latest of the four previous start dates plus the product of 1.4 times the F-F Lag. If not, the Finish Date in cell H19 is the Target Start Date plus the product of 1.4 times the sum of the duration and the S-S Lag.

Be very careful when you enter your Start and Finish Date formulas!

Because columns F and I are manual-entry columns, you can include the Current (or actual) Start and Finish dates for each activity. To do so, use the @DATE function or the model's macro. Release 2's /**R**ange **V**alue command was used for the sample model because we did not want any days late in figure 15.1.

Columns G and J reflect your Start and Finish Days Late, respectively. In cell G14, the formula is

G14: +F14-E14

(Activity 1's Current Date minus the Target Date.) Both columns contain this logic; you can repeat them by using the /Copy command.

Columns K, L, and M contain the S-S, F-S, and F-F Lags, in days. The range K14..M26 is a data-entry area.

Column OK represents the costs (dollars, man-hours, expendable supplies, and so on) associated with each activity. This column, which is also a data-entry column, should be completed before you calculate the model.

Cell O28 totals the costs with the formula

O28: @SUM(O14..O26)

The model will compute the project's duration and cost totals from the formulas and data, then place the final information above the general worksheet area. For example, Total Project Duration is calculated by the formula

D7: @SUM(D14..D26)

which is the total of column D. The Total Project Cost is computed by referencing the total of your Cost column, O:

D9: +O28

Your Project Duration Overrun (if any) is calculated using the equation

J7: +H26-@DATE(87,2,26)

in which H26 is the Target Finish Date for the project's last activity. This date is subtracted from the last activity's beginning Target Finish Date to determine any duration overrun.

Similarly, your project's cost overrun, if any, uses the formula

J9: +O28-740

in which cell O28 is the project's current cost and the value of 740 represents the beginning cost of your project.

These costs are summarized by department in the Cost Summary module.

Cost Summary

The example's Cost Summary module is located in cells Q10 through V22 (see fig. 15.2). Each group's costs are displayed by major project activity.

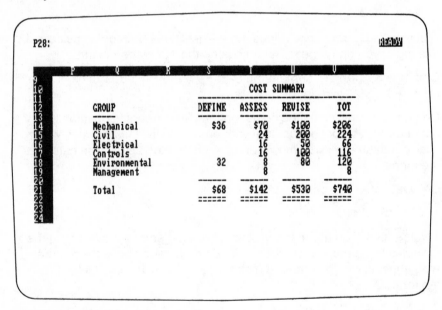

Fig. 15.2. The Cost Summary.

The structure of this module is simple. Group costs by project are calculated by referencing the appropriate cell in column O, Total Costs.

For example, the Mechanical Group's total Project Definition Costs are computed by the formula

S14: +O14

These costs, in turn, are totaled by Group and major project category. For example, the Mechanical Group's total cost for this project is calculated by the function

V14: @SUM(S14..U14)

This project's Total Definition Costs are computed with the equation

S21: @SUM(S14..S19)

Because all other totals in this section are calculated in a relative manner, the Cost Summary will be updated automatically whenever you recalculate the worksheet. As you can see, these summary totals are an excellent source for graphs (addressed in the "Using the Model" discussion later in this chapter). Before you turn to that section, take a brief look at the \d macro.

The \d Macro

The Project Manager's \d macro is located at cells V4 through X6 (see fig. 15.3). You can use this macro for entering multiple dates. Press Alt-D to invoke the macro. It will place the year portion of the date in the current cell location, pause while you furnish the month and day, and then finish entering the date. You may want to consider using this simple macro, which reduces the time it takes to perform this routine task, in your other spreadsheet applications.

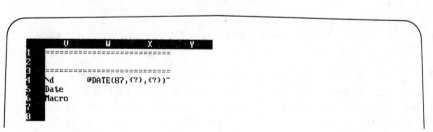

Fig. 15.3. The \d macro.

Now we'll show you how to use the Project Manager in your business.

Using the Model

As in previous chapters, the first step in using the model is to enter your project data. Enter the data in your Project Calculation Schedule section, using table 15.5 as a guide.

Table 15.5
Data Entry

Description	Location
Activity Number	Column A
Activity Description	Column B
Group Name	Column C
Duration (days)	Column D
Target Start Date	Column E
Current Start Date	Column F
Target Finish Date	Column H
Current Finish Date	Column I
S-S, F-S, F-F Lags	Columns K, L, M
Costs	Column O

Now press F9 (CALC) to calculate your project's Total Costs. Be sure to include this value in cell J9's formula.

If your original Current Start and Finish dates fluctuate, revise your model for these changes by entering the new date(s). Don't forget to recalculate the worksheet before you retrieve another file or end your 1-2-3 session.

Your Project Manager, which is an excellent source of graphs, will produce meaningful management reports from your Cost Summary. Consider, for example, the pie graph shown in figure 15.4.

This graph displays the percent of cost of your project by group. To produce this graph, you would issue the /Graph Type Pie command. The **X**-Range is your Group names (Q14..Q19), the **A**-Range is each group's total cost (V14..V19). The two titles are added by using the /Graph Options Titles First (and then Second) sequence of commands. If you then select View, your computer should generate the graph displayed in figure 15.4.

By changing the **X**-Range to your Activity Names (S12..V12) and the **A**-Range to the Activity Totals (S21..V21), you can produce the graph shown in figure 15.5.

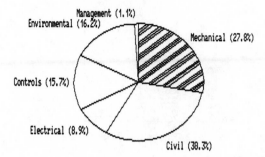

Fig. 15.4. Percent of Project Cost by Group.

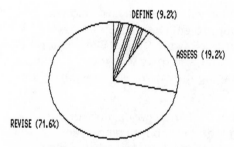

Fig. 15.5. Percent of Cost by Activity.

This graph, the converse of the first, displays the cost of the project divided by activity category.

Finally, figure 15.6 presents, in a stacked-bar format, the information displayed in the previous graphs.

To create this graph, you use the **/G**raph **T**ype **S**tacked-Bar command. As in the first graph, your Group names are the **X**-Range (Q14..Q19). This time, howe.er, the A, B, and C ranges will be the cost data in columns S, T, and U of the Cost Summary. In other words, the **A**-Range is S14..S19. As you can see, this graph has been enhanced with First and Second titles of "Impact Calculation" and "Costs Per Group"; the Activity descriptions (S12..V12) have been used as **L**egends.

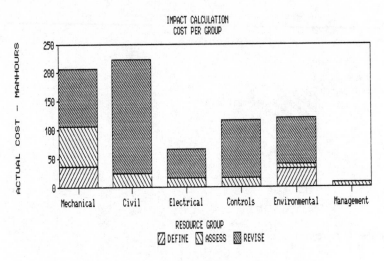

Fig. 15.6. Cost of Project in Dollars by Group and Activity.

Modifying the Model

If you believe there is a strong possibility that you may need to add additional groups or activities to your project after it is underway, consider placing your Cost Summary below the Project Calculation Schedule. In this manner, you can easily add rows with the /Worksheet Insert Row command, without damaging the model. Be sure to adjust your logic interties accordingly.

Finally, if you know the man-hour costs of each group, consider including your unit costs in column P and number of employees assigned from that group in column Q. In this fashion, you can have 1-2-3 calculate your total costs in column M from the product of columns P and Q. This is particularly useful if employees are reassigned to or from the project.

Conclusion

The Project Manager application gives you project-management capability with no additional software investment. The model informs you of your project cost, time, and any cost overruns. And as you have seen, you can use 1-2-3 graphics to display these costs in a number of ways. In sum, the Project Manager demonstrates 1-2-3's flexibility and power and can help you solve almost any business problem.

```
A1: [W6] \=
B1: [W18] \=
C1: \=
D1: [W6] \=
E1: [W12] \=
F1: [W12] \=
G1: [W6] \=
H1: [W12] \=
I1: [W12] \=
J1: [W6] \=
K1: [W7] \=
L1: [W7] \=
M1: [W7] \=
N1: [W4] \=
O1: \=
P1: \=
Q1: [W12] \=
R1: \=
S1: \=
T1: \=
U1: \=
V1: \=
AA1: '\d
AB1: '@DATE(87,{?},{?})~
A2: [W6] 'PROJECT MANAGER
D2: [W6] 'Copyright (C) Que Corporation 1987
A3: [W6] \=
B3: [W18] \=
C3: \=
D3: [W6] \=
E3: [W12] \=
F3: [W12] \=
G3: [W6] \=
H3: [W12] \=
I3: [W12] \=
J3: [W6] \=
K3: [W7] \=
L3: [W7] \=
M3: [W7] \=
N3: [W4] \=
O3: \=
P3: \=
Q3: [W12] \=
R3: \=
S3: \=
T3: \=
U3: \=
V3: \=
A5: [W6] 'PROJECT ENGINEERING IMPACT CALCULATION SCHEDULE
A7: [W6] 'TOTAL PROJECT DURATION =
D7: [W6] @SUM(D14..D26)
G7: [W6] 'DURATION OVERRUN
J7: (F0) [W6] +H26-@DATE(87,2,26)
K7: [W7] 'DAYS
```

```
A9: [W6] 'TOTAL PROJECT COST =
D9: (C0) [W6] +O28
G9: [W6] 'COST OVERRUN
J9: (C0) [W6] +O28-740
K9: [W7] 'MANHOURS
T10: "COST
U10: 'SUMMARY
A11: [W6] ' ACTIVITY
E11: [W12] '      START
F11: [W12] 'DATE
G11: [W6] 'DAYS
H11: [W12] '     FINISH
I11: [W12] 'DATE
J11: [W6] 'DAYS
L11: [W7] ^LAG
O11: '   TOTAL
S11: '  -------
T11: \-
U11: \-
V11: \-
A12: [W6] 'NO.
B12: [W18] 'DESCRIPTION
C12: 'GROUP
D12: [W6] 'DUR
E12: [W12] ^TARGET
F12: [W12] ^CURRENT
G12: [W6] 'LATE
H12: [W12] ^TARGET
I12: [W12] ^CURRENT
J12: [W6] 'LATE
K12: [W7] "S-S
L12: [W7] "F-S
M12: [W7] "F-F
O12: "COST
Q12: [W12] 'GROUP
S12: "DEFINE
T12: "ASSESS
U12: "REVISE
V12: "TOT
A13: [W6] \-
B13: [W18] \-
C13: \-
D13: [W6] \-
E13: [W12] \-
F13: [W12] \-
G13: [W6] \-
H13: [W12] \-
I13: [W12] \-
J13: [W6] \-
K13: [W7] \-
L13: [W7] \-
M13: [W7] \-
N13: [W4] \-
```

```
O13: \-
Q13: [W12] '-----
S13: "------
T13: "------
U13: "------
V13: "---
A14: [W6] 1
B14: [W18] 'DEFINE IMPACT
C14: 'MECH
D14: [W6] 3
E14: (D1) [W12] @DATE(87,1,2)
F14: (D1) [W12] @DATE(87,1,2)
G14: [W6] +F14-E14
H14: (D1) [W12] @DATE(87,1,6)
I14: (D1) [W12] 31783
J14: [W6] +I14-H14
K14: [W7] 0
L14: [W7] 0
M14: [W7] 0
O14: (C0) 36
Q14: [W12] 'Mechanical
S14: (C0) +O14
T14: (C0) +O15
U14: (C0) +O21
V14: (C0) @SUM(S14..U14)
A15: [W6] 2
B15: [W18] 'EVALUATE IMPACT
C15: 'MECH
D15: [W6] 6
E15: (D1) [W12] @IF($K$15>$L$15,$E$14+1.4*$K$15,1+$H$14+1.4*$L$15)
F15: (D1) [W12] 31784
G15: [W6] +F15-E15
H15: (D1) [W12] @IF($H$14+1.4*M15>E15+1.4*(D15+K15),$H$14+1.4*M15,
                   E15+1.4*(D15+K15))
I15: (D1) [W12] 31792.4
J15: [W6] +I15-H15
K15: [W7] 0
L15: [W7] 0
M15: [W7] 0
O15: 70
Q15: [W12] 'Civil
T15: +O16
U15: +O22
V15: @SUM(S15..U15)
A16: [W6] 3
B16: [W18] 'EVALUATE IMPACT
C16: 'CIVIL
D16: [W6] 4
E16: (D1) [W12] @IF($K$15>$L$15,$E$14+1.4*$K$15,1+$H$14+1.4*$L$15)
F16: (D1) [W12] 31784
G16: [W6] +F16-E16
H16: (D1) [W12] @IF($H$14+1.4*M16>E16+1.4*(D16+K16),$H$14+1.4*M16,
                   E16+1.4*(D16+K16))
```

I16: (D1) [W12] 31789.6
J16: [W6] +I16-H16
K16: [W7] 0
L16: [W7] 0
M16: [W7] 0
O16: 24
Q16: [W12] 'Electrical
T16: +O17
U16: +O23
V16: @SUM(S16..U16)
A17: [W6] 4
B17: [W18] 'EVALUATE IMPACT
C17: 'ELEC
D17: [W6] 3
E17: (D1) [W12] @IF($K$15>$L$15,$E$14+1.4*$K$15,1+$H$14+1.4*$L$15)
F17: (D1) [W12] 31784
G17: [W6] +F17-E17
H17: (D1) [W12] @IF($H$14+1.4*M17>E17+1.4*(D17+K17),$H$14+1.4*M17,
                    E17+1.4*(D17+K17))
I17: (D1) [W12] 31788.2
J17: [W6] +I17-H17
K17: [W7] 0
L17: [W7] 0
M17: [W7] 0
O17: 16
Q17: [W12] 'Controls
T17: +O18
U17: +O24
V17: @SUM(S17..U17)
A18: [W6] 5
B18: [W18] 'EVALUATE IMPACT
C18: 'CONT
D18: [W6] 3
E18: (D1) [W12] @IF($K$15>$L$15,$E$14+1.4*$K$15,1+$H$14+1.4*$L$15)
F18: (D1) [W12] 31784
G18: [W6] +F18-E18
H18: (D1) [W12] @IF($H$14+1.4*M18>E18+1.4*(D18+K18),$H$14+1.4*M18,
                    E18+1.4*(D18+K18))
I18: (D1) [W12] 31788.2
J18: [W6] +I18-H18
K18: [W7] 0
L18: [W7] 0
M18: [W7] 0
O18: 16
Q18: [W12] 'Environmental
S18: +O19
T18: +O20
U18: +O25
V18: @SUM(S18..U18)
A19: [W6] 6
B19: [W18] 'ASSESS IMPACTS
C19: 'ENV
D19: [W6] 5

E19: (D1) [W12] @IF(K19>L19,@MAX(E15..E18)+1.4*K19,1+@MAX(H15..H18)
                +1.4*L19)
F19: (D1) [W12] 31793.4
G19: [W6] +F19-E19
H19: (D1) [W12] @IF(@MAX(H15..H18)+1.4*M19>E19+1.4*(D19+K19),
                    @MAX(H15..H18)+1.4*M19,E19+1.4*(D19+K19))
I19: (D1) [W12] 31800.4
J19: [W6] +I19-H19
K19: [W7] 0
L19: [W7] 0
M19: [W7] 0
O19: 32
Q19: [W12] 'Management
T19: +O26
V19: @SUM(S19..U19)
A20: [W6] 7
B20: [W18] 'ISSUE ASSESSMENT
C20: 'ENV
D20: [W6] 2
E20: (D1) [W12] @IF(K20>L20,@MAX(E16..E19)+1.4*K20,1+@MAX(H16..H19)
                +1.4*L20)
F20: (D1) [W12] 31801.4
G20: [W6] +F20-E20
H20: (D1) [W12] @IF(@MAX(H16..H19)+1.4*M20>E20+1.4*(D20+K20),
                    @MAX(H16..H19)+1.4*M20,E20+1.4*(D20+K20))
I20: (D1) [W12] 31804.2
J20: [W6] +I20-H20
K20: [W7] 0
L20: [W7] 0
M20: [W7] 0
O20: 8
S20: "------
T20: "------
U20: "------
V20: "------
A21: [W6] 8
B21: [W18] 'REVISE DESIGN
C21: 'MECH
D21: [W6] 10
E21: (D1) [W12] @IF(K21>L21,@MAX(E17..E20)+1.4*K21,1+@MAX(H17..H20)
                +1.4*L21)
F21: (D1) [W12] 31805.2
G21: [W6] +F21-E21
H21: (D1) [W12] @IF(@MAX(H17..H20)+1.4*M21>E21+1.4*(D21+K21),
                    @MAX(H17..H20)+1.4*M21,E21+1.4*(D21+K21))
I21: (D1) [W12] 31819.2
J21: [W6] +I21-H21
K21: [W7] 0
L21: [W7] 0
M21: [W7] 0
O21: 100
Q21: [W12] 'Total
S21: (C0) @SUM(S14..S19)
T21: (C0) @SUM(T14..T19)

```
U21: (C0) @SUM(U14..U19)
V21: (C0) @SUM(V14..V19)
A22: [W6] 9
B22: [W18] 'REVISE DESIGN
C22: 'CIVIL
D22: [W6] 15
E22: (D1) [W12] @IF($K$22>$L$22,$E$21+1.4*$K$22,1+$H$20+1.4*$L$22)
F22: (D1) [W12] 31805.2
G22: [W6] +F22-E22
H22: (D1) [W12] @IF(@MAX(H18..H21)+1.4*M22>E22+1.4*(D22+K22),
                     @MAX(H18..H21)+1.4*M22,E22+1.4*(D22+K22))
I22: (D1) [W12] 31826.2
J22: [W6] +I22-H22
K22: [W7] 0
L22: [W7] 0
M22: [W7] 0
O22: 200
S22: "======
T22: "======
U22: "======
V22: "======
A23: [W6] 10
B23: [W18] 'REVISE DESIGN
C23: 'ELEC
D23: [W6] 8
E23: (D1) [W12] @IF($K$22>$L$22,$E$21+1.4*$K$22,1+$H$20+1.4*$L$22)
F23: (D1) [W12] 31805.2
G23: [W6] +F23-E23
H23: (D1) [W12] @IF(@MAX(H19..H20)+1.4*M23>E23+1.4*(D23+K23),
                     @MAX(H19..H20)+1.4*M23,E23+1.4*(D23+K23))
I23: (D1) [W12] 31816.4
J23: [W6] +I23-H23
K23: [W7] 0
L23: [W7] 0
M23: [W7] 0
O23: 50
A24: [W6] 11
B24: [W18] 'REVISE DESIGN
C24: 'CONT
D24: [W6] 10
E24: (D1) [W12] @IF($K$22>$L$22,$E$21+1.4*$K$22,1+$H$20+1.4*$L$22)
F24: (D1) [W12] 31805.2
G24: [W6] +F24-E24
H24: (D1) [W12] @IF(@MAX(H20..H21)+1.4*M24>E24+1.4*(D24+K24),
                     @MAX(H20..H21)+1.4*M24,E24+1.4*(D24+K24))
I24: (D1) [W12] 31819.2
J24: [W6] +I24-H24
K24: [W7] 0
L24: [W7] 0
M24: [W7] 0


O24: 100
A25: [W6] 12
```

B25: [W18] 'ASSESS REVISIONS
C25: 'ENV
D25: [W6] 5
E25: (D1) [W12] @IF(K25>L25,H23+1.4*K25,1+H23+1.4*L25)
F25: (D1) [W12] 31817.4
G25: [W6] +F25-E25
H25: (D1) [W12] @IF(@MAX(H21..H24)+1.4*M25>E25+1.4*(D25+K25),
                     @MAX(H21..H24)+1.4*M25,E25+1.4*(D25+K25))
I25: (D1) [W12] 31830.4
J25: [W6] +I25-H25
K25: [W7] 0
L25: [W7] 0
M25: [W7] 3
O25: 80
A26: [W6] 13
B26: [W18] 'APPROVE REVISIONS
C26: 'ENV
D26: [W6] 2
E26: (D1) [W12] @IF(K26>L26,H25+1.4*K26,1+H25+1.4*L26)
F26: (D1) [W12] 31831.4
G26: [W6] +F26-E26
H26: (D1) [W12] @IF(H25+1.4*M26>E26+1.4*(D26+K26),H25+1.4*M26,E26
                     +1.4*(D26+K26))
I26: (D1) [W12] 31834.2
J26: [W6] +I26-H26
K26: [W7] 0
L26: [W7] 0
M26: [W7] 0
O26: 8
O27: \-
O28: (C0) @SUM(O14..O26)
O29: \=

Index

B

H

I

S

T

More Computer Knowledge from Que

LOTUS SOFTWARE TITLES

1-2-3 QueCards	21.95
1-2-3 for Business, 2nd Edition	19.95
1-2-3 Business Formula Handbook	19.95
1-2-3 Command Language	19.95
1-2-3 Macro Library, 2nd Edition	19.95
1-2-3 Tips, Tricks, and Traps, 2nd Edition	19.95
Using 1-2-3, Special Edition	24.95
Using 1-2-3 Workbook and Disk, 2nd Edition	29.95
Using Lotus HAL	19.95
Using Symphony	23.95
Symphony: Advanced Topics	19.95
Symphony Macros and the Command Language	22.95
Symphony Tips, Tricks, and Traps	21.95

IBM TITLES

Networking IBM PCs, 2nd Edition	19.95
Using PC DOS, 2nd Edition	22.95

COMPUTER SYSTEMS TITLES

Amiga Programming Guide	18.95
CP/M Programmer's Encyclopedia	19.95
Managing Your Hard Disk	19.95
MS-DOS User's Guide, 2nd Edition	21.95
Using NetWare	24.95

APPLICATIONS SOFTWARE TITLES

Excel Macro Library	19.95
Multiplan Models for Business	15.95
Smart Tips, Tricks, and Traps	23.95
Using AppleWorks, 2nd Edition	19.95
Using Dollars and Sense	16.95
Using Dollars and Sense on the IBM	17.95
Using Enable	19.95
Using Excel	19.95
Using Javelin	21.95
Using Managing Your Money	17.95
Using Microsoft Works	18.95
Using Smart	22.95
Using SuperCalc4	18.95

WORD-PROCESSING AND DESKTOP PUBLISHING TITLES

Using DisplayWrite	19.95
Using DisplayWrite 4	19.95
Using Microsoft Word, 2nd Edition	19.95
Using MultiMate Advantage, 2nd Edition	18.95
Using PageMaker on the IBM	24.95
Using WordPerfect, 3rd Edition	19.95
Using WordPerfect Workbook and Disk	29.95
Using WordStar	18.95
WordPerfect Tips, Tricks, and Traps	19.95

DATABASE TITLES

dBASE III Plus Applications Library	19.95
dBASE III Plus Handbook, 2nd Edition	19.95
dBASE III Plus Advanced Programming, 2nd Edition	22.95
dBASE III Plus Tips, Tricks, and Traps	19.95
R:BASE System V Techniques and Applications	19.95
R:BASE System V User's Guide, 2nd Edition	19.95
Reflex Tips, Tricks, and Traps	19.95
Using Reflex	19.95
Using Paradox	21.95
Using Q & A	19.95

PROGRAMMING AND TECHNICAL TITLES

Advanced C: Techniques and Applications	21.95
C Programmer's Library	21.95
C Programming Guide, 2nd Edition	19.95
C Self-Study Guide	16.95
C Standard Library	21.95
Common C Functions	18.95
Debugging C	19.95
Turbo Pascal for BASIC Programmers	16.95
Turbo Pascal Program Library	19.95
Turbo Pascal Tips, Tricks, and Traps	19.95
Understanding UNIX: A Conceptual Guide	21.95
Understanding XENIX: A Conceptual Guide	21.95
Using Turbo Prolog	19.95

Que Order Line: **1-800-428-5331** All prices subject to change without notice.

OUTSTANDING BOOKS FROM QUE

1-2-3 Business Formula Handbook
by Ron Person

The *1-2-3 Business Formula Handbook*, a convenient desktop reference, helps you create the formulas you need for building your 1-2-3 models. More than 30 models show you how to create 1-2-3 formulas for financial analysis, business forecasts, investment analysis, and statistical and survey analysis. Each section explains thoroughly the 1-2-3 model, formulas used, and assumptions. You can easily duplicate the model or modify it for your applications. The *1-2-3 Business Formula Handbook* will save you time while you develop your skill in using complex 1-2-3 formulas.

1-2-3 Macro Library, 2nd Edition
by David P. Ewing

An enduring best-seller! Take advantage of 1-2-3, Release 2's macro capability, including its powerful command language, with *1-2-3 Macro Library*, 2nd Edition. This easy-to-use reference teaches the user how to create more than 100 macros for 1-2-3 spreadsheet, data management, and graphics applications. Readers will learn how to develop file management and print macros and design macros for special applications, such as using 1-2-3 to develop mail merge capabilities. And for 1-2-3, Release 1A users, references throughout the book and an appendix help create Release 1A macros. For those just getting started or looking for help with advanced macro applications, this comprehensive library provides all of the necessary information.

Using 1-2-3, 2nd Edition
by Geoffrey LeBlond and Douglas Cobb

Nationally acclaimed, *Using 1-2-3* is "the book" for every 1-2-3 user. Whether you are using Release 1A or 2, you will find *Using 1-2-3*, 2nd Edition, your most valuable source of information. Spreadsheet, database, graphics, and macro capabilities common to both Releases 1A and 2 or new to Release 2 are all covered in depth. Notations in the text and a tear-out command chart help you locate quickly the differences between Releases 1A and 2. Like thousands of other 1-2-3 users, you will consider this book indispensable.

> This title must surely be one of the greats when it comes to good books on 1-2-3.
> —*Computer Shopper*

1-2-3 Command Language
by Darien Fenn

1-2-3 Command Language introduces 1-2-3, Release 2 users to the powerful command language available in Release 2. In teaching how to program in 1-2-3, this book presents detailed descriptions of the syntax and function of each command and illustrates proper usage of the commands through numerous macro applications. *1-2-3 Command Language* helps the user learn techniques for developing, testing, debugging, and modifying many complex command language programs. Whether 1-2-3's command language is used to write simple programs for personal applications or to write complex programs for others, *1-2-3 Command Language* helps develop needed programming skills.

Mail to: Que Corporation • P.O. Box 90 • Carmel, IN 46032

Item	Title	Price	Quantity	Extension
196	1-2-3 Business Formula Handbook	$19.95		
44	1-2-3 Macro Libarary, 2nd Edition	$19.95		
130	Using 1-2-3, 2nd Edition	$21.95		
70	1-2-3 Command Language	$19.95		

Book Subtotal _____

Shipping & Handling ($2.50 per item) _____

Indiana Residents Add 5% Sales Tax _____

GRAND TOTAL _____

Method of Payment:

☐ Check   ☐ VISA   ☐ MasterCard   ☐ American Express

Card Number _____ Exp. Date _____

Cardholder's Name _____

Ship to _____

Address _____

City _____ State _____ ZIP _____

If you can't wait, call **1-800-428-5331** and order TODAY.

123FB2-872

All prices subject to change without notice.

REGISTER YOUR COPY OF
1-2-3 FOR BUSINESS, 2nd EDITION

Register your copy of *1-2-3 for Business,* 2nd Edition, and receive information about Que's newest products relating to Lotus 1-2-3. Complete this registration card and return it to Que Corporation, P.O. Box 90, Carmel, IN 46032.

Name _____

Address _____

City _____ State _____ ZIP _____

Phone _____

Where did you buy your copy of *1-2-3 for Business,* 2nd Edition?

_____

How do you plan to use the programs in this book?

_____

_____

_____

What other kinds of publications about Lotus products would you be interested in?

_____

_____

_____

_____

Which operating system do you use? _____

THANK YOU!

123FB2-872

FOLD HERE

Place
Stamp
Here

Que Corporation
P.O. Box 90
Carmel, IN 46032

Here's a tiny sample of the kinds of articles you'll read in every issue of *Absolute Reference*:

Discover the incredible power of macros—shortcuts for hundreds of applications and subroutines.
- A macro for formatting text
- Monitoring preset database conditions with a macro
- Three ways to design macro menus
- Building macros with string formulas
- Having fun with the marching macro
- Using the ROWs macro
- Generating a macro for tracking elapsed time

New applications and new solutions—every issue gives you novel ways to harness 1-2-3 and Symphony.
- Creating customized menus for your spreadsheets
- How to use criteria to unlock your spreadsheet program's data management power
- Using spreadsheets to monitor investments
- Improving profits with more effective sales forecasts
- An easy way to calculate year-to-date performance
- Using /Data Fill to streamline counting and range filling

Extend your uses—and your command—of spreadsheets.
- Printing spreadsheets sideways can help sell your ideas
- How to add goal-seeking capabilities to your spreadsheet

- Hiding columns to create custom worksheet printouts
- Lay out your spreadsheet for optimum memory management
- Toward an "intelligent" spreadsheet
- A quick way to erase extraneous zeros

Techniques for avoiding pitfalls and repairing the damage when disaster occurs.
- Preventing and trapping errors in your worksheet
- How to create an auditable spreadsheet
- Pinpointing specific errors in your spreadsheets
- Ways to avoid failing formulas
- Catching common debugging and data-entry errors
- Detecting data-entry errors
- Protecting worksheets from accidental (or deliberate) destruction
- Avoiding disaster with the /System command

Objective product reviews—we accept *no advertising,* so you can trust our editors' outspoken opinions.
- Metro Desktop Manager
- Freelance Plus
- Informix
- 4Word, InWord, Write-in
- Spreadsheet Analyst
- 101 macros for 1-2-3

Mail this card today for your free evaluation copy or call 1-800-277-7999.